CollegeBoard
connect to college success™

Real
SAT
Subject Tests™

Cover Design by Rich Koch

Copies of this book are available from your bookseller or may be ordered from College Board Publications, P.O. Box 869010, Plano, TX 75074-0998 [800 323-7155] $18.95 per copy.

Editorial inquiries concerning this book should be addressed to the College Board, SAT Program, 45 Columbus Avenue, New York, New York 10023-6992.

International Standard Book Number: 0-87447-757-3

Library of Congress Card Catalog Number: 99-085942

Printed in the United States of America

05   7 6 5 4 3

CONTENTS

The SAT Subject Tests™ v

How to Make the Most of the SAT Subject Tests ix

Getting Ready for the Tests xv

Psyching Yourself Up xxiii

The SAT Subject Test Development Committees 2002-03 xxvi

CHAPTER 1 Literature 1

CHAPTER 2 United States History 29

CHAPTER 3 World History 67

CHAPTER 4 Mathematics 115
      Math Level 1 120
      Math Level 2 153

CHAPTER 5 Biology E/M 191

CHAPTER 6 Chemistry 241

CHAPTER 7 Physics 279

CHAPTER 8 Chinese with Listening 317

CHAPTER 9 French 371
      French with Listening 403

CHAPTER 10 German 439
      German with Listening 475

CHAPTER 11 Italian 509

CHAPTER 12 Japanese with Listening 541

CHAPTER 13 Korean with Listening 579

CHAPTER 14 Latin 617

CHAPTER 15 Modern Hebrew 641

CHAPTER 16 Spanish 677
      Spanish with Listening 704

THE SAT SUBJECT TESTS™

Produced by the experts who create the SAT Reasoning Test™ and SAT Subject Tests™, this book provides information, guidance, and real practice to help students perform at their best on the tests.

About the SAT Subject Tests

Every year about 450,000 students who apply to college take SAT Subject Tests, formerly known as the College Board Achievement Tests. When colleges consider your application, they take into account many factors:

- your academic record
- your participation in school activities and sports
- letters of recommendation
- your best personal qualities
- your SAT Reasoning Test and SAT® Subject Test scores

Colleges require or recommend SAT Subject Tests because they measure your knowledge or skills in a particular subject and your ability to apply that knowledge.

Who Develops the Tests?

The SAT Subject Tests is a program of the College Board. Founded in 1900, the College Board is a not-for-profit educational association that supports academic preparation and transition to higher education for students around the world through the ongoing collaboration of its member schools, colleges, universities, educational systems, and organizations. Educational Testing Service (ETS) develops and administers the SAT Subject Tests for the College Board.

The College Board appoints a test development committee for each Subject Test. Committee members are typically teachers and college professors from institutions affiliated with the College Board. Test questions are written and reviewed by each Subject Test Committee, outside experts, and ETS staff.

Why this is the only book you'll need

Only *Real SAT Subject Tests* includes actual test questions from cover to cover. Every single question in this book was created for a Subject Test or has appeared on an actual test.

In addition to real practice tests, this book includes invaluable test-taking strategies from the people who know the SAT Subject Tests better than anyone else—the people who develop them. You'll find:

- descriptions of each test
- explanations for the types of questions in each test
- advice on preparing for the tests
- recently administered, full-length editions of 20 tests in 16 subjects
- answers to real test questions
- scoring instructions
- actual scores
- postage-paid mailer to request free listening test cassettes

This book contains information about the SAT Subject Tests. Although these tests are not expected to change in major ways during the next few years, occasional minor modifications may be made in the content, types of questions, or testing schedule.

For the most up-to-date information about the Subject Tests offered each year, go online at **www.collegeboard.com** or pick up a copy of *Taking the SAT Subject Tests*. This free booklet is available to every student who registers to take one or more Subject Tests. Copies are available in your high school guidance office or by calling the College Board SAT Program at 609 771-7600.

While the best preparation for each test is a solid course of study in that subject in high school, the practice questions in this book should help you identify your strengths and possible areas that may require more work. Use the information and practice tests in *Real SAT Subject Tests* to better understand what each test measures, the kinds of questions in each test, how the tests are scored, and how colleges use the scores.

The staff of the College Board hopes that you will find this book both easy to use and helpful. If you have specific comments or questions, please write to us at: The College Board Customer Service, 45 Columbus Avenue, New York, NY 10023-6992, or e-mail us at: inquiry@collegeboard.com.

How to Make the Most of the SAT Subject Tests

SAT Subject Tests measure your knowledge in particular subject areas and your ability to apply that knowledge. Subject Tests are independent of particular textbooks or methods of instruction. Although the types of questions change little from year to year, the content of the tests evolves to reflect current trends in high school curricula. The tests fall into five general subject areas:

ENGLISH	**LANGUAGES**
Literature	Chinese with Listening
	French
HISTORY and SOCIAL STUDIES	French with Listening
United States History	German
World History	German with Listening
	Italian
MATHEMATICS	Japanese with Listening
Math Level 1	Korean with Listening
Math Level 2	Latin
	Modern Hebrew
SCIENCE	Spanish
Biology E/M	Spanish with Listening
Chemistry	
Physics	

All SAT Subject Tests are one-hour, multiple-choice tests.

The Language Tests with Listening include Chinese, French, German, Japanese, Korean, and Spanish. All language tests have about a 20-minute listening section and a 40-minute reading section. *Note that the language tests with listening are offered only in November in designated test centers.* To take these tests, students MUST bring an acceptable cassette player with earphones to the test center.

The Math Tests have some questions that require you to use a scientific or graphing calculator.

The Biology E/M Test lets you choose questions with an ecological emphasis (Biology E) or a molecular emphasis (Biology M) in the same test. This means you have the opportunity to take the test you feel best prepared for. Biology E/M contains 80 questions: 60 are common to all test-takers. The remaining 20 questions emphasize either ecology/evolution or molecular/evolution.

How SAT Subject Test Scores Are Used

SAT Subject Test scores can help you present to the colleges to which you apply a personalized portfolio of your academic strengths. Some colleges require one or more of the Subject Tests for admission. Scores on these tests can help colleges assess how well prepared you are for different academic programs. Because SAT Subject Test scores are independent of specific textbooks, grading procedures, and methods of instruction, they are particularly suitable for admission. Colleges can compare your scores to the scores of students with different preparation and backgrounds. Used in conjunction with your high school record, results of tests like the SAT Reasoning Test, teacher recommendations, and other background information, Subject Test scores give colleges a reliable measure of your academic achievement. Many colleges and universities use the Subject Test scores not for admission, but rather to assist with placement and guidance.

Which Subject Tests Should You Take?

Before deciding which tests to take, make a tentative list of all the colleges you're thinking about. Then review their catalogs to find out whether or not they require Subject Test scores for admission and, if so, how many and which ones.

Use the list of colleges and their admissions requirements to help plan your high school course schedule. You may want to adjust your schedule in light of colleges' requirements. For example, a college to which you plan to apply may require a language Subject Test score for admission, or the college might exempt you from a freshman course requirement if you do well on a language Subject Test.

Many colleges that don't require Subject Test scores will still review them since they can give a fuller picture of your academic background. The content of high school courses and grading standards vary nationwide. Colleges use the tests to see how one student stacks up against another, regardless of textbooks used or method of instruction.

Getting Information about SAT Subject Tests Requirements

College catalogs include information about admissions requirements, including which Subject Tests are required. In addition, the College Board provides a number of resources you can search for information about Subject Test requirements at specific colleges:

- **Visit College Search at www.collegeboard.com.**
- Purchase a copy of the *College Handbook*.
- Visit the Web sites of various colleges and universities.

When to Take the Tests

If possible, take tests like U.S. History, Biology, Chemistry, and Physics right after the course ends, while the information is still fresh in your mind. On the other hand, you'll probably do better taking language tests after several years of study. Most students take Subject Tests toward the end of their junior year or at the beginning of their senior year.

This book tells you what preparation is recommended for each Subject Test. Before taking a test in a subject you haven't studied recently, review the course material thoroughly and methodically over several weeks. Also, ask your teacher's advice about the best time to take a test. Last-minute cramming won't help you do your best.

Deciding to Test Again

Before deciding whether or not to retest, you need to evaluate your scores. The best way to determine how well you really did on a Subject Test is to compare your scores to the admissions or placement requirements, or average scores, of the colleges to which you are applying. You may decide that with additional work you could do better taking the test again.

Registering for the Tests

You can register for the SAT Reasoning Test and SAT Subject Tests online by visiting the College Board's Web site at **www.collegeboard.com**. Registration Forms are also available in the SAT Program *Registration Bulletin* along with all the information you'll need to have your scores reported to the colleges you choose. Telephone reregistration is available if you have registered as a high school student for a previous SAT Reasoning Test or SAT Subject Test. Call 609 771-7600 to register.

Pick up a copy of the SAT Program *Registration Bulletin* in your school guidance office. If you're not currently in high school, you can get a copy at a local high school or by contacting the College Board SAT Program:

College Board SAT Program

P.O. Box 6200

Princeton, NJ 08541-6200

609 771-7600

www.collegeboard.com

When you register, you'll have to indicate the specific Subject Tests you plan to take on the test date you select. You may take one, two, or three tests on any given test date; your testing fee will vary accordingly. Except for the Language Tests with Listening, you may change your mind on the day of the test and select from any of the Subject Tests offered that day. **You must preregister for the listening tests.** Go to **www.collegeboard.com** or see the current *Registration Bulletin* for more information.

College Board Online®

www.collegeboard.com

Visit the College Board on the World Wide Web. You can register for SAT Program tests, get information on tests and services, try the "SAT Question of the Day™," browse the College Board Store where you can order *The College Handbook* and *The Official SAT Study Guide: For the New SAT™*, and send e-mails with your questions and concerns.

SAT SUBJECT TEST—SCHEDULE

Test Name	October	November	December	January	May	June
			Date			
Literature	•	•	•	•	•	•
United States (U.S.) History	•	•	•	•	•	•
World History			•			•
Math Level 1	•	•	•	•	•	•
Math Level 2	•	•	•	•	•	•
Biology E/M (Ecological/Molecular)	•	•	•	•	•	•
Chemistry	•	•	•	•	•	•
Physics	•	•	•	•	•	•
Languages: *Reading Only*						
French	•		•	•	•	•
German						•
Modern Hebrew						•
Italian			•			
Latin			•			•
Spanish	•		•	•	•	•
Languages: *Reading and Listening*						
Chinese		•				
French		•				
German		•				
Japanese		•				
Korean		•				
Spanish		•				

NOTES about the Subject Tests:

Students can take up to three SAT Subject Tests on a single test date.

Students must indicate which Subject Tests they plan to take when they register for a test. However, they can change which tests they take up to the test date—except for Language Tests with Listening.

Students may only use a calculator on the Math Level 1 and Math Level 2 Subject Tests. Both Math Level 1 and Math Level 2 have some questions that require the use of at least a scientific calculator. Students can take these tests without using a calculator, but it will put them at a disadvantage.

Students must cancel **all** Subject Tests for a single administration.

Getting Ready for the Tests

The best way to prepare for SAT Subject Tests is to become familiar with the organization and types of questions in each test you plan to take. Find out what will be expected of you on test day by taking the following steps to get ready:

Study the sample questions for the tests you plan to take. Sample questions give you a good idea of the kinds of questions you'll find on the tests. The more familiar you are with the sample questions, the more comfortable you'll feel when you see them on the actual test.

Study and understand the test directions. The directions for answering the questions in this book are the same as those in the test books. Learn the directions now. You will use less time reading them during the test and will have more time to answer questions.

Each Subject Test includes a background questionnaire on the first page of the test. You are asked to fill it out prior to taking the test. *The information is for statistical purposes only and will not influence your score on the test.* Your answers to the nine Row Q ovals will assist us in developing future versions of the test.

Test-Taking Strategies that Work

Follow these suggestions to increase your score as much as possible.

Before the Tests

Take the right tests at the right time. If possible take tests such as U.S. History, Biology, Chemistry, and Physics right after the course ends, when the content is still fresh in your mind. For other subjects, like languages, you would probably do better after you study the subject for two to four years. Most students take the Subject Tests toward the end of their junior year or at the beginning of their senior year.

Know what to expect. Make sure you know how the tests in which you are interested are organized, the type of test questions they include, and test day procedures.

Learn the directions now. Take some time to read the directions carefully for different types of questions. That way you won't lose time reading the directions on the day you take the Subject Tests. For every five minutes spent reading directions, five fewer minutes are available to answer questions.

Know how the tests are scored. You get one point for each right answer and lose a fraction of a point for each wrong answer. You neither gain nor lose points for omitting an answer. If you cannot eliminate any of the answer choices, it is to your benefit to omit the question.

Familiarize yourself with the SAT Subject Tests answer sheet. A set of sample answer sheets appears in the back of this book.

During the Tests

Answer all the easy questions you can before moving on to the harder ones. All questions are worth one point. So once you know where the easy and hard questions are located (see Pacing and Timing p. xviii), be sure to answer the easy questions before answering the harder, more time-consuming questions.

Eliminate choices. If you don't know the correct answer to a question, try eliminating wrong choices. It's sometimes easier to find the wrong answers than to find the correct one. On some questions, you can eliminate all the choices until you have only the one correct answer left. In other cases, eliminating choices can help you think your way through to the correct answer. If you can eliminate one choice as definitely wrong, guess an answer from the remaining choices.

Guess when you can eliminate at least one choice. If you can eliminate even one answer, you increase your chances of getting a question right. With each correct answer you gain one point; if you leave the answer blank, you get no points; if your answer is wrong, you only lose a fraction of a point.

Don't spend too much time on any one question. All questions are worth one point. If you can't answer a question without spending a long time figuring it out, go on to the next one. If you aren't sure how to answer a question, or you don't know where to begin, stop working on that question. You may have time to come back to it later.

You can omit questions. Many students who do well omit some of the questions. You can return to the ones you've skipped within the test if you finish before time is up.

Don't lose points to carelessness. No matter how frustrated you are, don't pass over questions without at least reading through them. Be sure to consider all of the choices in each question. You could lose points on easy questions through careless errors. Take each question as it comes and avoid careless mistakes:

- Answer the question asked.
- Read all the choices before selecting your answer.
- Try to work at an even, steady pace. Keep moving, but not so quickly that you make careless mistakes.

Use your test book as scratch paper. While you have to keep your *answer sheet* neat and free of stray marks, you can mark up the test book. You can write whatever you want, wherever you want, in the section of the book you're working on. Be sure to mark your answers on the separate answer sheet because you won't receive credit for anything written in the book.

Erasing all responses cancels all scores. If you erase all the responses to an individual Subject Test, it will be considered a request for cancellation, and scores from all Subject Tests taken on that day will be canceled.

Check your answer sheet regularly to make sure you are in the right place. Losing your place on the answer sheet can be a major problem that affects your score. To prevent this, check the number of the question and the number on the answer sheet every few questions. Check them carefully every time you skip a question.

Don't make extra marks on the answer sheet. The answer sheet is machine-scored, and the machine can't tell an answer from a doodle. If the machine reads what looks like two answers for one question, it will consider the question unanswered.

Recap: Test-Taking Rules

Before the Test

- Learn the directions.
- Know how the tests are scored.
- Familiarize yourself with the answer sheet.

During the Test

- Eliminate choices.
- Guess when you can eliminate at least one answer choice.
- Skip questions that are too hard and go back later, if you have time.
- Don't spend too much time on any one question.
- Don't lose points to carelessness.
- Answer all the easy questions you can before moving on to the harder ones.
- Use your test booklet as scratch paper.
- Check your answer sheet regularly.

Pacing and Timing

Pacing is based on the idea that each question on the test takes a certain amount of time to read and answer. If you had unlimited time, or very few questions to answer, pacing would not be a problem.

Good test-takers also develop a sense of timing to help them complete the test. The goal is to spend time on the questions that you are most likely to answer correctly and leave some time for review at the end of the testing period.

Strategies for Pacing

Following are some basic pacing strategies that will help ensure that you don't lose time during a Subject Test and that you'll have time to consider all the questions you may be able to answer:

Keep moving. Don't spend so much time puzzling out hard questions that you lose the time to find and answer the easier ones. Work on less time-consuming questions before moving on to the more time-consuming ones. Remember to mark the questions as you work on them, especially the ones to which you want to return. Also, cross out choices you can eliminate as you move through the test. This will save you time when you return to those questions later.

Keep track of time during the test. Each Subject Test requires one hour. You should develop the habit of occasionally checking your progress through the test, so that you know when you are one-fourth of the way through the hour, halfway through the hour, and when you have five minutes left. If you finish the test before the time is called, use the remaining time to check your answers and erase any stray marks on the answer sheet.

Remember that all questions are worth one point. The score value for a correct answer is the same regardless of the type of question or the difficulty of the question. So go through an entire section, answering questions that you know or can answer quickly and skipping questions that will need more time. Be careful to mark the skipped questions in your test book and leave the ovals on the answer sheet blank to avoid marking answers to the wrong questions.

A Recommended Approach to Pacing

Practice using the pacing approach that follows on the actual tests included in this book.

1. Set up a schedule for progress through the test. Know when you should be one-quarter of the way through and halfway through. Every now and then, check your progress against your schedule.

2. Begin to work as soon as the testing time begins. Keep your attention focused on the test. Don't daydream.

3. Don't ponder over alternatives on the first pass through a section. Answer questions you are sure of first; mark those questions you are unsure of in the test book so you can easily locate them later. When you skip questions, make sure to mark your answers to following questions in the appropriate ovals on the answer sheet.

4. Go back and try the questions you skipped, using guessing strategy if necessary.

5. In the last few minutes, check your answers to avoid careless mistakes.

6. Check your answer sheet to make sure that there are no stray marks and that all erasures are clean.

Recap: Pacing

- Keep moving.
- Spend time on the questions that you have the best chance of getting right.
- Keep track of time during the test.
- All questions are worth one point.

Guessing

Guessing on Subject Tests is a good idea if you have an effective strategy: *Eliminate all the answer choices that you know are wrong and guess from those remaining*.

Each correct answer on a Subject Test is worth one point. To correct for random guessing, a fraction of a point is subtracted for each incorrect answer to a multiple-choice question. Because of this correction for guessing, random guessing probably won't improve your score. However, if you can eliminate one or more choices as wrong, you improve your chances of guessing the right answer from the remaining choices. The more wrong choices you can eliminate, the better your chance of guessing the right answer.

Guessing Strategy

1. Guess only after you've tried your best to answer the question.
2. Eliminate choices that you know are wrong. Cross them out in your test book so that you can see clearly which choices are left. If you cannot eliminate one or more choices, guessing is probably not to your advantage.
3. After you have eliminated the choices that you know are wrong, guess from among the remaining answer choices. Your chances of getting the correct answer are improved.

Calculator Tips for Math Level 1 and Level 2 Tests

A calculator is required to solve some of the questions in Math Level 1 and Level 2. If you take these tests without a calculator, you will be at a disadvantage.

Use a calculator with which you are familiar and comfortable. Your degree of familiarity with the operation of a calculator may affect how well you do on these tests.

Make sure that your calculator is in good working condition before you take the tests. *No substitute calculators or batteries will be available at the test center.*

Remember that only some questions on these tests require the use of a calculator. Using your calculator too often can slow you down. First decide how you will solve a problem and then decide whether or not you will need the calculator.

Tips for Using Cassette Players for Language Tests with Listening

You must bring an acceptable cassette player with earphones to the test center. Put fresh batteries in your cassette player the day before the test. We recommend that you bring additional fresh batteries and a backup cassette player with earphones to the test center. Test center staff will NOT have batteries, cassette players, or earphones for your use.

Acceptable cassette players must be:

- personal (have earphones that let only you hear the recording)
- portable (small enough that the entire player can fit in your hand)
- battery-operated
- able to use a single (not dual) standard (2-1/2 inch by 4 inch) audiocassette not a mini- or microcassette.

If your cassette player has a programming feature that fast-forwards automatically to the next prompt, that feature must be deactivated before you start the test. You will not be allowed to share a cassette player with another test-taker.

Beginning with the November 2005 administration, portable CD players will be required instead of cassette players for language with listening tests.

After the Tests

About three weeks after you take the Subject Tests, your Score Report will be mailed to you, your high school, and colleges and scholarship programs you indicated on your Registration Form. Your Score Report will include your scores, percentiles, and interpretive information. Some scores may take longer to report because of such problems as late receipt of answer sheets or inconsistent student identification information. Scores are also available for a fee by telephone approximately two weeks after each SAT administration. The toll-free number is 800 728-7267. Dates on which scores are available and fees are listed on **www.collegeboard.com** and in the SAT Program *Registration Bulletin*.

Psyching Yourself Up

Your Subject Test results depend on how much you know and on how well you can put what you know to work. But your results can also reflect how you feel. Nerves, distractions, poor concentration, or a negative attitude can pull down your performance.

Relaxation Techniques

Being nervous is natural. Being nervous, by itself, isn't really a problem. A bit of a nervous edge can keep you sharp and focused. Too much nervousness, however, can keep you from concentrating and working effectively.

Here are some techniques that you can use to keep your nerves in check.

Before the Test

You can start your psychological preparation before the tests. Learn as much as you can about the tests well before you take them. Then, on the day before, briefly review the sample questions, explanations, and test directions in this book, on the College Board Web site, or in *Taking the SAT Subject Tests*. Cramming the night before the tests probably won't help your performance and might even make you more anxious. Instead, spend the evening relaxing and get a good night's sleep.

Have everything that you need for the test ready the night before:

- The appropriate ID, which must include your photo (for example, a school ID), or a brief description of yourself. The description must be on school stationery, and you must sign it in front of your principal or school counselor, who must also sign it.
- Admission ticket.
- No. 2 pencils and erasers.
- Calculator with fresh batteries if you are taking one of the Math Tests.
- Personal cassette player with fresh batteries if you are taking a Language Test with Listening.

Make sure you know the way to the test center and any special instructions for finding the entrance. Leave yourself plenty of time for mishaps and emergencies. If you're not there when the tests begin, you can't take them.

Think Positively

Getting down on yourself during the tests does more than make you feel bad. It can rob you of the confidence you need to solve problems. It can distract you. If you're thinking that you aren't doing well, you aren't thinking about the question in front of you. Think positive thoughts that will help you keep up your confidence and focus on each question.

Keep Yourself Focused

Try not to think about anything except the question in front of you.

If you catch yourself thinking about something else, bring your focus back to the test, and congratulate yourself. You have just demonstrated that you are in control.

Concentrate on Your Own Work

The first thing some students do when they get stuck on a question or find themselves running into a batch of tough questions is to look around to see how everyone else is doing. What they usually see is that others are filling in their answer sheets.

"Look at how well everyone else is doing....What's wrong with me?" If you start thinking this way, try to remember:

Everyone works at a different pace. Your neighbors may not be working on the question that puzzled you or even taking the same Subject Test.

Thinking about what someone else is doing doesn't help you answer even a single question. In fact, it takes away time you should be using on the test.

Put the Tests in Perspective

The SAT Reasoning Test and SAT Subject Tests are important, but how you do on the tests will not determine whether you get into college.

- Tests are only one factor in the college admissions decision.
- High school grades are considered more important than the SAT and the Subject Tests by most college admissions officers.
- Nonacademic admissions criteria are important, too. These include things like extracurricular activities and personal recommendations. College admissions officers at individual colleges will usually be glad to discuss the admissions

policies at their institutions with you.

- If you don't do as well as you wanted to, you can take the tests again.

Remember You're In Control

Developing a plan for taking SAT Subject Tests will keep you in control during the test: practice each type of question; learn how to pace yourself and guess wisely. If you're in control, you'll have the best chance of getting the best score you deserve.

The SAT Subject Test Development Committees 2002-03

2002–03 SAT BIOLOGY COMMITTEE

Professor Louise A. Paquin, Chair
McDaniel College, Westminster, MD
Professor William S. Bradshaw
Brigham Young University, Provo, UT
Ray A. Hill
Lowell College Preparatory, San Francisco, CA
John Zarnetske
Hoosick Falls Central School, Hoosick Falls, NY
Prue Talbot
University of California, Riverside, CA

2002–03 SAT CHEMISTRY COMMITTEE

Dr. Jo Allan Beran, Chair
Texas A&M University- Kingsville, Kingsville, TX
James D. Campbell
Brookline High School, Brookline, MA
Rose E. Hascom
Francis Parker School, San Diego, CA
Professor George E. Miller
University of California at Irvine, Irvine, CA
Ruiess Van Fossen Ramsey
Indiana University of Pennsylvania, Indiana, PA

2002–03 SAT CHINESE COMMITTEE

Scott McGinnis, Chair
National Foreign Language Center at University of Maryland, College Park, MD
Baozhang He
University of Florida, Gainesville, FL
Tianwei Xie
California State University: Long Beach, Long Beach, CA
Min Zhang
The Indiana Academy at Ball State University, Muncie, IN
Yunian Zhang
West Potomac High School, Alexandria, VA

2002–03 SAT FRENCH COMMITTEE

Marie-Thérèse Noiset, Chair
University of North Carolina, Charlotte, NC
Kitty Fair
Phillips Exeter Academy, Exeter, NH
Jacqueline Friedman
Horace Mann School, Riverdale, NY
Ndinzi Masagara
Youngstown State University, Youngstown, OH
François Wolman
Canyon High School, Canyon Country, CA

2002–03 SAT GERMAN COMMITTEE

Reinhard K. Zachau, Chair
University of the South, Sewanee, TN
John Lalande
State University of New York at Oswego, Oswego, NY
Glenn Levine
University of California: Irvine, Irvine, CA
Marlies Reppenhagen
Deering High School, Portland, ME
Gabriele Stracke
Shenendehowa High School East, Clifton Park, NY

2002–03 SAT MODERN HEBREW COMMITTEE

Dinah Haramati, Chair
Joel Braverman High School, Brooklyn, NY
Nancy Ezer
University of California: Los Angeles, Los Angeles, CA
Lee Goldberg
Highland Park High School, Highland Park, IL
Orna Kaplan
Milken Community High School, Los Angeles, CA
Vardit Ringvald
Brandeis University, Waltham, MA

2002–03 SAT ITALIAN COMMITTEE

Irene Marchegiani Jones, Chair
California State University: Long Beach, Long Beach, CA
Bruna Boyle
Narragansett High School, Narragansett, RI
Mariastella Cocchiara
Melrose High School, Melrose, MA
Erasmo Gerato
Florida State University, Tallahassee, FL
Alessandro Vettori
Rutgers University, New Brunswick, NJ

2002–03 SAT JAPANESE COMMITTEE

Hiroshi Nara, Chair
University of Pittsburgh, Pittsburgh, PA
Dan Dewey
University of Pittsburgh, Pittsburgh, PA
Virginia Marcus
Washington University, St. Louis, MO
Hiroko Muchnicki
Townsend Harris High School at Queens College , Flushing, NY
Hiroko T. Nomachi-Yuge
Venice High School, Los Angeles, CA

2002–03 SAT KOREAN COMMITTEE

Sung-Ock S. Sohn, Chair
University of California: Los Angeles, Los Angeles, CA
Cho Sungdai
State University of New York at Binghamton, Binghamton, NY
Eunice Lee
Torrance High School, Torrance, CA
Hyo Sang Lee
Indiana University, Bloomington, IN
Bongsoon Yow
Flushing High School, Flushing, NY

2002–03 SAT LATIN COMMITTEE

Mary Pendergraft, Chair
Wake Forest University, Winston-Salem, NC
Sue Gillen
White Plains High School, White Plains, NY
Edward Ligon
Roxbury Latin School, West Roxbury, MA
Sherwin Little
Indian Hill High School, Cincinnati, OH
Michele Salzman
University of California: Riverside, Riverside, CA

2002–03 SAT LITERATURE COMMITTEE

Joseph T. Skerrett, Sr., Chair
University of Massachusetts Amherst, Amherst, MA
C. Lok Chua
California State University, Fresno, CA
Idris Anderson
Crystal Springs Uplands Schools, Hillsborough, CA
Jerry W. Ward, Jr.
Dillard University, New Orleans, LA
Ruth W. Welborn
Stockbridge High School, Stockbridge, GA

2002–03 SAT MATHEMATICS COMMITTEE

Dr. Vincent P. Schielack, Jr., Chair
Texas A&M University, College Station, TX
Ann Davidian
General Douglas MacArthur High School, Levittown, NY
Roger Day
Illinois State University, Normal, IL
Christinia A. Frazier
Philadelphia High School for Girls, Philadelphia, PA
Marie M. Vaniskko
California State University: Stanislaus, Turlock, CA
David E. Williams
Suncoast High School, Rivera Beach, FL

2002–03 SAT PHYSICS COMMITTEE

Helene F. Perry, Chair
Loyola College in Maryland, Baltimore, MD
Dr. Robert G. Jacobsen
University of California: Berkeley, Berkeley, CA
John L. Kinard
Greenwood High School, Greenwood, SC
Professor Xinchou Lou
University of Texas at Dallas, Richardson, TX
Frank A. Norton
Cranbrook Kingswood School, Bloomfield Hills, MI

2002–03 SAT SPANISH COMMITTEE

Rodney Rodríguez, Chair
Manhattan College/College of Mount Saint Vincent, Riverdale, NY
Lori Langer de Ramírez
Herricks Public School, New Hyde Park, NY
Martha Mentch
Albuquerque Academy, Albuquerque, NM
Gilda Nissenberg
Dr. Michael M. Krop High School, Miami, FL
Carmen Silva-Corvalán
University of Southern California, Los Angeles, CA

2002–03 SAT U.S. HISTORY COMMITTEE

Professor Richard Weiss, Chair
University of California: Los Angeles, Los Angeles, CA
Charlotte Landreau
Highland Park Senior High School, St. Paul, MN
Daniel C. Littlefield
University of South Carolina, Columbia, SC
Cassandra A. Osborne
Oak Ridge High School, Oak Ridge, TN
Herbert E. Sloan
Barnard College, New York, NY

2002–03 SAT WORLD HISTORY COMMITTEE

Professor Howard Spodek, Chair
Temple University, Philadelphia, PA
Priscilla Campbell
East Hampton High School, East Hampton, NY
David Northrup
Boston College, Chestnut Hill, MA
George Rislov
Highland Park High School, Dallas, TX
Tara Sethia
California State Polytechnic University, Pomona, CA

Chapter 1
Literature

Purpose

The Literature Subject Test measures how well you have learned to read literary works from different periods and cultures. There is no prescribed or suggested reading list.

Format

This one-hour test consists of approximately 60 multiple-choice questions based on six to eight reading selections. About half of the selections are poetry and half are prose. Selections include complete short poems or excerpts from various works, including longer poems, stories, novels, nonfiction writing, and drama.

You are not expected to have read or studied particular poems or passages that appear on the test. Extensive knowledge of literary terminology is not essential, but the test does assume a good working knowledge of basic terminology (i.e., speaker, tone, image, irony, alliteration, stanza, etc.).

All questions are based on selections from original works written in English from the Renaissance to the present. The date printed at the end of each passage or poem is the original publication date, or in some cases, the estimated date of composition. The set of 4 to 12 questions per selection usually covers these aspects of a text:

- meaning—overall effect and argument or theme; and
- form—structure, genre, and method of organization (how one part develops from or differs from another).

A set of questions often covers these additional aspects:

- narrative voice—the characterization of the speaker, the possible distinction between the speaker and the author, the speaker's attitude;
- tone;
- characters represented—distinguishing traits and the techniques by which the character is presented and the traits revealed;

- characteristic use of language—imagery, figures of speech, and diction; and
- contextual meaning—specific words, phrases, and lines within a passage or poem.

Basis for Questions on the Literature Test

Source of Questions	Approximate Percentage of Test*
English Literature	40–50
American Literature	40–50
Other Literature Written in English	0–10

Chronology	
Renaissance and 17th Century	30
18th and 19th Centuries	30
20th Century	40

Genre	
Poetry	40–50
Prose	45–50
Drama and Other	0–10

*The distribution of passages may vary in different editions of the test. The chart above indicates typical or average content.

The Literature Subject Test included in this book contains 61 questions based on seven selections—a pair of excerpts from The Woman Warrior by Maxine Hong Kingston, "Against that time..." Sonnet #49 by William Shakespeare, "Ain't I a Woman?" by Sojourner Truth, "Permanently" by Kenneth Koch, an excerpt from Cranford by Elizabeth Gaskell, a pair of short poems by Ralph Waldo Emerson ("Limits") and Emily Dickinson ("The Rat is the concisest Tenant"), and an excerpt from A Tale of a Tub by Jonathan Swift. As frequently happens when tests are composed of lengthy sets of questions based on relatively few selections, the distribution of passages in a particular test differs somewhat from the typical or average content summarized in the chart. The test in this book, for example, contains more selections from the eighteenth- and nineteenth-century category than from the Renaissance and seventeenth-century category. Another Literature Subject Test may contain many selections from the twentieth-century category.

Recommended Preparation

- Close, critical reading in English and American literature from a variety of historical periods and genres is best.
- Have a working knowledge of basic literary terminology, such as speaker, tone, image, irony, alliteration, stanza, etc.
- There is no suggested reading list.
- Familiarize yourself with directions in advance. The directions in this book are identical to those that appear on the test.

Questions Used in the Literature Test

All of the questions in the Literature Subject Test are five-choice completion questions, such as:

- *Which of the following best describes the style of the passage?*
- *The style of the passage is best described as*

The questions fall into three categories:

- **regular multiple-choice questions**—choose the best response offered
- **NOT or EXCEPT questions**—from five choices you must select the inappropriate choice
- **Roman numeral questions**—one statement or a combination of statements may be the best response

All of the questions on the Literature Subject Test are grouped into sets based on poems or prose passages.

Score

The total score is reported on the 200-to-800 scale.

Sample Questions

The James Merrill poem below and many of the questions that follow it are fairly easy; however, some of the other passages and questions used in the Literature Subject Test are likely to be more difficult.

James Merrill was a twentieth-century American poet; therefore, according to the Basis for Questions chart on the preceding page, all of the questions on this poem would be classified as American Literature, Twentieth Century, Poetry.

The directions used in the test book precede the poem.

Directions: This test consists of selections from literary works and questions on their content, form, and style. After reading each passage or poem, choose the best answer to each question and fill in the corresponding oval on the answer sheet.

Note: Pay particular attention to the requirement of questions that contain the words NOT, LEAST, or EXCEPT.

Questions 1–6. Read the following poem carefully before you choose your answers.

Kite Poem

> *"One is reminded of a certain person,"*
> *Continued the parson, settling back in his chair*
> *With a glass of port, "who sought to emulate*
> *The sport of birds (it was something of a chore)*
> *(5) By climbing up on a kite. They found his coat*
> *Two counties away; the man himself was missing."*
> *His daughters tittered: it was meant to be a lesson*
> *To them—they had been caught kissing, or some such nonsense,*
> *The night before, under the crescent moon.*
> *(10) So, finishing his pheasant, their father began*
> *This thirty-minute discourse ending with*
> *A story improbable from the start. He paused for breath,*
> *Having shown but a few of the dangers. However, the wind*
> *Blew out the candles and the moon wrought changes*
> *(15) Which the daughters felt along their stockings. Then,*
> *Thus persuaded, they fled to their young men*
> *Waiting in the sweet night by the raspberry bed,*
> *And kissed and kissed, as though to escape on a kite.*

1. The attitude of the parson (line 2) toward the "certain person" (lines 1–6) is one of
   (A) admiration
   (B) anxiety
   (C) disdain
   (D) curiosity
   (E) grief

Choice (C) is the correct response to this question. In order to warn his daughters of the danger of imprudent behavior, the parson uses the tale of the person who climbed up on a kite. It is unlikely, given this purpose, that he would feel either "admiration," "anxiety," "curiosity," or "grief" for the man, and nothing in the poem suggests that the parson had any of these feelings. His attitude is one of disdain for a person whose behavior he regards as foolish.

2. The descriptive detail "settling back in his chair/With a glass of port" (lines 2–3) underscores the parson's
    (A) authority
    (B) complacency
    (C) hypocrisy
    (D) gentleness
    (E) indecisiveness

The poem suggests that the parson is a rather rigid, formal man given to lengthy moralizing. It can be inferred from the context that complacency is one element of his character; choice (B) is the correct response. There is no evidence in the poem that the parson is either hypocritical, gentle, or indecisive. Out of context, the quotation from the poem might be interpreted as behavior associated with someone in a position of authority. In context, however, the parson is more notable for his lack of authority—his daughters titter when he lectures and ignore his advice.

3. The chief reason the parson's daughters "tittered" (line 7) is that they
    (A) were embarrassed to have been caught kissing
    (B) knew where the missing man in their father's story was
    (C) wanted to flatter their father
    (D) did not take their father's lecture seriously
    (E) took cruel pleasure in the kite flyer's disaster

The most plausible explanation of why the daughters "tittered" is (D)—they did not take their father's lecture seriously. This view is supported by the daughters' actions—as soon as their father paused for breath, they did what his "thirty-minute discourse" warned them not to do. There is no indication in the poem that (B) or (E) is true, and if the daughters had wanted to flatter their father, as (C) claims, they certainly would not have tittered during his serious lecture. If (A) were true, it is unlikely that the daughters would have "fled to their young men" so quickly the second time.

4. The speaker's tone suggests that the reader should regard the parson's "thirty-minute discourse" (line 11) as

   (A) scholarly and enlightening

   (B) serious and important

   (C) entertaining and amusing

   (D) verbose and pedantic

   (E) grisly and morbid

The speaker's tone suggests that the reader should regard the parson's "thirty-minute discourse" as "verbose and pedantic," choice (D). The parson is presented as one who speaks at length, telling "improbable" stories and taking 30 minutes to show "but a few of the dangers" he wanted to warn his daughters about. He uses lengthy phrases such as "emulate/The sport of birds" when a simple verb such as "fly" would have sufficed. The parson might well have intended his discourse to seem "scholarly and enlightening," choice (A), and "serious and important," choice (B), but neither the daughters nor the speaker suggests that the parson succeeded, and the reader has no reason to assess the effectiveness of the discourse differently from the speaker and the daughters. The reader may be entertained and amused by the speaker's account of the discourse, but that response is not the same as being amused by the discourse itself, as (C) states. Choice (E) is implausible.

5. The daughters are "persuaded" (line 16) by

   (A) their own fear of danger

   (B) the fate of the kite flyer

   (C) their own natural impulses

   (D) the parson's authority

   (E) respect for their father

The daughters are "persuaded" by their own natural impulses, choice (C). According to the poem, "the moon wrought changes/Which the daughters felt along their stockings" (lines 14–15). These natural impulses were, ironically, more persuasive than the long discourse delivered by their father in an attempt to dissuade them. The daughters, like the kite flyer, are attracted to the possibility of "escape on a kite" (line 18) and are not deterred by solemn and tedious warnings of danger.

6. All of the following are elements of opposition in the development of the poem EXCEPT

   (A) indoors .. outdoors

   (B) talking .. kissing

   (C) caution .. adventure

   (D) work .. play

   (E) settling back .. flying

Choice (D) is the only opposition that is not evident in the poem. Actions such as "climbing up on a kite" and "kissing…under the crescent moon" might be regarded as forms of play, but the poem really does not offer any contrasting examples of work. Choices (A), (B), (C), and (E) illustrate the contrasting actions and attitudes of the parson on the one hand and the daughters or the kite flyer, or both, on the other.

Literature Test

The test that follows is an actual, recently administered SAT Subject Test in Literature. To get an idea of what a real administration is like, take the test under conditions as close as possible to those of a national administration:

- Set aside an hour when you can take the test uninterrupted. Make sure you complete the test in one sitting.

- Sit at a desk or table with no other books or papers. Dictionaries, other books, or notes are not allowed in the test room.

- Time yourself by placing a clock or kitchen timer in front of you.

- Tear out an answer sheet from the back of this book and fill it in just as you would on the day of the test. One answer sheet can be used for up to three Subject Tests.

- Read the instructions that precede the practice test. During the actual administration you will be asked to read them before answering test questions.

- After you finish the practice test, read the sections "How to Score the SAT Subject Test in Literature" and "Reviewing Your Performance on the Literature Subject Test."

- Actual test and answer sheets will indicate circles, not ovals.

Form K2-30AC

LITERATURE TEST

The top portion of the section of the answer sheet that you will use in taking the Literature test must be filled in exactly as shown in the illustration below. Note carefully that you have to do all of the following on your answer sheet.

1. Print LITERATURE on the line under the words "Subject Test (print)."

2. In the shaded box labeled "Test Code" fill in four ovals:

    —Fill in oval 3 in the row labeled V.

    —Fill in oval 1 in the row labeled W.

    —Fill in oval 1 in the row labeled X.

    —Fill in oval D in the row labeled Y.

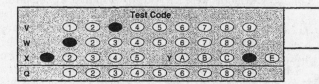

3. Please answer the two questions below by filling in the appropriate ovals in the row labeled Q on the answer sheet. The information you provide is for statistical purposes only and will not affect your score on the test.

Answer <u>both</u> questions on the basis of the authors and works read in your English classes in grade 10 to the present.

Question I

How many semesters of English courses that were predominantly devoted to the study of literature have you taken from grade 10 to the present? (If you are studying literature in the current semester, count the current semester as a full semester.) Fill in only <u>one</u> oval of ovals 1-3.

- One semester or less   —Fill in oval 1.
- Two semesters   —Fill in oval 2.
- Three semesters or more   —Fill in oval 3.

Question II

Of the following, which content areas made up a significant part (at least 10 percent) of the literature you read in your English classes in grades 10-12 ? Fill in as many ovals as apply.

- British and/or North American writers writing
    before 1800   —Fill in oval 4.
- European writers in translation   —Fill in oval 5.
- African American or Black Writers   —Fill in oval 6.
- Ethnic American writers (Hispanic American,
    Asian American, American Indian, etc.)   —Fill in oval 7.
- Latin American writers in translation   —Fill in oval 8.
- Writers from Africa or India writing
    in English   —Fill in oval 9.

When the supervisor gives the signal, turn the page and begin the Literature test. There are 100 numbered ovals on the answer sheet and 61 questions in the Literature test. Therefore, use only ovals 1 to 61 for recording your answers.

LITERATURE TEST

This test consists of selections from literary works and questions on their content, form, and style. After reading each passage or poem, choose the best answer to each question and fill in the corresponding oval on the answer sheet.

Note: Pay particular attention to the requirement of questions that contain the words NOT, LEAST, or EXCEPT.

Questions 1-8. Read the following excerpts carefully before you choose your answers.

(These excerpts are from a single chapter of a memoir written by the daughter of an immigrant family living in California during the 1940's and 1950's.)

EXCERPT 1

It was when I found out I had to talk that school became a misery, that the silence became a misery. I did not speak and felt bad each time that I did not speak. I
Line read aloud in first grade, though, and heard the barest
(5) whisper with little squeaks come out of my throat. "Louder," said the teacher, who scared the voice away again. The other Chinese girls did not talk either, so I knew the silence had to do with being a Chinese girl.

Reading out loud was easier than speaking because
(10) we did not have to make up what to say, but I stopped often, and the teacher would think I'd gone quiet again. I could not understand "I." The Chinese "I" has seven strokes, intricacies. How could the American "I," assuredly wearing a hat like the Chinese, have only
(15) three strokes, the middle so straight? Was it out of politeness that this writer left off strokes the way a Chinese has to write her own name small and crooked? No, it was not politeness; "I" is a capital and "you" is lowercase. I stared at that middle line and waited so
(20) long for its black center to resolve into tight strokes and dots that I forgot to pronounce it. The other troublesome word was "here," no strong consonant to hang on to, and so flat, when "here" is two mountainous ideographs.[1] The teacher, who had already told me every
(25) day how to read "I" and "here," put me in the low corner under the stairs again, where the noisy boys usually sat.

EXCERPT 2

After American school, we picked up our cigar boxes, in which we had arranged books, brushes, and
(30) an inkbox neatly, and went to Chinese school, from 5:00 to 7:30 p.m. There we chanted together, voices rising and falling, loud and soft, some boys shouting, everybody reading together, reciting together and not alone with one voice. When we had a memorization
(35) test, the teacher let each of us come to his desk and say the lesson to him privately, while the rest of the class practiced copying or tracing. Most of the teachers were men. The boys who were so well behaved in the Amer-

ican school played tricks on them and talked back to
(40) them. The girls were not mute. They screamed and yelled during recess, when there were no rules; they had fistfights. Nobody was afraid of children hurting themselves or of children hurting school property. The glass doors to the red and green balconies with the gold joy
(45) symbols were left wide open so that we could run out and climb the fire escapes. We played capture-the-flag in the auditorium, where Sun Yat-sen and Chiang Kai-shek's pictures[2] hung at the back of the stage, the Chinese flag on their left and the American flag on their
(50) right. We climbed on the teak ceremonial chairs and made flying leaps off the stage. One flag headquarters was behind the glass door and the other on stage right. Our feet drummed on the hollow stage. During recess the teachers locked themselves up in their office with
(55) the shelves of books, copybooks, inks from China. They drank tea and warmed their hands at a stove. There was no play supervision. At recess we had the school to ourselves, and also we could roam as far as we could go—downtown, Chinatown stores, home—as long as we returned before the bell rang.

(1976)

[1]ideographs: written symbols that represent a thing or an idea
[2]Sun Yat-sen (1866-1925) was known as the Father of the Chinese Republic. Chiang Kai-shek (1887-1975) led the Chinese Nationalist party in its military confrontations with Chinese communists.

1. In Excerpt 1, the speaker's perspective is best described as that of

    (A) a bewildered child
    (B) a scornful child
    (C) a cheerful child
    (D) an indignant adult
    (E) an authoritarian adult

GO ON TO THE NEXT PAGE

2. The statement that the teacher "scared the voice away again" (lines 6-7) suggests all of the following EXCEPT:

   (A) The child felt that her voice had a will of its own.
   (B) The child wanted to separate herself from her failure to read aloud.
   (C) The child had been similarly treated by the teacher before.
   (D) The teacher frightened the child deliberately.
   (E) The teacher intimidated rather than encouraged the child.

3. The speaker indicates that as a child she had difficulty understanding the English word "I" in a text because

   (A) she had not yet grasped the difference between lowercase and capital letters
   (B) the differences between the appearance of the English and Chinese "I" perplexed her
   (C) the American teacher did not try to explain the word "I"
   (D) she would daydream about the writer who used the pronoun "I"
   (E) the shape of the letter "I" seemed too complex to reflect a writer's ideas

4. In Excerpt 2, all of the following emphasize what the speaker sees as the positive qualities of the Chinese school EXCEPT

   (A) "not alone" (lines 33-34)
   (B) "gold joy symbols" (lines 44-45)
   (C) "wide open" (line 45)
   (D) "roam" (line 58)
   (E) "the bell" (line 60)

5. The arrangement of the stage at the Chinese school was probably intended to foster which of the following in the students?

   I. Awareness of the accomplishments of certain Chinese leaders
   II. Pride in their heritage
   III. Enthusiasm for performing

   (A) I only
   (B) II only
   (C) III only
   (D) I and II only
   (E) II and III only

6. All of the following are used to convey the speaker's impression of the Chinese school EXCEPT

   (A) images of movement
   (B) disdain for national symbols
   (C) depiction of children playing
   (D) references to large surrounding spaces
   (E) incongruity between purpose and use of the auditorium

7. All of the following contrasting features of the two schools are presented EXCEPT the

   (A) type of discipline
   (B) boys' treatment of teachers
   (C) nature of homework
   (D) behavior of Chinese girls
   (E) type of classroom participation

8. Although both excerpts are first-person accounts, they reveal which difference in perspective?

   (A) Excerpt 1 focuses on the thoughts of the child as an individual; Excerpt 2, on group activities.
   (B) Excerpt 1 focuses on the girls in the class; Excerpt 2, on the boys.
   (C) Excerpt 1 is critical of an English class; Excerpt 2, of a class at the Chinese school.
   (D) Excerpt 1 apologizes for the girl's poor performance in school; Excerpt 2 ignores her mistakes.
   (E) Excerpt 1 concentrates on what was taught; Excerpt 2, on how the students felt about school.

GO ON TO THE NEXT PAGE

Questions 9-18. Read the following poem carefully before you choose your answers.

> Against that time (if ever that time come)
> When I shall see thee frown on my defects,
> When as thy love hath cast his utmost sum,
> *Line* Called to that audit by advised respects—
> *(5)* Against that time when thou shalt strangely pass,
> And scarcely greet me with that sun, thine eye,
> When love, converted from the thing it was,
> Shall reasons find of settled gravity—
> Against that time do I ensconce me here
> *(10)* Within the knowledge of mine own desert,
> And this my hand against myself uprear,
> To guard the lawful reasons on thy part.
> To leave poor me thou hast the strength of laws,
> Since why to love I can allege no cause.

(1609)

9. The speaker of the poem is addressing

(A) an unspecified general audience
(B) a friend of the speaker's beloved
(C) a lover
(D) a former lover
(E) a legal adviser

10. The speaker imagines a time in the future when he might

(A) no longer be in love
(B) no longer be loved
(C) be even more deeply in love
(D) be able to explain why he is in love
(E) look back fondly on his present happiness

11. In lines 1-12, which of the following is a main verb?

(A) "come" (line 1)
(B) "shall see " (line 2)
(C) "shalt pass" (line 5)
(D) "shall find" (line 8)
(E) "do ensconce" (line 9)

12. In line 5, the adverb "strangely" means

(A) oddly
(B) for no good reason
(C) in a distant manner
(D) eerily
(E) haltingly

13. In lines 1, 5, and 9, "against" is best understood to mean

(A) in opposition to
(B) in repetition of
(C) in contrast to
(D) in preparation for
(E) in rejection of

14. The "reasons" mentioned in line 8 are best characterized as

(A) scientific explanations for a natural force
(B) arguments against rationality itself
(C) arguments for the importance of loving
(D) logical explanations for the absence of love
(E) counterarguments to the speaker's propositions

GO ON TO THE NEXT PAGE →

15. If the speaker is implying in line 10 that he is not deserving of love, which of the following most strongly supports the implication?

    (A) "defects" (line 2)
    (B) "utmost sum" (line 3)
    (C) "strangely" (line 5)
    (D) "love, converted" (line 7)
    (E) "settled gravity" (line 8)

16. The tone of the poem can best be described as

    (A) playful and lighthearted
    (B) hesitant and confused
    (C) confident and determined
    (D) reasoned and optimistic
    (E) self-deprecating and apprehensive

17. One theme of the poem appears to be that

    (A) unrequited love is still sweet
    (B) time transforms lust into love
    (C) the value of true love cannot be calculated
    (D) relationships should be controlled by laws
    (E) reason is insufficient to explain love

18. Which of the following best describes the language of the poem?

    (A) Concrete and matter-of-fact
    (B) Euphemistic and prosaic
    (C) Metaphoric and logical
    (D) Informal and conversational
    (E) Ironic and amused

GO ON TO THE NEXT PAGE

Questions 19-26. Read the following passage carefully before you choose your answers.

Well, children, where there is so much racket there must be something out of kilter. I think that 'twixt the Negroes of the South and the women at the North, all talking about rights, the White men will be in a fix
Line
(5) pretty soon. But what's all this here talking about?

That man over there says that women need to be helped into carriages, and lifted over ditches, and to have the best place everywhere. Nobody ever helps me into carriages, or over mud-puddles, or gives me any
(10) best place! And ain't I a woman? Look at me! Look at my arm! I have ploughed and planted, and gathered into barns, and no man could head me! And ain't I a woman? I could work as much and eat as much as a man—when I could get it—and bear the lash as well!
(15) And ain't I a woman? I have borne thirteen children, and seen them most all sold off to slavery, and when I cried out with my mother's grief, none but Jesus heard me! And ain't I a woman?

Then they talk about this thing in the head; what's
(20) this they call it? [Intellect, someone whispers.] That's it, honey. What's that got to do with women's rights or Negroes' rights? If my cup won't hold but a pint, and yours holds a quart, wouldn't you be mean not to let me have my little half-measure full?
(25) Then that little man in black there, he says women can't have as much rights as men, 'cause Christ wasn't a woman! Where did your Christ come from? Where did your Christ come from? From God and a woman! Man had nothing to do with Him.
(30) If the first woman God ever made was strong enough to turn the world upside down all alone, these women together ought to be able to turn it back, and get it right side up again! And now they is asking to do it, the men better let them.

Obliged to you for hearing me.

(c. 1851)

19. The speaker of the passage is principally concerned with

    (A) suggesting ways to overcome oppression
    (B) criticizing the male authorities who have worsened her plight
    (C) asserting her capabilities as a woman
    (D) arguing that religious doctrine provides the basis for human rights
    (E) opposing racial stereotyping

20. The second paragraph is characterized by which of the following?

    I. Emotionally charged illustrations
    II. Rhetorical questions
    III. Parallel sentence structure

    (A) I only
    (B) II only
    (C) I and II only
    (D) II and III only
    (E) I, II, and III

21. In the second paragraph, the speaker sees men's attitude toward women as

    (A) wrongheaded
    (B) cruel
    (C) admiring
    (D) condemnatory
    (E) wary

22. The speaker points to "That man" (line 6) and "that little man in black" (line 25) in order to

    (A) make her message appealing to men
    (B) dramatize the challenges to women in a society controlled by men
    (C) claim that only women can really understand what she is saying
    (D) prove that spiritual power is superior to temporal authority
    (E) show that men's ideas have made little real difference in women's lives

GO ON TO THE NEXT PAGE ➤

23. Which of the following most nearly represents the speaker's argument in the third paragraph?

    (A) Women and Black people are denied half of their human rights.
    (B) The heart is more important than the head in deciding on human rights.
    (C) Human rights should not be based on preconceptions about intellectual ability.
    (D) Intellectual progress is dependent on acknowledgment of human rights.
    (E) Only by using one's intellect can one earn full human rights.

24. The speaker's tone is best described as

    (A) self-effacing and reserved
    (B) self-conscious and mannered
    (C) self-assured and passionate
    (D) self-justifying and impersonal
    (E) self-reliant and aloof

25. The language and style of the passage are best described as

    (A) informal and disorganized
    (B) colloquial and rhetorical
    (C) formal and rhythmical
    (D) objective and logical
    (E) measured and cool

26. The speaker shapes her presentation as a

    (A) moral tale for young people
    (B) theoretical feminist tract
    (C) personal letter to a close friend
    (D) speech before a sympathetic audience
    (E) lecture for inattentive students

GO ON TO THE NEXT PAGE

Questions 27-34. Read the following poem carefully before you choose your answers.

Permanently

One day the Nouns were clustered in the street.
An Adjective walked by, with her dark beauty.
The Nouns were struck, moved, changed.
The next day a Verb drove up, and created the Sentence.

Line
(5) Each Sentence says one thing—for example, "Although it was a dark
      rainy day when the Adjective walked by, I shall remember the
      pure and sweet expression on her face until the day I perish
      from the green, effective earth."
Or, "Will you please close the window, Andrew?"
Or, for example, "Thank you, the pink pot of flowers on the window
      sill has changed color recently to a light yellow, due to the
      heat from the boiler factory which exists nearby."

In the springtime the Sentences and the Nouns lay silently on the
      grass.
A lonely Conjunction here and there would call, "And! But!"
(10) But the Adjective did not emerge.

As the Adjective is lost in the sentence,
So I am lost in your eyes, ears, nose, and throat—
You have enchanted me with a single kiss
Which can never be undone
Until the destruction of language.

(1962)

27. Which of the following best describes the nature of the poem as a whole?

(A) A pastoral fantasy
(B) A playful love poem
(C) A serious meditation on the nature of language
(D) A bitter satire on the pedantry of grammarians
(E) A narrative focused on a specific occasion

28. Which of the following does the first section (lines 1-4) imply?

(A) The adjective is shy and embarrassed.
(B) The adjective is essential to a sentence.
(C) The nouns are like young men idling on a street corner.
(D) The nouns are indifferent to their surroundings.
(E) The adjective brings forth both positive and negative aspects of nouns.

29. The first quoted sentence, " 'Although it was . . . earth' " (line 5), is characterized chiefly by

(A) active verbs
(B) lonely conjunctions
(C) syntax that parallels the third quoted sentence (line 7)
(D) an abundance of adjectives
(E) an implied insult to nouns and verbs

30. The diction of the third quoted sentence, " 'Thank you . . . nearby' " (line 7), is characterized by

(A) collective nouns
(B) complex metaphors
(C) forceful verbs
(D) abrupt contrasts
(E) stilted formality

GO ON TO THE NEXT PAGE

31. In line 12, the speaker uses "lost" to mean

    (A) reassured by
    (B) absorbed in
    (C) satisfied with
    (D) confused by
    (E) ignorant of

32. The "destruction of language" (line 15) metaphorically refers to the

    (A) end of a romance
    (B) end of time
    (C) misuse of words by poets
    (D) death of the speaker's loved one
    (E) substitution of action for words

33. The last three lines emphasize which of the following?

    (A) The steadfastness of the speaker's love
    (B) The inevitable destructiveness of time
    (C) The fragility of human language
    (D) The ambiguity of memory
    (E) The unpredictability of the speaker's emotions

34. The speaker's tone in the last section (lines 11-15) is

    (A) solemn and apologetic
    (B) proud and selfish
    (C) sincere and fervent
    (D) disheartened and resentful
    (E) cynical and ominous

GO ON TO THE NEXT PAGE

Questions 35-41. Read the following passage carefully before you choose your answers.

It seems that Miss Pole had a cousin, once or twice removed, who had offered to Miss Matty long ago. Now this cousin lived four or five
Line
(5) miles from Cranford on his own estate; but his property was not large enough to entitle him to a rank higher than yeoman or, rather, with something of the "pride which apes humility," he had refused to push himself on, as so many of his class had done, into the ranks of the
(10) squires. He would not allow himself to be called Thomas Holbrook, Esq; he even sent back letters with this address, telling the postmistress at Cranford that his name was Mr. Thomas Holbrook, yeoman. He rejected all domestic
(15) innovations: he would have the house-door stand open in summer and shut in winter, without knocker or bell to summon a servant. The closed fist or the knob of a stick did this office for him if he found the door locked. He
(20) despised every refinement which had not its root deep down in humanity. If people were not ill, he saw no necessity for moderating his voice. He spoke the dialect of the country in perfection and constantly used it in conversation; although
(25) Miss Pole (who gave me these particulars) added that he read aloud more beautifully and with more feeling than anyone she had ever heard except the late rector.
"And how came Miss Matilda not to marry
(30) him?" asked I.
"Oh, I don't know. She was willing enough, I think; but you know cousin Thomas would not have been enough of a gentleman for the rector and Miss Jenkyns."
(35) "Well! but they were not to marry him," said I, impatiently.
"No; but they did not like Miss Matty to marry below her rank. You know she was the rector's daughter, and somehow they are related
(40) to Sir Peter Arley: Miss Jenkyns thought a deal of that."
"Poor Miss Matty!" said I.
"Nay, now, I don't know anything more than that he offered and was refused. Miss Matty
(45) may not like him—and Miss Jenkyns might never have said a word—it's only a guess of mine."
"How old is he?" I asked after a pause of castle-building.
(50) "He must be about seventy, I think, my dear," said Miss Pole, blowing up my castle, as if by gunpowder, into small fragments.

(1853)

35. This passage is best characterized as

(A) an anecdotal description
(B) a personal confession
(C) an emotional narrative
(D) a humorous parody
(E) a formal report

36. The speaker uses the expression " 'pride which apes humility' " (line 7) to indicate that Mr. Holbrook

(A) is justly proud of the accuracy of his self-perception
(B) prefers his genuine humility to the pride of squires
(C) suspects that the two emotions are, in effect, identical
(D) takes pride in seeming self-abasing
(E) judges his own conduct by another's standards

37. The account of Mr. Holbrook's reaction to letters addressed to Thomas Holbrook, Esq., serves to

(A) demonstrate his regret that the world does not fit his high standards
(B) illustrate his sense of superiority to the employees of the post office
(C) mock his behavior by showing a foolish application of his values
(D) reveal his virtues to the reader in a single, highly detailed encounter
(E) deride his way of life by exposing his actual ambitions in society

38. Miss Pole's description of Mr. Holbrook's skill at reading aloud adds to the portrayal of his character by

(A) implying that his customary speech is partly an affectation
(B) suggesting that his education was unsuitable for a squire
(C) proving that his view of humanity was highly emotional
(D) betraying his secret desire to be the center of attention
(E) unmasking his true perception of himself as a gentleman

GO ON TO THE NEXT PAGE

39. The conversation indicates that the rector and Miss Jenkyns resembled Mr. Holbrook in their

(A) desire to criticize society
(B) consciousness of social rank
(C) respect for Miss Matty's personal wishes
(D) determination to disregard their civic duties
(E) confidence in their superiority to all others

40. In lines 51-52, the speaker compares Miss Pole's words to gunpowder in order to emphasize the

(A) conflict between Miss Pole's stated opinion and her actual feelings
(B) effect of the speaker's tendency to read hidden meanings into harmless words
(C) contradiction between the speaker's speculative tone and Miss Pole's authoritative words
(D) portrayal of the speaker's dismay that Miss Pole has deceived her
(E) suddenness with which the speaker's illusions vanish

41. Which of the following best represents the theme of the passage as a whole?

(A) The selfishness of a refusal to marry
(B) The exaggerated importance of class distinctions
(C) The necessity for family pride in a small community
(D) The difficulty of arranging an appropriate marriage
(E) The problems of a lonely farmer

GO ON TO THE NEXT PAGE ➔

Questions 42-51. Read the following poems carefully before you choose your answers.

Limits

Who knows this or that?
Hark in the wall to the rat:
Since the world was, he has gnawed;
Line Of his wisdom, of his fraud
(5) What dost thou know?
In the wretched little beast
Is life and heart,
Child and parent,
Not without relation
(10) To fruitful field and sun and moon.
What art thou? His wicked eye
Is cruel to thy cruelty.

(c.1841)

[The Rat is the concisest Tenant]

The Rat is the concisest Tenant.
He pays no Rent.
Repudiates the Obligation—
On Schemes intent

Line
(5) Balking our Wit
To sound or circumvent—
Hate cannot harm
A Foe so reticent—
Neither Decree prohibit him—
Lawfull as Equilibrium.

(c. 1876)

42. The title "Limits" refers primarily to the

(A) boundary between the natural and the super-natural
(B) limitations on animals' understanding of human beings
(C) border between the harmful and the benevolent in nature
(D) bounds of human understanding of the world
(E) finite resources of the natural world

43. In "Limits," the speaker refers to "fruitful field and sun and moon" (line 10) in order to

(A) present the rat as both eternal and bounded by time
(B) assert a connection between positive aspects of nature and the rat
(C) contrast the innocent plant world with the cruel animal world
(D) contrast the spacious natural world with the narrow indoor world of the rat
(E) contrast the destructiveness of the rat with the richness of nature

GO ON TO THE NEXT PAGE

44. Which of the following can be used to support the argument that in line 11 of "Limits," "thou" refers not to the rat but to a human being?

   I. The use of "his" in line 4
   II. The use of "thou" in line 5
   III. The use of "His" and "thy" in lines 11-12

   (A) III only
   (B) I and II only
   (C) I and III only
   (D) II and III only
   (E) I, II, and III

45. The last sentence (lines 11-12) of "Limits" suggests that

   (A) human beings see cruelty in the rat because of their own cruelty
   (B) nature intended the rat to be a cruel creature
   (C) if the rat could think in moral terms, it would see the evil in human beings
   (D) the cruelty of the rat provokes cruelty in humans
   (E) the rat's cruelty makes human behavior seem less wicked

46. In "The Rat is the concisest Tenant," the word "sound" (line 6) is best understood to be a

   (A) verb meaning "signal"
   (B) verb meaning "investigate"
   (C) verb meaning "make a noise"
   (D) noun meaning "noise"
   (E) noun meaning "channel"

47. Which of the following from "The Rat is the concisest Tenant" is most similar in its effect and meaning to the questions "Who knows this or that?" (line 1) and "What dost thou know?" (line 5) in "Limits"?

   (A) "He pays no Rent" (line 2)
   (B) "On Schemes intent" (line 4)
   (C) "Balking our Wit" (line 5)
   (D) "Hate cannot harm" (line 7)
   (E) "Lawfull as Equilibrium" (line 10)

48. The style of both poems can best be described as

   (A) logical and orderly
   (B) cryptic and spare
   (C) moralistic and allegorical
   (D) leisurely and descriptive
   (E) earthy and sardonic

49. Both poems imply all of the following EXCEPT:

   (A) Rats are usually considered to be disagreeable creatures.
   (B) Rats and humans are in conflict.
   (C) Rats are aware of human feelings toward them.
   (D) Rats behave in accordance with their nature.
   (E) Rats are part of the natural order.

50. Compared to the speaker in "Limits," the speaker in "The Rat is the concisest Tenant" sees the rat as

   (A) more unlike human beings
   (B) more clearly domesticated
   (C) more trusting
   (D) less harmful to human society
   (E) less intelligent in its relations with human beings

51. The two poems share which of the following themes?

   I. The limitations of human knowledge
   II. The unknowability of the natural world
   III. The importance of knowledge as a human trait

   (A) I only
   (B) I and II only
   (C) I and III only
   (D) II and III only
   (E) I, II, and III

GO ON TO THE NEXT PAGE

Questions 52-61. Read the following passage carefully before you choose your answers.

I have one word to say upon the subject of
profound writers, who are grown very numerous
of late; and I know very well, the judicious
Line world is resolved to list me in that number. I
(5) conceive therefore, as to the business of being
profound, that it is with writers as with wells—a
person with good eyes may see to the bottom of
the deepest, provided any water be there; and
that often, when there is nothing in the world at
(10) the bottom, besides dryness and dirt, though it
be but a yard and half under ground, it shall
pass, however, for wondrous deep, upon no
wiser a reason than because it is wondrous dark.
I am now trying an experiment very frequent
(15) among modern authors; which is to write upon
Nothing; when the subject is utterly exhausted,
to let the pen still move on; by some called the
ghost of wit, delighting to walk after the death
of its body. And to say the truth, there seems to
(20) be no part of knowledge in fewer hands, than
that of discerning when to have done. By the
time that an author has writ out a book, he and
his readers are become old acquaintances, and
grow very loth to part; so that I have sometimes
(25) known it to be in writing, as in visiting, where
the ceremony of taking leave has employed more
time than the whole conversation before.

(1704)

52. In terms of the comparison of writers to wells,
"water" (line 8) is best understood as

(A) imagination   (B) content   (C) style
(D) practical value   (E) mere appearance

53. Which of the following is the most appropriate
interpretation of the figurative language in
lines 6-8 ("it is . . . be there")?

(A) If the writing is truly profound, it is beyond
ordinary human understanding.
(B) If the writing has any substance, it can be
understood by an intelligent reader.
(C) The true meaning of a work is whatever an
intelligent reader wants it to be.
(D) If writing is to be truly profound, the ideas
must be conveyed in a complicated style.
(E) A complicated style of writing is often a
disguise for a shallow intelligence.

54. Given the terms of comparison in lines 6-13,
"dryness and dirt" (line 10) can be best
interpreted as

(A) inflexible beliefs
(B) conventional attitudes
(C) pornographic fancies
(D) barren thoughts
(E) down-to-earth realities

55. The speaker uses the words "wondrous" (lines 12
and 13) to convey

(A) the naïve enthusiasm of uncritical readers
(B) an awed response to genuine literary achieve-
ments
(C) critical approval of literary and philosophical
profundity
(D) the response the speaker wants others to have
toward the speaker's own works
(E) a perverse delight in light and shallow literature

56. In its metaphorical context, "body" (line 19)
refers to

(A) a completed text
(B) an author
(C) an edited and published work
(D) the author's talent
(E) the substance of the work

57. Which of the following best paraphrases the
sentence "And to say the truth . . . to have done"
(lines 19-21) ?

(A) Few authors know when to stop writing.
(B) Few authors really know how to express
themselves clearly.
(C) Authors seldom get their works into the
proper hands.
(D) Authors seldom know where to obtain the
knowledge they require.
(E) Authors seldom know anything about what
other authors have done.

GO ON TO THE NEXT PAGE

58. Which of the following best defines "his readers" in line 23 ?

    (A) The readers who have purchased the author's work
    (B) Friends the author has made through his writings
    (C) Loyal friends the author can depend upon to read his books
    (D) Acquaintances the author has sent his manuscript to
    (E) The readers the author imagines he is addressing as he writes

59. Given the speaker's attitude toward modern authors, the word "profound" (line 2) is best understood to mean

    (A) engagingly witty
    (B) authentically philosophical
    (C) intellectually pretentious
    (D) morbidly pessimistic
    (E) psychologically deep

60. Given the speaker's attitude toward modern authors and their readers, "judicious" (line 3) is best interpreted as

    (A) unnecessarily precise
    (B) acutely discriminating
    (C) intellectually challenging
    (D) critically inept
    (E) unpleasantly hypercritical

61. The second paragraph wittily illustrates

    (A) a philosophical argument on the nature of existence
    (B) the notion that most writers are truly profound
    (C) the nature of the relationship between writers and readers
    (D) the importance of leave-taking ceremonies as social convention
    (E) the very technique that the speaker is criticizing

STOP

IF YOU FINISH BEFORE TIME IS CALLED, YOU MAY CHECK YOUR WORK ON THIS TEST ONLY.
DO NOT TURN TO ANY OTHER TEST IN THIS BOOK.

ACKNOWLEDGEMENTS

Reprinted by permission of the publishers and Trustees of Amherst College from The Poems of Emily Dickinson, edited by Thomas H. Johnson, Cambridge, Mass.: The Belknap Press of Harvard University Press, Copyright 1951, (c)1955, 1979, 1983 by the President and Fellows of Harvard College.

How to Score the SAT Subject Test in Literature

When you take the SAT Subject Test in Literature, your answer sheet will be "read" by a scanning machine that will record your responses to the questions. Then a computer will compare your answers with the correct answers and produce your raw score. You get one point for each correct answer. For each wrong answer, you lose one-fourth of a point. Questions you omit (and any for which you mark more than one answer) are not counted. This raw score is converted to a scaled score that is reported to you and to the colleges you specify.

Worksheet 1. Finding Your Raw Test Score

STEP 1: Table A lists the correct answers for all the questions on the SAT Subject Test in Literature that is reproduced in this book. It also serves as a worksheet for you to calculate your raw score.

- Compare your answers with those given in the table.
- Put a check in the column marked "Right" if your answer is correct.
- Put a check in the column marked "Wrong" if your answer is incorrect.
- Leave both columns blank if you omitted the question.

STEP 2: Count the number of right answers.

Enter the total here: _____

STEP 3: Count the number of wrong answers.

Enter the total here: _____

STEP 4: Multiply the number of wrong answers by .250.

Enter the product here: _____

STEP 5: Subtract the result obtained in Step 4 from the total you obtained in Step 2.

Enter the result here: _____

STEP 6: Round the number obtained in Step 5 to the nearest whole number.

Enter the result here: _____

The number you obtained in Step 6 is your raw score.

TABLE A
Answers to the SAT Subject Test in Literature, Form K2-30AC, and Percentage of Students Answering Each Question Correctly

Question Number	Correct Answer	Right	Wrong	Percentage of Students Answering the Question Correctly*	Question Number	Correct Answer	Right	Wrong	Percentage of Students Answering the Question Correctly*
1	A			83	32	B			67
2	D			49	33	A			74
3	B			96	34	C			87
4	E			80	35	A			56
5	D			80	36	D			24
6	B			62	37	C			30
7	C			82	38	A			43
8	A			74	39	B			71
9	C			67	40	E			65
10	B			68	41	B			83
11	E			24	42	D			66
12	C			67	43	B			41
13	D			61	44	E			25
14	D			61	45	A			63
15	A			78	46	B			29
16	E			76	47	C			51
17	E			72	48	B			27
18	C			36	49	C			52
19	C			62	50	A			29
20	E			58	51	B			45
21	A			56	52	B			48
22	B			71	53	B			50
23	C			58	54	D			73
24	C			77	55	A			41
25	B			60	56	E			64
26	D			60	57	A			61
27	B			70	58	E			64
28	C			53	59	C			50
29	D			87	60	D			38
30	E			32	61	E			68
31	B			90					

*These percentages are based on an analysis of the answer sheets of a random sample of 9,644 students who took the original form of this test in June 1995, and whose mean score was 573. They may be used as an indication of the relative difficulty of a particular question. Each percentage may also be used to predict the likelihood that a typical SAT Subject Test in Literature candidate will answer that question correctly on this edition of the test.

Finding Your Scaled Score

When you take SAT Subject Tests, the scores sent to the colleges you specify are reported on the College Board scale, which ranges from 200 to 800. You can convert your practice test score to a scaled score by using Table B. To find your scaled score, locate your raw score in the left-hand column of Table B; the corresponding score in the right-hand column is your scaled score. For example, a raw score of 40 on this particular edition of the SAT Subject Test in Literature corresponds to a scaled score of 660.

Raw scores are converted to scaled scores to ensure that a score earned on any one edition of a particular Subject Test is comparable to the same scaled score earned on any other edition of the same Subject Test. Because some editions of tests may be slightly easier or more difficult than others, scaled scores are adjusted so that they indicate the same level of performance regardless of the edition of the test taken and the ability of the group that takes it. Thus, for example, a score of 400 on one edition of a test taken at a particular administration indicates the same level of achievement as a score of 400 on a different edition of the test taken at a different administration.

When you take the SAT Subject Tests during a national administration, your scores are likely to differ somewhat from the scores you obtain on the tests in this book. People perform at different levels at different times for reasons unrelated to the tests themselves. The precision of any test is also limited because it represents only a sample of all the possible questions that could be asked.

TABLE B
Scaled Score Conversion Table
Literature Subject Test (Form K2-30AC)

Raw Score	Scaled Score	Raw Score	Scaled Score	Raw Score	Scaled Score
61	800	32	590	3	330
60	800	31	580	2	320
59	800	30	570	1	310
58	800	29	560	0	300
57	800	28	550	−1	300
56	800	27	540	−2	290
55	790	26	530	−3	280
54	780	25	520	−4	270
53	780	24	510	−5	260
52	770	23	500	−6	250
51	760	22	490	−7	240
50	750	21	490	−8	240
49	740	20	480	−9	230
48	730	19	470	−10	220
47	720	18	460	−11	210
46	710	17	450	−12	200
45	700	16	440	−13	200
44	700	15	430	−14	200
43	690	14	420	−15	200
42	680	13	410		
41	670	12	410		
40	660	11	400		
39	650	10	390		
38	640	9	380		
37	630	8	370		
36	620	7	360		
35	620	6	350		
34	610	5	350		
33	600	4	340		

Reviewing Your Performance on the Literature Subject Test

After you score your test, analyze your performance—consider the following questions:

Did you run out of time before reaching the end of the test?

If so, you may need to pace yourself better. For example, maybe you spent too much time on one or two hard questions. A better approach might be to skip the questions you can't answer right away and try answering all the questions that remain on the test. Then if there's time, go back to the questions you skipped.

Did you take a long time reading the directions?

You will save time when you take the test by learning the directions to the Literature Subject Test ahead of time. Each minute you spend reading directions during the test is a minute that you could use to answer questions.

How did you handle questions you were unsure of?

If you were able to eliminate one or more of the answer choices as wrong and guess from the remaining ones, your approach probably worked to your advantage. On the other hand, making haphazard guesses or omitting questions without trying to eliminate choices could cost you valuable points.

How difficult were the questions for you compared with other students who took the test?

Table A shows you how difficult the multiple-choice questions were for the group of students who took this test during its national administration. The right-hand column gives the percentage of students who answered each question correctly.

A question answered correctly by almost everyone in the group is obviously an easy question. For example, 96 percent of the students answered question 3 correctly. But only 24 percent answered question 36 correctly.

Keep in mind that these percentages are based on just one group of students. They would probably be different if another group of students took the test.

If you missed several easy questions, go back and try to find out why: Did the questions cover material you haven't yet reviewed? Did you misunderstand the directions?

Chapter 2
United States History

Purpose

The emphasis of this test is on United States history from pre-Columbian times to the present as well as basic social science concepts, methods, and generalizations as they are found in the study of history. It is designed independent of any text book or instructional approach.

Format

This is a one-hour test with 90 to 95 multiple-choice questions. The questions cover political, economic, social, intellectual, and cultural history as well as foreign policy. The following chart shows you what content the test covers and the approximate percentages of questions covering that content.

Material Covered	Approximate Percentage of Test
Political History	32–36
Economic History	18–20
Social History	18–22
Intellectual and Cultural History	10–12
Foreign Policy	13–17

Social science concepts, methods, and generalizations are incorporated in the material above.

Periods Covered

Pre-Columbian history to 1789	20
1790 to 1898	40
1899 to the present	40

Recommended Preparation

The only essential preparation is a sound, one-year course in U.S. history at the college-preparatory level. Most of the test questions are based on material commonly taught in U.S. history courses in secondary schools, although some of the material may be covered in other social studies courses. Knowledge gained from social studies courses and from outside reading could be helpful. No one textbook or method of instruction is considered better than another.

The questions may:

1. Test recall of basic information and require you to know facts, terms, concepts, and generalizations.
2. Require you to analyze and interpret material such as graphs, charts, paintings, cartoons, photographs, and maps.
3. Test your understanding of important aspects of U.S. history.
4. Require you to relate to given data.
5. Require you to evaluate data for a given purpose, basing your judgment either on internal evidence, such as proof and logical consistency, or on external criteria, such as comparison with other works, established standards, and theories.

Familiarize yourself with directions in advance. The directions in this book are identical to those that appear on the test.

Score

The total score is reported on the 200-to-800 scale.

Sample Questions

The types of questions used in the test and the abilities they measure are described below. Questions may be presented as separate items or in sets based on quotations, maps, pictures, graphs, or tables.

Directions: Each of the questions or incomplete statements below is followed by five suggested answers or completions. Select the one that is best in each case and then fill in the corresponding oval on the answer sheet.

Some questions require you to know facts, terms, concepts, and generalizations. They test your recall of basic information and your understanding of significant aspects of U.S. history and the social studies. Question 1 is a sample of this type.

1. Harriet Tubman was known as the "Moses" of her people because she
   (A) helped slaves escape from the South
   (B) was instrumental in bringing about suffrage reform
   (C) advocated emigration to Africa for Black people
   (D) organized mass civil rights demonstrations
   (E) traveled as a lay minister preaching the gospel

To answer question 1, you need to know that Harriet Tubman was a notable African American abolitionist. As the use of the name "Moses" may help you to remember, Tubman led many slaves to freedom in the North along the route of the Underground Railroad as referred to in the correct answer (A). This achievement is not noted in any of the other choices which describe activities that Tubman did not pursue.

Some questions require you to analyze and interpret materials. Question 2, based on the chart below, illustrates a question that tests your ability to use these skills.

Popular Vote for Presidential Electors, Georgia, 1848 and 1852

	Democratic Electors	Whig Electors	Webster Electors
1848	44,809	47,538	———
1852	40,516	16,660	5,324

2. Using the table above, one might conclude that the most plausible explanation for the Georgia Democrats' victory in 1852, following their defeat in 1848, was that
   (A) many new voters increased the turnout in 1852, to the advantage of the Democrats
   (B) many voters abstained from voting in 1852, to the disadvantage of the Whigs
   (C) Webster, who had not run in 1848, drew sufficient votes from the Whigs to cost them the election of 1852
   (D) the Democrats, who had run a highly unpopular candidate in 1848, ran a highly popular candidate in 1852
   (E) the Democrats cast fraudulent ballots to increase their share of the votes in 1852

To answer question 2, you must analyze the electoral data given for 1848 and 1852, noting that the voter turnout dropped dramatically in 1852 and that the Whigs suffered a much larger decline in voter turnout than did the Democrats. As a consequence, the Whigs lost their majority position. Choices (A), (C), (D), and (E) are not logically consistent with this data. For example, choice (C) is incorrect because the table shows that the Democratic Electors received more votes than the Whig and Webster Electors combined. Choice (B) is the correct answer because it is the only plausible explanation for the change in the fortunes of the Georgia Democrats.

Other questions test both your ability to analyze material as well as your ability to recall information related to the materials, or to make inferences and interpolations based on the material. Questions 3, 4, 5, and 6 are illustrations of questions that test a combination of interpretation and recall.

3. "What is man born for but to be a reformer, a remaker of what man has made; a renouncer of lies; a restorer of truth and good, imitating that great Nature which embosoms us all, and which sleeps no moment on an old past, but every hour repairs herself, yielding every morning a new day, and with every pulsation a new life?"

    These sentiments are most characteristic of
    (A) fundamentalism
    (B) Social Darwinism
    (C) pragmatism
    (D) neoorthodoxy
    (E) transcendentalism

Several elements in the quotation suggest which option is the correct answer. The emphasis that the quotation places on reform, on nature as a source of moral truth, and on the infinite possibilities open to people mark it as an example of the thought of the transcendentalist movement. This combination of elements is not pertinent to any of the other choices. Even if you do not know the source of the material, your understanding of the nature of transcendentalism should lead you to choose (E), the correct answer.

Questions 4–5 refer to the following map.

4. The controversy with Great Britain over control of the shaded section was settled during the presidency of
   (A) John Quincy Adams
   (B) James K. Polk
   (C) Franklin Pierce
   (D) James Buchanan
   (E) Andrew Johnson

5. To the northwest of the area shown on the map is a continental territory purchased by Secretary of State William H. Seward from
   (A) Great Britain
   (B) Canada
   (C) Russia
   (D) France
   (E) Spain

To answer question 4, you must interpret the map and recognize the shaded section as part of the Oregon territory. Since the Oregon dispute with Great Britain was settled during the presidency of James K. Polk, choice (B) is the correct answer.

To answer question 5, you must go beyond the content of the map in order to determine that the territory referred to in the question is Alaska. If you recall that Secretary of State Seward purchased the territory from Russia in 1867, you can choose the correct answer, (C).

BORN TO COMMAND.

OF VETO MEMORY.

HAD I BEEN CONSULTED.

KING ANDREW THE FIRST.

Courtesy of the New York Historical Society

6. The point of view expressed by this cartoon would probably have met with the approval of

    (A) Daniel Webster

    (B) James K. Polk

    (C) Martin Van Buren

    (D) Roger B. Taney

    (E) Stephen A. Douglas

To answer question 6, you must first note the anti-Jackson tone of the cartoon, which portrays King Andrew the First trampling the Constitution of the United States. You must then decide which of the choices given opposed Jackson's use of the veto to return important bills to Congress. Only the Whig Daniel Webster fits that description, so choice (A) is correct. The others were Democrats who either supported Andrew Jackson or were politically active at a later time.

Some questions require you to select or relate hypotheses, concepts, principles, or generalizations to given data. The questions may begin with concrete specifics and ask for the appropriate concept, or they may begin with a concept and apply it to particular problems or situations. Thus, you may need to use inductive and deductive reasoning. Questions 7 and 8 are examples of questions in this category.

7. From 1870 to 1930, the trend in industry was for hours to be generally reduced, while both money wages and real wages rose. What factor was primarily responsible for this trend?

    (A) A reduction in profit margins

    (B) Minimum wage laws

    (C) Restriction of the labor supply

    (D) Increased output per hour of work

    (E) Right-to-work legislation

The best answer to this question is choice (D). To arrive at this answer, you must be aware that the trend referred to in the question came about primarily because of technological advances that resulted in increased productivity. None of the other answer choices satisfactorily accounts for all the conditions described in the question.

8. Which of the following wars of the United States would fit the description of a war neither lost nor won?

      I.   **The War of 1812**

     II.   **The Mexican War**

    III.   **The Spanish-American War**

    IV.   **The Second World War**

(A) I only

(B) II only

(C) I and III only

(D) II and IV only

(E) III and IV only

In answering question 8, you must recognize that a war not won, though not necessarily lost, is one in which a country either fails to achieve clear victory on the battlefield or fails to sign a peace treaty that is definitive and fulfills its goals. Only the War of 1812 is an illustration of the kind of war defined by the question. That war was ended by The Treaty of Ghent, which provided for the *Status quo ante bellum*, or a return to things as they had been before the war. Thus, (A) is the best answer.

Some questions require you to judge the value of data for a given purpose, either basing your judgment on internal evidence, such as accuracy and logical consistency, or on external criteria, such as accepted historical scholarship. Question 9 is an illustration of this kind of question.

9. Which of the following would most probably provide the widest range of information for a historian wishing to analyze the social composition of an American city in the 1880s?

   (A) The minutes of the city council

   (B) A debutante's diary

   (C) A manuscript census tabulating the residence, ethnicity, occupation, and wealth of each city resident

   (D) Precinct-level voting returns in a closely contested mayoral election held in a presidential election year

   (E) A survey of slum housing conditions carried out by a Social Gospel minister in the year following several epidemics

In answering this question, you must be able to eliminate from consideration choices that offer information about the city that is either irrelevant or less relevant than other options to understanding the social composition of the city, choices (A) and (D). You must also eliminate choices that offer relevant information but are limited to a particular section of the population of the city, choices (B) and (E). Choice (C), the correct answer, contains the widest range of information about the social composition of a city.

U.S. History Test

The test that follows is an actual, recently administered SAT Subject Test in U.S. History. To get an idea of what a real administration is like, take the test under conditions as close as possible to those of a national administration:

- Set aside an hour when you can take the test uninterrupted. Make sure you complete the test in one sitting.

- Sit at a desk or table with no other books or papers. Dictionaries, other books, or notes are not allowed in the test room.

- Time yourself by placing a clock or kitchen timer in front of you.

- Tear out an answer sheet from the back of this book and fill it in just as you would on the day of the test. One answer sheet can be used for up to three Subject Tests.

- Read the instructions that precede the practice test. During the actual administration you will be asked to read them before answering test questions.

- After you finish the practice test, read the sections "How to Score the SAT Subject Test in U.S. History" and "Reviewing Your Performance on the U.S. History Subject Test."

- Actual test and answer sheets will indicate circles, not ovals.

Form K-3RAC2

UNITED STATES HISTORY TEST

The top portion of the section of the answer sheet that you will use in taking the United States History Test must be filled in exactly as shown in the illustration below. Note carefully that you have to do all of the following on your answer sheet.

1. Print UNITED STATES HISTORY on the line under the words "Subject Test (print)."

2. In the shaded box labeled "Test Code" fill in four ovals:

   —Fill in oval 2 in the row labeled V.

   —Fill in oval 5 in the row labeled W.

   —Fill in oval 5 in the row labeled X.

   —Fill in oval C in the row labeled Y.

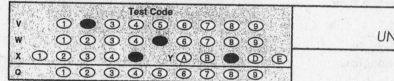

3. Please answer the two questions below by filling in the appropriate ovals in the row labeled Q on the answer sheet. The information you provide is for statistical purposes only and will not affect your score on the test.

Question I

How many semesters of United States History have you taken from grade 9 to the present? (If you are taking United States History this semester, count it as a full semester.) Fill in only one oval of ovals 1-4.

- One semester or less
- Two semesters
- Three semesters
- Four or more semesters

—Fill in oval 1.
—Fill in oval 2.
—Fill in oval 3.
—Fill in oval 4.

Question II

Which, if any, of the following social studies courses have you taken from grade 9 to the present? (Fill in ALL ovals that apply.)

- One or more semesters of government
- One or more semesters of economics
- One or more semesters of geography
- One or more semesters of psychology
- One or more semesters of sociology
  or anthropology

—Fill in oval 5.
—Fill in oval 6.
—Fill in oval 7.
—Fill in oval 8.

—Fill in oval 9.

If you have taken none of these social studies courses, leave the ovals 5 through 9 blank.

When the supervisor gives the signal, turn the page and begin the United States History Test. There are 100 numbered ovals on the answer sheet and 90 questions in the United States History Test. Therefore, use only ovals 1 to 90 for recording your answers.

39

UNITED STATES HISTORY TEST

1. Indentured servitude in the British colonies of North America was primarily a

   (A) method by which the colonies initially secured a workforce
   (B) device for preventing the emancipation of slaves
   (C) technique for regulating the size of the lower classes
   (D) means by which England rid itself of criminals
   (E) process by which young people learned skills

2. "My master used to ask us children, 'Do your folks pray at night?' We said 'No,' 'cause our folks had told us what to say. But the Lord have mercy, there was plenty of that going on. They'd pray, 'Lord, deliver us from under bondage.' "

   The statement above was probably made by a

   (A) Lowell mill worker who had escaped the poverty of a family farm
   (B) former indentured servant recalling praying for the end of the term of servitude
   (C) former slave criticizing the lack of religious worship in the quarters
   (D) former slave remembering the need to conceal one's thoughts under slavery
   (E) southern minister giving a sermon on prayer in the antebellum era

3. Which of the following was a major issue dividing the political parties during Andrew Jackson's presidency?

   (A) A national bank
   (B) Extension of the suffrage
   (C) Immigration
   (D) Military expenditures
   (E) Railroad construction

4. All of the following were true of the industrial working class of late-nineteenth-century America EXCEPT:

   (A) It was composed of native-born as well as immigrant workers.
   (B) Working-class neighborhoods were sometimes segregated ethnically.
   (C) Women and children frequently worked in factories.
   (D) Most workers belonged to unions.
   (E) Immigrants were hired primarily as unskilled and semiskilled workers.

5. The chief reason given by Woodrow Wilson for requesting a declaration of war against Germany in 1917 was the

   (A) refusal of Germany to accept the Fourteen Points as a basis for peace negotiations
   (B) need to establish a League of Nations after the war
   (C) resumption of unrestricted submarine warfare by Germany
   (D) economic rivalry between the United States and Germany
   (E) cultural ties between the United States and England

GO ON TO THE NEXT PAGE

K-3RAC2

6. "I have no doubt young criminals got their ideas of the romance of crime from moving pictures. I believe moving pictures are doing as much harm today as saloons did in the days of the open saloon, especially to the young. Movies are running day and night, Sunday and every other day, the year round, and in most jurisdictions without any regulation by censorship."

The speaker quoted above would most likely agree with which of the following statements?

(A) Blue laws should be repealed as unnecessary censorship.
(B) The content of movies needs to be monitored to prevent the corruption of youth.
(C) The censorship of technologies like radio and movies is not feasible.
(D) The culture of the 1920's was a vast improvement over the decadent "Gay Nineties."
(E) Outlawing movies would only cause a crime wave similar to that following Prohibition.

7. In the 50 years following the Second World War, inflation has meant a continuous increase in

(A) tax rates
(B) purchasing power
(C) exports
(D) prices
(E) stock market activity

8. Which of the following statements about social trends in the United States between 1945 and 1970 is INCORRECT?

(A) There was an overall increase in college enrollment.
(B) The proportion of blue-collar jobs in the economy decreased.
(C) Increasing numbers of African American children attended racially integrated schools.
(D) There was an exodus of population from the cities to the suburbs.
(E) More and more women abandoned paid employment in order to return to the home.

9. Which of the following was the stated reason for the Supreme Court ruling in the 1960's that prayer and formal religious instruction could not be required in public schools?

(A) Atheism and agnosticism had spread throughout American society.
(B) Church membership in America had declined rapidly.
(C) Prayer was no longer a significant way in which Americans expressed their religious faith.
(D) Prayer in public schools violated the principle of separation of church and state.
(E) Prayer in public schools encouraged the renewal of religious tests for public office.

GO ON TO THE NEXT PAGE

© 1991 The Pittsburgh Press

10. Which of the following best summarizes the idea expressed in the 1991 cartoon above?

(A) Although the President claimed otherwise, the primary interest of the United States in the Persian Gulf War was access to oil.

(B) The United States government was worried about the ecological impact of the oil spills that occurred during the Persian Gulf War.

(C) The United States was justified in using military force because doing so was necessary to keep the price of oil low.

(D) A glut of oil production in the Middle East was the main cause of the Persian Gulf War.

(E) The United States should avoid involvement in disputes between governments in the Middle East.

GO ON TO THE NEXT PAGE

11. Which of the following actions would be INCONSISTENT with the English policy of mercantilism as it was applied to the North American colonies?

    (A) Requiring the colonists to export specified products only to England
    (B) Encouraging the colonies to produce articles that England otherwise would have to import from Europe
    (C) Encouraging the settlement of colonies suitable for the growing of tropical and semitropical staple crops
    (D) Encouraging the colonies to produce articles also produced in England
    (E) Prohibiting the importation of goods into the colonies except in English ships

12. The Great Awakening was a movement that

    (A) strengthened the position of the established clergy
    (B) appealed only to the lower classes
    (C) denied individual responsibility
    (D) excluded women and African Americans from religious services
    (E) emphasized inner experience as the principal way of discovering truth

13. In the first half of the nineteenth century, all of the following goals had widespread support among women reformers EXCEPT the

    (A) abolition of slavery
    (B) right of women to vote
    (C) liberalization of abortion laws
    (D) passage of temperance laws
    (E) right of married women to own property

14. In the United States all of the following changed in significant ways between 1850 and 1900 EXCEPT the

    (A) scale of business enterprise
    (B) election of women to national office
    (C) legal status of the African American population
    (D) technology of communication
    (E) religious affiliation of the total population

15. The Interstate Commerce Act of 1887 sought to prevent

    (A) discrimination by the railroads against small customers
    (B) publication of railroad rate schedules
    (C) transportation of children across state lines for immoral purposes
    (D) shipment across state lines of goods produced in sweatshops
    (E) use of the federal mails for the dissemination of birth control information

16. Which of the following statements best represents the nativist attitude toward the influx of immigrants around 1900 ?

    (A) Slavs and Italians will be assimilated as easily into the American way of life as were earlier immigrant groups.
    (B) Ellis Island should be enlarged to accommodate the huge influx of immigrants who do not speak English.
    (C) Immigrants will work for low wages and break strikes, which will hurt all American workers.
    (D) Native-born Americans should organize to help find jobs and homes for new immigrants so that they can become citizens as quickly as possible.
    (E) Political machines in the large cities must be responsible for providing immigrants with food, shelter, and jobs in return for their votes.

17. Which statement best describes the treatment of Black soldiers in the United States Army during the First World War?

    (A) Black soldiers were integrated into White units on a basis of full military equality.
    (B) Black soldiers served in segregated units often commanded by White officers.
    (C) Black Americans were drafted into the armed forces but not allowed to enlist.
    (D) Black Americans were not allowed in the armed forces but were encouraged to move to factory jobs.
    (E) Because Black leaders opposed the war, the government placed Black soldiers only in noncombat positions.

GO ON TO THE NEXT PAGE

18. Which of the following had the widest audience among Americans in the 1920's?

    (A) Jazz festivals
    (B) Professional football
    (C) Television
    (D) Movies
    (E) Circuses

19. The economic policies of the New Deal are best described as a

    (A) carefully designed plan to change the United States business system from capitalism to socialism
    (B) series of hastily conceived temporary measures that pulled the economy out of the Depression by the start of President Franklin D. Roosevelt's third term
    (C) mixture of partly effective short-run measures against the Depression and enduring changes in the role of the federal government
    (D) program designed to equalize income for all Americans
    (E) political response to the demand for federal deficit spending voiced by Democratic party platforms since the candidacy of Woodrow Wilson

20. Which of the following did most to broaden participation in the political process?

    (A) The success of the States' rights movement
    (B) The Supreme Court decision in the case of *Brown* v. *Board of Education of Topeka*
    (C) The election of Franklin D. Roosevelt
    (D) The decline of the Ku Klux Klan
    (E) The Voting Rights Act of 1965

21. In the past 50 years in the House of Representatives, which of the following issues would most likely have resulted in a vote along party lines?

    (A) Federal aid to education
    (B) Civil rights legislation
    (C) Election of the Speaker of the House
    (D) Appropriations for foreign aid
    (E) Agricultural subsidies

22. From the sixteenth through the eighteenth century, the cultural patterns of the American Indians of the western plains were most dramatically influenced by

    (A) major changes in ecological conditions
    (B) contact with tribes from eastern coastal areas
    (C) the adoption of European military weaponry
    (D) the adoption of European agricultural techniques
    (E) the introduction of the horse by Spanish explorers

23. Many Americans believed the Articles of Confederation had which of the following problems?

    (A) They gave insufficient power to the central government.
    (B) They did not provide for a national legislature.
    (C) They could not be amended.
    (D) They were too long and complicated for the average person to understand.
    (E) They lacked a Bill of Rights.

24. An important reason why Thomas Jefferson recommended the purchase of Louisiana from France was his wish to

    (A) stimulate American manufacturing
    (B) enhance the role of Congress in acquiring new territories
    (C) embarrass the Federalists
    (D) secure western territory to help fulfill his ideal of an agrarian republic
    (E) follow advice given to him by Alexander Hamilton

25. In his book *Walden*, Henry David Thoreau did which of the following?

    (A) Described the unspoiled innocence of the American West.
    (B) Recorded his thoughts concerning the value of a life of simplicity and contemplation.
    (C) Argued that such modern inventions as the telegraph and the railroad were bringing about a higher quality of cultural life in America.
    (D) Offered his impressions of southern plantation life.
    (E) Portrayed a fictional utopian community where all live in peace and harmony.

GO ON TO THE NEXT PAGE

26. The primary reason the United States advanced the Open Door policy in 1899 was to

   (A) consolidate good relations between the United States and European countries holding leases in China
   (B) encourage Asian nations to protect Chinese interests
   (C) expand the effort of European nations to Westernize China
   (D) protect United States missionaries in China
   (E) protect United States trading opportunities in China

27. A major difference between the Ku Klux Klan of the Reconstruction period and the Klan of the 1920's was that the Klan of the 1920's

   (A) was hostile toward immigrants, non-Protestants, and African Americans
   (B) was not particularly hostile toward African Americans
   (C) expressed hostility only toward African Americans
   (D) practiced vigilantism
   (E) was confined to the South in its activities and membership

28. Which of the following contributed LEAST to the Great Depression?

   (A) Weaknesses in the banking system
   (B) Inflationary wage settlements
   (C) The depressed agricultural sector
   (D) Production in excess of consumption
   (E) The stock market crash

29. Prior to its declaration of war in December 1941, the United States government gave help to the Allies by

   (A) supplying war materials to the rebel forces in the Spanish Civil War
   (B) placing an embargo on the export of oil and metal to Fascist Italy
   (C) providing Lend-Lease aid
   (D) denying aid to the Soviet Union
   (E) encouraging the efforts of the America First Committee

30. Senator I: This amendment removes the incentive system from industry.

   Senator II: This amendment will abolish capitalism.

   Senator III: This amendment helps the worst elements in the country at the expense of the best elements in the country.

   This discussion would most likely have taken place during the debate on which of the following constitutional amendments?

   (A) Granting the vote to women
   (B) Extending due process of law to all citizens
   (C) Instituting direct election of senators
   (D) Creating a federal income tax
   (E) Abolishing slavery and indentured servitude

GO ON TO THE NEXT PAGE

Hy Rosen, in Albany *Times-Union*

31. Which of the following international incidents is the subject of the cartoon above?

    (A) The Soviet invasion of Finland in 1939
    (B) The Soviet blockade of Berlin in 1948
    (C) The Hungarian Revolution of 1956
    (D) The U-2 affair of 1960
    (E) The Cuban missile crisis of 1962

GO ON TO THE NEXT PAGE

32. Highly developed astronomy, mathematics, calendar systems, and agricultural techniques characterized the pre-Columbian cultures of

    (A) Mesoamerica
    (B) the Great Plains
    (C) the Eastern Woodlands
    (D) California
    (E) the Subarctic

33. The first decade of the English settlement at Jamestown is most notable for the

    (A) discovery of gold and precious metals
    (B) successful cultivation and export of tobacco
    (C) violent struggles between English and Spanish forces
    (D) harmonious relations between the native inhabitants and settlers
    (E) high mortality rate among the settlers

34. A principal consequence of the Northwest Ordinance of 1787 was that it

    (A) terminated the earlier system of land surveying established by the federal government for the territories
    (B) established a procedure for bringing new states into the Union as the equals of the older states
    (C) stimulated the formation of the first political parties organized on a national basis
    (D) encouraged the drafting of a new treaty with England on the disposition of the western territories
    (E) strengthened the role of the thirteen original states in Congress

35. As chief justice of the Supreme Court, John Marshall issued significant opinions on all of the following EXCEPT

    (A) judicial review
    (B) federal *versus* state power
    (C) the sanctity of contracts
    (D) the rights of slaves as persons
    (E) congressional control of interstate commerce

36. Of the following, which author was the first to create a western hero?

    (A) Mark Twain
    (B) Edgar Allan Poe
    (C) James Fenimore Cooper
    (D) Helen Hunt Jackson
    (E) Willa Cather

37. "If the Creator had separated Texas from the Union by mountain barriers, the Alps or the Andes, there might be plausible objections; but He has planed down the whole [Mississippi] Valley including Texas, and united every atom of the soil and every drop of the water of the mighty whole. He has linked their rivers with the great Mississippi, and marked and united the whole for the dominion of one government, the residence of one people."

    This quotation from the 1840's can be viewed as an expression of

    (A) the New Nationalism
    (B) popular sovereignty
    (C) Manifest Destiny
    (D) the Good Neighbor policy
    (E) the frontier thesis

38. At the start of the Civil War, the North had all of the following advantages EXCEPT

    (A) better military leaders
    (B) a more extensive railroad network
    (C) a larger population
    (D) more heavy industry
    (E) more abundant food resources

39. "Let it be understood that we cannot go outside of this alternative: liberty, inequality, survival of the fittest; not-liberty, equality, survival of the unfittest. The former carries society forward and favors all its best members; the latter carries society downward and favors all its worst members."

    These sentiments are most characteristic of

    (A) the Social Gospel
    (B) Social Darwinism
    (C) Socialism
    (D) Progressivism
    (E) Neoorthodoxy

GO ON TO THE NEXT PAGE

40. The participation of women in the labor force between 1880 and 1930 rose primarily because

    (A) most married women sought employment outside the home
    (B) new jobs for women were created in offices, stores, and factories
    (C) domestic service jobs increased
    (D) discrimination against women in professions such as medicine and law declined
    (E) equal pay acts encouraged more women to enter the workforce

41. All of the following accurately characterize the United States during the Second World War EXCEPT:

    (A) Some consumer goods were rationed.
    (B) Women entered the paid workforce in record numbers.
    (C) Southerners migrated to industrial cities in increased numbers.
    (D) The size and power of the federal government increased.
    (E) The gross national product and wage levels declined.

42. During the period from 1492 to 1700, French activity in the Americas was primarily directed toward

    (A) establishing trade with American Indians
    (B) plundering American Indian settlements for gold and silver
    (C) conquering Spanish and English colonies
    (D) encouraging the growth of permanent settlements
    (E) discovering a new route to Africa

43. During the years 1565-1763, Spanish Florida was important to Spain for which of the following reasons?

    (A) It was a major source of valuable tropical produce.
    (B) It was the center of the Catholic mission system in the New World.
    (C) It retarded English colonial expansion southward from the Carolinas.
    (D) It helped supply Spain with precious metals.
    (E) It shielded converted Catholic Indians from Protestant missionaries.

44. Colonists supported the American Revolution for all of the following reasons EXCEPT

    (A) the desire to preserve their local autonomy and way of life from British interference
    (B) strong resentment against the quartering of British troops in colonial homes
    (C) the desire for greater political participation in policies affecting the colonies
    (D) a strong interest in achieving a more even distribution of income among the colonists
    (E) a conviction that British ministers and other government officials were a corrupting influence on the colonists

45. The Supreme Court's dependency on the President to enforce its decisions is demonstrated by President Andrew Jackson's refusal to uphold

    (A) the right of antislavery societies to send abolitionist publications through the mails
    (B) land claims of the Cherokee Indians in Georgia
    (C) women's right to vote
    (D) a slave's right to freedom after being in free territory
    (E) payments made in paper money for public lands

GO ON TO THE NEXT PAGE

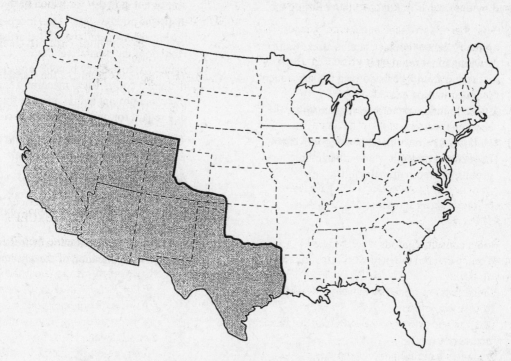

46. The entire shaded area in the map above was

    (A) ceded by Spain to the United States
    (B) once part of Mexico
    (C) claimed by the Confederacy
    (D) claimed by the Bear Flag Republic
    (E) known as the Gadsden Purchase

GO ON TO THE NEXT PAGE ➤

47. Which of the following best describes the role played by the People's (Populist) party during the 1890's?

   (A) An instrument to protect small businesses from governmental regulation
   (B) An organization foreshadowing the subsequent socialist movement
   (C) A vehicle for agrarian protest against the economic system
   (D) The political arm of the new labor movement
   (E) The medium through which urban ethnic groups entered national politics

48. "It seems to me . . . that the vital consideration connected with this problem of the trust is its effect upon our middle class — the independent, individual business person and the skilled artisan and mechanic. How does the trust affect them? . . . Their personal identity is lost. They become cogs and little wheels in a great complicated machine . . . . I favor complete and prompt annihilation of the trust — with due regard for property rights, of course."

The author of this statement would be likely to favor which of the following measures?

   (A) Nationalization of industry
   (B) A 100 percent inheritance tax
   (C) The rapid diffusion of mass-production techniques
   (D) Extensive distribution of free homestead land
   (E) Strict application of the Sherman Act

GO ON TO THE NEXT PAGE

Puck/Rothco Cartoons

49. The cartoon above is making the point that Woodrow Wilson

 (A) was the heir to the Populist tradition
 (B) was the last in a line of reform-minded Presidents that
    included William Howard Taft and Theodore Roosevelt
 (C) had a political philosophy that combined the tenets of the
    Republican and Progressive (Bull Moose) parties
 (D) owed his election to the presidency in 1912 to the split in
    the Republican party
 (E) owed his reelection to the presidency in 1916 to crossover
    votes by Republicans

GO ON TO THE NEXT PAGE

50. The primary purpose of the National Origins Act of 1924 was to

    (A) enumerate the populations of ethnic groups in the United States
    (B) limit immigration to the United States
    (C) help preserve American Indian culture
    (D) fund archaeological expeditions
    (E) support historical and genealogical research

51. Under Franklin D. Roosevelt's Good Neighbor policy, the United States stated its intention to refrain from intervening in the affairs of

    (A) Latin America
    (B) Europe
    (C) Canada
    (D) China
    (E) Japan

52. President Truman's foreign policy after the Second World War had as its expressed aim

    (A) preventive war
    (B) atomic proliferation
    (C) liberation of peoples under communist rule
    (D) massive retaliation against Soviet aggression
    (E) containment of international communism

53. The intellectual justification for revolutionary action contained in the Declaration of Independence was derived most directly from the work of

    (A) Rousseau
    (B) Locke
    (C) Montesquieu
    (D) Hobbes
    (E) Voltaire

GO ON TO THE NEXT PAGE

SLAVE IMPORTATIONS, 1500–1810

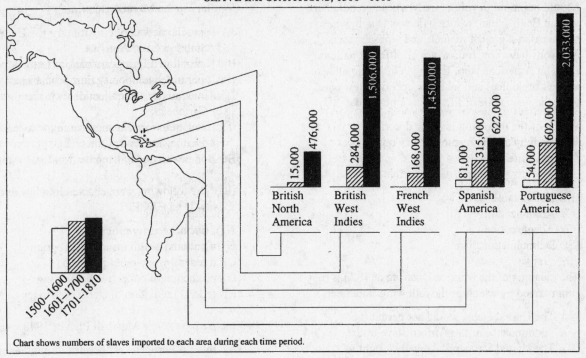

Chart shows numbers of slaves imported to each area during each time period.

Philip Curtin, *The Atlantic Slave Trade: A Census.*
Copyright © 1972 The University of Wisconsin Press.

54. The chart above lends support to which of the following
statements about slave importations between 1500 and 1810 ?

(A) Sugar-growing regions imported more slaves than did any
other region.

(B) The British imported more slaves to mainland colonies than
to island colonies.

(C) The British monopolized the African slave trade in the
eighteenth century.

(D) The importation of slaves decreased in proportion to the
increase in native-born slave populations.

(E) The importation of slaves increased at the same rate in each
region represented.

GO ON TO THE NEXT PAGE

55. "What then is the American, this new man? . . .
I could point out to you a family whose grandfather
was an Englishman, whose wife was Dutch, whose
son married a French woman, and whose present
four sons have now four wives of different nations.
He is an American who, leaving behind him all his
ancient prejudices and manners, receives new ones
from the new mode of life he has embraced. . . . "

Which of the following is being described in this
statement by an eighteenth-century observer of
American life?

(A) Social stratification
(B) Nativism
(C) Anglicization
(D) Acculturation
(E) Denominationalism

56. The meaning of the Monroe Doctrine of 1823 is best
summarized by which of the following statements?

(A) The United States would not permit the
continuance of the African slave trade.
(B) The United States proclaimed its right to
interfere in the internal affairs of neighboring
nations.
(C) The United States would fight the creation of
new colonies in the Western Hemisphere,
although it would not interfere with existing
ones.
(D) The United States would insist on a policy of
equal treatment in trade with the Far East.
(E) The United States would not extend diplomatic
recognition to any foreign government that
came to power by force.

57. All of the following are correct statements about
religious thought and expression in the nineteenth
century EXCEPT:

(A) The religions of American Indians emphasized
the sanctity of nature.
(B) The religion of slaves drew heavily on the Old
Testament story of the Exodus.
(C) Catholic priests worked to establish parochial
schools for the education of parish children.
(D) Deism and freethinking attracted wider support
among Protestants than did evangelicalism.
(E) Most Protestant denominations supported the
development of the temperance movement.

58. Which of the following is true about the Roosevelt
Corollary to the Monroe Doctrine?

(A) It proclaimed a policing role for the United
States in Latin America.
(B) It prohibited European loans to Latin America.
(C) It permitted temporary European armed
interventions to collect debts in the
Caribbean.
(D) It resulted from Japanese attempts to lease
territory in Lower California.
(E) It met with general approval in Latin America.

59. All of the following were enacted into law during
the New Deal EXCEPT

(A) a social security program
(B) a national health insurance program
(C) a federal work-relief program
(D) protection of collective bargaining
(E) federal regulation of stock exchanges

60. One purpose of the Marshall Plan of 1948 was to

(A) rebuild European economies through a joint
recovery program
(B) aid the depressed agricultural economies of
Latin American nations
(C) aid communist nations that would agree to
embrace democracy
(D) give military aid to those nations resisting
communist subversion
(E) help the peoples of Asia establish heavy
industries

61. The decline of sharecropping and of the crop-lien
system in the South after 1940 was due primarily to
which of the following?

(A) The New Deal's establishment of an agricul-
tural credit system for sharecroppers
(B) The political and social gains achieved by
Black people through the civil rights
movement
(C) The rise in cotton prices that freed sharecroppers
from debt
(D) The closing of many southern banks during the
Depression of the 1930's
(E) The increase in mechanization and the declining
demand for cotton

GO ON TO THE NEXT PAGE

62. Economic inequality in colonial North America was greatest

    (A) in the Carolina backcountry
    (B) in inland towns
    (C) in seaboard cities
    (D) among the Pennsylvania Dutch
    (E) in the Shenandoah Valley

63. All of the following were basic to seventeenth-century New England Puritanism EXCEPT

    (A) belief in the innate goodness of human nature
    (B) belief in the general principles of Calvinism
    (C) intolerance of outspoken religious dissenters
    (D) the necessity for a trained and educated ministry
    (E) the duty of merchants to sell wares at a just price

64. As a diplomat during the American Revolution, Benjamin Franklin played a part in which of the following?

    (A) Preventing the French government from joining with the British against the United States
    (B) Bringing Spain into the Revolutionary War on the side of the United States
    (C) Concluding a peace between Britain and France, thereby ending the war in Europe
    (D) Concluding an alliance between France and the United States
    (E) Preserving French neutrality during the war

65. All of the following were among the causes of the War of 1812 EXCEPT

    (A) British Orders-in-Council
    (B) British monopoly of the Atlantic slave trade
    (C) British violations of United States territorial waters
    (D) British impressment of United States seamen
    (E) the desire of some United States citizens to annex Canada

66. Which of the following was NOT prominently advocated during the reform era of the 1830's and 1840's?

    (A) Trust-busting
    (B) Temperance
    (C) Abolitionism
    (D) Free public education
    (E) Utopian communitarianism

67. Which of the following most accurately characterizes the slave system in the South between 1820 and 1860 ?

    (A) Slaves were so restricted that they were unable to develop their own social life and culture.
    (B) The high mortality and low birthrates of the slaves necessitated large slave importations.
    (C) Slaves were assisted in their work by substantial numbers of White wage earners, most of whom were foreign immigrants.
    (D) Slaves worked in a wide variety of skilled and unskilled occupations.
    (E) Slave owners had little incentive to keep their slaves healthy.

68. The first free immigrants whose right of entry into the United States was curtailed by federal legislation were

    (A) Africans
    (B) Asians
    (C) Latin Americans
    (D) Eastern and Southern Europeans
    (E) Western and Northern Europeans

69. The rapid rise in labor union membership in the late 1930's was mainly a result of the

    (A) spread of assembly-line production
    (B) merger of the AFL and the CIO
    (C) opposition of labor to Franklin D. Roosevelt's New Deal policies
    (D) organizing efforts of the Knights of Labor
    (E) passage of the Wagner Act

GO ON TO THE NEXT PAGE

THE SHIFTING FRONT IN KOREA*

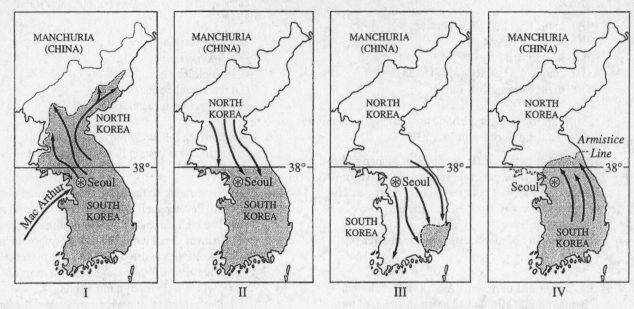

*Shaded areas represent position of UN forces.

70. Which of the following is the correct chronological sequence of
    the maps above?

    (A) I, II, IV, III
    (B) I, III, IV, II
    (C) II, III, I, IV
    (D) III, II, I, IV
    (E) IV, II, III, I

GO ON TO THE NEXT PAGE

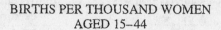

BIRTHS PER THOUSAND WOMEN
AGED 15–44

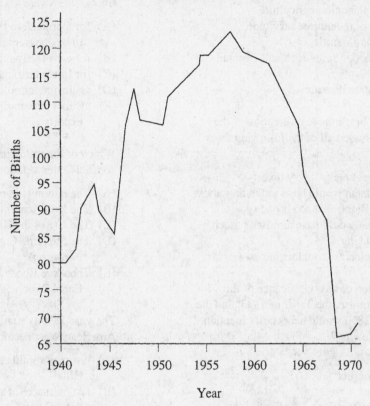

71. Which of the following statements is consistent with the data in the graph above?

   (A) The number of women having children rose during the Depression.
   (B) The wide availability of contraceptives led to a sharp decline in the birthrate during the 1960's.
   (C) Between 1955 and 1960 the United States had more women aged 15 to 44 than at any other time.
   (D) The number of single women having babies peaked in the 1960's.
   (E) The birthrate rose consistently between 1945 and 1960.

GO ON TO THE NEXT PAGE ➡

72. In the 1700's the southern Appalachian region was distinguished by

    (A) reliance on plantation agriculture
    (B) the absence of indentured servitude
    (C) numerous textile mills
    (D) large numbers of Scots-Irish and German settlers
    (E) high population densities

73. Anti-Federalist objections to ratification of the Constitution expressed all of the following fears EXCEPT:

    (A) Congress would levy heavy taxes.
    (B) The government would raise a standing army.
    (C) The Bill of Rights was too broad.
    (D) The President would have almost as much power as a king.
    (E) State governments would wither away.

74. A broad discussion of the significance of the Missouri Compromise, the Tariff of 1833, and the Compromise of 1850 would necessarily mention which of the following?

    (A) National debt
    (B) Religious conflict
    (C) The suffrage
    (D) The Monroe Doctrine
    (E) Sectional conflict

75. The Radical Republicans of America's post-Civil War period were radical in the sense that they favored

    (A) civil and political rights for Black people
    (B) the Reconstruction policies of President Andrew Johnson
    (C) nationalization of the railroad and coal industries
    (D) a government representing economic interests rather than geographical units
    (E) a guaranteed minimum income for former slaves

76. When American reformers in the late nineteenth century claimed that "the tariff is the mother of trusts," they were arguing

    (A) for a protective tariff and for an improvement in business ethics
    (B) for a protective tariff and against monopolies
    (C) for lower tariffs and against monopolies
    (D) against monopolies and against the sales tax
    (E) against monopolies and against taxes on exports

77. Which of the following events best supports a "class conflict" interpretation of American history?

    (A) The nationwide railroad strike of 1877
    (B) The Nullification crisis
    (C) The rise of the Know-Nothing party
    (D) The Supreme Court's decision in *Plessy* v. *Ferguson*
    (E) Theodore Roosevelt's "taking" of the Panama Canal Zone

78. The year 1890 is significant in the history of the American West because the

    (A) last major gold strike occurred in the Black Hills
    (B) last massacre of American Indians occurred at Sand Creek
    (C) most devastating blizzard ever to hit the Great Plains ended the long cattle drives
    (D) transcontinental railroad was officially completed
    (E) federal Census Office reported that a frontier line no longer existed

79. Organized labor opposed which of the following laws?

    (A) The Social Security Act
    (B) The Wagner Act
    (C) The Fair Labor Standards Act
    (D) The Taft-Hartley Act
    (E) The Employment Act of 1946

GO ON TO THE NEXT PAGE ➤

80. During the 1930's, which of the following was a fundamental political change that occurred among Black Americans?

    (A) A shift of Black voters from the two major parties to the minor parties
    (B) A shift of Black voters from the Republican party to the Democratic party
    (C) A great increase in the proportion of Black people who registered to vote
    (D) An increase in the importance of the Black vote in local elections in the South
    (E) A decrease in the participation of Black voters in federal elections

81. The United Nations was designed to maintain peace in the post-Second World War period through the implementation of

    (A) principles of free trade
    (B) bipolarity
    (C) collective security
    (D) bilateral treaties
    (E) regional pacts

82. Which of the following congressional actions resulted from an alleged attack on United States warships by North Vietnamese gunboats in 1964 ?

    (A) A declaration of war against North Vietnam
    (B) Passage of the War Powers Act
    (C) Authorization for air attacks against selected targets in China as well as in North Vietnam
    (D) A resolution urging the President to withdraw United States naval forces from Southeast Asian waters
    (E) The Tonkin Gulf Resolution

83. In the early decades of the republic, the intentions and expectations of the authors of the United States Constitution were most fully realized in the

    (A) respective roles of the executive and the legislative branches in conducting foreign policy
    (B) extensive role of the executive branch in drafting legislation
    (C) method of electing vice presidents
    (D) formation of political parties
    (E) elimination of property qualifications for voting

84. As secretary of the treasury, Alexander Hamilton did which of the following?

    (A) Sought to avoid a centralized banking system that could control the nation's currency.
    (B) Sought to link the interests of the national government and monied people.
    (C) Proposed to tax domestic manufactures to discourage the growth of factory towns.
    (D) Proposed to require the state governments to pay off the national debt.
    (E) Proposed to give away western land to small farmers to encourage settlement.

85. One of the goals of the Populist movement was

    (A) government control of railroads
    (B) collective ownership of farms
    (C) a strengthened electoral college
    (D) legislation to raise tariffs
    (E) abolition of income taxes

86. In *How the Other Half Lives*, Jacob Riis revealed the plight of

    (A) Black sharecroppers in the Deep South
    (B) Chinese workers in the railroad gangs of the West
    (C) European immigrants in the tenements of New York City
    (D) young boys in the Pennsylvania coal mines
    (E) American Indians in the Southwest

87. All of the following statements about the American economy during the First World War are correct EXCEPT:

    (A) Government boards were organized to manage crucial sectors of the economy.
    (B) Members of minority groups, especially Black people, moved into northern industrial cities to work in war factories.
    (C) The number of unionized workers increased.
    (D) The federal government expanded its prosecution of antitrust suits against large corporations.
    (E) Taxes were increased for corporations and wealthy individuals to help finance the war.

GO ON TO THE NEXT PAGE ▶

88. At the Yalta Conference in February 1945, Franklin D. Roosevelt's options were limited most seriously by which of the following?

    (A) Winston Churchill's suspicions of Roosevelt's motives and friendship
    (B) The poor health of Joseph Stalin
    (C) The rising tide of criticism of Roosevelt's leadership at home
    (D) The presence of Soviet troops in the Far East
    (E) The presence of Soviet troops in Poland

89. The American counterculture of the 1960's opposed

    (A) left-wing ideals of the 1930's and 1940's
    (B) modernist art and literature
    (C) the conservation movement
    (D) the materialism of American society
    (E) trade unionism

90. In the United States, the largest growth in population during the 1970's occurred in which of the following?

    (A) The Northeast Corridor from Boston to Washington, D.C.
    (B) States below the 37th parallel from Virginia to California
    (C) States of the upper Midwest from Ohio to Minnesota
    (D) The most heavily populated states, including New York, Pennsylvania, Illinois, and California
    (E) The regions concentrating on mature industries such as steel, automobiles, and major appliances

S T O P

IF YOU FINISH BEFORE TIME IS CALLED, YOU MAY CHECK YOUR WORK ON THIS TEST ONLY.
DO NOT TURN TO ANY OTHER TEST IN THIS BOOK.

How to Score the SAT Subject Test in U.S. History

When you take the SAT Subject Test in U.S. History, your answer sheet will be "read" by a scanning machine that will record your responses to each question. Then a computer will compare your answers with the correct answers and produce your raw score. You get one point for each correct answer. For each wrong answer, you lose one-fourth of a point. Questions you omit (and any for which you mark more than one answer) are not counted. This raw score is converted to a scaled score that is reported to you and to the colleges you specify.

Worksheet 1. Finding Your Raw Test Score

STEP 1: Table A lists the correct answers for all the questions on the SAT Subject Test in U.S. History that is reproduced in this book. It also serves as a worksheet for you to calculate your raw score.

- Compare your answers with those given in the table.
- Put a check in the column marked "Right" if your answer is correct.
- Put a check in the column marked "Wrong" if your answer is incorrect.
- Leave both columns blank if you omitted the question.

STEP 2: Count the number of right answers.

Enter the total here: _____

STEP 3: Count the number of wrong answers.

Enter the total here: _____

STEP 4: Multiply the number of wrong answers by .250.

Enter the product here: _____

STEP 5: Subtract the result obtained in Step 4 from the total you obtained in Step 2.

Enter the result here: _____

STEP 6: Round the number obtained in Step 5 to the nearest whole number.

Enter the result here: _____

The number you obtained in Step 6 is your raw score.

TABLE A
Answers to the SAT Subject Test in U.S. History, Form K-3RAC2
reformatted, and Percentage of Students Answering Each Question Correctly

Question Number	Correct Answer	Right	Wrong	Percentage of Students Answering the Question Correctly*	Question Number	Correct Answer	Right	Wrong	Percentage of Students Answering the Question Correctly*
1	A			66	32	A			70
2	D			85	33	E			45
3	A			69	34	B			45
4	D			71	35	D			45
5	C			74	36	C			45
6	B			95	37	C			65
7	D			78	38	A			57
8	E			63	39	B			69
9	D			96	40	B			51
10	A			90	41	E			54
11	D			68	42	A			47
12	E			54	43	C			51
13	C			68	44	D			62
14	B			76	45	B			56
15	A			65	46	B			61
16	C			86	47	C			26
17	B			83	48	E			42
18	D			35	49	D			49
19	C			58	50	B			53
20	E			79	51	A			61
21	C			59	52	E			54
22	E			56	53	B			57
23	A			54	54	A			58
24	D			67	55	D			40
25	B			57	56	C			45
26	E			73	57	D			51
27	A			59	58	A			65
28	B			33	59	B			34
29	C			73	60	A			37
30	D			74	61	E			41
31	E			69	62	C			32

Table A continued on next page

Table A continued from previous page

Question Number	Correct Answer	Right	Wrong	Percentage of Students Answering the Question Correctly*	Question Number	Correct Answer	Right	Wrong	Percentage of Students Answering the Question Correctly*
63	A			34	77	A			31
64	D			61	78	E			22
65	B			32	79	D			34
66	A			34	80	B			40
67	D			33	81	C			45
68	B			35	82	E			42
69	E			19	83	A			37
70	C			36	84	B			31
71	B			56	85	A			27
72	D			28	86	C			44
73	C			47	87	D			37
74	E			64	88	E			36
75	A			43	89	D			51
76	C			40	90	B			24

*These percentages are based on an analysis of the answer sheets of a random sample of 2,993 students who took the original form of this test in January 1997 and whose mean score was 556. They may be used as an indication of the relative difficulty of a particular question. Each percentage may also be used to predict the likelihood that a typical SAT Subject Test in U.S. History candidate will answer correctly that question on this edition of this test.

Finding Your Scaled Score

When you take SAT Subject Tests, the scores sent to the colleges you specify are reported on the College Board scale, which ranges from 200 to 800. You can convert your practice test score to a scaled score by using Table B. To find your scaled score, locate your raw score in the left-hand column of Table B; the corresponding score in the right-hand column is your scaled score. For example, a raw score of 60 on this particular edition of the SAT Subject Test in U.S. History corresponds to a scaled score of 680.

Raw scores are converted to scaled scores to ensure that a score earned on any one edition of a particular Subject Test is comparable to the same scaled score earned on any other edition of the same Subject Test. Because some editions of tests may be slightly easier or more difficult than others, College Board scaled scores are adjusted so that they indicate the same level of performance regardless of the edition of the test taken and the ability of the group that takes it. Thus, for example, a score of 400 on one edition of a test taken at a particular administration indicates the same level of achievement as a score of 400 on a different edition of the test taken at a different administration.

When you take the SAT Subject Tests during a national administration, your scores are likely to differ somewhat from the scores you obtain on the tests in this book. People perform at different levels at different times for reasons unrelated to the tests themselves. The precision of any test is also limited because it represents only a sample of all the possible questions that could be asked.

TABLE B
Scaled Score Conversion Table
U.S. History Subject Test (Form K-3RAC2)

Raw Score	Scaled Score	Raw Score	Scaled Score	Raw Score	Scaled Score
90	800	52	630	14	420
89	800	51	630	13	420
88	800	50	620	12	410
87	800	49	610	11	410
86	800	48	610	10	400
85	800	47	600	9	400
84	800	46	600	8	390
83	800	45	590	7	390
82	800	44	580	6	380
81	800	43	580	5	380
80	790	42	570	4	370
79	790	41	570	3	370
78	780	40	560	2	360
77	780	39	560	1	360
76	770	38	550	0	350
75	770	37	540	-1	350
74	760	36	540	-2	340
73	760	35	530	-3	340
72	750	34	530	-4	330
71	740	33	520	-5	330
70	740	32	520	-6	320
69	730	31	510	-7	320
68	730	30	510	-8	310
67	720	29	500	-9	310
66	720	28	490	-10	300
65	710	27	490	-11	300
64	700	26	480	-12	290
63	700	25	480	-13	280
62	690	24	470	-14	280
61	690	23	470	-15	270
60	680	22	460	-16	270
59	670	21	460	-17	260
58	670	20	450	-18	250
57	660	19	450	-19	250
56	660	18	440	-20	240
55	650	17	440	-21	230
54	640	16	430	-22	230
53	640	15	430		

Reviewing Your Performance on the U.S. History Subject Test

After you score your test, analyze your performance—consider the following questions:

Did you run out of time before reaching the end of the test?

If so, you may need to pace yourself better. For example, maybe you spent too much time on one or two hard questions. A better approach might be to skip the ones you can't answer right away and try answering all the questions that remain on the test. Then if there's time, go back to the questions you skipped.

Did you take a long time reading the directions?

You will save time when you take the test by learning the directions to the U.S. History Subject Test ahead of time. Each minute you spend reading directions during the test is a minute that you could use to answer questions.

How did you handle questions you were unsure of?

If you were able to eliminate one or more of the answer choices as wrong and guess from the remaining ones, your approach probably worked to your advantage. On the other hand, making haphazard guesses or omitting questions without trying to eliminate choices could cost you valuable points.

How difficult were the questions for you compared with other students who took the test?

Table A shows you how difficult the multiple-choice questions were for the group of students who took this test during its national administration. The right-hand column gives the percentage of students that answered each question correctly.

A question answered correctly by almost everyone in the group is obviously an easy question. For example, 96 percent of the students answered question 9 correctly. But only 19 percent answered question 69 correctly.

Keep in mind that these percentages are based on just one group of students. They would probably be different if another group of students took the test.

If you missed several easy questions, go back and try to find out why: Did the questions cover material you haven't yet reviewed? Did you misunderstand the directions?

Chapter 3
World History

Purpose

The World History Subject Test measures your understanding of the development of major world cultures and your use of historical techniques, including the application and weighing of evidence and the ability to interpret and generalize. The test covers all historical fields:

- political and diplomatic
- intellectual and cultural
- social and economic

Format

This one-hour test consists of 95 multiple-choice questions. Many of the questions are global in nature, dealing with issues and trends that have significance throughout the modern world. Some questions require:

- familiarity with terms commonly used in the social sciences
- understanding of cause-and-effect relationships
- knowledge of the history and geography necessary for understanding major historical developments

Other questions test:

- your grasp of concepts essential to historical analysis
- your capacity to interpret artistic materials
- your ability to assess quotations from speeches, documents, and other published materials
- your ability to use historical knowledge in interpreting data based on maps, graphs, and charts

Chronological Material Covered	Approximate Percentage of Test
Pre-history and Civilizations to the year 500 Common Era (C.E.)**	25
500–1500 C.E.	20
1500–1900 C.E.	25
Post–1900 C.E.	20
Cross-chronological	10

Geographical Material Covered	
Europe	25
Africa	10
Southwest Asia	10
South Asia	10
East Asia	10
The Americas (excluding the United States)	10
Global or comparative	25

**The SAT Subject Test in World History uses the chronological designations B.C.E. (before the common era) and C.E. (common era). These labels correspond to B.C. (before Christ) and A.D. (anno Domini), which are used in some history textbooks.

Recommended Preparation

You can prepare academically for the test by taking a one-year comprehensive course in world or global history at the college-preparatory level and through independent reading of materials on historic topics. Because secondary school programs differ, the World History Test does not emphasize any one textbook or particular course of study. Familiarize yourself with directions in advance. The directions in this book are identical to those that appear on the test.

Score

The total score is reported on the 200-to-800 scale.

Sample Questions

All questions on the World History Test are multiple-choice, requiring you to choose the best response from five choices. The following sample questions illustrate the types of questions on the test, their range of difficulty, and the abilities they measure. Questions may be presented as separate items or in sets based on quotations, maps, pictures, graphs, or tables.

Directions: Each of the questions or incomplete statements below is followed by five suggested answers or completions. Select the one that is best in each case and then fill in the corresponding oval on the answer sheet.

Questions 1 and 2 fall into the category of questions that require you to know social science terms, factual cause-and-effect relationships, geography, and other data necessary for understanding major historical developments.

1. Which of the following was immediately responsible for precipitating the French Revolution?
   (A) The threat of national bankruptcy
   (B) An attack upon the privileges of the middle class
   (C) The desire of the nobility for a written constitution
   (D) The suffering of the peasantry
   (E) The king's attempt to restore feudalism

To answer this question, you need to recall the circumstances that led in May 1789 to the first meeting of the French Estates-General in over a century and a half, an event that arrayed the Third Estate against the nobility and Louis XVI in the first stage of a political struggle that was to evolve into the French Revolution. With his debt-ridden government brought to a halt, the king, by mid-1788, was left with no other recourse than a promise to convene the Estates-General in the months ahead. The correct answer is (A).

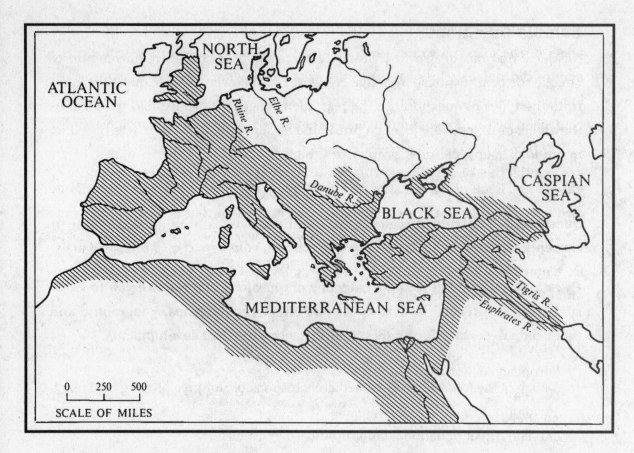

Question 2 refers to the map above.

2. The shaded area in the map above shows the extent of which of the following?

    (A) Irrigation agriculture in 1000 B.C.E.

    (B) Greek colonization in 550 B.C.E.

    (C) Alexander the Great's empire in 323 B.C.E.

    (D) The Roman Empire in 117 C.E.

    (E) The Byzantine Empire in 565 C.E.

Question 2 tests your knowledge of both history and geography. To answer this question you must know something about the extent to which irrigated farming was practiced in Africa, Europe, and Southwest Asia three thousand years ago, and you need to have a general idea of the extent of the territory controlled by four major ancient civilizations at specific points in time. Choice (A) can be eliminated because irrigation in this early period would have been confined to the regions along the major rivers of the Middle East and Southwest Asia. Choice (B) can be eliminated because Greek colonization was confined primarily to the eastern

Mediterranean and did not extend as far north in Europe as shown in the shaded areas of the map. Choice (C) can be eliminated because Alexander the Great's empire did not extend into either the western Mediterranean or northwestern Europe. Choice (D), the correct answer, outlines the greatest extent of territory controlled by the Roman Empire under the Emperor Trajan in the second century C.E. Choice (E) can be eliminated because the Byzantine Empire, with its capital in Constantinople, was confined primarily to the eastern Mediterranean area.

Questions 3–6 fall into the category of questions that test your understanding of concepts essential to history and social science, your capacity to interpret artistic materials, and your ability to assess quotations from speeches, documents, and other published materials.

3. Which of the following was introduced into the diet of Europeans only after European contact with the Americas in the fifteenth century?
    - (A) Tea
    - (B) Rice
    - (C) Cinnamon
    - (D) Sugar
    - (E) Potatoes

To answer this question you need to have some basic information about what has come to be known as the "Columbian Exchange," i.e., the enormous biological transfer that occurred as a result of the fifteenth- and sixteenth-century European voyages of discovery. Choice (A) can be ruled out because tea comes from China, not from the Americas, and was not widely used in Europe until the mid-seventeenth century. Choice (B) can be eliminated because the origin of rice culture has been traced to India. Rice was introduced into southern Europe in medieval times. Choice (C) can be eliminated because the cinnamon tree is native to South Asia and, like rice, has been known in Europe since medieval times. Choice (D) can be eliminated because sugarcane originated in what is now known as New Guinea, followed human migration routes from Southeast Asia through Southwest Asia to Europe and, although rare and expensive, was known to the European aristocracy in medieval times. Choice (E) is the correct answer. The potato is native to the Peruvian-Bolivian Andes and, after its "discovery" by the Europeans in the fifteenth century, became a staple of the European diet. The potato is now a major food crop worldwide.

Giraudon/Art Resource

4. The nineteenth-century wood-block print above is associated with the culture of

   (A) Japan

   (B) India

   (C) Iran

   (D) Myanmar (Burma)

   (E) Thailand

The correct answer choice to question 4 is (A) Japan. The scene depicted in this dramatic picture is world famous. Although the spatial arrangement and perspective are generally East Asian and the title at the upper left-hand corner is written in Chinese characters, also used in Japan, there are a number of characteristics that identify the picture as Japanese. The dramatic subject matter, with Mount Fuji in the background, is Japanese. In addition, colorful wood-block prints depicting famous scenery, beautiful women, warriors, and well-known theater subjects were popular in Japan from the seventeenth to the nineteenth centuries because they were widely affordable. This work is by the nineteenth-century artist Hokusai.

Questions 5 and 6 refer to the following passage.

We have heard that in your country opium is prohibited with the utmost strictness and severity—this is a strong proof that you know full well how hurtful it is to humankind. Since then you do not permit it to injure your own country, you ought not to have the injurious drug transferred to another country, and above all others, how much less to the Middle Kingdom!

5. The author of the diplomatic dispatch above most probably lived in which of the following countries?
   (A) Ghana
   (B) The Netherlands
   (C) Iran
   (D) China
   (E) Germany

The above discussion of the forced importation of opium suggests China's struggle against Great Britain, culminating in the Opium War of the mid-nineteenth century. The tone of the dispatch, expressing indignation at Great Britain's flaunting of Chinese law, is consistent with China's concern over growing opium addiction in China and with Chinese resistance to the British. From your study of China you will also remember that the Chinese used to refer to their country as the Middle Kingdom. Choice (D) is the answer to question 5.

6. The country that went to war in the nineteenth century over the issue raised in the dispatch was
   (A) France
   (B) Egypt
   (C) Great Britain
   (D) India
   (E) Japan

The answer to question 6 is (C) Great Britain. Great Britain was expanding its Asian trade and needed a product to exchange for Chinese goods. Opium from India was Great Britain's answer to this dilemma. The dispatch above was sent by a representative of the Chinese emperor to Queen Victoria shortly before the Opium War (1839–1842), in which China was defeated by the British and therefore was not able to enforce its prohibition against the importation of opium.

7. All of the following are "Pillars of Islam" EXCEPT

   (A) giving alms for the support of society's poor

   (B) praying five times a day in the direction of Mecca

   (C) fasting for one month of the year

   (D) making a pilgrimage to Mecca at least once during a lifetime

   (E) attending mosque prayers daily

Question 7 asks you to identify the exception in a series of true statements. In other words, you are being asked to locate the false answer among the five options. To answer this question, you need to draw on your knowledge of Islam. Choices (A) through (D) are true because they refer to four of the five "Pillars of Islam." Choice (E) is false because Muslims are not required to attend mosque prayers daily. The fifth pillar actually is the "profession of faith." In question 7 the correct answer choice is (E).

Questions posed in the negative, like this one, account for at most 25 percent of the test questions. Variations of this question format employ the capitalized words NOT or LEAST, as in the following examples: "Which of the following is NOT true?" "Which of the following is LEAST likely to occur?"

Questions based on graphs, charts, or cartoons require you to use historical knowledge in interpreting data. Questions 8–10 fall into this category.

ANNUAL PRODUCTION OF STEEL
(in thousands of metric tons)

Year				
1865	225	13	97	41
1870	286	68	169	83
1875	723	396	370	258
1880	1,320	1,267	660	388
1885	2,020	1,739	1,202	533
1890	3,637	4,346	2,161	566
1895	3,444	6,212	3,941	899
1900	5,130	10,382	6,645	1,565
1905	5,983	20,354	10,066	2,110
1910	6,374	26,512	13,698	3,506

8. Read from left to right, the column headings for the table above should be

    (A) Great Britain, United States, Germany, and France

    (B) Italy, Great Britain, Russia, and Germany

    (C) Germany, Great Britain, Russia, and France

    (D) Great Britain, United States, France, and Germany

    (E) Germany, Russia, Great Britain, and United States

The correct answer choice is (A). To answer this question, you need to know in which country the industrial revolution began and which other countries caught up early or late. Great Britain was industrialized by 1850, the United States and Germany were next, and France, Italy, and Russia followed later in the nineteenth century.

Questions containing charts and graphs require careful study and therefore may be more time-consuming than other types of questions. Remember to budget your time accordingly.

Questions 9 and 10 are based on the August 1914 *Punch* cartoon below.

BRAVO, BELGIUM !

9. The "No Thoroughfare" sign in the cartoon is a reference to

    (A) an international treaty guaranteeing the neutrality of Belgium

    (B) the heavy defensive fortifications built by Belgium in the preceding decade

    (C) a bilateral nonaggression pact between Belgium and Germany

    (D) an alliance between Belgium and France

    (E) the treacherous, swampy terrain on the Belgian-German border

10. This cartoon is a comment on Germany's attempt to
    (A) acquire valuable mineral resources in Belgium
    (B) invade France through Belgium
    (C) force Belgium to repeal tariffs on German goods
    (D) intimidate Belgium into signing a military alliance with Germany
    (E) pressure Belgium into withdrawing from the Triple Alliance

In this question set you are asked to interpret a British political cartoon published during the tense diplomatic period before the outbreak of the First World War. The correct answer to question 9 is (A), which refers to treaties signed by the Great Powers in 1839 guaranteeing the neutrality of Belgium and Luxembourg in the event of war. The set's second question focuses on Belgium's resistance to the more powerful Germany's threat of aggression if Belgium, situated between Germany and France, will not give transit to German troops. The correct answer for question 10 is (B).

11. Which of the following statements would be most difficult for historians to prove true or false?
    (A) There was little organized education in Europe during the Middle Ages.
    (B) Greece contributed more to Western civilization than Rome.
    (C) The invention of the steam engine influenced the way people lived.
    (D) Russia is territorially the largest country in the world.
    (E) The tourist industry in Europe increased markedly after the Second World War.

In a methodology question such as the one above, you must make the distinction between statements that are verifiable by fact and statements that are based on judgments. The latter are more difficult than the former to prove true or false because they are evaluations. In this question, choice (B) is the correct answer, since the assertion that Greece's contribution to Western civilization was greater than Rome's requires the most justification. Choice (B) is the most opinionated of the statements and therefore the one most difficult to prove or disprove.

12. The term "green revolution" refers to

    (A) protests against the placement of nuclear weapons in Europe

    (B) ecological changes in the ocean because of algae growth

    (C) increased agricultural output resulting from development of hybrid seeds and chemical fertilizers

    (D) expanded irrigation farming made possible by the construction of large dams

    (E) thinning of the atmospheric ozone layer resulting in changes in the growing season

The correct answer to question 12 is (C). To answer this question, you need to know about modern scientific breakthroughs in agricultural research that have allowed countries like India, formerly subject to terrible famines, to become self-sufficient in grain production.

World History Test

The test that follows is an actual, recently administered SAT Subject Test in World History. To get an idea of what a real administration is like, take the test under conditions as close as possible to those of a national administration:

- Set aside an hour when you can take the test uninterrupted. Make sure you complete the test in one sitting.

- Sit at a desk or table with no other books or papers. Dictionaries, other books, or notes are not allowed in the test room.

- Time yourself by placing a clock or kitchen timer in front of you.

- Tear out an answer sheet from the back of this book and fill it in just as you would on the day of the test. One answer sheet can be used for up to three Subject Tests.

- Read the instructions that precede the practice test. During the actual administration you will be asked to read them before answering test questions.

- After you finish the practice test, read the sections "How to Score the SAT Subject Test in World History" and "Reviewing Your Performance on the World History Subject Test."

- Actual test and answer sheets will indicate circles, not ovals.

Form 3SAC

WORLD HISTORY TEST

The top portion of the section of the answer sheet that you will use in taking the World History test must be filled in exactly as shown in the illustration below. Note carefully that you have to do all of the following on your answer sheet.

1. Print WORLD HISTORY on the line under the words "Subject Test (print)."

2. In the shaded box labeled "Test Code" fill in four ovals:

   —Fill in oval 1 in the row labeled V.

   —Fill in oval 7 in the row labeled W.

   —Fill in oval 3 in the row labeled X.

   —Fill in oval D in the row labeled Y.

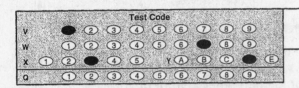

3. Please answer the three questions below by filling in the appropriate ovals in the row labeled Q on the answer sheet. The information you provide is for statistical purposes only and will not affect your score on the test.

Question I

How many semesters of world history, world cultures, or European history have you taken from grade 9 to the present? (If you are taking a course this semester, count it as a full semester.) Fill in only one oval of ovals 1-2.

- One semester or less   —Fill in oval 1.
- Two semesters or more   —Fill in oval 2.

Question II

For the courses in world history, world cultures, or European history you have taken, which of the following geographical areas did you study? Fill in all of the ovals that apply.

- Africa   —Fill in oval 3.
- Asia   —Fill in oval 4.
- Europe   —Fill in oval 5.
- Latin America   —Fill in oval 6.
- Middle East   —Fill in oval 7.

Question III

How recently have you studied world history, world cultures, or European history?

- I am currently enrolled in or have just completed such a course.   —Fill in oval 8.
- I have not studied this subject for 6 months or more.   —Fill in oval 9.

When the supervisor gives the signal, turn the page and begin the World History test. There are 100 numbered ovals on the answer sheet and 95 questions in the World History test. Therefore, use only ovals 1 to 95 for recording your answers.

WORLD HISTORY TEST

Directions: Each of the questions or incomplete statements below is followed by five suggested answers or completions. Select the one that is best in each case and then fill in the corresponding oval on the answer sheet.

Note: The World History Test uses the chronological designations B.C.E. (before the common era) and C.E. (common era). These labels correspond to B.C. (before Christ) and A.D. (anno Domini), which are used in some world history textbooks.

1. Which of the following best describes the Qur'an (Koran) ?

   (A) A ninth-century collection of Arabian poems and folktales
   (B) An Arabic mathematical treatise
   (C) An account of the lives of the Muslim prophets
   (D) Writings accepted by Muslims as God's revelations to Muhammad
   (E) An Arabic translation of the Old Testament

2. Which of the following escaped Western colonial control during the nineteenth and twentieth centuries?

   (A) Siam (Thailand)
   (B) Burma
   (C) The Philippines
   (D) India
   (E) Indochina

3. "Today China and Korea are no help at all to our country. . . . It follows that in making our present plans we have no time to await the development of neighboring countries and join them in reviving Asia. Rather, we should escape from them and join the company of Western civilized nations."

   The quotation above from a nineteenth-century Japanese author most clearly reflects which of the following developments in Japan?

   (A) Repudiation of the samurai tradition
   (B) Reimposition of the Tokugawa exclusion policy
   (C) Industrialization and institutional reform
   (D) Adoption of a foreign policy of nonalignment
   (E) Abolition of the monarchy

4. The Nazi-Soviet Nonaggression Pact of 1939 was significant primarily because it

   (A) eliminated causes of friction between Germany and the Soviet Union
   (B) showed that Hitler was not really anti-Communist
   (C) paved the way for agreement among the Axis powers
   (D) helped destroy the League of Nations
   (E) allowed either Germany or the Soviet Union to attack Poland without fearing the other

GO ON TO THE NEXT PAGE →

3SAC

Bibliothèque nationale, Paris.

5. Which of the following statements best describes the
   message of the illustration above?

   (A) The Church has compassion for people of all
       classes.
   (B) All members of society work together for
       common goals.
   (C) Lawyers are necessary for a society to function.
   (D) Farmers and workers support the privileged
       classes through their labors.
   (E) Diversity is one of the characteristic features of
       Western society.

GO ON TO THE NEXT PAGE →

6. In the ancient Mediterranean world, which of the following were primarily sea traders?

   (A) Assyrians
   (B) Hittites
   (C) Phoenicians
   (D) Hebrews
   (E) Egyptians

7. The bas-relief above is probably from

   (A) an Egyptian tomb
   (B) an Assyrian palace
   (C) a Hebrew temple
   (D) a Greek temple
   (E) a Roman triumphal arch

8. All human societies had mastered all of the following by the end of the Neolithic period EXCEPT

   (A) domestication of animals
   (B) the ability to control fire
   (C) hunting
   (D) writing
   (E) farming

9. Which of the following religions that originated outside Africa had the most influence in precolonial Africa?

   (A) Islam
   (B) Judaism
   (C) Christianity
   (D) Confucianism
   (E) Buddhism

10. The Maya of Mesoamerica are best known for their achievements in

   (A) shipbuilding and navigation
   (B) mathematics and astronomy
   (C) animal husbandry
   (D) carpentry
   (E) literature

GO ON TO THE NEXT PAGE

PERCENTAGE OF 18-22 YEAR OLDS OF WORKING-CLASS BACKGROUNDS
ENROLLED IN INSTITUTIONS OF HIGHER LEARNING IN 1960

Yugoslavia	56.0%
Czechoslovakia	39.3%
Poland	32.9%
Great Britain	25.0%
France	5.3%
West Germany	5.2%

---

11. Which of the following statements is supported by the table above?

    (A) A private enterprise system provided the greatest access for students to higher education.
    (B) European women and men had equal access to higher education.
    (C) In Eastern Europe the nationalization of industry had not displaced the former ruling classes from their social prominence.
    (D) Students from working-class backgrounds in Eastern Europe had greater access to higher education than did students from similar backgrounds in Western Europe.
    (E) Students in Eastern and Western Europe had approximately equal access to higher education.

---

12. The process of industrialization, as experienced in various parts of the world in the nineteenth and twentieth centuries, has required all of the following EXCEPT

    (A) a gold standard
    (B) technological know-how
    (C) domestic or foreign markets
    (D) capital investment
    (E) an adequate labor supply

13. "If a son has struck his father, they shall cut off his hand. If a nobleman has destroyed the eye of a member of the aristocracy, they shall destroy his eye. . . ."

    The quotation above is from the

    (A) Egyptian Book of the Dead
    (B) Law Code of Hammurabi
    (C) Zoroastrian Avesta
    (D) Analects of Confucius
    (E) Aryan Vedas

14. When the Roman Empire reached its greatest extent under the Emperor Trajan, about 117 C.E., it included or was bounded by portions of all of the following rivers EXCEPT the

    (A) Rhine
    (B) Thames
    (C) Seine
    (D) Vistula
    (E) Nile

15. Trade in which of the following items contributed to the wealth of the early West African kingdoms of Ghana, Mali, and Songhai?

    (A) Furs and cloth
    (B) Pottery and ivory
    (C) Gems and kola nuts
    (D) Gold and salt
    (E) Sugar and cattle

GO ON TO THE NEXT PAGE

Questions 16-17 are based on the map below.

16. The territorial divisions shown on the map reflect those that existed in

    (A) 1200
    (B) 1450
    (C) 1600
    (D) 1850
    (E) 1900

17. The three areas indicated by the emblem were territories that belonged to

    (A) France
    (B) Spain
    (C) the Netherlands
    (D) England
    (E) Portugal

GO ON TO THE NEXT PAGE →

18. Which of the following did the classical political economists of the early nineteenth century consider to be the most legitimate function of government?

    (A) The enactment of social legislation
    (B) The protection of home industries
    (C) Empire building
    (D) The regulation of business
    (E) The protection of private property

19. All of the following helped make possible the establishment of European colonies in Africa and Asia during the nineteenth century EXCEPT

    (A) the steamship
    (B) quinine
    (C) chemical defoliants
    (D) the telegraph
    (E) the railroad

20. "In the mid-nineteenth century, this nation produced approximately two-thirds of the world's coal, one-half of its iron, seventy percent of its steel, and one-half of its factory-produced textiles."

    The statement above describes

    (A) Great Britain
    (B) Prussia
    (C) France
    (D) Russia
    (E) the United States

21. "One opinion pervades the whole company, that they are on the eve of some great revolution in the government. Everything points to it: the confusion in the finances great, with a deficit impossible to provide for without the states-general of the kingdom, yet no ideas formed of what would be the consequence of their meeting; a prince on the throne, with excellent dispositions, but without the resources of a mind that could govern in such a moment without ministers; a court buried in pleasure and dissipation: a great ferment among all ranks of men."

    The passage above was probably written by a contemporary in

    (A) 1687
    (B) 1787
    (C) 1847
    (D) 1870
    (E) 1917

22. The success of the Bolshevik Revolution of November 1917 was in large part the result of

    (A) the overwhelming military power of the Bolshevik forces
    (B) active cooperation between the Bolsheviks and the German army
    (C) the Bolsheviks' determination to continue the war
    (D) the Bolsheviks' promise of peace, land, and bread
    (E) support for the Bolsheviks among many other political parties in Russia

GO ON TO THE NEXT PAGE

23. "When two elephants fight, no one gets hurt except the grass, which is trampled underfoot."

When Jomo Kenyatta, President of Kenya, made the statement above, he was referring to which of the following problems faced by newly independent African nations?

(A) The refusal of foreign settlers to return land to Africans
(B) Superpower rivalries in Africa
(C) Ethnic rivalries
(D) The conflict between Western and traditional codes of law
(E) Government acquisition of valuable agricultural land for game preserves

24. Which of the following has always been a central characteristic of the traditional Chinese family?

(A) Legal equality of husband and wife
(B) Separation of family life and religious rituals
(C) Physical separation of the elderly
(D) Freedom of choice in the selection of marriage partners
(E) Veneration of ancestral spirits

25. In the time of Pericles, which of the following were permitted to participate in the Athenian Assembly?

(A) All adults resident within the city walls
(B) All Greek males resident in Athens
(C) All who were willing to swear allegiance to the Athenian gods
(D) All adult males whose parents were of citizen descent
(E) All who could prove their fathers were Athenian

GO ON TO THE NEXT PAGE

Alinari/Art Resource

26. Bernini's altar canopy in St. Peter's at Rome, shown above, is an example of which of the following styles?

   (A) Gothic
   (B) Renaissance
   (C) Baroque
   (D) Neoclassical
   (E) Romanesque

GO ON TO THE NEXT PAGE

27. The rapid colonization of Africa by the European powers after 1880 was motivated primarily by

    (A) the demand for slaves to cultivate New World cotton and sugar
    (B) the desire for new markets, raw materials, and strategic advantage
    (C) the need to tap the hydroelectric potential of African rivers
    (D) the heavy demand for African workers in European factories
    (E) heightened interest by Europeans in tourism and big-game hunting

GO ON TO THE NEXT PAGE →

Reprinted by permission of the museum.

28. The illustration above showing the founding of a city
    is a primary source for the history of the

    (A) Aztecs
    (B) Egyptians
    (C) Hittites
    (D) Rajputs
    (E) Ashanti

GO ON TO THE NEXT PAGE

29. In 1644 China was conquered by

    (A) Muslim forces from Central Asia
    (B) European commercial and military groups led
         by Great Britain
    (C) the Tokugawa shogunate of Japan
    (D) Dutch imperial forces
    (E) Manchu armies that established the Qing
         (Ch'ing) dynasty

GO ON TO THE NEXT PAGE

<u>Questions 30-31</u> refer to the maps below.

POPULATION DENSITY OF EUROPE
AT THE TIME OF THE ROMAN EMPIRE
(number of inhabitants per square kilometer)

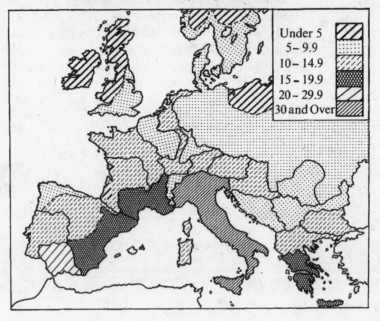

Under 5
5 – 9.9
10 – 14.9
15 – 19.9
20 – 29.9
30 and Over

TOWNS OF EUROPE AT THE
TIME OF THE ROMAN EMPIRE

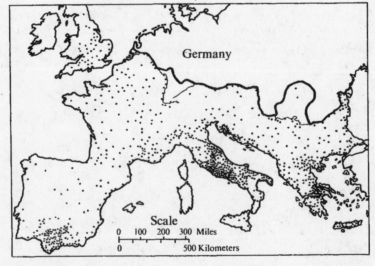

Germany

Scale

0   100   200   300   Miles

0   500 Kilometers

GO ON TO THE NEXT PAGE

30. The population density map indicates that during the period of the Roman Empire

    (A) Italy was overpopulated
    (B) central Europe was less densely populated than any other area of Europe
    (C) the Mediterranean area was more densely populated than any other area of Europe
    (D) more people lived in Spain than anywhere else
    (E) population density was highest in areas where the climate was coolest

31. The two maps together show that during the period of the Roman Empire

    (A) population density was highest in the most heavily urbanized areas
    (B) England was underpopulated because it had no towns
    (C) Greece had a higher population density than did Italy
    (D) most of the population of the empire lived in towns rather than in the countryside
    (E) there was a steady movement of people from the countryside into the towns

GO ON TO THE NEXT PAGE ➤

32. Which of the following helps to explain the relatively nonviolent nature of British political reform movements during the nineteenth century?

    (A) Police surveillance inhibited any revolutionary action.
    (B) Revolutionaries were subject to lifelong penal exile.
    (C) The tradition of reform by Parliament had been established.
    (D) The movements were dominated by intellectuals.
    (E) The leaders of the movements advocated passive resistance.

33. "God established kings as His ministers and rules peoples by them. . . . Thus princes act as ministers of God and as His lieutenants on earth."

    The passage above can be best described as a justification for

    (A) constitutional monarchy
    (B) rule by parliament
    (C) rule by the papacy
    (D) rule by the nobility
    (E) the divine right of kings

34. While holding to many of the teachings of both the Old Testament and the New Testament, Muslims reject belief in

    (A) monotheism
    (B) the divinity of Jesus
    (C) the teachings of Moses
    (D) God's covenant with Abraham
    (E) the prophets of the Old Testament

35. "This war served to diminish Britain's stature in the eyes of its own citizens and in those of the world. Guilt-ridden and anxious to achieve white solidarity, the British made immense concessions to the vanquished, which allowed the latter to maintain racial segregation and deny voting rights to the majority of the population."

    The war described above involved the

    (A) Scottish immigrants in Australia
    (B) English settlers in India
    (C) Dutch in Indonesia
    (D) Boers in South Africa
    (E) plantation owners in Trinidad

36. During the 1920's and early 1930's, Japanese citizens and United States citizens shared an enthusiasm for all of the following leisure activities EXCEPT

    (A) playing baseball
    (B) listening to the radio
    (C) watching movies
    (D) practicing martial arts
    (E) dancing the Charleston

37. All of the following were created in whole or in part from territory lost by Russia as a result of the First World War EXCEPT

    (A) Yugoslavia
    (B) Estonia
    (C) Poland
    (D) Latvia
    (E) Lithuania

GO ON TO THE NEXT PAGE

38. The English Bill of Rights of 1689 reaffirmed all of the following EXCEPT

    (A) the right to petition the king
    (B) freedom of debate in Parliament
    (C) freedom from cruel and unusual punishments
    (D) freedom to hold public office regardless of religious affiliation
    (E) the right of Parliament to authorize all taxation

39. Which of the following was an advocate of nationalist revolutions in the nineteenth century?

    (A) Cavour
    (B) Bismarck
    (C) Pugachev
    (D) Mazzini
    (E) Disraeli

40. In early Christian theology, belief in a divine plan governing worldly events and the acceptance of life's trials without undue complaint were most similar to which of the following ancient schools of philosophy?

    (A) Epicurean
    (B) Pythagorean
    (C) Stoic
    (D) Platonic
    (E) Aristotelian

41. During the eighteenth and early nineteenth centuries, one of the most important export commodities that British merchants purchased in China was

    (A) cocoa
    (B) tea
    (C) opium
    (D) crystallized sugar
    (E) cotton textiles

42. All of the following were agreed on at the Yalta conference in 1945 EXCEPT:

    (A) Free and unfettered elections would be held in Poland.
    (B) The Soviet Union would enter the war against Japan.
    (C) Germany would be divided into zones of occupation.
    (D) German war criminals would be tried and punished.
    (E) The Soviet Union would be given atomic information.

43. Which of the following is the correct chronological order, from earliest to latest, of the origins of the religions listed below?

    (A) Buddhism, Christianity, Islam
    (B) Buddhism, Islam, Christianity
    (C) Christianity, Buddhism, Islam
    (D) Christianity, Islam, Buddhism
    (E) Islam, Christianity, Buddhism

44. In the Mexican Revolution of 1910, the majority of the revolutionaries came from which of the following groups?

    (A) Russian-influenced army officers and radical clerics
    (B) Intellectuals and industrialists
    (C) Merchants and government bureaucrats
    (D) The urban upper class and large landowners
    (E) The urban working class and the peasantry

45. All of the following statements concerning the status of women in the former Soviet Union are correct EXCEPT:

    (A) Women shouldered a disproportionate share of home and family responsibilities.
    (B) Women had legal equality with men in the workplace.
    (C) Many women were members of the Central Committee of the Communist party.
    (D) The majority of Soviet physicians and surgeons were women.
    (E) Both men and women served in the Soviet military.

GO ON TO THE NEXT PAGE

46. All of the following were breaches of international treaty obligations in the 1930's EXCEPT the

  (A) rearmament of Germany
  (B) remilitarization of the Rhineland
  (C) annexation of Austria by Germany
  (D) occupation of Czechoslovakia by Germany
  (E) admission of the Soviet Union to the League of Nations

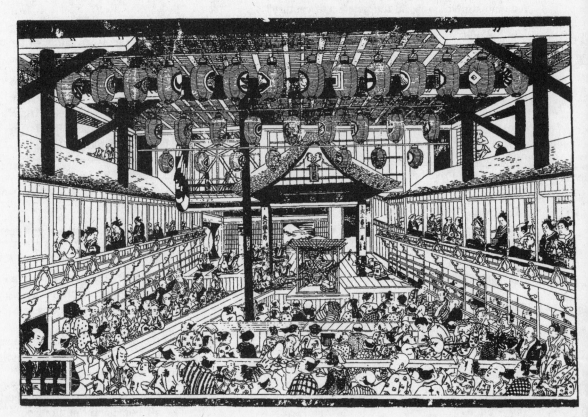

Courtesy of the Art Institute of Chicago, Clarence Buckingham Collection.

47. The picture above depicts a theatre performance in

  (A) India during the Gupta period
  (B) China during the Ming dynasty
  (C) Japan during the Tokugawa period
  (D) Indonesia under Dutch rule
  (E) the Philippines before Spanish rule

GO ON TO THE NEXT PAGE

48. Which of the following did Machiavelli advocate as a solution to Italy's political disunity and intercity warfare?

    (A) The establishment of order and unity by the French military
    (B) The negotiation of a truce among the warring city-states by the pope
    (C) The reestablishment of order by the Holy Roman Emperor
    (D) The destruction of the French troops and the establishment of order by the Spanish
    (E) The establishment of peace and political unity by a military leader from the Medici

49. Which of the following was brought under the control of the People's Republic of China in 1950-1951 ?

    (A) Tibet
    (B) Korea
    (C) Taiwan
    (D) Vietnam
    (E) Burma

50. The slave trade operated by Europeans and Americans during the late eighteenth and early nineteenth centuries had its most devastating impact on the people and cultures of

    (A) North Africa
    (B) West Africa
    (C) East Africa
    (D) South Africa
    (E) Central Africa

51. In ancient Athens, the means specifically provided for dealing with troublesome public figures was

    (A) ostracism
    (B) execution
    (C) flogging
    (D) trial by jury
    (E) human sacrifice to the gods

52. In the last quarter of the twentieth century, militant activists among the Sikhs in India and the Tamils in Sri Lanka have

    (A) been vigorous supporters of strong central governments in their countries
    (B) demanded special rights and autonomy for their ethnic groups
    (C) established fundamentalist Muslim groups working for the adoption of Islamic law
    (D) advocated the establishment of workers' republics based on class rather than ethnic interests
    (E) developed small communal settlements based on Christian liberation theology

53. "The preservation of peace forms the basis of our foreign policy. It is in the pursuit of this policy that we have chosen the policy of nonalignment. We believe, therefore, in nonaggression and noninterference by one country in the affairs of another. We are not a junior partner in this or that bloc; we control our own destiny."

    The man who made this statement in 1957 probably came from which of the following?

    (A) India
    (B) West Germany
    (C) Poland
    (D) North Korea
    (E) Taiwan

GO ON TO THE NEXT PAGE →

54. "The experience of several decades tells us to carry out the people's democratic dictatorship. That is, the right of reactionaries to voice their opinions must be abolished and only the people be allowed to have the right of voicing their opinion. Who are the 'people'? They are the working class, the peasant class, the petite bourgeoisie, and national bourgeoisie."

Which of the following national leaders most probably made this statement?

(A) Jawaharlal Nehru
(B) Mao Zedong (Mao Tse-tung)
(C) Haile Selassie
(D) Benito Mussolini
(E) Anwar Sadat

55. The eighteenth-century belief that God exists but does not interfere with the working of natural laws was a major tenet of

(A) Pietism
(B) Jansenism
(C) Methodism
(D) Quakerism
(E) Deism

56. The Peace of Augsburg in 1555 signaled a defeat for Roman Catholicism in Germany in that

(A) all church lands were confiscated by temporal rulers
(B) Roman Catholic churches became state churches separated from Rome
(C) each state was to be Roman Catholic or Lutheran according to the religion of its ruler
(D) Calvinism was recognized for the first time
(E) individual freedom of religious choice was accepted

57. The 1884-1885 Berlin Conference attempted to

(A) achieve political unification of all the German-speaking countries
(B) establish a free-trade zone in western Europe for agricultural commodities
(C) limit the arms buildup by the major European powers
(D) divide Africa into spheres of influence for European colonization
(E) outlaw socialist political parties and trade unions throughout Europe

58. "And I say also unto thee, that thou art Peter, and upon this rock I will build my church; and the gates of hell shall not prevail against it. And I will give unto thee the keys of the kingdom of heaven: and whatsoever thou shalt bind on earth shall be bound in heaven: and whatsoever thou shalt loose on earth shall be loosed also in heaven."

The quotation above is usually cited as the basis for

(A) papal supremacy
(B) claims of imperial supremacy
(C) the Crusades
(D) the building of St. Peter's Cathedral
(E) the sacraments

GO ON TO THE NEXT PAGE

59. Which of the following is an accurate statement about the right of Latin American women to vote?

    (A) It was won when Latin America gained its independence.
    (B) It has typically been won as a result of mass political action and civil disobedience.
    (C) It has been won only where socialist or Marxist governments have come to power.
    (D) It has been tied to property ownership in most countries.
    (E) It was generally won in the last half century.

60. "Atahualpa observed the greed with which [they] stole his personal table service. On the day after the massacre, [they] confiscated 800 pounds of gold, more than 3,500 pounds of silver, and 14 emeralds. . . . Although Atahualpa had paid his ransom, the invaders did not release him. . . . [After] a deathbed conversion to Christianity, [Atahualpa] was strangled by a rope twisted around his throat."

    The passage above describes the defeat of the

    (A) Khoisan peoples at the hands of the Boer settlers in southern Africa
    (B) Goths at the hands of the Romans under Valentinian I
    (C) Saxons at the hands of the Franks under Charlemagne
    (D) Saracens at the hands of the Crusaders under Richard the Lion-Hearted
    (E) Incas at the hands of the Spanish under Pizarro

61. Dramatic advancements in which of the following fields gave the greatest impetus to the scientific revolution of the seventeenth century?

    (A) Chemistry and biology
    (B) Physics and astronomy
    (C) Archaeology and geology
    (D) Medicine and theology
    (E) Astrology and alchemy

62. Which of the following results of the Paris Peace Conference of 1919 was a realization of one of President Wilson's Fourteen Points?

    (A) The unilateral disarmament of the Central Powers
    (B) Italy's acquisition of Trentino and Trieste
    (C) The cession of Germany's colonies to the victors
    (D) The re-creation of Poland as an independent country
    (E) Japan's acquisition of control over territory in China

63. Akbar, the Mughal ruler of India, strengthened the fabric of his state by

    (A) advocating religious tolerance
    (B) strictly enforcing fundamentalist Muslim law
    (C) persecuting Jesuit missionaries in India
    (D) crushing the Sikh forces in the northeast
    (E) developing a powerful navy

64. The state established as a result of the Iranian revolution in 1979 can best be described as a

    (A) radical Marxist regime
    (B) secular democratic republic
    (C) fundamentalist Islamic state
    (D) military dictatorship
    (E) constitutional monarchy

GO ON TO THE NEXT PAGE

THE THIRD-CLASS CARRIAGE

65. The painting above portrays an aspect of life in

   (A) Italy during the Renaissance
   (B) the Netherlands during the Reformation
   (C) Great Britain during the Enlightenment
   (D) France during the nineteenth century
   (E) the United States during the mid-twentieth century

GO ON TO THE NEXT PAGE

66. During the 1980's and continuing into the 1990's, the governments of Argentina, Brazil, and Chile began to move politically toward

    (A) communism
    (B) totalitarianism
    (C) corporatism
    (D) socialism
    (E) representative democracy

67.   As leaving aside worn-out garments,
           A person takes other, new ones,
        So leaving aside worn-out bodies,
           To other, new ones, goes the embodied soul.

    The passage quoted above represents a view of

    (A) baptism held by Christians
    (B) life after death held by Jews
    (C) becoming an ancestor held by Confucianists
    (D) reincarnation held by Hindus
    (E) the unending struggle for perfection held by Muslims

68. Which of the following nineteenth-century European movements used Darwin's theory of natural selection to support its policies?

    (A) Marxian socialism
    (B) Imperialism
    (C) Monarchism
    (D) Nationalism
    (E) Realism

69. Which of the following was a factor common to both the 1905 and the 1917 Russian Revolutions?

    (A) Military losses that created dissatisfaction with government policies
    (B) A liberal ideology that unified revolutionary forces
    (C) Military intervention by European powers
    (D) Successful exertion of government power over the revolutionaries
    (E) The pivotal role played by foreign advisors at the imperial court

70. When the Portuguese sailed around the Cape of Good Hope and entered the Indian Ocean in the late fifteenth century, they found

    (A) numerous ports under the control of merchants from Genoa and Venice
    (B) colonial domination of ports and sea lanes by the navy of the Ottoman Empire
    (C) a region where sea trade had not yet developed
    (D) a region defended and patrolled by fleets of the Chinese navy
    (E) a network of long-distance trade routes dominated by Muslim merchants

71. Greek city-states responded to the pressures of insufficient land and overpopulation by

    (A) regulating the age of marriage
    (B) conquering the kingdoms of Egypt and Phoenicia
    (C) sponsoring the colonization of overseas areas
    (D) reclaiming marsh areas
    (E) redistributing land

72. Which of the following statements is true of both Catherine the Great and Alexander I of Russia?

    (A) They encouraged hopes for internal reforms, which were not realized to any significant degree.
    (B) They were devoted to mystical religious doctrines.
    (C) They actively promoted the development of Russian industry.
    (D) They engaged in progressive emancipation of the Russian serfs.
    (E) They hailed the French Revolution as the triumph of the principles of liberty, equality, and fraternity.

GO ON TO THE NEXT PAGE

73. The Vedas are hymns and religious poems composed by

    (A) priests in the ancient cities of Mesopotamia
    (B) the Aryan groups that migrated to ancient India
    (C) the prophet Muhammad
    (D) Greek Stoics
    (E) Taoist monks in China

74. Which of the following best describes the orientation of President Salvador Allende when he nationalized mines and banks in Chile in the 1970's?

    (A) Capitalist
    (B) Marxist
    (C) Anarchist
    (D) Militarist
    (E) Nihilist

75. A major function of the Committee of Public Safety established in France in 1793 was to

    (A) expose and punish opponents of the Revolution
    (B) sue for peace with Austria and Prussia
    (C) ensure that the peasantry had sufficient supplies of grain
    (D) bring an end to the Reign of Terror
    (E) control revolutionary mobs in the streets of Paris

76. "He could reform the calendar, introduce a modified Roman script, and compel everyone to adopt surnames, but his impact on traditional attitudes — outside the main cities — was slight. His ambition to give his country a modern economy achieved only very limited success."

    The man described above is

    (A) Kemal Atatürk
    (B) Frederick the Great
    (C) Gandhi
    (D) Nasser
    (E) Hitler

77. The Great Leap Forward in China was primarily designed to do which of the following?

    (A) Achieve rapid industrialization of the Chinese economy
    (B) Oust the imperial government
    (C) Promote capitalism within the Chinese economy
    (D) Strengthen the Chinese so they could expel the Japanese from Manchuria
    (E) Expand Chinese influence in the Third World

78. Which of the following best describes nineteenth-century Zionism?

    (A) A political organization that advocated full civil rights for Jewish people everywhere in Europe
    (B) A Russian Jewish benevolent organization that advocated emigration to North America
    (C) A self-protection society in Germany and Austria-Hungary organized to combat anti-Semitism
    (D) An organization supporting the liberation of Alfred Dreyfus, the French officer imprisoned for treason
    (E) A movement among Jewish people in western and central Europe to create a separate Jewish state

79. Which of the following best describes the concept of karma in Hinduism?

    (A) The effect of personal actions on one's destiny
    (B) The pursuit of permissible pleasure
    (C) The cycle of birth and rebirth
    (D) The illusory world of the senses
    (E) The universal soul

GO ON TO THE NEXT PAGE ➤

80. All of the following were true of the New World colonies of Spain and Portugal EXCEPT:

    (A) Catholicism became the dominant religion.
    (B) Relations among ethnic groups were amicable.
    (C) Social and economic power was held by local elites.
    (D) The Crown attempted to govern through a centralized bureaucracy.
    (E) Autocracy was the rule in rural areas.

81. "Violence, intrigue, and bloody internecine rivalries characterized almost every accession to the throne. The odds against a prospective candidate's dying a natural death were astronomical. The army was biased in favor of choosing a successor from among its own generals."

    The situation described above obtained in

    (A) third-century Rome
    (B) tenth-century Germany
    (C) fifteenth-century England
    (D) seventeenth-century Spain
    (E) nineteenth-century Russia

82. Which of the following is the architectural feature LEAST likely to be found in Gothic cathedrals?

    (A) Elaborate stone sculptures
    (B) Rib vaulting
    (C) Domes
    (D) Flying buttresses
    (E) Large stained-glass windows

83. All of the following cities were under the control of the Ottoman Empire during the seventeenth and eighteenth centuries EXCEPT

    (A) Istanbul
    (B) Vienna
    (C) Jerusalem
    (D) Cairo
    (E) Athens

84. "Last summer the American barbarians arrived in the Bay of Uraga with four warships, bearing their President's message. Their deportment and manner of expression were exceedingly arrogant and the resulting insult to our national dignity was not small."

    The passage above is a local observer's account of

    (A) the first North American diplomatic mission to China
    (B) the first North American diplomatic mission to Samoa
    (C) the arrival of North American vessels in Hawaii
    (D) Stephen Decatur's mission to Tripoli to secure the release of North Americans captured by pirates
    (E) Admiral Perry's mission to open Japan to North American commercial interests

GO ON TO THE NEXT PAGE

85. Emmeline Pankhurst and her daughters, Christabel and Sylvia, were important figures in history because of their role in the struggle of British women to obtain

(A) the right to vote
(B) free access to birth control
(C) equal pay for equal work
(D) equal divorce rights
(E) protection for children working in factories

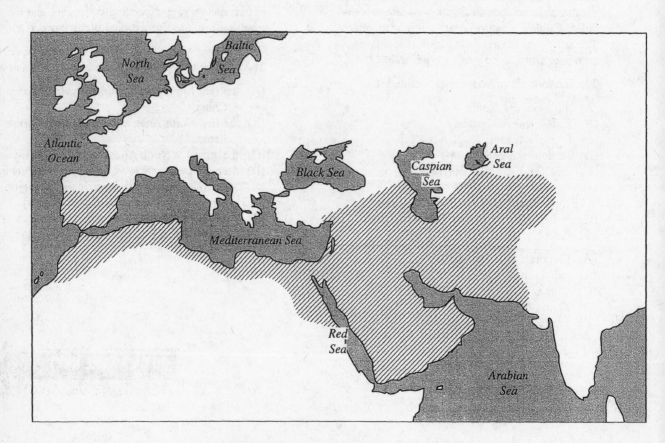

86. The lined portion of the map above indicates areas at the beginning of the ninth century included within the

(A) Byzantine Empire
(B) Islamic world
(C) Mongol dominions
(D) Holy Roman Empire
(E) Carolingian Empire

GO ON TO THE NEXT PAGE →

87. Which of the following best supports the argument that the First World War marked the end of the nineteenth century in Europe?

    (A) The increase in the number and types of military weapons
    (B) The introduction of mass conscription
    (C) The disappearance of large dynastic empires
    (D) The destruction of colonial empires
    (E) The creation of the European Common Market

88. Which of the following Russians is NOT correctly paired with his principal field of activity?

    (A) Turgenev..literature
    (B) Pushkin..painting
    (C) Pavlov..psychology
    (D) Mendeleyev..chemistry
    (E) Rimsky-Korsakov..music

89. Chinese government policy on population growth since the 1980's does which of the following?

    (A) Leaves decisions on family size to personal discretion.
    (B) Encourages population growth by offering subsidized day care to large families.
    (C) Allows religious groups to determine family size for their members.
    (D) Severely limits family size and punishes violators.
    (E) Encourages emigration from China to less populous neighboring nations.

90. "As the leading humanist of Northern Europe, he thought the aim of scholarship must be to free religious texts from corrupt translations and ignorant interpretations. Although a harsh critic of the Catholic church, he refused to participate in the destruction of Christian unity and became one of Martin Luther's harshest critics."

    The passage above best describes

    (A) John Calvin
    (B) Ulrich Zwingli
    (C) William Laud
    (D) John Knox
    (E) Desiderius Erasmus

91. Which of the following best describes the process by which China became a communist nation?

    (A) The Soviet army placed the Chinese communists in power.
    (B) The urban industrial workers revolted and took over the government.
    (C) The communist North invaded and took over the noncommunist South.
    (D) The communists won a plurality in the first free elections held after the fall of the Manchu dynasty.
    (E) The communists, supported by the peasantry, defeated the Nationalists.

GO ON TO THE NEXT PAGE →

Marburg/Art Resource

92. The statuary shown above was created during which
of the following periods?

    (A) Egyptian Old Kingdom
    (B) Archaic Greek
    (C) Late Roman
    (D) Medieval European
    (E) European High Renaissance

GO ON TO THE NEXT PAGE

93. Which of the following was viewed by eighteenth-century European society as a socially acceptable occupation for upper-class women?

    (A) Arts and letters
    (B) Banking and commerce
    (C) Engineering
    (D) Diplomacy
    (E) Theology

94. When the price of oil rose dramatically in 1973, which of the following was dependent on imported petroleum for nearly three-fourths of its energy?

    (A) Canada
    (B) The Soviet Union
    (C) China
    (D) Japan
    (E) The United States

95. The Truman Doctrine was proclaimed after tensions between the United States and the Soviet Union surfaced as a result of the civil war in which of the following countries?

    (A) Greece
    (B) The Philippines
    (C) Vietnam
    (D) India
    (E) Spain

STOP

IF YOU FINISH BEFORE TIME IS CALLED, YOU MAY CHECK YOUR WORK ON THIS TEST ONLY.
DO NOT TURN TO ANY OTHER TEST IN THIS BOOK.

How to Score the SAT Subject Test in World History

When you take an actual SAT Subject Test in World History, your answer sheet will be "read" by a scanning machine that will record your responses to each question. Then a computer will compare your answers with the correct answers and produce your raw score. You get one point for each correct answer. For each wrong answer, you lose one-fourth of a point. Questions you omit (and any for which you mark more than one answer) are not counted. This raw score is converted to a scaled score that is reported to you and to the colleges you specify.

Worksheet 1. Finding Your Raw Test Score

STEP 1: Table A lists the correct answers for all the multiple-choice questions on the SAT Subject Test in World History that is reproduced in this book. It also serves as a worksheet for you to calculate your raw multiple-choice score.

- Compare your answers with those given in the table.
- Put a check in the column marked "Right" if your answer is correct.
- Put a check in the column marked "Wrong" if your answer is incorrect.
- Leave both columns blank if you omitted the question.

STEP 2: Count the number of right answers.

Enter the total here: _____

STEP 3: Count the number of wrong answers.

Enter the total here: _____

STEP 4: Multiply the number of wrong answers by .250

Enter the product here: _____

STEP 5: Subtract the result obtained in Step 4 from the total you obtained in Step 2.

Enter the result here: _____

STEP 6: Round the number obtained in Step 5 to the nearest whole number.

Enter the result here: _____

The number you obtained in Step 6 is your raw score.

TABLE A
Answers to the SAT Subject Test in World History, Form 3SAC, and Percentage of Students Answering Each Question Correctly

Question Number	Correct Answer	Right	Wrong	Percentage of Students Answering the Question Correctly*	Question Number	Correct Answer	Right	Wrong	Percentage of Students Answering the Question Correctly*
1	D			87	36	D			52
2	A			37	37	A			48
3	C			77	38	D			44
4	E			60	39	D			24
5	D			86	40	C			41
6	C			64	41	B			52
7	B			39	42	E			69
8	D			76	43	A			37
9	A			70	44	E			75
10	B			77	45	C			21
11	D			88	46	E			69
12	A			81	47	C			69
13	B			83	48	E			45
14	D			30	49	A			42
15	D			49	50	B			67
16	C			65	51	A			38
17	E			58	52	B			50
18	E			30	53	A			39
19	C			54	54	B			33
20	A			57	55	E			50
21	B			48	56	C			51
22	D			68	57	D			38
23	B			53	58	A			35
24	E			84	59	E			57
25	D			47	60	E			66
26	C			26	61	B			59
27	B			84	62	D			46
28	A			85	63	A			36
29	E			70	64	C			55
30	C			74	65	D			52
31	A			63	66	E			70
32	C			54	67	D			85
33	E			90	68	B			44
34	B			75	69	A			50
35	D			56	70	E			29

Table A continued on next page

Table A continued from previous page

Question Number	Correct Answer	Right	Wrong	Percentage of Students Answering the Question Correctly*	Question Number	Correct Answer	Right	Wrong	Percentage of Students Answering the Question Correctly*
71	C			35	84	E			50
72	A			34	85	A			48
73	B			43	86	B			55
74	B			48	87	C			40
75	A			44	88	B			35
76	A			32	89	D			88
77	A			73	90	E			33
78	E			65	91	E			60
79	A			59	92	D			43
80	B			52	93	A			79
81	A			47	94	D			26
82	C			38	95	A			36
83	B			59					

*These percentages are based on an analysis of the answer sheets for a random sample of 4,591 students who took this form of the test in June 1996 and whose mean score was 580. They may be used as an indication of the relative difficulty of a particular question. Each percentage may also be used to predict the likelihood that a typical SAT Subject Test in World History candidate will answer correctly that question on this edition of this test.

Finding Your Scaled Score

When you take SAT Subject Tests, the scores sent to the colleges you specify are reported on the College Board scale, which ranges from 200 to 800. You can convert your practice test score to a scaled score by using Table B. To find your scaled score, locate your raw score in the left-hand column of Table B; the corresponding score in the right-hand column is your scaled score. For example, a raw score of 47 on this particular edition of the SAT Subject Test in World History corresponds to a scaled score of 600.

Raw scores are converted to scaled scores to ensure that a score earned on any one edition of a particular Subject Test is comparable to the same scaled score earned on any other edition of the same Subject Test. Because some editions of tests may be slightly easier or more difficult than others, scaled scores are adjusted so that they indicate the same level of performance regardless of the edition of the test taken and the ability of the group that takes it. Thus, for example, a score of 400 on one edition of a test taken at a particular administration indicates the same level of achievement as a score of 400 on a different edition of the test taken at a different administration.

When you take the SAT Subject Tests during a national administration, your scores are likely to differ somewhat from the scores you obtain on the tests in this book. People perform at different levels at different times for reasons unrelated to the tests themselves. The precision of any test is also limited because it represents only a sample of all the possible questions that could be asked.

TABLE B
Scaled Score Conversion Table
World History Subject Test (Form 3SAC)

Raw Score	Scaled Score	Raw Score	Scaled Score	Raw Score	Scaled Score
95	800	55	650	15	420
94	800	54	640	14	410
93	800	53	640	13	410
92	800	52	630	12	400
91	800	51	630	11	400
90	800	50	620	10	390
89	800	49	620	9	380
88	800	48	610	8	380
87	800	47	600	7	370
86	800	46	600	6	370
85	800	45	590	5	360
84	800	44	590	4	360
83	800	43	580	3	350
82	800	42	580	2	340
81	800	41	570	1	340
80	800	40	560	0	330
79	790	39	560	−1	320
78	780	38	550	−2	320
77	780	37	550	−3	310
76	770	36	540	−4	300
75	760	35	530	−5	300
74	760	34	530	−6	290
73	750	33	520	−7	280
72	740	32	520	−8	280
71	740	31	510	−9	270
70	730	30	500	−10	260
69	730	29	500	−11	260
68	720	28	490	−12	250
67	720	27	490	−13	250
66	710	26	480	−14	240
65	700	25	480	−15	240
64	700	24	470	−16	230
63	690	23	460	−17	220
62	690	22	460	−18	220
61	680	21	450	−19	210
60	680	20	450	−20	210
59	670	19	440	−21	200
58	670	18	440	−22	200
57	660	17	430	−23	200
56	660	16	420	−24	200

Reviewing Your Performance on the World History Subject Test

After you score your test, analyze your performance—consider the following questions:

Did you run out of time before reaching the end of the test?

If so, you may need to pace yourself better. For example, maybe you spent too much time on one or two hard questions. A better approach might be to skip the ones you can't answer right away and try answering all the questions that remain on the test. Then if there's time, go back to the questions you skipped.

Did you take a long time reading the directions?

You will save time when you take the test by learning the directions to the World History Subject Test ahead of time. Each minute you spend reading directions during the test is a minute you could use to answer questions.

How did you handle questions you were unsure of?

If you were able to eliminate one or more of the answer choices as wrong and guess from the remaining ones, your approach probably worked to your advantage. On the other hand, making haphazard guesses or omitting questions without trying to eliminate choices could cost you valuable points.

How difficult were the questions for you compared with other students who took the test?

Table A shows you how difficult the multiple-choice questions were for the group of students who took this test during its national administration. The right-hand column gives the percentage of students that answered each question correctly.

A question answered correctly by almost everyone in the group is obviously an easy question. For example, 90 percent of the students answered question 33 correctly. But only 21 percent answered question 45 correctly.

Keep in mind that these percentages are based on just one group of students. They would probably be different if another group of students took the test.

If you missed several easy questions, go back and try to find out why: Did the questions cover material you haven't reviewed yet? Did you misunderstand the directions?

Chapter 4
Mathematics

Purpose

There are two, one-hour subject tests in mathematics: Math Level 1 and Math Level 2. The purpose of these tests is to measure your knowledge of math through the first three years of college-preparatory mathematics for Level 1 and through precalculus for Level 2.

Format—Math Level 1 Subject Test

Math Level 1 is a one-hour broad survey test that consists of 50 multiple-choice questions. The test has questions on the following topics:

- algebra
- geometry (plane Euclidean geometry, coordinate geometry, three-dimensional geometry)
- basic trigonometry
- algebraic functions
- elementary statistics, including counting problems, probability, data interpretation, and measures of central tendency (mean, median, and mode)
- miscellaneous topics, including logic, elementary number theory, and arithmetic and geometric sequences

Format—Math Level 2 Subject Test

This one-hour test also contains 50 multiple-choice questions covering a variety of areas and topics:

- algebra
- geometry (coordinate geometry and three-dimensional geometry)
- trigonometry
- functions

- statistics, including probability, permutations, and combinations
- miscellaneous topics, including logic and proof, elementary number theory, sequences, and limits.

Recommended Preparation

Both tests require the use of a calculator at least at the level of a scientific calculator.

Familiarize yourself with directions in advance. The directions in this book are identical to those that appear on the test.

The SAT Subject Test in Math Level 2 is intended for students who have taken college-preparatory mathematics for more than three years: two years of algebra and one year of geometry, and elementary functions (precalculus) and/or trigonometry. You are not expected to have studied every topic on the test.

If you have studied trigonometry and elementary functions, have attained grades of B or better in these courses, and have skill in knowing when and how to use a scientific or graphing calculator, you should select the Level 2 test. If you are sufficiently prepared to take Level 2, but elect to take Level 1 in hopes of receiving high scores, you may not do as well as you expect.

Calculator Use

- **Both tests require the use of a scientific or graphing calculator.** It is not necessary to use a calculator to solve every question, but it is important to know when and how to use one. Students who take these tests without a calculator will be at a disadvantage.
- Both tests are developed with the expectation that most students are using graphing calculators. A graphing calculator may provide an advantage over a scientific calculator on some questions. However, you should bring the calculator with which you are most familiar.
- For 50 to 60 percent of the questions on Level 1 and 35 to 45 percent of the questions on Level 2, there is no advantage, perhaps even a disadvantage, to using a calculator. For 40 to 50 percent of the questions on Level 1 and 55 to 65 percent of the questions on Level 2, a calculator may be useful or necessary.

> *Calculator Policy: Currently students are not permitted to use a calculator on any Subject Test other than the Math Level 1 and Level 2 Tests.*

The questions on both tests are classified into three categories regarding calculator use:

CATEGORY 1: Calculator inactive—there is no advantage (perhaps even a disadvantage) to using a calculator.

CATEGORY 2: Calculator neutral—these problems can be solved without a calculator, but a calculator may be helpful.

CATEGORY 3: Calculator active—a calculator is very helpful or necessary to solve these problems.

You are permitted to use almost any scientific or graphing calculator on the Level 1 and Level 2 tests. You are NOT ALLOWED to use pocket organizers, "handheld" minicomputers, laptop computers, models with QWERTY (i.e., typewriter) keypads, electronic writing pads and pen-input devices, models with paper tapes, models that make noise or "talk," and calculators that require an external power source such as an electrical outlet. Students may not share calculators.

You should be thoroughly familiar with the operation of the calculator you plan to use on the test. Your degree of familiarity with the calculator may affect how well you do on the test.

To minimize the chance of a calculator malfunction, you should put in fresh batteries and make certain before the test that your calculator is in good working order. Test center staff cannot assist you if your calculator malfunctions. No batteries or calculators will be available at the test center for your use. You may bring batteries and a backup calculator to the test center. If your calculator malfunctions when you are taking Level 1 or Level 2 and you do not have a backup calculator, you must tell your test supervisor when the malfunction occurs in order to cancel scores on these tests only.

Comparing the Two Tests

The chart below shows approximately how the questions in each test are distributed among the major curriculum areas.

Topics Covered	Approximate Percentage of Test	
	Level 1	Level 2
Number and Operations	10–14	10–14
Operations, ratio and proportion, complex numbers, counting, elementary number theory, matrices, sequences, series, vectors		
Algebra and Functions	38–42	48–52
Expressions, equations, inequalities, representation and modeling, properties of functions (linear, polynomial, rational, exponential, *logarithmic*, *trigonometric*, *inverse trigonometric*, *periodic*, *piecewise*, *recursive*, *parametric*)		
Geometry and Measurement	38–42	28–32
Plane Euclidean/Measurement	18–22	—
Coordinate	8–12	10–14
Lines, parabolas, circles, *ellipses*, *hyperbolas*, symmetry, transformations, *polar coordinates*		
Three-dimensional	4–6	4–6
Solids, surface area and volume (cylinders, cones, pyramids, spheres, prisms), *coordinates in three dimensions*		
Trigonometry	6–8	12–16
Right triangles, identities, *radian*, *measure*, *law of cosines*, *law of sines*, *equations*, *double angle formulas*		
Data Analysis, Statistics, and Probability	6–10	6–10
Mean, median, mode, range, interquartile range, *standard deviation*, graphs and plots, regression (linear, *quadratic*, *exponential*), probability		

Areas of Overlap

The content of Level 1 overlaps somewhat with Level 2, especially in the following areas:

- elementary algebra
- three-dimensional geometry
- coordinate geometry
- statistics
- basic trigonometry

Differences Between the Tests

Although some questions may be appropriate for both tests, the emphasis for Level 2 is on more advanced content. The tests differ significantly in the following areas:

GEOMETRY   A significant percentage of the questions on Level 1 is devoted to plane Euclidean geometry, which is not tested directly on Level 2. The geometry questions on Level 2 cover topics such as *coordinate geometry*, *transformations*, and *three-dimensional geometry*.

TRIGONOMETRY   The trigonometry questions on Level 1 are primarily limited to *right triangle trigonometry* and the *fundamental relationships among the trigonometric ratios*. Level 2 places more emphasis on the *properties and graphs of the trigonometric functions, the inverse trigonometric functions, trigonometric equations and identities*, and *the laws of sines and cosines*.

FUNCTIONS   Level 1 contains mainly *algebraic* functions, whereas Level 2 also contains more advanced functions, such as *logarithmic* and *exponential functions*.

STATISTICS   The statistics questions on Level 1 include *probability*, *mean*, *median*, *mode*, *counting*, and *data interpretation*. Level 2 also has questions on *permutations*, *combinations*, and *standard deviation*.

Scores

The total score for each test is reported on the 200-to-800 scale. In general, because the content measured by Level 1 and Level 2 differs considerably, you should not use your score on one test to predict your score on the other.

Math Level 1

Sample Questions

All questions in the Math Level 1 and Level 2 Tests are multiple-choice questions in which you must choose the BEST response from the five choices offered. The directions that follow are the same as those that are in the Math Level 1 Test.

Directions: For each of the following problems, decide which is the BEST of the choices given. If the exact numerical value is not one of the choices, select the choice that best approximates this value. Then fill in the corresponding oval on the answer sheet.

Notes:

(1) A calculator will be necessary for answering some (but not all) of the questions in this test. For each question you will have to decide whether or not you should use a calculator. The calculator you use must be at least a scientific calculator; programmable calculators and calculators that can display graphs are permitted.

(2) The only angle measure used on this test is degree measure. Make sure your calculator is in the degree mode.

(3) Figures that accompany problems in this test are intended to provide information useful in solving the problems. They are drawn as accurately as possible EXCEPT when it is stated in a specific problem that its figure is not drawn to scale. All figures lie in a plane unless otherwise indicated.

(4) Unless otherwise specified, the domain of any function f is assumed to be the set of all real numbers x for which $f(x)$ is a real number.

(5) Reference information that may be useful in answering the questions in this test can be found on the page preceding Question 1.

Reference Information: The following information is for your reference in answering some of the questions in this test.

Volume of a right circular cone with radius r and height h: $V = \frac{1}{3}\pi r^2 h$

Lateral Area of a right circular cone with circumference of the base c and slant height ℓ: $S = \frac{1}{2}c\ell$

Volume of a sphere with radius r: $V = \frac{4}{3}\pi r^3$

Surface Area of a sphere with radius r: $S = 4\pi r^2$

Volume of a pyramid with base area B and height h: $V = \frac{1}{3}Bh$

Algebra

1. The rental cost of a certain video game is $6 per day for each of the first 2 days and $3 per day for each succeeding day. Which of the following is an expression for the cost, in dollars, of renting this video game for n days, if $n > 2$?

   (A) $5n$
   (B) $6 + 3(n-2)$
   (C) $12 + 3n$
   (D) $12 + (3n-2)$
   (E) $12 + 3(n-2)$

For the first two days the rental cost is $12. For the remaining $(n-2)$ days the rental cost is $3(n-2)$ dollars. Thus, the total cost, in dollars, of renting the video game for n days is $12 + 3(n-2)$, which is choice (E).

2. If $ax^2 + 12x + 9 = 0$ has $-\dfrac{3}{2}$ as its only solution, what is the value of a ?

    (A) $-\dfrac{3}{2}$

    (B) $-\dfrac{2}{3}$

    (C) 2

    (D) 3

    (E) 4

$$a\left(-\tfrac{3}{2}\right)^2 + 12\left(-\tfrac{3}{2}\right) + 9 =$$

$$\tfrac{3}{2} \times \tfrac{3}{2} = \tfrac{9}{4} \qquad \tfrac{24}{2}$$

$$21 - 12$$

$$\tfrac{9}{4}a - 12 + 9 = 0$$

One way to solve for a is to substitute $-\dfrac{3}{2}$ for x in the equation, which would

result in $a\left(-\dfrac{3}{2}\right)^2 + 12\left(-\dfrac{3}{2}\right) + 9 = 0$ or $\dfrac{9}{4}a - 9 = 0$. This equation yields $a = 4$, which

is choice (E). Another way to solve this question is to recognize that if a quadratic

equation of the form $ax^2 + bx + c = 0$ has only 1 root, then the discriminant,

$b^2 - 4ac$, is 0. Therefore, $12^2 - 4(a)(9) = 144 - 36a = 0$. Thus, $a = 4$. Alternately, if

you have a graphing calculator with a solver, you can use it to find the value of a

when $x = -\dfrac{3}{2}$.

Plane Geometry

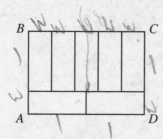

Figure 1

3. Rectangle *ABCD* in Figure 1 is formed from seven congruent rectangles and has perimeter 68. What is the area of rectangle *ABCD* ?

    (A) 98

    (B) 196

    (C) 280

    (D) 284

    (E) 476

Let ℓ and w represent the length and width, respectively, of each of the congruent rectangles and label the figure as shown below.

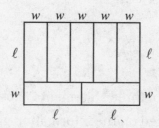

Since the perimeter of *ABCD* is 68, $7w + 4\ell = 68$. Also, $5w = 2\ell$ since $BC = AD$. You can substitute for ℓ in the first equation:

$$7w + 10w = 68$$
$$17w = 68$$
$$w = 4$$

If $w = 4$, then $\ell = 10$. The area of rectangle *ABCD* is $(w + \ell)(5w) = 14(20) = 280$. The correct answer is (C).

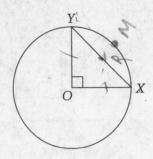

Figure 2

4. In Figure 2, X and Y are points on the circle with center O. Point M (not shown) is a point on the minor arc $\overset{\frown}{XY}$ such that $\overline{OM}$ intersects $\overline{XY}$ at point R (not shown). If $OX = 5$, which of the following must be true?

    I. $XY = 5\sqrt{2}$

    II. $XR = RY$

    III. $OM = 5$

    (A) I only

    (B) II only

    (C) III only

    (D) I and II

    (E) I and III

In this type of question, each of three statements, labeled I, II, and III, must be considered independently based on the information given. First, consider statement I. From the figure we know $\overline{OX} \perp \overline{OY}$. Since $\overline{OX}$ and $\overline{OY}$ are both radii and $OX = 5$, then $OY = 5$. Thus, $\overline{XY}$ is the hypotenuse of an isosceles right triangle and has length $5\sqrt{2}$, and statement I is true.

In statement II, we know that R is the point where $\overline{OM}$ intersects $\overline{XY}$. If M is closer to Y, then R is also closer to Y, and if M is closer to X, R is closer to X. Thus, it *cannot* be concluded that $XR = RY$.

In statement III, since we know the circle has radius 5 and that $\overline{OM}$ is a radius of the circle, statement III is true. Therefore, the correct choice is (E) because statements I and III *must* be true.

Coordinate Geometry

5. If one vertex of a square in the xy-plane has coordinates $(0,0)$, how many other vertices of the square must lie on either the x-axis or the y-axis?

    (A) None

    (B) One

    (C) Two

    (D) Three

    (E) Four

For this question it may be helpful to draw a figure:

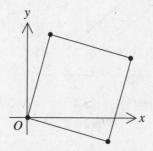

The figure above shows a square with no other vertices on the axes. Therefore, the correct choice is (A) since none of the other three vertices must be on the axes.

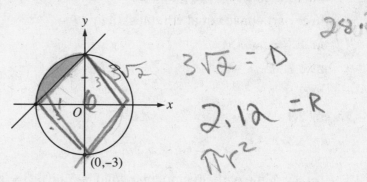

Figure 3

6. In Figure 3, the origin O is the center of the circle. What is the area of the shaded region?

    (A) 0.21

    (B) 0.29

    (C) 2.57

    (D) 14.35

    (E) 19.27

Figure 3 shows a circle with radius 3. The area of the shaded region is equal to the area of a quarter circle minus the area of the right triangle shown. Thus, the area of the shaded region is $\dfrac{9\pi}{4} - \dfrac{1}{2}(3)(3)$, which is approximately equal to 2.5686. The best answer is choice (C) 2.57.

Solid Geometry

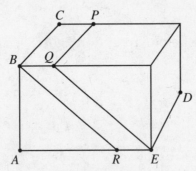

Note: Figure not drawn to scale.

Figure 4

7. Figure 4 shows a rectangular solid with $AB = 5$, $AE = 10$, and $ED = 6$. The solid is sliced by two parallel planes, one passing through points P, Q, and E and the other passing through points B, C, and R, dividing the solid into three parts. If the three parts have equal volumes, then $CP =$

   (A) 1.3
   (B) 1.7
   (C) 2
   (D) 2.9
   (E) 3.3

The total volume of the rectangular solid is $5 \times 10 \times 6 = 300$. Therefore, the volume of each part is 100. The volume of the piece containing points A, B, and R is found by multiplying the area of the base by the height of the piece. Thus, the volume is $\left(\dfrac{1}{2} \cdot 5 \cdot AR \right) \cdot 6$, which equals 100. The length of AR is $\dfrac{20}{3}$ and $RE = 10 - \dfrac{20}{3} = \dfrac{10}{3}$. Since the planes are parallel, $CP = BQ = RE$. Thus, $CP = \dfrac{10}{3}$ or 3.3. The correct answer is (E).

Trigonometry

8. In $\triangle ABC$, the measure of $\angle A$ is $50°$ and the length of side AB is 8. What is the length of the altitude from B to side AC?

   (A) 4.6

   (B) 5.1

   (C) 5.7

   (D) 6.1

   (E) 6.4

Although you don't know exactly what triangle ABC looks like, you can draw the following sketch.

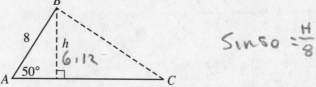

Let h be the length of the altitude from B to side AC. You need to use the properties of right triangle trigonometry to find h. Since $\sin 50° = \dfrac{h}{8}$, $h = 8 \sin 50°$, which is approximately equal to 6.128. The best answer is (D). Remember your calculator should always be in the degree mode for the Level 1 Test.

Algebraic Functions

9. If $f(g(x)) = 6x + 3$ and $(g(x)) = 2x + 1$, which of the following is $f(x)$?

   (A) 3

   (B) $3x$

   (C) $3(2x + 1)$

   (D) $3g(x)$

   (E) $g(3x)$

The problem involves the composition of two functions f and g. In this case, $g(x)$ is being used as the "input" value in function f. Because $(2x + 1)$ is the "input" value for f, you need to determine the rule $f(x)$ that would yield an "output" value of $6x + 3$. Since $6x + 3 = 3(2x + 1)$, the function that gives an "output" value equal to 3 times its "input" value is required. If x represents the "input" value for f, then $3x$ is the "output" value. Thus, $f(x) = 3x$, and the correct choice is (B).

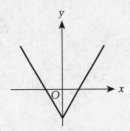

Figure 5

10. Figure 5 is the graph of $y = f(x)$. Which of the following is the graph of $y = |f(x)|$?

(A)

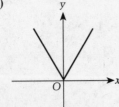

(B)

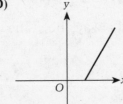

(C)

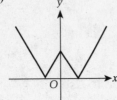

(D)

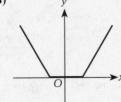

(E)

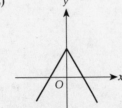

This problem can be solved by using the fact that the absolute value of any number is greater than or equal to 0. Since $|x| = -x$ when x is negative, all values of $|f(x)|$ where $f(x) < 0$ will be transformed to $-f(x)$ by the definition of absolute value. Thus the portion of the graph below the x-axis in Figure 5 (that is, where

$y = f(x) < 0)$ would be reflected in that axis to become positive. The correct choice is (A). You can use a graphing calculator to see what effect taking the absolute value of a function has on the graph of the function by graphing a function that extends below the *x*-axis and also graphing its absolute value.

Elementary Statistics

11. This year the owner of a firm paid each of his 50 employees the same salary as last year, but the owner, whose salary was greatest, increased his own salary from $200,000 to $225,000. How does this affect the mean and median of all the salaries of this year compared with those of last year?

    (A) The mean and the median stay the same.

    (B) The mean increases, but the median stays the same.

    (C) The mean stays the same, but the median increases.

    (D) The mean and median both increase.

    (E) It cannot be determined from the information given.

The mean salary equals the result when the sum of all 51 salaries is divided by 51. Since the sum of the salaries increased by $25,000, the mean salary increases. The median salary is the middle salary, when the salaries are ordered from least to greatest (or vice versa). Since the only salary that changed was the greatest salary, the median salary stays the same. Therefore, the correct choice is (B).

Miscellaneous

12. If p and r are different prime numbers, which of the following numbers must be odd?

   (A) pr

   (B) $2p + r$

   (C) $p + r + 1$

   (D) $pr - 1$

   (E) $2p + 2r + 1$

This is a number theory question. You need to think about all possible values for p and r, and then look at each of the answer choices to see if they *must* be odd. Since 2 is a prime number and a possible value for p or r, choice (A) could be even. Likewise, if p is odd and $r = 2$, choices (B) and (C) would be even. If both p and r are odd, choice (D) is even. For choice (E), $2p + 2r$ must be even for all values of p and r, so $2p + 2r + 1$ must be odd. The correct answer is (E).

Math Level 1 Test

The test that follows is an actual, recently administered SAT Subject Test in Math Level 1. To get an idea of what a real administration is like, take the test under conditions as close as possible to those of a national administration:

- Set aside an hour when you can take the test uninterrupted. Make sure you complete the test in one sitting.

- Sit at a desk or table with no other books or papers. Dictionaries, other books, or notes are not allowed in the test room.

- Remember to have a scientific or graphing calculator with you.

- Time yourself by placing a clock or kitchen timer in front of you.

- Tear out an answer sheet from the back of this book and fill it in just as you would on the day of the test. One answer sheet can be used for up to three Subject Tests.

- Read the instructions that precede the practice test. During the actual administration you will be asked to read them before answering test questions. Become familiar with the directions so you aren't seeing them for the first time during the actual administration.

- After you finish the practice test, read the sections "How to Score the SAT Subject Test in Math Level 1" and "Reviewing Your Performance on the Math Level 1 Subject Test."

- Actual test and answer sheets will indicate circles, not ovals.

Form 3TBC2

REFERENCE INFORMATION

THE FOLLOWING INFORMATION IS FOR YOUR REFERENCE IN ANSWERING SOME OF THE QUESTIONS IN THIS TEST.

Volume of a right circular cone with radius r and height h: $V = \frac{1}{3}\pi r^2 h$

Lateral Area of a right circular cone with circumference of the base c and slant height ℓ: $S = \frac{1}{2}c\ell$

Volume of a sphere with radius r: $V = \frac{4}{3}\pi r^3$

Surface Area of a sphere with radius r: $S = 4\pi r^2$

Volume of a pyramid with base area B and height h: $V = \frac{1}{3}Bh$

MATHEMATICS LEVEL IC TEST

The top portion of the section of the answer sheet that you will use in taking the Mathematics Level IC test must be filled in exactly as shown in the illustration below. Note carefully that you have to do all of the following on your answer sheet.

1. Print MATHEMATICS LEVEL IC on the line under the words "Subject Test (print)."

2. In the shaded box labeled "Test Code" fill in four ovals:

   —Fill in oval 3 in the row labeled V.

   —Fill in oval 2 in the row labeled W.

   —Fill in oval 5 in the row labeled X.

   —Fill in oval A in the row labeled Y.

3. Please answer Part I and Part II below by filling in the specified ovals in row Q that correspond to the courses you have taken or are presently taking, and the oval that corresponds to the type of calculator you are going to use to take this test. The information that you provide is for statistical purposes only and will not affect your score on the test.

Part I.   Which of the following describes a mathematics course you have taken or are currently taking? (FILL IN **ALL** OVALS THAT APPLY.)

- Algebra I or Elementary Algebra **OR** Course I of a college preparatory mathematics sequence —Fill in oval 1.

- Geometry **OR** Course II of a college preparatory mathematics sequence —Fill in oval 2.

- Algebra II or Intermediate Algebra **OR** Course III of a college preparatory mathematics sequence —Fill in oval 3.

- Elementary Functions (Precalculus) and/or Trigonometry **OR** beyond Course III of a college preparatory mathematics sequence —Fill in oval 4.

- Advanced Placement Mathematics (Calculus AB or Calculus BC) —Fill in oval 5.

Part II.   What type of calculator did you bring to use for this test? (FILL IN THE **ONE** OVAL THAT APPLIES.)

- 4-Function —Fill in oval 6.

- Scientific —Fill in oval 7.

- Graphing —Fill in oval 8.

- None (Forgot or do not have a calculator) —Fill in oval 9.

When the supervisor gives the signal, turn the page and begin the Mathematics Level IC test. There are 100 numbered ovals on the answer sheet and 50 questions in the Mathematics Level IC test. Therefore, use only ovals 1 to 50 for recording your answers.

MATHEMATICS LEVEL IC TEST

For each of the following problems, decide which is the BEST of the choices given. If the exact numerical value is not one of the choices, select the choice that best approximates this value. Then fill in the corresponding oval on the answer sheet.

Notes: (1) A calculator will be necessary for answering some (but not all) of the questions in this test. For each question you will have to decide whether or not you should use a calculator. The calculator you use must be at least a scientific calculator; programmable calculators and calculators that can display graphs are permitted.

(2) The only angle measure used on this test is degree measure. Make sure your calculator is in the degree mode.

(3) Figures that accompany problems in this test are intended to provide information useful in solving the problems. They are drawn as accurately as possible EXCEPT when it is stated in a specific problem that its figure is not drawn to scale. All figures lie in a plane unless otherwise indicated.

(4) Unless otherwise specified, the domain of any function f is assumed to be the set of all real numbers x for which $f(x)$ is a real number.

(5) Reference information that may be useful in answering the questions in this test can be found on the page preceding Question 1.

USE THIS SPACE FOR SCRATCHWORK.

1. If $2t + 3t = 4t + 6t - 10$, then $t =$

   (A) −1   (B) 0   (C) $\frac{1}{2}$ (D) 1   (E) 2

2. For all $x \neq 0, \dfrac{1}{\left(\dfrac{2}{x^2}\right)} =$

   (A) $\dfrac{x^2}{2}$ (B) $\dfrac{x^2}{4}$ (C) $\dfrac{2}{x^2}$ (D) $\dfrac{1}{2x^2}$ (E) $2x^2$

3. If $x = 1$, then $(x - 5)(x + 2) =$

   (A) −12   (B) −3   (C) −1   (D) 3   (E) 12

GO ON TO THE NEXT PAGE

3TBC2

USE THIS SPACE FOR SCRATCHWORK.

4. In rectangle $ABCD$ in Figure 1, what are the coordinates of vertex C ?

   (A) $(1, 4)$
   (B) $(1, 5)$
   (C) $(5, 7)$
   (D) $(7, 4)$
   (E) $(7, 5)$

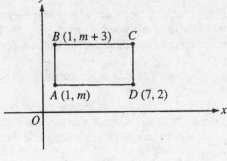

Figure 1

5. $(a + b + 2)(a + b + 2) =$

   (A) $(a + b)^2 + 4$
   (B) $(a + b)^2 + 4(a + b)$
   (C) $(a + b)^2 + 4(a + b) + 4$
   (D) $a^2 + b^2 + 4$
   (E) $a^2 + b^2 + 4ab$

6. At what point does the graph of $2x + 3y = 12$ intersect the y-axis?

   (A) $(0, -6)$
   (B) $(0, -2)$
   (C) $(0, 3)$
   (D) $(0, 4)$
   (E) $(0, 12)$

7. If $12x^2 = 7$, then $7\left(12x^2\right)^2 =$

   (A) 49
   (B) 84
   (C) 98
   (D) 144
   (E) 343

GO ON TO THE NEXT PAGE

MATHEMATICS LEVEL IC TEST — *Continued*

8. If lines ℓ and m are parallel and are intersected by line t, what is the sum of the measures of the interior angles on the same side of line t ?

   (A) 90°   (B) 180°   (C) 270°   (D) 360°   (E) 540°

9. If $x + y = 5$ and $x - y = 3$, then $x =$

   (A) 4   (B) 2   (C) 1   (D) 0   (E) −1

10. If the cube root of the square root of a number is 2, what is the number?

    (A)   16
    (B)   32
    (C)   36
    (D)   64
    (E)   256

11. Each face of the cube in Figure 2 consists of nine small squares. The shading on three of the faces is shown, and the shading on the other three faces is such that on opposite faces the reverse squares are shaded. For example, if one face has only the center square shaded, its opposite face will have eight of the nine squares shaded (the center square will not be shaded). What is the total number of shaded squares on all six faces of the cube?

    (A) 12   (B) 16   (C) 18   (D) 27   (E) 54

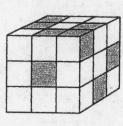

Figure 2

12. For three bins, A, B, and C, the volume of A is one-half that of B and the volume of B is two-thirds that of C. If A has a volume of 210 cubic meters, what is the volume of C, in cubic meters?

    (A) 630   (B) 315   (C) 280   (D) 140   (E) 70

GO ON TO THE NEXT PAGE

MATHEMATICS LEVEL IC TEST—*Continued*

USE THIS SPACE FOR SCRATCHWORK.

13. In Figure 3, when ray OA is rotated clockwise 7 degrees about point O, ray OA will be perpendicular to ray OB. What is the measure of $\angle AOB$ before this rotation?

(A) 97° (B) 90° (C) 87° (D) 83° (E) 80°

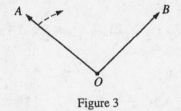

Figure 3

14. If $x + x + x = y$, then $x - y =$

(A) $-3x$ (B) $-2x$ (C) $-\frac{x}{2}$ (D) $\frac{2}{3}x$ (E) $2x$

15. If $f(x) = \frac{1}{x}$ for $x > 0$, then $f(1.5) =$

(A) $\frac{3}{4}$ (B) $\frac{2}{3}$ (C) $\frac{1}{2}$ (D) $\frac{1}{3}$ (E) $\frac{1}{4}$

16. If $15^m = 3^4 \cdot 5^4$, what is the value of m ?

(A) 4 (B) 8 (C) 16 (D) 32 (E) 128

17. What are all values of x for which $|x - 2| < 3$?

(A) $x < -1$ or $x > 5$
(B) $x < -1$
(C) $x > 5$
(D) $-5 < x < 1$
(E) $-1 < x < 5$

GO ON TO THE NEXT PAGE

MATHEMATICS LEVEL IC TEST—*Continued*

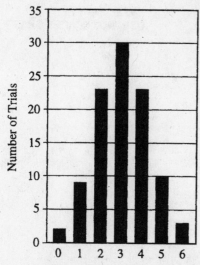

Number of Heads per 6–coin Toss

18. An algebra class conducted a coin-tossing experiment. Each trial of the experiment consisted of tossing 6 coins and counting the number of heads that resulted. The results for 100 trials are pictured in the graph above. In approximately what percent of the trials were there 3 <u>or more</u> heads?

(A) 32%   (B) 36%   (C) 50%   (D) 60%   (E) 66%

19. The circle in Figure 4 has center J and radius 6. What is the length of chord GH ?

(A) 6   (B) 8.49   (C) 10.39   (D) 12   (E) 16.97

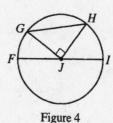

Figure 4

GO ON TO THE NEXT PAGE

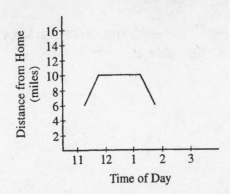

USE THIS SPACE FOR SCRATCHWORK.

20. The graph above shows the distance of Janet's car from her home over a period of time on a given day. Which of the following situations best fits the information?

(A) Janet leaves her workplace, drives to a restaurant for lunch, and then returns to her workplace.
(B) Janet leaves her workplace, drives home, and stays at home.
(C) Janet leaves home, drives to a friend's house, and stays at the friend's house.
(D) Janet drives from home to the grocery store and then returns home.
(E) Janet is at the grocery store, takes the groceries home, and then drives back to the grocery store.

$$X = \{2, 3, 4, 5, 6, 7, 8, 9\}$$
$$Y = \{0, 1\}$$
$$Z = \{0, 1, 2, 3, 4, 5, 6, 7, 8, 9\}$$

21. Before 1990, telephone area codes in the United States were three-digit numbers of the form xyz. Shown above are sets X, Y, and Z from which the digits x, y, and z, respectively, were chosen. How many possible area codes were there?

(A) 919   (B) 160   (C) 144   (D) 126   (E) 20

GO ON TO THE NEXT PAGE

MATHEMATICS LEVEL IC TEST—*Continued*

USE THIS SPACE FOR SCRATCHWORK.

22. In Figure 5, $\triangle ABC$ is equilateral and $EF \parallel DG \parallel AC$. What is the perimeter of the shaded region?

    (A) 4   (B) 6   (C) 8   (D) 9   (E) 10

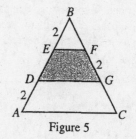

Figure 5

23. In Figure 6, two congruent circles are tangent to the number line at points 5 and 10, respectively, and tangent to rays from points 0 and 8, respectively. The circle at 10 is to be moved to the right along the number line, and the ray from point 8 is to be rotated so that it is tangent to the circle at its new position and $\tan x° = \tan y°$. How many units to the right must the circle be moved?

    (A) 1   (B) 2   (C) 3   (D) 4   (E) 5

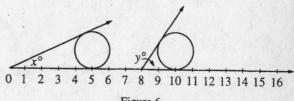

Figure 6

GO ON TO THE NEXT PAGE

IC IC IC IC IC IC IC IC IC

MATHEMATICS LEVEL IC TEST—*Continued*

USE THIS SPACE FOR SCRATCHWORK.

24. A beacon that rotates in a complete circle at a constant rate throws a single beam of light that is seen every 9 seconds at a point four miles away. How many degrees does the beacon turn in 1 second?

    (A) 6°   (B) 20°   (C) 40°   (D) 54°   (E) 60°

25. If $i^2 = -1$ and if $\left(\left(i^2\right)^3\right)^k = 1$, then the least positive integer value of k is

    (A) 1   (B) 2   (C) 4   (D) 6   (E) 8

26. In Figure 7, if $\theta = 44°$, what is the value of c ?

    (A) 6.94   (B) 7.19   (C) 9.66   (D) 10.36   (E) 13.90

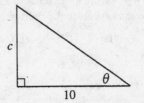

Note: Figure not drawn to scale.

Figure 7

GO ON TO THE NEXT PAGE

MATHEMATICS LEVEL IC TEST—*Continued*

USE THIS SPACE FOR SCRATCHWORK.

27. The thickness of concrete that lines a swimming pool is a function of the depth of the pool. If d represents the depth, in feet, of the pool and $t(d)$ represents the thickness, in inches, of the concrete, then $t(d) = \frac{1}{12}\left(d^2 - 2d + 6\right)$.

Of the following, which is the closest approximation to the thickness, in inches, of the concrete at a depth of 10 feet?

(A) 0.5   (B) 1.5   (C) 6.2   (D) 7.2   (E) 10.5

28. Of the following, which has the greatest value?

(A) 10^{100}

(B) 100^{10}

(C) $\left(10 \cdot 10^{10}\right)^{10}$

(D) $(100 \cdot 10)^{10}$

(E) 10,000,000,000

29. In the xy-plane, the points $O(0, 0)$, $P(-6, 0)$, $R(-7, 5)$, and $S(-1, 1)$ can be connected to form line segments. Which two segments have the same length?

(A) OP and OR
(B) OP and OS
(C) OR and RS
(D) OS and PR
(E) PR and PS

30. A total of 9 students took a test and their average (arithmetic mean) score was 86. If the average score for 4 of the students was 81, what was the average score for the remaining 5 students?

(A) 87   (B) 88   (C) 89   (D) 90   (E) 91

GO ON TO THE NEXT PAGE

MATHEMATICS LEVEL IC TEST—*Continued*

USE THIS SPACE FOR SCRATCHWORK.

31. Line ℓ has a positive slope and a negative y-intercept.
    Line m is parallel to ℓ and has a positive y-intercept.
    The x-intercept of m must be

    (A) negative and greater than the x-intercept of ℓ
    (B) negative and less than the x-intercept of ℓ
    (C) zero
    (D) positive and greater than the x-intercept of ℓ
    (E) positive and less than the x-intercept of ℓ

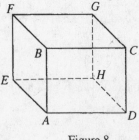

32. Figure 8 is a right rectangular prism. Which of the given points is
    located in the plane determined by the vertices G, H, and B ?

    (A) A (B) C (C) D (D) E (E) F

Figure 8

33. The sum of the two roots of a quadratic equation is 5 and their
    product is -6. Which of the following could be the equation?

    (A) $x^2 - 6x + 5 = 0$
    (B) $x^2 - 5x - 6 = 0$
    (C) $x^2 - 5x + 6 = 0$
    (D) $x^2 + 5x - 6 = 0$
    (E) $x^2 + 6x + 5 = 0$

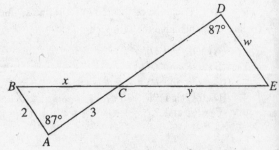

34. In Figure 9, triangles ABC and DEC are similar and $w = 5$.
    What is the value of $\dfrac{x}{y}$?

    (A) $\dfrac{2}{5}$ (B) $\dfrac{3}{5}$ (C) $\dfrac{2}{3}$ (D) $\dfrac{3}{2}$ (E) $\dfrac{5}{2}$

Note: Figure not drawn to scale.

Figure 9

35. $\left(\sin^2\theta + \cos^2\theta - 3\right)^4 =$

    (A) 256   (B) 81   (C) 64   (D) 32   (E) 16

GO ON TO THE NEXT PAGE

USE THIS SPACE FOR SCRATCHWORK.

36. In Figure 10, if $\triangle ABC$ is reflected across line ℓ, what will be the coordinates of the reflection of point A ?

    (A) $(5, 1)$ (B) $(8, 1)$ (C) $(9, 1)$ (D) $(11, 1)$ (E) $(13, 1)$

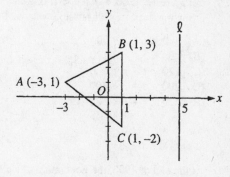

Figure 10

37. In Figure 11, the cube has edge of length 2. What is the distance from vertex A to the midpoint C of edge BD ?

    (A) $\sqrt{7}$
    (B) $2\sqrt{2}$
    (C) 3
    (D) 5
    (E) $\sqrt{29}$

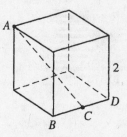

Figure 11

38. The line with equation $y = 7$ is graphed on the same xy-plane as the circle with center $(4, 5)$ and radius 3. What are the x-coordinates of the points of intersection of the line and the circle?

    (A) -5 and 5
    (B) -1 and 1
    (C) 1.35 and 6.65
    (D) 1.76 and 6.24
    (E) 2 and 6

GO ON TO THE NEXT PAGE

MATHEMATICS LEVEL IC TEST—*Continued*

USE THIS SPACE FOR SCRATCHWORK.

39. In Figure 12, if $60 < q + s < 160$, which of the
following describes all possible values of $t + r$?

(A) $\quad 0 < t + r < 60$
(B) $\quad 60 < t + r < 120$
(C) $120 < t + r < 200$
(D) $200 < t + r < 300$
(E) $420 < t + r < 520$

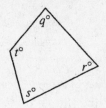

Figure 12

40. At the end of 1990, the population of a certain town
was 6,250. If the population increases at the rate of 3.5
percent each year, what will the population of the town
be at the end of 2005 ?

(A) 9,530
(B) 9,740
(C) 9,950
(D) 10,260
(E) 10,470

41. If points R, S, and T lie on a circle and if the center of the
circle lies on segment RT, then $\triangle RST$ must be

(A) acute
(B) obtuse
(C) right
(D) isosceles
(E) equilateral

42. The function f, where $f(x) = (1 + x)^2$, is defined for
$-2 \leq x \leq 2$. What is the range of f ?

(A) $0 \leq f(x) \leq 4$
(B) $0 \leq f(x) \leq 9$
(C) $1 \leq f(x) \leq 4$
(D) $1 \leq f(x) \leq 5$
(E) $1 \leq f(x) \leq 9$

GO ON TO THE NEXT PAGE

USE THIS SPACE FOR SCRATCHWORK.

43. In the right circular cylinder shown in Figure 13, P and O are the centers of the bases and segment AB is a diameter of one of the bases. What is the perimeter of $\triangle ABO$ if the height of the cylinder is 5 and the radius of the base is 3 ?

    (A) 11.83
    (B) 14.66
    (C) 16
    (D) 16.66
    (E) 17.66

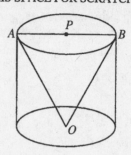

Figure 13

44. Sequential arrangements of squares are formed according to a pattern. Each arrangement after the first one is generated by adding a row of squares to the bottom of the previous arrangement, as shown in Figure 14. If this pattern continues, which of the following gives the number of squares in the nth arrangement?

    (A) $2n^2$

    (B) $2(2n-1)$

    (C) $n(n-1)$

    (D) $\frac{1}{2}n(n+1)$

    (E) $n(n+1)$

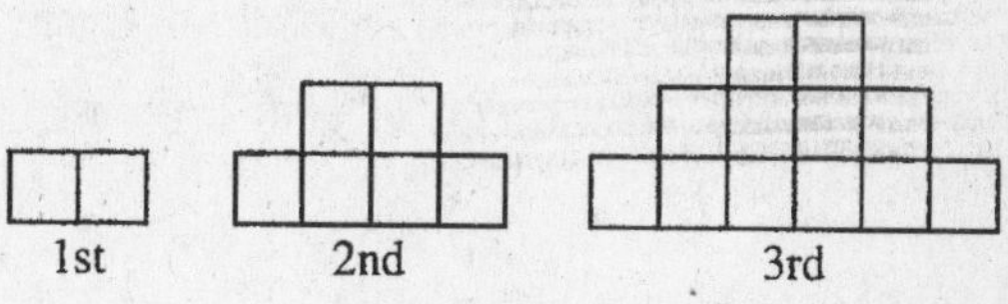

1st   2nd   3rd

Figure 14

45. If $f(x) = x^3 + 1$ and if f^{-1} is the inverse function of f, what is $f^{-1}(4)$?

    (A) 0.02   (B) 1.44   (C) 1.71   (D) 27   (E) 65

GO ON TO THE NEXT PAGE

USE THIS SPACE FOR SCRATCHWORK.

46. Two positive integers j and k satisfy the relation $j\mathbf{R}k$ if and only if $j = k^2 + 1$. If m, n, and p satisfy the relations $m\mathbf{R}n$ and $n\mathbf{R}p$, what is the value of m in terms of p ?

    (A) $p^2 + 1$

    (B) $p^2 + 2$

    (C) $\left(p^2 + 1\right)^2$

    (D) $\left(p^2 + 1\right)^2 + 1$

    (E) $\left(p^2 + 2\right)^2$

47. The area of parallelogram $ABCD$ in Figure 15 is

    (A) 12   (B) $6\sqrt{3}$ (C) 20   (D) $12\sqrt{3}$ (E) 24

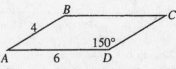

Figure 15

48. In Figure 16, the area of the shaded region bounded by the graph of the parabola $y = f(x)$ and the x-axis is 3. What is the area of the region bounded by the graph of $y = f(x - 2)$ and the x-axis?

    (A) 1   (B) $\dfrac{3}{2}$ (C) 2   (D) 3   (E) 6

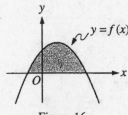

Figure 16

GO ON TO THE NEXT PAGE

USE THIS SPACE FOR SCRATCHWORK.

49. Marigolds are to be planted inside a circular flower garden so that there are 4 marigolds per square foot. The circumference of the garden is 20 feet. If marigolds are available only in packs of 6, how many packs of 6 flowers are needed?

   (A) 6 (B) 13 (C) 14 (D) 20 (E) 22

50. A solution is made by mixing concentrate with water. How many liters of concentrate should be mixed with 2 liters of water so that 32 percent of the solution is concentrate?

   (A) 0.63
   (B) 0.64
   (C) 0.68
   (D) 0.94
   (E) 1.06

STOP

IF YOU FINISH BEFORE TIME IS CALLED, YOU MAY CHECK YOUR WORK ON THIS TEST ONLY.
DO NOT TURN TO ANY OTHER TEST IN THIS BOOK.

How to Score the SAT Subject Test in Math Level 1

When you take the SAT Subject Test in Math Level 1, your answer sheet will be "read" by a scanning machine that will record your responses to each question. Then a computer will compare your answers with the correct answers and produce your raw score. You get one point for each correct answer. For each wrong answer, you lose one-fourth of a point. Questions you omit (and any for which you mark more than one answer) are not counted. This raw score is converted to a College Board scaled score that is reported to you and to the colleges you specify.

Worksheet 1. Finding Your Raw Test Score

STEP 1: Table A lists the correct answers for all the questions on the SAT Subject Test in Math Level 1 that is reproduced in this book. It also serves as a worksheet for you to calculate your raw score.

- Compare your answers with those given in the table.
- Put a check in the column marked "Right" if your answer is correct.
- Put a check in the column marked "Wrong" if your answer is incorrect.
- Leave both columns blank if you omitted the question.

STEP 2: Count the number of right answers.

Enter the total here: _____

STEP 3: Count the number of wrong answers.

Enter the total here: _____

STEP 4: Multiply the number of wrong answers by .250.

Enter the product here: _____

STEP 5: Subtract the result obtained in Step 4 from the total you obtained in Step 2.

Enter the result here: _____

STEP 6: Round the number obtained in Step 5 to the nearest whole number.

Enter the result here: _____

The number you obtained in Step 6 is your raw score.

TABLE A

Answers to the SAT Subject Test in Math Level 1, Form 3TBC2, and Percentage of Students Answering Each Question Correctly

Question Number	Correct Answer	Right	Wrong	Percentage of Students Answering the Question Correctly*	Question Number	Correct Answer	Right	Wrong	Percentage of Students Answering the Question Correctly*
1	E			92	26	C			68
2	A			76	27	D			72
3	A			93	28	C			52
4	E			91	29	E			57
5	C			65	30	D			53
6	D			77	31	B			58
7	E			86	32	A			51
8	B			77	33	B			24
9	A			88	34	A			51
10	D			80	35	E			49
11	D			78	36	E			38
12	A			75	37	C			34
13	A			80	38	D			25
14	B			75	39	D			37
15	B			86	40	E			25
16	A			71	41	C			25
17	E			71	42	B			14
18	E			65	43	E			51
19	B			80	44	E			42
20	A			72	45	B			28
21	B			68	46	D			32
22	E			66	47	A			19
23	C			60	48	D			19
24	C			72	49	E			22
25	B			63	50	D			27

* These percentages are based on an analysis of the answer sheets of a random sample of 9,999 students who took the original form of this test in December 1997, and whose mean score was 564. They may be used as an indication of the relative difficulty of a particular question. Each percentage may also be used to predict the likelihood that a typical SAT Subject Test in Math Level 1 candidate will answer correctly that question on this edition of the test.

Finding Your Scaled Score

When you take SAT Subject Tests, the scores sent to the colleges you specify are reported on the College Board scale, which ranges from 200 to 800. You can convert your practice test score to a scaled score by using Table B. To find your scaled score, locate your raw score in the left-hand column of Table B; the corresponding score in the right-hand column is your scaled score. For example, a raw score of 30 on this particular edition of the SAT Subject Test in Math Level 1 corresponds to a scaled score of 620.

Raw scores are converted to scaled scores to ensure that a score earned on any one edition of a particular Subject Test is comparable to the same scaled score earned on any other edition of the same Subject Test. Because some editions of tests may be slightly easier or more difficult than others, scaled scores are adjusted so that they indicate the same level of performance regardless of the edition of the test taken and the ability of the group that takes it. Thus, for example, a score of 400 on one edition of a test taken at a particular administration indicates the same level of achievement as a score of 400 on a different edition of the test taken at a different administration.

When you take the SAT Subject Tests during a national administration, your scores are likely to differ somewhat from the scores you obtain on the tests in this book. People perform at different levels at different times for reasons unrelated to the tests themselves. The precision of any test is also limited because it represents only a sample of all the possible questions that could be asked.

TABLE B

Scaled Score Conversion Table
Math Level 1 Test (Form 3TBC2)

Raw Score	Scaled Score	Raw Score	Scaled Score	Raw Score	Scaled Score
50	800	28	590	6	390
49	790	27	580	5	380
48	780	26	570	4	380
47	780	25	560	3	370
46	770	24	550	2	360
45	750	23	540	1	350
44	740	22	530	0	340
43	740	21	520	−1	340
42	730	20	510	−2	330
41	720	19	500	−3	320
40	710	18	490	−4	310
39	710	17	480	−5	300
38	700	16	470	−6	300
37	690	15	460	−7	280
36	680	14	460	−8	270
35	670	13	450	−9	260
34	660	12	440	−10	260
33	650	11	430	−11	250
32	640	10	420	−12	240
31	630	9	420		
30	620	8	410		
29	600	7	400		

Reviewing Your Performance on the Math Level 1 Subject Test

After you score your test, analyze your performance—consider the following questions:

Did you run out of time before reaching the end of the test?

If so, you may need to pace yourself better. For example, maybe you spent too much time on one or two hard questions. A better approach might be to skip the ones you can't answer right away and try answering all the questions that remain on the test. Then if there's time, go back to the questions you skipped.

Did you take a long time reading the directions?

You will save time when you take the test by learning the directions to the Math Level 1 Subject Test ahead of time. Each minute you spend reading directions during the test is a minute that you could use to answer questions. Also be familiar with what formulas are given at the front of the test so that you know when to refer to them during the test.

How did you handle questions you were unsure of?

If you were able to eliminate one or more of the answer choices as wrong and guess from the remaining ones, your approach probably worked to your advantage. On the other hand, making haphazard guesses or omitting questions without trying to eliminate choices could cost you valuable points.

How difficult were the questions for you compared with other students who took the test?

Table A shows you how difficult the multiple-choice questions were for the group of students who took this test during its national administration. The right-hand column gives the percentage of students that answered each question correctly.

A question answered correctly by almost everyone in the group is obviously an easy question. For example, 91 percent of the students answered question 4 correctly. But only 19 percent answered question 47 correctly.

Keep in mind that these percentages are based on just one group of students. They would probably be different if another group of students took the test.

If you missed several easy questions, go back and try to find out why: Did the questions cover material you haven't reviewed yet? Did you misunderstand the directions?

Math Level 2

Sample Questions

All questions in the Math Level 1 and Level 2 Tests are multiple-choice questions in which you must choose the BEST response from the five choices offered. The directions that follow are the same as those that are in the Level 2 test.

Directions: For each of the following problems, decide which is the BEST of the choices given. If the exact numerical value is not one of the choices, select the choice that best approximates this value. Then fill in the corresponding oval on the answer sheet.

Notes:

(1) A calculator will be necessary for answering some (but not all) of the questions in this test. For each question you will have to decide whether or not you should use a calculator. The calculator you use must be at least a scientific calculator; programmable calculators and calculators that can display graphs are permitted.

(2) For some questions in this test you may have to decide whether your calculator should be in the radian mode or the degree mode.

(3) Figures that accompany problems in this test are intended to provide information useful in solving the problems. They are drawn as accurately as possible EXCEPT when it is stated in a specific problem that its figure is not drawn to scale. All figures lie in a plane unless otherwise indicated.

(4) Unless otherwise specified, the domain of any function f is assumed to be the set of all real numbers x for which $f(x)$ is a real number.

(5) Reference information that may be useful in answering the questions in this test can be found on the page preceding Question 13.

Reference Information: The following information is for your reference in answering some of the questions in this test.

Volume of a right circular cone with radius r and height h: $V = \frac{1}{3}\pi r^2 h$

Lateral Area of a right circular cone with circumference of the base c and slant height ℓ: $S = \frac{1}{2}c\ell$

Volume of a sphere with radius r: $V = \frac{4}{3}\pi r^3$

Surface Area of a sphere with radius r: $S = 4\pi r^2$

Volume of a pyramid with base area B and height h: $V = \frac{1}{3}Bh$

Algebra

13. If $2^x = 3$, what does 3^x equal?

   (A) 5.7
   (B) 5.2
   (C) 2.0
   (D) 1.8
   (E) 1.6

A calculator is useful for this problem. To solve for x, you can take the natural log of both sides of the equation.

$$\ln 2^x = \ln 3$$
$$x \ln 2 = \ln 3$$
$$x = \frac{\ln 3}{\ln 2} = \frac{1.0986}{0.6931} \approx 1.5850$$
$$3^x \approx 5.7045$$

Since the directions to this test state, "If the exact numerical value is not one of the choices, select the choice that best approximates this value," the correct answer choice is (A).

You can also solve this problem by using a graphing calculator. First, graph $y_1 = 2^x$ and $y_2 = 3^x$. Using the trace feature, find an x-value that gives a y-value very close to 3 (for example, $y_1 = 3.0003$ at $x = 1.5851$). You may need to adjust the window to get very close. Move to y_2 and read off the y_2-value (in the example above, the y_2-value is 5.7054 which is approximately equal to 5.7, choice (A)).

Solid Geometry

Figure 6

14. In Figure 6, R and T are the midpoints of two adjacent edges of the cube. If the length of each edge of the cube is h, what is the volume of the pyramid $PRST$?

(A) $\dfrac{h^3}{24}$

(B) $\dfrac{h^3}{12}$

(C) $\dfrac{h^3}{8}$

(D) $\dfrac{h^3}{6}$

(E) $\dfrac{h^3}{4}$

The formula for the volume of the pyramid and several other formulae are given in the reference information at the beginning of the test. The volume of a pyramid is $\dfrac{1}{3}Bh$, where B is the area of the base of the pyramid and h is its height. It may be helpful to mark the figure to indicate those parts whose lengths are given or that can be deduced.

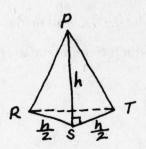

Since segment PS is perpendicular to the triangular base RST, its length h is the

height of the pyramid $PRST$. R and T are the midpoints of the two adjacent edges

of the cube; therefore, the lengths of segments RS and ST are both $\dfrac{h}{2}$.

Since $\triangle RST$ is a right triangle, its area is $\left(\dfrac{1}{2}\right)\left(\dfrac{h}{2}\right)\left(\dfrac{h}{2}\right) = \dfrac{h^2}{8}$. Thus the

volume of $PRST$ is $\left(\dfrac{1}{3}\right)\left(\dfrac{h^2}{8}\right)(h) = \dfrac{h^3}{24}$ and the correct choice is (A).

Coordinate Geometry

15. The graph of $\begin{cases} x = -t + 3 \\ y = 2t + 5 \end{cases}$ is a straight line whose y-intercept is

(A) $-\dfrac{5}{2}$

(B) $\dfrac{1}{2}$

(C) 3

(D) $\dfrac{11}{2}$

(E) 11

To answer this question, it would be helpful to write the parametric equations as

a single equation in terms of x and y. Since $t = 3 - x$ and $t = \dfrac{y-5}{2}$, then

$3 - x = \dfrac{y-5}{2}$ or $y = -2x + 11$. The y-intercept is the point with an x-coordinate of 0;

therefore, the y-intercept is 11. Another method of solution is to first observe

that at the y-intercept, x equals 0. Therefore, since $x = 0$, it follows that $t = 3$. For

$t = 3$, the y value is 11. Using a graphing calculator, you can set the calculator to

parametric mode. The two parametric equations can then be entered, graphed,

and traced to find the y-intercept. The correct answer is (E).

Trigonometry

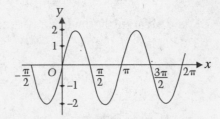

Figure 7

16. Which of the following equations has the graph shown in Figure 7?

    (A) $y = \sin\dfrac{x}{2} + 1$

    (B) $y = \sin 2x$

    (C) $y = 2\sin\dfrac{x}{2}$

    (D) $y = 2\sin x$

    (E) $y = 2\sin 2x$

The graph in Figure 7 is the graph of a sine function with amplitude 2 and period π. Therefore, the equation of the graph shown in Figure 7 is $y = 2\sin 2x$, which is choice (E).

    This problem can also be solved using a graphing calculator. However, to save time, you should first try to eliminate some of the choices. For example, choices (A) and (B) can be eliminated because each has an amplitude of 1 and the graph shows a sine function with an amplitude of 2. Also, choice (D) can be eliminated because it has a period of 2π. The remaining two choices can now be graphed and compared to the graph in Figure 7.

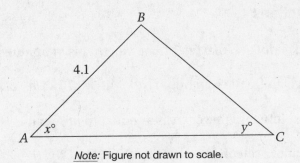

Note: Figure not drawn to scale.

Figure 8

17. In the triangle in Figure 8, $x = 36$ and $y = 30$. What is the length of side BC?

 (A) 3.5

 (B) 3.8

 (C) 4.8

 (D) 5.1

 (E) 7.5

This problem can be solved by using the law of sines with the calculator in degree mode.

$$\frac{\sin 30°}{4.1} = \frac{\sin 36°}{\text{length of side } BC}$$

The length of side $BC = \dfrac{(4.1)\sin 36°}{\sin 30°}$, which is approximately equal to 4.82.

Another method of solution is to draw a perpendicular from B to side AC and use right triangles. The correct choice is (C).

Elementary Functions

18. The total cost, in dollars, of a telephone call that is m minutes in length from City

    R to City T is given by the function $f(m) = 1.06(0.75 \times \lceil m \rceil + 1)$, where $m > 0$ and

    $\lceil m \rceil$ is the least integer greater than or equal to m. What is the total

    cost of a 5.5 minute telephone call from City R to City T?

    (A) $4.77
    (B) $5.04
    (C) $5.25
    (D) $5.56
    (E) $5.83

To solve this question, you need to evaluate $f(5.5) = 1.06(0.75\lceil 5.5 \rceil + 1)$. Since 6 is the least integer greater than 5.5, $\lceil 5.5 \rceil = 6$. Thus, $f(5.5) = 1.06(0.75(6)+1) = 5.83$. The correct choice is (E).

19. If $f(x) = 10^x$, where x is a real number, and if the inverse function of f is

    denoted by f^{-1}, then what is $\dfrac{f^{-1}(a)}{f^{-1}(b)}$ where $a > 1$ and $b > 1$?

    (A) $\log_{10} a - \log_{10} b$

    (B) $\log_{10}(a - b)$

    (C) $\dfrac{\log_{10} a}{\log_{10} b}$

    (D) $\dfrac{10^b}{10^a}$

    (E) $\log_{10} \dfrac{b}{a}$

Since the inverse of the exponential function $f(x) = 10^x$ is the logarithmic

function $f^{-1}(x) = \log_{10} x$, $\dfrac{f^{-1}(a)}{f^{-1}(b)} = \dfrac{\log_{10} a}{\log_{10} b}$ and the correct choice is (C).

20. If $f(x) = \dfrac{1-x}{x-1}$ for all $x \neq 1$, which of the following statements must be true?

I. $f(3) = f(2)$

II. $f(0) = f(2)$

III. $f(0) = f(4)$

(A) None

(B) I only

(C) II only

(D) II and III only

(E) I, II, and III

Realizing that $\dfrac{1-x}{x-1} = -1$ for all $x \neq 1$ greatly simplifies this problem. Since $f(0)$,

$f(2)$, $f(3)$, and $f(4)$ are all equal to -1, statements I, II, and III are all true and

the correct choice is (E). If you do not realize $f(x) = -1$, you can easily substitute

the numbers in f. Using a calculator may actually be a disadvantage to you if

you spend time substituting the numbers into an expression of this kind to find

the answer. However, if you have a graphing calculator, you can graph

$f(x) = \dfrac{1-x}{x-1}$ and see that the graph is a horizontal line crossing the y-axis at -1.

Therefore, $f(x) = -1$ for all values of x except 1.

Statistics

21. The probability that R hits a certain target is $\frac{3}{5}$ and, independently, the probability that T hits it is $\frac{5}{7}$. What is the probability that R hits the target and T misses it?

    (A) $\frac{4}{35}$

    (B) $\frac{6}{35}$

    (C) $\frac{3}{7}$

    (D) $\frac{21}{25}$

    (E) $\frac{31}{35}$

Since the two events are independent, the probability that R hits the target and T misses it is the product of the two probabilities. The former probability is given.

Since the probability that T hits the target is $\frac{5}{7}$, the probability that T misses the target is $1 - \frac{5}{7}$ or $\frac{2}{7}$. Therefore, $P = \left(\frac{3}{5}\right)\left(\frac{2}{7}\right) = \frac{6}{35}$. The correct choice is (B).

22. When five integers are arranged from least to greatest, the median is 4. If the only mode for this set of numbers is 6, what is the greatest sum that these five numbers can have?

    (A) 21
    (B) 22
    (C) 23
    (D) 24
    (E) 28

Since the median of the five integers is 4, the middle number in the list is 4. The two numbers greater than 4 are both 6 since the only mode for this set is 6; and so no other number can be repeated in the list.

The greatest sum results when the largest possible values are used for the two smaller numbers. Because 6 is the only mode, these two smaller numbers cannot be equal. Therefore, the five integers are 2, 3, 4, 6, and 6 and the sum of these five integers is 21. The correct choice is (A).

Miscellaneous

23. Two-thirds of the freshman class at a college were in the top 10 percent of their high school class. Half of the freshman class at this same college were in the top 3 percent of their high school class. What fraction of the freshman class were not in the top 3 percent of their high school class but were in the top 10 percent of their high school class?

(A) $\dfrac{1}{6}$

(B) $\dfrac{3}{10}$

(C) $\dfrac{1}{3}$

(D) $\dfrac{7}{10}$

(E) $\dfrac{5}{6}$

Since $\dfrac{1}{2}$ of the freshman class were in the top 3 percent of their high school class and $\dfrac{2}{3}$ of the class were in the top 10 percent of their high school class, then $\dfrac{2}{3} - \dfrac{1}{2}$ or $\dfrac{1}{6}$ of the freshman class were not in the top 3 percent but were in the top 10 percent of their high school class. The correct choice is (A).

It may also be helpful to sketch a figure:

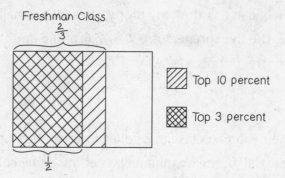

The fraction that is in the top 10 percent but not in the top 3 percent is $\frac{2}{3} - \frac{1}{2} = \frac{1}{6}$.

24. If $f(x) = \frac{x^2 - 16}{x - 4}$, what value does $f(x)$ approach as x approaches 4?

   (A) 0

   (B) 4

   (C) 8

   (D) 16

   (E) It does not approach a single number.

Since $\frac{x^2 - 16}{x - 4} = \frac{(x - 4)(x + 4)}{x - 4}$, the values of the function $\frac{x^2 - 16}{x - 4}$ are equal to

$x + 4$ for all values of x except 4. As x approaches 4, the values of the function

approach 8. The correct choice is (C). You could use a calculator to help you

arrive at this answer by substituting numbers very close to 4, such as 3.99 and

4.01, into the function $\frac{x^2 - 16}{x - 4}$ and see how the function behaves. If you have

a graphing calculator, you could graph $f(x) = \frac{x^2 - 16}{x - 4}$ and trace the graph

to obtain the answer. Your graphing calculator may not show that $f(x)$ is

undefined at $x = 4$.

Math Level 2 Test

The test that follows is an actual, recently administered SAT Subject Test in Math Level 2. To get an idea of what a real administration is like, take the test under conditions as close as possible to those of a national administration:

- Set aside an hour when you can take the test uninterrupted. Make sure you complete the test in one sitting.

- Sit at a desk or table with no other books or papers. Dictionaries, other books, or notes are not allowed in the test room.

- Remember to have a scientific or graphing calculator with you.

- Time yourself by placing a clock or kitchen timer in front of you.

- Tear out an answer sheet from the back of this book and fill it in just as you would on the day of the test. One answer sheet can be used for up to three Subject Tests.

- Read the instructions that precede the practice test. During the actual administration you will be asked to read them before answering test questions. Become familiar with the directions so you aren't seeing them for the first time during the actual administration.

- After you finish the practice test, read the sections "How to Score the SAT Subject Test in Math Level 2" and "Reviewing Your Performance on the Math Level 2 Subject Test."

- Actual test and answer sheets will indicate circles, not ovals.

Form 3RBC2

MATHEMATICS LEVEL IIC TEST

The top portion of the section of the answer sheet that you will use in taking the Mathematics Level IIC test must be filled in exactly as shown in the illustration below. Note carefully that you have to do all of the following on your answer sheet.

1. Print MATHEMATICS LEVEL IIC on the line under the words "Subject Test (print)."

2. In the shaded box labeled "Test Code" fill in four ovals:

   —Fill in oval 5 in the row labeled V.

   —Fill in oval 3 in the row labeled W.

   —Fill in oval 5 in the row labeled X.

   —Fill in oval E in the row labeled Y.

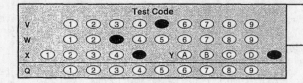

3. Please answer Part I and Part II below by filling in the specified ovals in row Q that correspond to the courses you have taken or are presently taking, and the oval that corresponds to the type of calculator you are going to use to take this test. The information that you provide is for statistical purposes only and will not affect your score on the test.

Part I.   Which of the following describes a mathematics course you have taken or are currently taking? (FILL IN **ALL** OVALS THAT APPLY.)

- Algebra I or Elementary Algebra **OR** Course I of a college preparatory mathematics sequence.   —Fill in oval 1.

- Geometry **OR** Course II of a college preparatory mathematics sequence.   —Fill in oval 2.

- Algebra II or Intermediate Algebra **OR** Course III of a college preparatory mathematics sequence.   —Fill in oval 3.

- Elementary Functions (Precalculus) and/or Trigonometry **OR** beyond Course III of a college preparatory mathematics sequence.   —Fill in oval 4.

- Advanced Placement Mathematics (Calculus AB or Calculus BC)   —Fill in oval 5.

Part II.   What type of calculator did you bring to use for this test? (FILL IN THE **ONE** OVAL THAT APPLIES.)

- 4-Function   —Fill in oval 6.

- Scientific   —Fill in oval 7.

- Graphing   —Fill in oval 8.

- None (Forgot or do not have a calculator)   —Fill in oval 9.

When the supervisor gives the signal, turn the page and begin the Mathematics Level IIC test. There are 100 numbered ovals on the answer sheet and 50 questions in the Mathematics Level IIC test. Therefore, use only ovals 1 to 50 for recording your answers.

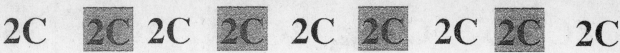
MATHEMATICS LEVEL IIC TEST

REFERENCE INFORMATION

THE FOLLOWING INFORMATION IS FOR YOUR REFERENCE IN ANSWERING SOME OF THE QUESTIONS IN THIS TEST.

Volume of a right circular cone with radius r and height h: $V = \frac{1}{3}\pi r^2 h$

Lateral Area of a right circular cone with circumference of the base c and slant height ℓ: $S = \frac{1}{2} c \ell$

Volume of a sphere with radius r: $V = \frac{4}{3}\pi r^3$

Surface Area of a sphere with radius r: $S = 4\pi r^2$

Volume of a pyramid with base area B and height h: $V = \frac{1}{3} Bh$

DO NOT DETACH FROM BOOK.

GO ON TO THE NEXT PAGE

MATHEMATICS LEVEL IIC TEST

For each of the following problems, decide which is the BEST of the choices given. If the exact numerical value is not one of the choices, select the choice that best approximates this value. Then fill in the corresponding oval on the answer sheet.

Notes: (1) A calculator will be necessary for answering some (but not all) of the questions in this test. For each question you will have to decide whether or not you should use a calculator. The calculator you use must be at least a scientific calculator; programmable calculators and calculators that can display graphs are permitted.

(2) For some questions in this test you may have to decide whether your calculator should be in the radian mode or the degree mode.

(3) Figures that accompany problems in this test are intended to provide information useful in solving the problems. They are drawn as accurately as possible EXCEPT when it is stated in a specific problem that its figure is not drawn to scale. All figures lie in a plane unless otherwise indicated.

(4) Unless otherwise specified, the domain of any function f is assumed to be the set of all real numbers x for which $f(x)$ is a real number.

(5) Reference information that may be useful in answering the questions in this test can be found on the page preceding Question 1.

USE THIS SPACE FOR SCRATCHWORK.

1. If $1 - \dfrac{1}{x} = 3 - \dfrac{3}{x}$, then $1 - \dfrac{1}{x} =$

   (A) $-\dfrac{1}{2}$ (B) 0 (C) $\dfrac{1}{2}$ (D) $\dfrac{2}{3}$ (E) 3

2. $a\left(\dfrac{1}{b} + \dfrac{1}{c}\right) =$

   (A) $\dfrac{a}{bc}$

   (B) $\dfrac{a}{b+c}$

   (C) $\dfrac{2a}{b+c}$

   (D) $\dfrac{ab+ac}{bc}$

   (E) $\dfrac{1}{ab+ac}$

GO ON TO THE NEXT PAGE

3RBC2

MATHEMATICS LEVEL IIC TEST—*Continued*

USE THIS SPACE FOR SCRATCHWORK.

3. Figure 1 shows one cycle of the graph of the function $y = \sin x$ for $0 \le x \le 2\pi$. If the minimum value of the function occurs at point P, then the coordinates of P are

(A) $\left(\dfrac{4\pi}{3}, -\pi\right)$

(B) $\left(\dfrac{4\pi}{3}, -1\right)$

(C) $\left(\dfrac{3\pi}{2}, -\pi\right)$

(D) $\left(\dfrac{3\pi}{2}, -1\right)$

(E) $\left(\dfrac{3\pi}{2}, 0\right)$

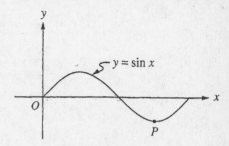

Figure 1

Note: Figure not drawn to scale.

4. If P and Q are different points in a plane, the set of all points in this plane that are closer to P than to Q is

(A) the region of the plane on one side of a line
(B) the interior of a square
(C) a wedge-shaped region of the plane
(D) the region of the plane bounded by a parabola
(E) the interior of a circle

5. If $\sqrt{6y} = 4.73$, then $y =$

(A) 0.62   (B) 1.93   (C) 3.73   (D) 5.33   (E) 11.59

➡ GO ON TO THE NEXT PAGE

MATHEMATICS LEVEL IIC TEST—*Continued*

USE THIS SPACE FOR SCRATCHWORK.

6. In Figure 2, $r \cos \theta =$

    (A) x
    (B) y
    (C) r
    (D) $x + y$
    (E) $r + y$

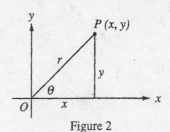

Figure 2

7. If $f(x) = \sqrt{0.3x^2 - x}$ and $g(x) = \dfrac{x + 1}{x - 1}$, then $g(f(10)) =$

    (A) 0.2   (B) 1.2   (C) 1.6   (D) 4.5   (E) 5.5

8. If n, p, and t are nonzero real numbers and if

$n^4 p^7 t^9 = \dfrac{4n^3 p^7}{t^{-9}}$, then $n =$

    (A) $\dfrac{1}{4}$ (B) $\dfrac{1}{2}$ (C) 4   (D) $4p^2 t^2$ (E) $4p^{18} t^{18}$

9. In the triangle in Figure 3, if $OA = AB$, what is the slope of segment AB ?

    (A) $\sqrt{2}$

    (B) $\dfrac{\sqrt{2}}{2}$

    (C) $-\dfrac{\sqrt{2}}{2}$

    (D) $-\sqrt{2}$

    (E) It cannot be determined from the information given.

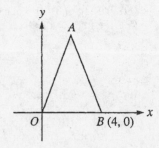

Figure 3

GO ON TO THE NEXT PAGE

USE THIS SPACE FOR SCRATCHWORK.

10. Where defined, $\csc(2\theta)\,\sin(2\theta) =$

(A) 1
(B) 0
(C) −1
(D) $2\csc(4\theta)$
(E) $2\sec(4\theta)$

11. The graph of $y = f(x)$ is shown in Figure 4. Which

of the following could be the graph of $y = |f(x)|$?

(A)
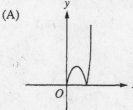

(B)
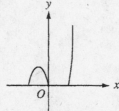

(C)
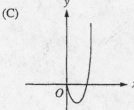

(D)
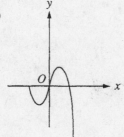

(E)
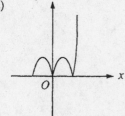

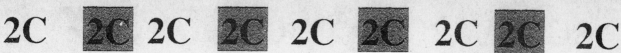

Figure 4

GO ON TO THE NEXT PAGE

MATHEMATICS LEVEL IIC TEST — *Continued*

USE THIS SPACE FOR SCRATCHWORK.

12. If 3 and −2 are both zeros of the polynomial $p(x)$, then a factor of $p(x)$ is

(A) $x^2 - 6$
(B) $x^2 - x - 6$
(C) $x^2 + 6$
(D) $x^2 + x - 6$
(E) $x^2 + x + 6$

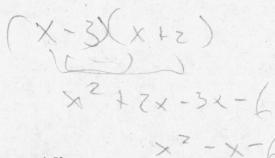

13. A kite string is attached to a peg in the ground. If 100 meters of kite string are played out on the kite and the string makes an angle of 49° with the ground, what is the distance, in meters, from the kite to the ground? (Assume that the string is taut and the ground is level.)

(A) 133   (B) 115   (C) 75   (D) 66   (E) 52

14. If $f(x) = 3x + 5$ and $f(g(1)) = 11$, which of the following could be $g(x)$?

(A) $7x - 5$
(B) $5x + 7$
(C) $5x - 7$
(D) $5x + 3$
(E) $-5x + 3$

GO ON TO THE NEXT PAGE

MATHEMATICS LEVEL IIC TEST—*Continued*

USE THIS SPACE FOR SCRATCHWORK.

15. Figure 5 shows a cube with edge of length 3 centimeters.
If points A and C are midpoints of the edges of the
cube, what is the perimeter of region $ABCD$?

(A)   6.71 cm
(B) 11.25 cm
(C) 13.42 cm
(D) 22.50 cm
(E) 45.00 cm

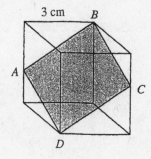

Figure 5

16. An equation of line ℓ in Figure 6 is

(A) $x = 2$
(B) $y = 2$
(C) $x = 0$
(D) $y = x + 2$
(E) $x + y = 2$

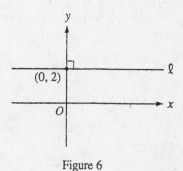

Figure 6

17. The mean weight of the 19 members of an algebra class
was 112 pounds. When a new student enrolled, the mean
decreased to 111 pounds. What was the weight, in
pounds, of the new student?

(A) 91   (B) 92   (C) 93   (D) 101   (E) 110

GO ON TO THE NEXT PAGE

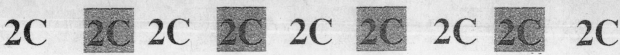

MATHEMATICS LEVEL IIC TEST — *Continued*

USE THIS SPACE FOR SCRATCHWORK.

18. If $0 < x < \pi$ and $\cos x = 0.875$, what is the value of

$\tan \left(\dfrac{x}{2}\right)$?

(A) 0.008
(B) 0.017
(C) 0.258
(D) 0.277
(E) 0.553

19. Recently 30,744 residents of Lyon County and 20,496 residents of Saline County voted on a referendum. A total of 38,430 residents of the two counties voted yes. If the same percentage of the voters in each county voted yes, how many of the residents of Lyon County voted yes?

(A)   7,686
(B) 10,248
(C) 15,372
(D) 17,934
(E) 23,058

20. If $f:(x, y) \rightarrow (x + 2y, y)$ for every pair (x, y) in the plane, for what points (x, y) is it true that $(x, y) \rightarrow (x, y)$?

(A) The set of points (x, y) such that $x = 0$
(B) The set of points (x, y) such that $y = 0$
(C) The set of points (x, y) such that $y = 1$
(D) $(0, 0)$ only
(E) $(-1, 1)$ only

GO ON TO THE NEXT PAGE

MATHEMATICS LEVEL IIC TEST—*Continued*

USE THIS SPACE FOR SCRATCHWORK.

21. What number should be added to each of the three numbers 1, 7, and 19 so that the resulting three numbers form a geometric progression?

    (A) 2　(B) 3　(C) 4　(D) 5　(E) 6

22. If $f(x) = ax^2 + bx + c$ for all real numbers x and if $f(0) = 1$ and $f(1) = 2$, then $a + b =$

    (A) −2　(B) −1　(C) 0　(D) 1　(E) 2

23. What is the degree measure of the largest angle of a triangle that has sides of length 7, 6, and 6 ?

    (A)　31.00°
    (B)　54.31°
    (C)　71.37°
    (D)　125.69°
    (E)　144.31°

24. What is the domain of $f(x) = \sqrt[3]{-x^2 + 13}$?

    (A)　$x > 0$
    (B)　$x > 2.35$
    (C)　$-2.35 < x < 2.35$
    (D)　$-3.61 < x < 3.61$
    (E)　All real numbers

GO ON TO THE NEXT PAGE

USE THIS SPACE FOR SCRATCHWORK.

25. If $\cos x = \tan x$, which of the following is a possible radian value of x ?

    (A) -1.00
    (B) -0.52
    (C) 0.00
    (D) 0.52
    (E) 0.67

26. Figure 7 shows a portion of the graph of $y = 3^x$. What is the sum of the areas of the three inscribed rectangles shown?

    (A) 4,698   (B) 1,638   (C) 819   (D) 182   (E) 91

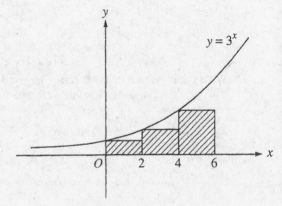

Figure 7

<u>Note:</u> Figure not drawn to scale.

◁GO ON TO THE NEXT PAGE

MATHEMATICS LEVEL IIC TEST—*Continued*

USE THIS SPACE FOR SCRATCHWORK.

27. When a certain radioactive element decays, the amount that exists at any time t can be calculated by the function $E(t) = ae^{\frac{-t}{1,000}}$, where a is the initial amount and t is the elapsed time in years. How many years would it take for an initial amount of 600 milligrams of this element to decay to 300 milligrams?

(A)   0.5
(B)   500
(C)   693
(D) 1,443
(E) 5,704

28. Which of the following lines are asymptotes of the graph of $y = \dfrac{1 + x}{x}$?

  I. $x = 0$
 II. $y = 0$
III. $y = 1$

(A) I only
(B) II only
(C) I and II only
(D) I and III only
(E) I, II, and III

29. If $f(2x + 1) = 2x - 1$ for all real numbers x, then $f(x) =$

(A) $-x + 1$

(B) $x - 1$

(C) $x - 2$

(D) $2x - 1$

(E) $\frac{1}{2}x - 1$

GO ON TO THE NEXT PAGE

MATHEMATICS LEVEL IIC TEST — *Continued*

USE THIS SPACE FOR SCRATCHWORK.

30. Which of the following could be the coordinates of the center of a circle tangent to the x-axis and the y-axis?

   (A) $(-1, 0)$
   (B) $(-1, 2)$
   (C) $(0, 2)$
   (D) $(2, -2)$
   (E) $(2, 1)$

31. What is the range of the function defined by

$$f(x) = \begin{cases} x^{\frac{1}{3}}, & x > 2 \\ 2x - 1, & x \leq 2 \end{cases} ?$$

   (A) $y > 2^{\frac{1}{3}}$

   (B) $y \leq 3$

   (C) $2^{\frac{1}{3}} < y < 3$

   (D) $y \geq 3$

   (E) All real numbers

32. If $3x - 4y + 7 = 0$ and $2y - x^2 = 0$ for $x \geq 0$, then $x =$

   (A) 1.27
   (B) 2.07
   (C) 2.77
   (D) 4.15
   (E) 5.53

GO ON TO THE NEXT PAGE

MATHEMATICS LEVEL IIC TEST—*Continued*

USE THIS SPACE FOR SCRATCHWORK.

33. If $f(x) = \log_2 x$ for $x > 0$, then $f^{-1}(x) =$

(A) 2^x

(B) x^2

(C) $\dfrac{x}{2}$

(D) $\dfrac{2}{x}$

(E) $\log_x 2$

34. If $x_0 = 0$ and $x_{n+1} = \sqrt{6 + x_n}$, then $x_3 =$

(A) 2.449
(B) 2.907
(C) 2.984
(D) 2.997
(E) 3.162

35. Figure 8 shows a triangle inscribed in a semicircle. What is the area of the triangle in terms of θ ?

(A) $\dfrac{\theta\pi}{2}$

(B) $\dfrac{\theta}{2}$

(C) $\tan \theta$

(D) $\sin \theta$

(E) $2 \sin \theta \cos \theta$

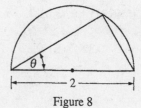

Figure 8

GO ON TO THE NEXT PAGE

MATHEMATICS LEVEL IIC TEST — *Continued*

USE THIS SPACE FOR SCRATCHWORK.

36. In a certain experiment, there is a 0.2 probability that any thermometer used is in error by more than 1°C. If 4 thermometers are used, what is the probability that all of them are in error by more than 1°C?

   (A) 0.0016
   (B) 0.0081
   (C) 0.16
   (D) 0.25
   (E) 0.80

37. If the magnitudes of vectors **a** and **b** are 5 and 12, respectively, then the magnitude of vector (**b** − **a**) could NOT be

   (A) 5
   (B) 7
   (C) 10
   (D) 12
   (E) 17

38. If $(6.31)^m = (3.02)^n$, what is the value of $\dfrac{m}{n}$?

   (A) −0.32   (B) 0.32   (C) 0.48   (D) 0.60   (E) 1.67

GO ON TO THE NEXT PAGE

MATHEMATICS LEVEL IIC TEST—*Continued*

USE THIS SPACE FOR SCRATCHWORK.

39. If $\arccos(\cos x) = 0$ and $0 \le x \le \dfrac{\pi}{2}$, then x could equal

(A) 0

(B) $\dfrac{\pi}{6}$

(C) $\dfrac{\pi}{4}$

(D) $\dfrac{\pi}{3}$

(E) $\dfrac{\pi}{2}$

40. If the 20th term of an arithmetic sequence is 100 and the 40th term of the sequence is 250, what is the first term of the sequence?

(A) -50
(B) -42.5
(C) 5
(D) 42.5
(E) 50

41. If n distinct planes intersect in a line, and another line ℓ intersects one of these planes in a single point, what is the <u>least</u> number of these n planes that ℓ could intersect?

(A) n (B) $n - 1$ (C) $n - 2$ (D) $\dfrac{n}{2}$ (E) $\dfrac{n-1}{2}$

GO ON TO THE NEXT PAGE

MATHEMATICS LEVEL IIC TEST—*Continued*

42. For all θ, $\sin \theta + \sin(-\theta) + \cos \theta + \cos(-\theta) =$

   (A) 0   (B) 2   (C) $2 \sin \theta$ (D) $2 \cos \theta$ (E) $2(\sin \theta + \cos \theta)$

43. $\dfrac{[(n-1)!]^2}{[n!]^2} =$

   (A) $\dfrac{1}{n}$

   (B) $\dfrac{1}{n^2}$

   (C) $\dfrac{n-1}{n}$

   (D) $\left(\dfrac{n-1}{n}\right)^2$

   (E) $(n-1)^2$

44. The radius of the base of a right circular cone is 6 and the radius of a parallel cross section is 4. If the distance between the base and the cross section is 8, what is the height of the cone?

   (A) 11

   (B) $13\frac{1}{3}$

   (C) 16

   (D) 20

   (E) 24

GO ON TO THE NEXT PAGE →

MATHEMATICS LEVEL IIC TEST — *Continued*

USE THIS SPACE FOR SCRATCHWORK.

45. An indirect proof of the statement "If $x = 2$, then $\sqrt{x}$ is <u>not</u> a rational number" could begin with the assumption that

(A) $x = \sqrt{2}$

(B) $x^2 = 2$

(C) $\sqrt{x}$ is rational

(D) $\sqrt{x}$ is not rational

(E) x is nonnegative

46. Suppose the graph of $f(x) = -x^2$ is translated 3 units left and 1 unit up. If the resulting graph represents $g(x)$, what is the value of $g(-1.6)$?

(A) 2.96
(B) −0.96
(C) −1.56
(D) −1.96
(E) −2.56

47. In how many ways can 10 people be divided into two groups, one with 7 people and the other with 3 people?

(A) 120   (B) 210   (C) 240   (D) 5,040   (E) 14,400

GO ON TO THE NEXT PAGE

USE THIS SPACE FOR SCRATCHWORK.

48. Which of the following has an element that is less than any other element in that set?

   I. The set of positive rational numbers

   II. The set of positive rational numbers r such that $r^2 \geq 2$

   III. The set of positive rational numbers r such that $r^2 > 4$

(A) None
(B) I only
(C) II only
(D) III only
(E) I and III

49. What is the length of the major axis of the ellipse whose equation is $60x^2 + 30y^2 = 150$?

(A) 1.26
(B) 2.50
(C) 3.16
(D) 4.47
(E) 5.00

50. Under which of the following conditions is $\dfrac{a - b}{ab}$ positive?

(A) $0 < a < b$
(B) $a < b < 0$
(C) $b < a < 0$
(D) $b < 0 < a$
(E) None of the above

S T O P

IF YOU FINISH BEFORE TIME IS CALLED, YOU MAY CHECK YOUR WORK ON THIS TEST ONLY.
DO NOT TURN TO ANY OTHER TEST IN THIS BOOK.

How to Score the SAT Subject Test in Math Level 2

When you take the SAT Subject Test in Math Level 2, your answer sheet will be "read" by a scanning machine that will record your responses to each question. Then a computer will compare your answers with the correct answers and produce your raw score. You get one point for each correct answer. For each wrong answer, you lose one-fourth of a point. Questions you omit (and any for which you mark more than one answer) are not counted. This raw score is converted to a scaled score that is reported to you and to the colleges you specify.

Worksheet 1. Finding Your Raw Test Score

STEP 1: Table A lists the correct answers for all the questions on the SAT Subject Test in Math Level 2 that is reproduced in this book. It also serves as a worksheet for you to calculate your raw score.

- Compare your answers with those given in the table.
- Put a check in the column marked "Right" if your answer is correct.
- Put a check in the column marked "Wrong" if your answer is incorrect.
- Leave both columns blank if you omitted the question.

STEP 2: Count the number of right answers.

Enter the total here: _____

STEP 3: Count the number of wrong answers.

Enter the total here: _____

STEP 4: Multiply the number of wrong answers by .250.

Enter the product here: _____

STEP 5: Subtract the result obtained in Step 4 from the total you obtained in Step 2.

Enter the result here: _____

STEP 6: Round the number obtained in Step 5 to the nearest whole number.

Enter the result here: _____

The number you obtained in Step 6 is your raw score.

TABLE A
Answers to the SAT Subject Test in Math Level 2, Form 3RBC2, and Percentage of Students Answering Each Question Correctly

Question Number	Correct Answer	Right	Wrong	Percentage of Students Answering the Question Correctly*	Question Number	Correct Answer	Right	Wrong	Percentage of Students Answering the Question Correctly*
1	B			79	26	D			66
2	D			81	27	C			57
3	D			89	28	D			56
4	A			52	29	C			54
5	C			94	30	D			84
6	A			84	31	E			48
7	C			89	32	C			52
8	C			80	33	A			52
9	E			82	34	C			42
10	A			84	35	E			34
11	E			74	36	A			60
12	B			84	37	A			24
13	C			85	38	D			45
14	A			89	39	A			56
15	C			71	40	B			28
16	B			96	41	B			22
17	B			80	42	D			56
18	C			85	43	B			51
19	E			65	44	E			32
20	B			59	45	C			28
21	D			64	46	B			33
22	D			79	47	A			26
23	C			67	48	A			14
24	E			61	49	D			24
25	E			68	50	C			45

*These percentages are based on an analysis of the answer sheets of a random sample of 9,983 students who took the original form of this test in June 1995, and whose mean score was 649. They may be used as an indication of the relative difficulty of a particular question. Each percentage may also be used to predict the likelihood that a typical SAT Subject Test in Math Level 2 candidate will answer correctly that question on this edition of the test.

Finding Your Scaled Score

When you take SAT Subject Tests, the scores sent to the colleges you specify are reported on the College Board scale, which ranges from 200 to 800. You can convert your practice test score to a scaled score by using Table B. To find your scaled score, locate your raw score in the left-hand column of Table B; the corresponding score in the right-hand column is your scaled score. For example, a raw score of 30 on this particular edition of the SAT Subject Test in Math Level 2 corresponds to a scaled score of 670.

Raw scores are converted to scaled scores to ensure that a score earned on any one edition of a particular Subject Test is comparable to the same scaled score earned on any other edition of the same Subject Test. Because some editions of tests may be slightly easier or more difficult than others, scaled scores are adjusted so that they indicate the same level of performance regardless of the edition of the test taken and the ability of the group that takes it. Thus, for example, a score of 400 on one edition of a test taken at a particular administration indicates the same level of achievement as a score of 400 on a different edition of the test taken at a different administration.

When you take the SAT Subject Tests during a national administration, your scores are likely to differ somewhat from the scores you obtain on the tests in this book. People perform at different levels at different times for reasons unrelated to the tests themselves. The precision of any test is also limited because it represents only a sample of all the possible questions that could be asked.

TABLE B

Scaled Score Conversion Table
Math Level 2 Test (Form 3RBC2)

Raw Score	Scaled Score	Raw Score	Scaled Score	Raw Score	Scaled Score
50	800	28	650	6	480
49	800	27	640	5	470
48	800	26	630	4	460
47	800	25	630	3	450
46	800	24	620	2	440
45	800	23	610	1	430
44	800	22	600	0	410
43	800	21	590	−1	390
42	790	20	580	−2	370
41	780	19	570	−3	360
40	770	18	560	−4	340
39	760	17	560	−5	340
38	750	16	550	−6	330
37	740	15	540	−7	320
36	730	14	530	−8	320
35	720	13	530	−9	320
34	710	12	520	−10	320
33	700	11	510	−11	310
32	690	10	500	−12	310
31	680	9	500		
30	670	8	490		
29	660	7	480		

Reviewing Your Performance on the Math Level 2 Subject Test

After you score your test, analyze your performance—consider the following questions:

Did you run out of time before reaching the end of the test?

If so, you may need to pace yourself better. For example, maybe you spent too much time on one or two hard questions. A better approach might be to skip the ones you can't answer right away and try answering all the questions that remain on the test. Then if there's time, go back to the questions you skipped.

Did you take a long time reading the directions?

You will save time when you take the test by learning the directions to the Math Level 2 Subject Test ahead of time. Each minute you spend reading directions during the test is a minute that you could use to answer questions. Also be familiar with what formulas are given at the front of the test so that you know when to refer to them during the test.

How did you handle questions you were unsure of?

If you were able to eliminate one or more of the answer choices as wrong and guess from the remaining ones, your approach probably worked to your advantage. On the other hand, making haphazard guesses or omitting questions without trying to eliminate choices could cost you valuable points.

How difficult were the questions for you compared with other students who took the test?

Table A shows you how difficult the multiple-choice questions were for the group of students who took this test during its national administration. The right-hand column gives the percentage of students that answered each question correctly.

A question answered correctly by almost everyone in the group is obviously an easy question. For example, 96 percent of the students answered question 16 correctly. But only 24 percent answered question 49 correctly.

Keep in mind that these percentages are based on just one group of students. They would probably be different if another group of students took the test.

If you missed several easy questions, go back and try to find out why: Did the questions cover material you haven't reviewed yet? Did you misunderstand the directions?

Chapter 5
Biology E/M

Purpose

The Biology E/M Test measures the knowledge students would be expected to have after successfully completing a college-preparatory course in high school and is designed to be independent of the particular textbook used or instructional approach of the biology course you have taken. The Biology E/M Test is for students taking a biology course that has placed particular emphasis on either ecological or molecular biology, with recognition that evolution is inherent in both. The test lets you choose the area in biology for which you feel best prepared. If you are unsure of the emphasis in your biology course, consult your teacher.

Format

The Biology E/M Test with either ecological (Biology-E) or molecular (Biology-M) emphasis has a common core of 60 questions, followed by 20 questions in each specialized section (Biology-E or Biology-M). Each student answers 80 questions. The content coverage for Biology E/M is listed in the following chart. Descriptions of these topics are also provided.

Biology E/M Test Topics Covered in Common Core	Approximate Percentage of E Test	Approximate Percentage of M Test
Cellular and Molecular Biology	15	27
Cell structure and organization, mitosis, photosynthesis, cellular respiration, enzymes, molecular genetics, biosynthesis, biological chemistry		

Ecology	23	13

Energy flow, nutrient cycles, populations, communities, ecosystems, biomes

Classical Genetics	15	20

Meiosis, Mendelian genetics, inheritance patterns, molecular genetics, population genetics

Organismal Biology	25	25

Structure, function, and development of organisms (with emphasis on plants and animals), animal behavior

Evolution and Diversity	22	15

Origin of life, evidence of evolution, natural selection, speciation, patterns of evolution, classification and diversity of prokaryotes, protists, fungi, plants and animals

Recommended Preparation

Before you take the Biology E/M Test, you should have completed a one-year course not only in biology but also in algebra so that you can understand simple algebraic concepts (including ratios and direct and inverse proportions) and apply such concepts to solving word problems. Success in high school biology courses typically requires good reasoning and mathematical skills. Your preparation in biology should have enabled you to develop these and other skills that are important to the study of biology.

Biology-E and Biology-M Skills Specifications	**Approximate Percentage of Test**
Knowledge of Fundamental Concepts:	30

remembering specific facts; demonstrating straightforward knowledge of information and familiarity with terminology

Application: 35

understanding concepts and reformulating information into other equivalent forms; applying knowledge to unfamiliar and/or practical situations; solving problems using mathematical relationships

Interpretation: 35

inferring and deducing from qualitative and quantitative data and integrating information to form conclusions; recognizing unstated assumptions

You should be able to recall and understand the major concepts of biology and to apply the principles you have learned to solve specific problems in biology. You should also be able to organize and interpret results obtained by observation and experimentation and to draw conclusions or make inferences from experimental data, including data presented in graphic and/or tabular form. Laboratory experience is a significant factor in developing reasoning and problem-solving skills. Although testing of laboratory skills in a multiple-choice test is necessarily limited, reasonable experience in the laboratory will help you prepare for the test.

You will not be allowed to use a calculator during the Biology E/M Test. Numerical calculations are limited to simple arithmetic. The metric system is used in these tests.

Familiarize yourself with directions in advance. The directions in this book are identical to those that appear on the test.

How to Choose Biology-E or Biology-M

- Take Biology-E if you feel more comfortable answering questions pertaining to biological communities, populations, and energy flow.
- Take Biology-M if you feel more comfortable answering questions pertaining to biochemistry, cellular structure and processes, such as respiration and photosynthesis.
- Indicate choice of Biology-E or Biology-M on your answer sheet on test day.

You can decide whether you want to take Biology-E or Biology-M on the test day by gridding the appropriate code for the test you have chosen on your answer sheet. *Only questions pertaining to the test code that is gridded on your answer sheet will be scored.*

Because there is a common core of questions, you are NOT allowed to take Biology-E and Biology-M on the same test date. You can take them on two different test dates.

Score

The total score for each test is reported on the 200-to-800 scale.

Sample Questions

Classification Questions

Each set of classification questions has five lettered choices in the heading that are used in answering all of the questions in the set. The choices may be statements that refer to concepts, principles, organisms, substances, or observable phenomena; or they may be graphs, pictures, equations, formulas, or experimental settings or situations.

Because the same five choices are applicable to several questions, classification questions usually require less reading than other types of multiple-choice questions. Answering a question correctly depends largely on the sophistication of the set of questions. One set may test recall; another may ask you to apply your knowledge to a specific situation or to translate information from one form to another (descriptive, graphical, mathematical). The directions for this type of question specifically state that you should not eliminate a choice simply because it is the correct answer to a previous question.

The following are directions for and an example of a classification set.

Core Section of Biology E/M

Directions: Each set of lettered choices below refers to the numbered statements immediately following it. Select the one lettered choice that best fits each statement and then fill in the corresponding oval on the answer sheet. A choice may be used once, more than once, or not at all in each set.

Questions 1–3 refer to the following pairs of organisms.

(A) Monerans and protists

(B) Angiosperms and gymnosperms

(C) Algae and fungi

(D) Ferns and mosses

(E) Monocots and dicots

1. Distinguished from each other by the presence or absence of a nuclear envelope

2. Distinguished from each other by the presence or absence of flowers

3. Distinguished from each other by the presence or absence of vascular tissue

The questions in this group are based on biological diversity and refer, in particular, to identification of distinguishing characteristics among certain groups of organisms that have arisen during evolutionary history.

Question 1 asks you to recognize that the absence of a nuclear envelope in cells separates prokaryotic cells from all other cells that do have a nuclear envelope, namely the eukaryotes. This characteristic is significant enough to place prokaryotes (bacteria, including cyanobacteria) in a separate taxonomic group, the kingdom Monera. The kingdom of protists consists mostly of unicellular forms with nuclear envelopes or simple multicellular forms that are descendants of unicellular protists. The correct answer to question 1 is (A).

Question 2 asks you to recognize that the presence or absence of flowers depends on whether seed plants produce seeds that are not enclosed in specialized structures or whether they are contained in specialized complex reproductive structures called ovaries. The former are called gymnosperms and appeared about 200 million years before the emergence of the flowering plants or angiosperms. The correct answer to question 2 is (B).

Question 3 is based on the recognition that the development of vascular tissue (phloem and xylem) was a major adaptation in the long evolution of photosynthetic organisms. Mosses were among the first autotrophs to display evolutionary adaptations to land existence, but they are usually less than 20 centimeters tall because they lack the woody tissue required to support tall plants on land. The evolutionary development of vascular tissue made possible the transporting of water and minerals and food between leaves and roots. Ferns are examples of vascular plants. The correct answer to question 3 is (D).

Five-Choice Questions

The five-choice question is written either as an incomplete statement or as a question. It is appropriate when: (1) the problem presented is clearly delineated by the wording of the question so that you are asked to choose not a universal solution but the best of the solutions offered; (2) the problem is such that you are required to evaluate the relevance of five plausible, or even scientifically accurate, options and to select the one most pertinent; (3) the problem has several pertinent solutions and you are required to select the one inappropriate solution that is presented. Such questions normally contain a word in capital letters such as NOT, LEAST, or EXCEPT.

A special type of five-choice question is used in some tests, including the SAT Subject Test in Biology E/M, to allow for the possibility of multiple correct answers. For these questions, you must evaluate each response independently of the others in order to select the most appropriate combination. In questions of this type several (usually three or four) statements labeled by Roman numerals are given with the question. One or more of these statements may correctly answer the question. You must select from among the five lettered choices that follow the one combination of statements that best answers the question. In the test, questions of this type are intermixed among the more standard five-choice questions. (Question 5 is an example of this type of question.)

In five-choice questions, you may be asked to convert the information given in a word problem into graphical form or to select and apply the mathematical relationship necessary to solve the scientific problem. Alternatively, you may be asked to interpret experimental data, graphical stimulus, or mathematical expressions.

When the experimental data or other scientific problems to be analyzed are comparatively extensive, it is often convenient to organize several five-choice questions into sets, that is, to direct each question in a set to the same material. This practice allows you to answer several questions based on the same material. In no case, however, is the answer to one question necessary for answering a subsequent question correctly. Each question in a set is independent of the others but refers to the same material given for the entire set.

The following are directions for and examples of five-choice questions.

Directions: Each of the questions or incomplete statements below is followed by five suggested answers or completions. Some questions pertain to a set that refers to a laboratory or experimental situation. For each question, select the one choice that is the best answer to the question and then fill in the corresponding oval on the answer sheet.

4. All of the following are population characteristics EXCEPT
   (A) number of individuals
   (B) phenotype
   (C) sex ratio
   (D) age distribution
   (E) death rate

Question 4 is a question on population ecology and asks you to consider what constitutes a population. An investigator necessarily has to define the limits of the population, but once those parameters are set, it is possible to study the variations in the time and space in the size and density of the population thus defined. A population can be characterized by the number of individuals present, the age distribution, the death rate within the population, and the sex ratio among the individuals. However, the phenotype is a characteristic of an organism and is observed at the level of the individual rather than at the level of a population; thus (B) is the correct answer to the question.

5. ATP is produced during which of the following processes?

    I. **Photosynthesis**
    II. **Aerobic respiration**
    III. **Fermentation**

(A) I only

(B) II only

(C) I and III only

(D) II and III only

(E) I, II, and III

This is a question on cellular and molecular biology that asks you to consider whether ATP is produced by more than one metabolic pathway. Each of the processes designated by a Roman numeral must be evaluated independently. In photosynthesis, solar energy captured by chlorophyll-containing plants creates a flow of electrons that results in the synthesis of ATP. Thus I is correct. Aerobic respiration, the process by which glucose is broken down to CO_2 and H_2O in the presence of O_2, is the most efficient mechanism by which cells produce the ATP they need to carry on their other metabolic activities. Thus II is also correct. Fermentation also involves the breakdown of glucose but without O_2. Under these conditions, substances such as lactic acid or ethyl alcohol and CO_2 are produced, together with limited quantities of ATP. Although the carbon-containing end products of fermentation still have much of the energy contained in the original glucose, fermentation permits a cell to produce some ATP under anaerobic conditions. Thus III is also correct and the answer to the question is (E).

Questions 6–8

In a breeding experiment using gray and white mice of unknown genotypes, the following results were obtained.

Cross	Parents Female		Male	Offspring Gray	White
I	Gray	X	White	82	78
II	Gray	X	Gray	118	39
III	White	X	White	0	50
IV	Gray	X	White	74	0

6. Heterozygous gray female parents occur in
   - (A) cross I only
   - (B) cross II only
   - (C) cross IV only
   - (D) crosses I and II only
   - (E) crosses II and IV only

7. If two gray progeny of cross IV mate with each other, what is the probability that any individual offspring will be gray?
   - (A) 100%
   - (B) 75%
   - (C) 50%
   - (D) 25%
   - (E) 0%

8. If the gray female from cross IV were mated with the gray male from cross II, then which of the following would most likely be true?
   - (A) All of the offspring would be gray.
   - (B) All of the offspring would be white.
   - (C) Half of the offspring would be gray.
   - (D) One-quarter of the offspring would be gray.
   - (E) One-quarter of the offspring would be white.

Questions 6–8 are on heredity. They refer to the experiment described in the introductory material. You are asked to draw conclusions from the results of the experiment and to predict the results of further experimentation on the basis of the information obtained.

Question 6 asks you to determine which gray female parents were heterozygous. First you must realize from the ratio of offspring obtained in all the crosses that gray coat color is dominant over white in these mice. Next, you should note that no white offspring were obtained in cross IV. Thus, the gray female in this cross was homozygous gray. In cross I, approximately 50 percent of the offspring were gray. Therefore, the gray female, mated with a white male, must have been heterozygous. In cross II, a gray female was mated with a gray male, and a 3:1 ratio of gray to white offspring was obtained. Therefore, both gray female and gray male parents were heterozygous. Thus heterozygous females occurred only in crosses I and II. Choice (D) is the answer.

Question 7 proposes a hypothetical mating between two gray progeny of cross IV. Since these progeny resulted from a cross between a gray female and a white male and no white offspring were produced, you can conclude that the female parent was homozygous gray and that all the offspring are heterozygous gray. Therefore, the mating of the gray progeny of cross IV will produce offspring in the ratio of 3 gray to 1 white. The probability, therefore, of an offspring of this cross being gray is 75 percent. The answer is (B).

Question 8 asks you to predict the results of a cross between the gray female from cross IV and the gray male from cross II. From the data given, you can determine that the gray female in cross IV is homozygous, and the male in cross II is heterozygous. Thus you could expect that all of the offspring from such a mating would be gray. The answer is (A).

Questions 9–11

Three students added equal volumes of pond water to each of four beakers (I–IV) and placed each in a different constant-temperature bath.

The baths were maintained at 5°C, 15°C, 25°C, and 35°C, respectively. The students then added 6 water fleas, *Daphnia pulex*, to each of the four beakers. After 1 hour, the students removed 3 *Daphnia pulex* from each beaker and each student immediately observed one *Daphnia pulex* under low-power magnification of a light microscope. (The transparent body of the *Daphnia pulex* can be seen easily under a light microscope.) Heart rates were recorded as beats per minute. The results of the experiment are summarized below.

Beaker	Temperature	Time Daphnia Added	Time Daphnia Removed	Heartbeats per Minute (average of 3 Daphnia)
I	5°C	2:00 p.m.	3:00 p.m.	41
II	15°C	2:10 p.m.	3:10 p.m.	119
III	25°C	2:20 p.m.	3:20 p.m.	202
IV	35°C	2:30 p.m.	3:30 p.m.	281

9. The independent variable in this experiment is the

(A) amount of light

(B) number of water fleas

(C) pH of the water

(D) temperature of the water

(E) average heart rate

10. If a graph is constructed using the data given in the table, it will most closely resemble which of the following?

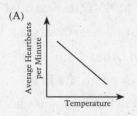

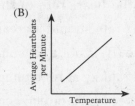

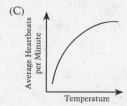

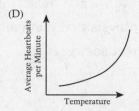

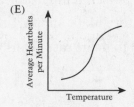

11. The data obtained in this experiment lend support to which of the following hypotheses?

(A) At 45°C the heart rate of Daphnia would be 320 beats/minute.

(B) Daphnia swim more slowly at high temperature.

(C) Metabolic rate in Daphnia is directly proportional to water temperature.

(D) Heart rate in Daphnia is inversely proportional to water temperature.

(E) Between 0°C and 5°C, the heart rate of Daphnia would remain constant.

Questions 9–11 describe an experiment that seeks to determine how the metabolism of water fleas is affected by temperature. The experimental setup states that equal volumes of pond water were added to each of four beakers and the same number of fleas were added to each beaker. Thus, in question 9, choices (B) and (C) are incorrect because both remained constant. Choice (A) is irrelevant in the case of water fleas, and choice (E) is the result the experiment seeks to measure. The only variable that changed during the course of the experiment was the temperature; thus (D) is the correct answer for question 9.

Question 10 requires examination of the data in the table. The results show that the average heartbeat per minute of these water fleas increased by about 80 heartbeats per every 10°C increase in temperature. This represents a linear increase of heartbeat with temperature and the only one of the five graphs given that shows this is choice (B); thus (B) is the correct answer to the question.

Question 11 asks students to evaluate which of the five choices given is a hypothesis that is supported by the data. Choice (A) is incorrect because, although there are no data for the heart rate of the fleas at 45°C, a reasonable inference would be that the heart rate should increase about 80 heartbeats above that at 35°C, to about 360. Choice (B) is not a reasonable hypothesis since the water fleas are likely to move more rapidly at high temperatures when the heart rate is higher. Choice (D) is incorrect because it directly contradicts the data and choice (E) is also incorrect because there is no reason to infer from the data that the heart rate would remain constant at lower temperatures. However, since heart rate increases linearly with temperature, data support the hypothesis that metabolic rate is also directly proportional to heart rate. Thus the correct answer is (C).

Biology-E Section

12. Which of the following individuals is most fit in evolutionary terms?
    (A) A child who does not become infected with any of the usual childhood diseases, such as measles or chicken pox
    (B) A woman of 40 with seven adult offspring
    (C) A woman of 80 who has one adult offspring
    (D) A 100-year-old man with no offspring
    (E) A childless man who can run a mile in less than five minutes

For question 12, you must know the premises upon which Darwin based his explanation of evolutionary change in terms of natural selection. To be fit in evolutionary terms means not only that organisms possessing favorable variations will be able to survive better than those with less favorable variations, but also that the most fit organism will have a higher ability to leave more viable offspring in the next generation. Thus a child who is resistant to certain diseases has not yet demonstrated fitness. Therefore, (A) is not the answer to this question. Similarly a person with no offspring has not demonstrated fitness, whether or not she or he is actively exercising. Thus (D) and (E) are incorrect. Finally a woman with numerous surviving offspring is more fit in the evolutionary sense than a woman with one surviving offspring, regardless of the life span of the woman. Thus (B) is a better answer than (C) and is the correct answer to this question.

Questions 13–15

Known numbers of seeds from two species (*X* and *Y*) of annual plants are mixed together in different proportions and planted in five small plots of soil in the spring. The plants grow, flower, and produce seeds. It is found that the percentage of seeds of species *X* and species *Y* in the harvest is usually different from the proportion that was planted, although the total number of seeds produced is the same as the number of seeds planted. The data are plotted on the graph below.

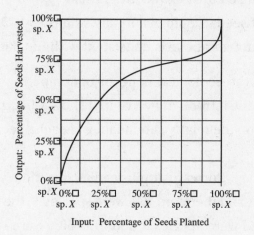

Input: Percentage of Seeds Planted

13. What mixture of seeds was harvested in the plot that was planted with 25 percent species *X* and 75 percent species *Y*?

	X	*Y*
(A)	25%	75%
(B)	40%	60%
(C)	50%	50%
(D)	60%	40%
(E)	75%	25%

14. What do the data indicate about the ecological relationship between species *X* and species *Y*?

(A) They are mutualistic for low percentages of *X* seeds.

(B) They are mutualistic for high percentages of *X* seeds.

(C) *X* and *Y* compete when both *X* and *Y* seeds are present.

(D) *Y* competes successfully against *X* at all percentages of *X* and *Y* seeds.

(E) *X* is a parasite of *Y* when *Y* is rare.

15. If you started out with 25 percent species X seeds and 75 percent species Y seeds and replanted a plot year after year with the seeds produced each autumn, what pattern would you expect to see in the mixture of the two species over the years of the experiment?

(A) Species X would increase to 100% while species Y would decrease to 0%.

(B) Species Y would increase to 100% while species X would decrease to 0%.

(C) One of the species would increase to 100% but which one depends on the initial mixture used to start the experiment.

(D) The mixture of seeds would eventually stabilize at 75% X and 25% Y.

(E) None of the patterns above is consistent with the data.

Questions 13–15 test the ecological concept of competition among species. The graph presented with the introductory material shows that the survival of either of two species depends on the relative abundance of each species at the time of seed planting.

Question 13 is a straightforward graph-reading question: when 25% of the seeds planted were species X and therefore 75% were species Y, the graph shows that 50% of the seeds harvested were species X and thus 50% were species Y. The correct answer is (C).

Question 14 asks you to draw a conclusion about the ecological relationship described in this experiment. In a mutualistic relationship, both species benefit but the data do not show that this is true at either low or high percentages of species X. Thus choices (A) and (B) can be eliminated. There is no evidence for parasitism so choice (E) can be eliminated. Competition is occurring but not in a manner such that one species is successful over the other no matter what the percentage of seeds of each species planted. Thus (D) is incorrect. The correct answer is (C).

In question 15, you are asked to predict the results of a proposed experiment. If you started by planting 25% species X seeds and 75% species Y seeds, you would recover 50% species X seeds and 50% species Y seeds at harvest time. If these seeds were replanted the following year, the graph shows about 70% species X and 30% species Y seeds would be harvested. Replanting these results year after year would increase the percentage of species X seeds harvested to 75% but there will be no further change in percentage of seeds planted and harvested. The percentage of seeds of each species would stabilize when 75% species X and 25% species Y are planted. Neither species would reach either 100% or 0% given the percentage of seeds from each species originally planted. Thus (A), (B), and (C) can be eliminated. The correct answer is (D). Choice (E) can be eliminated because the pattern in (D) is consistent with the data.

Biology-M Section

16. Which of the following most accurately reveals common ancestry among many different species of organisms?
    (A) The amino acid sequence of their cytochrome C
    (B) Their ability to synthesize hemoglobin
    (C) The percentage of their body weight that is fat
    (D) The percentage of their body surface that is used in gas exchange
    (E) The mechanism of their mode of locomotion

To assess common ancestry, or evolutionary relationship, among organisms, it is necessary to examine the similarities and differences among species for one or more structures that are homologous. For homologous structures—whether complex structures such as limbs or less complex structure such as a single gene product—the differences arise through the accumulation of mutations over time. Great similarity reflects a shorter time of divergence from a common ancestor. By this reasoning, only (A), examination of an enzyme of identical function in various organisms, represents a comparison of a homologous structure. Choice (B) can be ruled out because organisms either possess or lack the ability to synthesize hemoglobin; thus, this character allows one to sort organisms only into two groups, without providing information on relationships within those groups. Choice (C) can be ruled out because the amount of body fat is controlled physiologically, and varies within a single species. Choice (D) can be ruled out because gas exchange does not occur through the surface of some organisms that are only distantly related (e.g., mammals vs. insects) or occurs through the entire surface of many organisms that vary tremendously in relationship (e.g., all unicellular organisms). Choice (E) can be ruled out because many unrelated organisms do not move at all (e.g., plants vs. fungi), or derived their mode of locomotion independently (e.g., bats vs. birds vs. flying insects). The correct answer is (A).

Questions 17–19

Thymine is used by animal cells primarily for the synthesis of DNA. A group of sea urchin eggs was fertilized in sea water containing radioactive thymine. Following fertilization samples of embryos were removed at regular intervals and the radioactivity in the embryos' nucleic acid was measured in counts per minute. The results obtained are shown in the figure below.

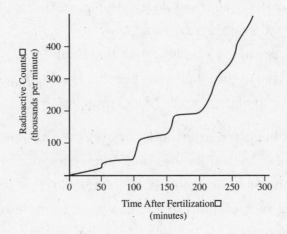

17. The increase in radioactivity of the embryos with time probably results from
    (A) synthesis of new proteins by the developing embryos
    (B) synthesis of radioactive thymine by the developing embryos
    (C) oxidation of radioactive thymine
    (D) incorporation of radioactive thymine in new cell membranes
    (E) incorporation of radioactive thymine in new DNA during replication

18. The time required for a complete cell division cycle in the sea urchin embryos studied in the experiment is approximately
    (A) 25 minutes
    (B) 50 minutes
    (C) 75 minutes
    (D) 100 minutes
    (E) 200 minutes

19. An appropriate control to show that this experiment measures DNA synthesis and not RNA synthesis would be to perform the same procedures but

 (A) not fertilize the eggs

 (B) sample the embryos at longer time intervals

 (C) add radioactive uracil instead of radioactive thymine

 (D) fertilize the eggs in sea water that does not contain radioactive thymine

 (E) count the number of cells in the embryos at the beginning and at the end of the experiment

Questions 17–19 describe an experiment that asks you to recognize that cell division occurs rapidly after fertilization and that DNA is synthesized when cells replicate. The introductory material tells you that animal cells use thymine primarily for DNA synthesis (thymine is one of the four bases contained in DNA).

To answer question 17, you need to realize that the use of radioactive thymine in the experimental design is needed as a means of measuring its uptake in the embryos. Thus (E) is the correct answer to the question. Radioactive thymine is not incorporated in embryonic cell membranes nor is it oxidized or synthesized by the embryos. Thus (B), (C), and (D) are all incorrect. The developing embryos do synthesize proteins but (A) is incorrect because thymine is not incorporated into proteins.

To answer question 18, you need to know that DNA is synthesized most rapidly during replication so that the largest increase in uptake of radioactive thymine would occur at that time. The graph indicates that the steepest jumps in radioactivity occur every 50 minutes so that would represent a complete cell division cycle. The correct answer is (B).

To answer question 19, you need to know that uracil is contained in RNA but thymine is not. Thus using radioactive thymine measures DNA synthesis and not RNA synthesis. Use of radioactive uracil would yield data that measures RNA synthesis. Thus (C) is the correct answer. Without the use of radioactive thymine in the sea water, the experimenter would have no mechanism for measuring any DNA synthesis at all, so (D) would not be an appropriate control. Collecting samples either at longer time intervals or only at the start and end of the experiment would provide less data and could not provide any appropriate control. Thus (B) and (E) are incorrect. Not fertilizing the eggs would provide no cell division whatsoever and so would provide no supporting evidence to show that the experiment measures DNA synthesis and not RNA synthesis. Thus (A) is also incorrect.

Biology E/M Test

The test that follows is an actual, recently administered SAT Subject Test in Biology E/M. To get an idea of what a real administration is like, take the test under conditions as close as possible to those of a national administration:

- Set aside an hour when you can take the test uninterrupted. Make sure you complete the test in one sitting.

- Sit at a desk or table with no other books or papers. Dictionaries, other books, or notes are not allowed in the test room.

- Time yourself by placing a clock or kitchen timer in front of you.

- Tear out an answer sheet from the back of this book and fill it in just as you would on the day of the test. One answer sheet can be used for up to three Subject Tests.

- Read the instructions that precede the practice test. During the actual administration you will be asked to read them before answering test questions.

- After you finish the practice test, read the sections "How to Score the SAT Subject Test in Biology-E" or "How to Score the SAT Subject Test in Biology-M " and "Reviewing Your Performance on the Biology E/M Subject Test."

- Actual test and answer sheets will indicate circles, not ovals.

Form 3UACZ

BIOLOGY–E TEST or BIOLOGY–M TEST

You MUST decide now whether you want to take a Biology Test with Ecological Emphasis (BIOLOGY-E) or Molecular Emphasis (BIOLOGY-M). The top portion of the section of the answer sheet that you will use in taking the Biology Test you have selected must be filled in exactly as shown in one of the illustrations below. Note carefully that you have to do all of the following on your answer sheet.

1. Print BIOLOGY-E or BIOLOGY-M on the line under the words "Subject Test (print)."

2. In the shaded box labeled "Test Code" fill in four ovals as follows:

For BIOLOGY-E

  — Fill in oval 1 in the row labeled V.
  — Fill in oval 9 in the row labeled W.
  — Fill in oval 4 in the row labeled X.
  — Fill in oval B in the row labeled Y.

For BIOLOGY-M

  — Fill in oval 5 in the row labeled V.
  — Fill in oval 7 in the row labeled W.
  — Fill in oval 5 in the row labeled X.
  — Fill in oval C in the row labeled Y.

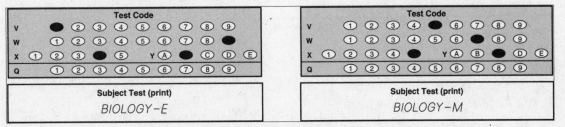

3. Please answer the questions below by filling in the appropriate ovals in the row labeled Q on the answer sheet. The information you provide is for statistical purposes only and will not affect your score on the test.

Question I   How many semesters of biology have you taken in high school? (If you are taking biology this semester, count it as a full semester.) Fill in only one oval of ovals 1-3.

    • One semester or less   — Fill in oval 1.
    • Two semesters   — Fill in oval 2.
    • Three semesters or more   — Fill in oval 3.

Question II   Which of the following best describes your biology course? Fill in only one oval of ovals 4-6.

    • General Biology   — Fill in oval 4.
    • Biology with emphasis on ecology   — Fill in oval 5.
    • Biology with emphasis on molecular biology   — Fill in oval 6.

Question III   Which of the following best describes your background in algebra? (If you are taking an algebra course this semester, count it as a full semester.) Fill in only one oval of ovals 7-8.

    • One semester or less   — Fill in oval 7.
    • Two semesters or more   — Fill in oval 8.

Question IV   Are you currently taking Advanced Placement Biology? If you are, fill in oval 9.

When the supervisor gives the signal, turn the page and begin the Biology Test. There are 100 numbered ovals on the answer sheet. There are 60 questions in the core Biology Test, 20 questions in the Biology-E section, and 20 questions in the Biology-M section. Therefore use ONLY ovals 1-80 (for Biology-E) OR ovals 1-60 plus 81-100 (for Biology-M) for recording your answers.

BIOLOGY E/M TEST

FOR BOTH BIOLOGY-E AND BIOLOGY-M, ANSWER QUESTIONS 1-60

Directions: Each set of lettered choices below refers to the numbered questions or statements immediately following it. Select the one lettered choice that best answers each question or best fits each statement and then fill in the corresponding oval on the answer sheet. A choice may be used once, more than once, or not at all in each set.

Questions 1-3

    (A) Carnivores
    (B) Decomposers
    (C) Herbivores
    (D) Producers
    (E) Omnivores

1. Bacteria that convert the excrement of cattle into simpler substances

2. Rotifers that eat unicellular green algae

3. Minnows that eat only insect larvae

Questions 4-7

    (A) Phagocytosis
    (B) Spermatogenesis
    (C) Parthenogenesis
    (D) Homeostasis
    (E) Peristalsis

4. The formation of male gametes

5. The action of smooth muscle in the digestive tract

6. The action of white blood cells in destroying pathogens

7. The maintenance of a constant internal salt concentration by brine shrimp

Questions 8-12

    (A) Hydrolysis
    (B) Dehydration synthesis
    (C) Ionization
    (D) Phosphorylation
    (E) Fermentation (anaerobic respiration)

8. $H_2CO_3 \longrightarrow H^+ + HCO_3^-$

9. Glucose $\longrightarrow$ alcohol + carbon dioxide

10. Fat + water $\longrightarrow$ fatty acids + glycerol

11. Glucose + fructose $\longrightarrow$ sucrose + water

12. Polypeptide + water $\longrightarrow$ amino acids

Questions 13-15

    (A) Linked genes
    (B) Sex-influenced traits
    (C) Autosomal recessive traits
    (D) Sex-linked traits
    (E) Lethal alleles

13. The inheritance of blue eye color in humans

14. The occurrence of type O blood in children born to parents who each have type A blood

15. The more frequent occurrence of pattern baldness in men than in women

GO ON TO THE NEXT PAGE

BIOLOGY E/M TEST—*Continued*

Directions: Each of the questions or incomplete statements below is followed by five suggested answers or completions. Some questions pertain to a set that refers to a laboratory or experimental situation. For each question, select
the one choice that is the best answer to the question and then fill in the corresponding oval on the answer sheet.

16. Which of the following constitutes a likely food chain?

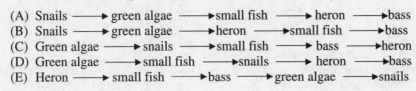

(A) Snails ⟶ green algae ⟶ small fish ⟶ heron ⟶ bass
(B) Snails ⟶ green algae ⟶ heron ⟶ small fish ⟶ bass
(C) Green algae ⟶ snails ⟶ small fish ⟶ bass ⟶ heron
(D) Green algae ⟶ small fish ⟶ snails ⟶ heron ⟶ bass
(E) Heron ⟶ small fish ⟶ bass ⟶ green algae ⟶ snails

17. Two animal populations are considered to be
of the same species if their members

(A) eat the same food
(B) can live in similar ecological niches
(C) can interbreed to produce live, fertile
offspring
(D) breed within the same geographic area
(E) migrate to new locations at the same time
of year

18. Which of the following are NOT members of
the Arthropoda?

(A) Grasshoppers
(B) Lobsters
(C) Centipedes
(D) Earthworms
(E) Spiders

19. Inbreeding tends to produce

(A) an increase in the frequency of certain
characteristics among the offspring
(B) offspring that are larger than normal
(C) heterozygous offspring
(D) increased strength and vigor in the offspring
(E) greater genetic diversity in the offspring

20. The main advantage in planting a legume such as
soybeans in a field one year and corn in the same
field the next year is that legumes

(A) use less water than corn does
(B) produce more oxygen than corn does
(C) increase the aeration of the soil
(D) increase the nitrogen content of the soil
(E) increase the phosphorus content of the soil

21. Two mature plants that are each 12 centimeters in
height are crossed and produce offspring ranging
from 4 to 18 centimeters in height when mature.
Of the following, which is the most likely explanation for these results?

(A) Tallness is dominant over shortness.
(B) Multiple genes affect height in plants.
(C) Height is a sex-linked trait in plants.
(D) Nondisjunction has occurred.
(E) A mutation has occurred.

GO ON TO THE NEXT PAGE

22. The two nucleotide chains of a DNA double helix are held together by hydrogen bonds between

    (A) sugars
    (B) phosphates
    (C) nitrogenous bases
    (D) amino acids
    (E) enzymes

23. Female moths release or secrete chemical substances that influence the behavior of male moths of the same species. Such substances are classified as

    (A) neurotransmitters
    (B) hormones
    (C) enzymes
    (D) flavins
    (E) pheromones

24. The human urinary bladder serves to

    (A) concentrate urine
    (B) store urine
    (C) reabsorb certain dissolved minerals
    (D) change urea to urine
    (E) detoxify certain components of excretion

25. The process by which a new allele of a gene arises within a population is

    (A) fertilization
    (B) independent assortment
    (C) mutation
    (D) genetic drift
    (E) natural selection

26. Of the following substances available to mammalian cells, which is most readily used as a source of energy?

    (A) Fat
    (B) Glycogen
    (C) Nucleic acid
    (D) Protein
    (E) Glucose

27. All of the following pairs of animals represent examples of similar ecological relationships EXCEPT

    (A) cat and sparrow
    (B) hawk and mouse
    (C) horse and donkey
    (D) lizard and grasshopper
    (E) fox and rabbit

28. Which of the following does NOT belong to the phylum Chordata?

    (A) Salamander
    (B) Frog
    (C) Octopus
    (D) Shark
    (E) Whale

GO ON TO THE NEXT PAGE

29. Which of the following biomes contains the greatest diversity of species?

    (A) Temperate forest
    (B) Temperate grassland
    (C) Boreal taiga
    (D) Tropical savanna
    (E) Tropical rain forest

30. A major ecological role of heterotrophs is to

    (A) recycle carbon and oxygen
    (B) control soil erosion
    (C) provide organic compounds for autotrophs
    (D) purify water
    (E) act as primary producers

31. A pea plant with the geonotype *Aa* for one trait and *Bb* for another trait is allowed to self-pollinate, and the characteristics of all the off-spring are recorded, with the results shown below.

    307 offspring with both dominant traits
    110 offspring with both recessive traits

    These results are most likely accounted for by which of the following?

    (A) Crossing-over occurred between the genes for these traits.
    (B) The genes for these traits are on the same chromosome.
    (C) The alleles for the traits segregated independently during meiosis.
    (D) Multiple alleles exist for these traits.
    (E) The traits are codominant.

ELECTRON MICROSCOPE

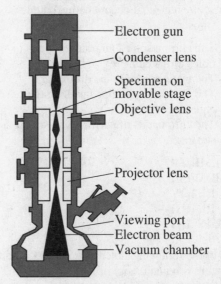

- Electron gun
- Condenser lens
- Specimen on movable stage
- Objective lens
- Projector lens
- Viewing port
- Electron beam
- Vacuum chamber

32. In the instrument shown above, which of the following serves as the energy source for the formation of the image?

    (A) Vacuum chamber
    (B) Condenser lens
    (C) Projector lens
    (D) Specimen
    (E) Electron gun

GO ON TO THE NEXT PAGE →

33. Which of the following represents the correct sequence of events that occurs within a cell during mitosis?

    I. The chromosomes migrate to opposite poles of the cell.
    II. The nuclear membrane disappears.
    III. The chromosomes line up along the equator of the cell.
    IV. The chromatids of each chromosome separate.

    (A) I, II, III, IV
    (B) I, II, IV, III
    (C) II, III, I, IV
    (D) II, III, IV, I
    (E) III, IV, II, I

34. Which of the following statements is NOT a part of Darwin's original theory of natural selection?

    (A) There is a struggle for survival.
    (B) Variations arise from gene mutation.
    (C) Variations are found among individuals in each species.
    (D) More organisms are born than can survive to reproduce.
    (E) Some variations are favorable to an organism and help it to survive.

35. Which of the following are the genotypes of a couple that have four children, each with a different blood type?

    (A) *AA* and *BO*
    (B) *AB* and *BO*
    (C) *AO* and *AB*
    (D) *AO* and *BO*
    (E) *AB* and *OO*

36. The presence of hydrochloric acid in the stomach of mammals is responsible for the

    (A) conversion of starch to sugar
    (B) conversion of pepsinogen to pepsin
    (C) secretion of bile
    (D) secretion of insulin
    (E) secretion of glucose

37. One important adaptation that developed in terrestrial arthropods such as insects, but not in aquatic arthropods such as crayfish, and that allowed the insects to invade the terrestial environment is

    (A) jointed appendages
    (B) digestive system
    (C) tracheal respiratory system
    (D) muscular system
    (E) central nervous system

38. Important functions of the stomata include which of the following?

    I. Transporting water to mesophyll cells
    II. Facilitating an exchange of carbon dioxide and oxygen
    III. Preventing excessive loss of water

    (A) I only
    (B) III only
    (C) I and II only
    (D) II and III only
    (E) I, II, and III

GO ON TO THE NEXT PAGE →

39. In humans, the rate of breathing is primarily controlled by the

    (A) cerebral cortex
    (B) medulla oblongata
    (C) cerebellum
    (D) pituitary gland
    (E) olfactory bulbs

40. Which of the following statements is true of most vitamins?

    (A) They catalyze the digestion of starches.
    (B) They have similar molecular structures.
    (C) They must be present in large amounts to be effective.
    (D) They cannot be synthesized by animals and therefore must be ingested.
    (E) All animals require the same vitamins.

41. Ferns (Pterophyta) have all of the following EXCEPT

    (A) seeds
    (B) xylem
    (C) true leaves
    (D) roots
    (E) chloroplasts

42. Which of the following colors of light is LEAST likely to be absorbed by an ordinary plant leaf?

    (A) Violet
    (B) Blue
    (C) Green
    (D) Yellow
    (E) Red

43. The largest population of omnivores can be supported if they secure their food predominantly from

    (A) primary producers
    (B) primary consumers
    (C) secondary consumers
    (D) decomposers
    (E) other omnivores

44. An earthworm and a snake both possess which of the following characteristics?

    (A) Radial symmetry
    (B) Dorsal tubular nervous system
    (C) Closed circulatory system
    (D) Chitinous exoskeleton
    (E) Scales

45. The trunk of a dicot tree grows in diameter largely from cell divisions that occur in the

    (A) apical meristem
    (B) vascular cambium
    (C) cortex
    (D) phloem
    (E) xylem

46. A mouse is placed in a maze containing food. The behavior of this mouse in its first search for food is an example of

    (A) conditioning
    (B) habituation
    (C) imprinting
    (D) insight
    (E) trial and error

GO ON TO THE NEXT PAGE

Questions 47-50

  An experiment was conducted to measure the rate of respiration by germinating pea seeds. Pea seeds were soaked in water overnight to initiate germination. The volume of germinating pea seeds was measured by water displacement. The germinating peas were placed in a respirometer containing a 5 mL solution of potassium hydroxide (KOH), which reacts with CO_2 and removes it from the gas phase. Nongerminating pea seeds equal to the total volume of the germinating pea seeds were placed in a second respirometer that also contained KOH. Stones equal in volume to the germinating pea seeds were placed in a third respirometer that also contained KOH. Each respirometer was sealed with an airtight stopper fitted with a graduated pipet. At the beginning of the experiment, several drops of water were placed in each of the three pipets so that the top of the water was at the zero mark. The respirometers were then allowed to stand for 2 hours. The diagrams below show the water levels in each of the pipets at the end of the 2-hour period.

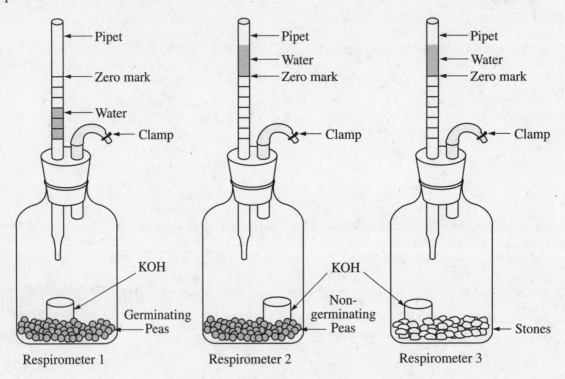

GO ON TO THE NEXT PAGE

47. The experiment is designed to test which of the following hypotheses?

    (A) Seeds consume oxygen when they germinate.
    (B) Seeds produce oxygen as they germinate.
    (C) Seeds break down water when they germinate.
    (D) The volume of CO_2 consumed is greater than the volume of O_2 produced when seeds germinate.
    (E) Water evaporates less rapidly from stones than from seeds.

48. Which of the following explains why the water level in respirometer 1 is lower than the water levels in respirometers 2 and 3 at the end of the 2-hour period?

    (A) The molecular structure of carbon dioxide is heavier than the molecular structure of oxygen.
    (B) The temperature of the germinating peas in respirometer 1 increased.
    (C) Oxygen produced in respirometer 1 dissolved in the KOH solution.
    (D) The carbon dioxide gas produced in respirometer 1 reacted with KOH, which reduced the volume of gas.
    (E) The amount of water vapor from the KOH in respirator 1 increased.

49. Which of the following is a possible explanation for the rise in the water levels in respirometers 2 and 3 ?

    (A) The atmospheric pressure decreased.
    (B) Respiration occurred in the nongerminating pea seeds
    (C) Photosynthesis occurred in the nongerminating pea seeds.
    (D) The abiotic stones underwent respiration in the presence of KOH.
    (E) The airtight seal in each of these respirometers was broken.

50. In order to measure the rate of respiration from the experiment, all of the following conditions must be met EXCEPT:

    (A) The respirometers must have the same volume.
    (B) The stoppers must fit tightly in the respirometers.
    (C) The volume of pea seeds, germinating and nongerminating, and the volume of stones must be equal.
    (D) The volume in the respirometers must be recorded several times at fixed intervals.
    (E) The temperature of each respirometer must fluctuate by 10°C.

GO ON TO THE NEXT PAGE

Questions 51-53 refer to the diagrams below, which illustrate the stages in the development of an ovum into an early embryo.

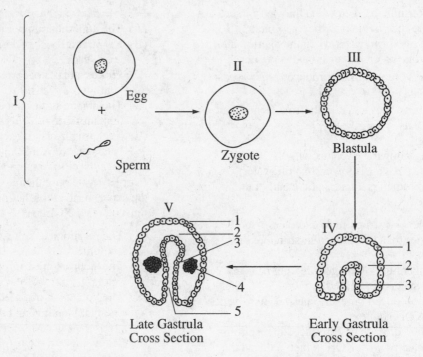

51. In the late gastrula (stage V), some of the cells of layer number 1 will differentiate and become the

    (A) skeleton
    (B) epidermis
    (C) circulatory system
    (D) reproductive system
    (E) excretory system

52. Which of the stages is characterized by haploid cells?

    (A) I
    (B) II
    (C) III
    (D) IV
    (E) V

53. The blastula (stage III) is the product of

    (A) transcription
    (B) many meiotic divisions
    (C) many mitotic divisions
    (D) conjugation
    (E) cellular fusion

GO ON TO THE NEXT PAGE

Questions 54-57 refer to an experiment in which people were asked to run on a treadmill moving at 18 kilometers per hour for 8 seconds, followed by rest periods of either 10 or 20 or 30 seconds each. The data shown in the graph below were recorded for each person as long as the person was able to keep pace with the treadmill, up to a maximum of 30 runs.

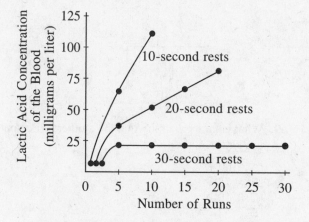

Rodolfo Margaria, "The Sources of Muscular Energy." *Scientific American*, March 1972. Reprinted by permission.

54. According to the data, when the rest period was 20 seconds, exhaustion occurred after how many runs?

(A) 5
(B) 10
(C) 15
(D) 20
(E) 30

55. An inference consistent with the data obtained is that lactic acid is

(A) formed in the blood during rest
(B) produced when oxygen intake is inadequate, as during continuous exercise
(C) removed from the blood faster during exercise than it is during rest
(D) unrelated to exercise rates
(E) decomposed readily when it reaches saturation levels in the blood

56. Which of the following statements about lactic acid is supported by the data in the graph?

(A) The more frequent the rest periods, the less the accumulation of lactic acid.
(B) The longer the period of rest, the less the accumulation of lactic acid.
(C) The greater the accumulation of lactic acid, the slower the person runs.
(D) For the runs with 30-second rest periods, exhaustion is reached at 23 milligrams of lactic acid per liter.
(E) There is no relationship between the lactic acid levels of the blood and the number of runs achieved.

57. According to the data, which of the following would maximize the amount of running a person could perform?

   I. Allowing running periods that are about 16 seconds long
   II. Allowing rest periods that are about 30 seconds long
   III. Setting the treadmill to move at a faster rate

(A) II only
(B) III only
(C) I and II only
(D) II and III only
(E) I, II, and III

GO ON TO THE NEXT PAGE

Questions 58-60

Tay-Sachs disease is a genetic defect controlled by a single pair of alleles. The recessive allele, when homozygous, causes the disease, which is characterized by the inability to synthesize a particular enzyme. For the three families depicted below, circles represent females and squares represent males. Symbols for individuals who have Tay-Sachs disease are shaded. Testing has shown that Person I and Person III are carriers of the Tay-Sachs allele and that Person II is not.

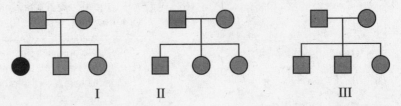

58. What is the probability that a child of Persons I and II will have Tay-Sachs disease?

    (A) 0
    (B) 25%
    (C) 33%
    (D) 50%
    (E) 75%

59. If Person I and Person III have a child, what is the probability that the child will <u>not</u> have Tay-Sachs disease?

    (A) 0
    (B) 25%
    (C) 33%
    (D) 50%
    (E) 75%

60. What is the probability that the mother of Person I is a carrier?

    (A) 100%
    (B) 75%
    (C) 50%
    (D) 33%
    (E) It cannot be determined from the information given.

If you are taking the Biology-E test, continue with questions 61-80.
If you are taking the Biology-M test, go to question 81 now.

BIOLOGY-E SECTION

Directions: Each of the questions or incomplete statements below is followed by five suggested answers or comple-tions. Some questions pertain to a set that refers to a laboratory or experimental situation. For each question, select the one choice that is the best answer to the question and then fill in the corresponding oval on the answer sheet.

61. Factors that influence population density include which of the following?

    I. Competition within the same species
    II. Competition among different species
    III. Predation

(A) II only
(B) III only
(C) I and II only
(D) II and III only
(E) I, II, and III

62. Today's worldwide human population can best be described as

(A) oscillating
(B) declining
(C) fluctuating near equilibrium
(D) growing arithmetically
(E) growing exponentially

63. Characteristics of the arctic tundra biome include which of the following?

    I. Long, cold winters
    II. Coniferous trees as the dominant species
    III. High levels of precipitation

(A) I only
(B) III only
(C) I and II only
(D) II and III only
(E) I, II, and III

64. All of the following processes occur as part of the carbon cycle EXCEPT

(A) organic decay
(B) forest fires
(C) photosynthesis
(D) respiration
(E) transpiration

65. Which of the following plays the greatest role in producing acid rain?

(A) Methane
(B) Sulfur dioxide
(C) Carbon dioxide
(D) Carbon monoxide
(E) Ozone

66. A trophic level within an ecosystem is best defined by the

(A) total chemical energy contained in nutrients within the ecosystem
(B) total available energy captured by photosynthesis within an ecosystem
(C) amount of pollution within the ecosystem
(D) main source of nutrition of the organisms within it
(E) density of the population relative to the carrying capacity of the environment

GO ON TO THE NEXT PAGE

Questions 67-70 refer to the following diagram, which shows the numbers of families of marine organisms over geologic time.

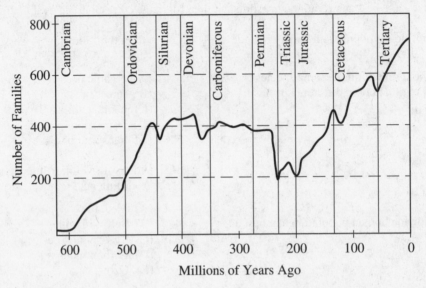

67. During the geological period that appears to have had the most severe mass extinction, approximately what percentage of the families of marine animals living at that time became extinct?

    (A) 1%
    (B) 10%
    (C) 33%
    (D) 50%
    (E) 98%

68. About the same number of families of marine organisms existed at the beginning of the Carboniferous period as at the end. Which of the following is the best hypothesis to explain this pattern?

    (A) Homeostasis stabilized the number of families.
    (B) The number of families that appeared was approximately equal to the number that became extinct.
    (C) Evolution did not occur during this period.
    (D) The mutations that occurred during this period were harmful.
    (E) The populations were too large to allow the appearance of new families.

69. The greatest number of families of marine animals existed on Earth during which of the following time periods?

    (A) The present time
    (B) 25 million years ago
    (C) 50 million years ago
    (D) 200 million years ago
    (E) 400 million years ago

70. Useful methods for obtaining the kind of data presented in the graph include which of the following?

    I. Analyses of geological formations
    II. Radioactive dating
    III. Study of fossils

    (A) II only
    (B) III only
    (C) I and II only
    (D) I and III only
    (E) I, II, and III

GO ON TO THE NEXT PAGE

Questions 71-75

An ecology class counted every tree in a 3-hectare woodland and measured each trunk's diameter at a height of 1 meter. By measuring annual growth rings in samples of trees cut in a nearby woodland, the class found that all of the species grew about 2 cm in diameter each year. It was also discovered that each tree species requires about 5 years to grow to a height of 1 meter. The measurements of the growth rings were converted into an approximate age for each tree. Data for the three most common species are graphed below. By interviewing nearby residents, the class learned that the 3-hectare site had been a hay field until 25 years ago.

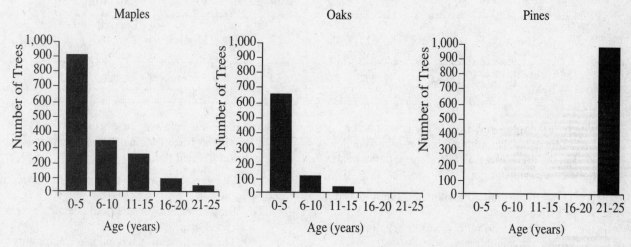

71. Trees of which of the following species are reproducing in the 3-hectare woodland?

(A) Maples only
(B) Oaks only
(C) Pines only
(D) Pines and oaks only
(E) Maples and oaks only

72. The age of the woodland is approximately equaled by the average age of which of the following populations?

(A) Maples only
(B) Oaks only
(C) Pines only
(D) Maples and pines only
(E) Oaks, maples, and pines

73. The data collected suggest that the woodland is undergoing

(A) desertification
(B) succession
(C) eutrophication
(D) biological magnification
(E) speciation

74. Some trees of which of the following species are about 2 meters tall?

(A) Maples only
(B) Oaks only
(C) Pines only
(D) Maples and oaks only
(E) Oaks and pines only

75. For the oldest trees, the diameter of the trunk at the height of one meter above the ground is closest to

(A) 10 cm
(B) 20 cm
(C) 25 cm
(D) 40 cm
(E) 75 cm

GO ON TO THE NEXT PAGE

Questions 76-80 refer to the study of three artificial ponds that are essentially identical in depth, surface area, volume, and site characteristics (soil type, elevation, slope orientation). The ponds differ in nutrients, turbidity, and the predominant organisms that cause the turbidity, as shown in the table below.

Location of Pond	Nitrogen Concentration (mg/m^3)	Phosphorus Concentration (mg/m^3)	Potassium Concentration (mg/m^3)	Turbidity	Predominant Organisms
Undisturbed field	517 ± 17	8 ± 2	844 ± 26	Very low	Autotrophs
Cow pasture	942 ± 88	11 ± 4	827 ± 32	Moderate	Decomposers and autotrophs
Cultivated field	$1,445 \pm 263$	87 ± 24	854 ± 81	Very high	Autotrophs

76. Which of the following most likely accounts for the difference in the predominant organisms in the pond in the undisturbed field and those in the pond in the cow pasture?

    (A) The difference in potassium concentration in the two ponds
    (B) The difference in phosphorus concentration in the two ponds
    (C) The greater input of organic matter into the pond in the cow pasture
    (D) The release of oxygen by the decomposers into the pond in the cow pasture
    (E) The release of methane by the autotrophs into the pond in the cow pasture

77. Which of the following best accounts for the relatively high concentration of phosphorus in the pond in the cultivated field?

    (A) Organic compounds in the pond have decomposed.
    (B) Runoff water from the field contains excess fertilizers.
    (C) The soil beneath the pond is releasing more phosphorus.
    (D) The high turbidity inhibits the evaporation of phosphorus into the atmosphere.
    (E) Nitrogen fixation promotes the release of phosphorus from plants in the field.

GO ON TO THE NEXT PAGE

78. The data suggest that the low turbidity in the pond in the undisturbed field can be the result of which of the following?

    I. Relatively limited availability of nitrogen and phosphorus for autotrophs

    II. Relatively limited availability of potassium for autotrophs

    III. Relatively high activity of decomposers

(A) I only
(B) II only
(C) III only
(D) I and II only
(E) I, II, and III

79. The most likely source of the additional nitrogen compounds in the cow pasture pond is

(A) animal excrement
(B) the trampled plants in the pasture
(C) the soil churned up by the cows' hooves
(D) the carbon-fixing actions of the autotrophs
(E) methane produced in the cows' stomachs

80. In a special study, 200 seedlings of the same species were divided into groups. The water from each pond was given to a different group of seedlings, and the fourth group was watered with distilled water. Each group received the same volume of water. After 2 months, which of the following is the most likely result?

(A) All four groups will have the same total biomass.
(B) The seedlings watered from the cow pasture pond will be dead.
(C) The seedlings watered from the cultivated field pond will have the greatest biomass.
(D) The seedlings watered with distilled water will have the greatest biomass.
(E) The seedlings watered from the pond in the undisturbed field will be greener.

STOP

IF YOU FINISH BEFORE TIME IS CALLED, YOU MAY CHECK YOUR WORK ON THE ENTIRE BIOLOGY-E TEST ONLY. DO NOT TURN TO ANY OTHER TEST IN THIS BOOK.

BIOLOGY-M SECTION

If you are taking the Biology-M test, continue with questions 81-100.
Be sure to start this section of the test by filling in oval 81 on your answer sheet.

<u>Directions</u>: Each of the questions or incomplete statements below is followed by five suggested answers or completions. Some questions pertain to a set that refers to a laboratory or experimental situation. For each question, select the one choice that is the best answer to the question and then fill in the corresponding oval on the answer sheet.

81. The initial role of chlorophyll in photosynthesis is to

    (A) absorb light energy

    (B) fix CO_2

    (C) convert ADP to ATP

    (D) synthesize glucose

    (E) oxidize water

82. Which of the following processes utilizes atmospheric oxygen?

    (A) Photosynthesis
    (B) Cellular respiration
    (C) Fermentation
    (D) Glycolysis
    (E) Hydrolysis

83. Which of the following characteristics directly contributes to the function of a protein?

    (A) Tertiary structure
    (B) Base pairing
    (C) Atomic mass
    (D) Nucleic acid composition
    (E) Type of peptide bonds

84. Which of the following is an end product of both cellular respiration and the light-dependent reactions of photosynthesis?

    (A) Glucose

    (B) CO_2

    (C) Chlorophyll

    (D) Oxygen

    (E) ATP

85. What is the maximum number of amino acids that could be incorporated into a polypeptide encoded by 15 nucleotides of messenger RNA?

    (A) 3
    (B) 5
    (C) 15
    (D) 30
    (E) 45

86. Solutions of lactose and lactase are placed together in a test tube. After 30 minutes at 37°C, lactose, lactase, and equal amounts of glucose and galactose are found in the tube. Which of the following is a reasonable interpretation of these data?

    (A) Lactose and lactase decompose at 37°C.
    (B) Lactose consists of glucose and galactose monosaccharide units.
    (C) Lactose consists only of galactose monosaccharide units that can further decompose into glucose.
    (D) The concentration of lactase at the end of the experiment is smaller than at the beginning.
    (E) The concentration of lactose is the same at the beginning and at the end of the experiment.

87. When a mutation in a particular gene prevents the synthesis of a particular enzyme, it is most likely that

    (A) the messenger RNA with the correct sequence for that enzyme is not produced
    (B) ATP will no longer be synthesized
    (C) the ribosomes of the cell become inactive
    (D) transfer RNA in the cell is no longer functional
    (E) some essential amino acids from the cell are missing

GO ON TO THE NEXT PAGE

Questions 88-90 refer to an experiment in which liver cells from a live culture were mechanically ruptured to release the cell components. The resulting suspension was centrifuged several times in succession to produce layers in which certain cell organelles predominated, as shown in the diagram below.

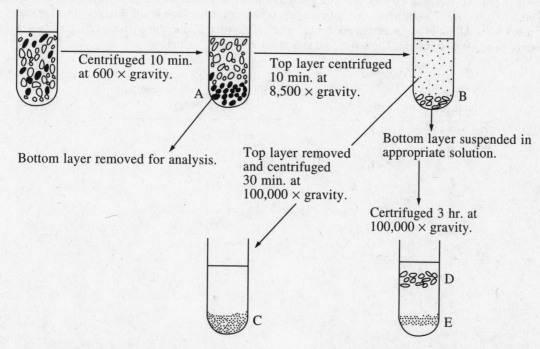

88. Upon analysis, layer A was found to have the highest proportion of DNA, indicating that the layer contained the major portion of the

    (A) mitochondria
    (B) nuclei
    (C) ribosomes
    (D) lysosomes
    (E) endoplasmic reticulum

89. Upon analysis, layer D was found to have the highest rate of oxygen uptake. This layer most likely contained

    (A) mitochondria
    (B) nuclei
    (C) ribosomes
    (D) lysosomes
    (E) endoplasmic reticulum

90. Upon analysis, layer C had the greatest concentration of RNA and was probably made up mostly of

    (A) mitochondria
    (B) nuclei
    (C) ribosomes
    (D) lysosomes
    (E) plasma membrane

GO ON TO THE NEXT PAGE

Questions 91-93 refer to the following laboratory experiment.

A student tests the effect of pH on the enzymatic activity of pepsin. Ten test tubes are set up, each with 5 milliliters of a gelatin (a protein) solution. To each tube, drops of hydrochloric acid or sodium hydroxide are added to adjust the pH. To each of tubes 1-5, 2 milliliters of a 5 percent pepsin solution added and 2 milliliters of distilled water added to each of tubes 6-10. All tubes are placed in an incubator at 37°C. After 1 hour, the contents of each tube are tested for the presence or absence of gelatin. The results are summarized in the table below.

Tube Number	pH	Presence of Gelatin at End of Incubation (relative units)
1	1.0	+ (Trace)
2	3.0	- (None)
3	5.0	+++
4	7.0	++++
5	9.0	++++
6	1.0	++++
7	3.0	++++
8	5.0	++++
9	7.0	++++
10	9.0	++++

GO ON TO THE NEXT PAGE

91. According to the data, the digestion of gelatin by pepsin is accomplished most effectively under which of the following conditions?

    (A) At any pH when the reaction is carried out for 12 hours at 37°C
    (B) At neutral pH only
    (C) At a pH between 8.0 and 11.0
    (D) In any acid medium
    (E) At a pH between 1.0 and 3.0

92. The experiment lends support to which of the following statements?

    (A) All foods are digested by pepsin.
    (B) Some enzymes operate most efficiently within a narrow range of pH.
    (C) The lower the pH, the better the digestive process.
    (D) Enzyme activity is not appreciably affected by variations in temperature.
    (E) Certain proteins are digested only in alkaline solutions of pepsin.

93. Which of the following graphs most closely represents the relationship between pH and the digestion of gelatin by pepsin?

(A)
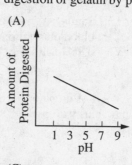

(B)
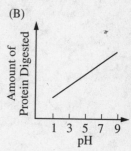

(C)
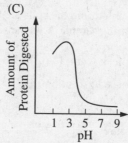

(D)
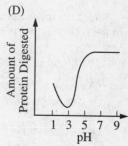

(E)
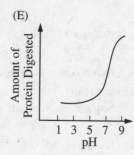

GO ON TO THE NEXT PAGE

Questions 94-97

Three blood samples are prepared according to the following procedure.

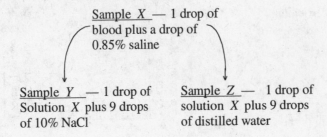

Sample X — 1 drop of
blood plus a drop of
0.85% saline

Sample Y — 1 drop of
Solution X plus 9 drops
of 10% NaCl

Sample Z — 1 drop of
solution X plus 9 drops
of distilled water

Slides are made of each sample and the cells are viewed microscopically. The concentration of solutes in the solution used in preparing sample X is the same as that of the red blood cells.

94. The blood cells in sample Z would

(A) look the same as those in solution Y
(B) undergo lysis
(C) shrink
(D) exhibit turgor pressure
(E) show wilting

95. Which of the following is true regarding the blood cells in sample Y ?

(A) The cells would look like those in sample X when viewed microscopically.
(B) The cells would lose water to the surrounding solution.
(C) The concentration of the NA^+ and Cl^- ions in the cells would decrease.
(D) The amount of NA^+ entering the cells will equal the amount of Cl^- leaving the cells.
(E) The cells would swell.

96. The cells in sample X are unaffected because

(A) sample X is unstable at temperatures below 37°
(B) sample X has a higher solute concentration than human plasma
(C) sample X has the same solute concentration as human plasma
(D) sample X has the same concentration as seawater from which animals evolved
(E) red blood cells are selectively impermeable to water

97. The results of the experiment illustrate which of the following processes?

(A) Dehydration
(B) Active transport
(C) Cellular homogeneity
(D) Osmosis
(E) Hydrolysis

GO ON TO THE NEXT PAGE

Questions 98-100

The gene for a certain protein has been isolated and sequenced from five different species. During their evolution from a common ancestor, these species have undergone only single-nucleotide mutations. A partial DNA sequence from each of the five species is

     I. 3'...AGTAC...5'

    II. 3'...AGTTC...5'

   III. 3'...AGTAT...5'

   IV. 3'...TGTTC...5'

    V. 3'...ACTTC...5'

98. The sequence 5'...UGAAG...3' would most likely represent an RNA sequence transcribed from which of the following species?

(A) I
(B) II
(C) III
(D) IV
(E) V

99. Which of the species would require the fewest point mutations in the original sequence in order to give rise to the new sequence 3'...GGTAT...5'?

(A) I
(B) II
(C) III
(D) IV
(E) V

100. Which is most likely to be the oldest species if 3'...AGAAC...5' were the partial DNA sequence of the common ancestor of the group?

(A) I
(B) II
(C) III
(D) IV
(E) V

STOP

IF YOU FINISH BEFORE TIME IS CALLED, YOU MAY CHECK YOUR WORK ON THE ENTIRE BIOLOGY-M TEST ONLY. DO NOT TURN TO ANY OTHER TEST IN THIS BOOK.

How to Score the SAT Subject Test in Biology-E

When you take the Biology-E Subject Test, your answer sheet will be "read" by a scanning machine that will record your responses to each question. Then a computer will compare your answers with the correct answers and produce your raw score. You get one point for each correct answer. For each wrong answer, you lose one-fourth of a point. Questions you omit (and any for which you mark more than one answer) are not counted. This raw score is converted to a scaled score that is reported to you and to the colleges you specify.

Worksheet 1. Finding Your Raw Test Score

STEP 1: Table A lists the correct answers for all the questions on the SAT Subject Test in Biology-E that is reproduced in this book. It also serves as a worksheet for you to calculate your raw score.

- Compare your answers with those given in the table.
- Put a check in the column marked "Right" if your answer is correct.
- Put a check in the column marked "Wrong" if your answer is incorrect.
- Leave both columns blank if you omitted the question.

STEP 2: Count the number of right answers.

Enter the total here: _____

STEP 3: Count the number of wrong answers.

Enter the total here: _____

STEP 4: Multiply the number of wrong answers by .250.

Enter the product here: _____

STEP 5: Subtract the result obtained in Step 4 from the total you obtained in Step 2.

Enter the result here: _____

STEP 6: Round the number obtained in Step 5 to the nearest whole number.

Enter the result here: _____

The number you obtained in Step 6 is your raw score.

How to Score the SAT Subject Test in Biology-M

When you take the Biology-M Subject Test, your answer sheet will be "read" by a scanning machine that will record your responses to each question. Then a computer will compare your answers with the correct answers and produce your raw score. You get one point for each correct answer. For each wrong answer, you lose one-fourth of a point. Questions you omit (and any for which you mark more than one answer) are not counted. This raw score is converted to a scaled score that is reported to you and to the colleges you specify.

Worksheet 1. Finding Your Raw Test Score

STEP 1: Table A lists the correct answers for all the questions on the SAT Subject Test in Biology-M that is reproduced in this book. It also serves as a worksheet for you to calculate your raw score.

- Compare your answers with those given in the table.
- Put a check in the column marked "Right" if your answer is correct.
- Put a check in the column marked "Wrong" if your answer is incorrect.
- Leave both columns blank if you omitted the question.

STEP 2: Count the number of right answers.

Enter the total here: _____

STEP 3: Count the number of wrong answers.

Enter the total here: _____

STEP 4: Multiply the number of wrong answers by .250.

Enter the product here: _____

STEP 5: Subtract the result obtained in Step 4 from the total you obtained in Step 2.

Enter the result here: _____

STEP 6: Round the number obtained in Step 5 to the nearest whole number.

Enter the result here: _____

The number you obtained in Step 6 is your raw score.

TABLE A
Answers to the SAT Subject Test in Biology E/M, Form 3UAC2 reformatted, and Percentage of Students Answering Each Question Correctly

Question Number	Correct Answer	Right	Wrong	Percentage of Students Answering the Question Correctly*	Question Number	Correct Answer	Right	Wrong	Percentage of Students Answering the Question Correctly*
1	B			95	31	B			19
2	C			83	32	E			75
3	A			78	33	D			52
4	B			93	34	B			56
5	E			71	35	D			45
6	A			60	36	B			41
7	D			79	37	C			73
8	C			75	38	D			45
9	E			81	39	B			38
10	A			42	40	D			47
11	B			48	41	A			41
12	A			42	42	C			55
13	C			48	43	A			46
14	C			68	44	C			23
15	B			47	45	B			27
16	C			85	46	E			61
17	C			87	47	A			40
18	D			63	48	D			53
19	A			73	49	A			47
20	D			59	50	E			70
21	B			59	51	B			60
22	C			50	52	A			54
23	E			67	53	C			55
24	B			71	54	D			71
25	C			65	55	B			83
26	E			67	56	B			78
27	C			71	57	A			70
28	C			41	58	A			44
29	E			88	59	E			53
30	A			36	60	A			44

*Table A continued on next pag

Table A continued from previous page

Question Number	Correct Answer	Right	Wrong	Percentage of Students Answering the Question Correctly*	Question Number	Correct Answer	Right	Wrong	Percentage of Students Answering the Question Correctly*
61	E			77	81	A			89
62	E			67	82	B			71
63	A			53	83	A			40
64	E			37	84	E			63
65	B			43	85	B			42
66	D			19	86	B			41
67	D			64	87	A			53
68	B			56	88	B			88
69	A			86	89	A			80
70	E			67	90	C			79
71	E			77	91	E			78
72	C			56	92	B			60
73	B			41	93	C			62
74	D			79	94	B			32
75	D			59	95	B			64
76	C			64	96	C			69
77	B			51	97	D			72
78	A			48	98	E			84
79	A			74	99	C			82
80	C			69	100	A			63

*These percentages are based on an analysis of the answer sheets for a random sample of 2,725 students who took the Biology-E test and 2,685 students who took the Biology-M test in November 1998. They may be used as an indication of the relative difficulty of a particular question. Each percentage may also be used to predict the likelihood that a typical SAT Subject Test in Biology E/M candidate will answer correctly that question on this edition of this test.

Finding Your Biology-E Scaled Score

When you take SAT Subject Tests, the scores sent to the colleges you specify are reported on the College Board scale, which ranges from 200 to 800. You can convert your practice test score to a scaled score by using Table B. To find your scaled score, locate your raw score in the left-hand column of Table B; the corresponding score in the right-hand column is your scaled score. For example, a raw score of 55 on this particular edition of the SAT Subject Test in Biology-E corresponds to a scaled score of 670.

Raw scores are converted to scaled scores to ensure that a score earned on any one edition of a particular Subject Test is comparable to the same scaled score earned on any other edition of the same Subject Test. Because some editions of tests may be slightly easier or more difficult than others, scaled scores are adjusted so that they indicate the same level of performance regardless of the edition of the test taken and the ability of the group that takes it. Thus, for example, a score of 400 on one edition of a test taken at a particular administration indicates the same level of achievement as a score of 400 on a different edition of the test taken at a different administration.

When you take the SAT Subject Tests during a national administration, your scores are likely to differ somewhat from the scores you obtain on the tests in this book. People perform at different levels at different times for reasons unrelated to the tests themselves. The precision of any test is also limited because it represents only a sample of all the possible questions that could be asked.

Finding Your Biology-M Scaled Score

When you take SAT Subject Tests, the scores sent to the colleges you specify are reported on the College Board scale, which ranges from 200 to 800. You can convert your practice test score to a scaled score by using Table C. To find your scaled score, locate your raw score in the left-hand column of Table C; the corresponding score in the right-hand column is your scaled score. For example, a raw score of 30 on this particular edition of the SAT Subject Test in Biology-M corresponds to a scaled score of 500.

Raw scores are converted to scaled scores to ensure that a score earned on any one edition of a particular Subject Test is comparable to the same scaled score earned on any other edition of the same Subject Test. Because some editions of tests may be slightly easier or more difficult than others, scaled scores are adjusted so that they indicate the same level of performance regardless of the edition of the test taken and the ability of the group that takes it. Thus, for example, a score of 400 on one edition of a test taken at a particular administration indicates the same level of achievement as a score of 400 on a different edition of the test taken at a different administration.

When you take the SAT Subject Tests during a national administration, your scores are likely to differ somewhat from the scores you obtain on the tests in this book. People perform at different levels at different times for reasons unrelated to the tests themselves. The precision of any test is also limited because it represents only a sample of all the possible questions that could be asked.

TABLE B
Scaled Score Conversion Table
Biology-E Subject Test (Form 3UAC2)

Raw Score	Scaled Score	Raw Score	Scaled Score	Raw Score	Scaled Score
80	800	45	600	10	370
79	800	44	600	9	360
78	800	43	590	8	360
77	800	42	590	7	350
76	800	41	580	6	340
75	800	40	570	5	340
74	800	39	570	4	330
73	800	38	560	3	330
72	790	37	550	2	320
71	780	36	550	1	310
70	780	35	540	0	300
69	770	34	530	−1	290
68	760	33	520	−2	280
67	760	32	510	−3	270
66	750	31	510	−4	270
65	740	30	500	−5	260
64	730	29	490	−6	250
63	730	28	480	−7	250
62	720	27	480	−8	240
61	710	26	470	−9	240
60	710	25	460	−10	240
59	700	24	460	−11	240
58	690	23	450	−12	230
57	690	22	440	−13	230
56	680	21	440	−14	230
55	670	20	430	−15	230
54	670	19	430	−16	230
53	660	18	420	−17	220
52	650	17	410	−18	220
51	640	16	410	−19	220
50	630	15	400	−20	220
49	630	14	400		
48	620	13	390		
47	610	12	380		
46	610	11	380		

TABLE C
Scaled Score Conversion Table
Biology-M Subject Test (Form 3UAC2)

Raw Score	Scaled Score	Raw Score	Scaled Score	Raw Score	Scaled Score
80	800	45	600	10	380
79	800	44	600	9	370
78	800	43	590	8	360
77	800	42	590	7	360
76	800	41	580	6	350
75	800	40	570	5	350
74	800	39	570	4	340
73	790	38	560	3	330
72	790	37	560	2	330
71	780	36	550	1	320
70	770	35	540	0	310
69	770	34	530	−1	310
68	760	33	530	−2	300
67	750	32	520	−3	290
66	750	31	510	−4	280
65	740	30	500	−5	270
64	730	29	490	−6	260
63	720	28	490	−7	250
62	720	27	480	−8	250
61	710	26	470	−9	250
60	700	25	470	−10	240
59	700	24	460	−11	240
58	690	23	460	−12	240
57	680	22	450	−13	240
56	680	21	440	−14	230
55	670	20	440	−15	230
54	660	19	430	−16	230
53	660	18	430	−17	230
52	650	17	420	−18	220
51	640	16	410	−19	220
50	630	15	410	−20	220
49	630	14	400		
48	620	13	400		
47	610	12	390		
46	610	11	380		

Reviewing Your Performance on the Biology E/M Subject Test

After you score your test, analyze your performance—consider the following questions:

Did you run out of time before reaching the end of the test?

If so, you may need to pace yourself better. For example, maybe you spent too much time on one or two hard questions. A better approach might be to skip the ones you can't answer right away and try answering all the questions that remain on the test. Then if there's time, go back to the questions you skipped.

Did you take a long time reading the directions?

You will save time when you take the test by learning the directions to the Biology-E/M Subject Test ahead of time. Each minute you spend reading directions during the test is a minute that you could use to answer questions.

How did you handle questions you were unsure of?

If you were able to eliminate one or more of the answer choices as wrong and guess from the remaining ones, your approach probably worked to your advantage. On the other hand, making haphazard guesses or omitting questions without trying to eliminate choices could cost you valuable points.

How difficult were the questions for you compared with other students who took the test?

Table A shows you how difficult the multiple-choice questions were for the group of students who took this test during its national administration. The right-hand column gives the percentage of students that answered each question correctly.

A question answered correctly by almost everyone in the group is obviously an easy question. For example, 93 percent of the students answered question 4 correctly. But only 19 percent answered question 31 correctly.

Keep in mind that these percentages are based on just one group of students. They would probably be different if another group of students took the test.

If you missed several easy questions, go back and try to find out why: Did the questions cover material you haven't reviewed yet? Did you misunderstand the directions?

Chapter 6
Chemistry

Purpose

This test measures the understanding of chemistry you would be expected to have after successfully completing a college-preparatory course in high school and is designed to be independent of the particular textbook or instructional approach used.

Format

This is a one-hour test with 85 multiple-choice questions. The test covers the topics listed in the chart. Different aspects of these topics are stressed from year to year. However, because high school courses differ, both in the amount of time devoted to each major topic and in the specific subtopics covered, it is likely that most students will encounter some questions on topics with which they are not familiar. Every edition of the test contains approximately five questions on equation balancing and/or predicting products of chemical reactions; these are distributed among the various content categories.

Topics Covered	Approximate Percentage of Test
I. Structure of Matter	25
Atomic theory and structure, including periodic relationships Chemical bonding and molecular structure Nuclear reactions	
II. States of Matter	15
Kinetic molecular theory of gases, gas laws, liquids, solids, and phase changes Solutions, including concentration units, solubility, conductivity, and colligative properties	

III. Reaction Types   14

Acids and bases, oxidation-reduction, precipitation

IV. Stoichiometry   12

Including the mole concept, Avogadro's number, empirical and
molecular formulas, percentage composition, stoichiometric
calculations, and limiting reagents

V. Equilibrium and Reaction Rates   7

Including mass action expressions, gas equilibria, ionic equilibria,
and Le Chatelier's principle; factors affecting rates of reaction

VI. Thermodynamics   6

Including energy changes in chemical reactions and physical
processes, Hess's Law, and randomness

VII. Descriptive Chemistry   13

Physical and chemical properties of elements and more familiar
compounds, chemical reactivity and products of chemical reactions
from organic chemistry and environmental chemistry

VIII. Laboratory   8

Equipment, measurement, procedures, observations, safety,
calculations, and interpretation of results

Skills Specifications   Approximate Percentage of Test

Recall of Knowledge   20

Remembering fundamental concepts and
specific information; demonstrating
familiarity with terminology

Application of Knowledge   45

Applying a single principle to unfamiliar and/or
practical situations; to obtain a qualitative
result or solve a quantitative problem

Synthesis of Knowledge   35

Inferring and deducing from qualitative data and/or
quantitative data; integrating two or more relationships
to draw conclusions or solve problems

*You will not be allowed to use a calculator during the test. Numerical
calculations are limited to simple arithmetic. In this test, the metric
system of units is used.*

Recommended Preparation

- Take a one-year introductory chemistry course at the college-preparatory level.
- Laboratory experience is a significant factor in developing reasoning and problem-solving skills and should help in test preparation even though laboratory skills can be tested only in a limited way in a multiple-choice test.
- Mathematics preparation that enables handling simple algebraic relationships and applying these to solving word problems will help.
- Familiarize yourself with the concepts of ratio and direct and inverse proportions, exponents, and scientific notation.
- Familiarize yourself with directions in advance. The directions in this book are identical to those that appear on the test.

You should have the ability to:

- recall and understand the major concepts of chemistry and to apply the principles to solve specific problems in chemistry.
- organize and interpret results obtained by observation and experimentation and to draw conclusions or make inferences from experimental data, including data presented in graphic and/or tabular form.

Other

- a periodic table indicating the atomic numbers and masses of elements is provided for all test administrations
- calculator use is not allowed during the test
- problem solving requires simple numerical calculations
- the metric system of units is used

Score

The total score is reported on the 200-to-800 scale.

Sample Questions

Three types of questions are used in the Chemistry Test: classification questions, relationship analysis questions, and five-choice completion questions.

Classification Questions

Each set of classification questions has, in the heading, five lettered choices that you will use to answer all of the questions in the set. The choices may be statements that refer to concepts, principles, substances, or observable phenomena; or they may be graphs, pictures, equations, numbers, or experimental settings or situations.

Because the same five choices are applicable to several questions, the classification questions usually require less reading than other types of multiple-choice questions. Answering a question correctly depends on the sophistication of the set of questions. One set may test your ability to recall information; another set may ask you to apply information to a specific situation or to translate information from one form to another (descriptive, graphical, mathematical). The directions for this type of question specifically state that you should not eliminate a choice simply because it is the correct answer to a previous question.

Following are the directions for and an example of a classification set.

Directions: Each set of lettered choices below refers to the numbered statements immediately following it. Select the one lettered choice that best fits each statement or answers each question and then fill in the corresponding oval on the answer sheet. A choice may be used once, more than once, or not at all in each set.

Questions 1–3 refer to the following aqueous solutions:

(A) 0.1 M HCl

(B) 0.1 M NaCl

(C) 0.1 M $HC_2H_3O_2$

(D) 0.1 M CH_3OH

(E) 0.1 M KOH

1. Is weakly acidic

2. Has the highest pH

3. Reacts with an equal volume of 0.05 M $Ba(OH)_2$ to form a solution with pH = 7

These three questions belong to the topic category of acids and bases and require you to apply knowledge in this area to the particular solutions specified in the five choices.

To answer the first question, you must recognize which of the choices above are acid solutions. Only (A) and (C) satisfy this requirement. Choice (B) refers to a neutral salt solution, (D) is a solution of an alcohol, and (E) is a basic solution. Both

(A) and (C) are acidic solutions, but (A) is a strong acid that is completely ionized in aqueous solution, while (C) is only partially ionized in aqueous solution. Since the concentrations of all the solutions are the same, you do not need to consider this factor. The hydrogen ion concentration of a 0.1-molar acetic acid solution is considerably smaller than 0.1-molar. The hydrogen ion concentration in (A) is equal to 0.1-molar. Thus (C) is a weakly acidic solution and is the answer to the question.

To answer the second question, you need to understand the pH scale, which is a measure of the hydrogen ion concentration in solution and is defined as $pH = -\log [H^+]$. The higher the pH, the lower the hydrogen ion concentration and the more basic the solution. Among the choices given above, (E) is the most basic solution and is the answer to this question.

To answer the third question, you need to know that acids react with bases to form salts and water. Since the question refers to equal volumes of each solution, assume 1 liter of each solution is available. Barium hydroxide solution is a strong base, i.e., is completely ionized in water, and 1 liter of $0.05\ M\ Ba(OH)_2$ provides 0.1 mole of OH^- ions in solution. When 1 liter of this solution is added to 1 liter of either $0.1\ M\ NaCl$, $0.1\ M\ CH_3OH$, or $0.1\ M\ KOH$ no reactions occur and the resulting solutions remain basic, i.e., the pH will be greater than 7 in each case. When 0.1 mole OH^- ions reacts with 0.1 mole of acetic acid, the resulting solution will also be basic and have a pH greater than 7 because acetic acid is a weak acid, i.e., is incompletely ionized in water. The acetic acid reacts with the OH^- ions as follows:

$$HC_2H_3O_2 + OH^- \rightleftarrows C_2H_3O_2^- + H_2O$$

The acetate salt formed hydrolyzes in water yielding a solution containing more OH^- ions than H^+ ions. When 1 liter of $0.05\ M\ Ba(OH)_2$ reacts with 1 liter of $0.1\ M\ HCl$, there is a reaction between 0.1 mole OH^- ions and 0.1 mole H^+ to form 0.1 mole H_2O. The resulting solution contains Ba^{2+} ions and Cl^- ions and equal concentrations of OH^- and H^+ ions. The solution formed is neutral and the pH is 7. Thus (A) is the answer to the question.

Relationship Analysis Questions

This type of question consists of a specific statement or assertion (Statement I) followed by an explanation of the assertion (Statement II). The question is answered by determining if the assertion and the explanation are each true statements and if so, whether the explanation (or reason) provided does in fact properly explain the statement given in the assertion.

This type of question tests your ability to identify proper cause-and-effect relationships. It probes whether you can assess the correctness of the original assertion and then evaluate the truth of the "reason" proposed to justify it. The analysis required by this type of question provides you with an opportunity to demonstrate developed reasoning skills and the scope of your understanding of a particular topic.

On the actual Chemistry Test, the following type of question must be answered on a special section (labeled "chemistry") at the lower left-hand corner of page 2 of your answer sheet. These questions will be numbered beginning with 101 and must be answered according to the following directions.

SAMPLE ANSWER GRID

Directions: Each question below consists of two statements, I in the left-hand column and II in the right-hand column. For each question, determine whether statement I is true or false and whether statement II is true or false and fill in the corresponding T or F ovals on your answer sheet. *Fill in oval CE only if statement II is a correct explanation of statement I.*

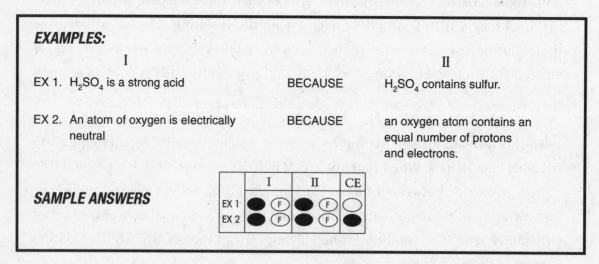

EXAMPLES:

	I		II
EX 1.	H_2SO_4 is a strong acid	BECAUSE	H_2SO_4 contains sulfur.
EX 2.	An atom of oxygen is electrically neutral	BECAUSE	an oxygen atom contains an equal number of protons and electrons.

SAMPLE ANSWERS

	I	II	CE
EX 1	● F	● F	○
EX 2	● F	● F	●

	I		II
4.	The electrolysis of a concentrated solution of sodium chloride produces chlorine	BECAUSE	sodium chloride is a covalent compound.

The above question has several components. Statement I, the assertion, has to do with an oxidation-reduction reaction, more specifically, an electrochemical reaction.

This statement is true because the electrolysis of a concentrated sodium chloride solution yields chlorine gas at the anode (oxidation) and hydrogen gas at the cathode (reduction). The electrolytic solution gradually becomes alkaline with the accumulation of hydroxide ions (i.e., OH⁻ ions) as the reaction proceeds.

Statement II, the reason, is false because the type of chemical bonding in sodium chloride is ionic. According to the directions for answering this question type, you should fill in the corresponding T and F ovals on your answer sheet.

	I		II
5.	Atoms of different elements can have the same mass number	BECAUSE	atoms of each element have a characteristic number of protons in the nucleus.

This is a question on atomic structure. The sum of the number of protons plus the number of neutrons contained in the nucleus of an atom is the mass number. However, atoms of the same element may have different numbers of neutrons in their nuclei and thus have different masses. Such atoms, which have the same number of protons but different numbers of neutrons, are called isotopes of an element ($^{12}_{6}C$ and $^{14}_{6}C$, for example). The existence of isotopes makes it possible for atoms of different elements, that is, with different numbers of protons, to have the same total mass or mass number ($^{14}_{6}C$ and $^{14}_{7}N$, for example). Thus Statement I is true. Statement II is also true because the number of protons in the nucleus of an atom is a characteristic feature that identifies each element. But it is not the reason that explains the existence of isotopes and so does not properly explain Statement I. Thus, to answer this question, you should fill in both T ovals for this question, but not the CE oval.

	I		II
6.	When the system $CO(g) + Cl_2(g) \rightleftarrows COCl_2(g)$ is at equilibrium and the pressure on the system is increased by decreasing the volume at constant temperature, more $COCl_2(g)$ will be produced	BECAUSE	an increase of pressure on a system will be relieved when the system shifts to a smaller total number of moles of gas.

Statement I is true because whenever stress is applied to a system at equilibrium the system will tend to shift to relieve the stress (Le Chatelier's principle). In the system described, the stress is caused by an increase in pressure resulting from a decrease in the volume and will be relieved by the reaction of some CO and Cl_2 to form more $COCl_2$. The new equilibrium that will be established will contain a smaller total number of moles of gas, thereby reducing the pressure stress. This is the explanation given in Statement II, which is not only true but also correctly explains the phenomenon described in Statement I. Thus, to answer this question correctly you should fill in both T ovals as well as the CE oval.

Five-Choice Completion Questions

The five-choice completion question is written either as an incomplete statement or as a question. It is appropriate when: (1) the problem presented is clearly delineated by the wording of the question so that you are asked to choose not a universal solution but the best of the solutions offered; (2) the problem is such that you are required to evaluate the relevance of five plausible, or even scientifically accurate, options and to select the one most pertinent; (3) the problem has several pertinent solutions and you are required to select the one inappropriate solution that is presented. Such questions normally contain a word in capital letters such as NOT, LEAST, or EXCEPT.

A special type of five-choice completion question is used in some tests, including the SAT Subject Test in Chemistry, to allow for the possibility of multiple correct answers. For these questions, you must evaluate each response independently of the others in order to select the most appropriate combination. In questions of this type several (usually three or four) statements labeled by Roman numerals are given with the question. One or more of these statements may correctly answer the question. You must select from among the five lettered choices that follow the one combination of statements that best answers the question. In the test, questions of this type are intermixed among the more standard five-choice completion questions. (Question 8 is an example of this type of question.)

In five-choice completion questions, you may be asked to convert the information given in a word problem into graphical form or to select and apply the mathematical relationship necessary to solve the scientific problem. Alternatively, you may be asked to interpret experimental data, graphical stimuli, or mathematical expressions.

When the experimental data or other scientific problems to be analyzed are comparatively extensive, it is often convenient to organize several five-choice completion questions into sets, that is, direct each question in a set to the same material. This practice allows you to answer several questions based on the same material. In no case, however, is the answer to one question necessary for answering a subsequent question correctly. Each question in a set is independent of the others and refers only to the material given for the entire set.

Directions: Each of the questions or incomplete statements below is followed by five suggested answers or completions. Select the one that is best in each case and fill in the corresponding oval on the answer sheet.

7. The hydrogen ion concentration of a solution prepared by diluting 50 milliliters of 0.100-molar HNO_3 with water to 500 milliliters of solution is

    (A) $0.0010\ M$

    (B) $0.0050\ M$

    (C) $0.010\ M$

    (D) $0.050\ M$

    (E) $1.0\ M$

This is a question that concerns solution concentrations. One way to solve the problem is through the use of ratios. In this question, a solution of nitric acid is diluted 10-fold; therefore, the concentration of the solution will decrease by a factor of 10, that is, from 0.100-molar to 0.010-molar. Alternatively, you could calculate the number of moles of H^+ ions present and divide this value by 0.50 liter: $(0.100 \times 0.050)/0.5 = M$ of the diluted solution. In either case, the correct answer is (C).

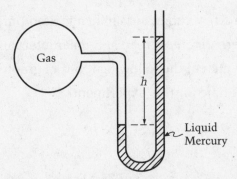

8. The bulb of the open-end manometer shown above contains a gas. True statements about this system include which of the following?

    I.   **Only atmospheric pressure is exerted on the exposed mercury surface in the right side of the tube.**

    II. **The gas pressure is greater than atmospheric pressure.**

    III. **The difference in the height, h, of mercury levels is equal to the pressure of the gas.**

(A) II only

(B) III only

(C) I and II only

(D) I and III only

(E) I, II, and III

This is a laboratory-oriented question pertaining to the measurement of gas pressures. It demands higher-level analytical skills that involve drawing conclusions from results obtained in an experiment. To answer this question correctly, you must first understand that, in an open type of manometer, the air exerts pressure on the column of liquid in the open side of the U-tube and the gas being studied exerts pressure on the other side of the U-tube. It is clear then that Statement I is true since the data given show that the manometer is open-ended and its right side is exposed to the atmosphere. Statement II is also a true statement because the level of liquid mercury is higher in the right side, which is exposed to the atmosphere, than in the left side, which is exposed to the gas. Thus the gas pressure is greater than atmospheric pressure. Statement III is not a correct statement because the pressure of the gas in the bulb, expressed in millimeters of mercury, is equal to the difference in height, h, of the two mercury levels, plus the atmospheric pressure. Thus only Statements I and II are correct and the answer to the question is (C).

9. A thermometer is placed in a test tube containing a melted pure substance. As slow cooling occurs, the thermometer is read at regular intervals until well after the sample has solidified. Which of the following types of graphs is obtained by plotting temperature versus time for this experiment?

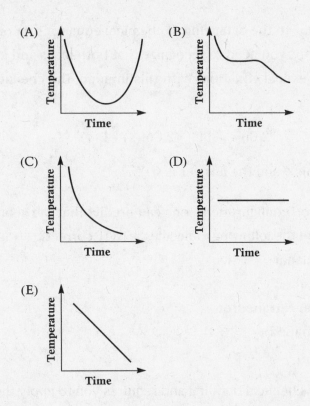

(A)

Temperature / Time

(B)

Temperature / Time

(C)

Temperature / Time

(D)

Temperature / Time

(E)

Temperature / Time

This is a question on states of matter. You must convert the description of the physical phenomenon given in the question to graphical form. When a liquid is cooled slowly, its temperature will decrease with time. Thus the first portion of a graph depicting this phenomenon must show a decrease when temperature is plotted against time. When a pure liquid substance reaches its fusion (melting) point, continued cooling will release heat with time as the substance solidifies. During this period there is no drop in temperature. After the substance has completely solidified, further cooling will cause an additional drop in temperature. The only graph shown that accurately depicts the events described is (B), which is the answer.

$$\ldots Cu^{2+} + \ldots I^- \rightarrow \ldots CuI(s) + \ldots I_2(s)$$

10. When the equation above is balanced and all coefficients are reduced to lowest whole-number terms, the coefficient for I^- is

(A) 1

(B) 2

(C) 3

(D) 4

(E) 5

This question pertains to the balancing of chemical equations. In order to answer this question correctly, you need to recognize that both mass and charge must be conserved in any chemical equation. With this in mind, the chemical equation is correctly written as

$$2\ Cu^{2+} + 4\ I^- \rightarrow 2\ CuI(s) + I_2(s)$$

The coefficient for I^- is 4 and the answer is (D).

11. From their electron configurations, one can predict that the geometric configuration for which of the following molecules is NOT correct?

(A) PF_3 trigonal planar
(B) CF_4 tetrahedral
(C) $CHCl_3$ irregular tetrahedron
(D) OF_2 bent (v-shaped)
(E) HF linear

This is a question on chemical bonding and requires you to apply the principles of molecular bonding. Each of the molecules given is correctly paired with the term describing its molecular geometry except (A). The geometry of PF_3 is not trigonal planar, but trigonal pyramidal, because this geometry corresponds to a maximum possible separation of the electron pairs around the central atom, phosphorus, and therefore yields the most stable configuration; the central atom of the molecule is surrounded by three single bonds and one unshared electron pair. Thus the answer is (A). Note that this is the type of question that asks you to identify the *one* solution to the problem that is *inappropriate*.

$$\ldots SO_2 + \ldots O_2 \rightarrow \ldots ?$$

12. According to the reaction above, how many moles of SO_2 are required to react completely with 1 mole of O_2?

(A) 0.5 mole
(B) 1 mole
(C) 2 moles
(D) 3 moles
(E) 4 moles

This is a question on descriptive chemistry that also tests your ability to balance chemical equations. The correct answer to this question depends first on your knowing that the combustion of sulfur dioxide, SO_2, produces sulfur trioxide, SO_3. The stoichiometry of the correctly balanced equation indicates that 2 moles of SO_2 are needed to react completely with 1 mole of O_2 to form 2 moles of SO_3. The answer is (C).

13. Analysis by mass of a certain compound shows that it contains 14.4 percent hydrogen and 85.6 percent carbon. Which of the following is the most informative statement that can properly be made about the compound on the basis of these data?

(A) It is a hydrocarbon.

(B) Its empirical formula is CH_2.

(C) Its molecular formula is C_2H_4.

(D) Its molar mass is 28 grams.

(E) It contains a triple bond.

This is a question on stoichiometry that tests the important skill of scientific reasoning based on experimental evidence. The question states that 100 percent of the composition of the compound analyzed can be accounted for with the elements hydrogen and carbon. Thus, this compound is a hydrocarbon and (A) is a correct statement. It is not the correct answer to the question, however, because you can deduce more specific conclusions about this compound from the information given. The relative percentage composition provides evidence that the atomic ratio of carbon to hydrogen in the compound must be 85.6/12.0 : 14.4/1.0 or 1:2. Therefore, you can conclude that the empirical formula for the compound is CH_2, a hydrocarbon. Thus (B) is a better answer than (A). Since you do not know the total number of moles of the compound used for analysis, you cannot calculate the molar mass or derive the molecular formula for this compound. Thus (C) and (D) cannot be determined from the information given and so they are not correct answers to the question. It is known, however, that a substance with an empirical formula of CH_2 cannot have a triple bond. Therefore, (E) is incorrect. The best answer to the question is (B).

Chemistry Test

The test that follows is an actual, recently administered SAT Subject Test in Chemistry. To get an idea of what a real administration is like, take the test under conditions as close as possible to those of a national administration:

- Set aside an hour when you can take the test uninterrupted. Make sure you complete the test in one sitting.

- Sit at a desk or table with no other books or papers. Dictionaries, other books, or notes are not allowed in the test room.

- Time yourself by placing a clock or kitchen timer in front of you.

- Tear out an answer sheet from the back of this book and fill it in just as you would on the day of the test. One answer sheet can be used for up to three Subject Tests.

- Read the instructions that precede the practice test. During the actual administration you will be asked to read them before answering test questions.

- After you finish the practice test, read the sections "How to Score the SAT Subject Test in Chemistry" and "Reviewing Your Performance on the Chemistry Subject Test."

- Actual test and answer sheets will indicate circles, not ovals.

Form 3PAC7

CHEMISTRY TEST

The top portion of the section of the answer sheet that you will use in taking the Chemistry test must be filled in exactly as shown in the illustration below. Note carefully that you have to do all of the following on your answer sheet.

1. Print CHEMISTRY on the line under the words "Subject Test (print)."

2. In the shaded box labeled "Test Code" fill in four ovals:

   —Fill in oval 2 in the row labeled V.

   —Fill in oval 2 in the row labeled W.

   —Fill in oval 4 in the row labeled X.

   —Fill in oval D in the row labeled Y.

3. Please answer the questions below by filling in the appropriate ovals in the row labeled Q on the answer sheet. The information you provide is for statistical purposes only and will not affect your score on the test.

Question I

How many semesters of chemistry have you taken in high school? (If you are taking chemistry this semester, count it as a full semester.) Fill in only <u>one</u> oval of ovals 1-3.

- One semester or less   —Fill in oval 1.
- Two semesters   —Fill in oval 2.
- Three semesters or more   —Fill in oval 3.

Question II

How recently have you studied chemistry?

- I am currently enrolled in or have   —Fill in oval 4. just completed a chemistry course.
- I have not studied chemistry for 6 months or more.   —Fill in oval 5.

Question III

Which of the following best describes your preparation in algebra? (If you are taking an algebra course this semester, count it as a full semester.) Fill in only <u>one</u> oval of ovals 6-8.

- One semester or less   —Fill in oval 6.
- Two semesters   —Fill in oval 7.
- Three semesters or more   —Fill in oval 8.

Question IV

Are you currently taking Advanced Placement Chemistry? If you are, fill in oval 9.

When the supervisor gives the signal, turn the page and begin the Chemistry test. There are a total of 85 questions in the Chemistry test (1-70 plus 101-115 on the special section at the bottom left-hand corner of the answer sheet.)

CHEMISTRY TEST

Material in the following table may be useful in answering the questions in this examination.

PERIODIC CHART OF THE ELEMENTS

1 H 1.0079																	2 He 4.003
3 Li 6.941	4 Be 9.012											5 B 10.81	6 C 12.011	7 N 14.007	8 O 16.00	9 F 19.00	10 Ne 20.179
11 Na 22.99	12 Mg 24.30											13 Al 26.98	14 Si 28.09	15 P 30.974	16 S 32.06	17 Cl 35.453	18 Ar 39.948
19 K 39.10	20 Ca 40.08	21 Sc 44.96	22 Ti 47.90	23 V 50.94	24 Cr 52.00	25 Mn 54.94	26 Fe 55.85	27 Co 58.93	28 Ni 58.70	29 Cu 63.55	30 Zn 65.38	31 Ga 69.72	32 Ge 72.59	33 As 74.92	34 Se 78.96	35 Br 79.90	36 Kr 83.80
37 Rb 85.47	38 Sr 87.62	39 Y 88.91	40 Zr 91.22	41 Nb 92.91	42 Mo 95.94	43 Tc (97)	44 Ru 101.1	45 Rh 102.91	46 Pd 106.4	47 Ag 107.868	48 Cd 112.41	49 In 114.82	50 Sn 118.7	51 Sb 121.75	52 Te 127.60	53 I 126.90	54 Xe 131.30
55 Cs 132.91	56 Ba 137.33	57 *La 138.91	72 Hf 178.49	73 Ta 180.95	74 W 183.85	75 Re 186.21	76 Os 190.2	77 Ir 192.2	78 Pt 195.09	79 Au 196.97	80 Hg 200.59	81 Tl 204.37	82 Pb 207.2	83 Bi 208.98	84 Po (209)	85 At (210)	86 Rn (222)
87 Fr (223)	88 Ra (226)	89 †Ac (227)															

*Lanthanum Series

58 Ce 140.12	59 Pr 140.91	60 Nd 144.24	61 Pm (145)	62 Sm 150.4	63 Eu 152.0	64 Gd 157.25	65 Tb 158.93	66 Dy 162.50	67 Ho 164.93	68 Er 167.26	69 Tm 168.93	70 Yb 173.04	71 Lu 174.97

†Actinium Series

90 Th 232.0	91 Pa 231.0	92 U 238.03	93 Np 237.0	94 Pu (244)	95 Am (243)	96 Cm (247)	97 Bk (247)	98 Cf (251)	99 Es (252)	100 Fm (257)	101 Md (258)	102 No (259)	103 Lr (260)

CHEMISTRY TEST

Note: For all questions involving solutions and/or chemical equations, assume that the system is in pure water unless otherwise stated.

Part A

Directions: Each set of lettered choices below refers to the numbered questions or statements immediately following it. Select the one lettered choice that best answers each question or best fits each statement, and then fill in the corresponding oval on the answer sheet. A choice may be used once, more than once, or not at all in each set.

Questions 1-4

(A) X_2Y

(B) XY

(C) XY_2

(D) XY_3

(E) XY_4

Which of the above represents the formula for the most common compound of X and Y, where X and Y represent given pairs of elements as indicated below?

	X	Y
1.	Mg	S
2.	Ca	F
3.	N	H
4.	Si	O

GO ON TO THE NEXT PAGE

Questions 5-9

(A) $Cr_2O_7^{2-}$

(B) H^+

(C) OH^-

(D) Cr^{3+}

(E) Ba^{2+}

Which of the above is the appropriate ion for each blank in the following series of reactions?

$$OH^- + \underline{(5)} \longrightarrow CrO_4^{2-} + H^+$$

$$\downarrow \underline{(6)}$$

$$BaCrO_4(s) \underset{\underline{(8)}}{\overset{\underline{(7)}}{\rightleftharpoons}} Ba^{2+} + Cr_2O_7^{2-} + H_2O$$
(yellow precipitate)

$$\downarrow SO_2(g), H^+$$

$$BaSO_4(s) + \underline{(9)} + H_2O$$

GO ON TO THE NEXT PAGE

CHEMISTRY TEST—*Continued*

Questions 10-12

    (A) s-s bonds

    (B) s-p bonds

    (C) p-p bonds

    (D) sp^3-p bonds

    (E) sp^2-sp^2 bonds

10. Describes the bonding in H_2

11. Describes the bonding in HF

12. Describes the bonding in F_2

Questions 13-15 refer to the following elements.

    (A) Lithium
    (B) Sodium
    (C) Potassium
    (D) Rubidium
    (E) Cesium

13. Which forms the smallest of the +1 ions?

14. Which has the largest atomic radius?

15. Which has the smallest first ionization energy?

Questions 16-19

    (A) Element with atomic number 2
    (B) Element with atomic number 7
    (C) Element with atomic number 19
    (D) Element with atomic number 35
    (E) Element with atomic number 74

16. An element that reacts vigorously with water

17. A transition element

18. An element whose chemical properties are similar to those of chlorine

19. An element that forms diatomic molecules that have triple bonds

GO ON TO THE NEXT PAGE

CHEMISTRY TEST—*Continued*

Questions 20-22 refer to the following processes.

    (A) Precipitation
    (B) Oxidation-reduction
    (C) Distillation
    (D) Hydration
    (E) Condensation

20. Electrolysis of water to form hydrogen and oxygen gases

21. Reaction of silver ion with chloride ion in water solution

22. Reaction of iron filings with powdered sulfur

Questions 23-25

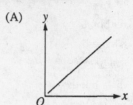 (A)
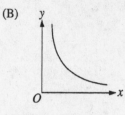 (B)

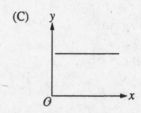 (C)
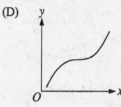 (D)

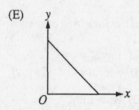 (E)

23. Could be a plot of the pressure of a gas (y) against the volume (x) for one mole of an ideal gas at fixed temperature

24. Could be a plot of the pressure of a gas (y) against the absolute temperature (x) for one mole of an ideal gas in a fixed volume

25. Could be the plot of the average molecular kinetic energy of molecules (y) against the absolute temperature (x) for one mole of an ideal gas

GO ON TO THE NEXT PAGE

CHEMISTRY TEST—*Continued*

PLEASE GO TO THE SPECIAL SECTION AT THE LOWER LEFT-HAND CORNER OF PAGE 2 OF YOUR ANSWER SHEET LABELED CHEMISTRY AND ANSWER QUESTIONS 101-115 ACCORDING TO THE FOLLOWING DIRECTIONS.

Part B

Directions: Each question below consists of two statements, I in the left-hand column and II in the right-hand column. For each question, determine whether statement I is true or false and whether statement II is true or false and fill in the corresponding T or F ovals on your answer sheet. Fill in oval CE only if statement II is a correct explanation of statement I.

EXAMPLES:

	I		II
EX 1.	H_2SO_4 is a strong acid	BECAUSE	H_2SO_4 contains sulfur.
EX 2.	An atom of oxygen is electrically neutral	BECAUSE	an oxygen atom contains an equal number of protons and electrons.

SAMPLE ANSWERS

	I	II	CE*
EX 1	● Ⓕ	● Ⓕ	○
EX 2	● Ⓕ	● Ⓕ	●

	I		II
101.	The shape of a water molecule is linear	BECAUSE	the bonds in a water molecule are nonpolar.
102.	Some alpha particles shot at a thin metal foil are reflected back toward the source	BECAUSE	alpha particles shot at thin metal foil sometimes approach the nuclei of the metal atoms head-on and are thus repelled.
103.	Potassium permanganate is a colored compound	BECAUSE	both potassium and manganese are metals.
104.	A molecule of silicon tetrachloride, $SiCl_4$, is nonpolar	BECAUSE	the four bonds in $SiCl_4$ are identical and the molecule has a tetrahedral structure.
105.	When solid KNO_3 dissolves in water, covalent bonds are broken	BECAUSE	solid KNO_3 dissociates into K^+ and NO_3^- ions in water.
106.	An element that has the electron configuration $1s^2\, 2s^2 2p^6\, 3s^2 3p^6 3d^3\, 4s^2$ is a transition element	BECAUSE	in atoms of transition elements, the $1s$, $2s$, $2p$, $3s$ and $3p$ orbitals are completely filled in the ground state.
107.	The reaction of hydrogen with oxygen to form water is an exothermic reaction	BECAUSE	water molecules have polar covalent bonds.

GO ON TO THE NEXT PAGE →

I   II

108. An element whose atoms have an outer   BECAUSE   metallic elements readily gain electrons.
     electron configuration $3s^1$ shows metallic
     properties

109. H_2O and H_2O_2 have the same empirical   BECAUSE   in H_2O and H_2O_2, oxygen has the same
     formula   oxidation state.

110. A salt whose water solution has a pH of 5   BECAUSE   a solution having a pH of 5 has a higher con-
     is basic   centration of H_3O^+ ions than of OH^- ions

111. A buret is normally used in volumetric   BECAUSE   a buret can accurately measure the volumes o
     titrations   a solution delivered.

112. The combustion of fuels containing sulfur   BECAUSE   sulfur oxides form acid solutions in water.
     leads to the production of acid rain

113. After a system has reached chemical   BECAUSE   reactions are not reversible at equilibrium.
     equilibrium, there is no change in the
     concentrations of reactants and products

114. At the same temperature and pressure,   BECAUSE   equal volumes of ideal gases at the same
     1 liter of hydrogen gas and 1 liter of neon   temperature and pressure contain the same
     gas have the same mass   number of moles.

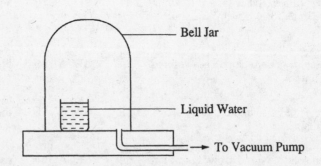

A container of water is placed inside an insulated bell jar as shown above. A vacuum pump lowers the
pressure.

115. When the pressure drops sufficiently,   BECAUSE   at the boiling point, the vapor pressure
     the water starts to boil   of the water equals the pressure inside the
                                                             bell jar.

**RETURN TO THE SECTION OF YOUR ANSWER SHEET YOU STARTED FOR CHEMIST
AND ANSWER QUESTIONS 26-70.**

GO ON TO THE NEXT PAGE

Part C

Directions: Each of the questions or incomplete statements below is followed by five suggested answers or completions. Select the one that is best in each case and then fill in the corresponding oval on the answer sheet.

---

26. A certain mass of carbon required 16 grams of oxygen to be converted into carbon monoxide, CO. If this same mass of carbon were to be converted into carbon dioxide, CO_2, the mass of oxygen required would be

    (A) 4.0 grams
    (B) 8.0 grams
    (C) 12 grams
    (D) 32 grams
    (E) indeterminable from the information given

27. $\ldots BCl_3(g) + \ldots H_2(g) \rightarrow \ldots HCl(g) + \ldots B(s)$

    When the equation for the reaction represented above is balanced and all coefficients are reduced to lowest whole-number terms, the coefficient for HCl is

    (A) 1   (B) 2   (C) 3   (D) 4   (E) 6

28. Petroleum is an important source for all of the following EXCEPT

    (A) paraffin wax
    (B) octane
    (C) ethylene
    (D) cellulose
    (E) lubricating oils

Porous Membrane

| NaCl Solution | Pure H_2O |

29. As shown in the figure above, two compartments are separated by a porous membrane that is permeable to ionic salts. A sodium chloride solution is placed in one compartment while distilled water is placed in the other. Factors that influence the initial rate at which the water diffuses into the compartment containing the NaCl solution include which of the following?

    I. Concentration of the sodium chloride solution
    II. Area of the porous membrane
    III. Temperature of the system

    (A) I only
    (B) II only
    (C) I and III only
    (D) II and III only
    (E) I, II, and III

30. $\ldots ClO^- \rightleftarrows \ldots ClO_3^- + \ldots Cl^-$

    When the equation for the reaction represented above is balanced with coefficients reduced to the lowest whole-number terms, correct statements include which of the following?

    I.   The coefficient for Cl^- is 4.
    II. The coefficient for ClO_3^- is 2.
    III. The coefficient for ClO^- is 3.

    (A) I only
    (B) II only
    (C) III only
    (D) I and II only
    (E) I, II, and III

GO ON TO THE NEXT PAGE

31. A student adds 0.1-molar HCl to 0.1-molar KOH until the resulting solution is neutral. When this solution is evaporated to dryness, the substance that remains can be correctly described as which of the following?

    I. A white, crystalline solid
    II. A covalent solid
    III. A water-soluble salt

    (A) I only
    (B) II only
    (C) III only
    (D) I and III only
    (E) I, II, and III

32. How many milliliters of 0.200-molar sodium hydroxide must be added to a 100-milliliter solution of 0.100-molar nitric acid to obtain a solution with a pH of 7 ?

    (A) 10.0 mL
    (B) 25.0 mL
    (C) 50.0 mL
    (D) 100. mL
    (E) 200. mL

33. Which of the following statements about catalysts is true?

    (A) They increase the value of the equilibrium constant.
    (B) They increase the amount of product present at equilibrium.
    (C) They increase the concentration of reactants.
    (D) They are permanently altered as the reaction proceeds.
    (E) They reduce the activation energy of the reaction.

34. Complete combustion of hydrocarbons produces

    (A) C_2H_5OH
    (B) $HC_2H_3O_2$
    (C) $H_2 + CH_3COOH$
    (D) $CO_2 + H_2O$
    (E) $CH_3CH_2CH_3 + CH_4$

35. The rate at which a solid dissolves in water is increased by which of the following?

    I. Increasing the surface area of the solid
    II. Raising the temperature of the water
    III. Stirring the mixture

    (A) I only
    (B) II only
    (C) I and II only
    (D) II and III only
    (E) I, II, and III

GO ON TO THE NEXT PAGE

36. $\ldots C(s) + \ldots H_2SO_4(\ell) \rightarrow \ldots CO_2(g) + \ldots SO_2(g) + \ldots H_2O(\ell)$

When the equation for the reaction represented above is balanced and the coefficients are reduced to the lowest whole-number terms, the coefficient for $SO_2(g)$ is

(A) 1   (B) 2   (C) 3   (D) 4   (E) 6

37. The ground state electron configuration of the silicon atom is characterized by which of the following?

    I. Partially filled $3p$ orbitals
   II. The presence of unpaired electrons
  III. Six valence electrons

(A) I only
(B) II only
(C) I and II only
(D) I and III only
(E) I, II, and III

38. Which of the following gases is LEAST dense when all are measured under the same conditions?

(A) CO_2 (B) Cl_2 (C) SO_2

(D) H_2 (E) NO

39. Which of the following best accounts for some of the nonideal behavior observed in real gases?

(A) Some gaseous molecules are not spherical.
(B) There are intermolecular attractive forces.
(C) The temperature is not kept constant.
(D) R, the gas constant, is not a true constant.
(E) Experimental errors are made in the measurement of the pressure and the volume.

GO ON TO THE NEXT PAGE

Questions 40-43 refer to the experiment shown below in which the vapor pressure of isopropanol was determined. Throughout the experiment, the temperature was held constant at 25°C, and the atmospheric pressure remained at 760 millimeters of Hg.

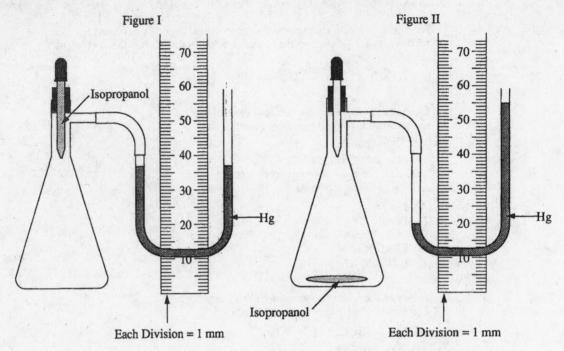

Figure I

Isopropanol

Hg

Each Division = 1 mm

Before injection of isopropanol

Figure II

Isopropanol

Hg

Each Division = 1 mm

After equilibrium is established

40. According to Figure I, the initial pressure inside the flask is

   (A) near zero (vacuum)
   (B) 27 mm Hg
   (C) 760 mm Hg
   (D) (760 − 27) mm Hg
   (E) (760 + 27) mm Hg

41. According to Figure II, the vapor pressure of isopropanol at 25° C was determined to be

   (A) 20 mm Hg
   (B) 35 mm Hg
   (C) 45 mm Hg
   (D) 725 mm Hg
   (E) 795 mm Hg

42. Which of the following is a possible source of error in the results of this experiment?

   (A) Inaccurate weighing of the isopropanol
   (B) The presence of bits of broken glass in the flask
   (C) Failure to correct for humidity
   (D) Misreading of the atmospheric pressure
   (E) Leakage around the rubber stopper

43. Which of the following changes in the experiment would cause the Hg levels in the U-tube to vary from those shown in Figure II ?

   (A) Replacing the flask with one that has a round bottom
   (B) Doubling the volume of liquid injected into the flask
   (C) Increasing the temperature of the system to 30° C
   (D) Replacing the air originally in the flask with helium gas at a pressure of 760 mm Hg
   (E) Increasing the diameter of the U-tube

GO ON TO THE NEXT PAGE

44. Filtration is a technique particularly suited to the separation of

    (A) two solids with different densities
    (B) two liquids with different molar masses
    (C) two liquids with different boiling points
    (D) a solid and a liquid
    (E) a gas and a liquid

45. In which of the following compounds does bromine have the highest positive oxidation state?

    (A) HBr
    (B) BrF_3
    (C) BrO_2
    (D) NaBrO
    (E) $NaBrO_3$

46. What is the empirical formula of a compound that contains 0.025 mole of Cd, 0.050 mole of C, and 0.100 mole of O ?

    (A) CdCO
    (B) $CdCO_2$
    (C) $CdCO_3$
    (D) CdC_2O_2
    (E) CdC_2O_4

47. The mass of 6.02×10^{23} molecules of a gas is 64.0 grams. What volume does 8.00 grams of the gas occupy at standard temperature and pressure?

    (A) 2.80 liters
    (B) 8.00 liters
    (C) 11.2 liters
    (D) 22.4 liters
    (E) 64.0 liters

48. Raising the temperature at which a chemical reaction proceeds may do all of the following EXCEPT

    (A) increase the molecular collision frequency
    (B) increase the number of molecules with energy greater than the activation energy
    (C) speed up the forward and reverse reactions
    (D) decrease the randomness of the system
    (E) change the relative concentrations of products to reactants that are present at equilibrium

49. To determine whether a water solution of $Na_2S_2O_3$ at room temperature is supersaturated, one can

    (A) heat the solution to its boiling point
    (B) add water to the solution
    (C) add a crystal of $Na_2S_2O_3$ to the solution
    (D) acidify the solution
    (E) cool the solution to its freezing point

GO ON TO THE NEXT PAGE

Questions 50-52

The following elements are listed in order of decreasing reactivity as they appear in the electro-chemical series.

Ca, Na, Mg, Zn, Fe, H, Cu, Hg, Ag, Au

50. The element that is the best reducing agent is

(A) Ca   (B) Au   (C) H   (D) Fe   (E) Cu

51. Of the following, the element that does NOT react with hydrochloric acid to produce hydrogen gas is

(A) Zn   (B) Fe   (C) Hg   (D) Ca   (E) Mg

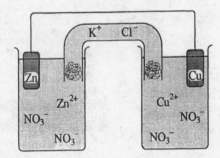

52. In the electrochemical cell shown above, which of the following half-reactions occurs at the anode?

(A) $Cu^{2+} + e \rightarrow Cu^{+}$

(B) $Zn(s) \rightarrow Zn^{2+} + 2e$

(C) $Zn^{2+} + 2e \rightarrow Zn(s)$

(D) $Cu(s) \rightarrow Cu^{2+} + 2e$

(E) $Cu^{2+} + 2e \rightarrow Cu(s)$

53. An atom contains 15 protons, 15 electrons, and 16 neutrons. Which of the following combinations of particles is an isotope of that atom?

	Protons	Electrons	Neutrons
(A)	16	16	17
(B)	15	16	16
(C)	15	15	15
(D)	14	15	16
(E)	14	14	15

54. What is the percent composition by mass of aluminum in a compound of aluminum and oxygen if the mole ratio of Al:O is 2:3 ?

(A) 37% Al
(B) 47% Al
(C) 53% Al
(D) 63% Al
(E) 74% Al

55. At constant temperature, the change of state of any substance from liquid to gas always includes which of the following?

  I. The breaking of covalent bonds
 II. An increase in the randomness of the system
III. The absorption of energy

(A) I only
(B) II only
(C) I and II only
(D) II and III only
(E) I, II, and III

GO ON TO THE NEXT PAGE

Questions 56-57

$$N_2(g) + 3 H_2(g) \rightarrow 2 NH_3(g) + 92 \text{ kilojoules}$$

56. Ammonia is produced from nitrogen and hydrogen by the exothermic reaction represented above. When 4 moles of ammonia are produced by the reaction, which of the following occurs?

(A) 46 kilojoules are absorbed.
(B) 92 kilojoules are absorbed.
(C) 184 kilojoules are absorbed.
(D) 92 kilojoules are given off.
(E) 184 kilojoules are given off.

57. According to the equation above, what mass of nitrogen gas is required to produce 68 grams of ammonia?

(A) 112 grams
(B) 56 grams
(C) 44 grams
(D) 28 grams
(E) 14 grams

58. The electron dot structure for the hydronium ion is

(A) H^+

(B) $\left[H : \ddot{O} : \right]^-$

(C) $\left[H : \ddot{O} : H \atop \ddot{H} \right]^+$

(D) $\left[{H \atop H : O : H \atop H} \right]^+$

(E) $\left[H : O : H \atop \ddot{H} \right]^+$

59. Which of the following does NOT react with a dilute H_2SO_4 solution?

(A) $NaNO_3$

(B) Na_2S

(C) Na_3PO_4

(D) Na_2CO_3

(E) $NaOH$

60. $\ldots AlCl_3(aq) + \ldots NH_3(aq) + \ldots H_2O \rightarrow$

Which of the following is one of the products obtained from the reaction above?

(A) AlN
(B) AlH_3
(C) Al
(D) $Al(NO_3)_3$
(E) $Al(OH)_3$

GO ON TO THE NEXT PAGE

61. A 0.1-molar solution of which of the following compounds has the lowest hydrogen ion concentration?

(A) HCl
(B) AlCl$_3$
(C) NaHCO$_3$
(D) NaOH
(E) HC$_2$H$_3$O$_2$ (acetic acid)

62.

Mixture	Milliliters of 0.1 M Pb(NO$_3$)$_2$	Milliliters of 0.1 M NaI
I	2	7
II	3	6
III	4	5
IV	5	4
V	6	3

Which of the mixtures listed above yields the maximum amount of precipitated PbI$_2$?

(A) I   (B) II   (C) III   (D) IV   (E) V

63. When HS$^-$ acts as a Brönsted base, which of the following is formed?

(A) S^{2-}

(B) H$^+$

(C) H$_2$S

(D) H$_2$S$_2$

(E) H$_3$S$^+$

64. $2 NO(g) + H_2(g) \rightleftharpoons N_2O(g) + H_2O(g) + 351$ kilojoules

If the total pressure on the system is increased when the reaction represented above is at equilibrium, which of the following occurs?

(A) The concentration of H$_2$O increases.
(B) The concentration of N$_2$O decreases.
(C) The rate of the reaction decreases.
(D) The temperature of the system decreases.
(E) The H$_2$ gas condenses.

GO ON TO THE NEXT PAGE

65. Neutralization of 500 milliliters of 2-molar NaOH requires the smallest volume of which of the following?

    (A) 1 M H_2SO_4

    (B) 1 M CH_3COOH

    (C) 1 M HCl

    (D) 1 M NH_3

    (E) 0.1 M H_2SO_4

66. Boron trifluoride, BF_3, is a nonpolar molecule, whereas ammonia, NH_3, is a polar molecule. The difference in polarities is related to the fact that

    (A) BF_3 has no hydrogen bonding and NH_3 does
    (B) BF_3 is triangular planar and NH_3 is pyramidal
    (C) BF_3 is a Lewis base and NH_3 is a Lewis acid
    (D) the B-F bond is less polar than the N-H bond
    (E) boron is more electronegative than nitrogen

$$\text{I.} \quad A + B \rightleftharpoons 2C + D$$
$$\text{II.} \quad 2C + D \rightleftharpoons A + B$$

67. If the equilibrium constant for the reaction represented by equation I above is 4.0×10^{-2}, what is the value of the equilibrium constant for the reaction represented by equation II ?

    (A) 16×10^{-4}

    (B) 4.0×10^{-2}

    (C) $\dfrac{1}{4.0}$

    (D) $\dfrac{1}{4.0 \times 10^{-2}}$

    (E) 4.0×10^{2}

68. A solution is made by adding 5.6 grams of KOH (molar mass 56 grams) to enough water to make 1.0 liter of solution. What is the approximate pH of the resulting solution?

    (A) 1
    (B) 3
    (C) 7
    (D) 9
    (E) 13

69.
$$H_2(g) + S(s) \rightleftharpoons H_2S(g)$$

What is the mass action expression (equilibrium constant expression) for the equilibrium mixture of solid sulfur, hydrogen gas, and hydrogen sulfide gas represented by the equation above?

    (A) $K = \dfrac{1}{[H_2]}$

    (B) $K = \dfrac{1}{[H_2S]}$

    (C) $K = \dfrac{[H_2S]}{[H_2]}$

    (D) $K = \dfrac{[H_2][S]}{[H_2S]}$

    (E) $K = \dfrac{[H_2S]}{[H_2][S]}$

70. A 1.0-liter sample of a 0.01-molar solution of $CaCl_2$ contains a total of

    (A) 0.04 mole of Ca^{2+}
    (B) 0.02 mole of Ca^{2+}
    (C) 0.01 mole of Cl_2
    (D) 0.01 mole of Cl^-
    (E) 0.02 mole of Cl^-

STOP

**IF YOU FINISH BEFORE TIME IS CALLED, YOU MAY CHECK YOUR WORK ON THIS TEST ONLY.
DO NOT TURN TO ANY OTHER TEST IN THIS BOOK.**

How to Score the SAT Subject Test in Chemistry

When you take the Chemistry Subject Test, your answer sheet will be "read" by a scanning machine that will record your response to each question. Then a computer will compare your answers with the correct answers and produce your raw score. You get one point for each correct answer. For each wrong answer, you lose one-fourth of a point. Questions you omit (and any for which you mark more than one answer) are not counted. This raw score is converted to a scaled score that is reported to you and to the colleges you specify.

Worksheet 1. Finding Your Raw Test Score

STEP 1: Table A lists the correct answers for all the questions on the SAT Subject Test in Chemistry that is reproduced in this book. It also serves as a worksheet for you to calculate your raw score.

- Compare your answers with those given in the table.
- Put a check in the column marked "Right" if your answer is correct.
- Put a check in the column marked "Wrong" if your answer is incorrect.
- Leave both columns blank if you omitted the question.

STEP 2: Count the number of right answers.

Enter the total here: _____

STEP 3: Count the number of wrong answers.

Enter the total here: _____

STEP 4: Multiply the number of wrong answers by .250.

Enter the product here: _____

STEP 5: Subtract the result obtained in Step 4 from the total you obtained in Step 2.

Enter the result here: _____

STEP 6: Round the number obtained in Step 5 to the nearest whole number.

Enter the result here: _____

The number you obtained in Step 6 is your raw test score.

TABLE A
Answers to the SAT Subject Test in Chemistry, Form 3PAC7 reformatted, and Percentage of Students Answering Each Question Correctly

Question Number	Correct Answer	Right	Wrong	Percentage of Students Answering the Question Correctly*	Question Number	Correct Answer	Right	Wrong	Percentage of Students Answering the Question Correctly*
1	B			88	33	E			73
2	C			82	34	D			69
3	D			78	35	E			66
4	C			66	36	B			67
5	A			45	37	C			52
6	E			88	38	D			75
7	B			41	39	B			58
8	C			35	40	C			56
9	D			39	41	B			24
10	A			90	42	E			54
11	B			79	43	C			55
12	C			64	44	D			83
13	A			85	45	E			52
14	E			84	46	E			76
15	E			55	47	A			52
16	C			62	48	D			55
17	E			84	49	C			63
18	D			89	50	A			47
19	B			71	51	C			56
20	B			40	52	B			28
21	A			53	53	C			64
22	B			51	54	C			42
23	B			38	55	D			45
24	A			59	56	E			64
25	A			44	57	B			45
26	D			78	58	C			56
27	E			87	59	A			16
28	D			66	60	E			41
29	E			51	61	D			35
30	C			75	62	B			36
31	D			54	63	C			50
32	C			55	64	A			44

Table A continued on next page

Table A continued from previous page

Question Number	Correct Answer	Right	Wrong	Percentage of Students Answering the Question Correctly*	Question Number	Correct Answer	Right	Wrong	Percentage of Students Answering the Question Correctly
65	A			27	106	T,T			30
66	B			45	107	T,T			32
67	D			54	108	T,F			48
68	E			34	109	F,F			61
69	C			44	110	F,T			60
70	E			49	111	T,T,CE			73
101	F,F			63	112	T,T,CE			70
102	T,T,CE			74	113	T,F			65
103	T,T			48	114	F,T			53
104	T,T,CE			63	115	T,T,CE			54
105	F,T			48					

*These percentages are based on an analysis of the answer sheets for a random sample of 2,382 students who took this form of the test in May 1994 and whose mean score was 598. They may be used as an indication of the relative difficulty of a particular question. Each percentage may also be used to predict the likelihood that a typical SAT Subject Test in Chemistry candidate will answer correctly that question on this edition of this test.

Finding Your Scaled Score

When you take SAT Subject Tests, the scores sent to the colleges you specify are reported on the College Board scale, which ranges from 200 to 800. You can convert your practice test score to a scaled score by using Table B. To find your scaled score, locate your raw score in the left-hand column of Table B; the corresponding score in the right-hand column is your scaled score. For example, a raw score of 60 on this particular edition of the SAT Subject Test in Chemistry corresponds to a scaled score of about 700.

Raw scores are converted to scaled scores to ensure that a score earned on any edition of a particular Subject Test is comparable to the same scaled score earned on any other edition of the same Subject Test. Because some editions of tests may be slightly easier or more difficult than others, scaled scores are adjusted so that they indicate the same level of performance regardless of the edition of the test taken and the ability of the group that takes it. Thus, for example, a score of 400 on one edition of a test taken at a particular administration indicates the same level of achievement as a score of 400 on a different edition of the test taken at a different administration.

When you take the SAT Subject Tests during a national administration, your score is likely to differ somewhat from the scores you obtain on the tests in this book. People perform at different levels at different times for reasons unrelated to the tests themselves. The precision of any test is also limited because it represents only a sample of all the possible questions that could be asked.

TABLE B
Scaled Score Conversion Table
Chemistry Subject Test (Form 3PAC7)

Raw Score	Scaled Score	Raw Score	Scaled Score	Raw Score	Scaled Score
85	800	49	640	13	440
84	800	48	640	12	440
83	800	47	630	11	430
82	800	46	620	10	430
81	800	45	620	9	420
80	800	44	610	8	420
79	800	43	610	7	410
78	800	42	600	6	410
77	790	41	600	5	400
76	790	40	590	4	390
75	780	39	590	3	390
74	780	38	580	2	380
73	770	37	580	1	380
72	770	36	570	0	370
71	760	35	560	−1	370
70	760	34	560	−2	360
69	750	33	550	−3	360
68	750	32	550	−4	350
67	740	31	540	−5	340
66	730	30	540	−6	340
65	730	29	530	−7	330
64	720	28	530	−8	330
63	720	27	520	−9	320
62	710	26	510	−10	320
61	710	25	510	−11	310
60	700	24	500	−12	310
59	700	23	500	−13	300
58	690	22	490	−14	300
57	690	21	490	−15	290
56	680	20	480	−16	280
55	670	19	480	−17	280
54	670	18	470	−18	270
53	660	17	470	−19	270
52	660	16	460	−20	260
51	650	15	450	−21	260
50	650	14	450		

Reviewing Your Performance on the Chemistry Subject Test

After you score your test, analyze your performance—consider the following questions:

Did you run out of time before reaching the end of the test?

If so, you may need to pace yourself better. For example, maybe you got bogged down on one or two hard questions. A better approach might be to skip the ones you can't answer right away and try answering all the questions that remain on the test. Then if there's time, go back to the questions you skipped.

Did you take a long time reading the directions?

You will save time when you take the test by learning the directions to the Chemistry Subject Test ahead of time. Each minute you spend reading directions during the test is a minute that you could be answering questions.

How did you handle questions you were unsure of?

If you were able to eliminate one or more of the answer choices as wrong and guess from the remaining ones, your approach probably worked to your advantage. On the other hand, making haphazard guesses or omitting questions without trying to eliminate choices could cost you valuable points.

How difficult were the questions for you compared with other students who took the test?

Table A shows you how difficult the multiple-choice questions were for the group of students who took this test during its national administration. The right-hand column gives the percentage of students that answered each question correctly.

A question answered correctly by almost everyone in the group is obviously an easy question. For example, 90 percent of the students answered question 10 correctly. But only 16 percent answered question 59 correctly.

Keep in mind that these percentages are based on just one group of students. They would probably be different if another group of students took the test.

If you missed several easy questions, go back and try to find out why: Did the questions cover material you haven't reviewed yet? Did you misunderstand the directions?

Chapter 7
Physics

Purpose

The Physics Subject Test measures the knowledge students would be expected to have after successfully completing a college-preparatory course in high school. The test is not based on any one textbook or instructional approach, but concentrates on the common core of material found in most texts.

Format

This one-hour test consists of 75 multiple-choice questions. Topics that are covered in most high school courses are emphasized. Because high school courses differ, both in percentage of time devoted to each major topic and in the specific subtopics covered, most students will find that there are some questions on topics with which they are not familiar.

Content of the Test

Topics Covered   Approximate Percentage of Test

I. Mechanics   36–42

A. Kinematics (such as velocity, acceleration, motion in one dimension, and motion of projectiles)

B. Dynamics (such as force, Newton's laws, and statics)

C. Energy and Momentum (such as potential and kinetic energy, work, power, impulse, and conservation laws)

D. Circular Motion and Rotation (such as uniform circular motion, centripetal force, torque, and angular momentum)

E. Vibrations (such as simple harmonic motion, mass on a spring, and the simple pendulum)

F. Gravity (such as the law of gravitation and orbits and Kepler's Laws)

II. Electricity and Magnetism 18–24

A. Electric Fields, Forces, and Potentials (such as Coulomb's law, induced charge, field and potential of groups of point charges, and charged particles in electric fields)

B. Magnetic Fields and Forces (such as permanent magnets, fields caused by currents, and particles in magnetic fields, Faraday's law, Lenz's law)

C. Capacitance (such as parallel-plate capacitors and transients)

D. Circuits and Circuit Elements (such as Ohm's law, Joule's law, resistors, lightbulbs, and series and parallel networks)

III. Waves 15–19

A. General Wave Properties (such as wave speed, frequency, wavelength, and Doppler effect)

B. Reflection and Refraction (such as Snell's law and changes in wavelength and speed)

C. Physical Optics (such as single-slit diffraction, double-slit interference, polarization, and color)

D. Ray Optics (such as image formation in mirrors and lenses and using pinholes)

IV. Heat and Thermodynamics 6–11

A. Thermal Properties (such as temperature, specific and latent heats, and thermal expansion)

B. Laws of Thermodynamics (such as first and second laws, internal energy, entropy, and heat engine efficiency)

V. Modern Physics 6–11

A. Quantum Phenomena (such as photons, photoelectric effect, and the uncertainty principle)

B. Atomic (such as the Rutherford and Bohr models, atomic energy levels, and atomic spectra)

C. Nuclear and Particle Physics (such as radioactivity, nuclear reactions and fundamental particles)

D. Relativity (such as time dilation, length contraction, and mass-energy equivalence)

VI. Miscellaneous   4–9

  A. General (such as history of physics and general
     questions that overlap several major topics)

  B. Analytical Skills (such as graphical analysis,
     measurement, and math skills)

  C. Contemporary Physics (such as astrophysics,
     biophysics, and superconductivity)

Note: Some questions may deal with laboratory skills in context.

Level of Concept Application	Approximate Percentage of Test
Recall (generally involves remembering and understanding concepts or information)	20–33
Single-concept problem (recall and use of a single physical relationship)	40–53
Multiple-concept problem (recall and integration of two or more physical relationships)	20–33

You may NOT use a calculator during the test. Numerical calculations are not emphasized and are limited to simple arithmetic. Metric units are used predominantly in this test.

Recommended Preparation

The test is intended for students who have completed a one-year introductory physics course at the college-preparatory level. You should be able to:

- recall and understand the major concepts of physics and to apply these physical principles you have learned to solve specific problems.
- understand simple algebraic, trigonometric, and graphical relationships, and the concepts of ratio and proportion and apply these to physics problems.

Although laboratory experience is a significant factor in developing reasoning and problem-solving skills, this multiple-choice test can measure laboratory skills only in a limited way such as asking you to interpret laboratory data on some questions.

Familiarize yourself with directions in advance. The directions in this book are identical to those that appear on the test.

Other

- the direction of any current is the direction of flow of positive charge (conventional current)
- calculator use is not allowed during the test
- numerical calculations are not emphasized and are limited to simple arithmetic
- predominantly uses the metric system

Score

The total score for each test is reported on the 200-to-800 scale.

Sample Questions

Two types of questions are used in the Physics Test—classification and five-choice completion questions.

Classification Questions

Each set of classification questions includes five lettered choices that you will use to answer all of the questions in the set (see sample questions 1–4). These choices appear before the questions in the set. In addition, there may be descriptive material that is relevant in answering the questions in the set. The choices may be words, phrases, sentences, graphs, pictures, equations, or data. The numbered questions themselves may also be any of these, or they may be given in the question format directly. To answer each question, select the lettered choice that provides the most appropriate response. You should consider all of the lettered choices before answering a question. The directions for this type of question state specifically that a choice cannot be eliminated just because it is the correct answer to a previous question.

Because the same five choices are applicable to several questions, the classification questions usually require less reading than other types of multiple-choice questions. Therefore, classification questions provide a quick means, in terms of testing time, of determining how well you have mastered the topics represented. The set of questions may ask you to recall appropriate information, or the set may ask you to apply information to a specific situation or to translate information between different forms (descriptive, graphical, mathematical). Thus, different types of abilities can be tested by this type of question.

Directions: Each set of lettered choices below refers to the numbered questions or statements immediately following it. Select the one lettered choice that best answers each question or best fits each statement and then fill in the corresponding oval on the answer sheet. A choice may be used once, more than once, or not at all in each set.

Questions 1–2:

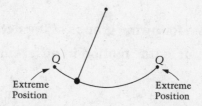

A small sphere attached to the end of a string swings as a simple pendulum. The sphere moves along the arc shown above. Consider the following properties of the sphere.

    (A) **Acceleration**
    (B) **Kinetic energy**
    (C) **Mass**
    (D) **Potential energy**
    (E) **Velocity**

1. Which property remains constant throughout the motion of the sphere?

2. Which property goes to zero and changes direction at each extreme position Q?

To answer question 1, you may know that in classical mechanics mass is a fundamental property of an object that does not depend on the position or velocity of the object. Thus the answer is (C). Alternately, you may realize that, since a pendulum during its motion repeatedly speeds up, slows down, and changes direction, the sphere's velocity, kinetic energy, and acceleration must also change. Also, since the height of the sphere varies, so must its potential energy. Thus you can also obtain the answer by the process of elimination.

    To answer question 2, you must know some specific details about the motion of the pendulum. At each extreme position Q, the velocity and the kinetic energy (which is proportional to the square of the speed) are both zero, but kinetic energy has magnitude only and thus no direction to change. Velocity does have direction, and in this case the velocity of the sphere is directed away from the center, or equilibrium position, just before the sphere reaches Q, but directed toward the center just after leaving Q. The velocity changes direction at each point Q, so the answer is (E). The only other choice that has direction is acceleration, but acceleration has its maximum magnitude at each point Q and is directed toward the center, both shortly before and shortly after the sphere is at Q.

Questions 3–4 relate to the following graphs of the net force *F* on a body *versus* time *t*, for the body in straight-line motion in different situations.

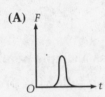

(A) *F*

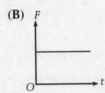

(B) *F*

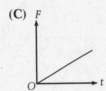

(C) *F*

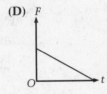

(D) *F*

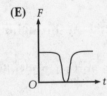

(E) *F*

For each of the following speed *v* versus time *t* graphs for the body, choose the graph above with which it is consistent.

3.

4.

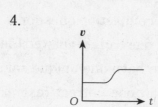

Questions 3 and 4 test the application of physical principles to information presented in graphical form. In each of these questions two concepts are involved. From Newton's second law we know that the net force on a body is equal to the body's acceleration multiplied by the body's mass, a constant. Thus graphs of acceleration versus time must have the same shape as the graphs of force versus time that are given in the options. We must also know that at a particular time the acceleration of a body in its direction of motion is equal to the rate of change of its speed, as determined by the slope of the speed v versus time t graph at that particular time. In question 3, the slope of the graph continually increases with increasing t; therefore, the body's acceleration and consequently the net force on the body must also increase continually. The only graph among the choices that shows this relationship is graph (C), the answer. In question 4, the graph initially shows a constant speed, implying an acceleration and net force of zero. Then the curve sharply increases for a brief time, implying a large positive acceleration and large net force. Finally the curve returns to constant speed, implying a return to a zero net force. Graph (A) is the answer because it is the only choice that shows a force that varies in this manner.

Five-Choice Completion Questions

The five-choice completion question is written either as an incomplete statement or as a question. In its simplest application, it poses a problem that intrinsically has a unique solution. It is also appropriate when: (1) the problem presented is clearly delineated by the wording of the question so that you choose not a universal solution but the best of the five offered solutions; (2) the problem is such that you are required to evaluate the relevance of five plausible, or scientifically accurate, choices and to select the one most pertinent; or (3) the problem has several pertinent solutions and you are required to select the one that is *inappropriate* or not correct from among the five choices presented. Questions of this latter type (see sample question 6) will normally contain a word in capital letters such as NOT, EXCEPT, or LEAST.

A special type of five-choice completion question is used in some tests to allow for the possibility of more than one correct answer. Unlike many quantitative problems that must by their nature have one unique solution, situations do arise in which there may be more than one correct response. In such situations, you should evaluate each response independently of the others in order to select the most appropriate combination (see sample question 7). In questions of this type, several (usually three) statements labeled by Roman numerals are given with the question. One or more of these statements may correctly answer the question. The statements are followed by five lettered choices, with each choice consisting of some combination of the Roman numerals that label the statements. You must select from among the five lettered choices the one that gives the combination of statements that best answers the question. In the test, questions of this type are intermixed among the more standard five-choice completion questions.

The five-choice completion question also tests problem-solving skills. With this type of question, you may be asked to convert the information given in a word problem into graphical forms or to select and apply the mathematical relationship necessary to solve the scientific problem. Alternatively, you may be asked to interpret experimental data, graphs, or mathematical expressions. Thus, the five-choice completion question can be adapted to test several kinds of abilities.

When the experimental data or other scientific problems to be analyzed are comparatively long, it is often convenient to organize several five-choice completion questions into sets, with each question in the set relating to the same common material that precedes the set (see sample questions 8–9). This practice allows you to respond to several questions based on information that may otherwise take considerable testing time to read and comprehend. Such sets also test how thorough your understanding is of a particular situation. Although the questions in a set may be related, you do not have to know the answer to one question in a set to answer a subsequent question correctly. Each question in a set can be answered directly from the common material given for the entire set.

Directions: Each of the questions or incomplete statements below is followed by five suggested answers or completions. Select the one that is best in each case and then fill in the corresponding oval on the answer sheet.

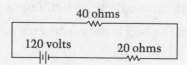

5. If the internal resistance of the 120-volt battery in the circuit shown above is negligible, the current in the wire is

   (A) 0 A

   (B) 2 A

   (C) 3 A

   (D) 6 A

   (E) 9 A

In question 5, you must apply two concepts to solve the problem. First, you must recognize that the two resistors are connected in series and thus are equivalent to a single resistor whose resistance is 60 ohms, the sum of the two component resistances. Next, applying Ohm's law, you will find that the current is given by the potential difference divided by this equivalent resistance. Thus, the answer is $\frac{120 \text{ volts}}{60 \text{ ohms}}$, which equals 2 amperes. Therefore, (B) is the answer.

6. All of the following are vector quantities EXCEPT

   (A) force

   (B) velocity

   (C) acceleration

   (D) power

   (E) momentum

Question 6 is a straightforward question that tests your knowledge of vector and scalar quantities. A vector quantity is one that has both magnitude and direction. All five quantities have a magnitude associated with them, but only quantities (A), (B), (C), and (E) also have a direction. Power, a rate of change of energy, is not a vector quantity, so the answer is (D).

7. A ball is thrown vertically upward. Air resistance is negligible. After leaving the hand, the acceleration of the ball is downward under which of the following conditions?

   I.   **On the way up**
   II.   **On the way down**
   III.   **At the top of its rise**

   (A) I only
   (B) III only
   (C) I and II only
   (D) II and III only
   (E) I, II, and III

In question 7, one or several of the phrases represented by the Roman numerals may be correct answers to the question. One must evaluate each in turn. When the ball is on the way up, its speed is decreasing so the acceleration of the ball must be directed in the direction opposite to the ball's velocity. Since the velocity is upward, the acceleration must be downward, making I correct. When the ball is on the way down, its speed is increasing, so its acceleration must be directed in the same direction as its velocity, which is downward. So II is also correct. Finally, at the top of the rise, the ball has an instantaneous speed of zero, but its velocity is changing from upward to downward, implying a downward acceleration and making III correct also. A simpler analysis would be to realize that in all three cases, the ball is acted on by the downward force of gravity and no other forces. By Newton's second law, the acceleration must be in the direction of the net force, so it must be downward in all three cases. Since the phrases in I, II, and III are each correct answers to the question, the correct response is (E).

Questions 8–9: In the following graph, the speed of a small object as it moves along a horizontal straight line is plotted against time.

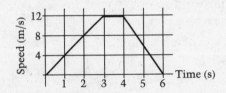

8. The magnitude of the acceleration of the object during the first 3 seconds is

    (A) 3 m/s^2
    (B) 4 m/s^2
    (C) 6 m/s^2
    (D) 12 m/s^2
    (E) 36 m/s^2

9. The average speed of the object during the first 4 seconds is
    (A) 1.9 m/s
    (B) 3.0 m/s
    (C) 4.0 m/s
    (D) 6.0 m/s
    (E) 7.5 m/s

Questions 8 and 9 are a set of questions, both based on the graph provided.

To answer question 8, you need to know that the magnitude of the acceleration is equal to the magnitude of the slope of a graph of speed *versus* time. In this situation, from time = 0 to time = 3 seconds, the graph has a constant slope of $\dfrac{12 \text{ m/s}}{3 \text{ s}} = 4 \text{ m/s}^2$, which is the magnitude of the acceleration. So the answer is (B).

The average speed of an object during a certain time is equal to the total distance traveled by the object during that time divided by the time. In question 9, the total distance traveled by the object during the first 4 seconds is equal to the area under the graph from time = 0 to time = 4 seconds. This area is $\dfrac{1}{2}$ (3 s)(12 m/s) + (1 s)(12 m/s) = 18 m + 12 m = 30 m. The average speed is therefore $\dfrac{30 \text{ m}}{4 \text{ s}} = 7.5 \text{ m/s}$, which is choice (E).

Physics Test

The test that follows is an actual, recently administered SAT Subject Test in Physics. To get an idea of what a real administration is like, take the test under conditions as close as possible to those of a national administration:

- Set aside an hour when you can take the test uninterrupted. Make sure you complete the test in one sitting.

- Sit at a desk or table with no other books or papers. Dictionaries, other books, or notes are not allowed in the test room.

- Do not use a calculator. Calculators are not allowed for the Physics Test.

- Time yourself by placing a clock or kitchen timer in front of you.

- Tear out an answer sheet from the back of this book and fill it in just as you would on the day of the test. One answer sheet can be used for up to three Subject Tests.

- Read the instructions that precede the practice test. During the actual administration you will be asked to read them before answering test questions.

- After you finish the practice test, read the sections "How to Score the SAT Subject Test in Physics" and "Reviewing Your Performance on the Physics Subject Test."

- Actual test and answer sheets will indicate circles, not ovals.

Form 3RAC2

PHYSICS TEST

The top portion of the section of the answer sheet that you will use in taking the Physics test must be filled in exactly as shown in the illustration below. Note carefully that you have to do all of the following on your answer sheet.

1. Print PHYSICS on the line under the words "Subject Test (print)."

2. In the shaded box labeled "Test Code" fill in four ovals:

   —Fill in oval 2 in the row labeled V.

   —Fill in oval 3 in the row labeled W.

   —Fill in oval 3 in the row labeled X.

   —Fill in oval C in the row labeled Y.

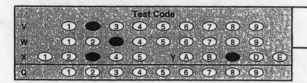

3. Please answer the three questions below by filling in the appropriate ovals in the row labeled Q on the answer sheet. The information you provide is for statistical purposes only and will not affect your score on the test.

Question I

How many semesters of physics have you taken in high school? (If you are taking physics this semester, count it as a full semester.) Fill in only <u>one</u> oval of ovals 1-3.

- One semester or less   —Fill in oval 1.
- Two semesters   —Fill in oval 2.
- Three semesters or more   —Fill in oval 3.

Question II

Which of the following describe courses you have taken or are taking now? (Fill in <u>all</u> ovals that apply.)

- Algebra I or Elementary Algebra   —Fill in oval 4.
- Geometry   —Fill in oval 5.
- Algebra II or Intermediate Algebra   —Fill in oval 6.
- Algebra III or Trigonometry or Precalculus   —Fill in oval 7.

Question III

Are you currently taking Advanced Placement Physics? If you are, fill in oval 8.

Leave oval 9 blank.

When the supervisor gives the signal, turn the page and begin the Physics test. There are 100 numbered ovals on the answer sheet and 75 questions in the Physics test. Therefore, use only ovals 1 to 75 for recording your answers.

PHYSICS TEST

Part A

Directions: Each set of lettered choices below refers to the numbered questions or statements immediately following it. Select the one lettered choice that best answers each question or best fits each statement, and then fill in the corresponding oval on the answer sheet. A choice may be used once, more than once, or not at all in each set.

Questions 1-3 relate to the following.

    (A) Electron
    (B) Proton
    (C) Neutron
    (D) Positron
    (E) Alpha particle

1. Which particle could NOT be deflected by a uniform magnetic field?

2. If all of the particles were in the same electric field, which would be accelerated in a direction opposite to the field?

3. If all of the particles were in the same uniform electric field, which would have the greatest force acting on it?

Questions 4-7 relate to the following equations or physical principles that might be used to solve certain problems.

    (A) Kinematic equations for constant acceleration
    (B) Newton's second law ($F = ma$)
    (C) Newton's third law (For every action there is an equal and opposite reaction.)
    (D) Conservation of mechanical energy
    (E) Conservation of linear momentum

Select the choice that should be used to provide the best and most direct solution to each of the following problems.

4. A marble is dropped from rest at a given height above the ground. Air resistance is negligible. How long is the marble in free fall?

5. A weight is dropped onto the bed of a toy flatcar that is initially coasting on a straight, horizontal, frictionless track. What is the speed of the flatcar after the weight has settled on it?

6. A frictionless pendulum of given length and mass is released from a horizontal position. What is the speed of the pendulum bob at the lowest position in its swing?

7. A brick of known weight is in free fall. While it is falling, what force does the brick exert on the Earth?

GO ON TO THE NEXT PAGE

3RAC2

Questions 8-9

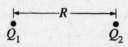

Two point charges, Q_1 and Q_2, are separated by a distance R, as shown above. The following choices refer to the electric force on Q_1 due to Q_2.

(A) It is quadrupled.
(B) It is doubled.
(C) It remains the same.
(D) It is halved.
(E) It is quartered.

8. What happens to the magnitude of the force on Q_1 if the sign of Q_1 is changed and Q_2 remains the same?

9. What happens to the magnitude of the force on Q_1 if Q_1 is doubled and Q_2 remains the same?

GO ON TO THE NEXT PAGE

Questions 10-12 relate to the following graphs

(A)   (B)   (C)   (D)   (E)

Select the graph above that best expresses each of the following relationships (y as a function of x).

	y		x
10.	Decay rate of nuclei in a radioactive sample	*vs.*	Time
11.	Kinetic energy of a relativistic particle	*vs.*	Speed of the particle
12.	Maximum kinetic energy of a photoelectron ejected from a metal plate	*vs.*	Frequency of the light incident on the plate

GO ON TO THE NEXT PAGE

Part B

> **Directions:** Each of the questions or incomplete statements below is followed by five suggested answers or completions. Select the one that is best in each case and then fill in the corresponding oval on the answer sheet.

13. You are in a glider that is traveling due east at 60 kilometers per hour relative to an air mass that is traveling due north at 60 kilometers per hour relative to the ground. Your motion relative to the ground is

    (A) due east
    (B) northeast
    (C) due north
    (D) southwest
    (E) due south

14. Each of the figures below shows the velocity **v** of a particle and the force or forces acting on the particle. Forces F_1 and F_2 have the same magnitude. In which figure is the particle's speed or direction NOT being changed?

    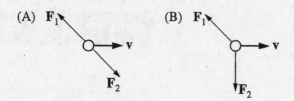

    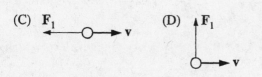

    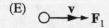

15. The magnitude of the electric force exerted by charged particle X on charged particle Y depends on which of the following?

    I. The magnitude of the charge on particle X
    II. The magnitude of the charge on particle Y
    III. The distance between particle X and particle Y

    (A) I only
    (B) III only
    (C) I and II only
    (D) II and III only
    (E) I, II, and III

Questions 16-17 refer to the electrical circuit shown below. Ammeter A reads 2.0 amperes.

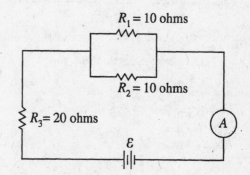

16. What is the voltage across R_3?

    (A) 10 V
    (B) 20 V
    (C) 30 V
    (D) 40 V
    (E) 80 V

17. What is the current in R_1?

    (A) 1.0 A
    (B) 2.0 A
    (C) 4.0 A
    (D) 10 A
    (E) 20 A

GO ON TO THE NEXT PAGE

Questions 18-19 refer to the following drawing of a wave.

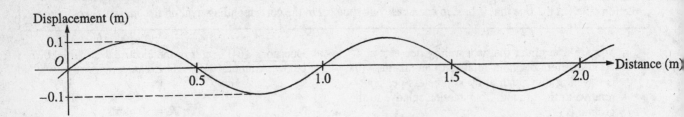

18. What is the wavelength of the wave?

   (A) 0.1 m
   (B) 0.2 m
   (C) 0.5 m
   (D) 1.0 m
   (E) 2.0 m

19. What is the amplitude of the wave?

   (A) 0.1 m
   (B) 0.2 m
   (C) 0.5 m
   (D) 1.0 m
   (E) It varies between −0.1 m and +0.1 m.

GO ON TO THE NEXT PAGE

Questions 20-22

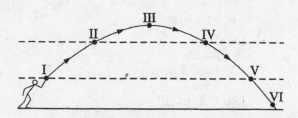

The sketch above shows the path of a heavy iron ball thrown by an athlete. The ground is level and the dashed lines are parallel to the ground. Assume that the frictional forces acting on the ball are negligible.

20. The speed of the ball at point I, when it leaves the hand of the athlete, is the same as its speed at point

(A) II
(B) III
(C) IV
(D) V
(E) VI

21. The potential energy of the ball is greatest at point

(A) I
(B) II
(C) III
(D) IV
(E) VI

22. Which of the following is a true statement about the acceleration of the ball during its flight?

(A) It is greatest at point I.
(B) It is greatest at point III.
(C) It is least at point III.
(D) It is least at point V.
(E) It is the same at all points.

23. Which of the following is true of the half-life of a particular radioactive isotope?

(A) It increases as the isotope decays.
(B) It increases as pressure increases.
(C) It increases as temperature increases.
(D) It decreases as the amount of the original substance increases.
(E) It remains constant.

24. All of the following statements concerning the structure of atoms are true EXCEPT:

(A) Two atoms can have the same atomic number and different mass numbers.
(B) Two atoms can have different atomic numbers and the same mass number.
(C) An atom can have an atomic number greater than its mass number.
(D) A hydrogen atom with one proton and no neutrons is an isotope of hydrogen.
(E) The number of neutrons in an atom can be less than the number of protons.

25. The fact that heat flows naturally from a hotter body to a cooler body is a consequence of which of the following principles of physics?

(A) Ideal gas law
(B) Conservation of charge
(C) Conservation of momentum
(D) First law of thermodynamics (conservation of energy)
(E) Second law of thermodynamics (entropy increase)

GO ON TO THE NEXT PAGE

26. A black metal ball and a black rubber ball of equal radius are both heated to the same temperature. A person who picks up the balls, one in each hand, finds that the metal ball feels hotter to the touch. Which of the following is a correct explanation of this phenomenon?

    (A) The density of the metal is higher; therefore the metal ball has a higher heat capacity.
    (B) The mass of the metal ball is higher; therefore the thermal energy of the metal ball is higher.
    (C) The specific heat of the metal is lower; therefore the thermal energy of the metal ball is higher.
    (D) The thermal conductivity of the metal is higher; therefore the metal ball conducts heat to the hand more quickly.
    (E) The melting point of the metal is higher; therefore the metal ball can absorb more heat from its surroundings.

28. Diffraction is a property of which of the following?

    I. Visible light
    II. Sound waves
    III. Radio waves

    (A) I only
    (B) II only
    (C) I and II only
    (D) I and III only
    (E) I, II, and III

29. Which of the following properties of light can be used to explain why the legs of a child standing waist deep in water, when viewed from above the water, appear to be shorter than they actually are?

    (A) Reflection
    (B) Absorption
    (C) Interference
    (D) Polarization
    (E) Refraction

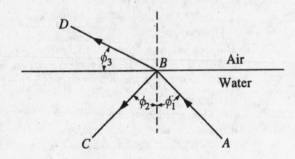

27. In the diagram above, the angle of reflection and the refracted ray are correctly labeled by which of the following?

	Angle of Reflection	Refracted Ray
(A)	ϕ_1	BC
(B)	ϕ_2	BC
(C)	ϕ_2	BD
(D)	ϕ_3	BC
(E)	ϕ_3	BD

GO ON TO THE NEXT PAGE

<u>Questions 30-31</u> refer to the diagram below, which represents a mass suspended on a spring. The mass oscillates between levels X and Z. Level Y is half-way between X and Z. Assume that gravitational potential energy is zero at Z and that there is no loss of energy from the system due to friction.

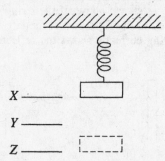

30. The net force acting on the mass is upward and at its greatest magnitude at what level?

    (A) X
    (B) Between X and Y
    (C) Y
    (D) Between Y and Z
    (E) Z

31. When the mass is at level X, it has

    (A) zero energy
    (B) zero acceleration
    (C) potential energy but not kinetic energy
    (D) kinetic energy but not potential energy
    (E) both potential energy and kinetic energy

32. A satellite is moving around the Earth in a circle. All forces on the satellite except the force of gravity are negligible. Which of the following is true of the acceleration resulting from the gravitational force?

    (A) It is constant in magnitude and direction.
    (B) It is constant in magnitude but not in direction.
    (C) It is zero.
    (D) It causes the speed of the satellite to increase.
    (E) It causes the speed of the satellite to decrease.

33. A spaceship orbits the Earth at constant speed in a circular path. An astronaut inside the spaceship releases a ball, but the ball shows no tendency to move away from the astronaut's hand. Which of the following best explains the behavior of the ball?

    (A) Any object moving in a circle around the Earth experiences no gravitational pull.
    (B) The gravitational pull of the spaceship on the ball exactly balances the gravitational pull of the Earth on the ball.
    (C) The mass of the ball is so small that the pull of gravity exerted on the ball by the Earth is negligible.
    (D) The force of gravity exerted on the ball by the Earth is extremely weak due to the great distance of the spaceship from the Earth.
    (E) The force of gravity exerted on the ball by the Earth causes the ball to move in the same circular path as the spaceship.

GO ON TO THE NEXT PAGE

Magnetic Field

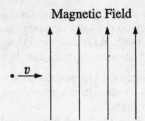

34. A proton of charge 1.6×10^{-19} coulomb moves through a vacuum with a speed v of 1×10^6 meters per second. It passes through a uniform magnetic field as shown above. If the force exerted on the proton is 8×10^{-15} newton, the magnitude of the magnetic field is most nearly

   (A) 1.3×10^{-27} T
   (B) 2×10^{-11} T
   (C) 5×10^{-10} T
   (D) 5×10^{-2} T
   (E) 20 T

35. A negatively charged rod is brought close to the knob of an uncharged electroscope and the leaves of the electroscope diverge, as shown above. The correct explanation for this phenomenon is that

   (A) both leaves become positively charged
   (B) both leaves become negatively charged
   (C) both leaves remain neutral
   (D) one leaf becomes positively charged and the other becomes negatively charged
   (E) one leaf becomes positively charged and the other remains neutral

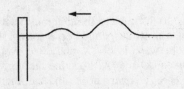

36. Two wave pulses travel toward the left on a taut string, as shown above. If the string is tightly attached to the rigid post at the left, which of the following correctly shows the reflection of these pulses?

(A)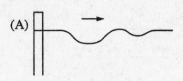

(B)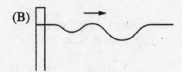

(C)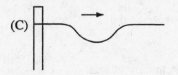

(D)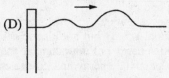

(E)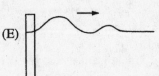

GO ON TO THE NEXT PAGE

37. A guitar string vibrates with a frequency of 400 hertz. If the tension in the string is increased but the length of the string is fixed, which of the following will change?

  I. The wavelength of the fundamental standing wave on the string
  II. The frequency of the fundamental standing wave on the string
  III. The pitch of the sound produced

  (A) I only
  (B) II only
  (C) I and III only
  (D) II and III only
  (E) I, II, and III

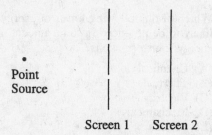

Point
Source

Screen 1   Screen 2

38. In a darkened room, monochromatic light from the point source shown above passes through two very narrow slits in screen 1. Which of the following best describes the interference pattern that is formed on screen 2 ?

  (A) A set of bright concentric circles
  (B) An array of bright dots
  (C) A continuous bright band dimming toward the middle
  (D) A set of bright parallel bars at right angles to the slits
  (E) A set of bright parallel bars parallel to the slits

39. If the mass of a body and the net force acting on the body are both doubled, the acceleration of the body is

  (A) quartered
  (B) halved
  (C) unchanged
  (D) doubled
  (E) quadrupled

40. An object starts from rest and accelerates at 4.0 meters per second squared. How far will it travel during the first 3.0 seconds?

  (A) 6.0 m
  (B) 18 m
  (C) 24 m
  (D) 36 m
  (E) 48 m

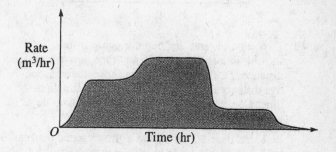

Rate
(m^3/hr)

O Time (hr)

41. The graph above shows the rate at which water is pumped into a tank (measured in cubic meters per hour) as a function of time (measured in hours). The shaded area under the curve is equal to the

  (A) average volume pumped in one hour
  (B) average rate of pumping in m^3/hr
  (C) average time required to pump 1 m^3
  (D) total volume of water pumped into the tank
  (E) total time required to fill the tank

GO ON TO THE NEXT PAGE

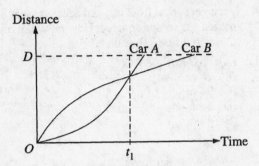

Distance

D ---- Car A Car B

O t_1 Time

42. Two cars, A and B, begin moving from a starting line at time $t = 0$ and race over a total distance D. The graph above shows their respective distances from the starting line as functions of time. Correct statements about the cars include which of the following?

I. At time t_1, car A has a greater speed than car B.
II. At time t_1, car A is closer to the finish line than car B.
III. Car A crosses the finish line first.

(A) I only
(B) II only
(C) I and III only
(D) II and III only
(E) I, II, and III

43. The second hand of a clock completes one revolution each minute. What is its frequency of rotation?

(A) 3,600 Hz
(B)   60 Hz
(C)   1 Hz
(D) 1/12 Hz
(E) 1/60 Hz

44. Halley's comet is in an elliptical orbit about the Sun and is visible from the Earth once every 76 years. Which of the following statements about the comet is true?

(A) The direction of the velocity of the comet and the direction of the force on the comet are the same.
(B) The speed of the comet is always minimum when the comet is closest to the Sun.
(C) The speed of the comet is always maximum when the comet is farthest from the Earth.
(D) The direction and the magnitude of the force on the comet are always changing.
(E) The direction of motion of the comet is always changing, but its speed is constant.

45. Which of the following forms of energy is most likely to be produced in some amount in nearly all energy transformations?

(A) Chemical
(B) Thermal
(C) Electrical
(D) Mechanical
(E) Sound

46. A source emits sound with a frequency of 7.0×10^3 hertz. If the speed of the sound is 3.5×10^2 meters per second, what is the wavelength of the sound?

(A) 4.1×10^{-7} m
(B) 5.0×10^{-2} m
(C) 2.0×10^{-1} m
(D) 2.0×10^5 m
(E) 2.5×10^6 m

GO ON TO THE NEXT PAGE

47. A plane mirror can be used alone to form a

    (A) magnified real image
    (B) diminished real image
    (C) magnified virtual image
    (D) diminished virtual image
    (E) virtual image neither magnified nor diminished

49. If electricity costs $0.10 per kilowatt-hour, how much does it cost for electricity to operate a 100-watt lightbulb for 10 hours?

    (A) $0.001
    (B) $0.01
    (C) $0.10
    (D) $1.00
    (E) $10.00

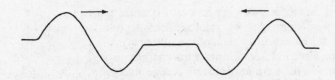

48. The figure above shows two pulses on a string approaching each other. Which of the following statements about the pulses is true?

    (A) They will reflect off each other, reversing their directions.
    (B) They will pass through each other without changing their directions.
    (C) They will completely cancel each other and afterward there will be no pulse on the string.
    (D) They will combine to form a single pulse with amplitude twice that of each original pulse.
    (E) They will combine to form a standing wave on the string.

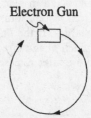

Electron Gun

50. An experiment involves the deflection of an electron beam by a uniform magnetic field as shown above. In what direction does the magnetic field point?

    (A) To the left in the plane of the page
    (B) To the right in the plane of the page
    (C) Upward in the plane of the page
    (D) Into the page
    (E) Out of the page

GO ON TO THE NEXT PAGE

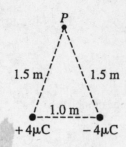

51. Charges of +4 microcoulombs and −4 microcoulombs are located 1.0 meter apart and fixed in place, as shown above. A third charge, of +1 microcoulomb, is released from rest at point *P*, which is located 1.5 meters from each of the other two charges. If the only forces acting are the electric forces between the charges, in which of the directions indicated below will the +1-microcoulomb charge start to move after release?

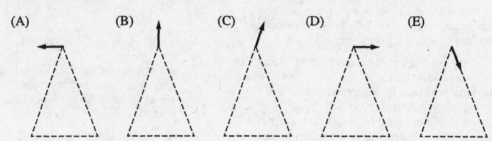

GO ON TO THE NEXT PAGE

52. The rate of heat loss through a wall by conduction is directly proportional to the area A of the wall, to the thermal conductivity k of the wall, and to the temperature difference across the wall, and is inversely proportional to the thickness D of the wall. If the outside temperature is T_1 and the room is maintained at temperature T_2, the rate of heat loss is given by which of the following?

    (A) $\dfrac{Ak(T_2 - T_1)}{D}$

    (B) $\dfrac{D}{Ak(T_2 - T_1)}$

    (C) $\dfrac{A + k + (T_2 - T_1)}{D}$

    (D) $Ak(T_2 - T_1) - \dfrac{1}{D}$

    (E) $A + k + (T_2 - T_1) + \dfrac{1}{D}$

53. A heat engine extracts 80 joules of energy from a hot reservoir, does work, then exhausts 60 joules of energy into a cold reservoir. What is the efficiency of the heat engine?

    (A) 25%
    (B) 33%
    (C) 43%
    (D) 57%
    (E) 75%

Questions 54-55 relate to the graph below, which shows the net force $\mathbf{F}$ in newtons exerted on a 1-kilogram block as a function of time t in seconds. Assume that the block is at rest at $t = 0$ and that $\mathbf{F}$ acts in a fixed direction.

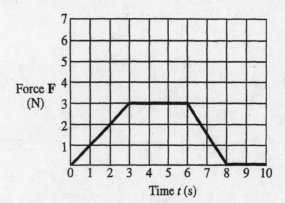

Time t (s)

54. The acceleration of the block at $t = 4$ seconds is

    (A) $\frac{1}{3}$ m/s^2

    (B) 1 m/s^2

    (C) 3 m/s^2

    (D) 9 m/s^2

    (E) 12 m/s^2

55. During which of the following time intervals is the speed of the block constant?

    (A) 0 to 3 s
    (B) 3 to 6 s
    (C) 6 to 8 s
    (D) 8 to 10 s
    (E) None of the time intervals

GO ON TO THE NEXT PAGE

56. Ball *X*, with a large mass, and ball *Y*, with a small mass, simultaneously roll with identical horizontal velocities off a tabletop. Air friction is negligible. Which of the following shows their subsequent trajectories?

(A)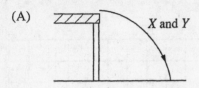

(B)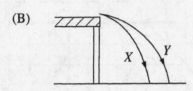

(C)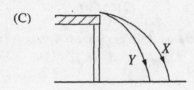

(D)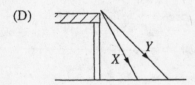

(E)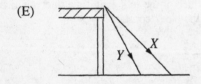

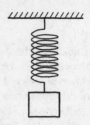

57. A mass is attached to one end of a spring. The other end of the spring is attached to the ceiling, as shown above. A person pulls the mass down and then releases it from rest. Just after the release, how do the energies of the system change?

	Kinetic Energy	Gravitational Potential Energy	Elastic Potential Energy
(A)	Increases	Increases	Increases
(B)	Increases	Increases	Decreases
(C)	Increases	Decreases	Increases
(D)	Increases	Decreases	Decreases
(E)	Decreases	Increases	Decreases

58. When a conductor is moved through a magnetic field, current is induced in the conductor. This phenomenon is used for practical purposes in the

(A) electric generator
(B) electric motor
(C) electroscope
(D) capacitor
(E) battery

GO ON TO THE NEXT PAGE

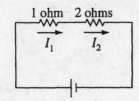

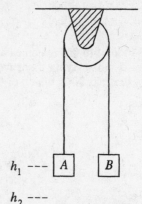

h_1 - - - [A]   [B]

h_2 - - -

59. In the circuit shown above, the current I_1 in the 1-ohm resistor is related to the current I_2 in the 2-ohm resistor by which of the following equations?

(A) $I_1 = \frac{1}{2}I_2$

(B) $I_1 = \frac{2}{3}I_2$

(C) $I_1 = I_2$

(D) $I_1 = \frac{3}{2}I_2$

(E) $I_1 = 2I_2$

60. An object is placed 10 centimeters from a converging lens of focal length 15 centimeters. If the image is 30 centimeters from the lens, what is the magnification?

(A) 0.5
(B) 1.5
(C) 2.0
(D) 3.0
(E) 5.0

61. The speed with which sound waves in the air pass a stationary observer depends on the

(A) speed of the air relative to the observer
(B) speed of the source relative to the air
(C) frequency of the source
(D) wavelength of the sound in the air
(E) intensity of the sound in the air

62. Two blocks of equal mass are attached to a string that passes over a frictionless pulley, as shown above, and are initially at rest with block A at height h_1. A small mass m is placed on top of block A, causing it to move downward. When block A reaches height h_2, the small mass m is lifted from block A. True statements about the motion of block A include which of the following?

I. It moves with constant velocity between heights h_1 and h_2.
II. It moves with constant acceleration between heights h_1 and h_2.
III. It comes to rest immediately after m is removed at height h_2.

(A) I only
(B) II only
(C) I and III only
(D) II and III only
(E) I, II, and III

63. A proton of mass 1.7×10^{-27} kilogram and speed 3×10^7 meters per second is moving in a circle of radius 200 meters. Which of the following is the best estimate of the order of magnitude of the magnetic force needed to maintain this motion?

(A) 10^{-20} N

(B) 10^{-14} N

(C) 10^{-8} N

(D) 10^{-4} N

(E) 10^0 N

GO ON TO THE NEXT PAGE

$$X + {}^{2}_{1}H \rightarrow {}^{4}_{2}He + {}^{1}_{0}n$$

64. In an attempt to use fusion as a source of energy, physicists are studying the reaction represented above. Particle X is which of the following?

(A) ${}^{1}_{1}H$

(B) ${}^{2}_{1}H$

(C) ${}^{3}_{1}H$

(D) ${}^{3}_{2}H$

(E) ${}^{-1}_{0}e$

65. On the basis of the Bohr model, it can be predicted that the internal energy of a hydrogen atom will

(A) increase when any frequency of light impinges on the atom
(B) change by any amount as a result of collisions with other hydrogen atoms
(C) change only as a result of the emission of light
(D) be restricted to certain discrete values
(E) always be the same

66. If thin metallic foil a few atoms thick is bombarded by a narrow beam of alpha particles, it will be observed that

(A) all particles pass through undeflected
(B) none of the particles are deflected through more than 45°
(C) most particles are deflected through more than 45°
(D) occasional particles are deflected through 180°
(E) all particles are deflected through 180°

View From Above

67. A child sits at the outer edge of a merry-go-round that rotates at constant speed. The child releases a ball at point P, shown above. As seen by a person who is at rest with respect to the Earth and looking down from above the merry-go-round, the path followed by the ball is shown by the arrow in which of the following?

(A)

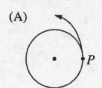

(B)

(C)

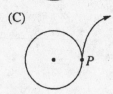

(D)

(E)

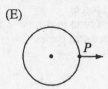

GO ON TO THE NEXT PAGE

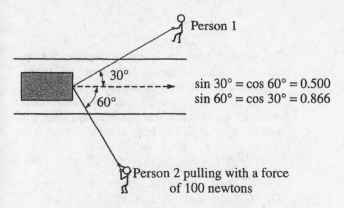

Person 1

30°

60°

$\sin 30° = \cos 60° = 0.500$
$\sin 60° = \cos 30° = 0.866$

Person 2 pulling with a force
of 100 newtons

68. Two people are pulling a box that is on a sheet of ice. The box moves in the direction shown by the broken line in the diagram above. If the ice offers no resistance and if Person 2 is pulling with a force of 100 newtons, with what force must Person 1 be pulling?

(A) 173 N
(B) 158 N
(C) 100 N
(D) 58 N
(E)   0 N

69. In the kinetic theory of gases, which of the following is true about the relationship between the speed of the molecules and the temperature of the gas?

(A) At any specified temperature, all molecules have the same speed.
(B) As the temperature of the gas is doubled, the speed of each molecule is also doubled.
(C) As the temperature of the gas is doubled, the speed of each molecule is halved.
(D) All molecules have speeds larger than a certain minimum and this minimum depends on the temperature of the gas.
(E) Molecular speeds are distributed over a wide range with a mean value that depends on the temperature of the gas.

70. How much heat is required to melt 1.0 kilogram of ice at 0°C and raise the temperature of the resulting water to 20°C? (Heat of fusion of ice = 3.3×10^5 joules per kilogram; specific heat of water = 4.2×10^3 joules per kilogram · °C)

(A) 4.1×10^5 J
(B) 3.3×10^5 J
(C) 8.7×10^4 J
(D) 8.4×10^4 J
(E) 7.5×10^3 J

71. Of the following observable phenomena, which can be explained by using the wave model of light, but not the particle model?

(A) Energy is transmitted by a light beam.
(B) Pressure is exerted by a light beam.
(C) A region receiving light from two small coherent sources can have points of zero intensity of light.
(D) All of the energy emitted by an atom as light can later be completely transferred to another atom.
(E) Light incident on a plane reflecting surface at a given angle is reflected at the same angle.

72. A ray of light obliquely incident on a plane boundary between air and glass is partially reflected and partially refracted. Which of the following characteristics is the same for both the incident ray and the refracted ray?

(A) Frequency
(B) Wavelength
(C) Speed
(D) Power transmitted
(E) Direction

GO ON TO THE NEXT PAGE

73. A 12-kilogram object initially has 24 joules of kinetic energy. How far will the object move against a net resisting force of 6 newtons?

    (A) 2 m
    (B) 4 m
    (C) 12 m
    (D) 16 m .
    (E) 24 m

74. Two bodies collide on a horizontal frictionless surface. Which of the following is true about the conservation of momentum and kinetic energy for such a collision?

	Momentum Conserved	Kinetic Energy Conserved
(A)	Always	Always
(B)	Always	Not always
(C)	Not always	Always
(D)	Not always	Not always
(E)	Not always	Never

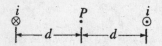

75. Two parallel wires are located a distance $2d$ apart and carry equal currents i in opposite directions perpendicular to the page, as shown above. The magnitude of the magnetic field at point P due to each wire alone is 2 tesla. The resultant magnetic field at point P due to both wires is

    (A) zero
    (B) 4 T perpendicular to the page
    (C) 4 T downward in the plane of the page
    (D) 4 T to the right in the plane of the page
    (E) 4 T to the left in the plane of the page

STOP

IF YOU FINISH BEFORE TIME IS CALLED, YOU MAY CHECK YOUR WORK ON THIS TEST ONLY.
DO NOT TURN TO ANY OTHER TEST IN THIS BOOK.

How to Score the SAT Subject Test in Physics

When you take an actual Physics Subject Test, your answer sheet will be "read" by a scanning machine that will record your responses to each question. Then a computer will compare your answers with the correct answers and produce your raw score. You get one point for each correct answer. For each wrong answer, you lose one-fourth of a point. Questions you omit (and any for which you mark more than one answer) are not counted. This raw score is converted to a scaled score that is reported to you and to the colleges you specify.

Worksheet 1. Finding Your Raw Test Score

STEP 1: Table A lists the correct answers for all the questions on the SAT Subject Test in Physics that is reproduced in this book. It also serves as a worksheet for you to calculate your raw score.

- Compare your answers with those given in the table.
- Put a check in the column marked "Right" if your answer is correct.
- Put a check in the column marked "Wrong" if your answer is incorrect.
- Leave both columns blank if you omitted the question.

STEP 2: Count the number of right answers.

Enter the total here: _____

STEP 3: Count the number of wrong answers.

Enter the total here: _____

STEP 4: Multiply the number of wrong answers by .250.

Enter the product here: _____

STEP 5: Subtract the result obtained in Step 4 from the total you obtained in Step 2.

Enter the result here: _____

STEP 6: Round the number obtained in Step 5 to the nearest whole number.

Enter the result here: _____

The number you obtained in Step 6 is your raw test score.

TABLE A

Answers to the SAT Subject Test in Physics, Form 3RAC2, and Percentage of Students Answering Each Question Correctly

Question Number	Correct Answer	Right	Wrong	Percentage of Students Answering the Question Correctly*	Question Number	Correct Answer	Right	Wrong	Percentage of Students Answering the Question Correctly*
1	C			74	33	E			67
2	A			62	34	D			28
3	E			34	35	B			76
4	A			92	36	A			51
5	E			66	37	D			35
6	D			62	38	E			47
7	C			42	39	C			90
8	C			71	40	B			66
9	B			61	41	D			85
10	D			67	42	C			68
11	C			50	43	E			67
12	B			36	44	D			52
13	B			86	45	B			80
14	A			72	46	B			48
15	E			86	47	E			81
16	D			65	48	B			46
17	A			58	49	C			64
18	D			87	50	D			37
19	A			76	51	D			49
20	D			89	52	A			74
21	C			92	53	A			36
22	E			66	54	C			80
23	E			74	55	D			60
24	C			56	56	A			62
25	E			53	57	B			58
26	D			60	58	A			55
27	C			56	59	C			45
28	E			48	60	D			46
29	E			90	61	A			21
30	E			73	62	B			65
31	C			82	63	B			30
32	B			53	64	C			62

Table A continued on next page

Table A continued from previous page

Question Number	Correct Answer	Right	Wrong	Percentage of Students Answering the Question Correctly*	Question Number	Correct Answer	Right	Wrong	Percentage of Students Answering the Question Correctly*
65	D			24	71	C			38
66	D			42	72	A			35
67	B			78	73	B			46
68	A			39	74	B			52
69	E			42	75	C			28
70	A			41					

* These percentages are based on an analysis of the answer sheets for a random sample of 3,239 students who took this form of the test in November 1995 and whose mean score was 653. They may be used as an indication of the relative difficulty of a particular question. Each percentage may also be used to predict the likelihood that a typical SAT Subject Test in Physics candidate will answer correctly that question on this edition of this test.

Finding Your Scaled Score

When you take SAT Subject Tests, the scores sent to the colleges you specify are reported on the College Board scale, which ranges from 200 to 800. You can convert your practice test score to a scaled score by using Table B. To find your scaled score, locate your raw score in the left-hand column of Table B; the corresponding score in the right-hand column is your scaled score. For example, a raw score of 60 on this particular edition of the SAT Subject Test in Physics corresponds to a scaled score of 780.

Raw scores are converted to scaled scores to ensure that a score earned on any one edition of a particular Subject Test is comparable to the same scaled score earned on any other edition of the same Subject Test. Because some editions of tests may be slightly easier or more difficult than others, scaled scores are adjusted so that they indicate the same level of performance regardless of the edition of the test taken and the ability of the group that takes it. Thus, for example, a score of 400 on one edition of a test taken at a particular administration indicates the same level of achievement as a score of 400 on a different edition of the test taken at a different administration.

When you take the SAT Subject Tests during a national administration, your scores are likely to differ somewhat from the scores you obtain on the tests in this book. People perform at different levels at different times for reasons unrelated to the tests themselves. The precision of any test is also limited because it represents only a sample of all the possible questions that could be asked.

TABLE B

Scaled Score Conversion Table
Physics Subject Test (Form 3RAC2)

Raw Score	Scaled Score	Raw Score	Scaled Score	Raw Score	Scaled Score
75	800	39	660	3	430
74	800	38	650	2	430
73	800	37	650	1	420
72	800	36	640	0	410
71	800	35	640	−1	410
70	800	34	630	−2	400
69	800	33	630	−3	390
68	800	32	620	−4	390
67	800	31	610	−5	380
66	800	30	610	−6	370
65	800	29	600	−7	370
64	800	28	600	−8	360
63	800	27	590	−9	350
62	790	26	580	−10	350
61	790	25	580	−11	340
60	780	24	570	−12	330
59	780	23	570	−13	330
58	770	22	560	−14	320
57	770	21	550	−15	310
56	760	20	540	−16	310
55	760	19	540	−17	300
54	750	18	530	−18	290
53	750	17	530	−19	290
52	740	16	520		
51	730	15	510		
50	730	14	510		
49	720	13	500		
48	720	12	490		
47	710	11	480		
46	700	10	480		
45	700	9	470		
44	690	8	470		
43	690	7	460		
42	680	6	450		
41	670	5	450		
40	670	4	440		

Reviewing Your Performance on the Physics Subject Test

After you score your test, analyze your performance—consider the following questions:

Did you run out of time before reaching the end of the test?

If so, you may need to pace yourself better. For example, maybe you spent too much time on one or two hard questions. A better approach might be to skip the ones you can't answer right away and try answering all the questions that remain on the test. Then if there's time, go back to the questions you skipped.

Did you take a long time reading the directions?

You will save time when you take the test by learning the directions to the Physics Subject Test ahead of time. Each minute you spend reading directions during the test is a minute that you could use to answer questions.

How did you handle questions you were unsure of?

If you were able to eliminate one or more of the answer choices as wrong and guess from the remaining choices, your approach probably worked to your advantage. On the other hand, making haphazard guesses or omitting questions without trying to eliminate choices could cost you valuable points.

How difficult were the questions for you compared with other students who took the test?

Table A shows you how difficult the multiple-choice questions were for the group of students who took this test during its national administration. The right-hand column gives the percentage of students that answered each question correctly.

A question answered correctly by almost everyone in the group is obviously an easy question. For example, 92 percent of the students answered question 21 correctly. But only 21 percent answered question 61 correctly.

Keep in mind that these percentages are based on just one group of students. They would probably be different if another group of students took the test.

If you missed several easy questions, go back and try to find out why: Did the questions cover material you haven't reviewed yet? Did you misunderstand the directions?

Chapter 8
Chinese with Listening

Purpose

This test measures your understanding of Mandarin Chinese in the context of contemporary Chinese culture. The questions on the test are written to reflect general trends in high school curricula and are independent of particular textbooks or methods of instruction.

Format

This is a one-hour test with about 20 minutes of listening comprehension and 40 minutes of usage and reading comprehension. There are 85 multiple-choice questions in three sections.

Listening Comprehension: These questions test the ability to understand the spoken language and are based on short, spoken dialogues and narratives primarily about everyday topics. There are two different kinds of listening comprehension questions: (A) a spoken statement, question, or exchange, followed by a choice of three possible responses (also spoken); (B) a spoken dialogue or monologue with a printed question or questions (in English) about what was said.

Usage: These questions ask you to select the answer that best completes a Chinese sentence in a way that is structurally and logically correct. Questions are written to reflect instructional practices of the curriculum. This section of the test is therefore presented in four columns across two pages of the test book to allow each question and its answer choices to be shown in four different ways of representing Chinese: traditional and simplified Chinese characters on the left page, and phonetic transcriptions in Pinyin romanization and the Chinese phonetic alphabet (Bopomofo) on the right page. You should choose the writing form you are most familiar with and read only from that column.

Reading Comprehension: Reading comprehension questions test your understanding of such points as main and supporting ideas, themes, and the setting of passages. Some of the passages are based on real-life materials such as timetables, forms, advertisements, notes, letters, diaries, and newspaper articles. All passages are printed in both traditional and simplified Chinese characters. While most questions deal with understanding of literal meaning, some inference questions may also be included. All reading comprehension questions are in English.

Skills Measured	Approximate Percentage of Test
Listening Comprehension	33
Usage	33
Reading Comprehension	33

Cassette Players

You must bring an acceptable cassette player with earphones to the test center. Put fresh batteries in your cassette player the day before the test. If you like, bring additional fresh batteries and a backup cassette player with earphones to the test center. Test center staff will NOT have batteries, cassette players, or earphones for your use.

Acceptable cassette players must be:

- personal (have earphones that let only you hear the recording)
- portable (small enough that the entire player can fit in your hand)
- battery-operated
- able to use a single (not dual) standard (2-1/2 inch by 4 inch) audiocassette— not a mini- or microcassette

If your cassette player has a programming feature that fast-forwards automatically to the next prompt, that feature must be deactivated before you start the test. You will not be allowed to share a cassette player with another test-taker.

Beginning with the November 2005 administration, portable CD players will be required instead of cassette players for language with listening tests.

Recommended Preparation

The best preparation is gradual development of competence in Chinese over a period of years. The test is appropriate for students who have studied Mandarin Chinese as a second or foreign language for two to four years in high school, or the equivalent. A practice cassette with sample questions is available from your school counselor. Familiarize yourself with the test directions in advance. The directions in this book are identical to those that appear on the test.

Scores

The total score is reported on the 200-to-800 scale. Listening, usage, and reading subscores are reported on the 20-to-80 scale.

The Chinese Subject Test with Listening is offered only at designated test centers on designated test dates. To take the test, you MUST bring an acceptable cassette player with earphones to the test center.

A cassette tape with listening questions is available for the Chinese Subject Test with Listening practice test in this book. To receive your copy, complete and mail the postcard in this book. If the postcard has been removed, call 212 649-8424, or write to:

The College Board
Subject Tests Language Listening Cassette
45 Columbus Avenue
New York, New York 10023-6992

You must indicate the SAT Language Test with Listening you plan to take.

Sample Questions

Following are some samples for each section of the SAT Subject Test in Chinese with Listening. All questions are multiple choice. You must choose the best response from the three or four choices offered for each question.

In an actual test administration, all spoken Chinese will be presented by tape playback. Text that appears in this book in brackets ([ ]) will be recorded in an actual test and it will not be printed in your test booklet. Spoken text appears in printed form here because a taped version is not available.

Please note that your answer sheet has five answer positions marked A, B, C, D, E, while the questions throughout this test contain only three or four choices. Be sure NOT to make any marks in column E, and do not make any marks in column D if there are only three choices given.

Sample Listening Questions

Please note that the cassette does not start here. Begin using the cassette when you start the actual practice test on page 329.

Part A

Directions: In this part of the test, you will hear short questions, statements, or commands in Mandarin Chinese followed by three responses in Mandarin Chinese designated (A), (B), and (C). You will hear the questions or statements, as well as the responses, just one time, and they are not printed in your test book. Therefore, you must listen very carefully. Select the best choice and fill in the corresponding oval on your answer sheet.

Question 1

| (Narrator) | [Number 1 |
| (Woman) | 請問圖書館在哪兒？ |

(Man)	(A) 圖書館九點開門。
	(B) 圖書館裡書很多。
	(C) 圖書館就在前面。]　　(5 seconds)

The correct answer is (C) because it responds to the question "where is the library?" Choice (A) is incorrect because it tells when the library opens, and (B) is incorrect because it tells what's inside the library.

Question 2

(Narrator)   [Number 2

(Man)   這本書貴不貴？

(Woman)   不貴，也不便宜。

(Man)   (A)   多久了？

                (B)   多少錢？

                (C)   多不多？]   (5 seconds)

The conversation concerns the price of a book. The man asks if the book is expensive, and the woman replies that it is neither expensive nor cheap. The correct answer is (B) because it asks how much the book costs. Choice (A) is incorrect because it asks about the length of time. Choice (C) is incorrect because it asks if there are many.

Part B

Directions: You will now hear a series of short selections. You will hear them only once, and they are not printed in your test booklet. After each selection, you will be asked to answer one or more questions about what you have just heard. These questions, each with four possible answers, are printed in your test booklet. Select the best answer to each question from among the four choices printed and fill in the corresponding oval on your answer sheet. You will have fifteen seconds to answer each question.

Questions 3–4

(Narrator)	[Questions 3 and 4. Listen to find out what the woman will do next summer.
(Woman)	你去過香港嗎？
(Man)	沒去過，可是我明年夏天從日本到中國去的時候會經過香港。
(Woman)	明年夏天我得留在美國上暑期班。哪兒都不能去。
(Narrator)	Now answer questions 3 and 4.] (30 seconds)

3. Where will the woman spend the summer next year?
   (A) In China
   (B) In Japan
   (C) In Hong Kong
   (D) In the United States

The woman states in the conversation that she will stay in the United States next summer, so the correct answer is (D). Choices (A), (B), and (C) are the places where the man will go next summer.

4. What will the woman do?
    (A) Visit friends
    (B) Go to school
    (C) Look for a job
    (D) Travel abroad

The correct answer is (B) because the woman states in the conversation that she will go to summer school. None of the other answer choices are mentioned by the woman in the conversation.

Sample Usage Questions

Directions: This section consists of a number of incomplete statements, each of which has four possible completions. Select the word or phrase that best completes the sentence structurally and logically and fill in the corresponding oval on your answer sheet.

This section of the test is presented in four columns to allow each question to be shown in four different ways of representing Chinese: traditional characters, simplified characters, Pinyin romanization, and the Chinese phonetic alphabet (Bopomofo). TO SAVE TIME, IT IS RECOMMENDED THAT YOU CHOOSE THE WRITING FORM WITH WHICH YOU ARE MOST FAMILIAR AND **READ ONLY FROM THAT COLUMN** AS YOU WORK THROUGH THIS SECTION OF THE TEST.

Question 5

5. 我很喜歡這部電影。

你 _____ ?

(A) 啊

(B) 嗎

(C) 吧

(D) 呢

5. 我很喜欢这部电影。

你 _____ ?

(A) 啊

(B) 吗

(C) 吧

(D) 呢

5. Wǒ hěn xǐhuan zhèi bù diànyǐng.

Nǐ _____ ?

(A) a

(B) ma

(C) ba

(D) ne

This question tests the use of sentence-final particles. Of the four answer choices, only (D) "ne" following the second-person singular pronoun "Nǐ" conveys the intended meaning "How about you?" as a question appended to the preceding statement, "I really like this movie."

Question 6

6. 他 ____ 生氣 ____
　　臉紅。

(A) 連 …… 都
(B) 一 …… 就
(C) 不跟 …… 一樣
(D) 雖然 …… 可是

6. 他 ____ 生气 ____
　　脸红。

(A) 连 …… 都
(B) 一 …… 就
(C) 不跟 …… 一样
(D) 虽然 …… 可是

6. Tā ____ shēngqì ____
　　liǎn hóng.

(A) lián …… dōu
(B) yī …… jiù
(C) bù gēn …… yíyàng
(D) suīrán …… kěshì

6. ㄊㄚ ____ ㄕㄥ ㄑㄧˋ ____
　　ㄌㄧㄢˇ ㄏㄨㄥˊ.

(A) ㄌㄧㄢˊ …… ㄉㄡ
(B) ㄧ …… ㄐㄧㄡˋ
(C) ㄅㄨˋ ㄍㄣ …… ㄧ ㄧㄤˋ
(D) ㄙㄨㄟ ㄖㄢˊ …… ㄎㄜˇ ㄕˋ

This question tests the use of sentence-linking constructions. Choice (B) is the correct answer because the nonmovable forwarding-linking adverb "yi" is paired with "jiu" to convey the meaning "as soon as … then." None of the other answer choices are structurally or logically correct in this context.

Sample Reading Questions

Directions: Read the following texts carefully for comprehension. Each is followed by one or more questions or incomplete statements. Select the answer or completion that is best according to the text and fill in the corresponding oval on the answer sheet.

This section of the test is presented in two writing systems: traditional characters and simplified characters. IT IS RECOMMENDED THAT YOU CHOOSE THE WRITING SYSTEM WITH WHICH YOU ARE MOST FAMILIAR AND **READ ONLY THAT VERSION** AS YOU WORK THROUGH THIS SECTION OF THE TEST.

Questions 7–8

國立台灣師範大學音樂系

張 鳴 欣

教授　作曲家

國立台灣師範大學
台北市和平東路一段162號

電話: 公(02)321-8400

国立台湾师范大学音乐系

张 鸣 欣

教授　作曲家

国立台湾师范大学
台北市和平东路一段162号

电话: 公(02)321-8400

7. What is this?

    (A) A business card

    (B) A thank-you note

    (C) A return envelope

    (D) A concert ticket

The text contains a person's name, workplace, profession, office address, and telephone number, all arranged in the standard format for an individual's business card. Therefore, the correct answer choice is (A).

8. The person named is a

    (A) professor

    (B) singer

    (C) conductor

    (D) journalist

The text of the business card shows that the person works in the music department of a university and gives the person's professional title as "professor and composer." Therefore, the correct answer choice is (A).

Chinese Test with Listening

The test that follows is an actual, recently administered SAT Subject Test in Chinese with Listening. To get an idea of what a real administration is like, take the test under conditions as close as possible to those of a national administration:

- Set aside an hour when you can take the test uninterrupted. Make sure you complete the test in one sitting.

- Sit at a desk or table with no other books or papers. Dictionaries, other books, or notes are not allowed in the test room.

- Time yourself by placing a clock or kitchen timer in front of you.

- Tear out an answer sheet from the back of this book and fill it in just as you would on the day of the test. One answer sheet can be used for up to three Subject Tests.

- Read the instructions that precede the practice test. During the actual administration you will be asked to read them before answering test questions.

- After you finish the practice test, read the sections "How to Score the SAT Subject Test in Chinese with Listening" and "Reviewing Your Performance on the Chinese Subject Test with Listening."

- Actual test and answer sheets will indicate circles, not ovals.

Form K-3RLC

CHINESE TEST WITH LISTENING

The top portion of the section of the answer sheet that you will use in taking the Chinese Test with Listening must be filled in exactly as shown in the illustration below. Note carefully that you have to do all of the following on your answer sheet.

1. Print **CHINESE WITH LISTENING** on the line under the words "Subject Test (print)."

2. In the shaded box labeled "Test Code" fill in four ovals:

    - Fill in oval 3 in the row labeled V.

    - Fill in oval 5 in the row labeled W.

    - Fill in oval 4 in the row labeled X.

    - Fill in oval D in the row labeled Y.

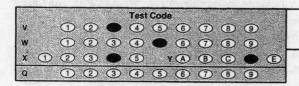

Please answer Part I and Part II below by filling in the appropriate ovals in the row labeled Q on your answer sheet. Select the answers that correspond to your Chinese language experience and to the Chinese language courses you have taken or are taking at present. The information that you provide is for statistical purposes only and will not affect your score on the test.

PART I   Fill in **ALL** the ovals that apply to your Chinese language experience.
(Choose <u>one or more</u>.)

Oval 1   You have lived in a place and/or a home in which <u>Mandarin Chinese</u> is used.

Oval 2   You have lived in a place and/or a home in which <u>Chinese other than Mandarin</u> is used.

Oval 3   You have studied Chinese language in an extracurricular (e.g., after-school, weekend, summer, or study-abroad) program.

Oval 4   You have studied Chinese language in kindergarten and/or grades 1 through 8.

Oval 5   You have studied Chinese language in grades 9 through 12.

PART II   How long (in academic years) have you studied Chinese language in grades 9 through 12 ?
(Choose <u>only one</u>.)

Oval 6   Less than 2 years

Oval 7   2 to $2\frac{1}{2}$ years

Oval 8   3 to $3\frac{1}{2}$ years

Oval 9   4 years

When the supervisor tells you to do so, turn the page and begin the Chinese Test with Listening. There are 100 numbered ovals on your answer sheet. Use <u>only ovals 1 to 85</u> to record your answers to the 85 questions in the Chinese Test with Listening.

CHINESE TEST WITH LISTENING

PLEASE NOTE THAT YOUR ANSWER SHEET HAS FIVE ANSWER POSITIONS, MARKED A, B, C, D, AND E, WHILE THE QUESTIONS THROUGHOUT THIS TEST CONTAIN ONLY THREE OR FOUR CHOICES. BE SURE NOT TO MAKE ANY MARKS IN COLUMN E, AND DO NOT MAKE ANY MARKS IN COLUMN D IF THERE ARE ONLY THREE CHOICES GIVEN.

SECTION I
LISTENING

Approximate time — 20 minutes

Questions 1 – 30

Part A

Directions: In this part of the test, you will hear short questions, statements, or commands in Mandarin Chinese, followed by three responses in Mandarin Chinese, designated (A), (B), and (C). You will hear the statements or questions, as well as the responses, just one time, and they are not printed in your test booklet. Therefore, you must listen very carefully. Select the best response and fill in the corresponding oval on your answer sheet. Now listen to the following example, but do not mark the answer on your answer sheet.

You will hear:

You will also hear:

The answer that most logically responds to the question is (C). Therefore, you should choose answer (C).

Now listen to the first exchange.

---

1. Mark your answer on your answer sheet.

2. Mark your answer on your answer sheet.

3. Mark your answer on your answer sheet.

4. Mark your answer on your answer sheet.

5. Mark your answer on your answer sheet.

6. Mark your answer on your answer sheet.

7. Mark your answer on your answer sheet.

8. Mark your answer on your answer sheet.

9. Mark your answer on your answer sheet.

10. Mark your answer on your answer sheet.

11. Mark your answer on your answer sheet.

12. Mark your answer on your answer sheet.

13. Mark your answer on your answer sheet.

14. Mark your answer on your answer sheet.

15. Mark your answer on your answer sheet.

16. Mark your answer on your answer sheet.

17. Mark your answer on your answer sheet.

18. Mark your answer on your answer sheet.

END OF PART A

K-3RLC

GO ON TO THE NEXT PAGE

Part B

Directions: You will now hear a series of short selections. You will hear them only once, and they are not printed in your test booklet. After each selection, you will be asked one or more questions about what you have just heard. These questions, each with four possible answers, are printed in your test booklet. Select the best answer to each question from among the four choices printed and fill in the corresponding oval on your answer sheet. You will have fifteen seconds to answer each question.

Now listen to the following example, but do not mark the answer on your answer sheet.

You will hear:

You will see:

What are the two people talking about?

(A) Food.
(B) Homework.
(C) History.
(D) Language.

The best answer to the question is (D), "Language." Therefore, you should choose answer (D).

Now listen to the first selection.

Questions 19 – 20

19. When did the trip to China take place?

(A) This year.
(B) Last year.
(C) Two years ago.
(D) Three years ago.

20. Why did the speaker prefer one city?

(A) There were many people to visit.
(B) It was a good place for shopping.
(C) She saw many historical sites.
(D) Her teacher was born there.

Questions 21 – 22

21. What function is the woman going to attend?

(A) A wedding reception.
(B) A birthday party.
(C) A family reunion.
(D) A graduation party.

22. When will she go?

(A) Thursday.
(B) Friday.
(C) Saturday.
(D) Sunday.

GO ON TO THE NEXT PAGE

Questions 23 – 24

23. What does the speaker do?

   (A) He cooks.
   (B) He cleans.
   (C) He rides horses.
   (D) He attends school.

24. What is the speaker's nickname?

   (A) Chen Da.
   (B) Xiao Ma.
   (C) Da Long.
   (D) Xiao Gao.

Questions 25 – 27

25. What kind of vehicle was involved in the accident?

   (A) A private car.
   (B) A taxicab.
   (C) A public bus.
   (D) A pickup truck.

26. What caused the accident?

   (A) The driver was too tired.
   (B) The driver drove too fast.
   (C) The road was slippery.
   (D) The road was blocked by a fallen tree.

27. When did the accident happen?

   (A) In the morning.
   (B) At noon.
   (C) In the afternoon.
   (D) At night.

Questions 28 – 30

28. What was found yesterday?

   (A) A wallet.
   (B) A key.
   (C) A watch.
   (D) A pair of glasses.

29. Where was the item found?

   (A) In the gym.
   (B) In the auditorium.
   (C) In the lab.
   (D) In the office.

30. When can the item be picked up?

   (A) During study hall.
   (B) Between classes.
   (C) After school.
   (D) During lunch.

END OF SECTION I
DO NOT GO ON TO SECTION II UNTIL YOU ARE TOLD TO DO SO.

Time for section II and III - 40 minutes
SECTION II
Usage

WHEN YOU BEGIN SECTION II, BE SURE THAT YOU MARK YOUR ANSWER TO THE FIRST USAGE
QUESTION BY FILLING IN ONE OF THE OVALS NEXT TO NUMBER 31 ON THE ANSWER SHEET.

Directions: This section consists of a number of incomplete statements, each of which has four possible
completions. Select the word or phrase that best completes the sentence structurally and logically and fill in the
corresponding oval on your answer sheet.

THIS SECTION OF THE TEST IS PRESENTED IN FOUR COLUMNS ACROSS TWO PAGES TO ALLOW
EACH QUESTION TO BE SHOWN IN FOUR WRITING SYSTEMS: TRADITIONAL CHARACTERS,
SIMPLIFIED CHARACTERS, PINYIN ROMANIZATION, AND THE CHINESE PHONETIC ALPHABET
(BOPOMOFO). TO SAVE TIME, IT IS RECOMMENDED THAT YOU CHOOSE THE WRITING SYSTEM
WITH WHICH YOU ARE MOST FAMILIAR AND **READ ONLY FROM THAT COLUMN** AS YOU
WORK THROUGH THIS SECTION OF THE TEST.

Example:

他＿＿有空＿＿喜歡看書。　　他＿＿有空＿＿喜欢看书。　　Tā ＿＿ yǒu kòng ＿＿ xǐhuan kànshū.

(A) 連 ..... 都　　　　　(A) 连 ..... 都　　　　　(A) lián ..... dōu

(B) 一 ..... 就　　　　　(B) 一 ..... 就　　　　　(B) yī ..... jiù

(C) 從 ..... 到　　　　　(C) 从 ..... 到　　　　　(C) cóng ..... dào

(D) 是 ..... 的　　　　　(D) 是 ..... 的　　　　　(D) shì ..... de

The best completion is answer (B). Therefore, you should choose answer (B) and fill in the corresponding
oval on your answer sheet. **Remember to work with one column only** and start by filling in one of the ovals
next to number 31 on your answer sheet.

GO ON TO THE NEXT PAGE

31. 他 ＿＿＿ 是我的弟弟，可是我不知道
他喜歡吃什麼。

 (A) 既然

 (B) 雖然

 (C) 必然

 (D) 居然

31. 他 ＿＿＿ 是我的弟弟，可是我不知道
他喜欢吃什么。

 (A) 既然

 (B) 虽然

 (C) 必然

 (D) 居然

32. 春節快到了，他想去買
＿＿＿ 衣服。

 (A) 新

 (B) 少

 (C) 老

 (D) 多

32. 春节快到了，他想去买
＿＿＿ 衣服。

 (A) 新

 (B) 少

 (C) 老

 (D) 多

33. 媽媽是醫生，爸爸 ＿＿＿ 是醫生。

 (A) 都

 (B) 再

 (C) 就

 (D) 也

33. 妈妈是医生，爸爸 ＿＿＿ 是医生。

 (A) 都

 (B) 再

 (C) 就

 (D) 也

34. 這雙皮鞋就二十塊錢？
真 ＿＿＿ ！

 (A) 方便

 (B) 便宜

 (C) 容易

 (D) 簡單

34. 这双皮鞋就二十块钱？
真 ＿＿＿ ！

 (A) 方便

 (B) 便宜

 (C) 容易

 (D) 简单

35. 我想今天他 ＿＿＿ 。

 (A) 會來兩點下午

 (B) 下午兩點會來

 (C) 兩點會來下午

 (D) 下午會來兩點

35. 我想今天他 ＿＿＿ 。

 (A) 会来两点下午

 (B) 下午两点会来

 (C) 两点会来下午

 (D) 下午会来两点

GO ON TO THE NEXT PAGE

31. Tā _____ shì wǒ de dìdi, kěshì wǒ bù zhīdao tā xǐhuan chī shénme.

    (A) jìrán

    (B) suīrán

    (C) bìrán

    (D) jūrán

31. ㄊㄚ _____ ㄕˋ ㄨㄛˇ ㄉㄜ ㄉㄧˋㄉㄧ, ㄎㄜˇㄕˋ ㄨㄛˇ ㄅㄨˋ ㄓ ㄉㄠ ㄊㄚ ㄒㄧˇㄏㄨㄢ ㄔ ㄕㄣˊㄇㄜ。

    (A) ㄐㄧˋ ㄖㄢˊ

    (B) ㄙㄨㄟ ㄖㄢˊ

    (C) ㄅㄧˋ ㄖㄢˊ

    (D) ㄐㄩ ㄖㄢˊ

32. Chūnjié kuài dào le, tā xiǎng qù mǎi _____ yīfu.

    (A) xīn

    (B) shǎo

    (C) lǎo

    (D) duō

32. ㄔㄨㄣ ㄐㄧㄝˊ ㄎㄨㄞˋ ㄉㄠˋ ㄌㄜ, ㄊㄚ ㄒㄧㄤˇ ㄑㄩˋ ㄇㄞˇ _____ ㄧ ㄈㄨ。

    (A) ㄒㄧㄣ

    (B) ㄕㄠˇ

    (C) ㄌㄠˇ

    (D) ㄉㄨㄛ

33. Māma shì yīshēng, bàba _____ shì yīshēng.

    (A) dōu

    (B) zài

    (C) jiù

    (D) yě

33. ㄇㄚ ㄇㄚ ㄕˋ ㄧ ㄕㄥ, ㄅㄚˋ ㄅㄚ _____ ㄕˋ ㄧ ㄕㄥ。

    (A) ㄉㄡ

    (B) ㄗㄞˋ

    (C) ㄐㄧㄡˋ

    (D) ㄧㄝˇ

34. Zhèi shuāng píxié jiù èrshí kuài qián? Zhēn _____ !

    (A) fāngbiàn

    (B) piányi

    (C) róngyì

    (D) jiǎndān

34. ㄓㄟˋ ㄕㄨㄤ ㄆㄧˊ ㄒㄧㄝˊ ㄐㄧㄡˋ ㄦˋ ㄕˊ ㄎㄨㄞˋ ㄑㄧㄢˊ? ㄓㄣ _____ !

    (A) ㄈㄤ ㄅㄧㄢˋ

    (B) ㄆㄧㄢˊ ㄧ

    (C) ㄖㄨㄥˊ ㄧˋ

    (D) ㄐㄧㄢˇ ㄉㄢ

35. Wǒ xiǎng jīntiān tā _____ .

    (A) huì lái liǎng diǎn xiàwǔ

    (B) xiàwǔ liǎng diǎn huì lái

    (C) liǎng diǎn huì lái xiàwǔ

    (D) xiàwǔ huì lái liǎng diǎn

35. ㄨㄛˇ ㄒㄧㄤˇ ㄐㄧㄣ ㄊㄧㄢ ㄊㄚ _____ 。

    (A) ㄏㄨㄟˋ ㄌㄞˊ ㄌㄧㄤˇ ㄉㄧㄢˇ ㄒㄧㄚˋ ㄨˇ

    (B) ㄒㄧㄚˋ ㄨˇ ㄌㄧㄤˇ ㄉㄧㄢˇ ㄏㄨㄟˋ ㄌㄞˊ

    (C) ㄌㄧㄤˇ ㄉㄧㄢˇ ㄏㄨㄟˋ ㄌㄞˊ ㄒㄧㄚˋ ㄨˇ

    (D) ㄒㄧㄚˋ ㄨˇ ㄏㄨㄟˋ ㄌㄞˊ ㄌㄧㄤˇ ㄉㄧㄢˇ

GO ON TO THE NEXT PAGE

36. 中國比美國 _____ 大。
    - (A) 再
    - (B) 連
    - (C) 更
    - (D) 如

36. 中国比美国 _____ 大。
    - (A) 再
    - (B) 连
    - (C) 更
    - (D) 如

37. 我 _____ 會說日語，可是現在
    忘了。
    - (A) 以前
    - (B) 以後
    - (C) 後來
    - (D) 從來

37. 我 _____ 会说日语，可是现在
    忘了。
    - (A) 以前
    - (B) 以后
    - (C) 后来
    - (D) 从来

38. 明天的會議希望你 _____ 來。
    - (A) 立刻
    - (B) 剛才
    - (C) 一定
    - (D) 以前

38. 明天的会议希望你 _____ 来。
    - (A) 立刻
    - (B) 刚才
    - (C) 一定
    - (D) 以前

39. 最近很忙，所以 _____。
    - (A) 我在一起不跟他
    - (B) 我一起不跟他在
    - (C) 我跟他在一起不
    - (D) 我跟他不在一起

39. 最近很忙，所以 _____。
    - (A) 我在一起不跟他
    - (B) 我一起不跟他在
    - (C) 我跟他在一起不
    - (D) 我跟他不在一起

40. 他們 _____ 地去參加畢業舞會。
    - (A) 真真假假
    - (B) 仔仔細細
    - (C) 清清楚楚
    - (D) 高高興興

40. 他们 _____ 地去参加毕业舞会。
    - (A) 真真假假
    - (B) 仔仔细细
    - (C) 清清楚楚
    - (D) 高高兴兴

GO ON TO THE NEXT PAGE

36. Zhōngguó bǐ Měiguó _____ dà.

    (A) zài

    (B) lián

    (C) gèng

    (D) rú

36. ㄓㄨㄥ ㄍㄨㄛ ㄅㄧ ㄇㄟ ㄍㄨㄛ _____ ㄉㄚ。

    (A) ㄗㄞ

    (B) ㄌㄧㄢ

    (C) ㄍㄥ

    (D) ㄖㄨ

37. Wǒ _____ huì shuō Rìyǔ, kěshì xiànzài wàng le.

    (A) yǐqián

    (B) yǐhòu

    (C) hòulái

    (D) cónglái

37. ㄨㄛ _____ ㄏㄨㄟ ㄕㄨㄛ ㄖ ㄩ, ㄎㄜ ㄕ ㄒㄧㄢ ㄗㄞ ㄨㄤ ㄌㄜ。

    (A) ㄧ ㄑㄧㄢ

    (B) ㄧ ㄏㄡ

    (C) ㄏㄡ ㄌㄞ

    (D) ㄘㄨㄥ ㄌㄞ

38. Míngtiān de huìyì xīwàng nǐ _____ lái.

    (A) lìkè

    (B) gāngcái

    (C) yídìng

    (D) yǐqián

38. ㄇㄧㄥ ㄊㄧㄢ ㄉㄜ ㄏㄨㄟ ㄧ ㄒㄧ ㄨㄤ ㄋㄧ _____ ㄌㄞ。

    (A) ㄌㄧ ㄎㄜ

    (B) ㄍㄤ ㄘㄞ

    (C) ㄧ ㄉㄧㄥ

    (D) ㄧ ㄑㄧㄢ

39. Zuìjìn hěn máng, suǒyǐ _____ .

    (A) wǒ zài yìqǐ bù gēn tā

    (B) wǒ yìqǐ bù gēn tā zài

    (C) wǒ gēn tā zài yìqǐ bù

    (D) wǒ gēn tā bú zài yìqǐ

39. ㄗㄨㄟ ㄐㄧㄣ ㄏㄣ ㄇㄤ, ㄙㄨㄛ ㄧ _____ 。

    (A) ㄨㄛ ㄗㄞ ㄧ ㄑㄧ ㄅㄨ ㄍㄣ ㄊㄚ

    (B) ㄨㄛ ㄧ ㄧ ㄑㄧ ㄅㄨ ㄍㄣ ㄊㄚ ㄗㄞ

    (C) ㄨㄛ ㄍㄣ ㄊㄚ ㄗㄞ ㄧ ㄑㄧ ㄅㄨ

    (D) ㄨㄛ ㄍㄣ ㄊㄚ ㄅㄨ ㄗㄞ ㄧ ㄑㄧ

40. Tāmen _____ de qù cānjiā bìyè wǔhuì.

    (A) zhēnzhēn–jiǎjiǎ

    (B) zǐzǐ–xìxì

    (C) qīngqīng–chǔchǔ

    (D) gāogāo–xìngxìng

40. ㄊㄚ ㄇㄣ _____ ㄉㄜ ㄑㄩ ㄘㄢ ㄐㄧㄚ ㄅㄧ ㄧㄝ ㄨ ㄏㄨㄟ。

    (A) ㄓㄣ ㄓㄣ ㄐㄧㄚ ㄐㄧㄚ

    (B) ㄗ ㄗ ㄒㄧ ㄒㄧ

    (C) ㄑㄧㄥ ㄑㄧㄥ ㄔㄨ ㄔㄨ

    (D) ㄍㄠ ㄍㄠ ㄒㄧㄥ ㄒㄧㄥ

GO ON TO THE NEXT PAGE

41. 只要你繼續學下去，＿＿。
    (A) 一定學得會
    (B) 會學一定得
    (C) 學得會一定
    (D) 得一定會學

41. 只要你继续学下去，＿＿。
    (A) 一定学得会
    (B) 会学一定得
    (C) 学得会一定
    (D) 得一定会学

42. 從你家到學校，開車要
    ＿＿時間？
    (A) 幾個
    (B) 怎麼
    (C) 哪位
    (D) 多少

42. 从你家到学校，开车要
    ＿＿时间？
    (A) 几个
    (B) 怎么
    (C) 哪位
    (D) 多少

43. 已經太晚了，我＿＿他＿＿來了。
    (A) 想……會
    (B) 想……不會
    (C) 不想……會
    (D) 不想……不會

43. 已经太晚了，我＿＿他＿＿来了。
    (A) 想……会
    (B) 想……不会
    (C) 不想……会
    (D) 不想……不会

44. 他今天很忙，所以＿＿看你。
    (A) 明天才来
    (B) 明天就走
    (C) 昨天才去
    (D) 昨天就到

44. 他今天很忙，所以＿＿看你。
    (A) 明天才来
    (B) 明天就走
    (C) 昨天才去
    (D) 昨天就到

45. ＿＿下星期一＿＿我們哪天
    都有空。
    (A) 不管……也
    (B) 無論……就
    (C) 除了……以外
    (D) 非要……不可

45. ＿＿下星期一＿＿我们哪天
    都有空。
    (A) 不管……也
    (B) 无论……就
    (C) 除了……以外
    (D) 非要……不可

GO ON TO THE NEXT PAGE →

41. Zhǐyào nǐ jìxù xué xiàqu, _____

    (A) yídìng xué de huì

    (B) huì xué yídìng de

    (C) xué de huì yídìng

    (D) de yídìng huì xué

41. ㄓˇ ㄧㄠˋ ㄋㄧˇ ㄐㄧˋ ㄒㄩˋ ㄒㄩㄝˊ ㄒㄧㄚˋ ㄑㄩ, _____。

    (A) ㄧˊ ㄉㄧㄥˋ ㄒㄩㄝˊ ㄉㄜ ㄏㄨㄟˋ

    (B) ㄏㄨㄟˋ ㄒㄩㄝˊ ㄧˊ ㄉㄧㄥˋ ㄉㄜ

    (C) ㄒㄩㄝˊ ㄉㄜ ㄏㄨㄟˋ ㄧˊ ㄉㄧㄥˋ

    (D) ㄉㄜ ㄧˊ ㄉㄧㄥˋ ㄏㄨㄟˋ ㄒㄩㄝˊ

42. Cóng nǐ jiā dào xuéxiào, kāichē yào

    _____ shíjiān?

    (A) jǐ gè

    (B) zěnme

    (C) něi wèi

    (D) duōshǎo

42. ㄘㄨㄥˊ ㄋㄧˇ ㄐㄧㄚ ㄉㄠˋ ㄒㄩㄝˊ ㄒㄧㄠˋ, ㄎㄞ ㄔㄜ ㄧㄠˋ

    _____ ㄕˊ ㄐㄧㄢ。

    (A) ㄐㄧˇ ㄍㄜˋ

    (B) ㄗㄣˇ ㄇㄜ

    (C) ㄋㄟˇ ㄨㄟˋ

    (D) ㄉㄨㄛ ㄕㄠˇ

43. Yǐjīng tài wǎn le, wǒ _____ tā _____ lái le.

    (A) xiǎng ...... huì

    (B) xiǎng ...... bú huì

    (C) bù xiǎng ...... huì

    (D) bù xiǎng ...... bú huì

43. ㄧˇ ㄐㄧㄥ ㄊㄞˋ ㄨㄢˇ ㄌㄜ, ㄨㄛˇ _____ ㄊㄚ _____ ㄌㄞˊ ㄌㄜ。

    (A) ㄒㄧㄤˇ ...... ㄏㄨㄟˋ

    (B) ㄒㄧㄤˇ ...... ㄅㄨˊ ㄏㄨㄟˋ

    (C) ㄅㄨˋ ㄒㄧㄤˇ ...... ㄏㄨㄟˋ

    (D) ㄅㄨˋ ㄒㄧㄤˇ ...... ㄅㄨˊ ㄏㄨㄟˋ

44. Tā jīntiān hěn máng, suǒyǐ _____ kàn nǐ.

    (A) míngtiān cái lái

    (B) míngtiān jiù zǒu

    (C) zuótiān cái qù

    (D) zuótiān jiù dào

44. ㄊㄚ ㄐㄧㄣ ㄊㄧㄢ ㄏㄣˇ ㄇㄤˊ, ㄙㄨㄛˇ ㄧˇ _____ ㄎㄢˋ ㄋㄧˇ。

    (A) ㄇㄧㄥˊ ㄊㄧㄢ ㄘㄞˊ ㄌㄞˊ

    (B) ㄇㄧㄥˊ ㄊㄧㄢ ㄐㄧㄡˋ ㄗㄡˇ

    (C) ㄗㄨㄛˊ ㄊㄧㄢ ㄘㄞˊ ㄑㄩˋ

    (D) ㄗㄨㄛˊ ㄊㄧㄢ ㄐㄧㄡˋ ㄉㄠˋ

45. _____ xià xīngqīyī _____ wǒmen něi tiān

    dōu yǒu kòng.

    (A) Bùguǎn ...... yě

    (B) Wúlùn ...... jiù

    (C) Chúle ...... yǐwài

    (D) Fēiyào ...... bùkě

45. _____ ㄒㄧㄚˋ ㄒㄧㄥ ㄑㄧ ㄧ _____ ㄨㄛˇ ㄇㄣˊ ㄋㄟˇ ㄊㄧㄢ

    ㄉㄡ ㄧㄡˇ ㄎㄨㄥˋ。

    (A) ㄅㄨˋ ㄍㄨㄢˇ ...... ㄧㄝˇ

    (B) ㄨˊ ㄌㄨㄣˋ ...... ㄐㄧㄡˋ

    (C) ㄔㄨˊ ㄌㄜ ...... ㄧˇ ㄨㄞˋ

    (D) ㄈㄟ ㄧㄠˋ ...... ㄅㄨˋ ㄎㄜˇ

GO ON TO THE NEXT PAGE

46. 時間過得真快，這個學期
  ____ 結束了。
  (A) 就要
  (B) 才要
  (C) 只是
  (D) 總是

46. 时间过得真快，这个学期
  ____ 结束了。
  (A) 就要
  (B) 才要
  (C) 只是
  (D) 总是

47. 我的字典不見了，怎麼也 ____。
  (A) 找別着
  (B) 找沒着
  (C) 找不着
  (D) 找得着

47. 我的字典不见了，怎么也 ____。
  (A) 找别着
  (B) 找没着
  (C) 找不着
  (D) 找得着

48. 學開車 ____ 並不難。
  (A) 其他
  (B) 其餘
  (C) 其中
  (D) 其實

48. 学开车 ____ 并不难。
  (A) 其他
  (B) 其余
  (C) 其中
  (D) 其实

49. 他的朋友 ____ 聰明 ____
  熱心幫助人。
  (A) 無論 ...... 也都
  (B) 以為 ...... 其實
  (C) 不但 ...... 而且
  (D) 即使 ...... 就是

49. 他的朋友 ____ 聪明 ____
  热心帮助人。
  (A) 无论 ...... 也都
  (B) 以为 ...... 其实
  (C) 不但 ...... 而且
  (D) 即使 ...... 就是

50. 你有沒有看到我的鉛筆？
  ____ 還在這兒的！
  (A) 現在
  (B) 剛才
  (C) 從此
  (D) 後來

50. 你有没有看到我的铅笔？
  ____ 还在这儿的！
  (A) 现在
  (B) 刚才
  (C) 从此
  (D) 后来

GO ON TO THE NEXT PAGE

340

46. Shíjiān guò de zhēn kuài, zhèige xuéqī

 _____ jiéshù le.

 (A) jiùyào

 (B) cáiyào

 (C) zhǐshì

 (D) zǒngshì

46. ㄕˊ ㄐㄧㄢ ㄍㄨㄛˋ ㄉㄜ˙ ㄓㄣ ㄎㄨㄞˋ, ㄓㄜˋ ㄍㄜ˙ ㄒㄩㄝˊ ㄑㄧ

 _____ ㄐㄧㄝˊ ㄕㄨˋ ㄉㄜ˙。

 (A) ㄐㄧㄡˋ ㄧㄠˋ

 (B) ㄘㄞˊ ㄧㄠˋ

 (C) ㄓˇ ㄕˋ

 (D) ㄗㄨㄥˇ ㄕˋ

47. Wǒ de zìdiǎn bú jiàn le, zěnme yě _____

 (A) zhǎo bié zháo

 (B) zhǎo méi zháo

 (C) zhǎo bu zháo

 (D) zhǎo de zháo

47. ㄨㄛˇ ㄉㄜ˙ ㄗˋ ㄉㄧㄢˇ ㄅㄨˊ ㄐㄧㄢˋ ㄉㄜ˙, ㄗㄣˇ ㄇㄜ˙ ㄧㄝˇ _____ 。

 (A) ㄓㄠˇ ㄅㄧㄝˊ ㄓㄠˊ

 (B) ㄓㄠˇ ㄇㄟˊ ㄓㄠˊ

 (C) ㄓㄠˇ ㄅㄨ˙ ㄓㄠˊ

 (D) ㄓㄠˇ ㄉㄜ˙ ㄓㄠˊ

48. Xué kāichē _____ bìng bù nán.

 (A) qítā

 (B) qíyú

 (C) qízhōng

 (D) qíshí

48. ㄒㄩㄝˊ ㄎㄞ ㄔㄜ _____ ㄅㄧㄥˋ ㄅㄨˋ ㄋㄢˊ。

 (A) ㄑㄧˊ ㄊㄚ

 (B) ㄑㄧˊ ㄩˊ

 (C) ㄑㄧˊ ㄓㄨㄥ

 (D) ㄑㄧˊ ㄕˊ

49. Tā de péngyou _____ cōngming _____

 rèxīn bāngzhù rén.

 (A) wúlùn ...... yě dōu

 (B) yǐwéi ...... qíshí

 (C) búdàn ...... érqiě

 (D) jíshǐ ...... jiùshì

49. ㄊㄚ ㄉㄜ˙ ㄆㄥˊ ㄧㄡ˙ _____ ㄘㄨㄥ ㄇㄧㄥˊ _____
 ㄖㄜˋ ㄒㄧㄣ ㄅㄤ ㄓㄨˋ ㄖㄣˊ。

 (A) ㄨˊ ㄌㄨㄣˋ ...... ㄧㄝˇ ㄉㄡ

 (B) ㄧˇ ㄨㄟˊ ...... ㄑㄧˊ ㄕˊ

 (C) ㄅㄨˊ ㄉㄢˋ ...... ㄦˊ ㄑㄧㄝˇ

 (D) ㄐㄧˊ ㄕˇ ...... ㄐㄧㄡˋ ㄕˋ

50. Nǐ yǒu méiyǒu kàn dào wǒ de qiānbǐ?

 _____ hái zài zhèr de!

 (A) Xiànzài

 (B) Gāngcái

 (C) Cóngcǐ

 (D) Hòulái

50. ㄋㄧˇ ㄧㄡˇ ㄇㄟˊ ㄧㄡˇ ㄎㄢˋ ㄉㄠˋ ㄨㄛˇ ㄉㄜ˙ ㄑㄧㄢ ㄅㄧˇ?
 _____ ㄏㄞˊ ㄗㄞˋ ㄓㄜˋ ㄦ ㄉㄜ˙。

 (A) ㄒㄧㄢˋ ㄗㄞˋ

 (B) ㄍㄤ ㄘㄞˊ

 (C) ㄘㄨㄥˊ ㄘˇ

 (D) ㄏㄡˋ ㄌㄞˊ

GO ON TO THE NEXT PAGE

51. 你怎麼 _____ 吃完了就馬上走。

 (A) 由於

 (B) 原來

 (C) 此外

 (D) 總是

52. 中國的出口貨品 _____
  美國的進口貨品。

 (A) 變化

 (B) 變成

 (C) 變通

 (D) 變形

53. 上海的天氣 _____ 北京那麼冷。

 (A) 跟

 (B) 比

 (C) 沒有

 (D) 不能

54. 真對不起，我把你看 _____
  張先生了。

 (A) 成

 (B) 到

 (C) 了

 (D) 過

55. 要是你想進一個好大學，
  你 _____ 用功不可。

 (A) 也

 (B) 都

 (C) 非

 (D) 再

51. 你怎么 _____ 吃完了就马上走。

 (A) 由于

 (B) 原来

 (C) 此外

 (D) 总是

52. 中国的出口货品 _____
  美国的进口货品。

 (A) 变化

 (B) 变成

 (C) 变通

 (D) 变形

53. 上海的天气 _____ 北京那么冷。

 (A) 跟

 (B) 比

 (C) 没有

 (D) 不能

54. 真对不起，我把你看 _____
  张先生了。

 (A) 成

 (B) 到

 (C) 了

 (D) 过

55. 要是你想进一个好大学，
  你 _____ 用功不可。

 (A) 也

 (B) 都

 (C) 非

 (D) 再

GO ON TO THE NEXT PAGE

51. Nǐ zěnme _____ chī wán le jiù mǎshàng zǒu.

    (A) yóuyú

    (B) yuánlái

    (C) cǐwài

    (D) zǒngshì

52. Zhōngguó de chūkǒu huòpǐn _____

    Měiguó de jìnkǒu huòpǐn.

    (A) biànhuà

    (B) biànchéng

    (C) biàntōng

    (D) biànxíng

53. Shànghǎi de tiānqì _____ Běijīng nàme lěng.

    (A) gēn

    (B) bǐ

    (C) méiyǒu

    (D) bù néng

54. Zhēn duìbuqǐ, wǒ bǎ nǐ kàn _____

    Zhāng xiānsheng le.

    (A) chéng

    (B) dào

    (C) le

    (D) guo

55. Yàoshi nǐ xiǎng jìn yí gè hǎo dàxué,

    nǐ _____ yònggōng bùkě.

    (A) yě

    (B) dōu

    (C) fēi

    (D) zài

END OF SECTION II

GO ON TO SECTION III.

SECTION III

READING COMPREHENSION

Suggested time — 25 minutes
Questions 56 – 85

WHEN YOU BEGIN THIS SECTION, BE SURE THAT YOU MARK YOUR ANSWER TO THE
FIRST QUESTION BY FILLING IN ONE OF THE OVALS NEXT TO NUMBER 56 ON YOUR
ANSWER SHEET.

Directions: Read the following texts carefully for comprehension. Each is followed by one or more
questions or incomplete statements. Select the answer or completion that is best according to the text
and fill in the corresponding oval on your answer sheet. There is no example for this part.

THIS SECTION OF THE TEST IS PRESENTED IN TWO WRITING SYSTEMS: TRADITIONAL
CHARACTERS AND SIMPLIFIED CHARACTERS. IT IS RECOMMENDED THAT YOU
CHOOSE THE WRITING SYSTEM WITH WHICH YOU ARE MORE FAMILIAR AND **READ
ONLY THAT VERSION** AS YOU WORK THROUGH THIS SECTION OF THE TEST.

Question 56

北海大學法文系教授	北海大学法文系教授
張立明	张立明
住址: 北海大學19樓5門502號 電話: 2012287-480 (辦公室)	住址: 北海大学19楼5门502号 电话: 2012287-480 (办公室)

56.   This business card belongs to a

    (A) professor
    (B) manager
    (C) physician
    (D) lawyer

GO ON TO THE NEXT PAGE ▶

Questions 57 – 59

星期天小李和他的老朋友
老張一起去飯店吃晚飯。小李
叫了一盤海鮮飯，老張叫了
一盤紅燒牛肉，一碗湯，和
四條春卷。

星期天小李和他的老朋友
老张一起去饭店吃晚饭。小李
叫了一盘海鲜饭，老张叫了
一盘红烧牛肉，一碗汤，和
四条春卷。

57. Where did the two friends go?

(A) To the fish market
(B) To a grocery store
(C) To Lao Zhang's home
(D) To a restaurant

58. On what day did the two friends go?

(A) Thursday
(B) Friday
(C) Saturday
(D) Sunday

59. What did Xiao Li choose?

(A) Beef
(B) Soup
(C) Seafood
(D) Vegetables

GO ON TO THE NEXT PAGE →

Question 60

王小姐：

　　　你媽媽剛才打電話來找你。
我告訴她你十分鐘後會回來。
她要你一回來就打電話給她。

李　3:45

王小姐：

　　　你妈妈刚才打电话来找你。
我告诉她你十分钟后会回来。
她要你一回来就打电话给她。

李　3:45

60. What should Ms. Wang do?

(A) Return the call.
(B) Wait for another call.
(C) Meet the caller in ten minutes.
(D) Talk to her father for more details.

Questions 61 – 62

元 元 小 吃
正宗台灣小吃
每週營業七天
上午十一點至晚上九點

元 元 小 吃
正宗台湾小吃
每周营业七天
上午十一点至晚上九点

61. When does the place open?

(A) Seven o'clock
(B) Nine o'clock
(C) Ten o'clock
(D) Eleven o'clock

62. This is an advertisement for a

(A) restaurant
(B) bakery
(C) supermarket
(D) drugstore

GO ON TO THE NEXT PAGE

Question 63

華東師範大學專家樓餐廳收據

客戶名稱_____			
品　　　名	@	數量	金　額
客飯		2	12.00
點心			
飲料			
水果			
總計(大寫)　壹拾貳元正			￥12.00
收款員　劉	日期九一年二月五日		

第二聯：餐廳收據

华东师范大学专家楼餐厅收据

客户名称_____			
品　　　名	@	数量	金　额
客饭		2	12.00
点心			
饮料			
水果			
总计(大写)　壹拾貳元正			￥12.00
收款员　刘	日期九一年二月五日		

第二联：餐厅收据

63.　This receipt is from a

(A)　cafeteria
(B)　bookstore
(C)　post office
(D)　grocery store

GO ON TO THE NEXT PAGE

<u>Question 64</u>

中國旅遊	
第一天	台北—香港—廣州
第二天	廣州—桂林
第三天	桂林
第四天	桂林—北京

中国旅游	
第一天	台北—香港—广州
第二天	广州—桂林
第三天	桂林
第四天	桂林—北京

64. Where does the tour originate?

(A) Beijing
(B) Guangzhou
(C) Taipei
(D) Hong Kong

GO ON TO THE NEXT PAGE ▶

Question 65 – 66

海 華 中 文 學 校 春季班
上課時間: 元月九日至六月十二日 (週六上午9:00 —12:00)
課程: 1. 中文課:聽、説、讀、寫、 作文等等。 2. 文化才藝選修課: 書法、 勞作、兒童繪畫班、 合唱、棋藝。

海 华 中 文 学 校 春季班
上课时间: 元月九日至六月十二日 (周六上午9:00 —12:00)
课程: 1. 中文课:听、说、读、写、 作文等等。 2. 文化才艺选修课:书法、 劳作、儿童绘画班、 合唱、棋艺。

65. When does this session end?

   (A) January
   (B) June
   (C) September
   (D) December

66. Which of the following courses is offered?

   (A) Cooking
   (B) Exercise
   (C) Dance
   (D) Singing

GO ON TO THE NEXT PAGE

<u>Questions 67 – 68</u>

在<u>中國</u>的馬路上有很多自行車。自行車雖然沒有汽車快，可是比汽車方便得多。第一，自行車很小，不要很大的停車場。第二，自行車不用汽油，可以減少空氣污染。第三，自行車很便宜，大家都能買得起。騎自行車上下班還可以鍛鍊身體。

在<u>中国</u>的马路上有很多自行车。自行车虽然没有汽车快，可是比汽车方便得多。第一，自行车很小，不要很大的停车场。第二，自行车不用汽油，可以减少空气污染。第三，自行车很便宜，大家都能买得起。骑自行车上下班还可以锻炼身体。

67. It can be inferred from the passage that the writer

(A) collects air samples
(B) does physical therapy
(C) designs mass transit systems
(D) prefers bicycles to cars

68. What is the main topic of the passage?

(A) An environmental issue
(B) A sale on fitness equipment
(C) A means of transportation
(D) A traffic problem

GO ON TO THE NEXT PAGE

Question 69

人立服裝店發票 上海南京西路17號						
貨 號	規 格	商 品	名 稱	數 量	單 價	售 價
		襯衫		1		16~

經手人 王明

九一 年九月七日

人立服裝店发票 上海南京西路17号						
货 号	规 格	商 品	名 称	数 量	单 价	售 价
		衬衫		1		16~

经手人 王明

九一 年九月七日

69. This is a receipt for a

(A) hat
(B) shirt
(C) jacket
(D) sweater

GO ON TO THE NEXT PAGE

Questions 70 – 71

今天早上文生五點半鐘就起
床了。吃了早飯以後，七點鐘
就離開家去學校。從八點鐘開
始，他上了英文課、數學課、
歷史課跟中文課，到十二點一
刻才吃中飯。下午他到圖書館
去找書，寫報告，到三點鐘才
回家。回家休息了一個鐘頭，
吃了一點東西，就立刻到超級
市場工作。從四點半開始一直
工作到晚上八點才下班回家。

今天早上文生五点半钟就起
床了。吃了早饭以后，七点钟
就离开家去学校。从八点钟开
始，他上了英文课、数学课、
历史课跟中文课，到十二点一
刻才吃中饭。下午他到图书馆
去找书，写报告，到三点钟才
回家。回家休息了一个钟头，
吃了一点东西，就立刻到超级
市场工作。从四点半开始一直
工作到晚上八点才下班回家。

70. Which of the following courses is NOT on Wen Sheng's schedule?

    (A) Chinese
    (B) History
    (C) Mathematics
    (D) Chemistry

71. Where was Wen Sheng at 5:30 p.m.?

    (A) At the supermarket
    (B) In the library
    (C) In class
    (D) At home

GO ON TO THE NEXT PAGE

Question 72

太平路郵電支局

郵政營業 8:00-18:30　電信營業 8:00-21:00

郵政編碼: 210002

太平路邮电支局

邮政营业 8:00-18:30　电信营业 8:00-21:00

邮政编码: 210002

72. This sign could be found outside a

(A) museum
(B) hospital
(C) post office
(D) bookstore

Question 73

糖醋排骨

排骨一斤　糖四湯匙
葱段少許　醋二湯匙
薑絲少許　酒一湯匙
鹽三茶匙　水一杯半

糖醋排骨

排骨一斤　糖四汤匙
葱段少许　醋二汤匙
姜丝少许　酒一汤匙
盐三茶匙　水一杯半

73. This is a portion of a

(A) menu
(B) recipe
(C) grocery list
(D) food label

GO ON TO THE NEXT PAGE

Questions 74 – 75

老張、小王、小李、和老陳，
他們四個人約好這個星期天一起
去黃山野餐，老陳負責準備飲
料，小王負責點心，小李和老張
準備三明治。他們打算星期天一
早就出發，要坐兩個鐘頭的車才
能到達黃山。

老张、小王、小李、和老陈，
他们四个人约好这个星期天一起
去黄山野餐，老陈负责准备饮
料，小王负责点心，小李和老张
准备三明治。他们打算星期天一
早就出发，要坐两个钟头的车才
能到达黄山。

74. How long will the bus ride take?

(A) One hour
(B) Two hours
(C) Three hours
(D) Four hours

75. What should Xiao Li bring to the picnic?

(A) Chips
(B) Drinks
(C) Dessert
(D) Sandwiches

GO ON TO THE NEXT PAGE

老王是我的朋友，他最喜歡的事就是運動。可是他的弟弟小王就不同了。小王的嗜好是看電視。老王也喜歡看電視，可是他只愛看喜劇，但是他的弟弟小王是什麼節目都看。談到運動，打球、游泳、爬山老王都喜歡；可是他最愛滑雪。小王只喜歡看電視上的運動節目，除了有時候出去走一走以外，大部份的時間都不喜歡出去走動。小王比老王胖，我想這也許是因爲他們兩個人有不同嗜好的緣故。

老王是我的朋友，他最喜欢的事就是运动。可是他的弟弟小王就不同了。小王的嗜好是看电视。老王也喜欢看电视，可是他只爱看喜剧，但是他的弟弟小王是什么节目都看。谈到运动，打球、游泳、爬山老王都喜欢；可是他最爱滑雪。小王只喜欢看电视上的运动节目，除了有时候出去走一走以外，大部份的时间都不喜欢出去走动。小王比老王胖，我想这也许是因为他们两个人有不同嗜好的缘故。

76. In what way are the brothers different?

    (A) One likes music and the other prefers reading.
    (B) They have different television viewing habits.
    (C) One jogs for exercise and the other prefers swimming.
    (D) They participate in different team sports.

77. What activity does Lao Wang enjoy most?

    (A) Skiing
    (B) Reading
    (C) Watching television
    (D) Mountain climbing

78. What else does the passage say about the brothers?

    (A) They spend little spare time together.
    (B) They do not make good roommates for each other.
    (C) They rarely attend each other's sporting events.
    (D) They look different physically.

GO ON TO THE NEXT PAGE

Question 79

新分店啓事

　　本公司爲擴展業務，自
四月十日起增設分店，擴
大社區服務。分店址爲上
海東路十號。尚祈舊雨新
知繼續指教。

　　　　中美貿易公司敬啓
　　　　一九九五年三月五日

新分店启事

　　本公司为扩展业务，自
四月十日起增设分店，扩
大社区服务。分店址为上
海东路十号。尚祈旧雨新
知继续指教。

　　　　中美贸易公司敬启
　　　　一九九五年三月五日

79. What is being announced?

(A) The opening of a branch office
(B) The temporary closing of a store
(C) The merging of two banks
(D) The relocation of a company

GO ON TO THE NEXT PAGE

Questions 80 – 83

下午去牙醫診所洗牙。一進
去，護士就叫我明明。其實我
的名字是英英。明明是我雙胞
胎的妹妹。我比明明高，又戴
了眼鏡，但還是有人把我認錯
成明明。我也懶得解釋了。在
候診室等了十分鐘才輪到我。
牙醫叫我張大嘴，要給我上麻
醉藥拔牙。我馬上從椅子上跳
了起來。指着我的眼鏡說：『我
是英英，我是來洗牙的。明明
是我妹妹。需要拔牙的是她，
不是我。』

下午去牙医诊所洗牙。一进
去，护士就叫我明明。其实我
的名字是英英。明明是我双胞
胎的妹妹。我比明明高，又戴
了眼镜，但还是有人把我认错
成明明。我也懒得解释了。在
候诊室等了十分钟才轮到我。
牙医叫我张大嘴，要给我上麻
醉药拔牙。我马上从椅子上跳
了起来。指着我的眼镜说："我
是英英，我是来洗牙的。明明
是我妹妹。需要拔牙的是她，
不是我。"

80. What is one difference between
    Mingming and Yingying?

    (A) They go to different dentists.
    (B) One is taller than the other.
    (C) They come from different families.
    (D) Their birthdays are ten days apart.

81. Who tells the story?

    (A) The nurse
    (B) The doctor
    (C) Mingming
    (D) Yingying

82. Where did Yingying go?

    (A) To buy glasses
    (B) To see a school nurse
    (C) To visit the dentist
    (D) To call her sister

83. What do we know about Yingying?

    (A) She wears glasses.
    (B) She is younger than Mingming.
    (C) She works at a doctor's office.
    (D) She needs to have her tooth pulled.

GO ON TO THE NEXT PAGE

Questions 84 – 85

每年八月底，我跟我的先生
都去海邊渡假。白天我們在海
邊曬太陽，晚上我們去音樂廳
聽音樂。每次我們都覺得一週
的假期太短了。

每年八月底，我跟我的先生
都去海边渡假。白天我们在海
边晒太阳，晚上我们去音乐厅
听音乐。每次我们都觉得一周
的假期太短了。

84. In which month does the couple go on vacation?

    (A) January
    (B) June
    (C) August
    (D) October

85. How long does their vacation last?

    (A) One weekend
    (B) One week
    (C) Two weeks
    (D) One month

END OF SECTION III

STOP

**IF YOU FINISH BEFORE TIME IS CALLED, YOU MAY CHECK YOUR WORK ON SECTIONS II AND III.
DO NOT TURN TO ANY OTHER TEST IN THIS BOOK.**

How to Score the SAT Subject Test in Chinese with Listening

When you take the SAT Subject Test in Chinese with Listening, you will receive an overall composite score as well as three subscores: one for the reading section, one for the listening section, and one for the usage section. The reading, listening, and usage scores are reported on the College Board's 20-to-80 scale. However, the composite score, which is the most significant of the scores reported to the colleges you specify, is in the form of the College Board's 200-to-800 scale.

Worksheet 1. Finding Your Raw Listening Subscore

STEP 1: Table A lists the correct answers for all the questions on the SAT Subject Test in Chinese with Listening that is reproduced in this book. It also serves as a worksheet for you to calculate your raw Listening subscore.

- Compare your answers with those given in the table.
- Put a check in the column marked "Right" if your answer is correct.
- Put a check in the column marked "Wrong" if your answer is incorrect.
- Leave both columns blank if you omitted the question.

STEP 2: Count the number of right answers for questions 1–18.

Enter the total here: _____

STEP 3: Count the number of wrong answers for questions 1–18.

Enter the total here: _____

STEP 4: Multiply the number of wrong answers from Step 3 by .500.

Enter the product here: _____

STEP 5: Subtract the result obtained in Step 4 from the total you obtained in Step 2.

Enter the result here: _____

STEP 6: Count the number of right answers for questions 19–30.

Enter the total here: _____

STEP 7: Count the number of wrong answers for questions 19–30.

Enter the total here: _____

STEP 8: Multiply the number of wrong answers from Step 7 by .333.

Enter the product here: _____

STEP 9: Subtract the result obtained in Step 8 from the total you obtained in Step 6.

Enter the result here: _____

STEP 10: Add the result obtained in Step 5 to the result obtained in Step 9.

Enter the sum here: _____

STEP 11: Round the number obtained in Step 10 to the nearest whole number.

Enter the result here: _____

The number you obtained in Step 11 is your raw Listening subscore.

Worksheet 2. Finding Your Raw Reading Subscore

STEP 1: Table A lists the correct answers for all the questions on the SAT Subject Test in Chinese with Listening that is reproduced in this book. It also serves as a worksheet for you to calculate your raw Reading subscore.

STEP 2: Count the number of right answers for questions 56–85.

Enter the total here: _____

STEP 3: Count the number of wrong answers for questions 56–85.

Enter the total here: _____

STEP 4: Multiply the number of wrong answers from Step 3 by .333.

Enter the product here: _____

STEP 5: Subtract the result obtained in Step 4 from the total you obtained in Step 2.

Enter the result here: _____

STEP 6: Round the number obtained in Step 5 to the nearest whole number.

Enter the result here: _____

The number you obtained in Step 6 is your raw Reading subscore.

Worksheet 3. Finding Your Raw Usage Subscore

STEP 1: Table A lists the correct answers for all the questions on the SAT Subject Test in Chinese with Listening that is reproduced in this book. It also serves as a worksheet for you to calculate your raw Usage subscore.

STEP 2: Count the number of right answers for questions 31–55.

Enter the total here: _____

STEP 3: Count the number of wrong answers for questions 31–55.

Enter the total here: _____

STEP 4: Multiply the number of wrong answers from Step 3 by .333.

Enter the product here: _____

STEP 5: Subtract the result obtained in Step 4 from the total you obtained in Step 2.

Enter the result here: _____

STEP 6: Round the number obtained in Step 5 to the nearest whole number.

Enter the result here: _____

The number you obtained in Step 6 is your raw Usage subscore.

Worksheet 4. Finding Your Raw Composite Score*

STEP 1: Enter your unrounded raw reading subscore from Step 5 of Worksheet 2 here: _____

STEP 2: Multiply your unrounded raw reading subscore by 1.056. Enter the product here: _____

STEP 3: Enter your unrounded raw listening subscore from Step 10 of Worksheet 1 here: _____

STEP 4: Multiply your unrounded raw listening subscore by .923. Enter the product here: _____

STEP 5: Enter your unrounded raw usage subscore from Step 5 of Worksheet 3 here: _____

STEP 6: Multiply your unrounded raw usage subscore by 1.024. Enter the product here: _____

STEP 7: Add the results obtained in Steps 2, 4, and 6. Enter the sum here: _____

STEP 8: Round the number obtained in Step 7 to the nearest whole number. Enter the result here: _____

The number you obtained in Step 8 is your raw composite score.

*This weighting reflects the amount of time spent on the two sections of the test—40 minutes on the reading and usage questions and 20 minutes on the listening questions. For those who are curious about how the calculation works, the weighting is done in standard deviation units, a measure of score variability. The weight given to the listening subscore is calculated by dividing the standard deviation of the reading subscore by the standard deviation of the listening subscore. The weight given to the usage subscore is calculated by dividing the standard deviation of the reading subscore by the standard deviation of the usage subscore. Weights are applied to the reading, listening, and usage sections so that the maximum raw composite score equals 87.

TABLE A
Answers to the SAT Subject Test in Chinese with Listening, Form K-3RLC, and Percentage of Students Answering Each Question Correctly

Question Number	Correct Answer	Right	Wrong	Percentage of Students Answering the Question Correctly*	Question Number	Correct Answer	Right	Wrong	Percentage of Students Answering the Question Correctly*
1	B			92	33	D			96
2	C			92	34	B			91
3	C			87	35	B			91
4	A			94	36	C			89
5	B			92	37	A			87
6	A			82	38	C			82
7	A			68	39	D			89
8	C			74	40	D			83
9	B			75	41	A			83
10	C			84	42	D			86
11	A			90	43	B			83
12	A			86	44	A			80
13	B			83	45	C			77
14	B			84	46	A			75
15	C			83	47	C			77
16	C			75	48	D			74
17	A			76	49	C			75
18	B			78	50	B			74
19	B			93	51	D			67
20	C			90	52	B			69
21	B			84	53	C			68
22	D			75	54	A			64
23	D			85	55	C			69
24	B			87	56	A			94
25	C			86	57	D			95
26	A			79	58	D			95
27	B			46	59	C			91
28	D			89	60	A			90
29	A			63	61	D			97
30	C			79	62	A			74
31	B			83	63	A			86
32	A			95	64	C			80

Table A continued on next page

Table A continued from previous page

Question Number	Correct Answer	Right	Wrong	Percentage of Students Answering the Question Correctly*	Question Number	Correct Answer	Right	Wrong	Percentage of Students Answering the Question Correctly*
65	B			94	76	B			84
66	D			82	77	A			76
67	D			89	78	D			71
68	C			81	79	A			60
69	B			64	80	B			87
70	D			80	81	D			82
71	A			69	82	C			82
72	C			80	83	A			62
73	B			66	84	C			96
74	B			90	85	B			64
75	D			71					

*These percentages are based on an analysis of the answer sheets for a random sample of 513 students who took this form of the test in November 1995 and whose mean score was 682. They may be used as an indication of the relative difficulty of a particular question. Each percentage may also be used to predict the likelihood that a typical SAT Subject Test in Chinese with Listening candidate will answer correctly that question on this edition of this test.

Finding Your Scaled Score

When you take SAT Subject Tests, the scores sent to the colleges you specify are reported on the College Board scale, which ranges from 200 to 800. Subscores are reported on a scale that ranges from 20 to 80. You can convert your practice test scores to scaled scores by using Tables B, C, D, and E. To find your scaled score, locate your raw score in the left-hand column of the Table; the corresponding score in the right-hand column is your scaled score. For example, in Table B a raw composite score of 47 on this particular edition of the SAT Subject Test in Chinese with Listening corresponds to a scaled score of 600.

Raw scores are converted to scaled scores to ensure that a score earned on any one edition of a particular Subject Test is comparable to the same scaled score earned on any other edition of the same Subject Test. Because some editions of tests may be slightly easier or more difficult than others, scaled scores are adjusted so that they indicate the same level of performance regardless of the edition of the test taken and the ability of the group that takes it. Thus, for example, a score of 400 on one edition of a test taken at a particular administration indicates the same level of achievement as a score of 400 on a different edition of the test taken at a different administration.

When you take the SAT Subject Tests during a national administration, your scores are likely to differ somewhat from the scores you obtain on the tests in this book. People perform at different levels at different times for reasons unrelated to the tests themselves. The precision of any test is also limited because it represents only a sample of all the possible questions that could be asked.

Your scaled composite score from Table B is _____ .

Your scaled listening score from Table C is _____ .

Your scaled reading score from Table D is _____ .

Your scaled usage score from Table E is _____ .

TABLE B
Scaled Score Conversion Table
Chinese Subject Test with Listening Composite Scores (Form K-3RLC)

Raw Score	Scaled Score	Raw Score	Scaled Score	Raw Score	Scaled Score
		47	600	7	360
		46	600	6	360
85	800	45	590	5	350
84	800	44	580	4	350
83	790	43	580	3	340
82	780	42	570	2	340
81	780	41	560	1	330
80	770	40	560	0	330
79	760	39	550	−1	330
78	750	38	540	−2	320
77	750	37	540	−3	320
76	740	36	530	−4	310
75	740	35	520	−5	310
74	730	34	510	−6	310
73	730	33	510	−7	300
72	720	32	500	−8	300
71	720	31	490	−9	300
70	720	30	490	−10	290
69	710	29	480	−11	280
68	710	28	480	−12	280
67	700	27	470	−13	270
66	700	26	460	−14	270
65	690	25	460	−15	260
64	690	24	450	−16	250
63	690	23	450	−17	250
62	680	22	440	−18	240
61	680	21	430	−19	240
60	670	20	430	−20	230
59	670	19	420	−21	220
58	660	18	420	−22	220
57	660	17	410	−23	210
56	650	16	410	−24	210
55	650	15	400	−25	200
54	640	14	400	−26	200
53	640	13	390	−27	200
52	630	12	390	−28	200
51	630	11	380	−29	200
50	620	10	380	−30	200
49	620	9	370	−31	200
48	610	8	370		

TABLE C
Scaled Score Conversion Table
Chinese Subject Test with Listening Listening Subscore (Form K-3RLC)

Raw Score	Scaled Score	Raw Score	Scaled Score	Raw Score	Scaled Score
30	80	15	57	0	38
29	78	14	55	−1	37
28	76	13	54	−2	36
27	74	12	53	−3	35
26	72	11	52	−4	34
25	71	10	50	−5	33
24	70	9	49	−6	32
23	68	8	48	−7	31
22	67	7	47	−8	30
21	66	6	45	−9	28
20	64	5	44	−10	26
19	63	4	43	−11	25
18	61	3	42	−12	23
17	60	2	41	−13	21
16	58	1	39		

TABLE D
Scaled Score Conversion Table
Chinese Subject Test with Listening Reading Subscore (Form K-3RLC)

Raw Score	Scaled Score	Raw Score	Scaled Score	Raw Score	Scaled Score
30	80	16	57	2	35
29	78	15	55	1	34
28	76	14	53	0	32
27	75	13	51	−1	31
26	74	12	49	−2	30
25	73	11	48	−3	28
24	72	10	46	−4	26
23	71	9	45	−5	24
22	69	8	44	−6	21
21	68	7	42	−7	20
20	66	6	41	−8	20
19	64	5	40	−9	20
18	62	4	38	−10	20
17	59	3	37		

TABLE E
Scaled Score Conversion Table
Chinese Subject Test with Listening Usage Subscore (Form K-3RLC)

Raw Score	Scaled Score	Raw Score	Scaled Score	Raw Score	Scaled Score
25	79	13	63	1	37
24	74	12	60	0	35
23	73	11	58	−1	33
22	72	10	56	−2	32
21	71	9	53	−3	30
20	70	8	51	−4	28
19	70	7	49	−5	26
18	69	6	47	−6	23
17	68	5	45	−7	21
16	67	4	43	−8	20
15	66	3	41		
14	64	2	39		

Reviewing Your Performance
on the Chinese Subject Test with Listening

After you score your test, analyze your performance—consider the following questions:

Did you run out of time before reaching the end of the test?

If so, you may need to pace yourself better. For example, maybe you spent too much time on one or two hard questions. A better approach might be to skip the ones you can't answer right away and try answering all the questions that remain on the test. Then if there's time, go back to the questions you skipped.

Did you take a long time reading the directions?

You will save time when you take the test by learning the directions to the Chinese Test with Listening ahead of time. Each minute you spend reading directions during the test is a minute that you could use to answer questions.

How did you handle questions you were unsure of?

If you were able to eliminate one or more of the answer choices as wrong and guess from the remaining ones, your approach probably worked to your advantage. On the other hand, making haphazard guesses or omitting questions without trying to eliminate choices could cost you valuable points.

How difficult were the questions for you compared with other students who took the test?

Table A shows you how difficult the multiple-choice questions were for the group of students who took this test during its national administration. The right-hand column gives the percentage of students that answered each question correctly.

A question answered correctly by almost everyone in the group is obviously an easy question. For example, 90 percent of the students answered question 20 correctly. But only 46 percent answered question 27 correctly.

Keep in mind that these percentages are based on just one group of students. They would probably be different if another group of students took the test.

If you missed several easy questions, go back and try to find out why: Did the questions cover material you haven't reviewed yet? Did you misunderstand the directions?

Chapter 9
French

Purpose

There are two French Subject Tests: French and French with Listening. Both tests evaluate your reading skills through precision of vocabulary and structure use and comprehension of a variety of texts. The French Subject Test with Listening measures your ability to understand spoken as well as written French.

Format

- The French Test takes one hour and includes 85 multiple-choice questions.
- The French Test with Listening also takes one hour with about 20 minutes for listening questions and 40 minutes for reading questions. There are 85 to 90 multiple-choice listening and reading questions.

Both tests evaluate your reading ability in three areas through a variety of questions requiring a wide-ranging knowledge of French:

Vocabulary-in-context questions test knowledge of words representing different parts of speech and some basic idioms within culturally authentic contexts.

Structure questions measure your ability to select an appropriate word or expression that is grammatically correct within a sentence. One part of the test contains vocabulary and structure questions embedded in longer paragraphs.

Reading comprehension questions test your understanding of such points as main and supporting ideas, themes, and setting of a passage. Selections are drawn from fiction, essays, historical works, newspaper and magazine articles, or everyday materials such as advertisements, timetables, forms, and tickets.

In addition to these reading questions, the French Test with Listening also measures your ability to understand the spoken language with three types of *listening questions*:

Type one asks you to identify the sentence that most accurately describes what is presented in a picture or a photograph or what someone in the picture or photograph might say.

Type two tests your ability to answer general content questions based on short dialogues or monologues.

Type three requires you to answer more specific questions based on longer dialogues or monologues.

French

Skills Measured	Approximate Percentage of Test
Vocabulary in Context	30
Structure	30–35
Reading Comprehension	40

French with Listening

Types of Questions		Approximate Percentage of Test
Listening Section		35
Pictures:	8–12 questions	
Short dialogues:	5–12 questions	
Long dialogues:	10–15 questions	
Reading Section		65
Vocabulary:	16–20 questions	
Structure:	16–20 questions	
Reading Comprehension:	20–25 questions	

Recommended Preparation

Both tests are written to reflect general trends in high school curricula and are independent of particular textbooks or methods of instruction. The French Tests are appropriate for you if you have studied the language for three or four years in high school, or the equivalent; however, if you have two years of strong preparation in French, you are also encouraged to take the tests. Your best preparation for the tests is a gradual development of competence in French over a period of years. Familiarize yourself with directions in advance. The directions in this book are identical to those that appear on the test.

French with Listening

- a practice cassette with sample questions is available from your school counselor

Cassette Players

You must bring an acceptable cassette player with earphones to the test center. Put fresh batteries in your cassette player the day before the test; and, if you like, bring additional fresh batteries and a backup cassette player with earphones to the test center. Test center staff will NOT have batteries, cassette players, or earphones for your use.

Acceptable cassette players must be:
- personal (have earphones that let only you hear the recording)
- portable (small enough that the entire player can fit in your hand)
- battery-operated
- able to use a single (not dual) standard (2-1/2 inch by 4 inch) audiocassette—not a mini- or microcassette

If your cassette player has a programming feature that fast-forwards automatically to the next prompt, that feature must be deactivated before you start the test. You will not be allowed to share a cassette player with another test-taker.

Beginning with the November 2005 administration, portable CD players will be required instead of cassette players for language with listening tests.

Scores

For both tests, the total score is reported on the 200-to-800 scale. For the listening test, listening and reading subscores are reported on the 20-to-80 scale.

Sample Reading Questions

Four types of reading questions are used in the French Tests. All questions in the tests are multiple-choice questions in which you must choose the BEST response from the four choices offered.

Please note that your answer sheet has five answer positions marked A, B, C, D, E, while the questions throughout this test contain only four choices. Be sure NOT to make any marks in column E.

Part A

Directions: This part consists of a number of incomplete statements, each having four suggested completions. Select the most appropriate completion and fill in the corresponding oval on the answer sheet.

1. J'ai perdu mon argent parce qu'il y avait un trou dans la ... de mon pantalon.

   (A) manche

   (B) jambe

   (C) poche

   (D) ceinture

This question tests vocabulary. You are asked to choose the appropriate noun from the four answer choices. The correct answer is (C) because pants have pockets in which people keep money. Choices (A) and (D) are not normally used to carry money, and (B) refers to a part of the body.

2. Charles avait tant mangé qu'il ne pouvait plus ... une bouchée.

   (A) soutenir

   (B) emporter

   (C) avaler

   (D) évaluer

In this question, you are asked to find the appropriate verb from the four answer choices. The correct answer is (C). The verb *avaler* is the only option that can be used correctly in connection with une *bouchée*. Choices (A), (B), and (D) are incorrect.

Part B

Directions: Each of the following sentences contains a blank. From the four choices given, select the one that can be inserted in the blank to form a grammatically correct sentence and fill in the corresponding oval on the answer sheet. Choice (A) may consist of dashes that indicate that no insertion is required to form a grammatically correct sentence.

3. Dans sa cuisine, il fallait toujours que tout _____ impeccable et reluisant.

    (A) est

    (B) soit

    (C) était

    (D) serait

The correct form of the verb *être* from the four answer choices is (B). You need to know that *il fallait que* in the sentence is the past tense of *il faut que*, an impersonal expression that is followed by a verb in the subjunctive. Choices (A), (C), and (D) are forms of *être* in the indicative and are therefore incorrect.

4. _____ est le meilleur joueur de cette équipe?

    (A) Qu'

    (B) Quelle

    (C) Qu'est-ce qu'

    (D) Qui

In this question you are asked to choose the appropriate pronoun from the four answer choices. The correct answer is (D). The question mark tells you that the missing pronoun is interrogative and the verb *est* tells you that it is the subject of the sentence. *Qui* is an interrogative pronoun and the subject. Choices (A), (B), and (C) are incorrect because (A) cannot be used as a subject, (B) is an interrogative adjective, and (C) is an interrogative pronoun used as a direct object.

The sample questions for Part C have the format used in the most recent editions of the test. Note that the Part C questions in the complete test printed in this book have a different format.

Part C

Directions: The paragraphs below contain blank spaces indicating omissions in the text. For some blanks it is necessary to choose the completion that is most appropriate to the meaning of the passage; for other blanks, to choose the one completion that forms a grammatically correct sentence. In some instances, choice (A) may consist of dashes that indicate that no insertion is required to form a grammatically correct sentence. In each case, indicate your answer by filling in the corresponding oval on the answer sheet. Be sure to read the paragraph completely before answering the questions related to it.

Dès que vous __5__ le temps de prendre contact avec elle, donnez-__6__ un coup de téléphone. Il faut l'avertir que tout soit arrangé et que j'arriverai __7__ vingt.

5. **(A)** auriez
   (B) ayez
   (C) aurez
   (D) aviez

6. **(A)** lui
   (B) elle
   (C) vous
   (D) la

7. **(A)** le
   (B) au
   (C) sur le
   (D) dans le

5. Expressions such as *quand* and *dès que* are followed by the future in French when the verb in the main clause is in the present tense, as it is here with the present imperative *donnez*. The correct answer is (C) *aurez*, the future tense of the verb *avoir*. Choice (A) *auriez* is the conditional, (B) *ayez* is the present subjunctive, and (D) *aviez* is the imperfect.

6. What is missing in this part of the sentence is an indirect object pronoun that refers back to *elle* (in *avec elle*). The indirect object indicates the person to whom the *coup de téléphone* should be given. The correct pronoun form is (A) *lui*. (B) *elle* is not correct because it is used for the subject of a sentence or after a preposition, (C) *vous* is incorrect because something should be given to the woman designated by *elle*, not the person spoken to, and (D) *la* is incorrect because it is the direct object pronoun, not the indirect object pronoun.

7. When giving arrival and departure dates in French (the sentence here provides an arrival date), the date is preceded by *le* without a preposition. Choice (A) *le* is the correct answer. The other suggested answers contain prepositions and are therefore incorrect.

Part D

Directions: Read the following selections carefully for comprehension. Each selection is followed by a number of questions or incomplete statements. Select the completion or answer that is best according to the selection and fill in the corresponding oval on the answer sheet.

«Image Center» est l'histoire d'une passion. Hésitant entre

l'art et la science, Sylvie Magnus, 24 ans, passe deux ans à

l'Ecole des Beaux Arts et complète sa formation à Londres,

Ligne où elle apprend les applications de l'informatique sur

(5) l'image. Et c'est le déclic, peindre avec la lumière, créer

des décors magiques pour des défilés de mode, ou des

effets spéciaux pour le cinéma, tout la fascine. Une étude

de marché lui apprend qu'il n'existe pas d'agence

spécialisée dans la conception de ces images. Sylvie décide

(10) donc de combler l'espace: elle crée, grâce à un prêt

de famille et à des subventions, la première agence

européenne conseil en image de synthèse: «Image Center».

8. Qu'est-ce que Sylvie Magnus a étudié après ses deux ans à l'Ecole des Beaux Arts?

    (A) Les arts décoratifs
    (B) La cinématographie
    (C) Les nouvelles technologies
    (D) La médicine

The text tells you that Sylvie Magnus studied computer graphics after finishing her fine arts education (*Sylvie Magnus passe deux ans à l'Ecole des Beaux Arts et complète sa formation à Londres, où elle apprend les applications de l'informatique sur l'image*, lines 2–5). The correct answer is therefore (C) *les nouvelles technologies*. The other options are incorrect.

9. A la ligne 10, «combler l'espace» veut dire

    (A) répondre à un besoin

    (B) louer un bureau

    (C) faire des recherches scientifiques

    (D) faire des subventions

The text states that Sylvie Magnus has learned that there was no agency that specialized in computer graphics and decided to create one. The correct answer is (A) *répondre à un besoin*, "respond to a need." The expression does not mean that she rented an office (B), did scientific research (C), or subsidized anything (D). On the contrary, she received a subsidy (line 11).

10. Comment est-ce que Sylvie Magnus a trouvé l'argent pour lancer «Image Center»?

    (A) Elle a travaillé dans un hôpital.

    (B) Elle en a gagné pendant la révolution.

    (C) Elle a organisé des défilés de mode.

    (D) Elle en a emprunté à ses parents.

The text tells you that *grâce à un prêt de famille* (lines 10–11) Sylvie Magnus was able to create her agency. The correct answer is (D) *Elle en a emprunté à ses parents*. She did not obtain the money by working in a hospital (A), earning it during a revolution (B), or organizing fashion shows (C).

Sondage

Vous, amateurs de télé—

Question 1

Utilisez-vous personnellement une télécommande?

Question 2

Vous-même, quand vous utilisez cette télécommande, vous vous en servez pour: couper le son et faire autre chose? changer de chaîne dès que le programme ne vous plaît pas? suivre plusieurs émissions en même temps? chercher une émission particulière? éviter la publicité? rechercher la publicité?

Résultats:	**en %**
Proportion des Français âgés de 15 ans et plus	
Question 1: qui utilisent personnellement une télécommande	*46*
Question 2: qui s'en servent pour	
—couper le son pour faire autre chose	26
—changer de chaîne dès que le programme ne leur plaît pas	43
—suivre plusieurs émissions en même temps	12
—chercher une émission particulière	31
—éviter la publicité	23
—rechercher la publicité	2

11. Qu'est-ce qu'une télécommande?

    (A) Une sorte de téléviseur

    (B) Une émission de télévision

    (C) Une sorte de publicité

    (D) Un appareil électronique

What a *télécommande* is must be inferred because it is not stated directly in the survey. The text tells you that, among other things, a *télécommande* can be used to change television channels and to cut the sound of a program. It is a remote control and (D) *Un appareil électronique* is the correct answer. It is not a kind of television set (A), nor a television program (B), nor publicity (C).

12. Selon ce sondage, on se sert le plus souvent d'une télécommande pour

    (A) acheter quelque chose

    (B) trouver une émission plus intéressante

    (C) pouvoir regarder deux émissions à la fois

    (D) vérifier le bon fonctionnement de son téléviseur

This question asks you what the remote control is most frequently used for, according to the survey results. You must select the use in the chart that was selected by the most respondents and has the highest percentage. This use is *changer de chaîne dès que le programme ne leur plaît pas*, or "change the channel as soon as they no longer like the program." Choice (B) *trouver une émission plus intéressante* ("find a more interesting program") is the correct answer. The other options were selected by a lower percentage of respondents.

French Test

The test that follows is an actual, recently administered SAT Subject Test in French. To get an idea of what a real administration is like, take the test under conditions as close as possible to those of a national administration:

- Set aside an hour when you can take the test uninterrupted. Make sure you complete the test in one sitting.

- Sit at a desk or table with no other books or papers. Dictionaries, other books, or notes are not allowed in the test room.

- Time yourself by placing a clock or kitchen timer in front of you.

- Tear out an answer sheet from the back of this book and fill it in just as you would on the day of the test. One answer sheet can be used for up to three Subject Tests.

- Read the instructions that precede the practice test. During the actual administration you will be asked to read them before answering test questions.

- After you finish the practice test, read the sections "How to Score the SAT Subject Test in French" and "Reviewing Your Performance on the French Subject Test."

- Actual test and answer sheets will indicate circles, not ovals.

Form 3RAC

FRENCH TEST

The top portion of the section of the answer sheet that you will use in taking the French test must be filled in exactly as shown in the illustration below. Note carefully that you have to do all of the following on your answer sheet.

1. Print FRENCH on the line under the words "Subject Test (print)."

2. In the shaded box labeled "Test Code" fill in four ovals:

   —Fill in oval 3 in the row labeled V.

   —Fill in oval 3 in the row labeled W.

   —Fill in oval 1 in the row labeled X.

   —Fill in oval B in the row labeled Y.

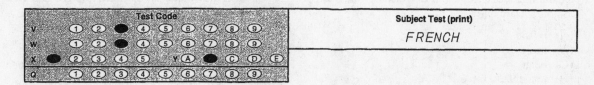

Please answer either Part I or Part II by filling in the specific oval in row Q. You are to fill in ONE and ONLY ONE oval as described below, to indicate how you obtained your knowledge of French. The information you provide is for statistical purposes only and will not influence your score on the test.

Part I   If your knowledge of French does not come primarily from courses taken in grades 9 through 12, fill in oval 9 and leave the remaining ovals blank, regardless of how long you studied the subject in school. For example, you are to fill in oval 9 if your knowledge of French comes primarily from any of the following sources: study prior to the ninth grade, courses taken at a college, or special study, living in a home in which French is the principal language spoken, or extensive residence abroad that includes significant experience in the French language.

Part II   If your knowledge of French does come primarily from courses taken in secondary school, fill in the oval that indicates the level of the French course in which you are currently enrolled. If you are not now enrolled in a French course, fill in the oval that indicates the level of the most advanced course in French that you have completed.

First year:	first or second half	—Fill in oval 1.
Second year:	first half	—Fill in oval 2.
	second half	—Fill in oval 3.
Third year:	first half	—Fill in oval 4.
	second half	—Fill in oval 5.
Fourth year:	first half	—Fill in oval 6.
	second half	—Fill in oval 7.
Advanced Placement course or a course at a level higher than fourth year, second half or high school course work plus a minimum of four weeks of study abroad		—Fill in oval 8.

When the supervisor gives the signal, turn the page and begin the French test. There are 100 numbered ovals on the answer sheet and 85 questions in the French test. Therefore, use only ovals 1 to 85 for recording your answers.

FRENCH TEST

PLEASE NOTE THAT YOUR ANSWER SHEET HAS FIVE ANSWER POSITIONS, MARKED A, B, C, D, E, WHILE THE QUESTIONS THROUGHOUT THIS TEST CONTAIN ONLY FOUR CHOICES. BE SURE <u>NOT</u> TO MAKE ANY MARKS IN COLUMN E.

Part A

<u>Directions:</u> This part consists of a number of incomplete statements, each having four suggested completions. Select the most appropriate completion and fill in the corresponding oval on the answer sheet.

---

1. Quand mes deux frères ont une discussion, c'est toujours Marc qui a . . .

    (A) raison
    (B) droit
    (C) beau
    (D) tendance

2. Il ne peut pas jouer au tennis aujourd'hui parce qu'il a mal au . . .

    (A) manche
    (B) bras
    (C) col
    (D) droit

3. Pour devenir chauffeur de taxi, on doit passer un examen de . . .

    (A) chauffage
    (B) génie
    (C) conduite
    (D) fin d'études

4. Je pars ce soir en voyage. Il faut que je fasse ma . . .

    (A) valeur
    (B) vérité
    (C) venue
    (D) valise

5. Pour ne plus avoir de . . . dans sa chambre, Julie a décidé de ranger ses affaires.

    (A) messe
    (B) désordre
    (C) salopettes
    (D) place

6. Quel est ce mot-là? Je n'arrive pas à déchiffrer votre . . .

    (A) stylo
    (B) écriture
    (C) lecture
    (D) pupitre

7. Ma soeur a eu de la peine à lire la carte sans ses . . .

    (A) spectacles
    (B) jumeaux
    (C) lunettes
    (D) glaces

8. Claude s'est . . . en passant trop près du feu.

    (A) brûlé
    (B) rafraîchi
    (C) gelé
    (D) mouillé

9. Le matin, j'allais . . . des fleurs pour en remplir les vases du salon.

    (A) peindre
    (B) admirer
    (C) cueillir
    (D) écraser

10. Au fond de la baie, les lumières du port . . . comme une couronne de diamants.

    (A) étincelaient
    (B) nageaient
    (C) voyageaient
    (D) pêchaient

3RAC

GO ON TO THE NEXT PAGE →

11. Marie-Claire achètera des cahiers à la . . .

  (A) blanchisserie
  (B) papeterie
  (C) charcuterie
  (D) bibliothèque

12. Il est très gentil, ce chien. Vous n'avez rien à . . .

  (A) oublier
  (B) craindre
  (C) garder
  (D) laisser

13. Ne sachant quel métier choisir, j'ai demandé . . . de ma mère.

  (A) l'envie
  (B) l'âme
  (C) l'avis
  (D) l'esprit

14. Lucienne ne m'a pas écrit. As-tu reçu de ses . . . ?

  (A) nouvelles
  (B) environs
  (C) rumeurs
  (D) courants

15. Tout à coup, dans le silence nocturne, un coup de tonnerre . . .

  (A) rentra
  (B) éternua
  (C) s'écria
  (D) éclata

16. Nicole s'est probablement couchée, puisque la lumière de la chambre est . . .

  (A) éteinte
  (B) brûlée
  (C) atteinte
  (D) brouillée

17. J'ai couru si vite que je suis arrivée chez toi tout . . .

  (A) épatée
  (B) essoufflée
  (C) égarée
  (D) emmêlée

18. Après avoir fini ses devoirs, Jeanne a poussé . . . de soulagement.

  (A) un soupir
  (B) un orage
  (C) une expression
  (D) une crise

19. La plage n'offrait aucun abri; il a . . . un trou dans le sable et s'y est couché.

  (A) croisé
  (B) creusé
  (C) foncé
  (D) fondé

20. Mes parents veulent que je fasse . . . d'un mois dans une entreprise française.

  (A) une course
  (B) un emploi
  (C) un stage
  (D) un temps

GO ON TO THE NEXT PAGE

Part B

Directions: Each of the following sentences contains a blank. From the four choices given, select the one that can be inserted in the blank to form a grammatically correct sentence and fill in the corresponding oval on the answer sheet. Choice (A) may consist of dashes that indicate that no insertion is required to form a grammatically correct sentence.

21. Il nous a parlé ------- ses longues années d'expérience dans l'enseignement.

    (A) de
    (B) en
    (C) vers
    (D) à

22. L'enfant ------- tellement qu'il n'a pas vu que ses parents étaient arrivés.

    (A) ayant pleuré
    (B) pleurerait
    (C) pleurait
    (D) aura pleuré

23. Vincent a peint ce portrait pour -------.

    (A) me
    (B) tu
    (C) les
    (D) elles

24. ------- est passé te voir hier soir, à l'heure du dîner?

    (A) Qu'est-ce qui
    (B) Qui
    (C) Laquelle
    (D) Qu'

25. Remplis les verres ------- eau, s'il te plaît.

    (A) d'
    (B) avec
    (C) en
    (D) l'

26. Elle est sortie ------- avoir entendu du bruit.

    (A) à
    (B) après
    (C) près d'
    (D) en

27. Il n'a répondu qu'en ------- mots.

    (A) peu
    (B) moins
    (C) quelques
    (D) aucun

28. L'avocate a ------- de plaider devant le juge.

    (A) fini
    (B) parti
    (C) venu
    (D) rentré

29. Je voulais voir les tableaux modernes avant de ------- le musée.

    (A) quitter
    (B) quittais
    (C) quitté
    (D) quittant

30. Il ne veut pas acheter ce pantalon ------- il lui aille très bien.

    (A) bien qu'
    (B) parce qu'
    (C) puisqu'
    (D) lorsqu'

GO ON TO THE NEXT PAGE

31. Je lui ai ------- parlé de mon séjour au Québec.

    (A) hier
    (B) souvent
    (C) après
    (D) là-bas

32. Il écrit moins ------- que moi.

    (A) rapide
    (B) beau
    (C) mauvais
    (D) bien

33. Jean-Pierre a choisi un sujet de thèse ------- aucun expert n'avait pensé.

    (A) ---
    (B) duquel
    (C) auquel
    (D) qu'

34. Est-ce que ton oncle Hans est déjà arrivé ------- Danemark?

    (A) du
    (B) de
    (C) à
    (D) en

GO ON TO THE NEXT PAGE

Part C

Directions: The paragraphs below contain blank spaces indicating omissions in the text. For some blanks, it is necessary to choose the completion that is most appropriate to the meaning of the passage; for other blanks, to choose the one completion that forms a grammatically correct sentence. In some instances, choice (A) may consist of dashes that indicate that no insertion is required to form a grammatically correct sentence. In each case, indicate you answer by filling in the corresponding oval on the answer sheet. Be sure to read the paragraph completely before answering the questions related to it.

Tous les mercredis, nous allions au marché dans une carriole à deux roues ------- par la petite ânesse Eglantine.

35. (A) chauffée
    (B) entraînée
    (C) conduite
    (D) tirée

L'été, Eglantine, ------- de son élégance et de son importance, portait un chapeau de paille fleuri noué sous le -------

36. (A) fatiguée
    (B) fière
    (C) reconnaissante
    (D) inquiète

37. (A) men‹
    (B) pied
    (C) geno
    (D) vent‹

muni de ------- pour ses longues oreilles. Quoi qu'on -------, elle n'hésitait ------- à s'arrêter au bord de la ------- si

38. (A) boucles
    (B) trous
    (C) gants
    (D) noeuds

39. (A) dise
    (B) disait
    (C) a dit
    (D) avait dit

40. (A) rien
    (B) encore
    (C) jamais
    (D) souvent

41. (A) maison
    (B) pelouse
    (C) paille
    (D) route

l'herbe lui paraissait tentante, pour ne repartir que quand elle ------- avait envie. Mais qu'un cheval ou un âne qui

42. (A) y
    (B) l'
    (C) lui
    (D) en

cheminait ------- nous tente de passer, Eglantine partait à un galop effréné qui nous ------- et menaçait de nous jeter

43. (A) derrière
    (B) contre
    (C) avant
    (D) entre

44. (A) secouait
    (B) balançait
    (C) berçait
    (D) soulageait

à bas.

GO ON TO THE NEXT PAGE

Cher client:

Le mois -------, nous vous avons adressé le catalogue de notre maison. ------- pas reçu de réponse, nous supposons

45. (A) tardif
    (B) dernier
    (C) proche
    (D) accordé

46. (A) N'ayant
    (B) N'ayons
    (C) N'avons
    (D) N'avoir

qu'il s'est ------- ou qu'il ------- a pas été remis. Nous joignons ------- un autre exemplaire à cette lettre en nous

47. (A) passé
    (B) laissé
    (C) égaré
    (D) promis

48. (A) ne vous
    (B) ne leur
    (C) n'en
    (D) ne lui

49. (A) si
    (B) combien
    (C) plus
    (D) donc

------- d'attirer votre attention sur les marques de nos machines et sur les facilités de paiement que nous accordons

50. (A) permettre
    (B) permettons
    (C) permettant
    (D) permettions

actuellement.

Trois enfants marchent ------- la plage. Ils s'avancent côte ------- côte, se tenant par la main. Ils ont à peu près la

51. (A) au loin
    (B) le long de
    (C) de travers
    (D) au niveau

52. (A) en
    (B) par
    (C) à
    (D) de

même -------, et sans doute aussi le même âge: une douzaine -------. Celui -------, cependant, est un peu plus petit

53. (A) taille
    (B) grosseur
    (C) pointure
    (D) largesse

54. (A) années
    (B) les années
    (C) des années
    (D) d'années

55. (A) du midi
    (B) de la moitié
    (C) du milieu
    (D) de la moyenne

------- les deux autres. Hormis ces trois enfants, toute la longue plage est déserte.

56. (A) que
    (B) ainsi
    (C) pareil
    (D) quoi

GO ON TO THE NEXT PAGE

Part D

Directions: Read the following texts carefully for comprehension. Each is followed by a number of questions or incomplete statements. Select the answer or completion that is best according to the text and fill in the corresponding oval on the answer sheet.

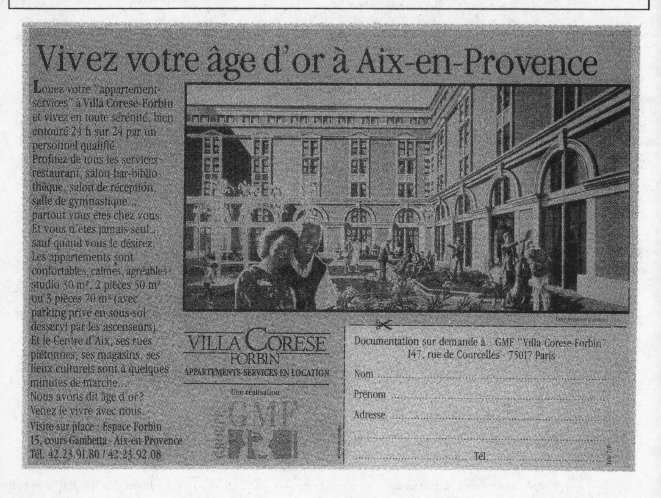

57. Cette publicité s'adresse surtout à des

 (A) familles nombreuses
 (B) personnes âgées
 (C) malades
 (D) artistes

58. On mentionne toutes les caractéristiques suivantes de la vie à Villa Corese-Forbin SAUF

 (A) son confort
 (B) sa situation
 (C) sa tranquillité
 (D) son prix

GO ON TO THE NEXT PAGE

QUESTION — Et que pensez-vous du «salaire maternel» pour les femmes qui restent chez elles avec leurs petits enfants? Il paraît quelque peu utopique. Croyez-vous que ce soit une solution possible?

RÉPONSE DE MME SIMONE VEIL — Non, je suis contre le «salaire maternel». Il exigerait des dépenses énormes et nos ressources sont restreintes. Etant donné la crise économique actuelle, il faut tenir compte des priorités. Nous devons nous occuper des retraités, des malades, et des handicapés. Nous devons penser aussi à l'avenir de ces femmes auxquelles aurait été accordé un «salaire maternel» pendant quelques années. Une fois leurs enfants grandis, et si elles ont à faire face à la solitude par veuvage ou divorce, ces femmes n'atteindraient sans formation professionnelle que des situations très modestes. Elles ne trouveraient pas de postes qui mèneraient à la possibilité d'avancement.

59. D'après le passage, quand on parle du «salaire maternel» on pense aux femmes qui

(A) sont malades ou handicapées
(B) ont reçu une formation professionnelle
(C) ont perdu leur mari
(D) ont des enfants

60. D'après le texte, une conséquence du salaire maternel est que la femme qui le reçoit risque plus tard de

(A) connaître le chômage
(B) n'obtenir qu'une situation inférieure
(C) devenir veuve
(D) souffrir de la solitude

61. Laquelle des phrases suivantes résume la pensée de Mme Veil?

(A) Les femmes devraient avoir la possibilité d'avancement professionnel.
(B) Le gouvernement ne donne pas assez d'argent aux femmes.
(C) La crise économique actuelle est causée par l'excès de naissances.
(D) L'aide aux femmes va provoquer la prochaine crise économique.

GO ON TO THE NEXT PAGE

Un bon tour

Un train est sur le point de partir. Les compartiments sont bondés. Un voyageur cherche vainement une place. Enfin il croit trouver un coin où se caser:

Ligne
(5) — Pardon, Monsieur, fait un grand homme, confortablement installé, la place est prise. Elle est à mon ami.

Et il montre du doigt une serviette de cuir noir qui, en effet, occupe la place.

Les autres voyageurs rient sous cape. Ils savent bien
(10) que le grand homme dit un mensonge.

Le chef de train donne le signal du départ.

— Diable! Votre ami devrait se dépêcher, dit le voyageur.

Le grand homme veut faire bonne mine à mauvais jeu.
(15) Il prend un air inquiet. Est-ce que son ami manquerait le train? Le convoi se met en marche. Ça y est, l'ami a manqué le train!

— Ah! Ma foi tant pis, fit le voyageur. Du moins il ne perdra pas sa serviette.
(20) Et il saisit l'objet, le lance par la fenêtre sur le quai, au grand ahurissement du propriétaire, le grand homme, honteux comme un renard qu'une poule aurait pris.

62. Le grand homme parle au voyageur qui arrive pour lui dire

 (A) que la place n'est pas libre
 (B) qu'il a trouvé une serviette de cuir
 (C) qu'il n'a pas de nouvelles de son ami
 (D) que c'est l'heure du départ

63. Que fait le grand homme dans le train?

 (A) Il cherche le compartiment.
 (B) Il reste assis.
 (C) Il descend du wagon.
 (D) Il s'éloigne des autres passagers.

64. Le grand homme répond au voyageur en

 (A) riant
 (B) se levant
 (C) se dépêchant
 (D) mentant

65. La phrase "Les autres voyageurs rient sous cape" à la ligne 9 signifie que les passagers rient

 (A) aux éclats
 (B) discrètement
 (C) de bon coeur
 (D) vainement

66. Qu'est-ce que le voyageur fait avec la serviette de cuir?

 (A) Il en découvre le contenu.
 (B) Il la jette dehors.
 (C) Il la laisse tomber par terre.
 (D) Il la cache sous la banquette.

67. Le titre de ce texte ("Un bon tour") évoque

 (A) un manège
 (B) un monument
 (C) une plaisanterie
 (D) un tour de force

GO ON TO THE NEXT PAGE

On parle toujours de la guerre de Troie parce qu'Homère l'a rendue célèbre dans *l'Iliade* et *l'Odyssée*. En réalité, elle n'était qu'un épisode de l'histoire de la Grèce. On a la
(5) certitude, maintenant, que la période la plus étonnante de la civilisation hellénique remonte aux XIVᵉ et XIIIᵉ siècles avant notre ère. A la fin du XIXᵉ siècle, les fouilles entreprises par l'Allemand Schliemann firent apparaître des
(10) vestiges importants de la civilisation grecque. Mais les textes historiques manquaient, et ce n'est qu'à partir de 1953, grâce au jeune savant anglais Michael Ventris, que l'on parvint à déchiffrer les tablettes et les inscriptions
(15) trouvées sur les vases.

Sur un sol difficile, balayé de tempêtes, les Grecs s'unirent, sous l'autorité d'un roi, pour s'enrichir par la conquête. Le roi décidait des guerres, commandait les chars, les cuirassés et
(20) les chevaux, attelés mais jamais montés. Il percevait les impôts en nature, métaux précieux ou vulgaires, étoffes, vivres. Les guerriers formaient l'aristocratie. Les artisans étaient prospères. L'élevage, le commerce des vins et
(25) des huiles parfumées enrichissaient les classes dirigeantes.

Toute civilisation, si brillante soit-elle, a son déclin. La Grèce ne fit pas exception, mais l'histoire de son passé prestigieux demeure, et n'est-ce pas la plus brillante des victoires?

68. D'après ce texte, il est évident que le mot "fouilles" à la ligne 8 se rapporte à la

   (A) visite de musées
   (B) construction de modèles de sites anciens
   (C) découverte d'objets anciens
   (D) reconstitution de langues disparues

69. La richesse des Grecs provenait

   (A) des fouilles
   (B) des conquêtes
   (C) de l'agriculture
   (D) de la pêche

70. On apprend qu'à l'époque en question les Grecs

   (A) étaient surtout des commerçants
   (B) ne connaissaient presque pas la guerre
   (C) ne montaient jamais à cheval
   (D) ne payaient pas d'impôts

71. Dans ce passage, il est évident que la guerre de Troie

   (A) est une guerre inventée par Homère
   (B) n'a aucune importance dans l'histoire grecque
   (C) n'est qu'un événement parmi d'autres dans une riche histoire
   (D) reste toujours incompréhensible pour l'homme moderne

72. C'est à partir de 1953 que l'on a réussi à

   (A) trouver des vestiges de la civilisation grecque
   (B) comprendre les cahiers historiques
   (C) démêler les secrets inscrits sur les objets antiques
   (D) mieux connaître la vie des empereurs

GO ON TO THE NEXT PAGE

IMPORTANT GROUPE INDRE
C.A. DE + 1 MILLIARD DE FRANCS

recherche

COMPTABLE

– **Formation supérieure type BTS, DECS.**

– **Professionnel performant.**

– **Expérience 5 ans minimum.**

Chargé de la comptabilité générale, des bilans, des déclarations fiscales.

Pratique de la comptabilité analytique et consolidation, souhaitée.

*Adresser CV + lettre manuscrite et prétentions à **AGENCE HAVAS**, BP 119, 36002 Châteauroux Cedex, sous réf. 4911, qui transmettra.*

---

73. Dans cette annonce publicitaire, qu'est-ce que la personne cherchée doit savoir faire?

   (A) Bien calculer
   (B) Comprendre les gens
   (C) Faire des discours
   (D) Ecrire clairement

74. Pour répondre à cette annonce, quel document faudra-t-il envoyer avec le curriculum vitae?

   (A) Une lettre de référence
   (B) Une demande d'inscription
   (C) Une lettre écrite à la main
   (D) Une déclaration d'impôts

GO ON TO THE NEXT PAGE ➤

On avait posé la lanterne tout près de ma tête — une de ces lanternes d'écurie, au pétrole, qui donnent plus de fumée que de lumière. J'ai essayé de me lever, sans
gne y réussir, mais je ne souffrais plus. Enfin, je me suis
(5) trouvé assis. De l'autre côté de la haie j'entendais geindre et souffler les bestiaux. Je me rendais parfaitement compte que même au cas où je parviendrais à me mettre debout, il était trop tard pour fuir, il ne me restait plus qu'à supporter patiemment la
10) curiosité de celui qui m'avait découvert, qui reviendrait bientôt chercher sa lanterne. J'ai pu me relever sur les genoux, et nous nous sommes trouvés brusquement face à face. J'avais reconnu Séraphita. Je lui ai souri. Je me suis aperçu alors qu'elle tenait à la main un seau rempli
15) d'eau, où nageait une espèce de chiffon, pas trop propre. "Une chance que je vous ai trouvé. En poursuivant les bêtes, mon sabot a roulé dans le chemin, je suis descendue, je vous croyais mort." — "Je vais mieux, je vais me lever." — "Vous tremblez trop,
20) m'a-t-elle dit, laissez-moi, j'ai l'habitude, oh là là!" Tout en parlant, elle me passait son chiffon sur le front, les joues. L'eau fraîche me faisait du bien, je me suis levé, mais je tremblais toujours aussi fort. Enfin ce frisson a cessé. Ma petite Samaritaine levait sa lanterne
25) à la hauteur de mon menton, pour mieux juger de son travail, je suppose. — "Si vous voulez, je vous accompagnerai jusqu'au bout du chemin. Prenez garde aux trous." Elle s'est rangée à mon côté, et quelques pas plus loin a mis sa main dans la mienne, sagement. Nous ne parlions ni l'un ni l'autre.

75. Le narrateur ne se lève pas parce qu'il

(A) souffre trop
(B) est endormi
(C) a peur des vaches
(D) est sans force

76. Qui a laissé la lanterne près du narrateur?

(A) Une inconnue
(B) Un chasseur
(C) Une fermière
(D) Un pasteur

77. Ce que dit la personne qui a trouvé le narrateur (lignes 16-18) indique

(A) qu'elle a perdu sa lanterne
(B) qu'elle l'a découvert par hasard
(C) qu'elle s'était égarée elle-même
(D) qu'elle cherchait de l'eau depuis longtemps

78. Quelle est la réaction du narrateur quand il voit la personne qui l'a trouvé?

(A) Il veut s'enfuir.
(B) Il commence à crier.
(C) Il est plutôt content.
(D) Il tombe à genoux.

79. Que fait la personne qui a trouvé le narrateur?

(A) Elle lui mouille le visage.
(B) Elle lui propose un chiffon.
(C) Elle lui donne à boire.
(D) Elle lui offre ses sabots.

80. Comment le narrateur réagit-il finalement après les soins qu'il a reçus?

(A) Il cesse de trembler.
(B) Il hausse son menton.
(C) Il laisse tomber le chiffon.
(D) Il remplit le seau d'eau.

81. Qu'est-ce que la fin de ce passage indique à propos du narrateur?

(A) Il ne sait pas où aller.
(B) Il aime bien faire des promenades.
(C) Il se méfie de son compagnon.
(D) Il se sent remis.

GO ON TO THE NEXT PAGE

Le ciel courroucé contre la France semblait avoir annoncé la date sanglante de la Révolution française par un orage effroyable arrivé juste un an auparavant. Le

Ligne dimanche 13 juillet 1788, le roi Louis XVI, revenant de
(5) Rambouillet où il avait couché, fut assailli d'une grêle épouvantable comme on n'en voit presque jamais. Le château royal de Rambouillet, situé à sept lieues de Versailles et sur la route de cette ville, a vu mourir François Ier en 1547. Sa situation était très agréable
(10) pour la chasse. Aussi, pendant quatre mois de l'année, Louis XVI y allait deux fois par semaine et n'en revenait qu'après avoir soupé, c'est-à-dire à quatre heures du matin. Ce jour-là tout le cortège fut obligé de se réfugier sous des hangars au village de Trappes, mais
(15) pas assez tôt pour que plusieurs cavaliers ne fussent blessés. Les campagnes étaient couvertes d'arbres renversés, d'oiseaux et de gibier écrasés. Je ne dirai pas le poids de plusieurs de ces glaçons ramassés longtemps après l'orage: on ne me croirait peut-être pas. Les
(20) moissons furent détruites, mais tous ces maux réunis ne pouvaient se comparer à ceux que Dieu nous réservait dans sa colère. C'était sur la terre qu'il voulait prendre les instruments de sa vengeance.

82. Le roi Louis XVI était à Rambouillet pour

(A) déjeuner
(B) prier
(C) mourir
(D) chasser

83. Quel événement est préfiguré dans cet extrait?

(A) Un bouleversement politique
(B) Les vacances du roi
(C) Un hiver rigoureux
(D) La mort de François Ier

84. Qu'est-ce qui a causé les dommages les plus sévères?

(A) La neige
(B) Le vent
(C) La grêle
(D) La pluie

85. On croyait que Dieu se vengeait contre

(A) les fermiers
(B) les cavaliers
(C) les animaux
(D) le pays

S T O P

IF YOU FINISH BEFORE TIME IS CALLED, YOU MAY CHECK YOUR WORK ON THIS TEST ONLY.
DO NOT TURN TO ANY OTHER TEST IN THIS BOOK.

How to Score the SAT Subject Test in French

When you take an actual SAT Subject Test in French, your answer sheet will be "read" by a scanning machine that will record your responses to each question. Then a computer will compare your answers with the correct answers and produce your raw score. You get one point for each correct answer. For each wrong answer, you lose one-third of a point. Questions you omit (and any for which you mark more than one answer) are not counted. This raw score is converted to a scaled score that is reported to you and to the colleges you specify.

Worksheet 1. Finding Your Raw Test Score

STEP 1: Table A lists the correct answers for all the questions on the SAT Subject Test in French that is reproduced in this book. It also serves as a worksheet for you to calculate your raw score.

- Compare your answers with those given in the table.
- Put a check in the column marked "Right" if your answer is correct.
- Put a check in the column marked "Wrong" if your answer is incorrect.
- Leave both columns blank if you omitted the question.

STEP 2: Count the number of right answers.

Enter the total here: _____

STEP 3: Count the number of wrong answers.

Enter the total here: _____

STEP 4: Multiply the number of wrong answers by .333.

Enter the product here: _____

STEP 5: Subtract the result obtained in Step 4 from the total you obtained in Step 2.

Enter the result here: _____

STEP 6: Round the number obtained in Step 5 to the nearest whole number.

Enter the result here: _____

The number you obtained in Step 6 is your raw score.

TABLE A
Answers to the SAT Subject Test in French, Form 3RAC, and Percentage of Students Answering Each Question Correctly

Question Number	Correct Answer	Right	Wrong	Percentage of Students Answering the Question Correctly*	Question Number	Correct Answer	Right	Wrong	Percentage of Students Answering the Question Correctly*
1	A			93	33	C			18
2	B			90	34	A			13
3	C			90	35	D			22
4	D			89	36	B			45
5	B			83	37	A			52
6	B			82	38	B			17
7	C			81	39	A			17
8	A			68	40	C			79
9	C			71	41	D			57
10	A			74	42	D			33
11	B			70	43	A			37
12	B			59	44	A			15
13	C			66	45	B			88
14	A			60	46	A			34
15	D			45	47	C			25
16	A			56	48	A			50
17	B			43	49	D			43
18	A			21	50	C			20
19	B			22	51	B			56
20	C			10	52	C			67
21	A			78	53	A			60
22	C			69	54	D			37
23	D			80	55	C			46
24	B			51	56	A			84
25	A			69	57	B			88
26	B			74	58	D			75
27	C			57	59	D			73
28	A			69	60	B			38
29	A			68	61	A			41
30	A			24	62	A			69
31	B			62	63	B			53
32	D			23	64	D			49

Table A continued on next page

Table A continued from previous page

Question Number	Correct Answer	Right	Wrong	Percentage of Students Answering the Question Correctly*	Question Number	Correct Answer	Right	Wrong	Percentage of Students Answering the Question Correctly*
65	B			63	76	C			28
66	B			57	77	B			57
67	C			61	78	C			52
68	C			57	79	A			20
69	B			63	80	A			51
70	C			17	81	D			26
71	C			39	82	D			54
72	C			55	83	A			26
73	A			67	84	C			44
74	C			31	85	D			53
75	D			47					

*These percentages are based on an analysis of the answer sheets for a random sample of 3,248 students who took this form of the test in December 1995 and whose mean score was 562. They may be used as an indication of the relative difficulty of a particular question. Each percentage may also be used to predict the likelihood that a typical SAT Subject Test in French candidate will answer correctly that question on this edition of this test.

Finding Your Scaled Score

When you take SAT Subject Tests, the scores sent to the colleges you specify are reported on the College Board scale, which ranges from 200 to 800. You can convert your practice test score to a scaled score by using Table B. To find your scaled score, locate your raw score in the left-hand column of Table B; the corresponding score in the right-hand column is your scaled score. For example, a raw score of 65 on this particular edition of the SAT Subject Test in French corresponds to a scaled score of 730.

Raw scores are converted to scaled scores to ensure that a score earned on any one edition of a particular Subject Test is comparable to the same scaled score earned on any other edition of the same Subject Test. Because some editions of tests may be slightly easier or more difficult than others, scaled scores are adjusted so that they indicate the same level of performance regardless of the edition of the test taken and the ability of the group that takes it. Thus, for example, a score of 400 on one edition of a test taken at a particular administration indicates the same level of achievement as a score of 400 on a different edition of the test taken at a different administration.

When you take the SAT Subject Tests during a national administration, your scores are likely to differ somewhat from the scores you obtain on the tests in this book. People perform at different levels at different times for reasons unrelated to the tests themselves. The precision of any test is also limited because it represents only a sample of all the possible questions that could be asked.

TABLE B
Scaled Score Conversion Table
French Subject Test (Form 3RAC)

Raw Score	Scaled Score	Raw Score	Scaled Score	Raw Score	Scaled Score
85	800	47	630	9	440
84	800	46	620	8	430
83	800	45	620	7	430
82	800	44	610	6	420
81	800	43	610	5	410
80	800	42	600	4	410
79	800	41	600	3	400
78	800	40	590	2	400
77	800	39	590	1	390
76	800	38	580	0	380
75	800	37	580	-1	380
74	790	36	570	-2	370
73	780	35	570	-3	370
72	780	34	560	-4	360
71	770	33	560	-5	350
70	760	32	550	-6	350
69	760	31	550	-7	340
68	750	30	540	-8	340
67	740	29	540	-9	330
66	740	28	540	-10	330
65	730	27	530	-11	320
64	720	26	530	-12	310
63	720	25	520	-13	310
62	710	24	520	-14	300
61	710	23	510	-15	300
60	700	22	510	-16	290
59	700	21	500	-17	280
58	690	20	500	-18	280
57	680	19	490	-19	270
56	680	18	490	-20	270
55	670	17	480	-21	260
54	670	16	480	-22	250
53	660	15	470	-23	250
52	660	14	470	-24	240
51	650	13	460	-25	240
50	640	12	450	-26	230
49	640	11	450	-27	230
48	630	10	440	-28	220

Reviewing Your Performance on the French Subject Test

After you score your test, analyze your performance—consider the following questions:

Did you run out of time before reaching the end of the test?

If so, you may need to pace yourself better. For example, maybe you spent too much time on one or two hard questions. A better approach might be to skip the ones you can't answer right away and try answering all the questions that remain on the test. Then if there's time, go back to the questions you skipped.

Did you take a long time reading the directions?

You will save time when you take the test by learning the directions to the French Subject Test ahead of time. Each minute you spend reading directions during the test is a minute that you could use to answer questions.

How did you handle questions you were unsure of?

If you were able to eliminate one or more of the answer choices as wrong and guess from the remaining ones, your approach probably worked to your advantage. On the other hand, making haphazard guesses or omitting questions without trying to eliminate choices could cost you valuable points.

How difficult were the questions for you compared with other students who took the test?

Table A shows you how difficult the multiple-choice questions were for the group of students who took this test during its national administration. The right-hand column gives the percentage of students that answered each question correctly.

A question answered correctly by almost everyone in the group is obviously an easy question. For example, 88 percent of the students answered question 57 correctly. But only 17 percent answered question 70 correctly.

Keep in mind that these percentages are based on just one group of students. They would probably be different if another group of students took the test.

If you missed several easy questions, go back and try to find out why: Did the questions cover material you haven't reviewed yet? Did you misunderstand the directions?

French with Listening

French with Listening is offered once a year only at designated test centers. To take the test you MUST bring an acceptable cassette player with earphones to the test center.

A cassette tape with listening questions is available for the French Subject Test with Listening practice test in this book. To receive your copy, complete and mail the postcard in this book. If the postcard has been removed, call 212 649-8424 or write to:

The College Board

Subject Tests Language Listening Cassette

45 Columbus Avenue

New York, New York 10023-6992

You must indicate the SAT Language Subject Test with Listening you plan to take.

Sample Listening Questions

The following three types of questions appear on the French Test with Listening. All questions in this section of the test are multiple-choice questions in which you must choose the BEST response from three or four choices offered. Text in brackets [ ] is recorded on the cassette tape. Please note that the cassette does not start here. Begin using the cassette when you start the actual practice test on page 412.

Part A

Please note that your answer sheet has five answer positions marked A, B, C, D, E, while the questions throughout this part contain only four choices. Be sure NOT to make any marks in column E.

Directions: For each item in this part, you will hear four sentences designated (A), (B), (C), and (D). They will not be printed in your test book. As you listen, look at the picture in your test book and select the choice that best reflects what you see in the picture or what someone in the picture might say. Then fill in the corresponding oval on the answer sheet. You will hear the choices only once. Now look at the following example.

You see:

You hear:

[**(A)**   Quelle joie d'être seul!

  (B)   Que c'est agréable de faire du vélo!

  (C)   Le moteur fait trop de bruit!

  (D)   Nous adorons la course à pied.]

Statement (B), "Que c'est agréable de faire du vélo!" best reflects what you see in the picture or what someone in the picture might say. Therefore, you should choose answer (B).

1. You see:

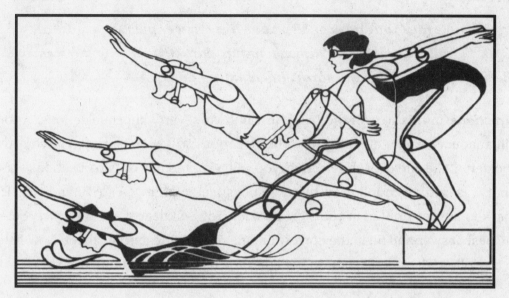

You hear:

[Numéro 1

(Woman)   **(A)**   Elle porte toujours un bonnet de bain.

             (B)   Elle a toujours peur de l'eau.

             (C)   Le ski nautique lui plaît beaucoup.

             (D)   Elle est en train de plonger dans l'eau.]

(7 seconds)

In question 1, you see a drawing that shows a slow motion scene of a girl diving into a pool. Answer (D) best reflects what can be seen in the picture and is therefore correct. Options (A), (B), and (C) are incorrect because the girl in the picture is not wearing a cap, does not seem to be afraid of water, and is not shown on water skis.

Part B

Please note that your answer sheet has five answer positions marked A, B, C, D, E, while the questions throughout this part contain only three choices. Be sure NOT to make any marks in column D or E.

Directions: In this part of the test you will hear several short selections. A tone will announce each new selection. The selections will not be printed in your test booklet. At the end of each selection, you will be asked one or two questions about what was said, each followed by three possible answers, (A), (B), and (C). The answers are not printed in your test booklet. You will hear them only *once*. Select the best answer and fill in the corresponding oval on the answer sheet. Now listen to the following example, but do not mark the answer on your answer sheet.

You hear:

   [(Tone)

   (Man B)   Papa, ta voiture est chez le garagiste.

   (Man A)   Mais pourquoi? Elle a toujours bien marché.

   (Man B)   Euh, en réalité, j'ai eu un accident.

   (Man A)   Quoi? Tu plaisantes, n'est-ce pas?

   (5 seconds)

   (Woman A)   Qu'est-ce qu'on peut dire de la voiture en question?

   (A) Elle est en réparation.

   (B) Elle est sur la route.

   (C) Elle est chez un ami.]

   (7 seconds)

The best answer to the question, "Qu'est-ce qu'on peut dire de la voiture en question?" is (A), "Elle est en réparation." Therefore, you should choose answer (A).

Questions 2–3

You hear:

[(Tone)

(Man) Votre passeport, madame.

(Woman) Voilà.

(Man) Et qu'est-ce que vous ferez au Canada?

(Woman) Je vais passer les vacances avec ma famille.

(Man) Très bien, madame. Je vous souhaite un bon séjour.]

(5 seconds)

2. [Numéro 2

(Man) Qui parle à cette femme?

(A) Un professeur.

(B) Un douanier.

(C) Un chauffeur.]

(7 seconds)

In question 2, you choose the person who is talking to the woman in the dialogue. The correct answer is (B) *Un douanier* because the woman is crossing the border into Canada. *Un professeur* or *un chauffeur* would not ask to see the woman's passport. Therefore, (A) and (C) are incorrect.

3. [Numéro 3

(Man) Qu'est-ce que la femme va faire?

(A) Obtenir un passeport.

(B) Chercher sa famille.

(C) Entrer au Canada.]

(7 seconds)

Question 3 asks what the woman is about to do. The correct answer is (C), which is the only logical answer according to the dialogue. After crossing the border, the woman will enter Canada. Choice (A) is incorrect because she already has a passport, and (B) is incorrect because she is vacationing with her family, not looking for them.

Part C

Please note that your answer sheet has five answer positions marked A, B, C, D, E, while the questions throughout this part contain only four choices. Be sure NOT to make any marks in column E.

Directions: You will now hear some extended dialogues or monologues. You will hear each only *once*. After each dialogue or monologue, you will be asked several questions about what you have just heard. These questions are also printed in your test book. Select the best answer to each question from among the four choices printed in your test book and fill in the corresponding oval on the answer sheet. There is no sample question for this part.

Questions 4–6

(Man)	[Dialogue numéro 1. Marie-Hélène et son amie Maude parlent de cinéma et de littérature.
(Woman A)	Tiens, Marie-Hélène, tu as acheté *Danse avec les loups* en anglais?
(Woman B)	Oui, j'ai acheté ce livre à Boston. Je me suis dit que c'était, euh, d'abord je n'avais pas vu le film et avant de voir le film j'avais vraiment envie de lire le livre; c'est tout. Et puis, tu sais, Maude, finalement je n'ai pas pu le lire, je n'ai pas eu le temps.
(Woman A)	Il faudra te dépêcher de le lire parce que le film est encore sur les écrans mais je ne sais pas combien de temps il va y rester. Il a beaucoup de succès, le film; le livre, je ne le connais pas. Il paraît qu'il est très très bien, le film, mais un peu long; moi, je compte aller le voir la semaine prochaine.]

4. **(Man)** [Qu'est-ce que Marie-Hélène déclare?]
   (12 seconds)
   Qu'est-ce que Marie-Hélène déclare?

   (A) Avoir vu un film.
   (B) Avoir l'intention de lire un livre.
   (C) Avoir lu un livre.
   (D) Avoir l'intention d'aller à Boston.

The correct answer is (B). Marie-Hélène states in the dialogue that she bought the book *Dances with Wolves* in Boston so that she could read it before seeing the movie. She also states *je n'ai pas pu le lire, je n'ai pas eu le temps* which means that she has not yet read the book. Choice (C) is therefore incorrect. Choices (A) and (D) are incorrect because she did not see the movie (A) and does not mention that she intends to go to Boston (D).

5. **(Man)** [Qu'est-ce que Maude avoue à son amie?]

(12 seconds)

Qu'est-ce que Maude avoue à son amie?

(A) Elle a lu le livre.

(B) Elle n'a pas encore vu le film.

(C) Elle n'a pas compris la critique.

(D) Elle a écouté la cassette.

The correct answer is (B). When Maude answers her friend, she tells her at the end: *Il paraît qu'il est très très bien, le film … je compte aller le voir la semaine prochaine*. Choice (A) is incorrect because Maude states the opposite (*le livre, je ne le connais pas*). According to the dialogue, Maude admits neither (C) nor (D); both options are therefore incorrect.

6. **(Man)** [Dans cette discussion, qu'est-ce qu'on peut dire des deux amies?]

(12 seconds)

Dans cette discussion, qu'est-ce qu'on peut dire des deux amies?

(A) Elles se font des compliments.

(B) Elles s'ignorent.

(C) Elles s'inquiètent.

(D) Elles partagent les mêmes goûts.

The correct answer is (D). It can be inferred from the dialogue that the two friends share the same interests, at least with regard to movies. Choices (A), (B), and (C) cannot be said about the two friends. They do not exchange compliments (A), do know each other (B), and do not become anxious or upset (C).

French Test with Listening

The test that follows is an actual, recently administered SAT Subject Test in French with Listening. To get an idea of what a real administration is like, take the test under conditions as close as possible to those of a national administration:

- Set aside an hour when you can take the test uninterrupted. Make sure you complete the test in one sitting.

- Sit at a desk or table with no other books or papers. Dictionaries, other books, or notes are not allowed in the test room.

- Time yourself by placing a clock or kitchen timer in front of you.

- Tear out an answer sheet from the back of this book and fill it in just as you would on the day of the test. One answer sheet can be used for up to three Subject Tests.

- Read the instructions that precede the practice test. During the actual administration you will be asked to read them before answering test questions.

- After you finish the practice test, read the sections "How to Score the SAT Subject Test in French with Listening" and "Reviewing Your Performance on the French Subject Test with Listening."

- Actual test and answer sheets will indicate circles, not ovals.

Form 30LC

FRENCH TEST WITH LISTENING

The top portion of the section of the answer sheet that you will use in taking the French test must be filled in exactly as shown in the illustration below. Note carefully that you have to do all of the following on your answer sheet.

1. Print FRENCH WITH LISTENING on the line under the words "Achievement Test Name."

2. In the shaded box labeled "Test Code" fill in four ovals:

—Fill in oval 5 in the row labeled V.

—Fill in oval 0 in the row labeled W.

—Fill in oval 1 in the row labeled X.

—Fill in oval 2 in the row labeled Y.

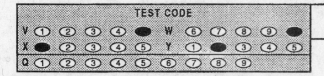

Please answer either Part I or Part II by filling in the specific oval in row Q. You are to fill in ONE and ONLY ONE oval, as described below, to indicate how you obtained your knowledge of French. The information you provide is for statistical purposes only and will not influence your score on the test.

Part I   If your knowledge of French does not come primarily from courses taken in grades 9 through 12, fill in oval 9 and leave the remaining ovals blank, regardless of how long you studied the subject in school. For example, you are to fill in oval 9 if your knowledge of French comes primarily from any of the following sources: study prior to the ninth grade, courses taken at a college, special study, living in a home in which French is the principal language spoken or extensive residence abroad that includes significant experience in the French language.

Part II   If your knowledge of French does come primarily from courses taken in secondary school, fill in the oval that indicates the level of the French course in which you are currently enrolled. If you are not now enrolled in a French course, fill in the oval that indicates the level of the most advanced course in French that you have completed.

First year:	first or second half	— fill in oval 1
Second year:	first half	— fill in oval 2
	second half	— fill in oval 3
Third year:	first half	— fill in oval 4
	second half	— fill in oval 5
Fourth year:	first half	— fill in oval 6
	second half	— fill in oval 7

Advanced Placement course
or a course at a level higher
than fourth year, second half
            or
high school course work plus
a minimum of four weeks of
study abroad   — fill in oval 8

When the supervisor gives the signal, turn the page and begin the French test. There are 100 numbered ovals on the answer sheet and 87 questions in the French test. Therefore, use only ovals 1 to 87 for recording your answers.

411

SECTION I

LISTENING

Approximate time—20 minutes

Questions 1-33

PLEASE NOTE THAT YOUR ANSWER SHEET HAS FIVE ANSWER POSITIONS MARKED A, B, C, D, E, WHILE THE QUESTIONS THROUGHOUT THIS PART CONTAIN ONLY FOUR CHOICES. BE SURE <u>NOT</u> TO MAKE ANY MARKS IN COLUMN E.

Part A

Directions: For each question in this part of the test, you will hear <u>four</u> sentences designated (A), (B), (C), and (D). The sentences will not be printed in your test book. You will hear them only once. As you listen to the four sentences, look at the picture in your test book and choose the sentence that best describes what you see in the picture. Then fill in the corresponding oval on the answer sheet. Now look at the sample picture in your test book.

Now listen to the four statements.

Statement (B), "Que c'est agréable de faire du vélo," best describes what you see in the picture. Therefore, you should choose answer (B).

3OLC

GO ON TO THE NEXT PAGE

1.

2.

3.

GO ON TO THE NEXT PAGE ➡

4.

5.

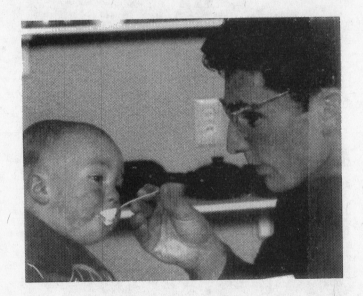

6.

GO ON TO THE NEXT PAGE

7.

8.

9.

GO ON TO THE NEXT PAGE

10.

GO ON TO THE NEXT PAGE

PLEASE NOTE THAT YOUR ANSWER SHEET HAS FIVE ANSWER POSITIONS MARKED A, B, C, D, E, WHILE THE QUESTIONS THROUGHOUT THIS PART CONTAIN ONLY THREE CHOICES. BE SURE NOT TO MAKE ANY MARKS IN COLUMNS D OR E.

Part B

Directions: In this part of the test you will hear several short selections. A tone will announce each new selection. The selections will not be printed in your test book, but each will be repeated. At the end of each selection, you will be asked one or two questions about what was said, each followed by three possible answers, (A), (B), and (C). The answers are not printed in your test book. You will hear them only once. Select the best answer and fill in the corresponding oval on the answer sheet. Now listen to the following example, but do not mark the answer on your answer sheet.

The best answer to the question, "Qu'est-ce qu'on peut dire de la voiture en question?" is (A), "Elle est en réparation." Therefore, you should choose answer (A).

Now listen to the first selection and then answer question Number 11.

11. Mark your answer on your answer sheet.
12. Mark your answer on your answer sheet.

13. Mark your answer on your answer sheet.
14. Mark your answer on your answer sheet.

15. Mark your answer on your answer sheet.
16. Mark your answer on your answer sheet.

17. Mark your answer on your answer sheet.
18. Mark your answer on your answer sheet.

19. Mark your answer on your answer sheet.
20. Mark your answer on your answer sheet.

21. Mark your answer on your answer sheet.
22. Mark your answer on your answer sheet.

GO ON TO THE NEXT PAGE

FRENCH TEST WITH LISTENING—*Continued*

PLEASE NOTE THAT YOUR ANSWER SHEET HAS FIVE ANSWER POSITIONS MARKED A, B, C, D, E, WHILE THE QUESTIONS THROUGHOUT THIS PART CONTAIN ONLY FOUR CHOICES. BE SURE <u>NOT</u> TO MAKE ANY MARKS IN COLUMN E.

Part C

Directions: You will now hear some extended dialogues. You will hear each only <u>once</u>. After each dialogue, you will be asked several questions about what you have just heard. These questions are also printed in your test book. Select the best answer to each question from among the four choices printed in your test book and fill in the corresponding oval on the answer sheet. There is no sample question for this part.

Now listen to the first dialogue and then answer question Number 23.

Dialogue numéro 1.

23. Quel genre d'étude Sabine a-t-elle choisi de faire?

(A) Des études de mathématiques.
(B) Des études scientifiques.
(C) Des études de géographie.
(D) Des études littéraires.

24. Qu'est-ce que Sabine voudrait devenir?

(A) Guide.
(B) Historienne.
(C) Professeur.
(D) Traductrice.

25. Qu'est-ce que Sabine aime faire?

(A) Travailler dans un bureau.
(B) Visiter des pays.
(C) Placer les gens.
(D) Peindre des tableaux.

Dialogue numéro 2.

26. Qu'est-ce qu'Ahmed est venu faire en France?

(A) Passer le bac.
(B) Travailler et faire des études supérieures.
(C) Apprendre le français.
(D) Retrouver sa femme et ses enfants.

27. Où Ahmed a-t-il fait ses études de lycée?

(A) Dans l'est du Maroc.
(B) Dans le Moyen Atlas.
(C) A Agadir.
(D) En France.

28. Pourquoi Ahmed a-t-il le droit d'enseigner en France?

(A) Il a le bac.
(B) Il a un doctorat.
(C) Il parle arabe.
(D) Il parle français.

29. Parmi ces sujets, lequel Ahmed enseigne-t-il?

(A) Le français.
(B) L'arabe.
(C) La géologie.
(D) L'histoire.

GO ON TO THE NEXT PAGE

Dialogue numéro 3.

30. Si Nicole n'allait pas à Prisunic, où est-ce qu'elle pourrait trouver la plupart des produits dont elle a besoin?

(A) Dans une pâtisserie.
(B) Dans une boucherie.
(C) Dans une charcuterie.
(D) Dans une crèmerie.

31. Quel est l'aspect désagréable du travail de Nicole?

(A) Il lui donne des migraines.
(B) Il lui donne faim.
(C) Il lui fait mal.
(D) Il lui donne soif.

32. Pourquoi Nicole veut-elle acheter des jus de fruits?

(A) Ils sont pratiques.
(B) Ils sont froids.
(C) Ils sont bon marché.
(D) Ils sont faciles à trouver.

33. Qu'est-ce que Nicole va faire tout de suite après être allée au supermarché?

(A) Rentrer chez elle.
(B) Aller chez le coiffeur.
(C) Aller à la poste.
(D) Boire un jus de fruits.

END OF SECTION I.
DO NOT GO ON TO SECTION II UNTIL YOU ARE TOLD TO DO SO.

SECTION II

READING

Time—40 minutes

Questions 34–87

WHEN YOU BEGIN THE READING SECTION, BE SURE THAT YOU MARK YOUR ANSWER TO THE FIRST READING QUESTION BY FILLING IN ONE OF THE OVALS NEXT TO NUMBER 34 ON THE ANSWER SHEET.

PLEASE NOTE THAT YOUR ANSWER SHEET HAS FIVE ANSWER POSITIONS MARKED A, B, C, D, E, WHILE THE QUESTIONS IN THIS SECTION OF THE TEST CONTAIN ONLY FOUR CHOICES, BE SURE NOT TO MAKE ANY MARKS IN COLUMN E.

Part A

Directions: This part consists of a number of incomplete statements, each having four suggested completions. Select the most appropriate completion and fill in the corresponding oval on the answer sheet.

---

34. Je n'ai pas pu . . . ma voiture parce qu'elle était trop vieille.

    (A) récolter
    (B) attraper
    (C) quitter
    (D) vendre

35. Je sais que tu es très sincère; n'aie pas . . . de dire la vérité.

    (A) honte
    (B) soif
    (C) besoin
    (D) envie

36. Ne fumez pas, je vous en prie; je ne peux pas . . . l'odeur de la fumée.

    (A) souffler
    (B) nettoyer
    (C) étendre
    (D) supporter

37. Tu as l'air fatigué. Va te . . .

    (A) lier
    (B) comporter
    (C) reposer
    (D) désoler

38. Puisqu'il faisait froid, Isabelle a mis son . . .

    (A) collier
    (B) manteau
    (C) mouchoir
    (D) couteau

39. Emile était si malade qu'il a dû garder le . . . pendant une semaine.

    (A) banc
    (B) mur
    (C) lit
    (D) plafond

40. Je viendrai te chercher à trois heures. Essaie d'être . . .

    (A) prêt
    (B) prochain
    (C) réduit
    (D) dressé

41. J'ai bien peur que ces gros nuages n'annoncent un . . .

    (A) mensonge
    (B) sondage
    (C) orage
    (D) dépannage

42. Je ne comprends rien au cours de chimie que . . . cette année.

    (A) je porte
    (B) j'attends
    (C) je suis
    (D) j'apprends

GO ON TO THE NEXT PAGE

Part B

Directions: Each of the following sentences contains a blank. From the four choices given, select the one that can be inserted in the blank to form a grammatically correct sentence and fill in the corresponding oval on the answer sheet. In some instances, choice (A) may consist of dashes that indicate that no insertion is required to form a grammatically correct sentence.

43. Eléonore et Monique se sont ------- après avoir fini leur travail.

(A) quittées
(B) quittée
(C) quittés
(D) quitté

44. Dans ------- université est-ce que tu comptes aller l'année prochaine?

(A) combien
(B) quelle
(C) comment
(D) quoi

45. En ce moment, je compte surtout sur ------- pour m'aider.

(A) leur
(B) te
(C) lui
(D) les

46. Cette année il y a eu de grands changements politiques ------- Europe.

(A) en
(B) à
(C) à l'
(D) dans

47. Va ------- à la bibliothèque rendre ce livre avant sept heures.

(A) rapide
(B) vite
(C) y
(D) vers

48. Il est absolument interdit ------- marcher sur la pelouse.

(A) ---
(B) de
(C) à
(D) pour

49. Bien que Didier ------- gentil, Lise refuse de sortir avec lui.

(A) est
(B) sera
(C) soit
(D) serait

50. Le Texas est le plus grand état ------- sud-ouest des Etats-Unis.

(A) du
(B) dans
(C) en
(D) à

51. Je vais ouvrir la fenêtre si vous ------- permettez.

(A) me le
(B) m'y
(C) m'en
(D) me la

GO ON TO THE NEXT PAGE

Part C

Directions: The paragraphs below contain blank spaces indicating omissions in the text. For some blanks, it is necessary to choose the completion that is most appropriate to the meaning of the passage; for other blanks, to choose the one completion that forms a grammatically correct sentence. In some instances, choice (A) may consist of dashes that indicate that no insertion is required to form a grammatically correct sentence. In each case, indicate your answer by filling in the corresponding oval on the answer sheet. Be sure to read the paragraph completely before answering the questions related to it.

Si nous ------- su que Mariette ------- régler l'addition, nous ------- tous commandé

52. (A) avons
    (B) avions
    (C) aurons
    (D) aurions

53. (A) va
    (B) alla
    (C) allait
    (D) est allé

54. (A) sommes
    (B) avons
    (C) serions
    (D) aurions

le plat ------- plus cher de la carte.

55. (A) ---
    (B) le
    (C) de
    (D) du

Dans ce petit restaurant de quartier, tout ------- la belle époque: les banquettes de velours -------

56. (A) évoquait
    (B) appelait
    (C) soutenait
    (D) désirait

57. (A) que
    (B) où
    (C) qui
    (D) dont

l'on ------- confortablement, les lampes de style 1900 qui ------- une lumière paisible et les murs rose saumon.

58. (A) se dénonçait
    (B) se renonçait
    (C) se débarrassait
    (D) s'enfonçait

59. (A) éteignaient
    (B) éclaboussaient
    (C) diffusaient
    (D) éclaircissaient

On ------- là-dedans comme on ouvre une vieille édition de Balzac ou comme on déchiffre ------- de cuisine

60. (A) entrait
    (B) entrera
    (C) entra
    (D) sera entré

61. (A) une recette
    (B) un billet
    (C) une lecture
    (D) un reçu

sortie d'un recueil ------- grand-mère.

62. (A) ---
    (B) de
    (C) après
    (D) depuis

GO ON TO THE NEXT PAGE

422

Elles s'étaient rencontrées il y a ------- années, à Montpellier où elles ------- passer trois ans à la Faculté de

63. (A) beaucoup des
    (B) de longs
    (C) bien des
    (D) longues

64. (A) doivent
    (B) devaient
    (C) devront
    (D) aient dû

Médecine. Diplômées depuis vingt ans, mariées, devenues mères de famille et divorcées ------- récemment,

65. (A) tant
    (B) juste
    (C) d'ici
    (D) tout

chacune d'elles était sûre qu'elle reconnaîtrait son amie ------- les années passées. Toutes deux avaient éprouvé

66. (A) depuis
    (B) sans
    (C) malgré
    (D) sauf

les joies et les peines ------- connaît presque toute femme moderne. A l'idée de ------- après une vingtaine

67. (A) quoi
    (B) que
    (C) dont
    (D) qui

68. (A) se revoir
    (B) se revoyant
    (C) revoir
    (D) revoyant

d'années, elles savouraient d'avance ce plaisir. Elles s'étaient ------- rendez-vous à la gare d'Austerlitz

69. (A) placé
    (B) trouvé
    (C) donné
    (D) appelé

------- elles s'étaient embarquées pour cette ville universitaire un après-midi d'automne inoubliable

70. (A) ce dont
    (B) qu'
    (C) laquelle
    (D) d'où

d'avant-guerre.

GO ON TO THE NEXT PAGE

Part D

Directions: Read the following selections carefully for comprehension. Each selection is followed by a number of questions or incomplete statements. Select the answer or completion that is best according to the selection and fill in the corresponding oval on the answer sheet.

Pour témoigner à un de nos professeurs de l'intérêt que nous prenions à son enseignement, nous lui avons offert une boîte de ses cigares préférés. Au dernier cours, le paquet, joliment ficelé, lui fut présenté. Il l'ouvrit,
Ligne
(5) mais sans un mot, sans le moindre signe de satisfaction; on crut même lire sur son visage une sorte de contrariété. Il fallut attendre la fin de l'heure pour savoir ce qu'il en pensait.

—Messieurs, dit-il alors, le règlement interdit
(10) formellement aux membres du corps enseignant d'accepter le moindre cadeau des étudiants. Votre charmante attention me touche, mais la règle est la règle. Il glissa alors la boîte sous son bras et ajouta:

—Il ne me reste donc qu'une chose à faire, emporter ces cigares chez moi et les brûler!

71. Dans ce passage, il s'agit d'un professeur qui

(A) ne fume pas
(B) ignore le règlement
(C) a le sens de l'humour
(D) ne sait pas exprimer sa gratitude

72. Les étudiants pensent que le cours donné par ce professeur est

(A) amusant
(B) curieux
(C) touchant
(D) intéressant

73. L'expression "corps enseignant" (ligne 10) veut dire

(A) l'armée
(B) les professeurs
(C) les ministres
(D) les médecins

74. La première réaction du professeur à la remise du cadeau est

(A) espérée
(B) décevante
(C) vive
(D) orgueilleuse

75. Selon ce que dit le professeur à la fin du passage, on suppose qu'il va

(A) profiter de son cadeau
(B) faire changer le règlement
(C) rendre les cigares
(D) donner de mauvaises notes aux étudiants

GO ON TO THE NEXT PAGE

424

Un jour d'automne, un après-midi qu'il faisait beau, je projetai une longue course du village que j'habitais au village voisin. Arrivé là, j'entrai dans un cabaret, je me reposai, je me rafraîchis. Le jour commençait à baisser, et je me disposais à regagner mon village lorsque j'entendis une femme qui poussait les cris les plus aigus. Je sortis; on s'était attroupé autour d'elle. Elle était à terre, elle s'arrachait les cheveux; elle disait en montrant les débris d'un grand pot: « je suis ruinée, je suis ruinée pour un mois; pendant ce temps qui est-ce qui nourrira mes pauvres enfants? Mon maître qui a l'âme plus dure qu'une pierre, ne me fera grâce d'un sou. » Tout le monde la plaignait mais personne ne mettait la main dans la poche. Je m'approchai brusquement et lui dit: « Ma bonne, qu'est-ce qui vous est arrivé? » — « Ce qui m'est arrivé! Est-ce que vous ne le voyez pas? On m'avait envoyée acheter un pot d'huile: j'ai fait un faux pas, je suis tombée, mon pot s'est cassé. » Dans ce moment arrivèrent les petits enfants de cette femme, ils étaient presque nus et les mauvais vêtements de leur mère montraient toute la misère de la famille. J'étais touché de compassion, les larmes me vinrent aux yeux. Je demandai à cette femme pour combien il y avait d'huile dans ce pot. « Pour combien? Pour neuf francs, pour plus que je ne saurais gagner en un mois. » A l'instant, ouvrant ma bourse et lui jetant des pièces d'argent, « tenez, ma bonne », lui dis-je, « en voilà douze », et, sans attendre ses remerciements, je repris le chemin du village.

76. Au début de ce passage, le projet du narrateur est de

    (A) se rafraîchir dans un cabaret
    (B) visiter plusieurs villages
    (C) faire une longue promenade
    (D) contempler la beauté d'un jour d'automne

77. Quand est-ce que le narrateur décide de rentrer chez lui?

    (A) Un peu avant midi
    (B) Vers la fin de l'après-midi
    (C) Après avoir bien dansé
    (D) Après avoir visité une amie

78. Pourquoi le narrateur est-il sorti du cabaret?

    (A) Le patron lui a dit de partir tout de suite.
    (B) Il avait peur de perdre son chemin.
    (C) Il avait trop bu et ne se sentait pas bien.
    (D) Il voulait savoir ce qui se passait dehors.

79. Les actions de la femme dans le passage montrent qu'elle

    (A) vend de l'huile au marché
    (B) cherche de l'eau à boire
    (C) est vraiment désespérée
    (D) est coiffeuse de profession

80. Qu'est-ce qui caractérise le maître de la femme?

    (A) Il a toujours la main dans la poche.
    (B) Il est peu charitable.
    (C) Il aime collectionner les pierres.
    (D) Il adore les petits enfants.

81. Qu'est-ce que le narrateur a fait après s'être approché de la femme?

    (A) Il lui a posé une question.
    (B) Il a caressé ses enfants.
    (C) Il est tombé.
    (D) Il a renversé le pot d'huile.

82. Quelle est la réaction des spectateurs à la chute de la femme?

    (A) Ils se moquent d'elle.
    (B) Ils lui parlent brusquement.
    (C) Ils ont pitié d'elle.
    (D) Ils l'aident à se relever.

83. L'expression "personne ne mettait la main dans la poche" (lignes 13-14) veut dire que les spectateurs

    (A) n'ont pas les mains froides
    (B) n'offrent rien à la dame
    (C) ont de bonnes manières
    (D) sont très honnêtes

84. L'expression "j'ai fait un faux pas" (lignes 17-18) veut dire que la femme

    (A) s'est mal soignée
    (B) s'est trompée de chemin
    (C) a été impolie
    (D) a perdu l'équilibre

85. Quelle a été la réaction du narrateur face à la pauvreté de la famille?

    (A) Il leur a donné des vêtements.
    (B) Il a été vivement ému.
    (C) Il n'a pas osé les regarder.
    (D) Il s'est plaint de la dureté du maître.

GO ON TO THE NEXT PAGE

Des trains et des hommes!

Le TGV postal! On croit rêver! Imaginez 65 tonnes de lettres enfermées dans les flancs protecteurs du bolide, lancées à 260 km/h entre Paris et Lyon, et vous vous ferez une idée juste de la Poste d'aujourd'hui.

86. La publicité suggère que la poste de nos jours est

   (A) démodée
   (B) efficace
   (C) imprévisible
   (D) fantaisiste

87. Lequel des noms suivants suggère que le train postal est comparé à une personne?

   (A) Tonnes
   (B) Lettres
   (C) Flancs
   (D) Idée

END OF SECTION II.

S T O P

IF YOU FINISH BEFORE TIME IS CALLED, YOU MAY CHECK YOUR WORK ON SECTION II OF THIS TES
DO NOT TURN TO ANY OTHER TEST IN THIS BOOK.

How to Score the SAT Subject Test in French with Listening

When you take the SAT Subject Test in French with Listening, you receive an overall composite score as well as two subscores: one for the reading section, one for the listening section.

The reading and listening subscores are reported on the College Board's 20-to-80 scale. However. the composite score, which is the most significant of the scores reported to the colleges you specify, is in the form of the College Board's 200-to-800 scale.

Worksheet 1. Finding Your Raw Listening Subscore

STEP 1: Table A lists the correct answers for all the questions on the SAT Subject Test in French with Listening that is reproduced in this book. It also serves as a worksheet for you to calculate your raw Listening subscore.

- Compare your answers with those given in the table.
- Put a check in the column marked "Right" if your answer is correct.
- Put a check in the column marked "Wrong" if your answer is incorrect.
- Leave both columns blank if you omitted the question.

STEP 2: Count the number of right answers for questions 1–10 and 23–33.

Enter the total here: _____

STEP 3: Count the number of wrong answers for questions 1–10 and 23–33.

Enter the total here: _____

STEP 4: Multiply the number of wrong answers from Step 3 by .333.

Enter the product here: _____

STEP 5: Subtract the result obtained in Step 4 from the total you obtained in Step 2.

Enter the result here: _____

STEP 6: Count the number of right answers for questions 11–22.

Enter the total here: _____

STEP 7: Count the number of wrong answers for questions 11–22.

Enter the total here: _____

STEP 8: Multiply the number of wrong answers from Step 7 by .500.

Enter the product here: _____

STEP 9: Subtract the result obtained in Step 8 from the total you obtained in Step 6.

Enter the result here: _____

STEP 10: Add the result obtained in Step 5 to the result obtained in Step 9.

Enter the result here: _____

STEP 11: Round the number obtained in Step 10 to the nearest whole number.

Enter the result here: _____

The number you obtained in Step 11 is your raw Listening subscore.

Worksheet 2. Finding Your Raw Reading Subscore

STEP 1: Table A lists the correct answers for all the questions on the SAT Subject Test in French with Listening that is reproduced in this book. It also serves as a worksheet for you to calculate your raw Reading subscore.

STEP 2: Count the number of right answers for questions 34–87.

Enter the total here: _____

STEP 3: Count the number of wrong answers for questions 34–87.

Enter the total here: _____

STEP 4: Multiply the number of wrong answers from Step 3 by .333.

Enter the product here: _____

STEP 5: Subtract the result obtained in Step 4 from the total you obtained in Step 2.

Enter the result here: _____

STEP 6: Round the number obtained in Step 5 to the nearest whole number.

Enter the result here: _____

The number you obtained in Step 6 is your raw Reading subscore.

Worksheet 3. Finding Your Raw Composite Score*

STEP 1: Enter your unrounded raw Reading subscore from Step 5
of Worksheet 2 here: _____

STEP 2: Enter your unrounded raw Listening subscore from Step 10
of Worksheet 1 here: _____

STEP 3: Multiply your unrounded raw Listening subscore by .7596.
Enter the product here: _____

STEP 4: Add the result obtained in Step 1 to the result obtained in Step 3.
Enter the result here: _____

STEP 5: Round the number obtained in Step 4 to the nearest whole number.
Enter the result here: _____

The number you obtained in Step 5 is your raw composite score.

*This weighting reflects the amount of time spent on the two sections of the test—40 minutes on the reading questions and 20 minutes on the listening questions. For those who are curious about how the calculation works, the weighting is done in standard deviation units, a measure of score variability. The weight given to the listening subscore is calculated by dividing the standard deviation of the reading subscore by two times the standard deviation of the listening subscore.

TABLE A
Answers to the SAT Subject Test in French with Listening, Form 3OLC reformatted, and Percentage of Students Answering Each Question Correctly

Question Number	Correct Answer	Right	Wrong	Percentage of Students Answering the Question Correctly*	Question Number	Correct Answer	Right	Wrong	Percentage of Students Answering the Question Correctly*
1	A			98	33	A			45
2	B			86	34	D			77
3	C			87	35	A			43
4	A			89	36	D			28
5	B			86	37	C			80
6	A			89	38	B			80
7	C			84	39	C			70
8	A			57	40	A			69
9	B			55	41	C			33
10	A			31	42	C			16
11	C			63	43	A			94
12	C			43	44	B			91
13	B			74	45	C			69
14	A			62	46	A			77
15	A			78	47	B			65
16	B			54	48	B			48
17	A			75	49	C			31
18	C			59	50	A			56
19	C			64	51	A			13
20	B			52	52	B			35
21	A			29	53	C			47
22	A			32	54	D			50
23	D			68	55	B			52
24	A			50	56	A			36
25	B			60	57	B			29
26	B			61	58	D			27
27	C			31	59	C			41
28	B			51	60	A			47
29	D			55	61	A			46
30	D			54	62	B			63
31	D			41	63	C			19
32	A			36	64	B			48

Table A continued on next page

Table A continued from previous page

Question Number	Correct Answer	Right	Wrong	Percentage of Students Answering the Question Correctly*	Question Number	Correct Answer	Right	Wrong	Percentage of Students Answering the Question Correctly*
65	D			30	77	B			62
66	C			23	78	D			59
67	B			22	79	C			81
68	A			36	80	B			49
69	C			22	81	A			71
70	D			55	82	C			54
71	C			52	83	B			80
72	D			55	84	D			42
73	B			77	85	B			48
74	B			48	86	B			22
75	A			40	87	C			60
76	C			51					

*These percentages are based on an analysis of the answer sheets for a random sample of 9,215 students who took this form of the test in November 1992 and whose mean score was 544. They may be used as an indication of the relative difficulty of a particular question. Each percentage may also be used to predict the likelihood that a typical SAT Subject Test in French with Listening candidate will answer correctly that question on this edition of this test.

Finding Your Scaled Score

When you take SAT Subject Tests, the scores sent to the colleges you specify are reported on the College Board scale, which ranges from 200 to 800. Subscores are reported on a scale that ranges from 20 to 80. You can convert your practice test scores to scaled scores by using Tables B, C, and D. To find your scaled score, locate your raw score in the left-hand column of the table; the corresponding score in the right-hand column is your scaled score. For example, in Table B a raw composite score of 47 on this particular edition of the SAT Subject Test in French with Listening corresponds to a scaled score of 640.

Raw scores are converted to scaled scores to ensure that a score earned on any one edition of a particular Subject Test is comparable to the same scaled score earned on any other edition of the same Subject Test. Because some editions of tests may be slightly easier or more difficult than others, scaled scores are adjusted so that they indicate the same level of performance regardless of the edition of the test taken and the ability of the group that takes it. Thus, for example, a score of 400 on one edition of a test taken at a particular administration indicates the same level of achievement as a score of 400 on a different edition of the test taken at a different administration.

When you take the SAT Subject Tests during a national administration, your scores are likely to differ somewhat from the scores you obtain on the tests in this book. People perform at different levels at different times for reasons unrelated to the tests themselves. The precision of any test is also limited because it represents only a sample of all the possible questions that could be asked.

Your scaled composite score from Table B is _____ .

Your scaled listening score from Table C is _____ .

Your scaled reading score from Table D is _____ .

TABLE B
Scaled Score Conversion Table
French Subject Test with Listening Composite Scores (Form 3OLC)

Raw Score	Scaled Score	Raw Score	Scaled Score	Raw Score	Scaled Score
79	800	43	610	7	400
78	800	42	600	6	400
77	800	41	600	5	390
76	800	40	590	4	390
75	800	39	580	3	380
74	800	38	580	2	380
73	800	37	570	1	370
72	800	36	570	0	370
71	800	35	560	-1	360
70	800	34	550	-2	350
69	790	33	550	-3	350
68	780	32	540	-4	340
67	780	31	540	-5	340
66	770	30	530	-6	330
65	760	29	520	-7	330
64	760	28	520	-8	320
63	750	27	510	-9	310
62	740	26	510	-10	310
61	730	25	500	-11	300
60	730	24	500	-12	300
59	720	23	490	-13	290
58	710	22	490	-14	280
57	710	21	480	-15	280
56	700	20	470	-16	270
55	690	19	470	-17	270
54	680	18	460	-18	260
53	680	17	460	-19	250
52	670	16	450	-20	250
51	660	15	450	-21	240
50	660	14	440	-22	230
49	650	13	440	-23	220
48	640	12	430	-24	220
47	640	11	430	-25	210
46	630	10	420	-26	200
45	620	9	410	-27	200
44	620	8	410	-28	200

TABLE C
Scaled Score Conversion Table
French Subject Test with Listening Listening Subscore (Form 3OLC)

Raw Score	Scaled Score	Raw Score	Scaled Score	Raw Score	Scaled Score
33	80	17	55	1	38
32	80	16	53	0	37
31	79	15	52	−1	36
30	76	14	51	−2	36
29	74	13	50	−3	35
28	72	12	49	−4	34
27	70	11	48	−5	33
26	68	10	47	−6	32
25	67	9	46	−7	31
24	65	8	45	−8	30
23	63	7	44	−9	29
22	62	6	43	−10	28
21	60	5	42	−11	27
20	59	4	41	−12	27
19	57	3	40	−13	26
18	56	2	39		

TABLE D
Scaled Score Conversion Table
French Subject Test with Listening Reading Subscore (Form 3OLC)

Raw Score	Scaled Score	Raw Score	Scaled Score	Raw Score	Scaled Score
54	80	29	62	4	42
53	80	28	61	3	41
52	80	27	60	2	40
51	80	26	59	1	39
50	80	25	59	0	39
49	80	24	58	-1	38
48	80	23	57	-2	37
47	80	22	56	-3	36
46	79	21	55	-4	35
45	78	20	54	-5	35
44	77	19	53	-6	34
43	76	18	53	-7	33
42	75	17	52	-8	32
41	74	16	51	-9	31
40	73	15	50	-10	31
39	72	14	49	-11	30
38	71	13	49	-12	29
37	70	12	48	-13	28
36	69	11	47	-14	27
35	68	10	46	-15	26
34	67	9	46	-16	25
33	66	8	45	-17	24
32	65	7	44	-18	23
31	64	6	43		
30	63	5	43		

Reviewing Your Performance on the French Subject Test with Listening

After you score your test, analyze your performance—consider the following questions:

Did you run out of time before reaching the end of the test?

If so, you may need to pace yourself better. For example, maybe you spent too much time on one or two hard questions. A better approach might be to skip the ones you can't answer right away and try answering all the questions that remain on the test. Then if there's time, go back to the questions you skipped.

Did you take a long time reading the directions?

You will save time when you take the test by learning the directions to the French Test with Listening ahead of time. Each minute you spend reading directions during the test is a minute that you could use to answer questions.

How did you handle questions you were unsure of?

If you were able to eliminate one or more of the answer choices as wrong and guess from the remaining ones, your approach probably worked to your advantage. On the other hand, making haphazard guesses or omitting questions without trying to eliminate choices could cost you valuable points.

How difficult were the questions for you compared with other students who took the test?

Table A shows you how difficult the multiple-choice questions were for the group of students who took this test during its national administration. The right-hand column gives the percentage of students that answered each question correctly.

A question answered correctly by almost everyone in the group is obviously an easy question.

For example, 89 percent of the students answered question 6 correctly. But only 22 percent answered question 67 correctly.

Keep in mind that these percentages are based on just one group of students. They would probably be different if another group of students took the test.

If you missed several easy questions, go back and try to find out why: Did the questions cover material you haven't reviewed yet? Did you misunderstand the directions?

Chapter 10
German

Purpose

There are two German Subject Tests: German and German with Listening. The reading-only test measures your ability to understand written German. German with Listening measures your ability to understand spoken and written German.

Format

- The German Test takes one hour and includes 80 to 85 multiple-choice questions.
- The German Test with Listening also takes one hour and includes 85 to 90 multiple-choice listening and reading questions. Listening questions require answers to questions based on shorter and longer listening selections.
- Both tests evaluate your reading ability through a variety of questions requiring a wide-ranging knowledge of German.
- Both tests comply with the German spelling reform (Rechtschreibreform) as much as possible. They evaluate reading ability in these areas:

Sentence completion and paragraph completion questions test vocabulary and grammar requiring you to know the meaning of words and idiomatic expressions in context and to identify usage that is structurally correct and appropriate. For each omission, you must select the choice that BEST fits each sentence.

Reading comprehension questions test your understanding of the content of various materials taken from sources such as advertisements, timetables, street signs, forms, and tickets. They also examine your ability to read passages representative of various styles and levels of difficulty. Each test edition has several prose passages followed by questions that test your understanding of the passage. The passages, mostly adapted from literary sources and newspapers or magazines, are generally one or two paragraphs in length and test whether you can identify the main idea or comprehend facts or details in the text.

The *listening* test also measures the ability to understand spoken language with two types of listening questions:

Type One: Contains short dialogues/monologues with one or two multiple-choice questions. Dialogues/monologues, questions, and answer choices are recorded. Questions are also printed in the test book.

Type Two: Contains longer dialogues and monologues with several multiple-choice questions. Dialogues/monologues and questions are only recorded and not printed in the test book. Answer choices are not recorded; they appear only in the test book.

German

Skills Measured	Approximate Percentage of Test
Vocabulary in Context and Structure in Context (grammar)	50
Reading Comprehension—(authentic stimulus materials and passages)	50

German with Listening

Test Sections	Approximate Percentage of Test
Listening Section (20 minutes)	35
Short dialogues/monologues	
Long dialogues/monologues	
Reading Section (40 minutes)	65
Vocabulary in Context	
Structure in Context (grammar)	
Reading Comprehension—(authentic stimulus materials and passages)	

Recommended Preparation

Both tests assume differences in language preparation; neither is tied to a specific textbook or method of instruction. The German tests are appropriate for students who have completed two, three, or four years of German language study in high school or the equivalent. Your best preparation for these tests is a gradual development of competence in German over a period of years. Familiarize yourself with directions in advance. The directions in this book are identical to those that appear on the test. For the German Test with Listening a practice cassette with sample questions is available from your school counselor.

Cassette Players

You must bring an acceptable cassette player with earphones to the test center. Put fresh batteries in your cassette player the day before the test. If you like, bring additional fresh batteries and a backup cassette player with earphones to the test center. Test center staff will NOT have batteries, cassette players, or earphones for your use.

Acceptable cassette players must be:
- personal (have earphones that let only you hear the recording)
- portable (small enough that the entire player can fit in your hand)
- battery-operated
- able to use a single (not dual) standard (2-1/2 inch by 4 inch) audiocassette—not a mini- or microcassette

If your cassette player has a programming feature that fast-forwards automatically to the next prompt, that feature must be deactivated before you start the test. You will not be allowed to share a cassette player with another test-taker.

Beginning with the November 2005 administration, portable CD players will be required instead of cassette players for language with listening tests.

Scores

For both tests, the total score is reported on the 200-to-800 scale. For the listening test, listening and reading subscores are reported on the 20-to-80 scale.

Sample Reading Questions

Please note that your answer sheet has five answer positions marked A, B, C, D, E, while the questions throughout this test contain only four choices. Be sure NOT to make any marks in column E.

Part A

Directions: This part consists of a number of incomplete statements, each having four suggested completions. Select the most appropriate completion and fill in the corresponding oval on the answer sheet.

Please note that the sentences are grouped by topic, as they are in current German Subject Tests, while the sentence completion questions in the practice tests are not presented in this format.

In den Ferien

1. Ich glaube, er kommt schon………Mittwoch zurück.
   - **(A)** nächstem
   - **(B)** nächster
   - **(C)** nächstes
   - **(D)** nächsten

Question 1: This question tests your knowledge of the correct weak adjective ending following a presupposed dative-preposition that would answer to the question "when" ("wann"). The correct answer is (D). You need to know that the gender of "Mittwoch" is masculine and that the correct preposition (eliminated here) would be "an." The entire prepositional phrase would be: an dem (am) nächsten Mittwoch; however, "am" or "an dem" is eliminated, an ellipsis very commonly used in temporal phrases. All other options (A), (B), and (C) cannot structurally be preceded by "am" or "an dem."

2. Diesen Sommer konnten die Touristen in Europa gar nicht über das Wetter………
   - **(A)** sagen
   - **(B)** kennen
   - **(C)** klagen
   - **(D)** denken

Question 2 tests your knowledge of verbs in combination with a negation and a preposition. You are asked to choose the verb that fits best. Choice (C) is the correct answer. Given the context (tourists could not complain about the weather in Europe this year), "klagen" is the only possible option that not only fits contextually but also structurally.

3. Annie ist die jüngste Tochter der Familie, bei………wir diesen Sommer gewohnt haben.

   (A) dem

   (B) denen

   (C) der

   (D) die

Question 3 asks you to choose the correct form of the relative pronoun "die" following the preposition "bei." You should know that "bei" asks for the dative and that the gender of "Familie," to which the relative pronoun refers, is feminine. Choice (C) is therefore the only possible answer, since "der" is the dative form of "die."

Part B

Directions: In each of the following paragraphs, there are numbered blanks indicating that words or phrases have been omitted. For each numbered blank, four completions are provided. First read through the entire paragraph. Then, for each numbered blank, choose the completion that is most appropriate and fill in the corresponding oval on the answer sheet.

<u>**Eine Geschäftsreise**</u>

Ich verabschiede mich jetzt, weil ich morgen _____

4. **(A)** gern

   (B) früh

   (C) schon

   (D) langsam

aufstehen muss, um _____ Berlin zu einer wichtigen

5. **(A)** auf

   (B) an

   (C) nach

   (D) zu

Konferenz _____.

6. **(A)** fährt

   (B) fahren

   (C) gefahren

   (D) zu fahren

Question 4 is a vocabulary question that tests your knowledge of adverbs. You are asked to choose the adverb that fits best. The correct answer is (B). Given the context (the person has to go on a business trip), "früh" is the most appropriate of the four choices to complement the verb "aufstehen."

In question 5, you are asked to choose the correct preposition, which here is part of an idiomatic expression. The correct answer is (C). You need to know that of the four choices only the preposition "nach" is appropriate in connection with a motion verb (fahren) and the name of a city (Berlin).

In question 6, you are asked to choose the correct form of the verb "fahren." The correct answer of the four answer choices is (D). The infinitive form of "fahren" with "zu" is required because the clause is introduced by "um." The other choices—(A) third person singular present tense, (B) infinitive without "zu," (C) past participle—are therefore not appropriate to form a grammatically correct sentence.

Part C

Directions: Read the following texts carefully for comprehension. Each is followed by a number of questions or incomplete statements. Select the answer or completion that is best according to the text and fill in the corresponding oval on the answer sheet.

Betreten der Baustelle verboten

Eltern haften für ihre Kinder!

7. Wo findet man dieses Schild?

    (A) Auf einem Kinderspielplatz

    (B) An einem Gefängnis

    (C) Vor einer Baumschule

    (D) Auf einem Bauplatz

Question 7 asks you where you would see such a sign. This sign tells you that you are not to enter the construction site. It continues that parents are responsible for their children's actions. "Bauplatz" in choice (D) is a synonym for "Baustelle"; both nouns, translated into English, mean construction site. Choice (D) is therefore the correct answer. Choice (A) refers to a playground (*Kinderspielplatz*), (B) to a prison (*Gefängnis*), and (C) to a nursery (*Baumschule*).

Der Frankfurter Sinkkasten ist ein Verein, der von drei jungen Leuten—Aina, Wolfgang und Werner—in einem Kellergewölbe am Main gegründet wurde, nachdem sie sich eines Tages entschlossen hatten, ihren Feierabend nicht weiter in Kneipen zu verbringen.

Der Sinkkasten verlangt einen Mitgliedsbeitrag von fünf Mark monatlich, obgleich es ihm gar nicht um Gewinne geht. Hier können aber endlich jeden Abend Jugendliche zusammenkommen und fröhlich sein. Im Sinkkasten treten außerdem viele prominente Musiker und Gruppen auf. Dazu kommen dann noch interessante Theateraufführungen. Oft werden den Gästen auch sehr gute Filme gezeigt. Junge Maler können hier ihre ersten Werke ausstellen, und regelmäßig dürfen die jungen Gäste selbst auch mal Künstler spielen: sie können beim freien Malen ihre bisher verborgenen Talente entdecken. Die schönsten Werke werden anschließend ausgestellt.

Das Programm ersetzt den Jugendlichen Theater, Kino und Kneipe zugleich. Deshalb kommen sie auch in Scharen! Längst hat es sich herumgesprochen, dass man im Sinkkasten ganz nette Leute kennenlernen kann. Die stadtverwaltung von Frankfurt am Main hat inzwischen den Sinkkasten schätzen gelernt: seit Anfang 1995 wird der Klub vom Kulturamt mit Geld unterstützt.

8. Was können die Gäste in diesem Klub tun?

   (A) Ihre eigenen Schöpfungen ausstellen

   (B) Endlich ihre Kochkunst zeigen

   (C) Ohne monatlichen Beitrag alles mitmachen

   (D) Die täglichen Hausaufgaben erledigen

In question 8 you are asked what club members and guests can do when visiting the "Sinkkasten." To answer this question, you have to read the second and third paragraph carefully. Nothing is mentioned with respect to choices (B) "Kochkunst" and (D) "Hausaufgaben." "Monatlicher Beitrag" in choice (C) is mentioned in the second paragraph ("Mitgliedsbeitrag ... monatlich"), but it is stated here that each member of the "Sinkkasten" has to contribute 5.-DM per month, while choice (C) describes exactly the opposite. Choice (A) *Ihre eigenen Schöpfungen ausstellen* is the only correct answer to the question and is supported by "regelmäßig dürfen die jungen Gäste selbst auch mal Künstler spielen:" ... up to ... "Die schönsten Werke werden anschließend ausgestellt."

9. Was kann man im allgemeinen über den Klub sagen?

   (A) Er ist das Kulturzentrum der Stadt Frankfurt.

   (B) Er ist finanzieller Mittelpunkt für die Stadtväter.

   (C) Er ist Anziehungspunkt für viele junge Leute.

   (D) Er ist als kultureller Treffpunkt nicht erfolgreich.

Question 9 asks what can be said in general about this club ("Der Sinkkasten"). The entire reading passage includes information about how and where young people used to spend their free time and how "der Sinkkasten" has changed their habits and what the club means to them. Choice (C) *Er ist Anziehungspunkt für viele junge Leute.* summarizes in one sentence this passage and is therefore the only correct answer. Choice (A) describes the club as the cultural center ("Kulturzentrum") of the city of Frankfurt, which is obviously never mentioned in the text. Choice (B) refers wrongly to the club as a financial center for representatives of the city government, and (D) claims erroneously that the club is unsuccessful as a cultural meeting place.

German Test

The test that follows is an actual, recently administered SAT Subject Test in German. To get an idea of what a real administration is like, take the test under conditions as close as possible to those of a national administration:

- Set aside an hour when you can take the test uninterrupted. Make sure you complete the test in one sitting.

- Sit at a desk or table with no other books or papers. Dictionaries, other books, or notes are not allowed in the test room.

- Time yourself by placing a clock or kitchen timer in front of you.

- Tear out an answer sheet from the back of this book and fill it in just as you would on the day of the test. One answer sheet can be used for up to three Subject Tests.

- Read the instructions that precede the practice test. During the actual administration you will be asked to read them before answering test questions.

- After you finish the practice test, read the sections "How to Score the SAT Subject Test in German" and "Reviewing Your Performance on the German Subject Test."

- Actual test and answer sheets will indicate circles, not ovals.

Form K-3OAC2

GERMAN TEST

The top portion of the section of the answer sheet that you will use in taking the German test must be filled in exactly as shown in the illustration below. Note carefully that you have to do all of the following on your answer sheet.

1. Print GERMAN on the line under the words "Subject Test (print)."

2. In the shaded box labeled "Test Code" fill in four ovals:

—Fill in oval 3 in the row labeled V.

—Fill in oval 4 in the row labeled W.

—Fill in oval 2 in the row labeled X.

—Fill in oval D in the row labeled Y.

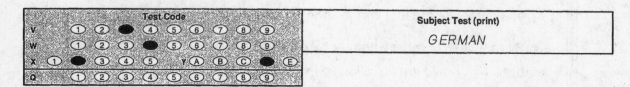

Please answer either Part I or Part II by filling in the specific oval in row Q. You are to fill in ONE and ONLY ONE oval, as described below, to indicate how you obtained your knowledge of German. The information you provide is for statistical purposes only and will not influence your score on the test.

Part I   If your knowledge of German does not come primarily from courses taken in grades 9 through 12, fill in oval 9 and leave the remaining ovals blank, regardless of how long you studied the subject in school. For example, you are to fill in oval 9 if your knowledge of German comes primarily from any of the following sources: study prior to the ninth grade, courses taken at a college, special study, living in a home in which German is the principal language spoken, or extensive residence abroad that includes significant experience in the German language.

Part II   If your knowledge of German does come primarily from courses taken in secondary school or the equivalent, fill in the oval that indicates the level of the German course in which you are currently enrolled. If you are not now enrolled in a German course, fill in the oval that indicates the level of the most advanced course in German that you have completed.

First year:	first or second half	—Fill in oval 1.
Second year:	first half	—Fill in oval 2.
	second half	—Fill in oval 3.
Third year:	first half	—Fill in oval 4.
	second half	—Fill in oval 5.
Fourth year:	first half	—Fill in oval 6.
	second half	—Fill in oval 7.

Advanced Placement course
or a course at a level higher
than fourth year, second half
or
high school course work plus
a minimum of four weeks of
study abroad   —Fill in oval 8.

When the supervisor gives the signal, turn the page and begin the German test. There are 100 numbered ovals on the answer sheet and 85 questions in the German test. Therefore, use only ovals 1 to 85 for recording your answers.

GERMAN TEST

PLEASE NOTE THAT YOUR ANSWER SHEET HAS FIVE ANSWER POSITIONS MARKED A, B, C, D, E, WHILE THE QUESTIONS THROUGHOUT THIS TEST CONTAIN ONLY FOUR CHOICES. BE SURE NOT TO MAKE ANY MARKS IN COLUMN E.

Part A

Directions: This part consists of a number of incomplete statements, each having four suggested completions. Select the most appropriate completion and fill in the corresponding oval on the answer sheet.

---

1. Wenn der Himmel ganz . . . ist, scheint die Sonne nicht.

   (A) blau
   (B) hell
   (C) sonnig
   (D) grau

2. Wohin hat Mutter mein Buch gelegt? Ah, . . . den Tisch!

   (A) am
   (B) aus
   (C) auf
   (D) um

3. Thomas trägt heute am rechten . . . einen schwarzen und am linken einen braunen Schuh.

   (A) Zeh
   (B) Fuß
   (C) Kopf
   (D) Hals

4. Das ist die . . . Antwort.

   (A) reichliche
   (B) rechtere
   (C) reiche
   (D) richtige

5. Herbert hatte sich den . . . Tag nicht wohl gefühlt.

   (A) ganzen
   (B) allen
   (C) vollen
   (D) hohlen

6. Können Sie mir bitte sagen, wieviel . . . es ist?

   (A) Zeit
   (B) Mal
   (C) Uhr
   (D) Stunde

7. Angelika ist so eigensinnig. Sie . . . einfach ihre Medizin nicht.

   (A) nehmen
   (B) nehmt
   (C) nehme
   (D) nimmt

8. Wir . . . unsere Freunde zum Abendessen ein.

   (A) erlaubten
   (B) baten
   (C) fragten
   (D) luden

9. Warum wird uns nicht . . . ?

   (A) halfen
   (B) geholfen
   (C) hilft
   (D) helfen

10. Familie Müller hatte uns . . . Sonntag zum Kaffee eingeladen.

    (A) morgen
    (B) ganzen
    (C) heutigen
    (D) letzten

11. In diesem Land . . . es sehr wenige Autos.

    (A) gibt
    (B) ist
    (C) sind
    (D) haben

GO ON TO THE NEXT PAGE

K-3OAC2

449

12. Heute . . . wieder ein interessanter Artikel in der Zeitung.

    (A) stellt
    (B) liest
    (C) steht
    (D) liegt

13. Ich bleibe noch hier, . . . Brigitte kommt.

    (A) dann
    (B) bis
    (C) sobald
    (D) ehe

14. Wo . . . man hier die Karten?

    (A) bekommen
    (B) bekommst
    (C) bekommt
    (D) bekomme

15. Sie . . . heute ihr schönstes Kleid.

    (A) paßt
    (B) fehlt
    (C) trägt
    (D) zieht

16. Peter ist schon lange ein guter . . . von uns.

    (A) Bekannter
    (B) Bekanntem
    (C) Bekannte
    (D) Bekannten

17. Es ist mir völlig . . . , was du machst!

    (A) egal
    (B) gültig
    (C) interessant
    (D) gleichzeitig

18. Die Torte sieht . . . schön aus, . . . sie schmeckt mir nicht.

    (A) sowohl. .als auch
    (B) zwar. .aber
    (C) weder. .noch
    (D) teils. .teils

19. Klaus und . . . Freundin sind eben angekommen.

    (A) ihrer
    (B) ihr
    (C) seiner
    (D) seine

20. Sie sitzt immer ganz . . . , weil sie alles hören will.

    (A) vorbei
    (B) dort
    (C) vorne
    (D) vorüber

21. Können Sie das auch . . . deutsch sagen?

    (A) an
    (B) auf
    (C) mit
    (D) zu

22. Er wollte . . . eine Woche in Dresden verbringen; mehr Zeit hatte er dieses Mal nicht.

    (A) höchstens
    (B) dauernd
    (C) meistens
    (D) gewöhnlich

23. Sie . . . eigentlich Ulrike, aber wir nennen sie Ulli.

    (A) heißt
    (B) ruft
    (C) schreit
    (D) spricht

24. Sie weiß . . . genau, was sie machen will.

    (A) viel
    (B) ganz
    (C) wenig
    (D) gut

25. Diese Studenten . . . gut Deutsch, denn sie haben fleißig gelernt.

    (A) wissen
    (B) kennen
    (C) können
    (D) kann

GO ON TO THE NEXT PAGE

26. Alles, . . . er sagte, war Quatsch.

    (A) das
    (B) daß
    (C) was
    (D) welches

27. Sie hat sich an diese schwere Arbeit . . .

    (A) gehabt
    (B) gewollt
    (C) gewöhnt
    (D) gezweifelt

28. Er tat, als ob er uns nicht . . .

    (A) sähe
    (B) siehst
    (C) sahen
    (D) sieh

29. Kann ich mal dein Deutschbuch benutzen? Ich habe meins in der Schule . . .

    (A) weggelassen
    (B) verlassen
    (C) ausgelassen
    (D) liegenlassen

30. Deine Bekannten sind sehr freundlich. Unter ihnen fühle ich mich so richtig . . .

    (A) schlecht
    (B) nett
    (C) wohl
    (D) feindlich

31. Meine Schwester hat Tiere gern; . . . möchte sie Tierärztin werden.

    (A) sogar
    (B) sonst
    (C) dann
    (D) deswegen

GO ON TO THE NEXT PAGE

GERMAN TEST—*Continued*

Part B

<u>Directions:</u> In each of the following paragraphs, there are numbered blanks indicating that words or phrases have been omitted. For each numbered blank, four completions are provided. First read through the entire paragraph. Then, for each numbered blank, choose the completion that is most appropriate and fill in the corresponding oval on the answer sheet.

Immer wenn ich einen aufregenden Film gesehen ------, muß ich im ganzen Haus ------ machen, alle Türen ------

32. (A) habe	33. (A) Fenster	34. (A) abschloß
(B) hast	(B) Licht	(B) abschließt
(C) hat	(C) Keller	(C) abgeschlossen
(D) hatte	(D) Birne	(D) abschließen

und ------ Radio anstellen, ------ sterbe ich vor Angst. Geht ------ das auch so?

35. (A) dem	36. (A) oder	37. (A) dir
(B) die	(B) sonst	(B) dich
(C) der	(C) denn	(C) es
(D) das	(D) und	(D) sie

Letzten Dienstag bekam er ------ seinem Bruder einen Brief, in ------ stand,

38. (A) bei	39. (A) die
(B) aus	(B) denen
(C) für	(C) dem
(D) von	(D) das

daß er sofort ------ Hause kommen müsse.

40. (A) zu
(B) nach
(C) von
(D) im

GO ON TO THE NEXT PAGE ➤

In der Hauptreisezeit, als die Stadt München voll von Touristen war, hatte sich ein ------- in

41. (A) Männer
    (B) Kind
    (C) Frau
    (D) Dame

der Altstadt verlaufen. Da es ------- dem dichten Verkehr den Weg nach Hause nicht mehr finden

42. (A) durch
    (B) trotz
    (C) in
    (D) von

konnte, stand das kleine ------- auf der Straße und ------- bitterlich.

43. (A) Junge   44. (A) weinte
    (B) Person   (B) hustete
    (C) Tier   (C) lächelte
    (D) Mädchen   (D) drehte

Dein Freund Günther hat gerade -------. Er wollte wissen, ------- du mit ------- ins

45. (A) angerufen   46. (A) wenn   47. (A) ihrer
    (B) anrufen   (B) da   (B) ihn
    (C) anzurufen   (C) weil   (C) ihm
    (D) rief an   (D) ob   (D) es

Kino gehen möchtest. Du hättest es ihm schon seit ------- versprochen.

48. (A) lange
    (B) langem
    (C) lang
    (D) langen

GO ON TO THE NEXT PAGE

Gestern ist meine Kusine aus Zürich ------- Besuch gekommen. Sie hat uns ------- etwas mitgebracht. Sie hat

49. (A) nach
    (B) für
    (C) zu
    (D) bei

50. (A) allen
    (B) alle
    (C) all
    (D) aller

mir einen ------- von Simmel geschenkt, denn sie weiß, daß ich den Autor ------- habe. Heute haben wir alles

51. (A) Zettel
    (B) Mantel
    (C) Fall
    (D) Roman

52. (A) den liebsten
    (B) lieben
    (C) am liebsten
    (D) lieber

mögliche -------; unter anderem wollen wir ins Museum und dann ins Kino gehen. Im ganzen will ich mich

53. (A) vorher
    (B) vor
    (C) voraus
    (D) bevor

aber völlig nach ihr richten.

GO ON TO THE NEXT PAGE

Part C

Directions: Read the following texts carefully for comprehension. Each is followed by a number of questions or incomplete statements. Select the answer or completion that is best according to the text and fill in the corresponding oval on the answer sheet.

---

 1. Programm

10.00 Tagesschau und Tagesthemen	17.55 Bayernstudio
10.23 Circus	18.05 Henry und ein linkes Bein
11.55 Umschau	18.30 Ein schönes Wochenende
12.10 Aus Forschung und Technik	19.50 Bayernstudio
12.55 Presseschau	19.57 Heute im Ersten
13.00 Tagesschau	20.00 Tagesschau
13.15 Videotext für alle	20.15 Spione und Agenten. Berüchtigt. Amerik. Spielfilm (1946). Regie: Alfred Hitchcock
14.30 Videotext für alle	21.55 Die Kriminalpolizei rät. Hinweise zur Verhinderung von Straftaten
14.50 Salto Mortale (11)	22.00 Tagesthemen
15.50 Tagesschau	22.30 ARD-Sport extra. Tennis-Davis-cup. USA – Bundesrepublik Deutschland
16.00 Pappi, was machst Du eigentlich den ganzen Tag (3)	0.30 ARD-Sommerkomödie. Feuer und Flamme. Franz. Spielfilm (1981)
16.15 Schwierig sich zu verloben. Spielfilm aus der DDR von 1982	2.15 Tagesschau
17.40 Julia und der Rentenkavalier (7). Schröder hat ein Kind gekriegt	2.20 Nachtgedanken. Späte Einsichten mit Hans Joachim Kulenkampff
17.45 Tagesschau	

54. Was ist das?

    (A) Ein Filmprogramm
    (B) Ein Konzertprogramm
    (C) Ein Fernsehprogramm
    (D) Ein Radioprogramm

GO ON TO THE NEXT PAGE

55. Wann kann man hier eine Theaterkarte kaufen?

    (A) Am Sonntag
    (B) Am Freitag
    (C) Am Dienstag
    (D) Am Abend

GO ON TO THE NEXT PAGE ➤

56. Was will die deutsche Bundespost fördern?

    (A) Alkoholfreie Getränke
    (B) Neue Nummernschilder
    (C) Vernünftiges Autofahren
    (D) Totales Alkoholverbot

GO ON TO THE NEXT PAGE

Die ganze deutsche Sprache in einem einzigen Band!

- Rechtschreibung ● Silben-
trennung ● Aussprache ● Stil
- Hochsprache ● Umgangssprache
- Fremdwörter ● Fachwörter
- Etymologie ● Synonyme
- mundartliche Besonderheiten usw.
  Alles in einem Band,
in einem Alphabet.

57. Wofür macht diese Anzeige Reklame?

    (A) Einen deutschen Roman
    (B) Die deutsche Sprache
    (C) Das deutsche Alphabet
    (D) Ein deutsches Wörterbuch

GO ON TO THE NEXT PAGE

Questions 58-59

Ilse Rössler

Zahnärztin

Sprechstunde nach Vereinbarung

Aufzug 3. ETAGE

58. Wann würde man Ilse Rössler aufsuchen?

(A) Wenn man sich ein Bein gebrochen hat
(B) Wenn man ein Zahnrad kaufen will
(C) Wenn man Zahnschmerzen hat
(D) Wenn man eine Rede halten muß

59. Was bedeutet das Wort „ETAGE"?

(A) Haushalt
(B) Stockwerk
(C) Bücherbrett
(D) Mietwohnung

GO ON TO THE NEXT PAGE

Es liegt bei Ihnen, gemütlich zu liegen.

Dieser Zug führt Schlafwagen und/oder Liegewagen. Sie können jetzt noch einen Bett- oder Liegewagenplatz reservieren. Fragen Sie den DSG-Schaffner nach einem freien Platz.

Speisen & Getränke

Die DSG hat für Sie den ganzen Tag und die ganze Nacht geöffnet. Gehen Sie zum DSG-Schaffner im Schlaf- oder Liegewagen.

60. Wann kann man im Schlaf- oder Liegewagen etwas zu essen bekommen?

(A) Nur morgens
(B) Nur abends
(C) Vierzehn Stunden lang
(D) Vierundzwanzig Stunden lang

GO ON TO THE NEXT PAGE

Questions 61-62

61. Was produziert diese Firma?

   (A) Maschinen
   (B) Stickers
   (C) Getränke
   (D) Kataloge

62. Was muß man machen, um die Produkte benutzen
    zu können?

   (A) Man muß sie wetterfest machen.
   (B) Man muß sie selbst produzieren.
   (C) Man muß sie nur festdrücken.
   (D) Man muß sie nur beschriften.

GO ON TO THE NEXT PAGE

461

Questions 63-64

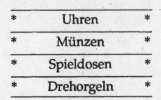

*	Uhren	*
*	Münzen	*
*	Spieldosen	*
*	Drehorgeln	*

FRANZ ANTHUBER 8000 MÜNCHEN 12 WESTENDSTRASSE 81

TELEFON (80 11) 53 36 67

63. Franz Anthuber ist

    (A) Kaufmann
    (B) Organist
    (C) Schauspieler
    (D) Jurist

64. Wo befindet sich dieses Geschäft?

    (A) In einer Stadt
    (B) Im Freien
    (C) Auf dem Lande
    (D) Auf dem Markt

GO ON TO THE NEXT PAGE

Questions 65-66

Dalmatiner

Ein Wurf neugeborener
Dalmatiner verblüfft:
Die Welpen sind voll-
kommen weiß. Erst nach
14 Tagen zeigen sich die ersten schwarzen
Tupfen, die dieser Rasse das aparte Aussehen
verleihen. Auch charakterlich ist der Dalmatiner eine ungewöhnliche Erscheinung: gelehrig,
treu und anpassungsfreudig, tadellos im
Benehmen, geduldig gegenüber Kindern. Für
die Stadtwohnung eignet er sich allerdings
nur, wenn er sehr viel Auslauf erhält.

65. Der Leser erfährt, daß Dalmatiner

    (A) schon bei der Geburt schwarz und weiß sind
    (B) wenig Auslauf brauchen
    (C) nach Jahren ganz schwarz werden
    (D) erst nach ein paar Wochen ihre Flecken bekommen

66. „Verblüfft" bedeutet hier soviel wie

    (A) überrascht
    (B) interessiert
    (C) erschreckt
    (D) langweilt

GO ON TO THE NEXT PAGE →

Questions 67-71

Im Jahre 1950 machte eine Berlinerin während einer Eisenbahnfahrt eine Wette. Damals mußte man noch die Fahrkarte am Ausgang abgeben. Die Berlinerin jedoch meinte, sie könnte ohne Fahrkarte den Bahnhof verlassen, und der Stationsvorsteher müßte sich noch bei ihr entschuldigen. Sie bat einen der Mitreisenden um seine Fahrkarte, plauderte lustig weiter und schrieb dabei unbemerkt die Buchstaben ihres Namens auf die Rückseite der Karte. Dann gab sie die Fahrkarte zurück. Natürlich hatte keiner der Mitreisenden gesehen, daß sie etwas auf die Rückseite der Karte schrieb. Bei der Ankunft des Zuges stieg sie aus, ging einige Zeit auf dem Bahnsteig auf und ab, kam als letzte durch den Ausgang und wollte ohne weiteres an dem Beamten vorübergehen.

Der Beamte rief ihr zu: „Bitte, Ihre Fahrkarte! Jeder Fahrgast muß im Besitz einer gültigen Fahrkarte sein!" Etwas verwundert antwortete die Berlinerin: „Meine Fahrkarte? Die habe ich Ihnen doch schon vorhin gegeben. Ich ging ja als eine der ersten durch den Ausgang! Erinnern Sie sich nicht? Ich mußte noch einmal zum Zug zurückgehen, weil ich etwas vergessen hatte!" Selbstverständlich erinnerte sich der Beamte nicht, verlangte noch einmal die Fahrkarte und wurde schließlich böse. Die Berlinerin wurde noch wütender, verlangte den Stationsvorsteher und sagte ihm ärgerlich: „Zum Glück kann ich die Wahrheit meiner Angaben beweisen. Ich schreibe immer auf die Rückseite meiner Fahrkarte die Buchstaben meines Namens." Die abgegebenen Karten wurden durchgesehen, und man fand die Karte mit ihrem Namen. Die beiden Beamten entschuldigten sich nunmehr, und die freche Berlinerin hatte ihre Wette gewonnen.

67. Die Berlinerin bat einen anderen Fahrgast um seine Karte, weil sie

(A) kein Geld hatte
(B) die Karte behalten wollte
(C) etwas vergessen hatte
(D) darauf schreiben wollte

68. Die Berlinerin kam

(A) als letzte durch den Ausgang
(B) mit einer Gruppe durch den Ausgang
(C) als erste durch den Ausgang
(D) nicht durch den Ausgang

69. Warum kontrollierte der Beamte die Fahrkarten?

(A) Er wollte sicher sein, daß jeder eine Karte gekauft hatte.
(B) Er wollte die Gepäckstücke der Reisenden untersuchen.
(C) Er wollte jedem Gast „eine gute Reise" wünschen.
(D) Er wollte nach der Reise etwas zu tun haben.

70. Warum konnte der Beamte sich nicht an die Berlinerin erinnern?

(A) Er hatte sie nur eine Fahrkarte kaufen sehen.
(B) Er hatte sie vorher nicht durch den Ausgang gehen sehen.
(C) Er hatte sie seit längerer Zeit nicht mehr gesehen.
(D) Er hatte sie auf Anhieb nicht erkennen können.

71. Warum kam der Stationsvorsteher?

(A) Er kannte die Berlinerin.
(B) Der Beamte wollte ihm eine Frage stellen.
(C) Die Berlinerin wollte ihn sprechen.
(D) Er war auf den Beamten böse.

GO ON TO THE NEXT PAGE

Tips zum Umweltschutz

Prüfen Sie, ob Wegwerferzeugnisse aus Papier—
Tischtücher, Handtücher, Becher, Teller, Servietten—
unbedingt verwendet werden müssen. Wenn überhaupt,
dann sollten Sie mit solchen Artikeln sehr sparsam
umgehen.

Altglas und Altpapier sollen nicht in die Mülltonne
wandern. Bringen Sie Altglas und Altpapier zu den
besonders gekennzeichneten Containern. Gemeinden
und Landkreise erteilen Auskunft, wo sich der nächste
Container befindet. Beachten Sie die Bekannt-
machungen über Altpapiersammlungen.

Abgefahrene Reifen haben in der Natur nichts zu
suchen. Tankstellen und Reifenhandel nehmen Altreifen
kostenlos oder gegen eine geringe Gebühr zurück. Im
übrigen können Sie Ihre Altreifen in vielen Fällen auch
bei kommunalen Sammelstellen abgeben. Nähere
Auskünfte, wo sich die nächste Sammelstelle befindet,
erteilt Ihnen die Kreisverwaltung.

Lassen Sie Ihr ausgedientes Auto nicht einfach auf
öffentlichen Straßen oder Plätzen oder irgendwo in der
freien Landschaft stehen. Bringen Sie Ihren alten
Wagen besser zum örtlichen Schrotthandel oder zu
einer Altautosammelstelle oder lassen Sie ihn abholen.
Viele Kreisverwaltungen bieten einen kostenlosen
Abholservice für Schrottfahrzeuge.

GO ON TO THE NEXT PAGE →

72. Für wen sind diese Tips?

    (A) Nur für reiche Leute
    (B) Hauptsächlich für Studenten
    (C) Eigentlich für alle Leute
    (D) Vor allem für Menschen ohne Autos

73. Besonders zu empfehlen sind Handtücher und Tischtücher aus

    (A) Papier
    (B) Stoff
    (C) Schrott
    (D) Altreifen

74. Mit Wegwerferzeugnissen sollte man sparsam sein, weil sie

    (A) nur für den täglichen Bedarf ausreichen
    (B) von schlechter Qualität sind
    (C) unbedingt verwendet werden müssen
    (D) zur Umweltbelastung beitragen

75. In vielen Landkreisen kann man unbrauchbare Autos

    (A) bei der Polizei stehen lassen
    (B) im Wald verstecken
    (C) umsonst abholen lassen
    (D) auf der Straße stehen lassen

GO ON TO THE NEXT PAGE

Wenn der Bus damals nicht vor dem Tor eines Porzellanwerkes gehalten hätte. . . . Das liegt etwa zwanzig Jahre zurück. Aus dem Sonneberger Bus stieg ein junges Mädchen. Ihr blieben fünfzehn Minuten bis zum Anschlußbus in die nächste Stadt, wo ein Betrieb Chemielaborantinnen suchte. Noch eine Woche zuvor hätte Dagmar das überhaupt nicht interessiert, denn sie wollte Ökonomie studieren. Dafür hatte sie mehrere Jahre lang in zwei Klassenzimmern gesessen, vormittags im Gymnasium, abends in der Volkshochschule. Dort lernte sie Sprachen, Schreibmaschine, Stenographie und Buchhaltung, weil ihr das für einen künftigen Beruf wichtig schien. Dagmar bekam schließlich ein sehr gutes Abiturzeugnis und einen Brief von der Universität: „. . . bedauern, Ihnen mitteilen zu müssen . . . abgelehnt . . ."

Das tat weh.

Dagmar entschied sich sehr praktisch: Wenn schon kein Ökonomiestudium an der Universität, dann wollte sie dorthin, wo sie der Ökonomie am nächsten kam— nämlich in die Industrie. In dem Nachbarort wurden Chemielaborantinnen gesucht, also machte sie sich auf den Weg. Nun stand sie zufällig an der Bushaltestelle vor einem Porzellanwerk. Der Aufenthalt brachte sie auf einen Gedanken. Vielleicht sollte sie gleich hier im Personalbüro nachfragen? Eine halbe Stunde später ging sie durch das Werktor mit einem Lehrvertrag als Technikerin.

76. Dagmar befand sich vor dem Tor eines Porzellanwerkes, weil sie

   (A) vorhatte, dort eine Stelle zu suchen
   (B) dort an der Haltestelle umsteigen sollte
   (C) Ökonomie studieren wollte
   (D) dort als Chemielaborantin arbeiten wollte

77. Obwohl mit einem Ökonomiestudium im Moment nichts anzufangen war, wollte Dagmar sofort ihr Wissen . . . erweitern.

   (A) in der Welt der Industrie
   (B) an der Universität
   (C) an der Bushaltestelle
   (D) im Personalbüro

78. Wieviel Jahre liegt Dagmars Entscheidung zurück?

   (A) Ein Jahr
   (B) Zwei Jahrzehnte
   (C) Zehn Jahre
   (D) Fünfzehn Minuten

79. Welcher Satz beschreibt Dagmar am besten?

   (A) Sie kann sich nicht entscheiden, welchen Beruf sie lernen will.
   (B) Es ist ihr völlig egal, welchen Beruf sie lernen wird.
   (C) Sie entscheidet sich schnell, wenn sich die richtige Gelegenheit findet.
   (D) Wenn sie nicht studieren kann, will sie auch nicht arbeiten.

80. Was hatte Dagmar nach dem Abitur studieren wollen?

   (A) Wirtschaftslehre
   (B) Pädagogik
   (C) Sozialwirtschaft
   (D) Kunstgeschichte

GO ON TO THE NEXT PAGE

Der Dichter Franz Werfel hat einmal ausgerechnet, daß wir volle zweieinhalb Jahre unseres Lebens ausschließlich dem Essen widmen. Auch andere prominente Leute hatten ähnliche Kalkulationen angestellt, und es gibt zahllose lustige Geschichten von berühmten Essern.

Immanuel Kant kümmerte sich bis in alle Einzelheiten um den Küchenzettel seines Haushalts. Er führte nicht nur eine Kartei, in der die Lieblingsspeisen seiner Freunde verzeichnet waren, sondern sprach oft mit weiblichen Besuchern über Rezepte.

Von Goethe sagt man, er habe zwar gelegentlich etwas Schlechtes geschrieben, aber nie etwas Schlechtes gegessen.

Max Reger galt bei seinen Freunden als Vielesser. Als ihm eine begeisterte Konzertbesucherin nach einer meisterhaften Interpretation des „Forellen-Quintetts" von Schubert sechs Forellen ins Haus schickte, bedankte sich der Meister mit dem Hinweis, er werde bei nächster Gelegenheit Haydns „Ochsen-Menuett" spielen.

Gioacchino Rossini war einer der fleißigsten Komponisten aller Zeiten, aber er gab selber zu, daß ihn die Kochkunst viel stärker als die Musik interessiert habe. Einmal speiste der kochende Komponist bei einer reichen, aber geizigen Dame, deren kleine Portionen ihm nicht gefielen. Als er sich hungrig verabschiedete, flötete die Dame: „Ich hoffe, Sie werden recht bald wieder bei mir speisen!" Rossini erwiderte: „Am liebsten sofort, wenn es Ihnen recht ist."

81. Worüber wird in dieser kleinen Geschichte hauptsächlich gesprochen?

   (A) Es gibt viele Rezepte auf der Welt.
   (B) Berühmte Leute kochen besonders gerne.
   (C) Man braucht viel Zeit zum Kochen.
   (D) Die Kochkunst interessiert berühmte Leute.

82. Was schrieb Kant sich auf?

   (A) Was er mit seinen Studenten besprach
   (B) Was seine Freunde gerne aßen
   (C) Wo der Einkaufszettel zu Hause lag
   (D) Was er am liebsten aß

83. Dieser Geschichte nach soll Goethe ab und zu

   (A) schlecht gegessen haben
   (B) gut geschlafen haben
   (C) etwas Schlechtes geschrieben haben
   (D) sehr wenig geschrieben haben

84. Was gab Reger seiner Bewunderin zu verstehen?

   (A) Er werde noch ein Musikstück schreiben.
   (B) Er werde die Freude am Essen verlieren.
   (C) Er wolle das Geschenk von Forellen nicht annehmen.
   (D) Er erwarte nächstes Mal einen Ochsen als Geschenk.

85. Rossini wollte bei seiner Gastgeberin länger bleiben, denn er

   (A) hatte immer noch großen Hunger
   (B) wollte sie um einige neue Rezepte bitten
   (C) wußte, daß sie eine gute Köchin war
   (D) wollte sie dazu bringen, mehr zu essen

STOP

IF YOU FINISH BEFORE TIME IS CALLED, YOU MAY CHECK YOUR WORK ON THIS TEST ONLY.
DO NOT TURN TO ANY OTHER TEST IN THIS BOOK.

How to Score the SAT Subject Test in German

When you take an actual SAT Subject Test in German, your answer sheet will be "read" by a scanning machine that will record your responses to each question. Then a computer will compare your answers with the correct answers and produce your raw score. You get one point for each correct answer. For each wrong answer, you lose one-third of a point. Questions you omit (and any for which you mark more than one answer) are not counted. This raw score is converted to a scaled score that is reported to you and to the colleges you specify.

Worksheet 1. Finding Your Raw Score

STEP 1: Table A lists the correct answers for all the questions on the SAT Subject Test in German that is reproduced in this book. It also serves as a worksheet for you to calculate your raw score.

- Compare your answers with those given in the table.
- Put a check in the column marked "Right" if your answer is correct.
- Put a check in the column marked "Wrong" if your answer is incorrect.
- Leave both columns blank if you omitted the question.

STEP 2: Count the number of right answers.

Enter the result here: _____

STEP 3: Count the number of wrong answers.

Enter the result here: _____

STEP 4: Multiply the number of wrong answers by .333.

Enter the result here: _____

STEP 5: Subtract the result obtained in Step 4 from the total you obtained in Step 2.

Enter the result here: _____

STEP 6: Round the number obtained in Step 5 to the nearest whole number.

Enter the result here: _____

The number you obtained in Step 6 is your raw score.

TABLE A
Answers to the SAT Subject Test in German, Form K-3OAC2, and Percentage of Students Answering Each Question Correctly

Question Number	Correct Answer	Right	Wrong	Percentage of Students Answering the Question Correctly*	Question Number	Correct Answer	Right	Wrong	Percentage of Students Answering the Question Correctly*
1	D			91	33	B			74
2	C			93	34	D			71
3	B			98	35	D			70
4	D			98	36	B			27
5	A			92	37	A			64
6	C			83	38	D			78
7	D			84	39	C			64
8	D			65	40	B			82
9	B			44	41	B			88
10	D			85	42	C			32
11	A			88	43	D			56
12	C			58	44	A			79
13	B			79	45	A			89
14	C			93	46	D			57
15	C			89	47	C			88
16	A			65	48	B			20
17	A			56	49	C			37
18	B			89	50	A			27
19	D			80	51	D			63
20	C			36	52	C			79
21	B			92	53	B			37
22	A			29	54	C			96
23	A			94	55	A			89
24	B			64	56	C			58
25	C			29	57	D			79
26	C			43	58	C			90
27	C			23	59	B			34
28	A			30	60	D			91
29	D			15	61	B			89
30	C			48	62	C			54
31	D			39	63	A			63
32	A			80	64	A			86

Table A continued on next page

Table A continued from previous page

Question Number	Correct Answer	Right	Wrong	Percentage of Students Answering the Question Correctly*	Question Number	Correct Answer	Right	Wrong	Percentage of Students Answering the Question Correctly*
65	D			77	76	B			20
66	A			36	77	A			52
67	D			51	78	B			63
68	A			60	79	C			43
69	A			84	80	A			46
70	B			60	81	D			60
71	C			64	82	B			51
72	C			91	83	C			77
73	B			10	84	D			34
74	D			40	85	A			38
75	C			61					

*These percentages are based on the analysis of the answer sheets for a random sample of 855 students who took this test in June 1995 and whose mean score was 556. They may be used as an indication of the relative difficulty of a particular question. Each percentage may also be used to predict the likelihood that a typical SAT Subject Test in German candidate will answer correctly that question on this edition of this test.

Finding Your Scaled Score

When you take SAT Subject Tests, the scores sent to the colleges you specify are reported on the College Board scale, which ranges from 200 to 800. You can convert your practice test score to a scaled score by using Table B. To find your scaled score, locate your raw score in the left-hand column of Table B; the corresponding score in the right-hand column is your scaled score. For example, a raw score of 65 on this particular edition of the SAT Subject Test in German corresponds to a scaled score of 690.

Raw scores are converted to scaled scores to ensure that a score earned on any one edition of a particular Subject Test is comparable to the same scaled score earned on any other edition of the same Subject Test. Because some editions of tests may be slightly easier or more difficult than others, scaled scores are adjusted so that they indicate the same level of performance regardless of the edition of the test taken and the ability of the group that takes it. Thus, for example, a score of 400 on one edition of a test taken at a particular administration indicates the same level of achievement as a score of 400 on a different edition of the test taken at a different administration.

When you take the SAT Subject Tests during a national administration, your scores are likely to differ somewhat from the scores you obtain on the tests in this book. People perform at different levels at different times for reasons unrelated to the tests themselves. The precision of any test is also limited because it represents only a sample of all the possible questions that could be asked.

TABLE B
Scaled Score Conversion Table
German Subject Test (Form K-3OAC2)

Raw Score	Scaled Score	Raw Score	Scaled Score	Raw Score	Scaled Score
85	800	47	570	9	340
84	800	46	570	8	340
83	790	45	560	7	330
82	790	44	550	6	330
81	780	43	540	5	320
80	780	42	540	4	310
79	770	41	530	3	310
78	770	40	520	2	300
77	760	39	520	1	300
76	760	38	510	0	290
75	750	37	500	−1	290
74	740	36	500	−2	280
73	740	35	490	−3	280
72	730	34	480	−4	270
71	730	33	480	−5	270
70	720	32	470	−6	260
69	720	31	460	−7	250
68	710	30	460	−8	250
67	700	29	450	−9	240
66	700	28	450	−10	240
65	690	27	440	−11	230
64	690	26	440	−12	230
63	680	25	430	−13	220
62	670	24	430	−14	220
61	670	23	420	−15	210
60	660	22	420	−16	200
59	660	21	410	−17	200
58	650	20	400	−18	200
57	640	19	400	−19	200
56	640	18	390	−20	200
55	630	17	390	−21	200
54	620	16	380	−22	200
53	620	15	380	−23	200
52	610	14	370	−24	200
51	600	13	360	−25	200
50	590	12	360	−26	200
49	590	11	350	−27	200
48	580	10	350	−28	200

Reviewing Your Performance on the German Subject Test

After you score your test, analyze your performance—consider the following questions:

Did you run out of time before reaching the end of the test?

If so, you may need to pace yourself better. For example, maybe you spent too much time on one or two hard questions. A better approach might be to skip the ones you can't answer right away and try answering all the questions that remain on the test. Then if there's time, go back to the questions you skipped.

Did you take a long time reading the directions?

You will save time when you take the test by learning the directions to the German Subject Test ahead of time. Each minute you spend reading directions during the test is a minute that you could use to answer questions.

How did you handle questions you were unsure of?

If you were able to eliminate one or more of the answer choices as wrong and guess from the remaining ones, your approach probably worked to your advantage. On the other hand, making haphazard guesses or omitting questions without trying to eliminate choices could cost you valuable points.

How difficult were the questions for you compared with other students who took the test?

Table A shows you how difficult the multiple-choice questions were for the group of students who took this test during its national administration. The right-hand column gives the percentage of students that answered each question correctly.

A question answered correctly by almost everyone in the group is obviously an easy question. For example, 92 percent of the students answered question 21 correctly. But only 15 percent answered question 29 correctly.

Keep in mind that these percentages are based on just one group of students. They would probably be different if another group of students took the test.

If you missed several easy questions, go back and try to find out why: Did the questions cover material you haven't yet reviewed? Did you misunderstand the directions?

German with Listening

German with Listening is offered once a year only at designated test centers. To take the test you MUST bring an acceptable cassette player with earphones to the test center.

A cassette tape with listening questions is available for the German Subject Test with Listening practice test in this book. To receive your copy, complete and mail the postcard in this book. If the postcard has been removed, call 212 649-8424 or write to:

The College Board

Subject Tests Language Listening Cassette

45 Columbus Avenue

New York, New York 10023-6992

You must indicate the SAT Language Test with Listening you plan to take.

Sample Listening Questions

Text in brackets [ ] is *only* recorded; it is not printed in your test book. The questions in Part A, however, will be recorded and printed in your test book. Please note that the cassette does not start here. Begin using the cassette when you start the actual practice test on page 481.

Please note that your answer sheet has five answer positions marked A, B, C, D, E. Because the questions throughout this test contain only three or four choices, do NOT make any marks in column E, and do not make any marks in column D if there are only three choices given.

Part A

Directions: In this part of the test you will hear several selections. They will not be printed in your test book. You will hear them *only once*. Therefore, you must listen very carefully. In your test book you will read one or two short questions about what was said. Another speaker will read the questions for you. Each question will be followed by *four* choices marked (A), (B), (C), and (D). The choices are not printed in your test book. You will hear them *once*. Select the best answer and fill in the corresponding oval on your answer sheet.

(Narrator)   [Questions 1 and 2 refer to the following exchange.]

(Woman)   [Könnten Sie mir bitte dieses Kleid heute noch reinigen.

(Man)   Das ist leider unmöglich. Wir machen in einer Stunde, um neunzehn Uhr, Feierabend.

(Woman)   Aber bitte, ich muss dieses Kleid unbedingt heute zum Konzert tragen!]

1. (Man)   [Wo findet dieser Dialog wohl statt?]

    Wo findet dieser Dialog wohl statt?

    (Woman)   [(A) In einer Reinigung.

        (B) In einem Konzertsaal.

        (C) In einer Boutique.

        (D) Auf einem Ball.]

(5 seconds)

In question 1, you are asked to choose from the four answer choices where the short dialogue you just heard takes place. The correct answer is (A) *In einer Reinigung*. You have to understand the verb "reinigen" and make the connection between "reinigen" mentioned in the dialogue and the noun "Reinigung" in one of the answer choices. Choices (B), (C), and (D) do not apply to "reinigen" and are therefore incorrect.

2. (Man)   [Welche Tageszeit ist est?]

    Welche Tageszeit ist est?

    (Woman)   [(A) Morgen.

        (B) Mittag.

        (C) Abend.

        (D) Nachtmittag.]

(5 seconds)

In question 2, you are asked to select from the four choices at which time of day the dialogue is taking place. The correct answer is (C) *Abend*. The man in the dialogue says that they "machen Feierabend" in an hour, at 7 p.m. Even if the German 24-hour clock is not known, the use of the word "Feierabend" can also lead to the correct answer. Choices (A), (B), and (D) are incorrect because there is no reference to morning, noon, or afternoon in the dialogue.

Part B

Directions: You will now listen to some extended dialogues or monologues. You will hear each *only once*. After each dialogue or monologue, you will be asked several questions about what you have just heard. These questions are not printed in your test book. From the four printed choices, select the best answer to each question and fill in the corresponding oval on the answer sheet. There is no sample question for this part.

Questions 3–5

(Narrator)	[Two students talk about Chris's year abroad.]
(Woman)	[Du, Chris, stimmt es? Du wirst das nächste Schuljahr in Amerika verbringen?
(Man)	Ja, ich soll bei einer Familie Lazarro in Los Angeles wohnen und mit ihrem Sohn Miguel zur Schule gehen.
(Woman)	Welche Fächer wirst du denn da haben?
(Man)	Weiß ich noch nicht, aber ich werde mit Miguel die 11. Klasse besuchen.
(Woman)	In amerikanischen Highschools wird auch viel Sport getrieben, nicht?
(Man)	Ja, Miguel soll sogar ein recht guter Schwimmer sein. Er hat schon einige Medaillen gewonnen.
(Woman)	Das ist ja was für dich! Du schwimmst doch auch so gern!
(Man)	Ja, aber jetzt muss ich zuerst noch fleißig Englisch üben. Ich will doch so viel wie möglich im Unterricht verstehen und mich natürlich auch mit meiner neuen Familie unterhalten können.

3. **(Man)**   [Was für eine Schule wird Chris in Amerika besuchen?]

   (12 seconds)

   (A) Eine Kunstakademie.

   (B) Eine Universität.

   (C) Eine Oberschule.

   (D) Eine Sportschule.

In question 3, you are asked to answer the question about what kind of school Chris will be going to in America. The correct answer is (C) *Eine Oberschule.* "Oberschule" is the German equivalent to high school mentioned in the dialogue.

It is also mentioned that he will be in eleventh grade, thus referring to "Oberschule" but not to the schools in (A), (B), and (D). These choices are therefore incorrect.

4. **(Man)**   [Warum glaubt Chris, dass Miguel ein guter Schwimmer ist?]

     (12 seconds)

     (A) Er besucht die Highschool.

     (B) Er hat Auszeichnungen gewonnen.

     (C) Er wohnt in Kalifornien.

     (D) Er ist im Fernsehen erschienen.

Question 4 asks why Chris thinks that Miguel is a good swimmer. The correct answer is (B) *Er hat Auszeichnungen gewonnen.* Chris states in the dialogue that Miguel has won several medals. The use of "Medaillen" (medals) is a more specific way to describe "Auszeichnungen," which is a more general term. It cannot be inferred from answer choices (A) and (C) that Miguel is a good swimmer, and (D) is not at all mentioned in the dialogue.

5. **(Man)**   [Was will Chris noch vor seiner Reise tun?]

     (12 seconds)

     (A) Studienfächer auswählen.

     (B) Medaillen gewinnen.

     (C) Englisch lernen.

     (D) Viel schwimmen.

Question 5 asks what Chris wants to do before he goes on his trip. The correct answer is (C) *Englisch lernen.* At the end of the dialogue, Chris says that he needs to practice English in order to understand as much as possible in class and to be able to talk with his new family. Since the activities in the other answer choices are not mentioned as something he wants to do before leaving, (A), (B) and (D) are incorrect.

Please note that the short rejoinders presented in Part A of the listening section in the practice test (beginning on page 481) are no longer included in current German Subject Tests with Listening. The German Subject Test with Listening also has a Reading Section. Please refer to pages 441–446 for Sample Reading Questions.

German Test with Listening

The test that follows is an actual, recently administered SAT Subject Test in German with Listening. To get an idea of what a real administration is like, take the test under conditions as close as possible to those of a national administration:

- Set aside an hour when you can take the test uninterrupted. Make sure you complete the test in one sitting.

- Sit at a desk or table with no other books or papers. Dictionaries, other books, or notes are not allowed in the test room.

- Time yourself by placing a clock or kitchen timer in front of you.

- Tear out an answer sheet from the back of this book and fill it in just as you would on the day of the test. One answer sheet can be used for up to three Subject Tests.

- Read the instructions that precede the practice test. During the actual administration you will be asked to read them before answering test questions.

- After you finish the practice test, read the sections "How to Score the SAT Subject Test in German with Listening" and "Reviewing Your Performance on the German Subject Test with Listening."

- Actual test and answer sheets will indicate circles, not ovals.

Form 3QLC

GERMAN TEST WITH LISTENING

The top portion of the section of the answer sheet that you will use in taking the German Test with Listening must be filled in exactly as shown in the illustration below. Note carefully that you have to do all of the following on your answer sheet.

1. Print GERMAN WITH LISTENING on the line under the words "Subject Test (print)."

2. In the shaded box labeled "Test Code" fill in four ovals:

   —Fill in oval 5 in the row labeled V.

   —Fill in oval 4 in the row labeled W.

   —Fill in oval 3 in the row labeled X.

   —Fill in oval E in the row labeled Y.

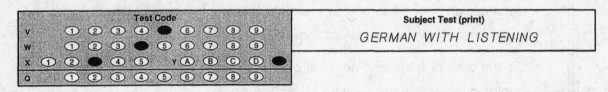

Please answer either Part I or Part II by filling in the specific oval in row Q. You are to fill in ONE and ONLY ONE oval, as described below, to indicate how you obtained your knowledge of German. The information you provide is for statistical purposes only and will not influence your score on the test.

Part I   If your knowledge of German does not come primarily from courses taken in grades 9 through 12, fill in oval 9 and leave the remaining ovals blank, regardless of how long you studied the subject in school. For example, you are to fill in oval 9 if your knowledge of German comes primarily from any of the following sources: study prior to the ninth grade, courses taken at a college, special study, living in a home in which German is the principal language spoken, or extensive residence abroad that includes significant experience in the German language.

Part II   If your knowledge of German does come primarily from courses taken in secondary school or the equivalent, fill in the oval that indicates the level of the German course in which you are currently enrolled. If you are not now enrolled in a German course, fill in the oval that indicates the level of the most advanced course in German that you have completed.

First year:	first or second half	—Fill in oval 1.
Second year:	first half	—Fill in oval 2.
	second half	—Fill in oval 3.
Third year:	first half	—Fill in oval 4.
	second half	—Fill in oval 5.
Fourth year:	first half	—Fill in oval 6.
	second half	—Fill in oval 7.

Advanced Placement course
or a course at a level higher
than fourth year, second half
or
high school course work plus
a minimum of four weeks of
study abroad   —Fill in oval 8.

When the supervisor gives the signal, turn the page and begin the German Test with Listening. There are 100 numbered ovals on the answer sheet and 88 questions in the German Test with Listening. Therefore, use only ovals 1 to 88 for recording your answers.

GERMAN TEST WITH LISTENING

PLEASE NOTE THAT YOUR ANSWER SHEET HAS FIVE ANSWER POSITIONS MARKED A, B, C, D, AND E. BECAUSE THE QUESTIONS THROUGHOUT THIS TEST CONTAIN ONLY THREE OR FOUR CHOICES, DO NOT MAKE ANY MARKS IN COLUMN E, AND DO NOT MAKE ANY MARKS IN COLUMN D IF THERE ARE ONLY THREE CHOICES GIVEN.

SECTION I

LISTENING

Approximate time — 20 minutes

Questions 1-33

Part A

Directions: In this part of the test you will hear statements or questions spoken in German, each followed by three responses also spoken in German. You will hear the statements or questions twice, but the responses will be spoken just one time. The sentences and responses you hear will not be written in your test booklet. Therefore, you must listen very carefully. Select the best answer and fill in the corresponding oval on the answer sheet. Now listen to this example.

You will hear: ● Ⓑ Ⓒ Ⓓ

You will also hear:

The best answer to the question „Wo wohnen Sie?" is choice (A) „In der Freistraße." Therefore, you should choose answer (A).

Now, let us begin this part with question Number 1.

1. Mark your answer on your answer sheet.

2. Mark your answer on your answer sheet.

3. Mark your answer on your answer sheet.

4. Mark your answer on your answer sheet.

5. Mark your answer on your answer sheet.

6. Mark your answer on your answer sheet.

7. Mark your answer on your answer sheet.

8. Mark your answer on your answer sheet.

9. Mark your answer on your answer sheet.

10. Mark your answer on your answer sheet.

GO ON TO THE NEXT PAGE

3QLC

Part B

Directions: In this part of the test you will hear several selections. They will not be printed in your test book. You will hear them <u>only once</u>. Therefore, you must listen very carefully. In your test book you will read one or two short questions about what was said. Another speaker will read the questions for you. Each question will be followed by <u>four</u> choices marked (A), (B), (C), and (D). The choices are <u>not</u> printed in your test book. You will hear them <u>once</u>. Select the best answer and fill in the corresponding oval on your answer sheet.

Listen to the following example.

You will hear:

You will hear and read: Was schenkt der Mann Lisa zum Geburtstag?

You will hear: Ⓐ ● Ⓒ Ⓓ

The best answer to the question „Was schenkt der Mann Lisa zum Geburtstag?" is (B), „Ein Buch." Therefore, you should choose option (B).

Now listen to the first selection.

---

11. Was gibt es diese Woche bei Hertie?

    Mark your answer on your answer sheet.

12. Warum fährt der junge Mann nicht mit?

    Mark your answer on your answer sheet.

    _____

13. Wo sind die beiden?

    Mark your answer on your answer sheet.

    _____

14. Worüber ist diese Sendung?

    Mark your answer on your answer sheet.

15. Wie wird es am Sonntag?

    Mark your answer on your answer sheet.

    _____

16. Wer spricht mit der Frau?

    Mark your answer on your answer sheet.

17. Was bestellt die Dame?

    Mark your answer on your answer sheet.

    _____

18. Wo sind die beiden Sprecher?

    Mark your answer on your answer sheet.

19. Was für einen Platz möchte die Frau?

    Mark your answer on your answer sheet.

    _____

20. Wo findet dieses Gespräch statt?

    Mark your answer on your answer sheet.

21. Was ist hier das Problem?

    Mark your answer on your answer sheet.

GO ON TO THE NEXT PAGE →

Part C

Directions: You will now listen to some extended dialogues or monologues. You will hear each only once. After each dialogue or monologue, you will be asked several questions about what you have just heard. These questions are not printed in your test book. From the four printed choices, select the best answer to each question and fill in the corresponding oval on the answer sheet. There is no sample question for this part.

Selection number 1

22. (A) Manchmal.
    (B) Täglich.
    (C) Später.
    (D) Öfter.

23. (A) Lederwaren.
    (B) Spielzeug.
    (C) Lebensmittel.
    (D) Schreibwaren.

24. (A) Briefe einwerfen.
    (B) Karten aussuchen.
    (C) Briefmarken sammeln.
    (D) Anrufe machen.

25. (A) Nudeln.
    (B) Eine Einkaufsliste.
    (C) Einen Brief.
    (D) Äpfel.

Selection number 2

26. (A) Ein junger Mann parkte vor dem Kölner Dom.
    (B) Ein junger Mann schenkte vielen Leuten Geld.
    (C) Ein junger Mann ging in den Kölner Dom.
    (D) Ein junger Mann verursachte einen Unfall.

27. (A) Amerikanisch.
    (B) Unglücklich.
    (C) Groß.
    (D) Schick.

28. (A) Sie liefen sofort zum Polizeipräsidium.
    (B) Sie gaben eine Spende.
    (C) Sie waren etwas skeptisch.
    (D) Sie schrieben ihm Empfehlungen.

29. (A) Wer dieser Mann wohl war.
    (B) Wo dieses seltsame Ereignis stattfand.
    (C) Ob die Geldscheine wohl echt sind.
    (D) Wer das Geld wohl angenommen hat.

GO ON TO THE NEXT PAGE

Selection number 3

30. (A) Den Kauf eines neuen Komputers.
    (B) Besetzung einer neuen IBM Stelle.
    (C) Heimarbeit mit Hilfe von Komputern.
    (D) Eröffnung einer IBM Branche in Holland.

31. (A) Höhere Produktivität.
    (B) Niedrigere Telefonrechnungen.
    (C) Höhere Gehälter.
    (D) Kürzeres Training.

32. (A) Sie ruft ständig ihre Sekretärin an.
    (B) Sie stellt zu Hause einfach ihren Komputer an.
    (C) Sie fährt sonntags ins Büro.
    (D) Sie besucht oft ihre Mitarbeiter zu Hause.

33. (A) Sie weiß es noch nicht genau.
    (B) Sie findet es sehr informativ.
    (C) Sie möchte mehr darüber erfahren.
    (D) Sie findet es sehr fortschrittlich.

END OF SECTION I.
DO NOT GO ON TO SECTION II UNTIL YOU ARE TOLD TO DO SO.

GO ON TO THE NEXT PAGE

SECTION II

READING

Time — 40 minutes

Questions 34-88

WHEN YOU BEGIN THE READING SECTION, BE SURE THAT YOU MARK YOUR ANSWER TO THE FIRST READING QUESTION BY FILLING IN ONE OF THE OVALS NEXT TO NUMBER 34 ON THE ANSWER SHEET.

Part A

Directions: This part consists of a number of incomplete statements, each having four suggested completions. Select the most appropriate completion and fill in the corresponding oval on the answer sheet.

---

34. Ist dieser . . . noch frei? — Ja, setzen Sie sich!

    (A) Teller
    (B) Platz
    (C) Ort
    (D) Weg

35. In der Schule lesen wir jetzt . . . Buch über Amerika.

    (A) ein
    (B) eines
    (C) einem
    (D) eins

36. Wenn er Geld hätte, . . . er ins Kino gehen.

    (A) werde
    (B) wäre
    (C) würde
    (D) hätte

37. Normalerweise fährt der Bus . . . zehn Minuten.

    (A) viele
    (B) alle
    (C) gleich
    (D) um

38. Warum bist du nicht früher gekommen? Jetzt . . . ich leider weggehen.

    (A) kann
    (B) mag
    (C) darf
    (D) muß

39. Es wird . . . Zeit, daß du ins Bett gehst!

    (A) größte
    (B) höchste
    (C) wirkliche
    (D) echte

40. Ich . . . , daß er gerne ins Gebirge geht.

    (A) wandere
    (B) steige
    (C) kenne
    (D) weiß

41. Es ist . . . , daß du nicht länger bleiben kannst.

    (A) schade
    (B) spät
    (C) ungern
    (D) leider

GO ON TO THE NEXT PAGE

42. Diese Bleistifte gehören . . .

    (A) mein
    (B) meine
    (C) mir
    (D) mich

43. Das ist nicht genug Salat. Wir brauchen eigentlich
    zwei . . .

    (A) Köpfen
    (B) Kopfe
    (C) Köpfe
    (D) Kopf

44. Er wußte immer noch nicht, wem . . .

    (A) er sollte danken
    (B) er hätte danken sollen
    (C) solle er danken
    (D) hat er danken sollen

45. Sie hat bestimmt nichts gegen dich. Das . . . du dir
    nur ein.

    (A) denkst
    (B) bildest
    (C) glaubst
    (D) machst

46. Die meisten Kinder lieben ihre Eltern . . .

    (A) sehr
    (B) viel
    (C) äußerst
    (D) bestens

47. Kann ich mir dieses Buch ausleihen? Ich . . . es
    bestimmt morgen zurück.

    (A) verstehe
    (B) nehme
    (C) bringe
    (D) lese

GO ON TO THE NEXT PAGE

Part B

Directions: In each of the following paragraphs, there are numbered blanks indicating that words or phrases have been omitted. For each numbered blank, four completions are provided. First read through the entire paragraph. Then, for each numbered blank, choose the completion that is most appropriate and fill in the corresponding oval on the answer sheet.

Schon immer wollte Anke einmal auf einem ------- arbeiten, ------- sie die Natur und auch

48.	(A) Gymnasium	49.	(A) daß
	(B) Bauernhof		(B) ob
	(C) Bergwerk		(C) als
	(D) Hotel		(D) weil

Tiere liebt. Später möchte sie einmal an der Universität studieren, um entweder Försterin oder

Tierärztin zu werden, aber im Moment ist die Wahl zwischen den ------- Berufen einfach zu

50. (A) beide
(B) beiden
(C) beides
(D) beider

------- . Um etwas Erfahrung zu sammeln, will sie im ------- Sommer vier Wochen ------- ihrem

51.	(A) schweres	52.	(A) kommen	53.	(A) bei
	(B) schwere		(B) kommend		(B) zu
	(C) schwerer		(C) kommende		(C) an
	(D) schwer		(D) kommenden		(D) vor

Onkel und ihrer Tante auf dem Lande in Bayern verbringen.

GO ON TO THE NEXT PAGE

Liebe Karin:

Ich studiere jetzt ------- der Universität Freiburg und wohne in ------- deutschen Studentenheim!

54. (A) zu
    (B) an
    (C) mit
    (D) unter

55. (A) einen
    (B) einer
    (C) einem
    (D) ein

Leider muß ich meine Wohnung mit anderen Studenten ------- . Meine Mitbewohner sind so

56. (A) trennen
    (B) teilen
    (C) suchen
    (D) leben

unordentlich, das gefällt mir gar nicht! Ich habe ------- gesagt, daß ich nichts ------- die

57. (A) ihn
    (B) sie
    (C) ihnen
    (D) ihrer

58. (A) für
    (B) gegen
    (C) über
    (D) durch

Unordnung in ihren eigenen Zimmern habe, aber unser gemeinsames Wohnzimmer muß ordentlich sein.

Herzlichst,

Dein Bryan

GO ON TO THE NEXT PAGE

Karla hatte eigentlich vor, erst nach einer Stelle zu ------- und später weiter zu studieren, aber

          59. (A) geben
              (B) machen
              (C) erfinden
              (D) suchen

------- gefiel kein Angebot. Deshalb ------- sie sich, ihre Ausbildung ------- Bibliothekarin erst

60.	(A) ihr	61.	(A) entschied	62.	(A) wie
	(B) sie		(B) beschloß		(B) als
	(C) ihrer		(C) verstand		(C) für
	(D) ihrem		(D) glaubte		(D) die

einmal zu beenden, auch ------- sie sich dafür ------- leihen mußte.

63.	(A) wann	64.	(A) Buch
	(B) dann		(B) Zahl
	(C) wenn		(C) Papier
	(D) denn		(D) Geld

GO ON TO THE NEXT PAGE

Part C

Directions: Read the following texts carefully for comprehension. Each is followed by a number of questions or incomplete statements. Select the answer or completion that is best according to the text and fill in the corresponding oval on your answer sheet.

Questions 65-66

Symphoniekonzert
Studentenorchester der
Heinrich - Heine - Universität
Düsseldorf

G. Rossini: Ouvertüre zur Oper "Die diebische Elster"
Ch. Koechlin: "Sur les flots lointaines"
J. Haydn: Konzert für Cello und Orchester, C-Dur, Hob VII b: 1
F. Schubert: Symphonie Nr. 4, C-Moll, "Die Tragische"

Solist: Jochen Fuchs
Dirigentin: Silke Löhr

4.7.90   20.00

Neues Gewandhaus Leipzig,
Großer Saal

Vorverkauf: Studentenrat der Karl-Marx-Universität
Leipzig, Hauptgebäude 2. Etage

65. Wann findet dieses Konzert statt?

(A) Am zwanzigsten Juli
(B) Am zwanzigsten April
(C) Am siebten April
(D) Am vierten Juli

66. Wo kann man Karten im voraus kaufen?

(A) Im Neuen Gewandhaus
(B) Im Großen Saal
(C) Beim Studentenrat
(D) Bei der Dirigentin

GO ON TO THE NEXT PAGE ▶

> ## Gute Werbung = höherer Umsatz

67. Was bedeutet diese Gleichung?

    (A) Wenn man gut wirbt, kann man mehr Produkte verkaufen.
    (B) Wenn man gut wirbt, kann man wenig Geld verdienen.
    (C) Wenn man keine Werbung macht, kann man hohen Profit
        machen.
    (D) Wenn man billige Waren hat, kann man mehr Produkte
        verkaufen.

GO ON TO THE NEXT PAGE →

Questions 68-72

Manche mögen's scharf

Chilis haben die kulinarische Welt in Brand gesetzt

Es müssen mutige Menschen gewesen sein, die die ersten Paprikaschoten aßen, und noch tapferer diejenigen, die sich an die zweiten wagten. Dennoch haben die pikanten Gebilde rund um den Erdball eine kulinarische Revolution verursacht.

Sämtliche 300 bis 7000 Pfefferschotensorten—die Zahlen variieren je nachdem, wo der Spezialist zu Hause ist, den man befragt—stammen aus Amerika; sie waren in Mittelamerika, Mexiko und den Vereinigten Staaten schon lange Volks- nahrungsmittel, ehe Kolumbus in der Neuen Welt an Land ging.

Außerhalb jenes Kontinents fand man Chilis zuerst unter den spanischen Entdeckern. Die Gewürzhändler fanden sehr schnell heraus, daß sie damit über eine «heiße" Ware verfügten.

Im 15. Jahrhundert überquerten getrocknete Pfefferschoten und -samen den Pazifischen Ozean. Schon bald gediehen die unempfindlichen Pflanzen auch in Südostasien, in China, Indien sowie dem heutigen Pakistan und Indonesien, wo sie schnell Bestandteile der jeweiligen Küche wurden. Von Asien aus verbreiteten sich die Chilis über Afrika und kamen als Paprika und Cayennepfeffer in die europäischen Haushalte. Die Bundesrepublik Deutschland importiert jährlich rund 6500 Tonnen Paprika und Cayennepfeffer.

Pfefferschoten gibt es in vielen verschiedenen Größen, Farben, Ge- schmacksrichtungen und Schärfegraden.

Was macht die Chilis scharf? Eine teuflische Chemikalie namens Capsaicin, eine kristalline Substanz, die vor allem in den Scheidewänden und Samen der Frucht zu finden ist. Vielfach wird behauptet, grüne Pfefferschoten seien schärfer als rote. In Wahrheit verändert sich der Capsaicingehalt der Pfefferschote nach eingetretener Reife nicht mehr, und reif kann schon die noch grüne Frucht sein. Eine grüne Schote enthält nicht soviel Fruchtzucker wie eine rote, und ihre Schärfe wird deshalb nicht durch den Zucker verdeckt, aber beide sind gleich scharf.

Ganz gleich, welche Farbe die Pfefferschote hat, sie kann einem in jedem Fall zusetzen, wenn Capsaicintropfen auf die Haut oder in die Augen spritzen. Wer Chilis berührt hat, sollte sich anschließend sofort die Hände mit Seife waschen.

68. Warum war es erstaunlich, daß Menschen Paprikaschoten aßen?

   (A) Sie waren so scharf.
   (B) Sie waren schön.
   (C) Sie waren interessant.
   (D) Sie waren knallrot.

69. Die vielen Pfeffersorten kamen ursprünglich aus

   (A) Afrika
   (B) Südostasien
   (C) Spanien
   (D) Amerika

70. Wann wurden die ersten Paprikaschoten gegessen?

   (A) Erst vor ein paar Jahren
   (B) Lange bevor Kolumbus in die Neue Welt
       segelte
   (C) Zur Zeit des amerikanischen Bürgerkrieges
   (D) Erst im 19. Jahrhundert

71. Womit könnte man „heiß" (im dritten Abschnitt) ersetzen?

   (A) Sehr leidenschaftlich
   (B) Nicht eßbar
   (C) Besonders bitter
   (D) Gut verkäuflich

72. Warum sind viele Paprikaschoten scharf?

   (A) Sie enthalten eine besondere Chemikalie.
   (B) Sie wachsen auf besonderem Boden.
   (C) Sie werden unreif geerntet.
   (D) Sie kommen aus Afrika.

GO ON TO THE NEXT PAGE →

Gewinnen Sie ein Mainzer Ausbauhaus

Die Bausparkasse Mainz verlost ein Ausbauhaus im Wert von 68 058.–DM.

So wie die Gewinner-Familie unserer letzten Verlosung können auch Sie sich schon bald über Ihr eigenes Haus freuen. Senden Sie den Gewinn-Scheck gleich ab–und nehmen Sie teil an der Hausverlosung. Gleichzeitig erfahren Sie alles darüber, wie Sie sich den Traum vom eigenen Haus erfüllen können:

- *Das Mainzer Ausbauhaus ist außen komplett fertig.*
  Für den Innenausbau, geschützt vor Wind und Wetter, gibt es preisgünstige Ausbaupakete.
- *Durch Eigenleistung sparen Sie leicht bis zu 30% der Baukosten.*
  Besondere handwerkliche Kenntnisse sind dazu nicht erforderlich, denn ausführliche Anleitungen zeigen Ihnen Schritt für Schritt, was zu tun ist.
- *Wählen Sie unter 15 verschiedenen Mainzer Ausbauhäusern Ihr Traumhaus aus.*
  Schon ab 53 735.–DM erhalten Sie ein Mainzer Ausbauhaus geliefert und fachmännisch aufgestellt.
- *Ab 10% Eigenkapital stehen Ihnen die Türen zum eigenen Haus offen.*
  Die Bausparkasse Mainz bietet Ihnen nicht nur preiswerte Ausbauhäuser, sondern auch eine Finanzierung, die speziell für Bauherren mit durchschnittlichem Einkommen und wenig Eigenkapital entwickelt worden ist.
- *Nutzen Sie Ihre große Chance jetzt. Nehmen Sie teil an der Hausverlosung.*
  Senden Sie Ihren Gewinn-Scheck gleich heute noch ab.

Teilnahmebedingungen:

Einsendeschluß ist der 30. September dieses Jahres (Poststempel). Die Verlosung erfolgt unter juristischer Aufsicht.

Teilnahmeberechtigt ist jeder über 18 Jahre mit Wohnsitz in der Bundesrepublik Deutschland. Jeder Einsender kann nur einmal an der Verlosung teilnehmen. Die Mitarbeiter der Bausparkasse Mainz und angeschlossenen Organisationen sowie deren Angehörige sind von der Teilnahme ausgeschlossen.

GO ON TO THE NEXT PAGE

73. Was muß der Gewinner eines Ausbauhauses noch machen?

    (A) Das Dach decken
    (B) Das Haus transportieren
    (C) Die Innenräume fertigstellen
    (D) Nur noch Fenster und Türen kaufen

74. Was muß der Gewinner haben, um sich das Haus bauen zu lassen?

    (A) Ein Grundstück
    (B) Viel Eigenkapital
    (C) Einen oder mehrere Baupartner
    (D) Sehr gute handwerkliche Kenntnisse

75. Wer darf an der Verlosung teilnehmen?

    (A) Deutsche, die im Ausland wohnen
    (B) Jeder, der einen Gewinn-Scheck hat
    (C) Einwohner der BRD, die volljährig sind
    (D) Mitarbeiter der Bausparkasse Mainz

76. Was muß man haben, um das Haus zu gewinnen?

    (A) Sehr viel Glück
    (B) Ausgezeichnete Baukenntnisse
    (C) Ein hohes Einkommen
    (D) Wenigstens 30% Eigenkapital

77. Aus der Anzeige können wir entnehmen, daß die Bausparkasse durch die Verlosung

    (A) Mainz in ein Bauzentrum verwandeln will
    (B) Reklame für sich selber machen will
    (C) Nachteile der Eigenleistung hervorheben will
    (D) Mitarbeiter an dem Gewinn beteiligen will

GO ON TO THE NEXT PAGE →

Questions 80-81

Siemens Mobiltelefone. Ihre Unabhängigkeits- erklärung.

78. Was bedeutet hier Unabhängigkeit?

(A) Man kann billiger telefonieren.
(B) Man ist bei Siemens angestellt.
(C) Man kann durch Joggen fit bleiben.
(D) Man ist nicht an einen Ort gebunden.

– 14.00	**Europamagazin**
– 14.30	**Hallo Spencer Serie**
– 15.00	**Formel Eins Hitparade**
– 16.30	**Magazin**
	Moderation: Antje-Katrin Kühnemann
	und Winfried Göpfert
	• Operation mit Laserstrahlen
– 16.40	**Magisches Intermezzo**
	Mikro-Magie und Partyzauberei
	Von José Aldini
– 17.55	**Tagesschau**
– 18.00	**Sportschau-Telegramm**

79. Professor Göpfert sieht sich gerne mal Hokuspokus an. Welche Sendung würden Sie empfehlen?

(A) Europamagazin
(B) Magazin
(C) Magisches Intermezzo
(D) Sportschau

Universitätsstraße 7 · 7800 Freiburg
Telefon 0761 / 3 99 79

80. Was erfahren wir aus dieser Anzeige?

(A) Axmann erhöht alle Preise.
(B) Axmann hat das Geschäft aufgegeben.
(C) Axmann macht einen Sommerschlußverkauf.
(D) Axmann wird in ein anderes Gebäude ziehen.

81. Was für ein Geschäft ist Axmann?

(A) Ein Lebensmittelgeschäft
(B) Ein Schreibwarengeschäft
(C) Ein Möbelgeschäft
(D) Ein Baugeschäft

GO ON TO THE NEXT PAGE ➤

Questions 82-87

In einer kleinen Provinzstadt hatte ein Zirkus seine Zelte aufgestellt. Das Programm bestand, wie es sich für einen guten Wanderzirkus gehört, aus Weltsensationen, heroischen Aufführungen und dem spannendsten Boxkampf aller Zeiten. Sogar einen weltberühmten Magier und einen unglaublichen Feuerschlucker hatte man angekündigt.

Aber es kam kein Mensch. Man setzte die Eintrittspreise stark herunter. Es kam immer noch niemand. Schließlich hängte die Direktion Plakate auf mit der Bekanntmachung: „Eintritt frei!" Das half. Jetzt kamen mehr Zuschauer als der Zirkus Plätze hatte, und man stellte noch weitere Bänke dazu.

Nach der Vorstellung drängten alle eilig zum Ausgang. Dort, an der Tür, standen schweigend die Boxer und ließen ihre Muskeln spielen. Über ihnen hing ein Plakat: „Ausgang: DM 1.- pro Person!" Alle zahlten. Nachts baute der Zirkus schnell seine Zelte ab und fuhr weiter.

82. Die Geschichte handelt von

(A) einem berühmten Boxer
(B) einer kleinen Provinzstadt
(C) einem cleveren Wanderzirkus
(D) einem berühmten Feuerschlucker

83. Man setzte die Eintrittspreise herab, weil

(A) es keine Bänke gab
(B) keine Leute kamen
(C) es keine Plakate gab
(D) ein Zauberer fehlte

84. Der Zirkus wurde so voll, daß man

(A) die Vorstellung absagen mußte
(B) gar keine Karten verkaufte
(C) mehr Sitzplätze brauchte
(D) den Eintritt verbot

85. Die Boxer standen am Ausgang, um

(A) den Besuchern Geld abzunehmen
(B) ein Plakat hochzuhalten
(C) die Besucher zu begrüßen
(D) jeder Person DM 1.- zu geben

86. Wann baute der Zirkus seine Zelte ab?

(A) Zwei Nächte später
(B) Innerhalb einer Stunde
(C) Früh am nächsten Morgen
(D) Noch in derselben Nacht

87. Warum fuhr der Zirkus wohl weiter?

(A) Aus Freude über die guten Einnahmen
(B) Aus Angst vor den verärgerten Bürgern
(C) Aus Rache an den sparsamen Zuschauern
(D) Aus Interesse an neuen Plätzen

GO ON TO THE NEXT PAGE

88. Was soll der Leser dieser Anzeige tun?

   (A) Fotos machen
   (B) Tourist werden
   (C) Reklame machen
   (D) Brücken kaufen

END OF SECTION II

S T O P

IF YOU FINISH BEFORE TIME IS CALLED, YOU MAY CHECK YOUR WORK ON SECTION II OF THIS TEST.
DO NOT TURN TO ANY OTHER TEST IN THIS BOOK.

How to Score the SAT Subject Test in German with Listening

When you take the SAT Subject Test in German with Listening, you will receive an overall composite score as well as two subscores: one for the reading section, one for the listening section.

The reading and listening scores are reported on the College Board's 20-to-80 scale. However, the composite score, which is the most significant of the scores reported to the colleges you specify, is in the form of the College Board's 200-to-800 scale.

Worksheet 1. Finding Your Raw Listening Subscore

STEP 1: Table A lists the correct answers for all the questions on the SAT Subject Test in German with Listening that is reproduced in this book. It also serves as a worksheet for you to calculate your raw Listening subscore.

- Compare your answers with those given in the table.
- Put a check in the column marked "Right" if your answer is correct.
- Put a check in the column marked "Wrong" if your answer is incorrect.
- Leave both columns blank if you omitted the question.

STEP 2: Count the number of right answers for questions 1–10.

Enter the result here: _____

STEP 3: Count the number of wrong answers for questions 1–10.

Enter the result here: _____

STEP 4: Multiply the number of wrong answers from Step 3 by .500.

Enter the product here: _____

STEP 5: Subtract the result obtained in Step 4 from the total you obtained in Step 2.

Enter the result here: _____

STEP 6: Count the number of right answers for questions 11–33.

Enter the result here: _____

STEP 7: Count the number of wrong answers for questions 11–33.

Enter the result here: _____

STEP 8: Multiply the number of wrong answers from Step 7 by .333.

Enter the product here: _____

STEP 9: Subtract the result obtained in Step 8 from the total obtained in Step 6.

Enter the result here: _____

STEP 10: Add the result obtained in Step 5 to the result obtained in Step 9.

Enter the result here: _____

STEP 11: Round the number obtained in Step 10 to the nearest whole number.

Enter the result here: _____

The number you obtained in Step 11 is your raw Listening subscore.

Worksheet 2. Finding Your Raw Reading Subscore

STEP 1: Table A lists the correct answers for all the questions on the SAT Subject Test in German with Listening that is reproduced in this book. It also serves as a worksheet for you to calculate your raw Reading subscore.

STEP 2: Count the number of right answers for questions 34–88.

Enter the result here: _____

STEP 3: Count the number of wrong answers for questions 34–88.

Enter the result here: _____

STEP 4: Multiply the number of wrong answers from Step 3 by .333.

Enter the product here: _____

STEP 5: Subtract the result obtained in Step 4 from the total you obtained in Step 2.

Enter the result here: _____

STEP 6: Round the number obtained in Step 5 to the nearest whole number.

Enter the result here: _____

The number you obtained in Step 6 is your raw Reading subscore.

Worksheet 3. Finding Your Raw Composite Score*

STEP 1: Enter your unrounded raw Reading subscore from Step 5 of Worksheet 2 here:_____

STEP 2: Multiply your unrounded raw Reading subscore by 1.072.

Enter the product here: _____

STEP 3: Enter your unrounded raw Listening subscore from Step 10 of Worksheet 1 here:_____

STEP 4: Multiply your unrounded raw Listening subscore by .8810.

Enter the product here: _____

STEP 5: Add the result obtained in Step 2 to the result obtained in step 4.

Enter the result here: _____

STEP 6: Round the number obtained in Step 5 to the nearest whole number.

Enter the product here: _____

The number you obtained in Step 6 is your raw composite score.

*This weighting reflects the amount of time spent on the two sections of the test—40 minutes on the reading questions and 20 minutes on the listening questions. For those who are curious about how the calculation works, the weighting is done in standard deviation units, a measure of score variability. The weight given to the listening subscore is calculated by dividing the standard deviation of the reading subscore by two times the standard deviation of the listening subscore. Weights are then applied to both reading and listening sections so that the maximum raw composite score equals 88.

TABLE A
Answers to the SAT Subject Test in German with Listening, Form 3QLC, and Percentage of Students Answering Each Question Correctly

Question Number	Correct Answer	Right	Wrong	Percentage of Students Answering the Question Correctly*	Question Number	Correct Answer	Right	Wrong	Percentage of Students Answering the Question Correctly*
1	A			94	33	D			49
2	B			94	34	B			90
3	A			55	35	A			77
4	C			84	36	C			70
5	B			90	37	B			25
6	C			66	38	D			79
7	A			80	39	B			38
8	B			86	40	D			85
9	A			74	41	A			89
10	C			80	42	C			71
11	B			84	43	C			38
12	A			66	44	B			27
13	C			23	45	B			16
14	C			85	46	A			25
15	D			60	47	C			86
16	C			61	48	B			59
17	A			10	49	D			84
18	C			89	50	B			85
19	B			87	51	D			81
20	B			61	52	D			52
21	D			73	53	A			84
22	B			81	54	B			78
23	C			54	55	C			49
24	A			85	56	B			47
25	D			67	57	C			40
26	B			66	58	B			63
27	D			61	59	D			27
28	C			30	60	A			26
29	A			41	61	A			38
30	C			29	62	B			40
31	A			77	63	C			43
32	B			77	64	D			41

Table A continued on next page

Table A continued from previous page

Question Number	Correct Answer	Right	Wrong	Percentage of Students Answering the Question Correctly*	Question Number	Correct Answer	Right	Wrong	Percentage of Students Answering the Question Correctly*
65	D			70	77	B			20
66	C			92	78	D			45
67	A			63	79	C			82
68	A			74	80	D			21
69	D			78	81	C			30
70	B			85	82	C			70
71	D			31	83	B			71
72	A			85	84	C			57
73	C			49	85	A			41
74	A			28	86	D			65
75	C			51	87	B			37
76	A			51	88	C			35

*These percentages are based on an analysis of the answer sheets for a random sample of 994 students who took this form of the test in November 1994 and whose mean score was 534. They may be used as an indication of the relative difficulty of a particular question. Each percentage may also be used to predict the likelihood that a typical SAT Subject Test in German with Listening candidate will answer correctly that question on this edition of this test.

Finding Your Scaled Score

When you take SAT Subject Tests, the scores sent to the colleges you specify are reported on the College Board scale, which ranges from 200 to 800. Subscores are reported on a scale that ranges from 20 to 80. You can convert your practice test scores to scaled scores by using Tables B, C, and D. To find your scaled score, locate your raw score in the left-hand column of the table; the corresponding score in the right-hand column is your scaled score. For example, in Table B a raw composite score of 47 on this particular edition of the SAT Subject Test in German with Listening corresponds to a scaled score of 560.

Raw scores are converted to scaled scores to ensure that a score earned on any one edition of a particular Subject Test is comparable to the same scaled score earned on any other edition of the same Subject Test. Because some editions of tests may be slightly easier or more difficult than others, scaled scores are adjusted so that they indicate the same level of performance regardless of the edition of the test taken and the ability of the group that takes it. Thus, for example, a score of 400 on one edition of a test taken at a particular administration indicates the same level of achievement as a score of 400 on a different edition of the test taken at a different administration.

When you take the SAT Subject Tests during a national administration, your scores are likely to differ somewhat from the scores you obtain on the tests in this book. People perform at different levels at different times for reasons unrelated to the tests themselves. The precision of any test is also limited because it represents only a sample of all the possible questions that could be asked.

Your scaled composite score from Table B is _____ .

Your scaled listening score from Table C is _____ .

Your scaled reading score from Table D is _____ .

TABLE B:
Scaled Score Conversion Table
German Subject Test with Listening Composite Scores (Form 3QLC)

Raw Score	Scaled Score	Raw Score	Scaled Score	Raw Score	Scaled Score
88	800	48	560	8	360
87	800	47	560	7	360
86	800	46	550	6	350
85	790	45	540	5	350
84	790	44	540	4	340
83	780	43	530	3	340
82	780	42	520	2	330
81	770	41	520	1	320
80	770	40	510	0	320
79	760	39	510	−1	310
78	760	38	500	−2	300
77	750	37	500	−3	300
76	750	36	490	−4	290
75	740	35	480	−5	280
74	740	34	480	−6	280
73	730	33	470	−7	270
72	730	32	470	−8	260
71	720	31	460	−9	250
70	720	30	460	−10	250
69	710	29	450	−11	240
68	700	28	450	−12	230
67	700	27	440	−13	230
66	690	26	440	−14	220
65	680	25	430	−15	220
64	680	24	430	−16	210
63	670	23	420	−17	210
62	670	22	420	−18	210
61	660	21	420	−19	200
60	650	20	410	−20	200
59	640	19	410	−21	200
58	640	18	400	−22	200
57	630	17	400	−23	200
56	620	16	400	−24	200
55	610	15	390	−25	200
54	600	14	390	−26	200
53	600	13	380	−27	200
52	590	12	380	−28	200
51	580	11	370	−29	200
50	580	10	370	−30	200
49	570	9	370	−31	200

TABLE C
Scaled Score Conversion Table
German Subject Test with Listening Listening Subscore (Form 3QLC)

Raw Score	Scaled Score	Raw Score	Scaled Score	Raw Score	Scaled Score
33	80	17	48	1	35
32	78	16	47	0	34
31	76	15	46	−1	33
30	74	14	45	−2	31
29	72	13	44	−3	31
28	70	12	43	−4	30
27	68	11	42	−5	29
26	66	10	42	−6	28
25	63	9	41	−7	27
24	60	8	40	−8	26
23	58	7	40	−9	25
22	56	6	39	−10	24
21	54	5	38	−11	23
20	52	4	38	−12	22
19	51	3	37	−13	21
18	50	2	36		

TABLE D
Scaled Score Conversion Table
German Subject Test with Listening Reading Subscore (Form 3QLC)

Raw Score	Scaled Score	Raw Score	Scaled Score	Raw Score	Scaled Score
55	80	30	59	5	38
54	80	29	58	4	37
53	79	28	57	3	36
52	78	27	56	2	35
51	78	26	55	1	34
50	77	25	54	0	33
49	76	24	53	−1	32
48	75	23	52	−2	31
47	75	22	51	−3	30
46	74	21	51	−4	29
45	73	20	50	−5	28
44	72	19	49	−6	27
43	72	18	48	−7	26
42	71	17	47	−8	25
41	70	16	46	−9	24
40	69	15	45	−10	23
39	68	14	45	−11	22
38	67	13	44	−12	21
37	66	12	43	−13	20
36	65	11	42	−14	20
35	64	10	42	−15	20
34	63	9	41	−16	20
33	62	8	40	−17	20
32	61	7	39	−18	20
31	60	6	39		

Reviewing Your Performance on the German Subject Test with Listening

After you score your test, analyze your performance—consider the following questions:

Did you run out of time before reaching the end of the test?

If so, you may need to pace yourself better. For example, maybe you spent too much time on one or two hard questions. A better approach might be to skip the ones you can't answer right away and try answering all the questions that remain on the test. Then if there's time, go back to the questions you skipped.

Did you take a long time reading the directions?

You will save time when you take the test by learning the directions to the German Subject Test with Listening ahead of time. Each minute you spend reading directions during the test is a minute that you could use to answer questions.

How did you handle questions you were unsure of?

If you were able to eliminate one or more of the answer choices as wrong and guess from the remaining ones, your approach probably worked to your advantage. On the other hand, making haphazard guesses or omitting questions without trying to eliminate choices could cost you valuable points.

How difficult were the questions for you compared with other students who took the test?

Table A shows you how difficult the multiple-choice questions were for the group of students who took this test during its national administration. The right-hand column gives the percentage of students that answered each question correctly.

A question answered correctly by almost everyone in the group is obviously an easy question. For example, 89 percent of the students answered question 18 correctly. But only 16 percent answered question 45 correctly.

Keep in mind that these percentages are based on just one group of students. They would probably be different if another group of students took the test.

If you missed several easy questions, go back and try to find out why: Did the questions cover material you haven't reviewed yet? Did you misunderstand the directions?

Chapter 11
Italian

Purpose

The Italian Subject Test measures your ability to understand written Italian. The test allows for variation in language preparation and is independent of particular textbooks used or methods of instruction. The test measures reading proficiency based on communicative materials authentic to the Italian culture.

Format

This is a one-hour test with 80 to 85 multiple-choice questions. Test questions are written to reflect current trends in high school curricula and test reading skills and familiarity with the language structure.

Areas of Evaluation:

Questions range in difficulty from elementary through advanced, although most questions are at the intermediate level. The test measures reading proficiency through a variety of questions requiring a broad knowledge of the language.

The test includes three parts:

Part A: sentence completion questions test your knowledge of high-frequency vocabulary and appropriate idiomatic expressions in the context of paragraphs.

Part B: structure questions arranged in sets of cultural themes, test your familiarity with the language structure.

Part C: reading comprehension tests your understanding of the content of various selections taken from sources such as newspaper and magazine articles, prose fiction, historical works, advertisements, tickets, brochures, forms, and schedules. Commonly taught grammatical constructions are tested, and all questions reflect current standard Italian.

Skills Measured	Approximate Percentage of Test
Vocabulary in Context	30
Structure in Blank	30
Reading Comprehension	40

Recommended Preparation

You should:

- Take two to four years of Italian language study in high school, or the equivalent.
- Develop competence in Italian over a period of years.
- Familiarize yourself with directions in advance. The directions in this book are identical to those that appear on the test.

Score

The total score is reported on the 200-to-800 scale.

Sample Questions

Please note that your answer sheet has five answer positions marked A, B, C, D, E, while the questions throughout this test contain only four choices. Be sure NOT to make any marks in column E.

Part A

Directions: In each of the following passages there are numbered blanks indicating that words or phrases have been omitted. For each numbered blank, four completions are provided. First read through the entire passage. Then, for each numbered blank, choose the completion that is most appropriate given the context of the entire passage and fill in the corresponding oval on the answer sheet.

Un piccolo villaggio siciliano

Baria Dorica è il nome di un piccolo villaggio estivo situato sulla costa siciliana. Tutte le __1__ del villaggio danno sulla piazzetta, dove si trova l'unico locale pubblico: il bar, che fa anche da panineria, pizzeria e panetteria.

La piazzetta è un luogo ___2___ riservato solamente ai pedoni e i bambini vi possono correre e giocare liberamente. La sera, i ragazzini formano dei gruppetti sparsi qua e là e ___3___ animatamente degli eventi della giornata. Fino a tarda sera tutto è animato e risuona di voci.

1. **(A)** macchine

   (B) strade

   (C) luci

   (D) corriere

2. **(A)** silenzioso

   (B) solitario

   (C) sicuro

   (D) privato

3. **(A)** cantano

   (B) leggono

   (C) parlano

   (D) pensano

In question 1, you have to choose the appropriate noun from the four answer choices. The correct answer is (B). Only *strade* can be used in connection with *danno sulla piazzetta* to form a meaningful sentence.

In question 2, you have to choose from the four answer choices the adjective that fits best according to the context. The correct answer is (C). The place in question can be considered *un luogo sicuro* since it is *riservato ai pedoni*, which means that there is no car traffic. Choices (A), (B), and (D) are incorrect because they are contradictory to what is said in the passage.

In question 3, you have to choose the appropriate verb from the four answer choices. The correct answer is (C). The verb *parlare* is the only verb that fits logically. The other options are not appropriate in this context even if (B) and (D) are verbs that could be used in connection with *eventi della giornata*.

Part B

Directions: In each sentence or dialogue below you will find a blank space indicating that a word or phrase has been omitted. Following each sentence are four completions. Of the four choices, select the one that best completes the sentence *structurally and logically* and fill in the corresponding oval on the answer sheet. The questions are grouped by topic but are not to be read as one passage. In some instances, choice (A) may consist of dashes; by choosing this option, you are indicating that no insertion is required to form a grammatically correct sentence.

<u>La spesa</u>

4. Molte turiste preferiscono comprare — — — — — — — — regali nei negozi del centro.
   - **(A)** il loro
   - **(B)** il suo
   - **(C)** i loro
   - **(D)** i suoi

In this question, you are asked to choose the correct possessive adjective from the four answer choices. The correct answer is (C). The possessive adjective *i loro* is used when the subject is third person, plural (*Molte turiste*), and the object is masculine, plural (*regali*). Choice (A) is incorrect because *il* refers to an object in the singular; choice (B) is incorrect because *il suo* refers to a third person, singular, subject, and an object in the singular; choice (D) is incorrect because it refers to a third person, singular, subject.

5. Dopo—le camicie, il cliente saluta e esce.
   - **(A)** aver comprato
   - **(B)** comprava
   - **(C)** abbia comprato
   - **(D)** comprerà

In question 5, you have to choose from the four answer choices the form of the verb *comprare* that fits in the sentence grammatically. The correct answer is (A). The verb *comprare* is in a subordinate clause introduced by *Dopo*. You need to know that *dopo* is used with a verb in the past infinitive. The other options are incorrect because the verb *comprare* is (B) in the imperfect, (C) in the past subjunctive, and (D) in the future tense.

Part C

Directions: Read the following texts carefully for comprehension. Each text is followed by a number of questions or incomplete statements. Select the answer or completion that is best according to the text and fill in the corresponding oval on the answer sheet.

Questions 6–7

QUEL FANTASTICO VENERDI' DI REPUBBLICA.

"Il Venerdì", tutte le settimane con Repubblica, vi porta attualità, grandi reportages, viaggi, inchieste e interviste: centotrentadue pagine a colori tutte per voi. "Il Venerdì" è in edicola ogni venerdì insieme a Repubblica e Affari& Finanza. Il tutto, per sole lire mille.

la Repubblica

6. In quest' annuncio, che cos' è "Il Venerdì"?

   (A) Un libro

   (B) Un settimanale

   (C) Un notiziario

   (D) Un' inchiesta

7. Come si ottiene "Il Venerdì"?

   (A) Si deve andare in un negozio.

   (B) Si deve comprare *la Repubblica*.

   (C) Si devono spendere due mila lire.

   (D) Si deve aspettare la fine del mese.

Question 6 asks what *"Il Venerdì"* is. The text mentions *tutte le settimane* and also *"Il Venerdì" è in edicola ogni venerdì.* The correct answer is (B) *Un settimanale.* Choices (A), (C), and (D) are incorrect within the context of the ad.

Question 7 asks about how you obtain *"Il Venerdì".* The text mentions *"Il Venerdì" (…) con Repubblica*, and also *(…) insieme a Repubblica*, so the correct answer is (B) *Si deve comprare la Repubblica.* Choices (A), (C), and (D) are incorrect within the context of the ad.

Questions 8–10

È "Ferragosto", festa nazionale, e se ne sono andati tutti. Restano solo alcune auto, abbandonate lo scorso inverno, ancora più solitarie sotto il sole d'agosto.

E incredibile, poter attraversare Milano in un quarto d'ora, da un capo all'altro. E poi fermarsi e parcheggiare dove si vuole. Bellissimo, ma per fare che cosa, se è tutto chiuso da una settimana? …

Vado all'edicola e la trovo sprangata. Il tabaccaio più vicino adesso si trova a un chilometro di distanza, e non ha più francobolli. Se in questo momento si fulmina una lampadina di casa sono perduto, non saprei dove comprarne una. Fortuna che per cibi e bevande mi ero fatto una scorta. L'assedio durerà fino al giorno 20, e occorre resistere.

Del resto non mi è mai piaciuto lo spettacolo di questo fuggi fuggi, di questo esodo di massa, come se a Milano fosse scoppiata un'epidemia di peste.

8. L'autore del brano si lamenta perchè
   - **(A)** la città è affollata
   - **(B)** è difficile attraversare la città
   - **(C)** gli abitanti se ne vanno
   - **(D)** c'è la peste

9. Secondo il brano durante il "Ferragosto" è probabile che chi ha una macchina possa
   - **(A)** comprare la benzina a buon mercato
   - **(B)** avere difficoltà nel parcheggiare
   - **(C)** muoversi facilmente in auto per la città
   - **(D)** stare in coda per un'ora per arrivare in centro

10. L'autore non morirà di fame perchè
   - **(A)** sua moglie gli ha lasciato cibi e bevande
   - **(B)** suo cognato ha un ristorante
   - **(C)** ha deciso di non fare più la dieta
   - **(D)** ha già comprato provviste sufficienti

Question 8 tests literal comprehension and refers to the reason for the author's complaint. The first line of the passage states ...*se ne sono andati tutti*, so the correct answer is (C) *gli abitanti se ne vanno*. Choices (A), (B), and (D) are incorrect within the context of this passage.

Question 9 tests literal comprehension and refers to an important detail mentioned in the text. In the second paragraph, the author states ...*È incredibile, poter attraversare Milano in un quarto d'ora, (…)* and also *(…) parcheggiare dove si vuole*. The correct answer is (C) *muoversi facilmente in auto per la città*. Choices (A), (B), and (D) are incorrect within the context of the passage.

Question 10 tests literal comprehension and refers to another important detail mentioned in the text. In the third paragraph, the author states *per cibi e bevande mi ero fatto una scorta*, so the correct answer is (D) *ha già comprato provviste sufficienti*. Choices (A), (B), and (C) are incorrect within the context of the passage.

Italian Test

The test that follows is an actual, recently administered SAT Subject Test in Italian. To get an idea of what a real administration is like, take the test under conditions as close as possible to those of a national administration:

- Set aside an hour when you can take the test uninterrupted. Make sure you complete the test in one sitting.

- Sit at a desk or table with no other books or papers. Dictionaries, other books, or notes are not allowed in the test room.

- Time yourself by placing a clock or kitchen timer in front of you.

- Tear out an answer sheet from the back of this book and fill it in just as you would on the day of the test. One answer sheet can be used for up to three Subject Tests.

- Read the instructions that precede the practice test. During the actual administration you will be asked to read them before answering test questions.

- After you finish the practice test, read the sections "How to Score the SAT Subject Test in Italian" and "Reviewing Your Performance on the Italian Subject Test."

- Actual test and answer sheets will indicate circles, not ovals.

Form 3QAC

ITALIAN TEST

The top portion of the section of the answer sheet that you will use in taking the Italian test must be filled in exactly as shown in the illustration below. Note carefully that you have to do all of the following on your answer sheet.

    1. Print ITALIAN on the line under the words "Subject Test (print)."

    2. In the shaded box labeled "Test Code" fill in four ovals:

        —Fill in oval 1 in the row labeled V.

        —Fill in oval 4 in the row labeled W.

        —Fill in oval 2 in the row labeled X.

        —Fill in oval B in the row labeled Y.

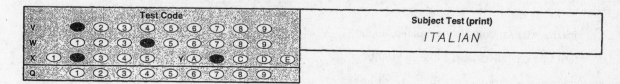

Please answer either Part I or Part II by filling in the specific oval in row Q. You are to fill in ONE and ONLY ONE oval, as described below, to indicate how you obtained your knowledge of Italian. The information you provide is for statistical purposes only and will not influence your score on the test.

Part I   If your knowledge of Italian <u>does not</u> come primarily from courses taken in grades 9 through 12, fill in <u>oval 9</u> and leave the remaining ovals blank, regardless of how long you studied the subject in school. For example, you are to fill in oval 9 if your knowledge of Italian comes primarily from any of the following sources: study prior to the ninth grade, courses taken at a college, special study, extensive residence abroad, or living in a home in which Italian is the principal language spoken.

Part II   If your knowledge of Italian <u>does</u> come primarily from courses taken in secondary school, fill in the oval that indicates the level of the Italian course in which you are currently enrolled. If you are not now enrolled in an Italian course, fill in the oval that indicates the level of the most advanced course in Italian that you have completed.

First year:	first or second half	—Fill in oval 1.
Second year:	first half	—Fill in oval 2.
	second half	—Fill in oval 3.
Third year:	first half	—Fill in oval 4.
	second half	—Fill in oval 5.
Fourth year:	first half	—Fill in oval 6.
	second half	—Fill in oval 7.
Course at a level higher than fourth year, second half or high school course work plus a minimum of four weeks of study abroad		—Fill in oval 8.

When the supervisor gives the signal, turn the page and begin the Italian test. There are 100 numbered ovals on the answer sheet and 82 questions in the Italian test. Therefore, use only ovals 1 to 82 for recording your answers.

ITALIAN TEST

PLEASE NOTE THAT YOUR ANSWER SHEET HAS FIVE ANSWER POSITIONS, MARKED A, B, C, D, AND E, WHILE THE QUESTIONS THROUGHOUT THIS TEST CONTAIN ONLY FOUR CHOICES. BE SURE <u>NOT</u> TO MAKE ANY MARKS IN COLUMN E.

Part A

<u>Directions:</u> In each of the following passages, there are numbered blanks indicating that words or phrases have been omitted. For each numbered blank, four completions are provided. First read through the entire passage. Then, for each numbered blank, choose the completion that is most appropriate given the context of the entire passage and fill in the corresponding oval on the answer sheet.

<u>L'isola d'Elba</u>

La settimana passata, con alcune amiche, siamo andate a fare una gita all'isola d'Elba. A Piombino abbiamo preso la nave traghetto e in __(1)__ di un'ora siamo arrivate a Portoferraio. __(2)__ scese dalla nave siamo andate alla parte alta della città. Volevamo infatti visitare la casa in cui __(3)__ Napoleone durante il suo confino sull' isola. La casa è molto interessante da vedere e offre una meravigliosa __(4)__ sui due lati dell'isola.

Abbiamo preso l'autobus per fare __(5)__ dell'isola. Arrivate a Procchio il mare era così bello e azzurro __(6)__ abbiamo deciso di fare un bagno. Abbiamo passato __(7)__ una bella giornata!

1. (A) vece
   (B) fondo
   (C) luogo
   (D) poco più

2. (A) Prima
   (B) Ancora
   (C) Appena
   (D) Quando

3. (A) era partito
   (B) aveva abitato
   (C) aveva comprato
   (D) aveva ascoltato

4. (A) vista
   (B) uscita
   (C) discesa
   (D) scena

5. (A) una camminata
   (B) una partita
   (C) un viaggio
   (D) un giro

6. (A) che
   (B) quando
   (C) dunque
   (D) insomma

7. (A) meno
   (B) come
   (C) davvero
   (D) soltanto

GO ON TO THE NEXT PAGE →

3QAC

La pasta

Pasta, pane, verdura, frutta, olio di oliva e vino sono i (8) principali di quella "dieta mediterranea", priva di grassi animali e di zucchero, che sta conquistando il mondo perchè:

• sconfigge il colesterolo

• (9) maggior potere di recupero, forza ed energia agli atleti

• è di facile assimilazione

• rende la vita (10) e più piacevole

Lo hanno riconosciuto:

• l'istituto superiore di sanità

• dietologi di tutto il mondo

La pasta, (11) , è il prodotto più semplice che ci sia.

8. (A) pasti
   (B) componenti
   (C) costi
   (D) menù

9. (A) diminuisce
   (B) impedisce
   (C) fornisce
   (D) assimila

10. (A) più breve
    (B) più sana
    (C) meno noiosa
    (D) insopportabile

11. (A) generalmente
    (B) velocemente
    (C) attentamente
    (D) raramente

GO ON TO THE NEXT PAGE

Giuseppe Verdi

Giuseppe Verdi, il più amato musicista italiano, __(12)__ nel 1813 a Roncole di Busseto, paesino in provincia di Parma. Di famiglia molto modesta, egli riuscì a seguire la sua vocazione per la __(13)__ grazie all'aiuto del Comune del suo paese e di un ricco commerciante locale, del quale __(14)__ sposò la figlia.

Nel 1873, in occasione della morte di Alessandro Manzoni, celebre __(15)__ del romanzo *I promessi sposi*, Verdi scrisse una *Messa da Requiem*. Dopo la composizione di opere famosissime, come *La traviata* e *Il trovatore*, __(16)__ di 74 anni Verdi compose l'*Otello* e, qualche anno dopo, il *Falstaff*. Queste due ultime opere sono considerate dai critici fra le migliori che siano __(17)__ state scritte. Le opere di Giuseppe Verdi sono anche oggi rappresentate sulle scene dei maggiori __(18)__ d'opera del mondo.

12. (A) nacque
    (B) passò
    (C) gridò
    (D) giacque

13. (A) poesia
    (B) musica
    (C) religione
    (D) storia

14. (A) sempre
    (B) già
    (C) poi
    (D) ancora

15. (A) autore
    (B) compositore
    (C) editore
    (D) lettore

16. (A) alla fine
    (B) a metà
    (C) all'età
    (D) all'inizio

17. (A) finora
    (B) allora
    (C) spesso
    (D) quasi

18. (A) schermi
    (B) cinema
    (C) locali
    (D) teatri

GO ON TO THE NEXT PAGE

L'inglese degli Stati Uniti alla televisione italiana

Imparare l'inglese dalla televisione con le frasi rubate alla vita __(19)__ degli americani. È l'idea di un programma che andrà __(20)__ su Italia 1, tutti i giorni, da lunedì a sabato, a __(21)__ dall'11 settembre.

Quest'anno Italia 1 ha girato New York con le sue __(22)__ , riprendendo scene di vita quotidiana. Poi, durante le 54 puntate in studio, i conduttori della trasmissione spiegheranno le frasi, le espressioni __(23)__ dei personaggi intervistati, __(24)__ il confronto con l'inglese scolastico.

19. (A) mensile
    (B) semestrale
    (C) annuale
    (D) quotidiana

20. (A) in barca
    (B) in voga
    (C) in onda
    (D) in ballo

21. (A) arrivare
    (B) andare
    (C) cominciare
    (D) sentire

22. (A) telecamere
    (B) antenne
    (C) immagini
    (D) televisioni

23. (A) cariche
    (B) idiomatiche
    (C) statiche
    (D) simmetriche

24. (A) prendendo
    (B) mettendo
    (C) facendo
    (D) inventando

GO ON TO THE NEXT PAGE

Part B

Directions: In each sentence or dialogue below, you will find a blank space indicating that a word or phrase has been omitted. Following each sentence are four completions. Of the four choices, select the one that best completes the sentence structurally and logically and fill in the corresponding oval on the answer sheet. In some instances, choice (A) consists of dashes; by choosing this option, you are indicating that no insertion is required to form a grammatically correct sentence. The questions are grouped by topic but are not to be read as one passage.

A letto!

25. Bambini, su, è tardi; ------- siete lavati i denti?

    (A) ci
    (B) vi
    (C) mi
    (D) ti

26. Non trovo il mio spazzolino; ------- l'ha preso?

    (A) chi
    (B) che
    (C) cui
    (D) quale

27. C'è ------- che è ancora sveglio; chi è?

    (A) ogni
    (B) qualche
    (C) qualcuno
    (D) ciascuno

28. Ho promesso che vi ------- una fiaba.

    (A) avrei raccontato
    (B) avevo raccontato
    (C) avessi raccontato
    (D) abbia raccontato

Al ristorante

29. Per secondo, vorrei una cotoletta ------- milanese.

    (A) al
    (B) alle
    (C) allo
    (D) alla

30. Come contorno, preferisco un po' di spinaci e ------- patatine fritte.

    (A) della
    (B) delle
    (C) del
    (D) dell'

31. Da -------, mi piacerebbe del vino bianco, freddo.

    (A) bevo
    (B) berrò
    (C) bevevo
    (D) bere

32. Cameriere, il servizio e la mancia sono -------?

    (A) incluso
    (B) inclusa
    (C) incluse
    (D) inclusi

GO ON TO THE NEXT PAGE

Al circo

33. Gli elefanti che ho visto al circo ------- proprio enormi.

    (A) era
    (B) eravamo
    (C) eravate
    (D) erano

34. Quale spettacolo ti è piaciuto ------- più?

    (A) da
    (B) di
    (C) per
    (D) in

A scuola

35. Fa con calma; ------- devi diplomare.

    (A) ti
    (B) vi
    (C) loro
    (D) mi

36. Ragazzi, lasciate gli stivali ------- corridoio.

    (A) -----
    (B) col
    (C) sul
    (D) nel

37. Non voglio che ------- una sola parola!

    (A) dite
    (B) diceste
    (C) direste
    (D) diciate

Vacanze

38. Papà, ------- andiamo quest'anno? Al mare?

    (A) quando
    (B) mentre
    (C) là
    (D) dove

39. Marco, tua sorella ha fatto la sua valigia e tu devi fare -------!

    (A) tua
    (B) la tua
    (C) tuo
    (D) il tuo

40. Laura ------- per la Francia la settimana prossima.

    (A) partiva
    (B) è partita
    (C) sta partendo
    (D) partirà

41. Sì, è vero. Se fossi ricca ------- un piccolo aeroplano.

    (A) compro
    (B) compri
    (C) comprerò
    (D) comprerei

42. Invece di mettere in valigia ------- sandali, ci ha messo solo scarpe.

    (A) alcune
    (B) dai
    (C) dei
    (D) qualche

GO ON TO THE NEXT PAGE ➤

In treno

43. ------- che binario parte il treno?

    (A) Da
    (B) Di
    (C) Con
    (D) Per

44. ------- persone vanno a Firenze con lei?

    (A) Chi
    (B) Coloro
    (C) Quante
    (D) Quale

45. A che ora ------- il treno ieri?

    (A) è arrivato
    (B) arriva
    (C) arriverebbe
    (D) arriverà

46. Il biglietto, ------- compro in anticipo.

    (A) la
    (B) lo
    (C) il
    (D) le

47. I passeggeri sono pregati di non -------.

    (A) fuma
    (B) fumano
    (C) fumava
    (D) fumare

48. ------- scompartimento è molto comodo.

    (A) Questo
    (B) Questa
    (C) Quest'
    (D) Questi

GO ON TO THE NEXT PAGE

Part C

Questions 49-52

Saranno sani.
Con Montefiore Dieterba. Pensato per dare ai bambini un futuro di salute.

Alcuni dei problemi fisici più diffusi fra gli adulti – obesità, carie, colesterolo, diabete – sono in gran parte il risultato di un'alimentazione errata nei primi anni di vita: cibo in eccesso e con ingredienti in dosi non equilibrate.

Montefiore Dieterba non è un biscotto comune perché studiato a misura di un bambino che cresce. Scegli la salute, scegli Montefiore Dieterba. Perché prevenire significa anche educare subito il tuo bambino a una sana abitudine alimentare.

49. Secondo l'annuncio, questo prodotto dà ai bambini

(A) fama mondiale
(B) tante vitamine
(C) un futuro sano
(D) biscotti adulti

50. Secondo l'annuncio, l'alimentazione data ai bambini è spesso

(A) poco grassa
(B) priva di zuccheri
(C) equilibrata
(D) sbagliata

51. Questo prodotto incoraggia i genitori a

(A) mettersi a dieta
(B) curare l'alimentazione dei figli
(C) preparare il proprio futuro
(D) mangiare più biscotti Montefiore

52. Montefiore non è un biscotto comune perchè

(A) è preparato con ingredienti sani
(B) ha un eccesso di additivi
(C) è diffuso fra gli adulti
(D) previene la carie

GO ON TO THE NEXT PAGE

<u>Questions 53-57</u>

Mia madre vedeva le sue amiche: sempre le stesse. A parte la Frances, e alcune altre che eran mogli di amici di mio padre, mia madre le sue amiche se le

Linea sceglieva giovani, un bel po' più giovani di lei:

(5) giovani signore sposate da poco, e povere: a loro poteva dare consigli, suggerire delle sartine. Le facevano orrore "le vecchie", come lei diceva, alludendo a gente che aveva press'a poco la sua età. Le facevano orrore i ricevimenti. Se una delle sue anziane

(10) conoscenze le mandava a dire che sarebbe venuta a farle visita, era presa dal panico. "Allora oggi non potrò andare a spasso!" diceva disperata. Quelle amiche giovani, invece, poteva tirarsele dietro a spasso, o al cinematografo; erano maneggevoli e disponibili, e

(15) pronte a mantenere con lei un rapporto senza cerimonie; e se avevano bambini piccoli, meglio, perchè lei amava molto i bambini. Accadeva a volte che il pomeriggio, queste amiche venissero a trovarla tutte insieme.

53. Che tipo di amiche preferiva la madre della scrittrice?

(A) Della sua età
(B) Anziane
(C) Le mogli degli amici del marito
(D) Parecchio più giovani

54. Perchè la madre frequentava anche amiche povere?

(A) Perchè erano amiche di suo padre
(B) Per offrir loro suggerimenti
(C) Per evitare di camminare
(D) Perchè erano vedove

55. Che cosa faceva orrore alla madre?

(A) Andare a spasso
(B) Le strade vuote
(C) I ricevimenti
(D) I cinematografi

56. Che tipo di rapporto stabiliva la madre con le amiche?

(A) Ossessivo
(B) Informale
(C) Disperato
(D) Senza rispetto

57. Cosa facevano occasionalmente le amiche della madre?

(A) Facevano ceremonie.
(B) Le lasciavano i bambini il pomeriggio.
(C) La andavano a visitare tutte insieme.
(D) Uscivano tutte insieme.

GO ON TO THE NEXT PAGE

Questions 58-61

UNIVERSITA' DEGLI STUDI DI URBINO
ASSOCIAZIONE AMICI DEL TEATRO

CONCERTO BAROCCO

Flauto: Elisabetta Donnanno
Violino: Massimiliano Poderi
Clavicembalo: Simona Bruscoli

**MERCOLEDI' 5 LUGLIO 1989 ORE 21
SALA CECCARINI — PIAZZA DELLE ERBE
URBINO**

Ingresso gratuito

PROGRAMMA

J. S. Bach	*Sonata in Sol min. BWV 1020 per flauto e cembalo*
C. P. E. Bach	*Sonata in La min. W 49/1 per clavicembalo*
D. Scarlatti	*Sonata in Sol. magg. per clavicembalo*
J. S. Bach	*Sonata N. 4 in Do min. per violino e cembalo concertante*

58. Dove ha luogo il concerto?

   (A) In una sala
   (B) In una chiesa
   (C) In piazza
   (D) All'università

59. Quando ha luogo il concerto?

   (A) La mattina del mercoledì
   (B) Ogni mercoledì
   (C) Mercoledì alle cinque del pomeriggio
   (D) Mercoledì alle nove di sera

60. Quanto costa l'ingresso?

   (A) L. 10.000
   (B) Niente
   (C) Non c'è scritto.
   (D) È soltanto per invito.

61. Quanti pezzi suonerà la flautista?

   (A) Uno
   (B) Due
   (C) Tre
   (D) Quattro

GO ON TO THE NEXT PAGE

Questions 62-64

In fondo al sentiero, dopo gli aranceti, c'era una pianura e in mezzo alla pianura una casetta che un tempo doveva essere stata dipinta di rosa e adesso, per *Linea* l'umidità e la vecchiezza, era in cattive condizioni. Una (5) scala esterna saliva al secondo piano, dove c'era una terrazza con un'arcata dalla quale pendevano trecce di peperoni, di pomodori e di cipolle. Davanti alla casa, in cortile, c'era una quantità di fichi sparsi a seccare al sole. Una casa di contadini, abitata. La contadina che venne (10) subito fuori era una vecchia magra da far paura, dal naso lungo, a becco, dagli occhi infossati, dalla fronte bassa e calva, che pareva quella di un falco. Disse "Chi siete, che volete?", e aveva in mano un bastone, come per difendersi.

62. Di che colore era originariamente la casa?

(A) Grigia
(B) Rosa
(C) Bianca
(D) Arancione

63. Che cosa pendeva dalla terrazza?

(A) Fiori
(B) Fichi
(C) Cipolle
(D) Arance

64. A che cosa somigliava il viso della contadina?

(A) Ad un uccello
(B) Ad un bastone
(C) Ad un fico
(D) Ad un peperone

Questions 65-66

TOSCA FONDELLI

PARRUCCHIERA

Via Pantaneto, 9 - Siena - Tel. 28.74.55

N. RICEVUTA	DATA	
1716	17-07-90	
	SERVIZI PRESTATI	CORRISPETTIVI
	Shampoo speciale	
	Messa in piega	
l	Messa in piega a phon	17.000
l	Taglio	10.000
	Pettinatura	
l	Lozione	5.000
	Balsamo	
TOTALE CORRISPETTIVI (IVA INCLUSA) L.		32.000
XA 3178 **90**	RICEVUTA FISCALE (Art. 2 D.M. 02.07.80)	

65. Tosca Fondelli è un posto dove una persona va a

(A) farsi tagliare i capelli
(B) farsi imbalsamare
(C) comprare giocattoli
(D) comprare prodotti da toletta

66. Questo documento è stato ottenuto in seguito ad

(A) una consumazione
(B) una ordinazione
(C) un ricevimento
(D) un pagamento

GO ON TO THE NEXT PAGE ➜

Question 67

Questions 68-70

Gli italiani non sono poi così malati di televisione come sono indotti a pensare dal dilagare delle mode e dei divi da tv. Infatti accendono il televisore tre ore al giorno. In base ad un'inchiesta realizzata da un'agenzia per conto della Mondadori e pubblicata sull'ultimo numero del settimanale *Epoca*, il telespettatore medio italiano sarebbe spesso distratto da altre attività, anche nelle tre ore al giorno che dedica alla televisione. Dall'inchiesta risulta che, in generale, questo e non di più è il tempo che l'italiano trascorre davanti al televisore acceso. Per oltre il 60 per cento di questo tempo, mangia, chiacchiera, fa pulizie e sonnecchia.

Linea
(5)

(10)

Rinascita *in abbonamento* **l'occasione per non perdere un numero**

Rinascita:

acquistatela in edicola.

---

67. Quest'annuncio tratta di

   (A) un teatro
   (B) un corso
   (C) una ditta
   (D) una rivista

68. Il brano dice che gli italiani, in generale, sono

   (A) malati di televisione
   (B) stufi della televisione
   (C) poco fanatici della televisione
   (D) davanti alla televisione giorno e notte

69. Cosa fanno spesso gli italiani quando hanno il televisore acceso?

   (A) Svolgono varie attività.
   (B) Ascoltano la musica.
   (C) Cambiano i canali.
   (D) Registrano altri programmi.

70. Quest'opinione sul comportamento dei telespettatori italiani viene da

   (A) l'italiano medio
   (B) uno studio statistico
   (C) un programma televisivo
   (D) un malato di televisione

GO ON TO THE NEXT PAGE ➤

Questions 71-73

In studio Cristiana del Melle e Riccardo Bonacina

71. Cosa è "Il coraggio di vivere"?

(A) Una rappresentazione teatrale
(B) Una trasmissione televisiva
(C) Un programma radiofonico
(D) Un'opera lirica moderna

72. Di cosa tratta "Il coraggio di vivere"?

(A) Di fantascienza
(B) Di racconti gialli
(C) Di episodi di vita vissuta
(D) Di episodi della storia italiana

73. Quando viene rappresentato "Il coraggio di vivere"?

(A) Ogni Natale
(B) Un sabato al mese
(C) Ogni sera alle 20,30
(D) Una volta alla settimana

GO ON TO THE NEXT PAGE ➤

Questions 74-76

Come prepararsi a visite inattese di ospiti in guanti neri.

Vacanze, week-end. Si parte felici, ma in fondo al cuore c'è una piccola apprensione: sarà al sicuro quello che lasciamo qui? La casa, i quadri, i gioielli della nonna.

Basta poco per assicurarsi la serenità. Sarà utile assicurarsi? Certamente sì. Con FATA in particolare.

Ideale per tutelare la tua proprietà sia in città che in campagna.

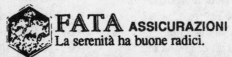 **FATA ASSICURAZIONI**
La serenità ha buone radici.

74. Secondo la pubblicità, chi sono gli ospiti in guanti neri?

(A) Le persone che vanno in vacanza
(B) Quelli che puliscono la casa
(C) I ladri che entrano in casa
(D) Le persone che lavorano in campagna

75. Che cosa vende FATA?

(A) Guanti neri
(B) Assicurazioni
(C) Case
(D) Gioielli e quadri

76. FATA protegge

(A) i viaggi
(B) le buone radici
(C) la proprietà
(D) i furti

GO ON TO THE NEXT PAGE →

Questions 77-80

Non amo particolarmente la geografia, non ho mai osservato un atlante più del tempo necessario per averne un'informazione, non mi ha mai interessato *Linea* "leggere" notizie su un fiume o su una montagna, ma (5) "guardare" quel fiume o quella montagna. Per questo seguo sempre con interesse i servizi televisivi o cinematografici o soltanto fotografici quando hanno come argomento il territorio ripreso dall'alto. Mi sembra infatti che una città, una regione, o una (10) montagna osservata dall'alto, ti appartenga subito e globalmente. In un secondo tempo ci potrà essere l'occasione per conoscere a distanza ravvicinata una strada, un monumento, un torrente e così via. Escludo però la possibilità di osservare da vicino, di frequentare (15) un ghiacciaio, una piccola isola, un tratto di mare inaccessibile.

Per questo ho più volte provato emozione guardando dal finestrino dell'aereo l'Elba, la Sardegna, le Alpi, l'Etna, la laguna di Venezia e Roma. Se l'arrivo a (20) Fiumicino non è dal mare, il sorvolare una parte della città non può non creare curiosità. Di volta in volta si riconosce un monumento, un ponte sul Tevere, una periferia. Chi, atterrando o decollando da una città, tiene la tapparella del finestrino abbassata o non ha più (25) curiosità è male per lui, o non ha mai saputo che, al di là dell'età, si possono coltivare stupori infantili.

77. Per l'autore, le caratteristiche di un terreno si osservano meglio

(A) da vicino
(B) da lontano
(C) di sotto
(D) da dentro

78. Quando l'aereo si avvicina a una città, l'autore prova il sentimento di

(A) curiosità
(B) paura
(C) confusione
(D) noia

79. Che succede all'autore quando guarda dall'alto?

(A) Si addormenta.
(B) Rimane indifferente.
(C) Pensa alla sua casa.
(D) Si commuove.

80. Secondo il brano, l'autore ama

(A) studiare la geografia
(B) vedere le cose da un aereo
(C) visitare alcune isole
(D) andare in montagna

GO ON TO THE NEXT PAGE

Questions 81-82

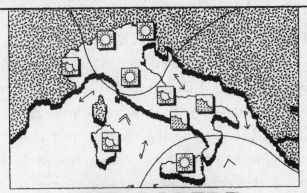

PER SAPERE CHE TEMPO FARA' NON GUARDATE QUI SOPRA.

LEGGETE QUI SOTTO.

Se invece di previsioni volete certezze, rivolgetevi a Delchi: in fatto di clima è uno vero specialista.

Delchi, nato con il condizionamento, ha conquistato il controllo del clima di qualsiasi ambiente grazie alle continue innovazioni tecnologiche e alla ricerca di nuove soluzioni per nuovi stili di vita.

Per questo è importante rivolgersi a chi ha la competenza e la professionalità per farlo.

Per esempio a Delchi, il numero uno in Europa.

CHIAMATA GRATUITA NUMEROVERDE 1678-34048

Ⓓ Delchi   LO SPECIALISTA DELLA CLIMATIZZAZIONE.

81. Di che cosa si occupa Delchi?

(A) Di carte geografiche
(B) Di condizione muscolare
(C) Di condizionatori d'aria
(D) Di previsioni meteorologiche

82. Cosa pensa sia importante per il consumatore la ditta Delchi?

(A) Leggere la cartina
(B) Telefonare all'ufficio
(C) Cambiare stile di vita
(D) Rivolgersi ad uno specialista

S T O P

IF YOU FINISH BEFORE TIME IS CALLED, YOU MAY CHECK YOUR WORK ON THIS TEST ONLY.
DO NOT TURN TO ANY OTHER TEST IN THIS BOOK.

How to Score the SAT Subject Test in Italian

When you take an actual SAT Subject Test in Italian, your answer sheet will be "read" by a scanning machine that will record your responses to each question. Then a computer will compare your answers with the correct answers and produce your raw score. You get one point for each correct answer. For each wrong answer, you lose one-third of a point. Questions you omit (and any for which you mark more than one answer) are not counted. This raw score is converted to a scaled score that is reported to you and to the colleges you specify.

Worksheet 1. Finding Your Raw Test Score

STEP 1: Table A lists the correct answers for all the questions on the SAT Subject Test in Italian that is reproduced in this book. It also serves as a worksheet for you to calculate your raw score.

- Compare your answers with those given in the table.
- Put a check in the column marked "Right" if your answer is correct.
- Put a check in the column marked "Wrong" if your answer is incorrect.
- Leave both columns blank if you omitted the question.

STEP 2: Count the number of right answers.

Enter the total here: _____

STEP 3: Count the number of wrong answers.

Enter the total here: _____

STEP 4: Multiply the number of wrong answers by .333.

Enter the product here: _____

STEP 5: Subtract the result obtained in Step 4 from the total you obtained in Step 2.

Enter the result here: _____

STEP 6: Round the number obtained in Step 5 to the nearest whole number.

Enter the result here: _____

The number you obtained in Step 6 is your raw score.

TABLE A
Answers to the SAT Subject Test in Italian, Form 3QAC, and
Percentage of Students Answering Each Question Correctly

Question Number	Correct Answer	Right	Wrong	Percentage of Students Answering the Question Correctly*	Question Number	Correct Answer	Right	Wrong	Percentage of Students Answering the Question Correctly*
1	D			83	33	D			94
2	C			34	34	B			79
3	B			96	35	A			82
4	A			61	36	D			86
5	D			65	37	D			30
6	A			68	38	D			96
7	C			64	39	B			64
8	B			91	40	D			63
9	C			40	41	D			58
10	B			60	42	C			37
11	A			95	43	A			67
12	A			87	44	C			78
13	B			87	45	A			87
14	C			48	46	B			88
15	A			46	47	D			81
16	C			57	48	A			95
17	A			37	49	C			80
18	D			88	50	D			42
19	D			64	51	B			44
20	C			37	52	A			61
21	C			77	53	D			67
22	A			70	54	B			61
23	B			65	55	C			58
24	C			51	56	B			49
25	B			87	57	C			49
26	A			83	58	A			23
27	C			82	59	D			86
28	A			40	60	B			77
29	D			44	61	A			81
30	B			91	62	B			78
31	D			74	63	C			74
32	D			67	64	A			31

Table A continued on next page

Table A continued from previous page

Question Number	Correct Answer	Right	Wrong	Percentage of Students Answering the Question Correctly*	Question Number	Correct Answer	Right	Wrong	Percentage of Students Answering the Question Correctly*
65	A			80	74	C			50
66	D			62	75	B			77
67	D			45	76	C			63
68	C			52	77	B			41
69	A			70	78	A			58
70	B			45	79	D			31
71	B			75	80	B			48
72	C			58	81	C			27
73	D			61	82	D			52

* These percentages are based on an analysis of the answer sheets of a random sample of 305 students who took the original form of this test in December 1994, and whose mean score was 585. They may be used as an indication of the relative difficulty of a particular question. Each percentage may also be used to predict the likelihood that a typical SAT Subject Test in Italian candidate will answer correctly that question on this edition of this test.

Finding Your Scaled Score

When you take SAT Subject Tests, the scores sent to the colleges you specify are reported on the College Board scale, which ranges from 200 to 800. You can convert your practice test score to a scaled score by using Table B. To find your scaled score, locate your raw score in the left-hand column of Table B; the corresponding score in the right-hand column is your scaled score. For example, a raw score of 57 on this particular edition of the SAT Subject Test in Italian corresponds to a scaled score of 670.

Raw scores are converted to scaled scores to ensure that a score earned on any one edition of a particular Subject Test is comparable to the same scaled score earned on any other edition of the same Subject Test. Because some editions of tests may be slightly easier or more difficult than others, scaled scores are adjusted so that they indicate the same level of performance regardless of the edition of the test taken and the ability of the group that takes it. Thus, for example, a score of 400 on one edition of a test taken at a particular administration indicates the same level of achievement as a score of 400 on a different edition of the test taken at a different administration.

When you take the SAT Subject Tests during a national administration, your scores are likely to differ somewhat from the scores you obtain on the tests in this book. People perform at different levels at different times for reasons unrelated to the tests themselves. The precision of any test is also limited because it represents only a sample of all the possible questions that could be asked.

TABLE B
Scaled Score Conversion Table
Italian Subject Test (Form 3QAC)

Raw Score	Scaled Score	Raw Score	Scaled Score	Raw Score	Scaled Score
82	800	44	590	6	320
81	790	43	580	5	310
80	780	42	570	4	300
79	780	41	570	3	290
78	770	40	560	2	290
77	770	39	550	1	280
76	760	38	550	0	270
75	760	37	540	−1	260
74	750	36	530	−2	260
73	750	35	530	−3	250
72	740	34	520	−4	250
71	740	33	510	−5	240
70	730	32	500	−6	230
69	730	31	500	−7	230
68	720	30	490	−8	220
67	720	29	480	−9	220
66	710	28	480	−10	210
65	710	27	470	−11	210
64	700	26	460	−12	200
63	700	25	450	−13	200
62	690	24	450	−14	200
61	690	23	440	−15	200
60	680	22	430	−16	200
59	680	21	430	−17	200
58	670	20	420	−18	200
57	670	19	410	−19	200
56	660	18	400	−20	200
55	650	17	400	−21	200
54	650	16	390	−22	200
53	640	15	380	−23	200
52	640	14	370	−24	200
51	630	13	370	−25	200
50	620	12	360	−26	200
49	620	11	350	−27	200
48	610	10	350		
47	610	9	340		
46	600	8	330		
45	590	7	320		

Reviewing Your Performance on the Italian Subject Test

After you score your test, analyze your performance—consider the following questions:

Did you run out of time before reaching the end of the test?

If so, you may need to pace yourself better. For example, maybe you spent too much time on one or two hard questions. A better approach might be to skip the ones you can't answer right away and try answering all the questions that remain on the test. Then if there's time, go back to the questions you skipped.

Did you take a long time reading the directions?

You will save time when you take the test by learning the directions to the Italian Subject Test ahead of time. Each minute you spend reading directions during the test is a minute that you could use to answer questions.

How did you handle questions you were unsure of?

If you were able to eliminate one or more of the answer choices as wrong and guess from the remaining ones, your approach probably worked to your advantage. On the other hand, making haphazard guesses or omitting questions without trying to eliminate choices could cost you valuable points.

How difficult were the questions for you compared with other students who took the test?

Table A shows you how difficult the multiple-choice questions were for the group of students who took this test during its national administration. The right-hand column gives the percentage of students that answered each question correctly.

A question answered correctly by almost everyone in the group is obviously an easy question. For example, 96 percent of the students answered question 3 correctly. But only 23 percent answered question 58 correctly.

Keep in mind that these percentages are based on just one group of students. They would probably be different if another group of students took the test.

If you missed several easy questions, go back and try to find out why: Did the questions cover material you haven't reviewed yet? Did you misunderstand the directions?

Chapter 12
Japanese with Listening

Purpose

This test measures your ability to communicate in Japanese in a culturally appropriate way.

Format

This is a one-hour test with about 20 minutes of listening and 40 minutes of usage and reading. There are 80 to 85 multiple-choice listening, reading, and usage questions written with high school curricula in mind. Questions represent situations you might readily encounter and reflect realistic and commonplace communication. Questions range in difficulty from elementary through advanced, although most are in the intermediate level. The test has a variety of questions requiring a wide-ranging knowledge of the Japanese language.

Listening Comprehension: You will hear listening comprehension selections on tape only once. These selections are based on short, spoken dialogues and narratives primarily about everyday topics. A brief explanation about each selection and the question(s) are given in English. Explanations are also printed in your test book.

Usage: These questions require you to complete Japanese sentences in a way that is appropriate in terms of structure (grammar), vocabulary, and context. Usage questions are printed in three different ways of representing Japanese. In the center column, the Japanese is presented in standard Japanese script and all *kanji* are supplied with *furigana*. In the other two columns, the Japanese is written in the two most common types of romanization (*rōmaji*). To the left, a modified Hepburn system is used. In that system, the Japanese word for "bicycle" is written as *jitensha*. In the right-hand column, a modified *kunrei-shiki* is used. In that system, the same Japanese word for "bicycle" is written as *ziteñsya*. You should choose the writing system you are familiar with and read only from that column on the test.

Reading Comprehension: These questions are in English and test your understanding of such points as main and supporting ideas. The selections in this section are taken from materials you might encounter in everyday situations, such as notes, menus, newspaper articles, advertisements, and letters. The test is written in *katakana*, *hiragana*, and *kanji* without *furigana*.

Skills Measured	Approximate Percentage of Test
Listening Comprehension	35
Usage	30
Reading Comprehension	35

Recommended Preparation

The best preparation is gradual development of competence in Japanese over a period of years. The test is appropriate for students who have studied Japanese as a second or foreign language for two, three, or four years in high school or the equivalent. You are more likely to perform successfully if you have completed at least two full years of Japanese language study. A practice cassette with sample questions is available from your school counselor. Familiarize yourself with directions in advance. The directions in this book are identical to those that appear on the test.

Cassette Players

You must bring an acceptable cassette player with earphones to the test center. Put fresh batteries in your cassette player the day before the test and, if you like, bring additional fresh batteries and a backup cassette player with earphones to the test center. Test center staff will NOT have batteries, cassette players, or earphones for your use.

Acceptable cassette players must be:
- personal (have earphones that let only you hear the recording)
- portable (small enough that the entire cassette player can fit in your hand)
- battery-operated
- able to use a single (not dual) standard (2-1/2 inch by 4 inch) audiocassette— not mini- or microcassette

If your cassette player has a programming feature that fast-forwards automatically to the next prompt, that feature must be deactivated before you start the test. You will not be allowed to share a cassette player with another test-taker.

Beginning with the November 2005 administration, portable CD players will be required instead of cassette players for language with listening tests.

Score

The total score is reported on the 200-to-800 scale. Listening, usage, and reading subscores are reported on the 20-to-80 scale.

Test development was supported by funding from the National Endowment for the Humanities to the College Board and the National Foreign Language Center.

The Japanese Subject Test with Listening is offered once a year only at designated tests centers. To take the test you MUST bring an acceptable cassette player with earphones to the test center.

A cassette tape with listening questions is available for the Japanese Subject Test with Listening practice test in this book. To receive your copy, complete and mail the postcard in this book. If the postcard has been removed, call 212 649-8424 or write to:

The College Board
Subject Tests Language Listening Cassette
45 Columbus Avenue
New York, New York 10023-6992

You must indicate the SAT Language Test with Listening you plan to take.

Sample Questions

Please note that your answer sheet has five answer positions marked A, B, C, D, E, while the questions throughout this test contain only four choices. Be sure NOT to make any marks in column E.

Sample Listening Question

Please note that the cassette does not start here. Begin using the cassette when you start the actual practice test on page 548.

Directions: In this section of the test you will hear short dialogues and monologues. You will hear them **only once**, and they are not printed in your test booklet. At the end of each selection, you will be asked questions about what was said. Now listen to the following example.

(Narrator)   [Listen to the following conversation in an office.

(Man)   明日家に電話してくださいませんか。

(Woman)   ええ、いいですよ。　電話番号は？

(Man)   あ、書きましょう。

(Narrator)   Question 1. What does the man ask the woman to do?]
(16 seconds)

1. **(A)** Tell him her phone number.
   (B) Call him at home.
   (C) Check with him tomorrow at work.
   (D) Write down her phone number.

This question tests students' knowledge of request forms. Choice (B) is the correct answer because this indicates the man's request. Choices (A), (C), and (D) are incorrect because they are not stated by the man.

Sample Usage Question

Directions: This section consists of a number of incomplete statements, each of which has four suggested completions. In some instances, choice (A) may consist of dashes that indicate that no insertion is required to form a correct sentence. Select the choice that best completes the sentence structurally and logically and fill in the corresponding oval on the answer sheet.

This section of the test is presented in three columns that provide identical information. Look at the example below and choose the one column of writing with which you are most familiar in order to answer this question. **DO NOT WASTE TIME BY SWITCHING FROM COLUMN TO COLUMN IN THIS SECTION.**

2. Sore wa totemo kirei – – – hana desu ne.	2. それはとてもきれい----- 花_{はな}ですねえ。	2. Sore wa totemo kiree – – – hana desu nee.
(A) – – –	**(A)** – – –	**(A)** – – –
(B) no	**(B)** の	**(B)** no
(C) ni	**(C)** に	**(C)** ni
(D) na	**(D)** な	**(D)** na

This question tests the proper usage of *kirei*. Choice (D) is the correct answer because *na* is always used to connect *kirei* with the noun that it modifies (in this case *hana*). Choices (A), (B), and (C) are incorrect because they do not follow this rule.

Sample Reading Question

Directions: Read the following texts carefully for comprehension. Each text is followed by one or more questions or incomplete statements based on its content. Select the answer or completion that is best according to the text and fill in the corresponding oval on the answer sheet.

This is a note to Akio from his mother.

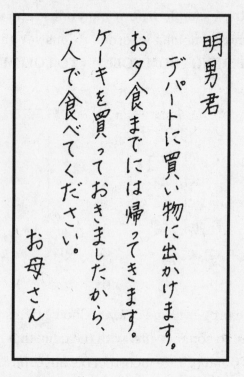

3. What does Akio's mother tell him to do?

(A) Come home by dinner time

(B) Eat the cake she bought

(C) Buy some cake

(D) Have dinner by himself

To answer this question, students must know the content of the request, including the identity of the object about which the request is made. This is a request to eat the cake the writer bought. Choice (B) is the correct answer because it explicitly reflects the content of the written request. Choices (A), (C), and (D) are all incorrect because the note does not request Akio to come home by dinner time, buy cake, or have dinner by himself.

Japanese Test with Listening

The test that follows is an actual, recently administered SAT Subject Test in Japanese with Listening. To get an idea of what a real administration is like, take the test under conditions as close as possible to those of a national administration:

- Set aside an hour when you can take the test uninterrupted. Make sure you complete the test in one sitting.

- Sit at a desk or table with no other books or papers. Dictionaries, other books, or notes are not allowed in the test room.

- Time yourself by placing a clock or kitchen timer in front of you.

- Tear out an answer sheet from the back of this book and fill it in just as you would on the day of the test. One answer sheet can be used for up to three Subject Tests.

- Read the instructions that precede the practice test. During the actual administration you will be asked to read them before answering test questions.

- After you finish the practice test, read the sections "How to Score the SAT Subject Test in Japanese with Listening" and "Reviewing Your Performance on the Japanese Subject Test with Listening."

- Actual test and answer sheets will indicate circles, not ovals.

Form 3PLC

JAPANESE TEST WITH LISTENING

PLEASE NOTE THAT YOUR ANSWER SHEET HAS FIVE ANSWER POSITIONS
MARKED A, B, C, D, AND E, WHILE THE QUESTIONS THROUGHOUT THIS
TEST CONTAIN ONLY FOUR CHOICES. BE SURE NOT TO MAKE ANY MARKS
IN COLUMN E.

SECTION I
Listening
Approximate time – 20 minutes

Directions: In this section of the test you will hear short dialogues and monologues. You will hear them only once, and they are not printed in your test booklet. At the end of each selection, you will be asked questions about what was said. Now listen to the following example, but do not mark the answer on your answer sheet.

You will hear:

Listen to this short conversation between two acquaintances.

    (A)   By bus.
    (B)   By car.
    (C)   By train.
    (D)   On foot.

The best answer to the question is (A), By bus. Therefore, you would select choice (A) and fill in the corresponding oval on the answer sheet. Now listen to the first selection.

Listen to this short telephone conversation.

1. (A) In a dormitory.
   (B) In a library.
   (C) In a train station.
   (D) In a telephone booth.

Listen to this exchange between a mother and her son.

2. (A) Disappointed.
   (B) Skeptical.
   (C) Enthusiastic.
   (D) Indifferent.

3. (A) An eye exam.
   (B) A school test.
   (C) A new game.
   (D) Sports results.

Listen to find out what the woman is offering her guest.

4. (A) Something to drink.
   (B) Something to read.
   (C) Something to wear.
   (D) Something to look at.

Listen to this person's self-introduction.

5. (A) Researcher.
   (B) Office worker.
   (C) High school student.
   (D) College student.

This conversation is taking place in a theater lobby.

6. (A) The left entrance.
   (B) The right entrance.
   (C) The front entrance.
   (D) The back entrance.

Listen to a conversation about going out to lunch.

7. (A) She doesn't like to eat out.
   (B) Most of the restaurants are new.
   (C) She doesn't know the area.
   (D) There aren't many that are well known.

8. (A) The most famous.
   (B) The one that the man always goes to.
   (C) The only one the woman knew about.
   (D) A new one.

GO ON TO THE NEXT PAGE →

This is a conversation about a library.

9. (A) Behind the station.
   (B) Behind the bank.
   (C) Across from the station.
   (D) In front of the bank.

Listen to two people talking about a concert.

10. (A) Go to the concert in his place.
    (B) Go to a concert with him.
    (C) Go to the concert by herself.
    (D) Go to a concert with his friend.

11. (A) The man's friend.
    (B) The man, the woman, and their friend.
    (C) The woman's friend.
    (D) The woman and her friend.

12. (A) 1:00 p.m. the following day.
    (B) 4:00 p.m. the following day.
    (C) 1:00 p.m. two days later.
    (D) 4:00 p.m. two days later .

Two people at a station are talking.

13. (A) A typhoon is coming.
    (B) The weather in Tokyo has been bad.
    (C) The man missed his train.
    (D) The train is late.

Now listen to the message Ms. Kojima left on an answering machine.

14. (A) To ask Mr. Brown to lend her his notes.
    (B) To find out why Mr. Brown wasn't in class.
    (C) To invite Mr. Brown to go to Nagoya.
    (D) To tell Mr. Brown about a note she received.

Listen to find out whom the people are talking about.

15. (A) Americans who stay in Japan for a long time.
    (B) Japanese who just came back from America.
    (C) Americans who just came back from Japan.
    (D) Japanese who go to American universities.

This conversation was heard on the way to school.

16. (A) Cloudy.
    (B) Windy.
    (C) Raining.
    (D) Snowing.

The next conversation is taking place in a store.

17. (A) A small briefcase.
    (B) A large briefcase.
    (C) A small book cover.
    (D) A large book cover.

This conversation was overheard in a coffee shop.

18. (A) It will take a long time to get home.
    (B) It's too late to go home.
    (C) She can stay a little while longer.
    (D) She must return home right away.

Listen to this coversation about food.

19. (A) He eats about equal amounts of meat and fish.
    (B) He likes fish better than he likes meat.
    (C) He doesn't eat as much meat as he eats fish.
    (D) He likes meat better than he likes fish.

Listen to find out where the men are talking.

20. (A) At a doctor's office.
    (B) At a shoe store.
    (C) At an umbrella shop.
    (D) At a drugstore.

Listen to this conversation in a department store.

21. (A) A customer and a store employee.
    (B) A sister and a brother.
    (C) Two friends.
    (D) A manager and his employee.

22. (A) Near the escalator.
    (B) By the elevator.
    (C) In the computer department.
    (D) At the information desk.

GO ON TO THE NEXT PAGE

A man and a woman are talking about the woman's family.

23. (A) One.
    (B) Two.
    (C) Three.
    (D) Four.

24. (A) He wishes he had a large family.
    (B) He is pleased he has a family in America.
    (C) He wishes he were in America.
    (D) He is happy to be an only child.

Listen to a conversation about a young person.

25. (A) The woman's son.
    (B) The man's son.
    (C) The woman's daughter.
    (D) The man's daughter.

26. (A) The person started a new job.
    (B) The person was transferred.
    (C) The person entered a university.
    (D) The person got married this year.

Listen to this discussion of the woman's concern.

27. (A) Whether she wants to go to college.
    (B) Whether her sister wants to go to college.
    (C) Whether she can get into college.
    (D) Whether her sister can get into college.

Listen to these people making plans.

28. (A) All going home together.
    (B) Not going to the mountains.
    (C) Staying home together.
    (D) Going to the beach or mountains.

29. (A) Reluctant.
    (B) Indifferent.
    (C) Sympathetic.
    (D) Enthusiastic.

Listen to this conversation about an unidentified place.

30. (A) It is beautiful and largely unpopulated.
    (B) It has nice scenery but there are too many people.
    (C) The people there are wonderful.
    (D) It is not very quiet.

END OF SECTION I.
DO NOT GO ON TO SECTION II UNTIL YOU ARE TOLD TO DO SO.

TIME FOR SECTIONS II AND III - 40 minutes
SECTION II
Usage

WHEN YOU BEGIN SECTION II, BE SURE THAT YOU MARK YOUR ANSWER TO THE FIRST USAGE QUESTION BY FILLING IN ONE OF THE OVALS NEXT TO NUMBER 31 ON THE ANSWER SHEET.

Directions: This section consists of a number of incomplete statements, each of which has four suggested completions. In some instances, choice (A) may consist of dashes that indicate that no insertion is required to form a correct sentence. Select the choice that best completes the sentence structurally and logically and fill in the corresponding oval on the answer sheet.

THIS SECTION OF THE TEST IS PRESENTED IN THREE COLUMNS THAT PROVIDE IDENTICAL INFORMATION. LOOK AT THE EXAMPLE BELOW AND CHOOSE THE ONE COLUMN OF WRITING WITH WHICH YOU ARE MOST FAMILIAR IN ORDER TO ANSWER THE QUESTION. DO NOT WASTE TIME BY SWITCHING FROM COLUMN TO COLUMN IN THIS SECTION.

Example:

Tōkyō wa -----

arimasu.

(A) Doitsu de

(B) Mekishiko o

(C) Furansu e

(D) Nihon ni

とうきょう
東京は-----

あります。

(A) ドイツで

(B) メキシコを

(C) フランスへ

にほん
(D) 日本に

Tookyoo wa -----

arimasu.

(A) Doitu de

(B) Mekisiko o

(C) Hurañsu e

(D) Nihoñ ni

The best completion is choice (D). Therefore, you would select choice (D) and fill in the corresponding oval on the answer sheet.

31. Ginkō wa ano mise no

tonari ni ----- .

(A) desu

(B) arimasu

(C) imasu

(D) orimasu

ぎんこう   みせ
31. 銀行はあの店の

となりに ----- 。

(A) です

(B) あります

(C) います

(D) おります

31. Giñkoo wa ano mise no

tonari ni ----- .

(A) desu

(B) arimasu

(C) imasu

(D) orimasu

GO ON TO THE NEXT PAGE

32. ----- shiroi tatemono ga

Takashi-san no gakkō?

  (A) Ano

  (B) Are no

  (C) Asoko

  (D) Anna no

32. ----- 白い建物が

隆さんの学校？

  (A) あの

  (B) あれの

  (C) あそこ

  (D) あんなの

32. ----- siroi tatemono ga

Takasi-sañ no gakkoo?

  (A) Ano

  (B) Are no

  (C) Asoko

  (D) Añna no

---

33. Masako-san wa

----- ni kimasu.

  (A) kyō

  (B) san-ji

  (C) ichi-nichi

  (D) rainen

33. 正子さんは

----- に来ます。

  (A) 今日

  (B) 三時

  (C) 一日

  (D) 来年

33. Masako-sañ wa

----- ni kimasu.

  (A) kyoo

  (B) sañ-zi

  (C) iti-niti

  (D) raineñ

---

34. Ni-kai ni ----- irasshaimasu ka?

  (A) dore ka

  (B) dore ga

  (C) donata ga

  (D) donata de

34. 二階に ----- いらっしゃいますか。

  (A) どれか

  (B) どれが

  (C) どなたが

  (D) どなたで

34. Ni-kai ni ----- irassyaimasu ka?

  (A) dore ka

  (B) dore ga

  (C) donata ga

  (D) donata de

---

35. Enpitsu wa -----

kaimashita ka?

  (A) nan-bon

  (B) nan-satsu

  (C) nan-mai

  (D) nan-dai

35. えんぴつは -----

買いましたか。

  (A) 何本

  (B) 何冊

  (C) 何枚

  (D) 何台

35. Eñpitu wa -----

kaimasita ka?

  (A) nañ-boñ

  (B) nañ-satu

  (C) nañ-mai

  (D) nañ-dai

GO ON TO THE NEXT PAGE

36. ----- imasen.

(A) Mō kyō made

(B) Mata ato

(C) Motto ato

(D) Mada kyō wa

36. ----- いません。

(A) もう今日^{きょう}まで

(B) またあと

(C) もっとあと

(D) まだ今日^{きょう}は

36. ----- imaseñ.

(A) Moo kyoo made

(B) Mata ato

(C) Motto ato

(D) Mada kyoo wa

---

37. Doitsugo ga ----- .

(A) shitte imasu

(B) kikimashita

(C) hanashimashita

(D) wakarimasu

37. ドイツ語^ごが ----- 。

(A) 知^しっています

(B) 聞^ききました

(C) 話^{はな}しました

(D) 分^わかります

37. Doitugo ga ----- .

(A) sitte imasu

(B) kikimasita

(C) hanasimasita

(D) wakarimasu

---

38. Gakkō no mae ----- .

(A) to yūbinkyoku ga arimasu

(B) ga yūbinkyoku ni arimasu

(C) yūbinkyoku ni arimasu

(D) ni yūbinkyoku ga arimasu

38. 学校^{がっこう}の前^{まえ} ----- 。

(A) と郵便局^{ゆうびんきょく}があります

(B) が郵便局^{ゆうびんきょく}にあります

(C) 郵便局^{ゆうびんきょく}にあります

(D) に郵便局^{ゆうびんきょく}があります

38. Gakkoo no mae ----- .

(A) to yuubiñkyoku ga arimasu

(B) ga yuubiñkyoku ni arimasu

(C) yuubiñkyoku ni arimasu

(D) ni yuubiñkyoku ga arimasu

---

39. Sukiyaki to tenpura de wa,

----- ii desu ka?

(A) dochira ni

(B) dore de mo

(C) dochira ga

(D) dore ga

39. すきやきと天^{てん}ぷらでは、

----- いいですか。

(A) どちらに

(B) どれでも

(C) どちらが

(D) どれが

39. Sukiyaki to teñpura de wa,

----- ii desu ka?

(A) dotira ni

(B) dore de mo

(C) dotira ga

(D) dore ga

GO ON TO THE NEXT PAGE ➡

40. A! Hon o wasurete ----- .

(A) ageta

(B) shimatta

(C) oita

(D) mita

40. あ！本をわすれて ----- 。

(A) あげた

(B) しまった

(C) おいた

(D) みた

40. A! Hoñ o wasurete ----- .

(A) ageta

(B) simatta

(C) oita

(D) mita

41. Kore mo sore ----- kudasai.

(A) o

(B) mo

(C) to

(D) wa

41. これもそれ ----- 下さい。

(A) を

(B) も

(C) と

(D) は

41. Kore mo sore ----- kudasai.

(A) o

(B) mo

(C) to

(D) wa

42. Kodomo ga ōkiku ----- .

(A) ni narimashita

(B) ni shimashita

(C) narimashita

(D) imashita

42. 子供が大きく ----- 。

(A) になりました

(B) にしました

(C) なりました

(D) いました

42. Kodomo ga ookiku ----- .

(A) ni narimasita

(B) ni simasita

(C) narimasita

(D) imasita

43. Asoko ni ----- .

(A) resutoran deshita

(B) tabemashita

(C) imashita

(D) deshita

43. あそこに ----- 。

(A) レストランでした

(B) 食べました

(C) いました

(D) でした

43. Asoko ni ----- .

(A) resutorañ desita

(B) tabemasita

(C) imasita

(D) desita

GO ON TO THE NEXT PAGE

44. Ashita no gēmu -----

ikitai to omou kedo . . .

(A) ga mite

(B) ni mite

(C) ga mi ni

(D) o mi ni

44. 明日のゲーム -----

行きたいと思うけど . . .

(A) が見て

(B) に見て

(C) が見に

(D) を見に

44. Asita no geemu -----

ikitai to omou kedo . . .

(A) ga mite

(B) ni mite

(C) ga mi ni

(D) o mi ni

---

45. Kirei da kara,

shashin o ----- .

(A) irimasu

(B) torimashō

(C) hoshii desu

(D) arimasen ka

45. きれいだから、

写真を ----- 。

(A) いります

(B) 撮りましょう

(C) ほしいです

(D) ありませんか

45. Kiree da kara,

syasiñ o ----- .

(A) irimasu

(B) torimasyoo

(C) hosii desu

(D) arimaseñ ka

---

46. Nihongo de sore

----- iimasu ka?

(A) ga nani mo

(B) o nan to

(C) wa nani ga

(D) to nani wa

46. 日本語でそれ

----- 言いますか。

(A) がなにも

(B) をなんと

(C) はなにが

(D) となには

46. Nihoñgo de sore

----- iimasu ka?

(A) ga nani mo

(B) o nañ to

(C) wa nani ga

(D) to nani wa

---

47. Kono mado ga akete ----- .

(A) arimashita

(B) okimashita

(C) shimashita

(D) imashita

47. この窓が開けて ----- 。

(A) ありました

(B) おきました

(C) しました

(D) いました

47. Kono mado ga akete ----- .

(A) arimasita

(B) okimasita

(C) simasita

(D) imasita

GO ON TO THE NEXT PAGE

555

48. Kinō gohyaku-nin

shika ----- .

(A) wa kimashita

(B) mo kimasen deshita

(C) kimasen deshita

(D) kimashita

48. 昨日五百人

しか ----- 。

(A) は来ました

(B) も来ませんでした

(C) 来ませんでした

(D) 来ました

48. Kinoo gohyaku-niñ

sika ----- .

(A) wa kimasita

(B) mo kimaseñ desita

(C) kimaseñ desita

(D) kimasita

49. Kono sakana wa atarashikute

----- desu nē.

(A) oishiku

(B) oishisa

(C) oishikute

(D) oishisō

49. この魚は新しくて

----- ですねえ。

(A) おいしく

(B) おいしさ

(C) おいしくて

(D) おいしそう

49. Kono sakana wa atarasikute

----- desu nee.

(A) oisiku

(B) oisisa

(C) oisikute

(D) oisisoo

50. Is-shūkan ni -----

mimasu.

(A) ichi-do ni

(B) ichi-do-goro

(C) ichi-do-gurai

(D) ichi-do shika

50. 一週間に -----

見ます。

(A) 一度に

(B) 一度ごろ

(C) 一度ぐらい

(D) 一度しか

50. Is-syuukañ ni -----

mimasu.

(A) iti-do ni

(B) iti-do-goro

(C) iti-do-gurai

(D) iti-do sika

51. Dono basu ni -----

ii desu ka?

(A) noreba

(B) noru no wa

(C) notte iku

(D) notte itte wa

51. どのバスに -----

いいですか。

(A) 乗れば

(B) 乗るのは

(C) 乗って行く

(D) 乗って行っては

51. Dono basu ni -----

ii desu ka?

(A) noreba

(B) noru no wa

(C) notte iku

(D) notte itte wa

GO ON TO THE NEXT PAGE

52. ----- kudasai.

(A) wasurenakute

(B) wasurenai

(C) wasurenai de

(D) wasurenaku

52. ----- ください。

(A) 忘れなくて

(B) 忘れない

(C) 忘れないで

(D) 忘れなく

52. ----- kudasai.

(A) wasurenakute

(B) wasurenai

(C) wasurenai de

(D) wasurenaku

53. Miruku ----- tsukurimashita.

(A) ni

(B) ga

(C) de

(D) shika

53. ミルク ----- 作りました。

(A) に

(B) が

(C) で

(D) しか

53. Miruku ----- tukurimasita.

(A) ni

(B) ga

(C) de

(D) sika

END OF SECTION II.
GO ON TO SECTION III.

Directions: Read the following texts carefully for comprehension. Each text is followed by one or more questions or incomplete statements based on its content. Select the answer or completion that is best according to the text and fill in the corresponding oval on the answer sheet. There is no example for this section.

This is an entry from Makoto's diary.

六月十九日　日曜日　雨

木下君と東公園へ行くつもりだったが、雨だったから二人で映画を見ることにした。帰りに、新しくできた店でアイスクリームを食べた。

54. What did Makoto do?

(A) He spent the day alone.
(B) He went to a park with a friend.
(C) He pursued his original plan.
(D) He ate ice cream after the movies.

This is a want ad in a newspaper.

求む

シェフ	男	二名
レジ	女	一名
ウエイトレス	女	六名
キッチンヘルパー	男	五名

毎週火曜日定休
レストラン北山　町田駅付近
(0427) 22-8800　森川まで

55. What job openings does the restaurant have for male job seekers?

(A) One manager and eight waiters
(B) One cashier and six waiters
(C) Two chefs and five kitchen helpers
(D) Two chefs and seven kitchen helpers

56. Which days will the employees not work?

(A) Every Monday
(B) Every Tuesday
(C) Every other Thursday
(D) Saturday and Sunday

57. Where is the restaurant located?

(A) In the station building
(B) On Mount Kitayama
(C) Near Machida Station
(D) In the northern section of Machida

GO ON TO THE NEXT PAGE ▶

This is a letter from a friend.

青木さん

　来月の八日から三日間仕事でそちらへ行くことになりました。
九日と十日の夜はあいているので、もしおひまなら、ぜひ
お会いしたいのですが。駅前のスカイホテルに泊まっています
から、電話してください。(078-54-2929)

安田

58. The purpose of Yasuda's trip is to

(A) go on vacation
(B) take a field trip
(C) return home
(D) do business

59. Yasuda wants to see Aoki on the

(A) third
(B) sixth or seventh
(C) eighth
(D) ninth or tenth

60. Yasuda asks Aoki to

(A) call him at work
(B) call him at the hotel
(C) write back
(D) meet him at the station

GO ON TO THE NEXT PAGE →

This is a note to Takahashi.

高橋さん
　すみませんが、あとで学校の方まで
　行ってきてください。

　　六日午後一時

　　　　　　　　　　森田

61. What is Takahashi likely to do after reading this note?

(A) Meet Morita at one o'clock
(B) Accept Morita's apology
(C) Come at the latest by the sixth
(D) Go to the school

GO ON TO THE NEXT PAGE

This is a menu.

キッチン長寿亭
東京都港区六本木2-2-2

イトーピア六本木ビル1F

TEL 583-5279

*ライス

1.	ドライカレー	600
2.	カレーライス	480
3.	ピラフ	600
4.	チキンライス	600

*トースト

1.	トースト	180
2.	ピザトースト	500
3.	ハムトースト	470
4.	ツナトースト	470
5.	チーズトースト	450

*サンドウィッチ

6.	ハムサンド	450
7.	ツナサンド	450
8.	タマゴサンド	450
9.	ミックスサンド	450

*ホット

1.	コーヒー	300
2.	アメリカン	300
3.	レモンティー	300
4.	ミルクティー	300
5.	ミルク	300
6.	ココア	350
7.	カフェ・オレ	350
8.	ウィンナ・コーヒー	350

*アイス

1.	アイスコーヒー	320
2.	アイスティー	320
3.	アイスミルクティー	320
4.	アイスミルク	320
5.	アイスココア	400
6.	アイス・オーレ	400
7.	アイス・ウィンナー	400

*ジュース

1.	レモン・スカッシュ	400
2.	オレンジ・ジュース	400
3.	トマト・ジュース	400
4.	ジンジャーエール	350
5.	コーラ	350
6.	ソーダ水	350

62. Which of the following kinds of sandwich is available?

(A) Vegetable
(B) Chicken
(C) Beef
(D) Tuna

63. Which of the following kinds of juice is served?

(A) Grape
(B) Tomato
(C) Pineapple
(D) Apple

GO ON TO THE NEXT PAGE

This is a letter from Carol.

広美さん

　私は高校で三年前から日本語を勉強しています。来年は大学ですが、もちろん大学でも日本語を続けるつもりです。いつか日本へ行ってみたいです。

　月曜日から金曜日まで学校へ行って、金、土、日の夜はレストランで働いています。仕事は大変ですが、チップがたくさんもらえるので好きです。お金をためて、赤いスポーツカーを買いたいと思っています。

　じゃあ、手紙を下さい。

　　　　　八月三十日

　　　　　　　　　　　　　　　　　　キャロル

64. When does Carol work?

(A) Every night
(B) Monday through Friday
(C) Friday, Saturday, and Sunday nights
(D) During lunchtime

65. Why does Carol like her job?

(A) She can practice Japanese.
(B) It pays for her studies.
(C) It is easy.
(D) She gets a lot of tips.

66. Carol is working in order to

(A) pay for Japanese lessons
(B) save money to go to Japan
(C) pay for her college education
(D) buy a car for herself

GO ON TO THE NEXT PAGE

This comes from a magazine.

あなたのアイデアを
　　お待ちしています。

この雑誌について、あなたの
アイデアとご意見を600字以内に
書いて、十月八日までにお送り
ください。

67. What is the purpose of this notice?

(A) To solicit readers' comments
(B) To sell magazine subscriptions
(C) To collect names for a mailing list
(D) To notify readers of the next publication date

This is a note left on the door of a dormitory room.

京子さん
　ちょっと近くのスーパーへ買物に
行って来ますから、中に入って
待っていてくださいね。
　　　　　　2:30 P.M.
　　　　みどり

68. The purpose of the note is to ask Kyōko to

(A) meet Midori at the store
(B) wait in Midori's room until Midori returns
(C) wait for Midori before going shopping
(D) come to Midori's room after Midori returns

GO ON TO THE NEXT PAGE ➤

This is a note to Yamamoto.

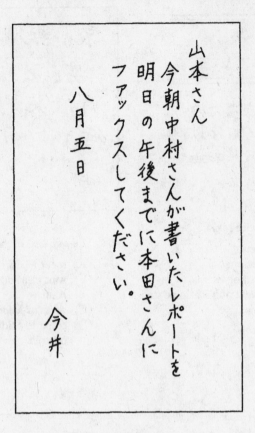

山本さん
今朝中村さんが書いたレポートを
明日の午後までに本田さんに
ファックスしてください。

八月五日

今井

69. What is Yamamoto asked to do?

(A) Send a fax to Honda before writing to Nakamura
(B) Fax Nakamura's report to Honda
(C) Write a report about Nakamura for Honda
(D) Write a report about Honda for Nakamura

70. When does Yamamoto have to carry out this task?

(A) By this morning
(B) By this afternoon
(C) By tomorrow morning
(D) By tomorrow afternoon

GO ON TO THE NEXT PAGE ➤

This is a letter from a Japanese student to a student in the United States.

ジム君

　ぼくの名前は川村明といいます。今日学校の先生からジム君の手紙をもらいました。日本人のペンパルを探しているそうですね。ぼくも外国の友達がほしかったので、とてもうれしいです。

　ジム君の日本語が上手なのでびっくりしました。何年習っているんですか。話すのも上手ですか。君の手紙を見て、ぼくももっと英語を勉強しようと思いました。

　ぼくはテニスが大好きで、週に三、四回やります。ジム君の趣味は何ですか。

　では返事を楽しみに待っています。

川村明

---

71. The writer is surprised that Jim

(A) wants a Japanese pen pal
(B) studied Japanese for many years
(C) writes Japanese well
(D) wants to speak Japanese

72. What does the writer say he wants?

(A) To study English harder
(B) To have Jim write back in English
(C) To write to Jim in English next time
(D) To play tennis more often

73. What does the writer ask Jim?

(A) How often he will write letters
(B) What his favorite foods are
(C) What his hobbies are
(D) If he wants to have a friend from another country

GO ON TO THE NEXT PAGE

This is a note.

明日の朝までに使った部屋を
かたづけなさい。いいですね。

74. For whom is the note intended?

   (A) A child
   (B) A wife
   (C) A mother
   (D) A boss

The following are messages found on a desk.

森先生へ

—旅行社の野口さんから電話。来週の火曜日の飛行機の予約がとれた
　そうです。　　　　　　　　　　　　　　　　　　　　　9:30 a.m.

—原さんがコンサートの切符を持っていらっしゃいました。テーブルの上に
　おいておきました。　　　　　　　　　　　　　　　　　3:40 p.m.

—古田さんから電話。来週のパーティーの時間と場所を明日知らせてください。
　　　　　　　　　　　　　　　　　　　　　　　　　　4:35 p.m.
　　　　　　　　　　　　　　　　　　　　　　　　　　山中

75. Ms. Noguchi called because she wants

   (A) to inform Mr. Mori that his reservation has
       been made
   (B) to meet Mr. Mori next Tuesday
   (C) to make arrangements for a trip
   (D) Mr. Mori to reserve airplane tickets for
       Tuesday

76. Ms. Yamanaka left the concert ticket

   (A) in a drawer
   (B) on the table
   (C) next to the telephone
   (D) on top of the television set

77. Mr. Furuta wants to know

   (A) who will come to the party
   (B) the time and place of the party
   (C) if the party has been canceled
   (D) if Mr. Hara will come to the party

GO ON TO THE NEXT PAGE ➡

This is a newspaper article.

先生が
タクシードライバーに

林さんは三十八才の時に、学校の教師をやめて、タクシーの運転手になった。運転手十五年。銀座、新宿を中心に夜の町を走っている。

78. What is the topic of the article?

(A) Having a second job
(B) Planning for retirement
(C) Improving one's standard of living
(D) Changing careers

79. What is Hayashi's present occupation?

(A) Teacher
(B) Auto mechanic
(C) Taxi driver
(D) Student

This is an excerpt from a children's story.

犬がいなくなったので、子供が悲しがって泣いていました。

80. How does the child feel?

(A) Angry
(B) Sad
(C) Envious
(D) Rejected

STOP

IF YOU FINISH BEFORE TIME IS CALLED, YOU MAY CHECK YOUR WORK ON SECTIONS II AND III.
DO NOT TURN TO ANY OTHER TEST IN THIS BOOK.

How to Score the SAT Subject Test in Japanese with Listening

When you take the SAT Subject Test in Japanese with Listening, you will receive an overall composite score as well as three subscores: one for the reading section, one for the listening section, and one for the usage section. The reading, listening, and usage scores are reported on the College Board's 20-to-80 scale. However, the composite score, which is the most significant of the scores reported to the colleges you specify, is in the form of the College Board's 200-to-800 scale.

Worksheet 1. Finding Your Raw Listening Subscore

STEP 1: Table A lists the correct answers for all the questions on the SAT Subject Test in Japanese with Listening that is reproduced in this book. It also serves as a worksheet for you to calculate your raw Listening subscore.

- Compare your answers with those given in the table.
- Put a check in the column marked "Right" if your answer is correct.
- Put a check in the column marked "Wrong" if your answer is incorrect.
- Leave both columns blank if you omitted the question.

STEP 2: Count the number of right answers for questions 1–30.

Enter the total here: _____

STEP 3: Count the number of wrong answers for questions 1–30.

Enter the total here: _____

STEP 4: Multiply the number of wrong answers from Step 3 by .333.

Enter the product here: _____

STEP 5: Subtract the result obtained in Step 4 from the total you obtained in Step 2.

Enter the total here: _____

STEP 6: Round the number obtained in Step 5 to the nearest whole number.

Enter the total here: _____

The number you obtained in Step 6 is your raw Listening subscore.

Worksheet 2. Finding Your Raw Reading Subscore

STEP 1: Table A lists the correct answers for all the questions on the SAT Subject Test in Japanese with Listening that is reproduced in this book. It also serves as a worksheet for you to calculate your raw Reading subscore.

STEP 2: Count the number of right answers for questions 54–80.

Enter the total here: _____

STEP 3: Count the number of wrong answers for questions 54–80.

Enter the total here: _____

STEP 4: Multiply the number of wrong answers by .333.

Enter the product here: _____

STEP 5: Subtract the result obtained in Step 4 from the total you obtained in Step 2.

Enter the result here: _____

STEP 6: Round the number obtained in Step 5 to the nearest whole number.

Enter the result here: _____

The number you obtained in Step 6 is your raw Reading subscore.

Worksheet 3. Finding Your Raw Usage Subscore

STEP 1: Table A lists the correct answers for all the questions on the SAT Subject Test in Japanese with Listening that is reproduced in this book. It also serves as a worksheet for you to calculate your raw Usage subscore.

STEP 2: Count the number of right answers for questions 31–53.

Enter the total here: _____

STEP 3: Count the number of wrong answers for questions 31–53.

Enter the total here: _____

STEP 4: Multiply the number of wrong answers by .333.

Enter the product here: _____

STEP 5: Subtract the result obtained in Step 4 from the total you obtained in Step 2.

Enter the result here: _____

STEP 6: Round the number obtained in Step 5 to the nearest whole number.

Enter the result here: _____

The number you obtained in Step 6 is your raw Usage subscore.

Worksheet 4. Finding Your Raw Composite Score*

STEP 1: Enter your unrounded raw reading subscore from Step 5 of Worksheet 2 here:_____

STEP 2: Enter your unrounded raw listening subscore from Step 5 of Worksheet 1 here:_____

STEP 3: Multiply your unrounded raw listening subscore by 1.035.

Enter the product here: _____

STEP 4: Enter your unrounded raw usage subscore from Step 5 of Worksheet 3 here:_____

STEP 5: Multiply your unrounded raw usage subscore by 1.226.

Enter the product here: _____

STEP 6: Add the results obtained in Steps 1, 3, and 5.

Enter the sum here: _____

STEP 7: Round the number obtained in Step 6 to the nearest whole number.

Enter the result here: _____

The number you obtained in Step 7 is your raw composite score.

*This weighting reflects the amount of time spent on the two sections of the test—40 minutes on the reading and usage questions and 20 minutes on the listening questions. For those who are curious about how the calculation works, the weighting is done in standard deviation units, a measure of score variability. The weight given to the listening subscore is calculated by dividing the standard deviation of the reading subscore by the standard deviation of the listening subscore. The weight given to the usage subscore is calculated by dividing the standard deviation of the reading subscore by the standard deviation of the usage subscore.

TABLE A

Answers to the SAT Subject Test in Japanese with Listening, Form 3PLC, and Percentage of Students Answering Each Question Correctly

Question Number	Correct Answer	Right	Wrong	Percentage of Students Answering the Question Correctly*	Question Number	Correct Answer	Right	Wrong	Percentage of Students Answering the Question Correctly*
1	B			93	33	B			67
2	A			83	34	C			33
3	B			92	35	A			70
4	A			68	36	D			59
5	D			51	37	D			54
6	B			80	38	D			85
7	C			73	39	C			73
8	B			58	40	B			46
9	B			35	41	B			29
10	B			75	42	C			48
11	A			78	43	C			41
12	A			45	44	D			49
13	D			55	45	B			57
14	A			53	46	B			30
15	D			46	47	A			24
16	B			47	48	C			34
17	A			28	49	D			57
18	D			69	50	C			49
19	C			48	51	A			23
20	D			69	52	C			65
21	A			87	53	C			20
22	D			59	54	D			86
23	A			28	55	C			93
24	A			49	56	B			76
25	B			45	57	C			56
26	A			49	58	D			65
27	D			50	59	D			86
28	D			59	60	B			87
29	D			42	61	D			50
30	A			30	62	D			79
31	B			82	63	B			95
32	A			75	64	C			67

Table A continued on next page

Table A continued from previous page

Question Number	Correct Answer	Right	Wrong	Percentage of Students Answering the Question Correctly*	Question Number	Correct Answer	Right	Wrong	Percentage of Students Answering the Question Correctly*
65	D			65	76	B			76
66	D			61	77	B			73
67	A			51	78	D			46
68	B			43	79	C			59
69	B			62	80	B			70
70	D			35					
71	C			45					
72	A			42					
73	C			69					
74	A			41					
75	A			26					

*These percentages are based on an analysis of the answer sheets for a random sample of 955 students who took this form of the test in April 1993 and whose mean score was 534. They may be used as an indication of the relative difficulty of a particular question. Each percentage may also be used to predict the likelihood that a typical SAT Subject Test in Japanese with Listening candidate will answer correctly that question on this edition of this test.

Finding Your Scaled Score

When you take SAT Subject Tests, the scores sent to the colleges you specify are reported on the College Board scale, which ranges from 200 to 800. Subscores are reported on a scale that ranges from 20 to 80. You can convert your practice test scores to scaled scores by using Tables B, C, D, and E. To find your scaled score, locate your raw score in the left-hand column of the table; the corresponding score in the right-hand column is your scaled score. For example, in Table B a raw composite score of 47 on this particular edition of the SAT Subject Test in Japanese with Listening corresponds to a scaled score of 590.

Raw scores are converted to scaled scores to ensure that a score earned on any one edition of a particular Subject Test is comparable to the same scaled score earned on any other edition of the same Subject Test. Because some editions of tests may be slightly easier or more difficult than others, scaled scores are adjusted so that they indicate the same level of performance regardless of the edition of the test taken and the ability of the group that takes it. Thus, for example, a score of 400 on one edition of a test taken at a particular administration indicates the same level of achievement as a score of 400 on a different edition of the test taken at a different administration.

When you take the SAT Subject Tests during a national administration, your scores are likely to differ somewhat from the scores you obtain on the tests in this book. People perform at different levels at different times for reasons unrelated to the tests themselves. The precision of any test is also limited because it represents only a sample of all the possible questions that could be asked.

Your scaled composite score from Table B is _____ .

Your scaled listening score from Table C is _____ .

Your scaled reading score from Table D is _____ .

Your scaled usage score from Table E is _____ .

TABLE B
Scaled Score Conversion Table
Japanese Subject Test with Listening Composite Scores (Form 3PLC)

Raw Score	Scaled Score	Raw Score	Scaled Score	Raw Score	Scaled Score
86	800	47	590	8	340
85	800	46	580	7	330
84	800	45	580	6	330
83	800	44	570	5	320
82	800	43	560	4	310
81	800	42	560	3	310
80	800	41	550	2	300
79	790	40	540	1	300
78	790	39	540	0	290
77	780	38	530	−1	280
76	770	37	520	−2	280
75	770	36	520	−3	270
74	760	35	510	−4	260
73	750	34	510	−5	260
72	750	33	500	−6	250
71	740	32	490	−7	240
70	730	31	490	−8	240
69	730	30	480	−9	230
68	720	29	470	−10	230
67	720	28	470	−11	220
66	710	27	460	−12	210
65	700	26	450	−13	210
64	700	25	450	−14	200
63	690	24	440	−15	200
62	680	23	440	−16	200
61	680	22	430	−17	200
60	670	21	420	−18	200
59	660	20	420	−19	200
58	660	19	410	−20	200
57	650	18	400	−21	200
56	650	17	400	−22	200
55	640	16	390	−23	200
54	630	15	380	−24	200
53	630	14	380	−25	200
52	620	13	370	−26	200
51	610	12	370	−27	200
50	610	11	360	−28	200
49	600	10	350	−29	200
48	590	9	350		

TABLE C

Scaled Score Conversion Table
Japanese Subject Test with Listening Listening Subscore (Form 3PLC)

Raw Score	Scaled Score	Raw Score	Scaled Score	Raw Score	Scaled Score
30	80	16	57	2	33
29	80	15	55	1	32
28	78	14	53	0	30
27	76	13	52	−1	29
26	74	12	50	−2	27
25	72	11	48	−3	26
24	70	10	46	−4	25
23	69	9	45	−5	23
22	67	8	43	−6	22
21	65	7	41	−7	20
20	63	6	40	−8	20
19	62	5	38	−9	20
18	60	4	36	−10	20
17	58	3	35		

TABLE D

Scaled Score Conversion Table
Japanese Subject Test with Listening Reading Subscore (Form 3PLC)

Raw Score	Scaled Score	Raw Score	Scaled Score	Raw Score	Scaled Score
27	80	14	53	1	33
26	76	13	52	0	32
25	73	12	50	−1	30
24	70	11	49	−2	28
23	68	10	47	−3	27
22	66	9	46	−4	25
21	64	8	44	−5	24
20	63	7	42	−6	22
19	61	6	41	−7	21
18	59	5	39	−8	20
17	58	4	38	−9	20
16	56	3	36		
15	55	2	35		

TABLE E

Scaled Score Conversion Table
Japanese Subject Test with Listening Usage Subscore (Form 3PLC)

Raw Score	Scaled Score	Raw Score	Scaled Score	Raw Score	Scaled Score
23	80	12	61	1	38
22	80	11	59	0	36
21	80	10	56	−1	34
20	78	9	54	−2	32
19	76	8	52	−3	31
18	73	7	50	−4	29
17	71	6	48	−5	27
16	69	5	46	−6	25
15	67	4	44	−7	23
14	65	3	42	−8	21
13	63	2	40		

Reviewing Your Performance
on the Japanese Subject Test with Listening

After you score your test, analyze your performance—consider the following questions:

Did you run out of time before reaching the end of the test?

If so, you may need to pace yourself better. For example, maybe you spent too much time on one or two hard questions. A better approach might be to skip the ones you can't answer right away and try answering all the questions that remain on the test. Then if there's time, go back to the questions you skipped.

Did you take a long time reading the directions?

You will save time when you take the test by learning the directions to the Japanese Test with Listening ahead of time. Each minute you spend reading directions during the test is a minute that you could use to answer questions.

How did you handle questions you were unsure of?

If you were able to eliminate one or more of the answer choices as wrong and guess from the remaining ones, your approach probably worked to your advantage. On the other hand, making haphazard guesses or omitting questions without trying to eliminate choices could cost you valuable points.

How difficult were the questions for you compared with other students who took the test?

Table A shows you how difficult the multiple-choice questions were for the group of students who took this test during its national administration. The right-hand column gives the percentage of students that answered each question correctly.

A question answered correctly by almost everyone in the group is obviously an easy question. For example, 95 percent of the students answered question 63 correctly. But only 20 percent answered question 53 correctly.

Keep in mind that these percentages are based on just one group of students. They would probably be different if another group of students took the test.

If you missed several easy questions, go back and try to find out why: Did the questions cover material you haven't reviewed yet? Did you misunderstand the directions?

Chapter 13
Korean with Listening

Purpose

This test measures your understanding of Korean and your ability to engage in purposeful communication in the context of contemporary Korean culture.

Format

This is a one-hour test with about 20 minutes of listening and 40 minutes of usage and reading. There are 80 to 85 multiple-choice questions.

Listening comprehension questions test your ability to understand the spoken language. They are based on short, spoken Korean dialogues and narratives primarily about everyday topics. All listening questions and possible answers are in English. The questions will be spoken on an audiocassette. They will also be printed in the test book.

Usage questions are written entirely in *Hangŭl* and require you to complete Korean sentences or phrases so that they are structurally and logically correct. Areas covered include vocabulary, honorifics, and various aspects of structure.

Reading questions test your understanding of such points as main and supporting ideas. All the passages in this section are written in *Hangŭl* and all the questions are in English. Most questions deal with understanding literal meaning, although some inference questions may be included. The Korean selections are drawn from authentic materials, such as notes, diaries, menus, newspaper articles, advertisements, letters, and literary texts.

Skills Measured	Approximate Percentage of Test
Listening Comprehension	35
Usage	30
Reading Comprehension	35

Recommended Preparation

This test is appropriate for students who have studied Korean as a second or foreign language for two to four years in high school, or the equivalent.

The best preparation is gradual development of competence in Korean over a period of years. You should also familiarize yourself with directions in advance. The directions in this book are identical to those that appear on the test.

Cassette Players

You must bring an acceptable cassette player with earphones to the test center. Put fresh batteries in your cassette player the day before the test and, if you like, bring additional fresh batteries and a backup cassette player with earphones to the test center. Test center staff will NOT have batteries, cassette players, or earphones for your use.

Acceptable cassette players must be:

- personal (have earphones that let only you hear the recording)
- portable (small enough that the entire player can fit in your hand)
- battery-operated
- able to use a single (not dual) standard (2 1/2 by 4 inches) audiocassette—not a mini- or microcassette

If your cassette player has a programming feature that fast-forwards automatically to the next prompt, that feature must be deactivated before you start the test. You will not be allowed to share a cassette player with another test-taker.

Beginning with the November 2005 administration, portable CD players will be required instead of cassette players for language with listening tests.

Score

The total score is reported on the 200-to-800 scale. Listening, usage, and reading subscores are reported on the 20-to-80 scale.

The Korean Subject Test with Listening is offered only once a year at designated test centers. To take the test, you MUST bring an acceptable cassette player with earphones to the test center.

A cassette tape with listening questions is available for the Korean Subject Test with Listening in this book. To receive your copy, complete and mail the postcard in this book. If the postcard has been removed, call 212 649-8424 or write to:

The College Board

Subject Tests Language Listening Cassette

45 Columbus Avenue

New York, New York 10023-6992

You must indicate the SAT Language Test with Listening you plan to take.

Sample Listening Questions

Please note that the cassette does not start here. Begin using the cassette when you start the actual practice test on page 586.

Please note that your answer sheet has five answer positions marked A, B, C, D, E, while the questions throughout this test contain only four choices. Be sure NOT to make any marks in column E.

Directions: In this part of the test you will hear several spoken selections. They will not be printed in your test book. You will hear them only once. After each selection you will be asked one or more questions about what you have just heard. These questions, with four possible answers, are printed in your test booklet. Select the best answer to each question from among the four choices printed and fill in the corresponding oval on your answer sheet.

(Narrator)   [Listen to this short exchange between friends. Then

answer Question 1.

(Man)   이번 방학에 뭐 해요?
(Woman)   방학에요? 일하려고 해요.
(Man)   그럼 일자리는 구했어요?
(Woman)   지금 찾는 중이에요.
                일자리 있으면 소개해 주세요.
(Man)   요새는 일자리 구하기가
                어려운데.

(Narrator)   Question 1. What is the woman doing now?] (16 seconds)

1. **(A)** Looking for work.
    (B) Looking for an apartment.
    (C) Writing a paper.
    (D) Preparing for summer school.

The answer is (A) Looking for work. This question requires the students' knowledge of vocabulary and expressions such as "–는 중이다," which conveys an action currently taking place.

Sample Usage Questions

Directions: This section consists of a number of incomplete statements, each of which has four suggested completions. Select the word or words that best complete the sentence structurally and logically and fill in the corresponding oval on the answer sheet.

2. 영수: 철수 일어났어요?
    철수 누나: 아니오.
               _____ 안 일어났어요.

    (A) 방금
    (B) 금방
    (C) 아직
    (D) 먼저

The answer is (C) 아직. To answer this question, students need to understand the usage of the adverb "아직," which best completes the sentence in the given context.

Sample Reading Questions

Directions: Read the following selections carefully for comprehension. Each selection is followed by one or more questions or incomplete statements based on its content. Choose the answer or completion that is best according to the selection and fill in the corresponding oval on the answer sheet.

Questions 3–4

> 행사 : 수미의 첫돌 잔치
> 장소 : 서울시 종로구 신영동
>   신영 아파트 234호
> 날짜 : 오월 삼십일 토요일
> 시간 : 저녁 여섯시 반

3. What is the occasion?
   (A) Baby shower
   (B) Baby's one hundredth day
   (C) Baby's first birthday
   (D) Nursery school graduation

4. The event will start at
   (A) 5:00 p.m.
   (B) 5:30 p.m.
   (C) 6:00 p.m.
   (D) 6:30 p.m.

The questions test the students' comprehension of vocabulary and time-related expressions. The answer to question 3 is (C) Baby's first birthday. The answer to question 4 is (D) 6:30 P.M.

Korean Test with Listening

The test that follows is an actual, recently administered SAT Subject Test in Korean with Listening. To get an idea of what a real administration is like, take the test under conditions as close as possible to those of a national administration:

- Set aside 60 minutes when you can take the test uninterrupted. Make sure you complete the test in one sitting.

- Sit at a desk or table with no other books or papers. Dictionaries, other books, or notes are not allowed in the test room.

- Time yourself by placing a clock or kitchen timer in front of you.

- Tear out an answer sheet from the back of this book and fill it in just as you would on the day of the test. One answer sheet can be used for up to three Subject Tests.

- Read the instructions that precede the practice test. During the actual administration you will be asked to read them before answering test questions.

- After you finish the practice test, read the sections "How to Score the SAT Subject Test in Korean with Listening" and "Reviewing Your Performance on the SAT Subject Test in Korean with Listening."

- Actual test and answer sheets will indicate circles, not ovals.

KOREAN TEST WITH LISTENING

The top portion of the section of the answer sheet that you will use in taking the Korean Test with Listening must be filled in exactly as shown in the illustration below. Note carefully that you have to do all of the following on your answer sheet.

1. Print KOREAN WITH LISTENING on the line under the words "Subject Test (print)."

2. In the shaded box labeled "Test Code" fill in four ovals:

   —Fill in oval 1 in the row labeled V.
   —Fill in oval 8 in the row labeled W.
   —Fill in oval 4 in the row labeled X.
   —Fill in oval A in the row labeled Y.

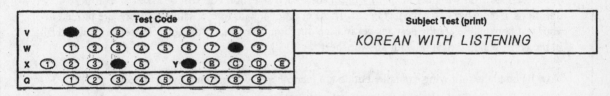

Please answer all questions that apply by filling in the specific ovals in the row Q.
The information you provide is for statistical purposes only and will not affect your score on the test.

I. Where have you learned Korean? (Fill in ALL ovals that apply.)

   • If you have learned Korean at home,   —Fill in oval 1.
   • If you have studied Korean in a US high school,   —Fill in oval 2.
   • If you have studied Korean in a Korean Language
       School while attending grades K-8,   —Fill in oval 3.
   • If you have studied Korean in a Korean Language
       School while attending grades 9-12,   —Fill in oval 4.
   • If you have lived in Korea longer than one year
       after age ten,   —Fill in oval 5.

II. How long did you study Korean while in grades 9-12 ? (Fill in the ONE oval that applies.)

   • Less than 2 years   —Fill in oval 6.
   • 2 to 2-1/2 years   —Fill in oval 7.
   • 3 to 3-1/2 years   —Fill in oval 8.
   • More than 3-1/2 years   —Fill in oval 9.

When the supervisor gives the signal, turn the page and begin the Korean Test with Listening. There are 100 numbered ovals on the answer sheet and 80 questions in the Korean Test with Listening. Therefore, use only ovals 1 to 80 for recording your answers.

KOREAN TEST WITH LISTENING

PLEASE NOTE THAT YOUR ANSWER SHEET HAS FIVE ANSWER POSITIONS MARKED A, B, C, D, AND E, WHILE THE QUESTIONS THROUGHOUT THIS TEST CONTAIN ONLY FOUR CHOICES. BE SURE <u>NOT</u> TO MAKE ANY MARKS IN COLUMN E.

SECTION I
LISTENING
Approximate time — 20 minutes
Questions 1–31

<u>Directions:</u> In this part of the test you will hear several spoken selections. They will not be printed in your test book. You will hear them <u>only once</u>. After each selection you will be asked one or more questions about what you have just heard. These questions, with four possible answers, are printed in your test booklet. Select the best answer to each question from among the four choices printed and fill in the corresponding oval on your answer sheet.

Now listen to the following example, but do not mark the answer on your answer sheet.

You will hear:

You will hear and see: What is the woman going to do during the vacation?

Sample Answer
(A) ● (C) (D)

You will see: (A)   Stay home.
                       (B)   Go to Korea.
                       (C)   Go to school.
                       (D)   Study Korean.

The best answer to the question is (B) "Go to Korea." Therefore, you should select choice (B) and fill in the corresponding oval on the answer sheet. Now listen to the first selection.

---

1. What is the man looking for?

   (A)   His wallet.
   (B)   His watch.
   (C)   His glasses.
   (D)   His book.

2. Where did the man find the item he was looking for?

   (A)   On his desk.
   (B)   Next to his briefcase.
   (C)   Next to his wallet.
   (D)   Inside his briefcase.

GO ON TO THE NEXT PAGE ➡

3TLC

3. How many people are in the group?

   (A) 2
   (B) 3
   (C) 4
   (D) 5

4. Why do they have to wait?

   (A) They could not find a parking space.
   (B) They are too early.
   (C) They did not make a reservation.
   (D) Their reservation was cancelled.

_____

5. Where do the speakers most likely work?

   (A) At a sporting goods store.
   (B) At a computer store.
   (C) At a business office.
   (D) At a doctor's office.

6. What is their main complaint?

   (A) The customers are too demanding.
   (B) The coworkers are not cooperative.
   (C) Their computer is not working fast
         enough.
   (D) Their work requires long sitting hours.

7. How did they decide on the place to go after
   work?

   (A) They looked it up in the phone book.
   (B) Their friend had recommended.
   (C) The man had been there before.
   (D) They have seen an ad on television.

8. Why couldn't the woman sleep late?

   (A) She had to attend classes.
   (B) She had to make a phone call.
   (C) She wanted to catch an early train.
   (D) She had an appointment.

9. What time did the woman get up?

   (A) 7:00.
   (B) 7:30.
   (C) 8:00.
   (D) 8:30.

_____

10. What did they decide to do for dinner?

   (A) They are going to have pizza delivered.
   (B) They are going to make something at
         home.
   (C) They are going to eat out.
   (D) They are going to have leftovers.

11. What do they think about pizza?

   (A) It's inexpensive.
   (B) Delivery is convenient.
   (C) It's too much bother to make.
   (D) It's generally not good for you.

GO ON TO THE NEXT PAGE ➤

12. What did the clerk recommend?

    (A) A conservative style watch.
    (B) A traveler's watch.
    (C) A popular style watch.
    (D) A digital watch.

13. How much did the customer pay for the watch?

    (A) $200.
    (B) $225.
    (C) $450.
    (D) $900.

14. How long is the discount valid?

    (A) Today only.
    (B) This week only.
    (C) For two more weeks.
    (D) For the entire month.

15. Where is the conversation taking place?

    (A) At an insurance agency.
    (B) At a doctor's office.
    (C) At a lawyer's office.
    (D) At a school administrative office.

16. What does the man ask the woman to do?

    (A) To show her passport.
    (B) To bring her resume.
    (C) To fill out a form.
    (D) To sign a check.

17. How long does the woman have to wait?

    (A) 5 minutes.
    (B) 10 minutes.
    (C) 15 minutes.
    (D) 20 minutes.

18. Where does this announcement take place?

    (A) At a subway station.
    (B) On an airplane.
    (C) On a tour bus.
    (D) At a ferry pier.

19. What is the subject of this announcement?

    (A) Safety rules.
    (B) Tourist sites.
    (C) Destination change.
    (D) Construction sites.

20. How are the passengers advised to go to Pusan?

    (A) By going to Chejudo and taking the next plane.
    (B) By going to Chejudo and taking the boat.
    (C) By getting off at Taegu and taking the train.
    (D) By getting off at Taegu and taking the bus.

21. When is the man going to Mexico?

    (A) Tomorrow.
    (B) The day after tomorrow.
    (C) A week from tomorrow.
    (D) In two weeks.

22. How long will the man stay in Mexico?

    (A) About 14 days.
    (B) About 20 days.
    (C) About a month.
    (D) About two months.

23. What is the woman's reaction to the man's trip?

    (A) She thinks that he is too busy to go away.
    (B) She wishes she could go in his place.
    (C) She envies him for going on a trip.
    (D) She hopes that he will bring back lots of pictures.

GO ON TO THE NEXT PAGE

24. Where is the father?

    (A) He is at a meeting.
    (B) He is on an overseas trip.
    (C) He is at a banquet.
    (D) He is at a retirement party.

25. What is the father's occupation?

    (A) A businessman.
    (B) A university professor.
    (C) A financial consultant.
    (D) A computer programmer.

26. What should the father do early the next day?

    (A) Come to the caller's office.
    (B) Come to the caller's home.
    (C) Telephone the caller at his office.
    (D) Telephone the caller at his home.

---

27. How much was the postage?

    (A) One third as much as the price of the book.
    (B) Half as much as the price of the book.
    (C) As much as the price of the book.
    (D) Twice as much as the price of the book.

28. What type of mailing did the man request?

    (A) Overnight.
    (B) Airmail.
    (C) Surface mail.
    (D) Book rate.

29. Who left the message?

    (A) Michael's teacher.
    (B) Michael's mother.
    (C) Michael's girlfriend.
    (D) Michael's sister.

30. What is the message?

    (A) The caller is asking to buy the ticket to the concert.
    (B) The concert will be held at a local church.
    (C) Michael's teacher will lecture right after the concert.
    (D) Michael will be performing with other students.

31. When is the concert to be held?

    (A) Saturday at 1:30 P.M.
    (B) Saturday at 5:30 P.M.
    (C) Sunday at 1:30 P.M.
    (D) Sunday at 5:30 P.M.

END OF SECTION I.
DO NOT GO ON TO SECTION II UNTIL YOU ARE TOLD TO DO SO.

SECTION II

USAGE

Time — 40 minutes for Sections II and III

Questions 32-52

WHEN YOU BEGIN THE USAGE SECTION, BE SURE THAT YOU MARK YOUR ANSWER TO THE FIRST USAGE QUESTION BY FILLING IN ONE OF THE OVALS NEXT TO NUMBER 32 ON THE ANSWER SHEET.

Part A

<u>Directions:</u> This section consists of a number of incomplete statements, each of which has four suggested completions. Select the word or words that best complete the sentence structurally and logically and fill in the corresponding oval on the answer sheet.

---

32. 나는 네가 서울에 돌아오기를
    손꼽아 기다리고 _____.

    (A) 잇다
    (B) 이다
    (C) 잊다
    (D) 있다

33. 너는 먹는 데에 별로
    관심이 _____ 것 같다.

    (A) 나는
    (B) 없는
    (C) 많은
    (D) 아닌

34. 강 _____ 바다가 넓다.

    (A) 이지만
    (B) 보다는
    (C) 으로는
    (D) 이기에

35. 날씨가 너무 추워서
    장갑을 _____고
    털 구두를 _____고 나갔어요.

    (A) 입.....신
    (B) 끼.....신
    (C) 끼.....입
    (D) 쓰.....차

36. 미나: "배가 _____ 식사부터
    먼저 할까?"

    준호: "그래, 그러자.
    점심을 일찍 먹어서
    배가 고픈데."

    (A) 고프길래
    (B) 고프더니
    (C) 고프고
    (D) 고프면

GO ON TO THE NEXT PAGE

37. 어제 _____ 일기예보에 의하면,
내일도 눈이 _____고 한다.

   (A) 듣는.....내렸다
   (B) 들은.....내렸었다
   (C) 듣는.....내렸겠다
   (D) 들은.....내리겠다

38. 네, 알겠습니다.
그럼 제가 사장님 _____
전화 드리겠습니다.

   (A) 집으로
   (B) 댁으로
   (C) 곳으로
   (D) 쪽으로

39. 이 식당 김치는 좀
맵_____어요.

   (A) 워
   (B) 지
   (C) 겠
   (D) 웠

40. 철수가 언제 우체국에 _____고
물었어요.

   (A) 간다
   (B) 가자
   (C) 가겠다
   (D) 가느냐

41. 그 _____ 수준이면 프로야구
선수가 될 수 있겠어요.

   (A) 밖에
   (B) 정도
   (C) 까지
   (D) 보다

42. 지난 토요일에 나는
동생하고 운전을 _____
멀리 사는 친구 집에
놀_____ 갔다.

   (A) 했어.....러
   (B) 해서.....러
   (C) 했어.....로
   (D) 해서.....로

43. 언니는 오늘 첫 출근을 _____,
아침부터 일찍 일어나
준비_____ 바쁩니다.

   (A) 하게 돼서.....하느라고
   (B) 하느라고.....하게 돼서
   (C) 하게 돼서.....하길래
   (D) 하느라고.....하기로

GO ON TO THE NEXT PAGE →

Part B

Directions: In each of the following paragraphs there are numbered blanks indicating that words or phrases have been omitted. For each numbered blank, four completions are provided. First read through the entire paragraph. Then, for each numbered blank, choose the completion that is most appropriate and fill in the corresponding oval on the answer sheet.

학업도 중요____, 그 보다 더 중요한 것은
44

운동이나 음악 등 여러 가지 활동을 ____
45

건강한 몸과 마음을 만들어 나가는

것이라고 ____.
46

44.
   (A) 하니까
   (B) 하지만
   (C) 하든지
   (D) 하듯이

45.
   (A) 통해
   (B) 위해
   (C) 의해
   (D) 대해

46.
   (A) 된다
   (B) 본다
   (C) 있다
   (D) 든다

GO ON TO THE NEXT PAGE

할머니, 안녕하셨습니까?

할머니께서 다녀 ____ 벌써
47

일 년이 ____. 할머니의 모습이 자꾸
48

떠올라 편지를 씁니다. 할머니를 ____
49

갔던 벚꽃 놀이가 잊혀지지 않습니다.

그 때 ____ 주시던 한국의 옛날
50

이야기도 귀에 ____ 남아 있습니다.
51

여름 방학이 되면 할머니를 ____
52

가겠습니다.

그럼 안녕히 계십시오.

47. (A) 가실 때
    (B) 가실 지
    (C) 가신 때
    (D) 가신 지

48. (A) 됩니다
    (B) 갑니다
    (C) 납니다
    (D) 듭니다

49. (A) 가지고
    (B) 데리고
    (C) 드리고
    (D) 모시고

50. (A) 들러
    (B) 들려
    (C) 들어
    (D) 들여

51. (A) 생생하여
    (B) 생생하게
    (C) 생생하고
    (D) 생생하나

52. (A) 볼게
    (B) 뵙게
    (C) 보러
    (D) 뵈러

END OF SECTION II.
GO ON TO SECTION III.

SECTION III

READING COMPREHENSION

Questions 53-80

> **Directions:** Read the following selections carefully for comprehension. Each selection is followed by one or more questions or incomplete statements based on its content. Choose the answer or completion that is best according to the selection and fill in the corresponding oval on the answer sheet.

Questions 53-55

> 영어를 한국어로,
> 한국어는 영어로,
> 번역할 수 있는 사람을 구함.
> 대학생이면 더욱 환영함.
> 시간제 일거리로 좋음.
> 시간당 만원.
> 운전 면허 소지자 우대.
> 연락처 829-3100

53. The advertiser is looking for

   (A) a college student
   (B) a translator
   (C) a Korean tutor
   (D) an English tutor

54. What is the pay?

   (A) 10,000 won per hour
   (B) 10,000 won per week
   (C) 100,000 won per hour
   (D) 100,000 won per week

55. Preference will be given to a person with

   (A) a driver's licence
   (B) previous experience
   (C) a college degree
   (D) full-time availability

GO ON TO THE NEXT PAGE

Questions 56-58

아버지께서는 내가 지난 학기에 우수한 성적을 받았다고,
내가 원하던 회고 귀엽게 생긴 강아지를 사 주셨습니다.
나는 학교에서 돌아와 숙제를 하고 나면 강아지에게
먹이를 줍니다. 강아지는 작년에 어머니께서 선물로
주신 검은 고양이와도 사이좋게 놀곤 합니다.

56. Father bought a puppy for the writer as a gift for

   (A) an excellent grade
   (B) doing chores
   (C) graduation
   (D) her birthday

57. When does the writer give food to the puppy?

   (A) Early morning
   (B) After lunch
   (C) After school
   (D) Before doing homework

58. What color is the cat?

   (A) White
   (B) Brown
   (C) Black
   (D) Grey

GO ON TO THE NEXT PAGE

Questions 59-60

```
진열품 가구 대폭 할인
새 것과 다름없는 품질
고급 목재 사용
침실용, 거실용, 사무실용 등
다양한 품목 취급


할인 기간: 11월 15일-20일
특별 할인 가격: 정가의 반값
```

59. What is being advertised?

   (A)   Appliances
   (B)   Bedding
   (C)   Upholstery
   (D)   Furniture

60. The advertisement offers

   (A)   free delivery
   (B)   buy one, get one free
   (C)   half off the regular price
   (D)   no payment for half a year

GO ON TO THE NEXT PAGE

Questions 61-62

이 제품으로는
사무실에서 더러워진 손, 얼굴 등을
깨끗이. 닦을 수 있습니다.
운전할 때 얼굴이나 손은 물론 차내의 더러운 곳도
깨끗이 닦을 수 있습니다.
운동 후 얼굴이나 손의 땀을 시원하게
닦아 낼 수 있습니다.
여행할 때 씻기가 불편 할 때도
항상 편리하게 쓰실 수 있습니다.

61. What is being advertised?

   (A) Tissue
   (B) Perfume
   (C) Shampoo
   (D) Lotion

62. Why is the item recommended?

   (A) It has many uses.
   (B) It does not cost much.
   (C) It comes in many fragrances.
   (D) It is good for sensitive skin.

GO ON TO THE NEXT PAGE

　진영이는 석 달 전에 한국말을 배우러 한국에 계시는
삼촌댁으로 갔어요. 처음 한 달 동안은 말이 통하지 않아
고생을 많이 했어요. 그러나 이제는 학교에서 친구도
사귀고 한국 생활을 즐기게 되었어요. 주말에는 친구들과
함께 등산도 가고 수영도 즐겨 합니다. 그러나 영화나
운전은 그렇게 즐기지 않아요. 삼촌이 휴가를 받으시면
진영이는 삼촌을 모시고 미국으로 돌아오겠다고 해요.

63. When did Chinyŏng go to Korea?

   (A)   Three weeks ago
   (B)   One month ago
   (C)   Three months ago
   (D)   Six months ago

64. What two activities does Chinyŏng enjoy
doing on weekends?

   (A)   Mountain climbing and swimming
   (B)   Mountain climbing and going to the
         movies
   (C)   Going to the movies and swimming
   (D)   Driving and going to the movies

65. With whom will Chinyŏng be returning to the
United States?

   (A)   A friend
   (B)   His aunt
   (C)   His uncle
   (D)   A cousin

GO ON TO THE NEXT PAGE →

Questions 66-67

오는 7월 5일 토요일 오후 6시에 친지 여러분을
모시고 조촐한 모임을 가지려고 합니다. 그 동안
우리 식구가 바라던 작은 집을 장만하게 되어
이것을 여러분과 축하하기 위해서입니다. 뒷장에
자세한 약도가 그려져 있고 전화 번호도 있습니다.
음식은 모두 준비되어 있으니 아무것도 가져오시지
마십시오. 차편이 필요하신 분이나 못 오실 분은
전화로 연락해 주시기 바랍니다.

66. The note is an invitation to a

(A) wedding anniversary
(B) family reunion
(C) birthday party
(D) housewarming party

67. In the note, you are asked to call if you

(A) can bring a dish
(B) can give someone a ride
(C) cannot attend
(D) cannot understand the directions

GO ON TO THE NEXT PAGE

Questions 68-69

This is a diary of an elementary school student.

6월 15일 수요일 맑음

이 달은 환경 보호의 달이다. 오늘 영어 시간에 짧은 영화를 보았다. 온갖 동물과 식물에 관한 과학 영화였는데, 동물과 식물 중에는 사람들이 먹을 수 있는 것이 많다고 배웠다. 육지뿐만 아니라 바다 속에도 먹을 수 있는 동식물이 많이 있다는 것도 알게 되었다. 바다도 우리에게 여러모로 도움을 준다고 느꼈다. 우리 모두 육지와 바다를 깨끗하게 하며 자연을 보호해야 되겠다고 새삼 느꼈다.

GO ON TO THE NEXT PAGE

68. What was the movie about?

    (A) Space and planets
    (B) Animals and plants
    (C) Science and English
    (D) Moon and Earth

69. What does the writer realize is important?

    (A) The English language
    (B) The study of science
    (C) Our environment
    (D) Our diet

GO ON TO THE NEXT PAGE

Questions 70-72

워싱톤 지역 친선 피크닉

지루했던 겨울도 이제는 가고 기다리던 봄이 찾아왔습니다.
화창한 봄날씨에 온 가족과 화목하게 모여서 즐거운 하루를
보내시지 않겠습니까?
바쁜 생활 속에 밤낮으로 부모님들이 일만 하다 보면
아이들은 모르는 사이에 타인처럼 자라나기 쉽습니다. 또한
우리 지역의 이웃들과도 대화를 통해 사귈 수 있는 기회를
마련하였습니다.

날짜: 1996년 4월 20일(토요일)
시간: 오전 10시 - 오후 3시
장소: 워싱톤 시 공원
점심: 각자 도시락 마련
음료수: 학부모회 제공
참가비: 가족당 5불(상품과 운동, 게임 마련)

70. What does the sponsor try to achieve through
the event?

(A) Strengthening of family and community ties
(B) Raising funds for community activities
(C) Recruiting athletes through sports
       competition
(D) Celebrating a Korean holiday

71. The fee collected for this event is used to pay for

(A) professional entertainers
(B) prizes and games
(C) the use of the park
(D) a picnic lunch

72. Who is responsible for the picnic lunch?

(A) The community sponsor
(B) The city
(C) Each family
(D) The grocers' association

GO ON TO THE NEXT PAGE

Questions 73-75

옛날에는 사람들이 자동차 대신 말을 타고 다녔다. 옛날 사람들은 말을 아주 좋아했던 것 같다. 꿈에 말을 보면 좋은 일이 생기고 꿈에 말을 타면 반가운 편지가 온다고 믿었으니까. 옛날에는 결혼식날 신랑은 백마를 타고 신부집에 갔다고 한다. 신랑이 탄 말이 신부집 앞에서 크게 울면 첫아들을 낳는다고 좋아했다. 정월 보름날 말에게 여러 가지 곡식으로 먹이를 주었을 때 말이 가장 먼저 먹는 것을 그 해에 심으면 풍년이 든다고 믿었다.

73. According to the story, a person who sees a horse in a dream will

   (A) receive a letter
   (B) receive a gift
   (C) have good luck
   (D) have a visitor

74. When the horse that carries the groom arrives at the bride's house and brays out, the new couple will

   (A) enjoy good fortune forever
   (B) live a long life together
   (C) have an abundant harvest
   (D) have a son as their first child

75. What did people believe would happen when they fed the horse a variety of grains on January 15 ?

   (A) The horse will select the best crop to be planted.
   (B) The horse will breed many offspring.
   (C) The family will have lots of children.
   (D) The first son will become rich and famous.

GO ON TO THE NEXT PAGE

영민아, 잘 있었니?

나는 지난 토요일 우리 식구들과 함께 산에 놀러
갔었어. 점심때가 되어, 개울가에 자리를 잡고
어머니가 정성스럽게 준비하신 점심을 먹었단다.
정말 꿀맛이었어. 나는 어머니께 감사하는 마음을
표하기 위해 "우리 엄마가 만드신 음식이 이 세상에서
제일 맛있어요."하고 큰 소리로 외쳤지. 어머니께서
빙긋이 웃으시더구나.

밥을 먹고 냇물에 발을 담그고 있자니 뭔가
간지러운 거야. 그래서 내려다보니 작은 송사리 떼가
몰려다니고 있잖아. 동생은 신이 나서 빈 병을
가져다가 고기를 잡겠다고 야단이더구나. 그렇지만
고기가 얼마나 빠른지 다 도망가는 거야. 나는
동생을 위로하기 위해 이렇게 말했어. "동수는
자연 보호주의자구나. 고기를 한 마리도 안 잡네."
울상이 됐던 동생이 겸연쩍었는지 씩 웃더니 훌쩍
숲쪽으로 뛰어가더구나. 나는 동생이 사라지는
나무숲을 바라보며 자연의 소중함을 다시 한 번
느꼈어.

그럼 잘 있어. 또 연락할게.

1995년 6월 17일
민희가

GO ON TO THE NEXT PAGE →

76. Where did Minhi's family go last Saturday?

    (A) To an amusement park
    (B) To a restaurant
    (C) To a beach
    (D) To the mountains

77. How did Minhi express her feelings toward her mother?

    (A) She shouted that mother was a good cook.
    (B) She ate all the food that her mother prepared.
    (C) She prepared lunch for her mother.
    (D) She washed the dishes after lunch.

78. What happened to Minhi's feet in the water?

    (A) They were stung by jellyfish.
    (B) They slipped and slid.
    (C) They were cut by broken glass.
    (D) They were tickled by little fish.

79. Why did Minhi call her brother an environmentalist?

    (A) He did not want to catch fish.
    (B) He is active in the environmental movement.
    (C) Minhi wanted to console him.
    (D) Minhi misunderstood him.

80. Which best describes Minhi's personality?

    (A) Caring
    (B) Quiet
    (C) Aggressive
    (D) Unpredictable

END OF SECTION III.

STOP

IF YOU FINISH BEFORE TIME IS CALLED, YOU MAY CHECK YOUR WORK
ON SECTIONS II AND III OF THIS TEST.
DO NOT TURN TO ANY OTHER TEST IN THIS BOOK.

How to Score the SAT Subject Test in Korean with Listening

When you take the SAT Subject Test in Korean with Listening, you will receive an overall composite score as well as three subscores: one for the reading section, one for the listening section, and one for the usage section. The reading, listening, and usage scores are reported on the College Board's 20-to-80 scale. However, the composite score, which is the most significant of the scores reported to the colleges you specify, is in the form of the College Board's 200-to-800 scale.

Worksheet 1. Finding Your Raw Listening Subscore

STEP 1: Table A lists the correct answers for all the questions on the SAT Subject Test in Korean with Listening that is reproduced in this book. It also serves as a worksheet for you to calculate your raw Listening subscore.

- Compare your answers with those given in the table.
- Put a check in the column marked "Right" if your answer is correct.
- Put a check in the column marked "Wrong" if your answer is incorrect.
- Leave both columns blank if you omitted the question.

STEP 2: Count the number of right answers for questions 1–31.

Enter the total here:_____

STEP 3: Count the number of wrong answers for questions 1–31.

Enter the total here:_____

STEP 4: Multiply the number of wrong answers from Step 3 by .333.

Enter the product here: _____

STEP 5: Subtract the result obtained in Step 4 from the total you obtained in Step 2.

Enter the total here:_____

STEP 6: Round the number obtained in Step 5 to the nearest whole number.

Enter the total here:_____

The number you obtained in Step 6 is your raw Listening subscore.

Worksheet 2. Finding Your Raw Reading Subscore

STEP 1: Table A lists the correct answers for all the questions on the SAT Subject Test in Korean with Listening that is reproduced in this book. It also serves as a worksheet for you to calculate your raw Reading subscore.

STEP 2: Count the number of right answers for questions 53–80.
Enter the total here:_____

STEP 3: Count the number of wrong answers for questions 53–80.
Enter the total here:_____

STEP 4: Multiply the number of wrong answers from Step 3 by .333.
Enter the product here: _____

STEP 5: Subtract the result obtained in Step 4 from the total you obtained in Step 2.
Enter the result here: _____

STEP 6: Round the number obtained in Step 5 to the nearest whole number.
Enter the result here: _____

The number you obtained in Step 6 is your raw Reading subscore.

Worksheet 3. Finding Your Raw Usage Subscore

STEP 1: Table A lists the correct answers for all the questions on the SAT Subject Test in Korean with Listening that is reproduced in this book. It also serves as a worksheet for you to calculate your raw Usage subscore.

STEP 2: Count the number of right answers for questions 32–52.
Enter the total here:_____

STEP 3: Count the number of wrong answers for questions 32–52.
Enter the total here:_____

STEP 4: Multiply the number of wrong answers from Step 3 by .333.
Enter the product here: _____

STEP 5: Subtract the result obtained in Step 4 from the total you obtained in Step 2.
Enter the result here: _____

STEP 6: Round the number obtained in Step 5 to the nearest whole number.
Enter the result here: _____

The number you obtained in Step 6 is your raw Usage subscore.

Worksheet 4. Finding Your Raw Composite Score*

STEP 1: Enter your unrounded raw reading subscore from Step 5 of Worksheet 2 here:_____

STEP 2: Multiply your unrounded raw reading subscore by 1.0010.

Enter the product here: _____

STEP 3: Enter your unrounded raw listening subscore from Step 5 of Worksheet 1 here:_____

STEP 4: Multiply your unrounded raw listening subscore by 1.0720.

Enter the product here: _____

STEP 5: Enter your unrounded raw usage subscore from Step 5 of Worksheet 3 here:_____

STEP 6: Multiply your unrounded raw usage subscore by 0.8920.

Enter the product here: _____

STEP 7: Add the results obtained in Steps 2, 4, and 6.

Enter the sum here:_____

STEP 8: Round the number obtained in Step 7 to the nearest whole number.

Enter the result here: _____

The number you obtained in Step 8 is your raw composite score.

*This weighting reflects the amount of time spent on the two sections of the test—40 minutes on the reading and usage questions and 20 minutes on the listening questions. For those who are curious about how the calculation works, the weighting is done in standard deviation units, a measure of score variability. The weight given to the listening subscore is calculated by dividing the standard deviation of the reading subscore by the standard deviation of the listening subscore. The weight given to the usage subscore is calculated by dividing the standard deviation of the reading subscore by the standard deviation of the usage subscore.

TABLE A

Answers to the SAT Subject Test in Korean with Listening, Form 3TLC, and Percentage of Students Answering Each Question Correctly

Question Number	Correct Answer	Right	Wrong	Percentage of Students Answering the Question Correctly*	Question Number	Correct Answer	Right	Wrong	Percentage of Students Answering the Question Correctly*
1	C			99	33	B			94
2	D			96	34	B			92
3	B			99	35	B			92
4	C			98	36	D			77
5	C			84	37	D			81
6	D			99	38	B			67
7	C			79	39	C			54
8	D			91	40	D			63
9	A			97	41	B			87
10	B			98	42	B			53
11	D			99	43	A			76
12	C			93	44	B			94
13	B			85	45	A			58
14	B			74	46	B			45
15	B			71	47	D			89
16	C			88	48	A			92
17	B			79	49	D			82
18	B			37	50	B			53
19	C			91	51	B			85
20	D			93	52	D			62
21	B			88	53	B			96
22	A			88	54	A			91
23	C			72	55	A			63
24	A			83	56	A			98
25	B			46	57	C			92
26	D			91	58	C			87
27	C			52	59	D			80
28	B			74	60	C			83
29	B			62	61	A			87
30	D			83	62	A			97
31	C			62	63	C			78
32	D			83	64	A			94

Table A continued on next page

Table A continued from previous page

Question Number	Correct Answer	Right	Wrong	Percentage of Students Answering the Question Correctly*	Question Number	Correct Answer	Right	Wrong	Percentage of Students Answering the Question Correctly*
65	C			95	76	D			98
66	D			85	77	A			95
67	C			87	78	D			94
68	B			96	79	C			75
69	C			95	80	A			93
70	A			93					
71	B			83					
72	C			65					
73	C			85					
74	D			90					
75	A			85					

*These percentages are based on an analysis of the answer sheets for a random sample of 745 students who took this form of the test in November 1997 and whose mean score was 595. They may be used as an indication of the relative difficulty of a particular question. Each percentage may also be used to predict the likelihood that a typical SAT Subject Test in Korean with Listening candidate will answer correctly that question on this edition of this test.

Finding Your Scaled Score

When you take SAT Subject Tests, the scores sent to the colleges you specify are reported on the College Board scale, which ranges from 200 to 800. Subscores are reported on a scale that ranges from 20 to 80. You can convert your practice test scores to scaled scores by using Tables B, C, D, and E. To find your scaled score, locate your raw score in the left-hand column of the table; the corresponding score in the right-hand column is your scaled score. For example, a raw composite score of 47 on this particular edition of the SAT Subject Test in Korean with Listening corresponds to a scaled score of 600.

Raw scores are converted to scaled scores to ensure that a score earned on any one edition of a particular Subject Test is comparable to the same scaled score earned on any other edition of the same Subject Test. Because some editions of tests may be slightly easier or more difficult than others, scaled scores are adjusted so that they indicate the same level of performance regardless of the edition of the test taken and the ability of the group that takes it. Thus, for example, a score of 400 on one edition of a test taken at a particular administration indicates the same level of achievement as a score of 400 on a different edition of the test taken at a different administration.

When you take the SAT Subject Tests during a national administration, your scores are likely to differ somewhat from the scores you obtain on the tests in this book. People perform at different levels at different times for reasons unrelated to the tests themselves. The precision of any test is also limited because it represents only a sample of all the possible questions that could be asked.

Your scaled composite score from Table B is _____.

Your scaled listening score from Table C is _____.

Your scaled reading score from Table D is_____.

Your scaled usage score from Table E is _____.

TABLE B
Scaled Score Conversion Table Korean Subject Test
with Listening Composite Scores (Form 3TLC)

Raw Score	Scaled Score	Raw Score	Scaled Score	Raw Score	Scaled Score
80	800	44	580	8	340
79	800	43	580	7	330
78	800	42	570	6	330
77	800	41	560	5	320
76	800	40	560	4	310
75	790	39	550	3	310
74	790	38	540	2	300
73	780	37	540	1	290
72	770	36	530	0	290
71	770	35	520	-1	280
70	760	34	520	-2	270
69	750	33	510	-3	270
68	750	32	500	-4	260
67	740	31	500	-5	250
66	730	30	490	-6	240
65	730	29	480	-7	240
64	720	28	480	-8	230
63	710	27	470	-9	220
62	710	26	460	-10	220
61	700	25	460	-11	210
60	690	24	450	-12	200
59	690	23	440	-13	200
58	680	22	430	-14	200
57	670	21	430	-15	200
56	670	20	420	-16	200
55	660	19	410	-17	200
54	650	18	410	-18	200
53	640	17	400	-19	200
52	640	16	390	-20	200
51	630	15	390	-21	200
50	620	14	380	-22	200
49	620	13	370	-23	200
48	610	12	370	-24	200
47	600	11	360	-25	200
46	600	10	350	-26	200
45	590	9	350		

TABLE C

Scaled Score Conversion Table
Korean Subject Test with Listening Listening Subscore (Form 3TLC)

Raw Score	Scaled Score	Raw Score	Scaled Score	Raw Score	Scaled Score
31	80	16	53	2	32
29	80	15	51	1	32
28	79	14	49	0	31
27	77	13	46	-1	30
26	75	12	45	-2	29
25	73	11	42	-3	28
24	72	10	41	-4	27
23	69	9	40	-5	26
22	66	8	38	-6	25
21	64	7	36	-7	24
20	63	6	35	-8	23
19	61	5	34	-9	22
18	58	4	33	-10	21
17	55	3	33		

TABLE D

Scaled Score Conversion Table
Korean Subject Test with Listening Reading Subscore (Form 3TLC)

Raw Score	Scaled Score	Raw Score	Scaled Score	Raw Score	Scaled Score
28	80	15	56	2	41
27	76	14	55	1	40
26	74	13	54	0	39
25	72	12	53	-1	37
24	70	11	51	-2	36
23	67	10	51	-3	34
22	66	9	50	-4	33
21	65	8	49	-5	32
20	63	7	48	-6	30
19	62	6	47	-7	29
18	61	5	46	-8	27
17	60	4	44	-9	26
16	58	3	43		

TABLE E

Scaled Score Conversion Table
Korean Subject Test with Listening Usage Subscore (Form 3TLC)

Raw Score	Scaled Score	Raw Score	Scaled Score	Raw Score	Scaled Score
21	80	11	66	1	47
20	79	10	64	0	45
19	78	9	62	-1	44
18	77	8	60	-2	43
17	75	7	58	-3	42
16	73	6	57	-4	40
15	72	5	54	-5	38
14	71	4	52	-6	36
13	69	3	50	-7	34
12	67	2	49		

Reviewing Your Performance
on the Korean Subject Test with Listening

After you score your test, analyze your performance—consider the following questions:

Did you run out of time before reaching the end of the test?

If so, you may need to pace yourself better. For example, maybe you spent too much time on one or two hard questions. A better approach might be to skip the ones you can't answer right away and try answering all the questions that remain on the test. Then if there's time, go back to the questions you skipped.

Did you take a long time reading the directions?

You will save time when you take the test by learning the directions to the Korean Test with Listening ahead of time. Each minute you spend reading directions during the test is a minute that you could use to answer questions.

How did you handle questions you were unsure of?

If you were able to eliminate one or more of the answer choices as wrong and guess from the remaining ones, your approach probably worked to your advantage. On the other hand, making haphazard guesses or omitting questions without trying to eliminate choices could cost you valuable points.

How difficult were the questions for you compared with other students who took the test?

Table A shows you how difficult the multiple-choice questions were for the group of students who took this test during its national administration. The right hand column gives the percentage of students that answered each question correctly.

A question answered correctly by almost everyone in the group is obviously an easy question. For example, 95 percent of the students answered question 65 correctly. But only 37 percent answered question 18 correctly.

Keep in mind that these percentages are based on just one group of students. They would probably be different if another group of students took the test.

If you missed several easy questions, go back and try to find out why: Did the questions cover material you haven't reviewed yet? Did you misunderstand the directions?

Chapter 14
Latin

Purpose

This test measures wide-ranging knowledge of Latin. It is written to reflect general trends in high school curricula and is independent of particular textbooks or methods of instruction.

Format

This one-hour test includes 70 to 75 multiple-choice questions.

Areas of Evaluation

- *Forms*—select appropriate grammatical forms of Latin words
- *Derivatives*—choose Latin words from which English words are derived
- *Translation*—translate from Latin to English
- *Sentence completion*—complete Latin sentences
- *Substitution*—choose alternate ways of expressing the same thought in Latin
- *Reading Comprehension*—answer a variety of questions based on short passages of prose or poetry

The reading comprehension part has 30 to 37 questions based on three to five reading passages and one or two poetry passages. A set of questions following a poetry passage always includes one question requiring you to scan the first four feet of a line of dactylic hexameter verse or to determine the number of elisions in a line.

Skills Measured	Approximate Percentage of Test
Grammar and Syntax	30
Derivatives	5
Translation and Reading Comprehension	65

Recommended Preparation

The test is intended for students who have studied Latin for two to four years in high school (the equivalent of two to four semesters in college). The best way to prepare is by gradually developing competence in sight-reading Latin over a period of years. You may also prepare for the Latin Test as you would for any comprehensive test that requires knowledge of facts and concepts and the ability to apply them, thereby acquiring the equivalent of two to four years of classroom preparation. Familiarize yourself with directions in advance. The directions in this book are identical to those that appear on the test.

Score

The total score is reported on the 200-to-800 scale.

Sample Questions

> *Please note that your answer sheet has five answer positions marked A, B, C, D, E, while the questions throughout this test contain only four choices. Be sure NOT to make any marks in column E.*

Forms

This type of question asks you to select a specific grammatical form of a Latin word. Any form of a noun, pronoun, adjective, adverb, or verb can be asked for.

Directions: In the statement below, you are asked to give a specific form of the underlined word. Select the correct form from the choices given. Then fill in the corresponding oval on the answer sheet.

1. The future indicative of <u>potest</u> is
    (A) <u>potuerat</u>
    (B) <u>poterat</u>
    (C) <u>potuerit</u>
    (D) <u>poterit</u>

In this question, you are asked to identify the future indicative of a very common irregular verb. The answer is (D). Choice (A) is the pluperfect tense, (B) the imperfect, and (C) the future perfect.

Derivatives

In this type of question, you are given an English sentence with one word underlined. You must choose the Latin word from which the underlined English word is derived.

Directions: The English sentence below contains a word that is underlined. From among the choices, select the Latin word to which the underlined word is related by derivation. Then fill in the corresponding oval on the answer sheet.

2. The goalkeeper was out of <u>position</u>.
    (A) <u>populus</u>
    (B) <u>pons</u>
    (C) <u>possum</u>
    (D) <u>pōnō</u>

The English word "position" is derived from *positus*, the past participle of the Latin verb *pōnō*, "to put or place." So, (D) is the answer. *Position* is not derived from the nouns *populus* and *pons*, which mean "people" and "bridge," nor from the verb *possum*, which means "to be able." Note that you will need to know the various forms of different Latin verbs to answer these questions.

Translation

You must choose the correct translation of the underlined Latin word or words. This type of question is more complex than the previous types, as it is based on the syntax of a complete Latin sentence.

Directions: In this section, part or all of the sentence is underlined. From among the choices, select the best translation for the underlined word or words. Then fill in the corresponding oval on the answer sheet.

3. Dux dīxit <u>sē mīlitēs laudātūrum esse</u>.
    (A) that they would praise the soldiers
    (B) that the soldiers had praised him
    (C) that he would praise the soldiers
    (D) that the soldiers should be praised

Real SAT Subject Tests

To answer this question correctly, you must know that the underlined part of the sentence is testing an indirect statement that depends on the verb *dīxit*. The answer is (C) "that he would praise the soldiers." The singular form of the future participle, *laudātūrum*, tells you that *sē* (he) is the subject of the indirect statement; therefore *mīlitēs* must be the direct object. The past tense of *dīxit* tells you that "would praise" is the correct translation of *laudātūrum esse*. None of the incorrect choices (A), (B), and (D) has both the correct subject of the indirect statement and the correct translation of the verb.

Sentence Completion

This type of question contains a Latin sentence in which a word or phrase has been omitted. You must select the Latin word or phrase that best fits grammatically into the sentence.

Directions: The sentence below contains a blank space indicating that a word or phrase has been omitted. For each blank, four completions are provided. Choose the word or phrase that best completes the sentence and fill in the corresponding oval on the answer sheet.

4. Ē castrīs ... nōluit.

    (A) ēgressus est

    (B) ēgredere

    (C) ut ēgrediātur

    (D) ēgredī

To answer this question correctly, you must be able to translate the words *Ē castrīs ... nōluit* ("He did not wish ... from the camp") and then select the only choice that can be added to these two words to make a complete, grammatical Latin sentence. Here the correct choice is (D) *ēgredī*, the infinitive, since *nōlō* takes the infinitive. (A) is incorrect because it is the present perfect form, (B) because it is the imperative, and (C) because *nōlō* does not take *ut* and the subjunctive. Note that *ēgredior* is a deponent verb.

Substitution

This type of question contains a complete Latin sentence, part or all of which is underlined. You are asked to select the substitution that is closest in meaning to the underlined words.

Directions: In the sentence below, part of the sentence is underlined. Select from the choices the expression that, when substituted for the underlined portion of the sentence, changes the meaning of the sentence LEAST. Then fill in the corresponding oval on the answer sheet.

5. Vēnit Rōmam ad <u>mātrem videndam</u>.

    (A) <u>cum mātrem vīdisset</u>

    (B) <u>mātre vīsā</u>

    (C) <u>quī mātrem vīdit</u>

    (D) <u>mātris videndae causā</u>

In this example, the underlined portion is translated: "to see his/her mother." You must select the answer choice whose translation is closest in meaning to this underlined part. The correct choice is (D) *mātris videndae causā*, which also expresses purpose or intention. None of the other choices does so.

Reading Comprehension

This type of question presents you with a series of short passages of prose or poetry followed by several questions. These questions test either grammatical points (9 below), translation of a phrase or clause (7, 8, and 10), grammatical reference (6), or summary/comprehension. In addition, poetry passages always have one question on the scansion of the first four feet of a line of dactylic hexameter verse.

Note: The passages have titles, include definitions of uncommon words that appear in the text, and are adapted from Latin authors. There are approximately three to five passages with a total of 32 to 37 questions on the test. At least one (and no more than two) poetry passage appears on the test.

Directions: Read the following text carefully for comprehension. The text is followed by a number of questions or incomplete statements. Select the answer or completion that is best according to the text and fill in the corresponding oval on the answer sheet.

An enemy attack

Sabīnī multi, ut ad moenia Rōmae venīrent, illōs in agrīs vīventēs oppugnābant. Agrī dēlēbantur; terror urbī iniectus (injectus) est. Tum plēbs benignē arma cēpit ad Sabīnōs repellendōs. Recūsantibus[1] frūstrā senātōribus, duo tamen exercitūs magnī cōnscrīptī sunt.

[1]recūsō, recūsāre: oppose

6. The word vīventēs (line 1) refers to

   (A) Sabīnī (line 1)

   (B) moenia (line 1)

   (C) illōs (line 1)

   (D) agrīs (line 1)

The word *vīventēs* refers to (C) *illōs*. Choice (B) cannot be the correct answer because *moenia* is neuter plural, and (D) *agrīs* is incorrect because the fields cannot be living somewhere. The sense of the sentence tells you that (A) *Sabīnī* is incorrect and that the words *illōs in agrīs vīventēs* belong together.

7. The sentence Sabīnī ... oppugnābant (lines 1–2) tells us that the

   (A) Sabines wanted to get to the city walls

   (B) Sabines were the people living in the fields

   (C) Romans wanted to go nearer to the city walls

   (D) Romans wanted to attack the people living in the fields

To answer this question correctly, you must know that *Sabīnī* is the subject of the sentence and that *illōs in agrīs vīventēs* is the object. You must also understand the purpose clause *ut ad moenia Rōmae venīrent* in line 1. The correct answer is (A). The Sabines are therefore not the people living in the fields (B), nor is it the Romans who want to get nearer to the city walls (C) or to attack the people living in the fields (D).

8. The sentence <u>Agrī</u> ... <u>iniectus (injectus) est</u> (line 2) tells us that the

    (A) Sabines were destroyed in the fields

    (B) Sabines were frightened of the city

    (C) fearful city was destroyed

    (D) city was filled with fear

The sentence tells us that the fields were destroyed and that fear was "thrown into" the city. The correct answer is therefore (D).

9. The subject of <u>cēpit</u> (line 3) is

    (A) <u>terror</u> (line 2)

    (B) <u>plēbs</u> (line 3)

    (C) <u>arma</u> (line 3)

    (D) he (understood)

The correct answer is (B) *plēbs*, which is in the nominative case and the subject of the sentence. Choice (A) *terror* is the subject of the previous clause and (C) *arma* is the object of *cēpit*. Choice (D) "he (understood)" is not the subject of this sentence, since there is an expressed subject.

10. The sentence <u>Recūsantibus</u> ... <u>conscrīptī sunt</u> (lines 3–4) tells us that

    (A) armies were raised for the senators

    (B) armies were raised in vain

    (C) the senators prevented the raising of armies

    (D) the senators did not want armies to be raised

The ablative absolute *Recūsantibus frūstrā senātōribus* tells us that the armies were raised with the senators resisting in vain. The correct answer is therefore (D) "the senators did not want the armies to be raised."

Latin Test

The test that follows is an actual, recently administered SAT Subject Test in Latin. To get an idea of what a real administration is like, take the test under conditions as close as possible to those of a national administration:

- Set aside an hour when you can take the test uninterrupted. Make sure you complete the test in one sitting.

- Sit at a desk or table with no other books or papers. Dictionaries, other books, or notes are not allowed in the test room.

- Time yourself by placing a clock or kitchen timer in front of you.

- Tear out an answer sheet from the back of this book and fill it in just as you would on the day of the test. One answer sheet can be used for up to three Subject Tests.

- Read the instructions that precede the practice test. During the actual administration you will be asked to read them before answering test questions.

- After you finish the practice test, read the sections "How to Score the SAT Subject Test in Latin" and "Reviewing Your Performance on the Latin Subject Test."

- Actual test and answer sheets will indicate circles, not ovals.

Form 3PAC2

LATIN TEST

The top portion of the section of the answer sheet that you will use in taking the Latin test must be filled in exactly as shown in the illustration below. Note carefully that you have to do all of the following on your answer sheet.

    1. Print LATIN on the line under the words "Subject (print)."

    2. In the shaded box labeled "Test Code" fill in four ovals:

        —Fill in oval 4 in the row labeled V.

        —Fill in oval 2 in the row labeled W.

        —Fill in oval 2 in the row labeled X.

        —Fill in oval C in the row labeled Y.

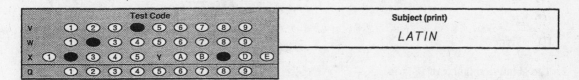

In the group of nine ovals labeled Q, you are to fill in ONE and ONLY ONE oval, as described below, to indicate how you obtained your knowledge of Latin. The information you provide is for statistical purposes only and will not influence your score on the test.

Part I   If your knowledge of Latin does not come primarily from courses taken in grades 9 through 12, fill in oval 9 and leave the remaining ovals blank, regardless of how long you studied the subject in school. For example, you are to fill in oval 9 if your knowledge of Latin comes primarily from any of the following sources: study prior to the ninth grade, courses taken at a college, or special study.

Part II   If your knowledge of Latin does come primarily from courses taken in grades 9 through 12, fill in the oval that indicates the level of the Latin course in which you are currently enrolled. If you are not now enrolled in a Latin course, fill in the oval that indicates the level of the most advanced course in Latin that you have completed.

First year:	first or second half	—fill in oval 1
Second year:	first half	—fill in oval 2
	second half	—fill in oval 3
Third year:	first half	—fill in oval 4
	second half	—fill in oval 5
Fourth year:	first half	—fill in oval 6
	second half	—fill in oval 7
Advanced Placement course or a course at a level higher than fourth year, second half		—fill in oval 8

When the supervisor gives the signal, turn the page and begin the Latin test. There are 100 numbered ovals on the answer sheet and 70 questions in the Latin test. Therefore, use only ovals 1 to 70 for recording your answers.

LATIN TEST

PLEASE NOTE THAT YOUR ANSWER SHEET HAS FIVE ANSWER POSITIONS MARKED A, B, C, D, E, WHILE THE QUESTIONS THROUGHOUT THIS TEST CONTAIN ONLY FOUR CHOICES. BE SURE <u>NOT</u> TO MAKE ANY MARKS IN COLUMN E.

<u>Note:</u> In some questions in this test, variations of Latin terms will appear in parentheses.

Part A

<u>Directions:</u> In each statement below, you are asked to give a specific form of the underlined word. Select the correct form from the choices given. Then fill in the corresponding oval on the answer sheet.

---

1. The accusative plural of <u>haec</u> is

    (A) <u>hae</u>

    (B) <u>hīs</u>

    (C) <u>hās</u>

    (D) <u>hārum</u>

2. The ablative singular of <u>fēlīx</u> is

    (A) <u>fēlīcem</u>

    (B) <u>fēlīcī</u>

    (C) <u>fēlīcibus</u>

    (D) <u>fēlīcis</u>

3. The superlative of <u>pulchrē</u> is

    (A) <u>pulchrius</u>

    (B) <u>pulcherrimī</u>

    (C) <u>pulcherrimē</u>

    (D) <u>pulcher</u>

4. The imperfect passive subjunctive of <u>ferō</u> is

    (A) <u>ferēbar</u>

    (B) <u>feror</u>

    (C) <u>ferrer</u>

    (D) <u>ferar</u>

5. The vocative singular of <u>fīlius</u> is

    (A) <u>fīlī</u>

    (B) <u>fīliī</u>

    (C) <u>fīlius</u>

    (D) <u>fīliō</u>

6. The nominative plural of <u>vīs</u> is

    (A) <u>vīrēs</u>

    (B) <u>vī</u>

    (C) <u>vīs</u>

    (D) <u>vīrī</u>

7. The future perfect of <u>audīris</u> is

    (A) <u>audiēris</u>

    (B) <u>audītūrus es</u>

    (C) <u>audiendus es</u>

    (D) <u>audītus eris</u>

8. The comparative of <u>breviter</u> is

    (A) <u>brevissimē</u>

    (B) <u>brevior</u>

    (C) <u>brevius</u>

    (D) <u>brevis</u>

GO ON TO THE NEXT PAGE

3PAC2

Part B

Directions: Each of the following English sentences contains a word that is underlined. From among the choices, select the Latin word to which the underlined word is related by derivation. Then fill in the corresponding oval on the answer sheet.

9. The statue has been placed on a new <u>pedestal</u>.

    (A) <u>pendō</u>

    (B) <u>pēs</u>

    (C) <u>pandō</u>

    (D) <u>podium</u>

10. She lives in another <u>section</u> of town.

    (A) <u>sextus</u>

    (B) <u>sequor</u>

    (C) <u>sēcūrus</u>

    (D) <u>secō</u>

11. Only a few passengers <u>survived</u> the plane crash.

    (A) <u>vītō</u>

    (B) <u>vīvō</u>

    (C) <u>videō</u>

    (D) <u>vocō</u>

12. The speaker's concluding statement was <u>cogent</u>.

    (A) <u>cognoscō</u>

    (B) <u>cōgitō</u>

    (C) <u>cōgō</u>

    (D) <u>cognōmen</u>

GO ON TO THE NEXT PAGE

627

Part C

Directions: In each of the sentences below, part or all of the sentence is underlined. From among the choices, select the best translation for the underlined word or words. Then fill in the corresponding oval on the answer sheet.

13. Agricolae quam celerrimē labōrant.

    (A) They work as quickly as the farmers.
    (B) How quickly they work for the farmers.
    (C) The farmers work as quickly as possible.
    (D) The work of the farmer is swift.

14. Viātōrēs mediā nocte vēnērunt.

    (A) after midnight
    (B) in the middle of the night
    (C) for half the night
    (D) most of the night

15. Claudia Rōmam rediit.

    (A) in Rome
    (B) to Rome
    (C) from Rome
    (D) at Rome

16. Hostibus victīs, mīlitēs sē ad castra retulerant.

    (A) After the enemy had been defeated
    (B) To conquer the enemy
    (C) Since the enemy had won
    (D) Although they would defeat the enemy

17. Pāreāmus lēgibus.

    (A) We obey
    (B) We will obey
    (C) Let us obey
    (D) We must obey

18. Putāvimus puerōs dōna ad puellās mīsisse.

    (A) Gifts were thought to have been sent by the boys to the girls.
    (B) The girls thought that the boys would send gifts.
    (C) We thought the boys should send gifts to the girls.
    (D) We thought that the boys had sent gifts to the girls.

19. Omnia mūtantur.

    (A) They change all things.
    (B) They are changed by all things.
    (C) All things are changed.
    (D) Let all things be changed.

20. Nisi māximō studiō labōrēs, haec facere nōn possīs.

    (A) this woman
    (B) these women
    (C) these things
    (D) to this

21. Sī Cicerō Rōmae remansisset, facta Brūtī laudāvisset.

    (A) he would praise
    (B) he praised
    (C) he had praised
    (D) he would have praised

22. Eī persuāsimus ut ad castra redīret.

    (A) Him
    (B) We
    (C) They
    (D) Them

23. Dīxistī tē oppidum occupātūrum esse.

    (A) I said that you took the town.
    (B) I said that the town would be taken by you.
    (C) You said that you would take the town.
    (D) You said the town would be taken.

24. Negāvit omnēs mīlitēs interfectōs esse.

    (A) would be killed
    (B) had to be killed
    (C) were being killed
    (D) had been killed

25. Fugientēs vulnerātī sunt.

    (A) Those who had run away
    (B) Those who were ready to run away
    (C) Those who were running away
    (D) Those who would have run away

26. Timet ut Caesar veniat.

    (A) He is afraid that Caesar is not coming.
    (B) He is afraid that Caesar is coming.
    (C) Caesar is afraid to come.
    (D) Caesar is not afraid to come.

GO ON TO THE NEXT PAGE

LATIN TEST—*Continued*

Part D

Directions: Each of the sentences below contains a blank space indicating that a word or phrase has been omitted. For each blank, four completions are provided. Choose the word or phrase that best completes the sentence and fill in the corresponding oval on the answer sheet.

27. Amīcī, mēcum . . . !

    (A) veniō
    (B) venīre
    (C) vēnī
    (D) venīte

28. Trēs fīliae . . . sunt.

    (A) eum
    (B) eī
    (C) eās
    (D) eā

29. Rēx crēdit līberōs ab hostibus . . .

    (A) cēpērunt
    (B) captōs esse
    (C) captī sunt
    (D) cēpisse

30. Claudia scrībit . . . causā.

    (A) docet
    (B) docēre
    (C) docendī
    (D) docentia

31. Rogat cūr sacrificium . . .

    (A) perficīs
    (B) perficiās
    (C) perficerēs
    (D) perficere

32. . . . fruēbāris?

    (A) Quō
    (B) Cui
    (C) Quid
    (D) Quae

33. Amīcī . . . in urbe vīdī fēlīcēs erant.

    (A) quis
    (B) quī
    (C) cui
    (D) quōs

GO ON TO THE NEXT PAGE

LATIN TEST—*Continued*

Directions: In each of the sentences below, part or all of the sentence is underlined. Select from the choices the expression that, when substituted for the underlined portion of the sentence, changes the meaning of the sentence LEAST. Then fill in the corresponding oval on the answer sheet.

34. Cum Cicerō consul erat, Pompēius (Pompējus) pīrātās vīcit.

    (A) Quod Cicerō consul est

    (B) Sī Cicerō consul sit

    (C) Cicerō consul

    (D) Cicerōne consule

35. Imperātor decem mīlitēs mittet quī urbem capiant.

    (A) ad urbem capiendam

    (B) urbe captā

    (C) ad urbem captam

    (D) urbem capī

36. Caesar mīlitēs ut oppugnārent rogāvit.

    (A) Caesar ab mīlitibus ut oppugnārent petīvit.

    (B) Caesar mīlitēs oppugnantēs rogāvit.

    (C) Mīlitēs Caesarem oppugnāre iussērunt (jussērunt).

    (D) Caesar mīlitēs oppugnāre nōluit.

37. Illud aedificium multōs annōs permanēbit.

    (A) Hōc

    (B) Id

    (C) Haec

    (D) Idem

38. Hae litterae mihi scrībendae sunt.

    (A) Hae litterae mihi scrīptae sunt.

    (B) Hās litterās scrībere dēbeō.

    (C) Hās litterās ego scrībam.

    (D) Hae sunt meae litterae scrīptae.

GO ON TO THE NEXT PAGE →

Part F

Directions: Read the following texts carefully for comprehension. Each is followed by a number of questions or incomplete statements. Select the answer or completion that is best according to the text and fill in the corresponding oval on the answer sheet.

A politician for the people

Gaius (Gajus) Gracchus dābat cīvitātem omnibus Italicīs, extendēbat eam paene usque Alpīs, dīvidēbat agrōs, vetābat quemquam cīvem plūs quingentīs iūgeribus (jūgeribus)[1] habēre. Nova etiam constituēbat
Line
(5) portōria[2], novīs colōniīs replēbat prōvinciās, iūdicia (jūdicia) ā senātū transferēbat ad equitēs, et frūmentum plebī darī instituerat. Nihil immōtum, nihil tranquillum, nihil quiētum, nihil dēnique in eōdem statū relinquēbat.

[1]iugera, iugerum (jugera, jugerum), n.pl.: acres
[2]portōrium, portōriī, n.: customs, duty

39. The case of Italicīs (line 2) is

    (A) nominative
    (B) genitive
    (C) ablative
    (D) dative

40. In line 2, the word eam refers to

    (A) Gracchus (line 1)

    (B) cīvitātem (line 1)

    (C) paene (line 2)

    (D) cīvem (line 3)

41. In line 3, quemquam is translated

    (A) whomever
    (B) although
    (C) however
    (D) any

42. From the first sentence (lines 1-4) we learn that Gracchus

    (A) forbade citizens from owning any land beyond the Alps
    (B) extended the borders of Italy beyond the Alps
    (C) forced all the citizens to live on farms
    (D) limited the amount of land citizens could own

43. Nova (line 4) modifies

    (A) portōria (line 5)

    (B) prōvinciās (line 5)

    (C) iūdicia (jūdicia) (lines 5-6)

    (D) senātū (line 6)

44. In line 5, the phrase novīs colōniīs is translated

    (A) with new colonies
    (B) in new colonies
    (C) after new colonies
    (D) beyond new colonies

45. The case and number of iūdicia (jūdicia) (lines 5-6) are

    (A) ablative singular
    (B) nominative singular
    (C) accusative plural
    (D) nominative plural

GO ON TO THE NEXT PAGE →

46. The words <u>ā senātū</u> (line 6) are translated

    (A) with the senate
    (B) from the senate
    (C) by the senate
    (D) at the senate

47. In lines 6-7, the phrase <u>frūmentum . . . instituerat</u> tells us that

    (A) Gracchus established a grain supply for the plebs to give away
    (B) the plebs had decided that grain should be given away
    (C) a grain supply was established for the plebs
    (D) Gracchus and the plebs created a steady supply of grain

48. According to the second sentence (lines 4-7), Gracchus wanted the law courts to be administered by the

    (A) provinces
    (B) senate
    (C) equites
    (D) plebs

49. The last sentence (lines 7-8), implies that Gracchus was

    (A) very energetic
    (B) honored with a statue
    (C) nearing retirement
    (D) extremely talkative

50. From this passage, we learn that Gracchus made changes in all of the following EXCEPT

    (A) landownership
    (B) colonization
    (C) law courts
    (D) military service

GO ON TO THE NEXT PAGE ➡

An explanation of thunder

Principiō tonitrū[1] quatiuntur[2] caerula[3] caelī.
Nec fit enim sonitus caelī dē parte serēnā,
vērum ubicumque[4] magis densō sunt agmine nūbēs[5],
tam magis hinc magnō fremitus[6] fit murmure saepe.

[1]tonitrus, tonitrūs, m.: thunder
[2]quatiō, quatere: shake
[3]caerula, caerulōrum, n. pl.: blue depths
[4]ubicumque: wherever
[5]nūbēs, nūbis, f.: cloud
[6]fremitus, fremitūs, m.: rumbling

51. Line 1 is translated

  (A) At first the blue depths of the sky are shaken
      by thunder
  (B) At first the blue heavens are shaken to their
      thundering depths
  (C) At first let the blue depths of the sky be
      shaken by thunder
  (D) At first the heavenly thunder shook the blue
      depths

52. The metrical pattern of the first four feet of
    line 1 is

  (A) $-\cup\cup\mid-\cup\cup\mid--\mid--$

  (B) $-\cup\cup\mid-\cup\cup\mid-\cup\cup\mid--$

  (C) $--\mid--\mid-\cup\cup\mid-\cup\cup$

  (D) $--\mid-\cup\cup\mid--\mid-\cup\cup$

53. Line 2 tells us that

  (A) no part of the sky ever makes a calm sound
  (B) sounds are made in many parts of the calm sky
  (C) sounds are made when part of the sky is calm
  (D) a sound is not made in a calm part of the sky

54. In line 4, hinc means

  (A) from here
  (B) this
  (C) however
  (D) to it

55. The word magnō (line 4) modifies

  (A) agmine (line 3)

  (B) fremitus (line 4)

  (C) murmure (line 4)

  (D) saepe (line 4)

56. In line 4, the tense and mood of fit are

  (A) present subjunctive
  (B) perfect indicative
  (C) present indicative
  (D) future indicative

GO ON TO THE NEXT PAGE

A superstitious emperor

Tonitrua[1] et fulmina tam valdē[2] timēbat ut ad
omnem māiōris (mājōris) tempestātis suspīciōnem
in tūtum locum sē reciperet. Somnia neque sua
neque aliēna dē sē neglegēbat; nam dīcunt eum
Line ōlim ante proelium grave, cum constituisset nōn
(5) ēgredī tabernāculō[3] propter morbum, tamen
ēgressum esse amīcī somniō monitum. Auspicia
quaedam ut certissima observābat; sī māne[4] suum
calceum[5] sinistrum prō dextrō forte indueret[6], ut
malum iūdicābat (jūdicābat).

[1]tonitrua, tonitruōrum, n. pl.: thunder
[2]valdē: greatly
[3]tabernāculum, tabernāculī, n.: tent
[4]māne: in the morning
[5]calceus, calceī, m.: shoe
[6]induō, induere: put on

57. The case and number of <u>fulmina</u> (line 1) are

 (A) nominative singular
 (B) accusative singular
 (C) nominative plural
 (D) accusative plural

58. The sentence <u>Tonitrua . . . reciperet</u> (lines 1-3) tells
    us that, at the approach of a storm, the emperor

 (A) watched the thunder and lightning for omens
 (B) retreated into a safe place
 (C) became suspicious of all around him
 (D) immediately hid himself under his bed

59. In lines 3-4 (<u>Somnia . . . neglegēbat</u>), we learn that
    the emperor

 (A) was not worried by other people's dreams
 (B) neglected others on account of his dreams
 (C) despised those who ignored their dreams
 (D) was interested in all dreams about himself

60. In line 5, <u>cum</u> is translated

 (A) with
 (B) although
 (C) because
 (D) whenever

61. The word <u>ēgredī</u> (line 6) is translated

 (A) to leave
 (B) they left
 (C) having been left
 (D) to be left

62. The word <u>suum</u> (line 8) is translated

 (A) his
 (B) their
 (C) its
 (D) your

63. The passage tells us that the emperor

 (A) lost a battle because of superstition
 (B) asked a friend to take the auspices
 (C) thought it was a bad omen to put on the wrong
     shoe
 (D) believed that thunder caused illness

GO ON TO THE NEXT PAGE

The care of flocks in hot weather

At cum longa diēs sitientēs[1] afferet aestus[2],
nunc ad silvās mitte gregēs, nunc longius herbās
quaere; sed ante diem[3] pecus exeat: ūmida[4] dulcēs
efficit aura cibōs, quotiens fugientibus ventīs
frīgida nocturnō tanguntur pascua[5] rōre[6].

[1]sitiens, sitientis: thirsty
[2]aestus, aestūs, f.: hot spell
[3]diēs, diēī, m.: here means daybreak
[4]ūmidus, ūmida, ūmidum: moist, damp
[5]pascua, pascuōrum, n. pl: pastures
[6]rōs, rōris, m.: dew

64. In line 1, cum is translated

(A) although
(B) with
(C) as
(D) when

65. In line 2, mitte gregēs is translated

(A) by sending the flocks
(B) send the flocks
(C) having sent the flocks
(D) to send the flocks

66. In line 3, pecus exeat is translated

(A) he will leave the herd
(B) he leaves the herd
(C) let the herd depart
(D) the herd will depart

67. The first three feet of line 4 are scanned

(A) $-\cup\cup|--|--$

(B) $--|--|-\cup\cup$

(C) $-\cup\cup|-\cup\cup|-\cup\cup$

(D) $--|-\cup\cup|-\cup\cup$

68. The words fugientibus ventīs (line 4) are translated

(A) while the winds are fleeing
(B) after the winds flee
(C) by fleeing the winds
(D) in order to flee the winds

69. The word frīgida (line 5) modifies

(A) aura (line 4)
(B) nocturnō (line 5)
(C) pascua (line 5)
(D) rōre (line 5)

70. In the clause ūmida . . . rōre (lines 3-5), the poet states that

(A) a moist breeze makes the animals' food sweet
(B) the night air makes the animals cold
(C) animals should eat at night
(D) animals should be exposed to cool winds

S T O P

IF YOU FINISH BEFORE TIME IS CALLED, YOU MAY CHECK YOUR WORK ON THIS TEST ONLY.
DO NOT TURN TO ANY OTHER TEST IN THIS BOOK.

How to Score the SAT Subject Test in Latin

When you take an actual SAT Subject Test in Latin, your answer sheet will be "read" by a scanning machine that will record your responses to each question. Then a computer will compare your answers with the correct answers and produce your raw score. You get one point for each correct answer. For each wrong answer, you lose one-third of a point. Questions you omit (and any for which you mark more than one answer) are not counted. This raw score is converted to a scaled score that is reported to you and to the colleges you specify.

Worksheet 1. Finding Your Raw Test Score

STEP 1: Table A lists the correct answers for all the questions on the SAT Subject Test in Latin that is reproduced in this book. It also serves as a worksheet for you to calculate your raw score.

- Compare your answers with those given in the table.
- Put a check in the column marked "Right" if your answer is correct.
- Put a check in the column marked "Wrong" if your answer is incorrect.
- Leave both columns blank if you omitted the question.

STEP 2: Count the number of right answers.

Enter the total here: _____

STEP 3: Count the number of wrong answers.

Enter the total here: _____

STEP 4: Multiply the number of wrong answers by .333.

Enter the product here: _____

STEP 5: Subtract the result obtained in Step 4 from the total you obtained in Step 2.

Enter the result here: _____

STEP 6: Round the number obtained in Step 5 to the nearest whole number.

Enter the result here: _____

The number you obtained in Step 6 is your raw score.

TABLE A
Answers to the SAT Subject Test in Latin, Form 3PAC2, and Percentage of Students Answering Each Question Correctly

Question Number	Correct Answer	Right	Wrong	Percentage of Students Answering the Question Correctly*	Question Number	Correct Answer	Right	Wrong	Percentage of Students Answering the Question Correctly*
1	C			82	36	A			38
2	B			82	37	B			34
3	C			87	38	B			28
4	C			46	39	D			58
5	A			50	40	B			73
6	A			47	41	D			37
7	D			47	42	D			32
8	C			37	43	A			89
9	B			67	44	A			68
10	D			59	45	C			49
11	B			83	46	B			65
12	C			46	47	C			78
13	C			84	48	C			69
14	B			94	49	A			67
15	B			81	50	D			94
16	A			73	51	A			88
17	C			68	52	B			58
18	D			77	53	D			69
19	C			75	54	A			47
20	C			72	55	C			57
21	D			75	56	C			47
22	A			70	57	D			36
23	C			54	58	B			56
24	D			54	59	D			42
25	C			73	60	B			47
26	A			33	61	A			46
27	D			75	62	A			77
28	B			44	63	C			73
29	B			48	64	D			72
30	C			44	65	B			60
31	B			34	66	C			57
32	A			28	67	C			47
33	D			35	68	A			37
34	D			51	69	C			57
35	A			46	70	A			66

*These percentages are based on an analysis of the answer sheets for a random sample of 688 students who took this form of the test in December 1993 and whose mean score was 573. They may be used as an indication of the relative difficulty of a particular question. Each percentage may also be used to predict the likelihood that a typical SAT Subject Test in Latin candidate will answer correctly that question on this edition of this test.

Finding Your Scaled Score

When you take SAT Subject Tests, the scores sent to the colleges you specify are reported on the College Board scale, which ranges from 200 to 800. You can convert your practice test score to a scaled score by using Table B. To find your scaled score, locate your raw score in the left-hand column of Table B; the corresponding score in the right-hand column is your scaled score. For example, a raw score of 47 on this particular edition of the SAT Subject Test in Latin corresponds to a scaled score of 670.

Raw scores are converted to scaled scores to ensure that a score earned on any one edition of a particular Subject Test is comparable to the same scaled score earned on any other edition of the same Subject Test. Because some editions of tests may be slightly easier or more difficult than others, scaled scores are adjusted so that they indicate the same level of performance regardless of the edition of the test taken and the ability of the group that takes it. Thus, for example, a score of 400 on one edition of a test taken at a particular administration indicates the same level of achievement as a score of 400 on a different edition of the test taken at a different administration.

When you take the SAT Subject Tests during a national administration, your scores are likely to differ somewhat from the scores you obtain on the tests in this book. People perform at different levels at different times for reasons unrelated to the tests themselves. The precision of any test is also limited because it represents only a sample of all the possible questions that could be asked.

TABLE B
Scaled Score Conversion Table
Latin Subject Test (Form 3PAC2)

Raw Score	Scaled Score	Raw Score	Scaled Score	Raw Score	Scaled Score
70	800	38	600	6	410
69	800	37	590	5	410
68	800	36	580	4	400
67	800	35	580	3	400
66	800	34	570	2	390
65	800	33	560	1	390
64	800	32	550	0	380
63	800	31	550	−1	380
62	790	30	540	−2	380
61	780	29	530	−3	370
60	770	28	530	−4	370
59	760	27	520	−5	360
58	750	26	520	−6	360
57	740	25	510	−7	350
56	740	24	500	−8	350
55	730	23	500	−9	340
54	720	22	490	−10	340
53	710	21	490	−11	330
52	710	20	480	−12	330
51	700	19	480	−13	320
50	690	18	470	−14	320
49	680	17	460	−15	310
48	670	16	460	−16	310
47	670	15	460	−17	300
46	660	14	450	−18	300
45	650	13	450	−19	300
44	640	12	440	−20	290
43	640	11	440	−21	290
42	630	10	430	−22	280
41	620	9	430	−23	270
40	610	8	420		
39	600	7	420		

Reviewing Your Performance on the Latin Subject Test

After you score your test, analyze your performance—consider the following questions:

Did you run out of time before reaching the end of the test?

If so, you may need to pace yourself better. For example, maybe you spent too much time on one or two hard questions. A better approach might be to skip the ones you can't answer right away and try answering all the questions that remain on the test. Then if there's time, go back to the questions you skipped.

Did you take a long time reading the directions?

You will save time when you take the test by learning the directions to the Latin Subject Test ahead of time. Each minute you spend reading directions during the test is a minute that you could use to answer questions.

How did you handle questions you were unsure of?

If you were able to eliminate one or more of the answer choices as wrong and guess from the remaining ones, your approach probably worked to your advantage. On the other hand, making haphazard guesses or omitting questions without trying to eliminate choices could cost you valuable points.

How difficult were the questions for you compared with other students who took the test?

Table A shows you how difficult the multiple-choice questions were for the group of students who took this test during its national administration. The right-hand column gives the percentage of students that answered each question correctly.

A question answered correctly by almost everyone in the group is obviously an easy question. For example, 94 percent of the students answered question 14 correctly. But only 28 percent answered question 32 correctly.

Keep in mind that these percentages are based on just one group of students. They would probably be different if another group of students took the test.

If you missed several easy questions, go back and try to find out why: Did the questions cover material you haven't reviewed yet? Did you misunderstand the directions?

CHAPTER 15
Modern Hebrew

Purpose

The Modern Hebrew Subject Test measures competence in Modern Hebrew and allows for variation in language preparation.

Format

This one-hour test consists of 85 multiple-choice questions. The test evaluates your mastery of vocabulary, structure, and reading comprehension through questions that require a wide-ranging knowledge of the language.

The test evaluates reading ability in three areas:

Vocabulary: These types of questions test knowledge of words representing different parts of speech and some basic idioms within culturally authentic contexts.

Structure: This kind of question tests grammar, including parts of speech as well as your ability to recognize appropriate language patterns.

Reading Comprehension: These questions test your understanding of passages of varying levels of difficulty. These passages, most of which are vocalized, are generally adapted from literary sources and newspaper or magazine articles. Authentic material such as advertisements have been added to the test. (A sample advertisement appears in the Sample Questions below.) While some passages have biblical references, no material in the test is written in biblical Hebrew.

Skills Measured	Approximate Percentage of Test
Vocabulary in Context	30
Structure in Context (grammar)	30
Reading Comprehension	40

Recommended Preparation

The Modern Hebrew Test allows for variation in language preparation. It is independent of particular textbooks or methods of instruction. You should:

- Take two to four years of Hebrew language study in high school or the equivalent.
- Obtain gradual development of competence in Hebrew over a period of years.
- Familiarize yourself with directions in advance. The directions in this book are identical to those that appear on the test.

Score

The total score is reported on the 200-to-800 scale.

Sample Questions

The three types of multiple-choice questions used in the test are:

- sentence completion questions
- paragraph completion questions
- questions based on a series of passages that test your understanding of those passages

Please note that your answer sheet has five answer positions marked A, B, C, D, E, while the questions throughout this test contain only four choices. Be sure NOT to make any marks in column E.

Sentence Completion

This type of question tests vocabulary mastery and requires the student to know the meaning of words and idiomatic expressions in context. Other sentence completion questions test mastery of structure and require students to identify usage that is structurally correct.

Directions: This part consists of a number of incomplete statements, each having four suggested completions. Select the most appropriate completion and fill in the corresponding oval on the answer sheet.

1. הוּא בָּא מֵאֵירוֹפָּה וְקָשֶׁה לוֹ _____

   לְחֹם בְּיִשְׂרָאֵל.

   (A) לְהִתְרַגֵּל

   (B) לְהִתְבַּיֵּשׁ

   (C) לְהִשְׁתַּזֵּף

   (D) לְהִתְיַבֵּשׁ

2. הַמִּשְׁפָּחָה שֶׁלָּנוּ _____ בִּכְפָר קָטָן.

   (A) גָּרִים

   (B) גָּרוֹת

   (C) גָּרָה

   (D) לָגוּר

Question 1 tests how well you have mastered vocabulary. Choice (A) is correct. All four choices are verbs, but (A) is the only one which expresses idiomatically that it is difficult for the person to *get used* to the hot weather in Israel. The other options are inappropriate verbs in this particular context.

Question 2 tests command of structure. To answer correctly you need to recognize correct noun-verb agreement. The noun *family* is feminine singular and (C) is the feminine singular verb. The other options are verbs of the same root but do not agree with the noun.

Paragraph Completion

In paragraph completion questions, you are presented with a paragraph(s) from which words have been omitted. You must select the option that is most appropriate to the context. The main difference between sentence completion and paragraph completion is that the paragraph enables you to answer correctly based on the content of the entire passage rather than a single sentence.

Directions: In each of the following paragraphs there are numbered blanks indicating that words or phrases have been omitted. For each numbered blank, four completions are provided; only one is correct. First read through the entire passage. Then for each numbered blank, choose the completion that is most appropriate and fill in the corresponding oval on the answer sheet.

בְּלֵיל הַסֵּדֶר יָשַׁב סַבָּא בְּרֹאשׁ הַשֻּׁלְחָן

(3) _____ כָּל בְּנֵי הַמִּשְׁפָּחָה.

אֲנַחְנוּ, הַנְּכָדִים הַצְּעִירִים, יָשַׁבְנוּ קָרוֹב

(4) _____, וְכָל אֶחָד מֵאִתָּנוּ

(5) _____ בְּיָדוֹ הַגָּדָה מְצֻיֶּרֶת.

כְּשֶׁסַּבָּא (6) _____ שֶׁכָּל אֶחָד

מֵהַיְלָדִים יִקְרָא שׁוּרוֹת (7) _____

מִן הַהַגָּדָה, (8) _____ לִפְתֹּחַ אֶת

הַסֵּפֶר שֶׁלִּי, וְקָרָאתִי בּוֹ בְּשֶׁקֶט לְעַצְמִי,

כְּדֵי שֶׁלֹּא (9) _____ כְּשֶׁיַּגִּיעַ תּוֹרִי.

3. (A) כְּשֶׁסְּבִיבוֹ
(B) כְּשֶׁעָלָיו
(C) כְּשֶׁבְּתוֹכוֹ
(D) כְּשֶׁבִּשְׁבִילוֹ

4. (A) מִמֶּנּוּ
(B) אֵלָיו
(C) שֶׁלּוֹ
(D) אוֹתוֹ

.5 (A) הִשְׁמִיעַ

(B) הִבִּיט

(C) הִקְשִׁיב

(D) הֶחֱזִיק

.6 (A) כִּבֵּד

(B) דִּבֵּר

(C) בִּקֵּשׁ

(D) סִפֵּר

.7 (A) מְעַט

(B) אַחְדוֹת

(C) קְצָת

(D) עֲשָׂרוֹת

.8 (A) הִפְסַקְתִּי

(B) שָׁכַחְתִּי

(C) הִשְׁאַרְתִּי

(D) מִהַרְתִּי

.9 (A) אָטְעֶה

(B) טוֹעֶה

(C) יִטְעֶה

(D) טָעִיתִי

The answer to question 3 is (A). You must find the correct preposition among the four prepositions that appear with the masculine singular. Choice (A) meaning *around him* is the only choice that fits in this context.

Question 4 tests another preposition, and the correct answer is (B). The children sat close to *him*.

The answer to question 5 is (D). This is a vocabulary question, and you are to choose the answer that means *held*.

The correct choice in question 6 is (C), which is the only verb that fits idiomatically in the sentence, "Grandfather *asked*."

In question 7 you are to choose the correct adjective to describe the noun *lines*, which is feminine plural, and (B) meaning *several or a few* is the right choice.

Question 8 tests vocabulary. You are to find the appropriate verb. The correct answer is (D). The verb *I hurried* is the only option that can be used correctly in this context.

In question 9 you are to choose the right tense of the verb *to make a mistake, to err*. The correct answer is (A), which is future tense for first person singular.

Reading Comprehension

This part examines your ability to read passages representative of various styles and levels of difficulty. Each SAT Subject Test in Modern Hebrew has several prose passages followed by questions that test understanding. Some are short newspaper items and/or ads; some are textual passages, one of which is unvocalized. The passages are generally adapted from literary sources. Most of the questions focus on main and supporting ideas. These questions test whether you comprehend the main idea and some facts and details contained in the text. The ad and the passage that follow are samples of the material that appears in the test.

Directions: Read the following passages carefully for comprehension. Each is followed by a number of questions or incomplete statements. Select the completion or answer that is best according to the passage and fill in the corresponding oval on the answer sheet.

דרושים מורים למתמטיקה ולמדע לכיתות ה-ו,

לחצי משרה או למשרה מלאה.

דרישות: תואר ראשון בתחום מתאים,

ותעודת הוראה.

בית ספר תומר, רח׳ בן יהודה.

טלפון: 556677.

10. הַפִּרְסוֹמֶת מוֹדִיעָה עַל

(A) מוֹרִים שֶׁמְּחַפְּשִׂים עֲבוֹדָה

(B) מְקוֹמוֹת עֲבוֹדָה לְמוֹרִים

(C) סְפָרֵי לִמוּד לְמָתֶמָטִיקָה וּמַדָּע

(D) תְּעוּדוֹת לְמוֹרִים

11. לְפִי הַפִּרְסוֹמֶת דְּרוּשִׁים

(A) מוֹרִים בְּאַרְצוֹת-הַבְּרִית

(B) כִּתּוֹת גְּדוֹלוֹת

(C) סְפָרֵי לִמוּד

(D) בַּעֲלֵי תּוֹאַר רִאשׁוֹן

12. 556677 הוּא מִסְפָּר הַטֶּלֶפוֹן שֶׁל

(A) הַמּוֹרָה

(B) בֵּית סָפָר תּוֹמֶר

(C) בֶּן יְהוּדָה

(D) הַכִּתָּה

Questions 10–12 ask details about the advertisement.

To answer Question 10, you need to know what is advertised in the ad. The correct answer is (B) because the school is looking for teachers.

Question 11 asks what are the requirements. Teachers holding a B.A. in Hebrew, their first academic degree, is correctly expressed in (D).

Question 12 checks if the reader understood whose phone number is given. The correct answer is (B) the Tomer School.

לְאַחֲרוֹנָה, הִתְחִילָה הַטֶּלֶוִיזְיָה הַיִשְׂרְאֵלִית
לְשַׁדֵּר כָּל יוֹם חֲדָשׁוֹת בַּשָּׂפָה הָאַנְגְּלִית. הַתָּכְנִית
מְשֻׁדֶּרֶת בְּשָׁעָה שְׁמוֹנָה בָּעֶרֶב וְהִיא נִמְשֶׁכֶת
חֲמֵשׁ-עֶשְׂרֵה דַּקּוֹת. תָּכְנִית הַחֲדָשׁוֹת בָּאַנְגְּלִית
זָכְתָה לְהַצְלָחָה גְדוֹלָה מִשּׁוּם שֶׁהִיא מְשַׁדֶּרֶת
אֶת הַחֲדָשׁוֹת בְּסִגְנוֹן אָמֶרִיקֶנִי וְיֵשׁ בָּהּ לְפָחוֹת
עֶשְׂרָה נוֹשְׂאִים שׁוֹנִים.
קַרְיָנֵי-הַחֲדָשׁוֹת הֵם אֲנָשִׁים נְעִימִים עִם
חִיּוּךְ עַל הַפָּנִים. בִּמְיֻחָד מָצְאָה-חֵן בְּעֵינַי
הַיִשְׂרְאֵלִים הַקַּרְיָנִית סוּזָאן, יְלִידַת בּוֹסְטוֹן,
בִּגְלַל סִגְנוֹנָהּ הַמְיֻחָד. סוּזָאן שֶׁלָּמְדָה עִבְרִית
בְּאַרְצוֹת-הַבְּרִית, בָּאָה לְיִשְׂרָאֵל לִשְׁנַת לִמּוּדִים
וְהֶחְלִיטָה לְהִשָּׁאֵר. לְאַחַר שֶׁעָלְתָה לָאָרֶץ
הִיא לָמְדָה תִּקְשֹׁרֶת בָּאוּנִיבֶרְסִיטָה הָעִבְרִית
בִּירוּשָׁלַיִם.

.13 אֵיךְ קִבְּלוּ הַיִשְׂרְאֵלִים אֶת הַתָּכְנִית?

(A) הֵם הִתְנַגְּדוּ לִשְׂפַת-הַחֲדָשׁוֹת

(B) הֵם הִתְפַּלְּאוּ עַל שְׁעַת-הַחֲדָשׁוֹת

(C) הֵם בִּטְּלוּ אֶת הַתָּכְנִית

(D) הֵם קִבְּלוּ אוֹתָהּ בְּהִתְלַהֲבוּת

.14 הַתָּכְנִית הִצְלִיחָה כִּי

(A) הָיְתָה עֲשִׁירָה וּמְעַנְיֶנֶת

(B) שֻׁדְּרָה פַּעֲמַיִם בְּיוֹם

(C) נֶעֶרְכָה עַל-יְדֵי הָאוּנִיבֶרְסִיטָה

(D) הַהִתְקַשְּׁרוּת הָיְתָה טוֹבָה

.15 מַדּוּעַ הִצְלִיחָה סוּזַאן כְּקַרְיָנִית?

(A) כִּי הִיא לָמְדָה עִבְרִית בְּאַרְצוֹת-הַבְּרִית

(B) כִּי הִיא הֶחֱלִיטָה לַעֲלוֹת לְיִשְׂרָאֵל

(C) כִּי הִיא נוֹלְדָה בְּבּוֹסְטוֹן

(D) כִּי הִגִּישָׁה יְדִיעוֹת בְּאֹפֶן מְעַנְיֵן

Questions 13–15 refer to the passage on the Israeli television's recently initiated news broadcast.

Question 13 asks how the Israelis accepted the new program. The passage describes the new program as having *gained much success*, thus option (D) *they received it with enthusiasm* is the correct answer. The remaining three options do not answer the question correctly.

Question 14 asks the reason for its success, and the correct answer is (A) *It was rich and interesting*. The passage describes the reason as: *It deals with at least ten different topics*. The other three options are not the reasons for the program's success.

Question 15 asks the reason for the success of the broadcast's announcer. The correct answer is (D) *She delivered the news in an interesting manner*. The passage talks about *her special style*. The other options give additional details about her but are not the reason for her success.

Modern Hebrew Test

The test that follows is an actual, recently administered SAT Subject Test in Modern Hebrew. To get an idea of what a real administration is like, take the test under conditions as close as possible to those of a national administration:

- Set aside an hour when you can take the test uninterrupted. Make sure you complete the test in one sitting.

- Sit at a desk or table with no other books or papers. Dictionaries, other books, or notes are not allowed in the test room.

- Time yourself by placing a clock or kitchen timer in front of you.

- Tear out an answer sheet from the back of this book and fill it in just as you would on the day of the test. One answer sheet can be used for up to three Subject Tests.

- Read the instructions that precede the practice test. During the actual administration you will be asked to read them before answering test questions.

- After you finish the practice test, read the sections "How to Score the SAT Subject Test in Modern Hebrew" and "Reviewing Your Performance on the Modern Hebrew Subject Test."

- Actual test and answer sheets will indicate circles, not ovals.

Form 3PAC

MODERN HEBREW TEST

The top portion of the section of the answer sheet that you will use in taking the Modern Hebrew test must be filled in exactly as shown in the illustration below. Note carefully that you have to do all of the following on your answer sheet.

1. Print MODERN HEBREW on the line under the words "Subject Test (print)."

2. In the shaded box labeled "Test Code" fill in four ovals:

    —Fill in oval 1 in the row labeled V.

    —Fill in oval 3 in the row labeled W.

    —Fill in oval 4 in the row labeled X.

    —Fill in oval C in the row labeled Y.

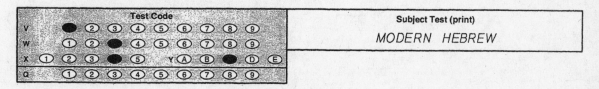

Please answer either Part I or Part II by filling in the specific oval in row Q. <u>The information you provide is for statistical purposes only and will not influence your score on the test.</u>

Part I   If your knowledge of Hebrew comes <u>primarily</u> from extensive residence in Israel after age 10, courses taken in college, or from living in a home where Hebrew is the principal language spoken, fill in <u>oval 9</u> and skip the remaining questions on this page.

Part II   If your knowledge of Hebrew comes <u>primarily</u> from courses taken in grades 9 through 12, fill in the oval that represents the total number of years you have studied Hebrew. Fill in only <u>one</u> of ovals 1-7. (Leave oval 8 blank).

Less than 2 years	Fill in oval 4.
2 - 2 1/2 years	Fill in oval 5.
3 - 3 1/2 years	Fill in oval 6.
4 years	Fill in oval 7.
If you have studied Hebrew in a Jewish/Hebrew Day School up to the 8th grade only,	Fill in oval 1.
If you have studied Hebrew in a Jewish/Hebrew Day School <u>and</u> less than 2 years in high school,	Fill in oval 2.
If you have studied Hebrew in a Jewish/Hebrew Day School <u>and</u> 2 or more years of study beyond 8th grade,	Fill in oval 3.

When the supervisor gives the signal, turn the page and begin the Modern Hebrew test. There are 100 numbered ovals on the answer sheet and 85 questions in the Modern Hebrew test. Therefore, use only ovals 1 to 85 for recording your answers.

MODERN HEBREW TEST

PLEASE NOTE THAT YOUR ANSWER SHEET HAS FIVE ANSWER POSITIONS MARKED A, B, C, D, E, WHILE THE QUESTIONS THROUGHOUT THIS TEST CONTAIN ONLY FOUR CHOICES. BE SURE <u>NOT</u> TO MAKE ANY MARKS IN COLUMN E.

Be sure to note that the questions are numbered on the RIGHT side of each column and begin on the RIGHT side of the page.

Part A

<u>Directions:</u> This part consists of a number of incomplete statements, each having four suggested completions. Select the most appropriate completion and fill in the corresponding oval on the answer sheet.

1. דָּנִי שָׁאַל אֶת הוֹרָיו אִם _____ לוֹ לִנְהֹג בַּמְּכוֹנִית שֶׁלָּהֶם.
   (A) בָּרוּר
   (B) נָכוֹן
   (C) מֻתָּר
   (D) יִתָּכֵן

2. יֵשׁ לִי _____ לֶאֱכֹל גְּלִידָה.
   (A) חֵלֶק
   (B) חֹם
   (C) חֹשֶׁךְ
   (D) חֵשֶׁק

3. דָּוִד _____ מִמֶּנִּי סְלִיחָה אַחֲרֵי שֶׁפָּגַע בִּי.
   (A) שָׁאַל
   (B) נָתַן
   (C) אָמַר
   (D) בִּקֵּשׁ

4. אֲנִי לֹא יָכֹל לָבוֹא הַיּוֹם לַפְּגִישָׁה כִּי אִמִּי רוֹצָה שֶׁאֲנִי _____ הָעֶרֶב.
   (A) לוֹמֵד
   (B) יִלְמַד
   (C) לִלְמֹד
   (D) אֶלְמַד

5. רָחֵל קִוְּתָה שֶׁכָּל חֲבֵרֶיהָ _____ לַמְּסִבָּה, אֲבָל רַק אֶחָד מֵהֶם הִגִּיעַ.
   (A) יָבוֹאוּ
   (B) בָּאִים
   (C) לָבוֹא
   (D) בָּאוּ

GO ON TO THE NEXT PAGE ➡

3PAC

MODERN HEBREW TEST—*Continued*

6. הַמַּדְרִיךְ שָׁלַח אֶת הַתַּיָּרוֹת לַכְּנֶסֶת אַךְ לֹא
הִסְבִּיר _____ אֵיךְ לְהַגִּיעַ לְשָׁם.

   (A) לָהֶן

   (B) אִתָּן

   (C) אוֹתָן

   (D) בִּשְׁבִילָן

7. כַּאֲשֶׁר דָּנִי חָלָה _____ בְּבֵיתוֹ.

   (A) בִּקַּרְתִּי

   (B) שִׁקַּרְתִּי

   (C) שִׁלַּמְתִּי

   (D) טִיַּלְתִּי

8. _____ אַתְּ מְחַכָּה?

   (A) בְּמִי

   (B) מִי

   (C) לְמִי

   (D) אֶת מִי

9. הַסְּטוּדֶנְטִים לֹא הִצְלִיחוּ בַּמִּבְחָן, מִפְּנֵי שֶׁלֹּא
_____ הֵיטֵב.

   (A) הִשְׁתַּמְּשׁוּ

   (B) הִתְבַּלְבְּלוּ

   (C) הִתְכּוֹנְנוּ

   (D) הִתְכַּתְבוּ

10. הַתַּלְמִידִים מְחַכִּים שֶׁהַמּוֹרָה הַחֲדָשָׁה
_____ לָהֶם אֶת תָּכְנִית הַלִּמּוּדִים.

   (A) יַגִּיד

   (B) מַגִּיד

   (C) לְהַגִּיד

   (D) תַּגִּיד

11. הַתַּלְמִידוֹת חִכּוּ _____ הַשִּׁעוּר, אֲבָל
הַמּוֹרָה לֹא הִגִּיעַ.

   (A) הַתְחָלוֹת

   (B) לְהַתְחָלָה

   (C) לְהַתְחָלַת

   (D) הַתְחָלַת

12. הַתַּיָּרִים יָצְאוּ מֵאַרְצוֹת הַבְּרִית וְהִגִּיעוּ לְיִשְׂרָאֵל
תּוֹךְ שְׁתַּיִם-עֶשְׂרֵה שָׁעוֹת, כִּי הֵם בָּאוּ _____.

   (A) בָּאֳנִיָּה

   (B) בְּרַכֶּבֶת

   (C) בְּמָטוֹס

   (D) בִּמְכוֹנִית

GO ON TO THE NEXT PAGE →

13. חִבַּרְתִּי הַטּוֹבָה _____ מְאֹד לִפְנֵי נְסִיעָתָה הָרִאשׁוֹנָה לָאָרֶץ.

   (A) מִתְרַגֶּשֶׁת
   (B) מִתְקַשֶּׁרֶת
   (C) מִתְקַדֶּמֶת
   (D) מִתְנַהֶגֶת

14. הִתְנַהֲגוּתוֹ שֶׁל הָאָדָם תְּלוּיָה _____ שֶׁהוּא קִבֵּל בַּבַּיִת.

   (A) בַּשּׁוּק
   (B) בְּשִׁתּוּף
   (C) בַּחִנּוּךְ
   (D) בַּדִּבּוּר

15. הֵם פּוֹתְחִים אֶת הַסִּפְרִיָּה שִׁשָּׁה יָמִים בְּשָׁבוּעַ, וְרַק בְּשַׁבָּת הִיא _____ .

   (A) סְגוּרָה
   (B) לִסְגֹּר
   (C) סָגְרוּ
   (D) סוֹגֶרֶת

16. אֲנָשִׁים נוֹסְעִים בַּדֶּרֶךְ כְּלָל בִּזְהִירוּת, כִּי הֵם מְפַחֲדִים _____ .

   (A) מִמִּלְחָמוֹת
   (B) מִתְּאוּנוֹת
   (C) מִבְּחִינוֹת
   (D) מִפְּגִישׁוֹת

17. הָרוֹפְאִים עֲדַיִן אֵינָם יוֹדְעִים מַה _____ שֶׁל הַתְּרוּפָה הַחֲדָשָׁה עַל הַלֵּב.

   (A) הַהַגְדָּלָה
   (B) הַהַשְׁפָּעָה
   (C) הַהַצָּעָה
   (D) הַהַחְלָטָה

18. הַשּׁוֹטֵר _____ אֶת הָאִישׁ בִּגְנֵבָה, וְהַשּׁוֹפֶטֶת דָּנָה אוֹתוֹ לְמַאֲסָר.

   (A) הִזְמִין
   (B) הֶאֱשִׁים
   (C) הֶעֱבִיד
   (D) הִשְׁלִים

GO ON TO THE NEXT PAGE

‏19. הַיֶדַע שֶׁלָּה בְּשָׂפוֹת וּבְכַלְכָּלָה _____ לָה בַּעֲבוֹדָתָהּ.
(A) עֶזְרָה
(B) עָזְרוּ
(C) עוֹזְרִים
(D) עָזַר

‏20. הַמֶּמְשָׁלָה פִּרְסְמָה _____ מְיֻחֶדֶת עַל שִׂיחוֹת הַשָּׁלוֹם.
(A) הַגְדָּרָה
(B) הוֹדָעָה
(C) מְצִיאָה
(D) יְשִׁיבָה

‏21. מֹשֶׁה לֹא רָצָה _____ לְשִׁמְעוֹן אֶת הַכֶּסֶף שֶׁהוּא חַיָּב לוֹ.
(A) לְהַחְזִיר
(B) לַחֲזֹר
(C) לְהַשְׁלִים
(D) לִזְכֹּר

‏22. אִילָן לֹא יָשַׁן מַסְפִּיק בַּלַּיְלָה וְלָכֵן הַבִּיט בִּי בְּעֵינַיִם _____ .
(A) עֲיֵפִים
(B) עֲיֵפוֹת
(C) מְעַיֵּף
(D) מְעַיְּפוֹת

‏23. בַּחֹרֶף, כְּשֶׁקַּר בַּחוּץ, _____ לָנוּ לִלְבֹּשׁ בְּגָדִים חַמִּים.
(A) צָרִיךְ
(B) יָכוֹל
(C) כְּדַאי
(D) מֻכְרָח

‏24. הַרְבֵּה אֲנָשִׁים יוֹצְאִים בְּיוֹם שִׁשִּׁי לָעֶרֶךְ _____ לְשַׁבָּת.
(A) מְנוּחָה
(B) בְּנִיָּה
(C) קְנִיּוֹת
(D) שְׁבִיתוֹת

‏25. אִמָּא שֶׁלִּי _____ מָחָר לַבֹּקֶר אֶצְלֵנוּ.
(A) יָבוֹא
(B) תָּבוֹאִי
(C) תָּבוֹא
(D) לָבוֹא

GO ON TO THE NEXT PAGE ➜

26. יְלָדִים, _____ מִיָּד אֶת הַדֶּלֶת!

    (A) סְגֹר

    (B) סִגְרוּ

    (C) סוֹגְרִים

    (D) סָגְרוּ

27. כְּשֶׁחַנָּה הָיְתָה יַלְדָּה קְטַנָּה _____ לָהּ בְּעָיוֹת בַּלִּמּוּדִים.

    (A) הָיִית

    (B) הָיָה

    (C) הָיְתָה

    (D) הָיוּ

28. הִיא עוֹבֶדֶת _____ הֶחָדָשׁ בְּחֵיפָה.

    (A) בְּבֵית-חוֹלִים

    (B) בְּבֵית-הַחוֹלִים

    (C) בְּבָתֵּי-חוֹלִים

    (D) בְּבָתֵּי-הַחוֹלִים

29. אַבָּא אָמַר לְיוֹרָם: "בְּכָל פַּעַם שֶׁאֲנִי _____ לְךָ כֶּסֶף, אַתָּה מְבַזְבֵּז אוֹתוֹ מִיָּד.".

    (A) מַלְוֶה

    (B) לֹוֶה

    (C) מְלַוֶּה

    (D) הַלְוָה

30. רוּת סִפְּרָה לָנוּ עַל _____ הַיָּפִים שֶׁל בְּנָהּ.

    (A) מִכְתָּבֶיהָ

    (B) מִכְתָּבָיו

    (C) מִכְתָּבִים

    (D) מִכְתְּבֵיהֶם

GO ON TO THE NEXT PAGE →

Part B

Directions: In each of the following paragraphs there are numbered blanks indicating that words or phrases have been omitted. For each numbered blank, four completions are provided. First read through the entire paragraph. Then, for each numbered blank, choose the completion that is most appropriate and fill in the corresponding oval on the answer sheet.

בִּשָׁנִים הָרִאשׁוֹנוֹת לְאַחַר קוּם הַמְּדִינָה

(31) ‏_____ לָאָרֶץ עוֹלִים חֲדָשִׁים מֵאֲרָצוֹת

(32) ‏_____ . אַנְשֵׁי הַחִנּוּךְ לֹא יָדְעוּ אֵיךְ

(33) ‏_____ אֶת הַתַּרְבֻּיּוֹת שֶׁל הָעוֹלִים הָאֵלֶּה.

חֵלֶק מֵאַנְשֵׁי הַחִנּוּךְ אָמְרוּ שֶׁצָּרִיךְ לִבְנוֹת תַּרְבּוּת

(34) ‏_____ אֲחִידָה וַחֲדָשָׁה. אֲחֵרִים אָמְרוּ,

שֶׁאָסוּר לְבַטֵּל אֶת הַתַּרְבֻּיּוֹת שֶׁהָעוֹלִים

הַחֲדָשִׁים הֵבִיאוּ, אֶלָּא לְהֵפֶךְ: כָּל (35) ‏_____

תְּטַפַּח אֶת תַּרְבּוּתָהּ, (36) ‏_____ עַל הַמִּנְהָגִים

הַמְּיֻחָדִים לָהּ. כַּיּוֹם (37) ‏_____ לְמַזֵּג אֶת

שְׁתֵּי הַדְּרָכִים: מִזּוּג תַּרְבֻּיּוֹת תּוֹךְ שְׁמִירָה עַל

הַמְּיֻחָד בְּכָל אַחַת (38) ‏_____ .

---

34. (A) יִשְׂרְאֵלִיּוֹת
(B) יִשְׂרְאֵלִיִּים
(C) יִשְׂרְאֵלִית
(D) יִשְׂרְאֵלִי

35. (A) עַם
(B) מְדִינָה
(C) אֶרֶץ
(D) קְבוּצָה

36. (A) וְיִשְׁמֹר
(B) וְלִשְׁמֹר
(C) וְתִשְׁמֹר
(D) וְנִשְׁמֹר

37. (A) נִסִּיתִי
(B) מְנַסִּים
(C) נִסָּה
(D) מְנַסָּה

38. (A) מֵהֶן
(B) מֵאִתְּכֶם
(C) מֵאִתָּנוּ
(D) מֵהֶם

---

31. (A) מַגִּיעִים
(B) יַגִּיעוּ
(C) לְהַגִּיעַ
(D) הִגִּיעוּ

32. (A) שׁוֹנוֹת
(B) רִאשׁוֹנוֹת
(C) אַחֲרוֹנוֹת
(D) קוֹדְמוֹת

33. (A) לְשַׂמֵּחַ
(B) לְאַחֵד
(C) לְטַפֵּל
(D) לְסַפֵּר

GO ON TO THE NEXT PAGE ➤

כְּשֶׁהָיִיתִי בַּת תֵּשַׁע (39) _____ הַגְּדוֹלָה

הָיְתָה בַּת אַרְבַּע-עֶשְׂרֵה, נָסַעְנוּ (40) _____

לְבַקּוּר אֵצֶל הַדּוֹדָה שֶׁלָּנוּ בַּכְּפָר. זוֹ הָיְתָה

(41) _____ הָרִאשׁוֹנָה שֶׁרָאִינוּ מִקָּרוֹב אֵיךְ

חַיִּים אַנְשֵׁי הָאֲדָמָה: הֵם קָמִים (42) _____

בַּבֹּקֶר לַעֲבוֹדָה וּמַקְדִּימִים (43) _____ לִישׁוֹן.

בַּכְּפָר (44) _____ חֲבֵרִים חֲדָשִׁים. בַּבְּקָרִים

עָזַרְנוּ (45) _____ קְצָת בַּעֲבוֹדָה בַּשָּׂדֶה,

וּבָעֲרָבִים שֶׁחַקְנוּ (46) _____ בַּחֲצֵרוֹת.

42. (A)	מְאַחֵר	39. (A)	וְאָבִי
(B)	מְקֻדָּם	(B)	וַאֲחוֹתִי
(C)	לְפָנַי	(C)	וְאִמִּי
(D)	רִאשׁוֹן	(D)	וְאָחִי
43. (A)	שׁוֹכֵב		
(B)	שׁוֹכְבִים		
(C)	לִשְׁכַּב		
(D)	שְׁכִיבָה		
44. (A)	שְׁכָחְנוּ	40. (A)	שְׁתֵּי
(B)	נִשְׁאַרְנוּ	(B)	שְׁתַּיִם
(C)	הִכַּרְנוּ	(C)	שְׁתֵּיהֶן
(D)	שִׁלַּמְנוּ	(D)	שְׁתֵּינוּ
45. (A)	אוֹתָם	41. (A)	הַפַּעַם
(B)	לָהֶם	(B)	הַיּוֹם
(C)	מֵהֶם	(C)	הַשָּׁבוּעַ
(D)	בָּהֶם	(D)	הַזְּמַן
46. (A)	אִתּוֹ		
(B)	אִתְּכֶם		
(C)	אִתָּנוּ		
(D)	אַתֶּם		

▶ GO ON TO THE NEXT PAGE

הַנְּסִיעָה לִירוּשָׁלַיִם נִמְשְׁכָה (47) _____

וָחֵצִי. הָיָה אָז חֹרֶף, אֲבָל מֶזֶג-הָאֲוִיר הָיָה קַיִצִי

(48) _____ . אֲנַחְנוּ, שֶׁהִגַּעְנוּ אַרְצָה מִצְּפוֹן

אַרְצוֹת הַבְּרִית, נֶהֱנִינוּ מְאֹד (49) _____

בְּאֶמְצַע הַחֹרֶף. כָּל הַנּוֹסְעִים בָּאוֹטוֹבּוּס הִסְתַּכְּלוּ

עָלֵינוּ (50) _____ כִּי לָבַשְׁנוּ מְעִילִים

(51) _____, כְּפָפוֹת-חֹרֶף וְכוֹבְעֵי-צֶמֶר. אֵינֶנִּי

יוֹדֵעַ בְּדִיּוּק מָה הֵם חָשְׁבוּ עָלֵינוּ, אֲבָל לִי זֶה לֹא

הָיָה אִכְפַּת. אֲנִי הִרְגַּשְׁתִּי כְּאִלּוּ (52) _____

הַבַּיְתָה, אִם כִּי זֶה הָיָה בִּקּוּרִי (53) _____

בְּיִשְׂרָאֵל.

50. (A) בְּתֵאָבוֹן
(B) בְּסַקְרָנוּת
(C) בְּקוֹל
(D) בְּשָׁלוֹם

51. (A) קָרִים
(B) רֵיקִים
(C) כְּבֵדִים
(D) גְּשׁוּמִים

52. (A) הוֹשַׁבְתִּי
(B) הֻשַׁבְתִּי
(C) שַׁבְתִּי
(D) יָשַׁבְתִּי

53. (A) הָרִאשׁוֹן
(B) אֶחָד
(C) הָרִאשׁוֹנָה
(D) אַחַת

47. (A) זְמָן
(B) שָׁעָה
(C) שְׁלֹשָׁה
(D) אַחַת

48. (A) וּצְפוֹנִי
(B) וְחָרְפִּי
(C) וְטָעִים
(D) וְנָעִים

49. (A) מֵהַשֶּׁפַע
(B) מֵהַחֹם
(C) מֵהַחֹשֶׁךְ
(D) מֵהַשֶּׁקֶט

GO ON TO THE NEXT PAGE

הַפִּינִיקִים הָיוּ עַם, שֶׁחַי לִפְנֵי שְׁלֹשֶׁת אֲלָפִים

(54) _____ עַל חוֹף הַיָּם הַתִּיכוֹן. הֵם הָיוּ

סוֹחֲרִים וְאַנְשֵׁי יָם. בְּאַחַת מִנְּסִיעוֹתֵיהֶם הֵם פָּגְשׁוּ

אֲנָשִׁים שֶׁהִשְׁתַּמְּשׁוּ בְּאָלֶף-בֵּית. (55) _____

הֵהֵם כָּתְבוּ הָאֲנָשִׁים בִּכְתַב סִמָּנִים: לְכָל מִלָּה

הָיָה סִמָּן, וְהָיָה קָשֶׁה לִזְכֹּר אֵיךְ לִכְתֹּב מִלִּים

(56) _____ . הַפִּינִיקִים קִבְּלוּ אֶת הַכְּתָב הַזֶּה,

(57) _____ יָכְלוּ לִכְתֹּב כָּל (58) _____

שֶׁרָצוּ. הֵם הֵבִיאוּ אֶת הַכְּתָב הַזֶּה לְכָל מָקוֹם

שֶׁנָּסְעוּ.

56. (A) רַבִּים

(B) רַבָּה

(C) רַב

(D) רַבּוֹת

57. (A) וּבְעֶזְרָתָם

(B) וּבְעֶזְרָתָהּ

(C) וּבְעֶזְרָתוֹ

(D) וּבְעֶזְרָתָן

58. (A) הַדָּבָר

(B) דָּבָר

(C) דְּבָרִים

(D) דִּבְרֵי

54. (A) שְׁנַת

(B) שָׁנָה

(C) שָׁנוֹת

(D) שְׁנָתַיִם

55. (A) בַּיּוֹם

(B) בַּזְּמַן

(C) בַּיָּמִים

(D) בַּתְּקוּפוֹת

GO ON TO THE NEXT PAGE

Part C

Directions: Read the following passages carefully for comprehension. Each passage is followed by a number of questions or incomplete statements. Select the answer or completion that is best according to the passage and fill in the corresponding oval on the answer sheet.

וְהָרֵי תַחֲזִית מֶזֶג הָאֲוִיר: הַיּוֹם יָרְדוּ גְּשָׁמִים
חֲזָקִים. יִהְיוּ גַּם רוּחוֹת חֲזָקוֹת. הַנֶּהָגִים צְרִיכִים
לְהִזָּהֵר מִסַּכָּנַת הַחְלָקָה בִּכְבִישׁ רָטֹב. הַנֶּהָגִים
מִתְבַּקְשִׁים לֹא לַעֲצֹר בְּאֹפֶן פִּתְאוֹמִי. כְּבִישִׁים
אֲחֵרִים יִסָּגְרוּ לִתְנוּעָה, וְיֵשׁ לְחַפֵּשׂ בִּמְקוֹמָם
דְּרָכִים אֲחֵרוֹת. בְּמֶשֶׁךְ הַלַּיְלָה יִתְחַזְּקוּ הַגְּשָׁמִים,
וְעִם בֹּקֶר הֵם יַחְלְשׁוּ. בְּסוֹף הַשָּׁבוּעַ יִהְיֶה מֶזֶג
אֲוִיר נָאֶה.

59. לְפִי הַקֶּטַע, מֶזֶג הָאֲוִיר יִגְרֹם

(A) לִבְעָיוֹת תְּנוּעָה בַּדְּרָכִים

(B) לְהַחְלָשַׁת הָרוּחוֹת

(C) לְהַצְלָחַת הַחַקְלָאוּת

(D) לִבְנִיַּת כְּבִישִׁים חֲדָשִׁים

60. מְצַפִּים שֶׁמֶזֶג הָאֲוִיר יִשְׁתַּנֶּה בְּקָרוֹב

(A) לְטוֹבָה

(B) לִבְרִיאוּת

(C) לָאַחֲרוֹנָה

(D) לִגְדֻלָּה

GO ON TO THE NEXT PAGE ➤

הַשָּׁבוּעַ הַחֵלּוּ מְכִירוֹת "סוֹף הָעוֹנָה" בַּחֲנֻיּוֹת
הַבְּגָדִים וְהַנַּעֲלַיִם. הֲנָחָה שֶׁל 20 אֲחוּזִים תִּהְיֶה
בִּמְחִירֵי מוּצָרִים אֵלֶּה. בְּכָךְ הִקְדִּימוּ הַסּוֹחֲרִים
אֶת הַמְּכִירוֹת הַמּוּזָלוֹת בְּחָדְשַׁיִם לְעֻמַּת הַשָּׁנִים
הַקּוֹדְמוֹת. הַסּוֹחֲרִים נַעֲנוּ לִפְנִיַּת שַׂר-הָאוֹצָר
לְהַקְדִּים אֶת הַמְּכִירוֹת וְלַעֲזֹר לְהִלָּחֵם
בָּאִינְפְלַצְיָה.

הִתְאַחֲדוּת הַסּוֹחֲרִים מְבָרֶרֶת אֶת הָאֶפְשָׁרוּת
לְהַרְחִיב אֶת מִבְצַע הַהוֹזָלוֹת גַּם לַעֲנָפִים אֲחֵרִים.

61. בְּאֵלּוּ מִן הַחֲנֻיּוֹת הַבָּאוֹת הוּזְלוּ הַמְּחִירִים?

    (A) הַלְבָּשָׁה

    (B) אֶלֶקְטְרוֹנִיקָה

    (C) מִשְׂחָקִים

    (D) מַכֹּלֶת

62. לְעֻמַּת שָׁנִים אֲחֵרוֹת, הַמְּכִירוֹת הַשָּׁנָה הֵחֵלּוּ

    (A) בְּהַרְחָבָה

    (B) יוֹתֵר בְּיֹקֶר

    (C) מֻקְדָּם יוֹתֵר

    (D) בְּהַצְלָחָה

63. בַּעֲלֵי הַחֲנֻיּוֹת הִסְכִּימוּ לְהַתְחָלַת מְכִירוֹת אֵלּוּ מִסִּבּוֹת

    (A) חִנּוּכִיּוֹת

    (B) דָּתִיּוֹת

    (C) כַּלְכָּלִיּוֹת

    (D) בִּלְתִּי יְדוּעוֹת

GO ON TO THE NEXT PAGE ➤

בָּעִתּוֹנוּת הוֹפִיעוּ לָאַחֲרוֹנָה מַאֲמָרִים רַבִּים
עַל הַסַּכָּנָה שֶׁבְּשִׁזּוּף. קוֹרֵאת מְדָאֶגֶת כּוֹתֶבֶת
בְּמִכְתָּב לַמַּעֲרֶכֶת, שֶׁרָאוּי הָיָה לְקַיֵּם יוֹתֵר
פְּעֻלוֹת הַסְבָּרָה בְּקֶשֶׁר לַסַּכָּנָה בְּקֶרֶב תַּלְמִידֵי
בָּתֵּי הַסֵּפֶר. לְדַעְתָּהּ, יֵשׁ לִפְעֻלוֹת כָּאֵלֶּה
הַשְׁפָּעָה רַבָּה. כְּהוֹכָחָה הִיא מְבִיאָה אֶת
הָעֻבְדָּה שֶׁהַיְלָדִים מְבִינִים אֶת הַסַּכָּנָה שֶׁבְּעִשּׁוּן
וְזֹאת כְּתוֹצָאָה מִפְּעֻלוֹת הַהַסְבָּרָה שֶׁעָסְקוּ רַבּוֹת
בַּנּוֹשֵׂא.

64. מַהִי הַסִּבָּה הָעִקָּרִית לַדְּאָגָה הַמֻּבַּעַת
בַּמַּאֲמָר?

(A) רִבּוּי הַמְעַשְׁנִים

(B) נִזְקֵי הַשֶּׁמֶשׁ

(C) כְּתִיבַת מַאֲמָרִים

(D) עִסּוּק בַּנּוֹשֵׂא

65. הַכּוֹתֶבֶת מַאֲמִינָה שֶׁאֶפְשָׁר לְשַׁפֵּר אֶת
הַמַּצָּב בְּעֶזְרַת

(A) הַרְצָאוֹת עַל הָעִשּׁוּן

(B) נְאוּמִים בַּכְּנֶסֶת

(C) חִנּוּךְ הַנֹּעַר

(D) הַגְבָּרַת הַשִּׁזּוּף

66. אֵיזוֹ דֻּגְמָה לְהַצְלָחָה מְבִיאָה הַכּוֹתֶבֶת?

(A) הַמַּאֲמָר עַל בָּתֵּי-הַסֵּפֶר

(B) הַמִּכְתָּבִים לָעִתּוֹנִים

(C) הַסֻּכּוֹת עַל שְׂפַת הַיָּם

(D) הַהַסְבָּרָה בְּקֶשֶׁר לְסִיגָרְיּוֹת

GO ON TO THE NEXT PAGE ➡

בֹּקֶר אֶחָד בִּקֵּשׁ אַבָּא שֶׁבְּדַרְכִּי לְבֵית הַסֵּפֶר
אָבִיא לוֹ אֶת הַשּׁוֹפָר הַגָּדוֹל מִבֵּית הַכְּנֶסֶת
שֶׁבַּכְּרֶם הַתֵּימָנִים. הָיָה זֶה שׁוֹפָר גָּדוֹל וְנֶהְדָּר
שֶׁתְּרוּעָתוֹ חֲזָקָה וּמְעוֹרֶרֶת כָּבוֹד, אַךְ יַחַד עִם
זֹאת הָיָה נוֹחַ לִתְקִיעָה בְּשֶׁל הַפִּיָּה הָרְחָבָה
שֶׁבּוֹ. אַבָּא סִפֵּר לִי רַבּוֹת עַל הַחֲשִׁיבוּת שֶׁל
הַשּׁוֹפָר הַזֶּה. אֶת הַשּׁוֹפָר עָשׂוּ מִקַּרְנָיו שֶׁל אַיִל
מֵהָרֵי יְהוּדָה. סָבִי קָנָה אוֹתוֹ וְתָרַם אוֹתוֹ לְבֵית
הַכְּנֶסֶת שֶׁבַּכְּרֶם הַתֵּימָנִים.

הִתְמַלֵּאתִי שִׂמְחָה כְּשֶׁחָשַׁבְתִּי שֶׁאָבוֹא לְבֵית
הַסֵּפֶר עִם הַשּׁוֹפָר. תֵּאַרְתִּי לְעַצְמִי אֵיךְ יַבִּיטוּ
בִּי כָּל הַיְלָדִים בְּסַקְרָנוּת וּבְקִנְאָה. אֲבָל אָבִי
צִוָּה עָלַי לְהַסְתִּיר אֶת הַשּׁוֹפָר בְּיַלְקוּטִי וְלֹא
לְהַרְאוֹת אוֹתוֹ לְאִישׁ עַד בּוֹאִי הַבַּיְתָה.

בַּלַּיְלָה הַהוּא הִתְהַפַּכְתִּי בְּמִטָּתִי וְשָׁמַעְתִּי
קוֹלוֹת שׁוֹפָר. חָלַמְתִּי עַל הַשּׁוֹפָר הַגָּדוֹל שֶׁל
בֵּית הַכְּנֶסֶת שֶׁבַּכְּרֶם הַתֵּימָנִים. רָאִיתִי אֶת סָבִי
הַצַּדִּיק עוֹלֶה לִירוּשָׁלַיִם כְּשֶׁזְּקָנוֹ הַלָּבָן מִתְבַּדֵּר
בָּרוּחַ, לִמְצֹא אֶת הַשּׁוֹפָר שֶׁיָּבִיא בִּתְקִיעָתוֹ אֶת
הַמֶּלֶךְ הַמָּשִׁיחַ.

מַה שֶּׁעָבַר עָלַי בְּאוֹתוֹ יוֹם שׁוּב אֵינִי זוֹכֵר.
אֲנִי זוֹכֵר רַק שֶׁהִסְתּוֹבַבְתִּי כָּל שְׁעוֹת הַבֹּקֶר
כְּחוֹלֵם, תּוֹעֶה בִּרְחוֹבוֹת עִירִי כְּשֶׁהַשּׁוֹפָר בְּיָדִי,
וְעוֹבְרִים וְשָׁבִים נֶעֱצָרִים וּמַבִּיטִים בִּי בְּתִמָּהוֹן.
יַלְדָּה אַחַת הִצְבִּיעָה עָלַי בְּיָדָהּ וְאָמְרָה לְאִמָּהּ:
"רְאִי, אִמָּא, יֶלֶד עִם שׁוֹפָר"!

67. מַה בִּקֵּשׁ הָאָב מִן הַמְּסַפֵּר?
(A) לִקְנוֹת שׁוֹפָר בַּדֶּרֶךְ לְבֵית הַסֵּפֶר
(B) לִתְרֹם אֶת הַשּׁוֹפָר לְבֵית הַכְּנֶסֶת
(C) לְהָבִיא אֶת הַשּׁוֹפָר לְבֵית הַסֵּפֶר
(D) לָקַחַת אֶת הַשּׁוֹפָר מִבֵּית הַכְּנֶסֶת

68. מֶה הָיָה הַקֶּשֶׁר שֶׁל הַמְּסַפֵּר אֶל הַשּׁוֹפָר?
(A) אָבִיו עָשָׂה אוֹתוֹ מִקַּרְנָיו שֶׁל אַיִל.
(B) אָבִיו קָנָה אוֹתוֹ מִבֵּית הַכְּנֶסֶת.
(C) הוּא קִבֵּל אוֹתוֹ בִּירוּשָׁה מִסָּבוֹ.
(D) סָבוֹ נָתַן אוֹתוֹ בְּמַתָּנָה לְבֵית הַכְּנֶסֶת.

69. מֶה הָיָה מְיֻחָד בַּשּׁוֹפָר?
(A) הוּא הָיָה כָּבֵד מְאֹד.
(B) הָיָה לוֹ קוֹל מַרְשִׁים.
(C) הָיָה קָשֶׁה לְהַחֲזִיק אוֹתוֹ.
(D) הוּא הָיָה הַיָּחִיד בָּעִיר.

70. הַמְּסַפֵּר שָׂמַח לְמַלֵּא אֶת בַּקָּשַׁת אָבִיו, כִּי הוּא
(A) אָהַב לַעֲזֹר לְאָבִיו
(B) יָדַע שֶׁחֲבֵרָיו יְקַנְאוּ בּוֹ
(C) רָצָה לִתְקֹעַ בַּשּׁוֹפָר
(D) נֶהֱנָה מֵהַחִפּוּשׂ מִלִּמּוּדִים

71. בַּחֲלוֹמוֹ בַּלַּיְלָה הַיֶּלֶד רָאָה אֶת סָבוֹ
(A) תּוֹקֵעַ בַּשּׁוֹפָר
(B) מִסְתּוֹבֵב בְּחוּצוֹת הָעִיר
(C) מְחַפֵּשׂ אַחַר הַשּׁוֹפָר
(D) מְסַפֵּר עַל חֲשִׁיבוּת הַשּׁוֹפָר

GO ON TO THE NEXT PAGE →

מְיוֹמָנָהּ שֶׁל יָעֵל דַּיָּן

יַלְדוּתִי עָבְרָה עָלַי בְּבָתִּים וּבִמְקוֹמוֹת שׁוֹנִים בָּאָרֶץ.

הַבַּיִת בְּתֵל־אָבִיב הָיָה בַּיִת שֶׁכֻּלָּנוּ אֲהַבְנוּהוּ, וְהוּא נִשְׁאַר כָּזֶה עַד שֶׁהוֹרַי הִתְגָּרְשׁוּ. לַעֲמַת זֹאת, הַבַּיִת בַּמּוֹשָׁב יִשָּׁאֵר תָּמִיד מָקוֹם הַיַּלְדוּתִי הָאָהוּב. אַף־עַל־פִּי שֶׁיָּדַעְנוּ שֶׁלֹּא נָגוּר בּוֹ שׁוּב, הוּא שֶׁנָּתַן לִי בִּטָּחוֹן, קִרְבָה לָאֲדָמָה וְהַרְגָּשָׁה שֶׁיֵּשׁ לִי שָׁרָשִׁים בַּמָּקוֹם. אֶת הַבַּיִת בִּירוּשָׁלַיִם כִּמְעַט שָׁכַחְנוּ. גַּם בִּירוּשָׁלַיִם וְגַם בַּמּוֹשָׁב הָיוּ לִי סַבָּא וְסָבְתָּא, וְאֶצְלָם תָּמִיד הִרְגַּשְׁתִּי כְּמוֹ בַּבַּיִת.

רֹב שְׁנוֹת נְעוּרַי גַּרְתִּי בַּבַּיִת בְּתֵל־אָבִיב שֶׁהָיָה בִּשְׁכוּנָה צְהֻלָּה. הַשְּׁכוּנָה נִבְנְתָה בִּשְׁבִיל קְצִינֵי צַהַ״ל. בַּבַּיִת הָיוּ שְׁלֹשָׁה חַדְרֵי שֵׁנָה, מִטְבָּח קָטָן, חֲדַר מְגוּרִים וְגַן גָּדוֹל. בְּשָׁנִים אֵלֶּה הִקְדַּשְׁתִּי זְמַן רַב יוֹתֵר לַלִּמּוּדִים, וְהִתְחַלְתִּי לִכְתֹּב בְּעִתּוֹן. רָצִיתִי לַעֲבֹד קָשֶׁה וּלְהוֹכִיחַ שׁוּב וָשׁוּב, שֶׁאֲנִי יְכוֹלָה לְהַצְלִיחַ בִּזְכוּת עַצְמִי.

מֵאָז וּמִתָּמִיד יָדַעְתִּי שֶׁאַהֲבָתָם שֶׁל הוֹרַי הִיא כֻּלָּהּ שֶׁלִּי, וְלֹא הִרְגַּשְׁתִּי צֹרֶךְ לִבְחֹן אוֹתָהּ. מַה שֶׁהָיָה עָלַי לְהַרְאוֹת הוּא מַה שֶׁאֲנִי עַצְמִי יְכוֹלָה לַעֲשׂוֹת.

73. הַמְּסַפֶּרֶת הִרְגִּישָׁה קֶשֶׁר חָזָק לְבֵיתָהּ בַּמּוֹשָׁב, כִּי הוּא

(A) מָקוֹם שֶׁהִיא מְקַנָּה לַחֲזֹר וְלָגוּר בּוֹ

(B) מָקוֹם שֶׁהוֹרֶיהָ גָּרִים בּוֹ עַד הַיּוֹם

(C) נָתַן לָהּ אֶפְשָׁרוּת לְבַקֵּר שׁוּב בַּכְּפָר

(D) נָתַן לָהּ הַרְגָּשָׁה שֶׁהִיא שַׁיֶּכֶת לַמָּקוֹם

74. הַמְּסַפֶּרֶת קִוְּתָה

(A) לִחְיוֹת בְּקִבּוּץ בָּאָרֶץ

(B) לֹא לְקַבֵּל עֶזְרָה מֵהַצָּבָא

(C) לַעֲבֹר לְבַיִת גָּדוֹל בָּעִיר

(D) לֹא לְהֵעָזֵר בִּבְנֵי מִשְׁפַּחְתָּהּ

72. הַמְּסַפֶּרֶת נוֹלְדָה, כְּשֶׁהוֹרֶיהָ גָּרוּ

(A) בְּתֵל־אָבִיב

(B) בַּמּוֹשָׁב

(C) בִּירוּשָׁלַיִם

(D) בַּקִּבּוּץ

GO ON TO THE NEXT PAGE →

75. הַמְּסַפֶּרֶת הִרְגִּישָׁה שֶׁהוֹרֶיהָ

    (A) עֲסוּקִים מִדַּי

    (B) אוֹהֲבִים אוֹתָהּ מְאֹד

    (C) אֵינָם מְרֻצִּים מִמַּעֲשֶׂיהָ

    (D) דּוֹרְשִׁים שֶׁתִּתְעַבֵּד קָשֶׁה

76. מִן הַסִּפּוּר נִרְאָה שֶׁהַמְּסַפֶּרֶת

    (A) הִצְטַעֲרָה עַל הַצֹּרֶךְ לַעֲבֹר דִּירָה

    (B) הָיְתָה עֲצוּבָה מִפְּנֵי שֶׁהוֹרֶיהָ נִפְרְדוּ

    (C) מְנַסָּה לְהַסְבִּיר מַה הִשְׁפִּיעַ עָלֶיהָ

    (D) מַסְבִּירָה מַדּוּעַ הֶחֱלִיפָה אֶת שְׁמָהּ

GO ON TO THE NEXT PAGE ➤

בְּכָל הַכְּפָרִים לֹא נִמְצָא סוּס יָפֶה כְּמוֹ סוּסוֹ
שֶׁל זַלְמָן. קַלְמָן, שְׁכֵנוֹ הֶעָשִׁיר שֶׁל זַלְמָן, אָמַר
לוֹ: "מְכֹר לִי אֶת סוּסְךָ, וְכָל אֲשֶׁר תְּבַקֵּשׁ אֶתֵּן
לְךָ." זַלְמָן עָנָה: "הַסּוּס יָקָר לִי מִבֵּיתִי וּמֵאִשְׁתִּי
וּמִבָּנַי. לֹא אֶמְכֹּר לְךָ אוֹתוֹ בְּשׁוּם מְחִיר".
הִצְטַעֵר קַלְמָן וְהֶחְלִיט לָקַחַת אֶת הַסּוּס בְּעָרְמָה.
יוֹם אֶחָד, כְּשֶׁרָכַב זַלְמָן עַל סוּסוֹ הָעִירָה,
הִתְחַפֵּשׂ קַלְמָן לְעָנִי חוֹלֶה, לָבַשׁ בְּגָדִים קְרוּעִים
וְשָׁכַב עַל הַדֶּרֶךְ. כַּאֲשֶׁר הִתְקָרֵב זַלְמָן, קָרָא
קַלְמָן: "רַחֵם עָלַי, נִפַלְתִּי וְאֵינֶנִּי יָכוֹל לָקוּם,
וַאֲנִי רָעֵב וְחוֹלֶה".
רִחֵם זַלְמָן עַל הָאִישׁ בְּצָרָה, וְיָרַד מֵסוּסוֹ
כְּדֵי לַעֲזֹר לוֹ. קָפַץ קַלְמָן עַל הַסּוּס, הִכָּה בּוֹ,
וְהַסּוּס רָץ וְהִתְרַחֵק מִזַּלְמָן. אָז קָרָא קַלְמָן
בְּקוֹל גָּדוֹל: "הִנֵּה סוּסְךָ בְּיָדַי לֹא אַחֲזִיר לְךָ
אוֹתוֹ". הִכִּיר זַלְמָן אֶת קוֹל קַלְמָן וְאָמַר:
"אָנָּא, קַלְמָן, עֲשֵׂה אִתִּי חֶסֶד וְאַל תְּסַפֵּר לְאִישׁ
אֵיךְ בָּא סוּסִי לְיָדְךָ, כִּי אִם יִשְׁמְעוּ הָאֲנָשִׁים אֶת
הַדָּבָר הַזֶּה, הֵם יַפְסִיקוּ לַעֲזֹר לַעֲנִיִּים".
כְּשֶׁשָּׁמַע קַלְמָן אֶת בַּקָּשַׁת זַלְמָן, הִתְחָרֵט
עַל מַעֲשָׂיו וְהֵשִׁיב לְזַלְמָן אֶת סוּסוֹ.

77. מַה הִצִּיעַ קַלְמָן לְזַלְמָן בְּעַד סוּסוֹ?

(A) בְּגָדִים קְרוּעִים

(B) בַּיִת יָקָר

(C) מְעַט כֶּסֶף

(D) כָּל מַה שֶׁיִּרְצֶה

78. זַלְמָן לֹא הִסְכִּים לִמְכֹּר לוֹ אֶת סוּסוֹ, כִּי

(A) הַסּוּס הָיָה חָשׁוּב לוֹ מִכֹּל

(B) לֹא הָיָה לוֹ סוּס אַחֵר

(C) הוּא שִׁלֵּם בְּעַד סוּסוֹ כֶּסֶף רַב

(D) הַמְּחִיר לֹא הִסְפִּיק לוֹ

GO ON TO THE NEXT PAGE →

79. קַלְמָן לָבַשׁ בְּגָדִים קְרוּעִים וְשָׁכַב עַל הַדֶּרֶךְ כְּדֵי

(A) שֶׁכֻּלָּם יַחְשְׁבוּ שֶׁזַּלְמָן הוּא אָדָם אַכְזָרִי

(B) שֶׁאֲנָשִׁים יַעַבְרוּ בַּדֶּרֶךְ וְיִתְּנוּ לוֹ כֶּסֶף

(C) שֶׁזַּלְמָן יְרַחֵם עַל הֶעָנִי וְיַעֲצֹר

(D) שֶׁהוּא יוּכַל לַעֲשׂוֹת חֶסֶד עִם זַלְמָן

80. מַדּוּעַ בָּרַח הַסּוּס מִזַּלְמָן?

(A) כִּי קַלְמָן רָכַב עָלָיו

(B) כִּי הוּא רָאָה סוּס אַחֵר

(C) כִּי הָיָה לוֹ כְּאֵב בָּרֶגֶל

(D) כִּי זַלְמָן הָיָה בְּצָרָה

81. אֵיךְ הֵגִיב זַלְמָן עַל הַמַּעֲשֶׂה שֶׁל קַלְמָן?

(A) הוּא בִּקֵּשׁ מִקַּלְמָן שֶׁלֹּא יְסַפֵּר אֵיךְ קִבֵּל אֶת הַסּוּס.

(B) הוּא צָחַק וְאָמַר שֶׁזֶּה לֹא הַסּוּס שֶׁרָצָה קַלְמָן.

(C) הוּא כָּעַס עָלָיו וְהֵרִים אֶת יָדוֹ לְהַכּוֹת אוֹתוֹ.

(D) הוּא סִפֵּר לְכֻלָּם עַל מַעֲשָׂיו הָרָעִים שֶׁל קַלְמָן.

82. מִמַּה פָּחַד זַלְמָן יוֹתֵר מִכֹּל?

(A) שֶׁכָּל אַנְשֵׁי הַכְּפָר יִצְחֲקוּ מִמֶּנּוּ

(B) שֶׁהוּא יִשָּׁאֵר בַּמִּדְבָּר וְיָמוּת בָּרָעָב

(C) שֶׁלֹּא יִרְאֶה יוֹתֵר אֶת סוּסוֹ הָאָהוּב

(D) שֶׁלֹּא יְרַחֲמוּ יוֹתֵר עַל עֲנִיִּים

GO ON TO THE NEXT PAGE ➡

שדכן בא אל אל בחור אחד לשדכו. כעס עליו
הבחור ואמר: "מאה פעמים אמרתי לך, שלא
אקח אישה על-ידי שדכן. רק באהבה אתחתן".
ענה לו השדכן: "על-כן באתי אליך. שמע
היטב: האב הוא בן שבעים, ועשיר גדול הוא,
והנערה בת יחידה, אין לה אח או אחות. יש
לה גם דוד עשיר שאין לו בנים. הייתכן שלא
תאהב נערה נפלאה כזאת?"

83. לפי דעתו של הבחור, מי שמתחתן על-ידי
שדכן

(A) מתחתן בגלל אהבת הכסף

(B) מתחתן בגלל הגיל

(C) אינו מתחתן מתוך אהבה

(D) מתחתן ומתגרש

84. מדוע כועס הבחור על השדכן?

(A) כי השדכן הציע לו בחורות לא
מוצלחות

(B) כי השדכן מבקש מחיר גבוה

(C) כי הבחור לא רוצה להתחתן
על-ידי שדכנים

(D) כי ההבחור לא רוצה אישה עשירה

85. מדוע מציין השדכן את גילו של
אבי-הנערה?

(A) כי זה גיל שלא רבים מגיעים אליו

(B) כי לאב לא נשארו הרבה שנים
לחיות

(C) כי לא נעים לשדכן לציין את גיל
הנערה

(D) כדי להראות שבמשפחת הנערה
מאריכים ימים

STOP

IF YOU FINISH BEFORE TIME IS CALLED, YOU MAY CHECK YOUR WORK ON THIS TEST ONLY.
DO NOT TURN TO ANY OTHER TEST IN THIS BOOK.

How to Score the SAT Subject Test in Modern Hebrew

When you take an actual SAT Subject Test in Modern Hebrew, your answer sheet will be "read" by a scanning machine that will record your responses to each question. Then a computer will compare your answers with the correct answers and produce your raw score. You get one point for each correct answer. For each wrong answer, you lose one-third of a point. Questions you omit (and any for which you mark more than one answer) are not counted. This raw score is converted to a scaled score that is reported to you and to the colleges you specify.

Worksheet 1. Finding Your Raw Test Score

STEP 1: Table A lists the correct answers for all the questions on the SAT Subject Test in Modern Hebrew that is reproduced in this book. It also serves as a worksheet for you to calculate your raw multiple-choice score.

- Compare your answers with those given in the table.
- Put a check in the column marked "Right" if your answer is correct.
- Put a check in the column marked "Wrong" if your answer is incorrect.
- Leave both columns blank if you omitted the question.

STEP 2: Count the number of right answers.

Enter the total here: _____

STEP 3: Count the number of wrong answers.

Enter the total here: _____

STEP 4: Multiply the number of wrong answers by .333.

Enter the product here: _____

STEP 5: Subtract the result obtained in Step 4 from the total you obtained in Step 2.

Enter the result here: _____

STEP 6: Round the number obtained in Step 5 to the nearest whole number.

Enter the result here: _____

The number you obtained in Step 6 is your raw score.

TABLE A

Answers to the SAT Subject Test in Modern Hebrew, Form 3PAC, and Percentage of Students Answering Each Question Correctly

Question Number	Correct Answer	Right	Wrong	Percentage of Students Answering the Question Correctly*	Question Number	Correct Answer	Right	Wrong	Percentage of Students Answering the Question Correctly*
1	C			94	33	B			57
2	D			90	34	C			82
3	D			97	35	D			80
4	D			90	36	C			66
5	A			92	37	B			75
6	A			93	38	A			78
7	A			93	39	B			97
8	C			92	40	D			94
9	C			85	41	A			98
10	D			86	42	B			97
11	C			90	43	C			47
12	C			83	44	C			86
13	A			68	45	B			72
14	C			80	46	D			90
15	A			85	47	B			89
16	B			62	48	D			94
17	B			72	49	B			87
18	B			82	50	B			93
19	D			50	51	C			85
20	B			64	52	C			49
21	A			39	53	A			70
22	B			79	54	B			87
23	C			60	55	C			91
24	C			70	56	D			66
25	C			87	57	C			32
26	B			67	58	B			90
27	D			52	59	A			91
28	B			41	60	A			87
29	A			38	61	A			93
30	B			25	62	C			57
31	D			90	63	C			60
32	A			91	64	B			25

Table A continued on next page

Table A continued from previous page

Question Number	Correct Answer	Right	Wrong	Percentage of Students Answering the Question Correctly*	Question Number	Correct Answer	Right	Wrong	Percentage of Students Answering the Question Correctly*
65	C			71	76	C			79
66	D			53	77	D			94
67	D			86	78	A			94
68	D			90	79	C			91
69	B			83	80	A			86
70	B			89	81	A			92
71	C			73	82	D			89
72	B			62	83	C			92
73	D			89	84	C			93
74	D			62	85	B			90
75	B			80					

*These percentages are based on an analysis of the answer sheets for a random sample of 288 students who took this form of the test in June 1993 and whose mean score was 564. They may be used as an indication of the relative difficulty of a particular question. Each percentage may also be used to predict the likelihood that a typical SAT Subject Test in Modern Hebrew candidate will answer correctly that question on this edition of this test.

Finding Your Scaled Score

When you take SAT Subject Tests, the scores sent to the colleges you specify are reported on the College Board scale, which ranges from 200 to 800. You can convert your practice test score to a scaled score by using Table B. To find your scaled score, locate your raw score in the left-hand column of Table B; the corresponding score in the right-hand column is your scaled score. For example, a raw score of 67 on this particular edition of the SAT Subject Test in Modern Hebrew corresponds to a scaled score of 590.

Raw scores are converted to scaled scores to ensure that a score earned on any one edition of a particular Subject Test is comparable to the same scaled score earned on any other edition of the same Subject Test. Because some editions of tests may be slightly easier or more difficult than others, scaled scores are adjusted so that they indicate the same level of performance regardless of the edition of the test taken and the ability of the group that takes it. Thus, for example, a score of 400 on one edition of a test taken at a particular administration indicates the same level of achievement as a score of 400 on a different edition of the test taken at a different administration.

When you take the SAT Subject Tests during a national administration, your scores are likely to differ somewhat from the scores you obtain on the tests in this book. People perform at different levels at different times for reasons unrelated to the tests themselves. The precision of any test is also limited because it represents only a sample of all the possible questions that could be asked.

TABLE B

Scaled Score Conversion Table
Modern Hebrew Subject Test: (Form 3PAC)

Raw Score	Scaled Score	Raw Score	Scaled Score	Raw Score	Scaled Score
85	800	47	470	9	320
84	800	46	470	8	310
83	780	45	460	7	310
82	760	44	460	6	300
81	740	43	450	5	300
80	720	42	450	4	290
79	710	41	450	3	280
78	700	40	440	2	280
77	680	39	440	1	270
76	670	38	430	0	260
75	660	37	430	-1	250
74	650	36	430	-2	250
73	640	35	420	-3	240
72	630	34	420	-4	230
71	620	33	420	-5	220
70	610	32	410	-6	210
69	600	31	410	-7	200
68	600	30	410	-8	200
67	590	29	400	-9	200
66	580	28	400	-10	200
65	570	27	400	-11	200
64	570	26	390	-12	200
63	560	25	390	-13	200
62	550	24	390	-14	200
61	540	23	380	-15	200
60	540	22	380	-16	200
59	530	21	370	-17	200
58	530	20	370	-18	200
57	520	19	370	-19	200
56	510	18	360	-20	200
55	510	17	360	-21	200
54	500	16	350	-22	200
53	500	15	350	-23	200
52	490	14	340	-24	200
51	490	13	340	-25	200
50	480	12	330	-26	200
49	480	11	330	-27	200
48	470	10	320	-28	200

Reviewing Your Performance
on the Modern Hebrew Subject Test

After you score your test, analyze your performance—consider the following questions:

Did you run out of time before reaching the end of the test?

If so, you may need to pace yourself better. For example, maybe you spent too much time on one or two hard questions. A better approach might be to skip the ones you can't answer right away and try answering all the questions that remain on the test. Then if there's time, go back to the questions you skipped.

Did you take a long time reading the directions?

You will save time when you take the test by learning the directions to the Modern Hebrew Subject Test ahead of time. Each minute you spend reading directions during the test is a minute that you could use to answer questions.

How did you handle questions you were unsure of?

If you were able to eliminate one or more of the answer choices as wrong and guess from the remaining choices, your approach probably worked to your advantage. On the other hand, making haphazard guesses or omitting questions without trying to eliminate choices could cost you valuable points.

How difficult were the questions for you compared with other students who took the test?

Table A shows you how difficult the multiple-choice questions were for the group of students who took this test during its national administration. The right-hand column gives the percentage of students that answered each question correctly.

A question answered correctly by almost everyone in the group is obviously an easy question. For example, 98 percent of the students answered question 41 correctly. But only 25 percent answered question 64 correctly.

Keep in mind that these percentages are based on just one group of students. They would probably be different if another group of students took the test.

If you missed several easy questions, go back and try to find out why:
Did the questions cover material you haven't reviewed yet? Did you misunderstand the directions?

Chapter 16
Spanish

Purpose

There are two Spanish Subject Tests: Spanish and Spanish with Listening. The reading-only test measures your ability to understand written Spanish. The Spanish Subject Test with Listening measures your ability to understand spoken and written Spanish.

Format

- The Spanish Test takes one hour and includes 85 multiple-choice questions.
- The Spanish with Listening Test also takes one hour, with about 20 minutes for listening questions and 40 minutes for the reading section; it includes 85 multiple-choice listening and reading questions.
- Both tests evaluate your reading skills through precision of vocabulary, structure use, and comprehension of a variety of texts.

Reading Section

Reading questions implicitly test vocabulary throughout the test, but some questions specifically test word meaning in the context of a sentence that reflects spoken or written language. Understanding of various parts of speech (nouns, verbs, adjectives, adverbs, etc.) and idiomatic expressions is tested. The reading section also asks:

Structure Questions. These questions ask you to identify usage that is both structurally correct and contextually appropriate. Other reading questions test vocabulary and grammatical usage in longer paragraphs.

Reading Questions. These questions are based on selections from prose fiction, historical works, newspaper and magazine articles, as well as advertisements, flyers, and letters. They test points such as main and supporting ideas, themes, style, tone, and the spatial and temporal settings of a passage.

Listening Section

The listening section has three parts:

Part A asks you to identify the sentence that most accurately describes what is presented in a photograph or what someone in the photograph might say.

Part B questions test your ability to identify a plausible continuation of a short conversation.

Part C requires that you answer comprehension questions based on more extensive listening selections.

Spanish

Skills Measured	Approximate Percentage of Test
Vocabulary and Structure	33
Paragraph Completion	33
Reading Comprehension	33

Spanish with Listening

Types of Questions	Approximate Percentage of Test
Listening Section (about 20 minutes)	40
(about 30 questions)	
Pictures	
Rejoinders	
Selections	
Reading Section (40 minutes)	60
(about 55 questions)	
Vocabulary and Structure	
Paragraph Completion	
Reading Comprehension	

Recommended Preparation

Both tests reflect general trends in high school curricula and are independent of particular textbooks or methods of instruction. You should:

- Take three to four years of study in high school or the equivalent (two years for outstanding students)
- Develop competence in Spanish over a period of years
- Familiarize yourself with directions in advance. The directions in this book are identical to those that appear on the test.

Spanish Test with Listening

A practice cassette with sample questions is available from your school counselor.

Cassette Players

You must bring an acceptable cassette player with earphones to the test center. Put fresh batteries in your cassette player the day before the test and, if you like, bring additional fresh batteries and a backup cassette player with earphones to the test center. Test center staff will NOT have batteries, cassette players, or earphones for your use.

Acceptable cassette players must be:

- personal (have earphones that let only you hear the recording)
- portable (small enough that the entire cassette player can fit in your hand)
- battery-operated
- able to use a single (not dual) standard (2-1/2 inch by 4 inch) audiocassette not a mini- or microcassette

If your cassette player has a programming feature that fast-forwards automatically to the next prompt, that feature must be deactivated before you start the test. You will not be allowed to share a cassette player with another test-taker.

Beginning with the November 2005 administration, portable CD players will be required instead of cassette players for language with listening tests.

Scores

For both tests, the total score is reported on the 200-to-800 scale. For the listening test, listening and reading subscores are reported on the 20-to-80 scale.

Sample Reading Questions

Please note that your answer sheet has five answer positions marked A, B, C, D, E, while the questions throughout this test contain only four choices. Be sure NOT to make any marks in column E.

Part A

Directions: This part consists of a number of incomplete statements, each having four suggested completions. Select the most appropriate completion and fill in the corresponding oval on the answer sheet.

1. Juan Pablo tuvo que esperar unos minutos antes de tomar la sopa porque estaba demasiado_____

   (A) caliente

   (B) calurosa

   (C) mojada

   (D) perfumada

2. Me gustó tanto la novela de Isabel Allende que _____ voy a recomendar a mis amigos.

   (A) le

   (B) lo

   (C) me la

   (D) se la

Question 1 tests how well you have mastered vocabulary. Choice (A) *caliente* is the correct choice. To answer correctly, you need to know that the only adjective that fits the context of the sentence is (A) *caliente*. The wrong choices, (B), (C), and (D), are inappropriate adjectives for describing soup in this context.

   Question 2 tests command of structure. Choice (D) *se la* is the correct choice. To answer correctly, you need to know the correct object pronoun usage and choose an indirect object with a singular, feminine direct object pronoun in the correct sequence. Choices (A), (B), and (C) have either an indirect object pronoun that would not agree with the plural indirect object, *mis amigos*, or a direct object pronoun that would not agree with the singular, feminine direct object, *la novela*.

6. ¿Para qué hay que mandar 75 pesetas?

(A) Para pagar el costo de correos

(B) Para recibir cupones de pedido

(C) Para comprar un periódico catalán

(D) Para pagar un anuncio ilustrado

Question 6 asks about a specific detail mentioned in the ad: the reason for sending 75 pesetas. In the text, *más 75.-Ptas. en sellos por gastos de envío* refers to shipping charges, so the correct answer is (A). Choices (B), (C), and (D) are incorrect within the context of the ad.

Questions 7–9

Un aire marino, pesado y fresco, entró en mis pulmones con la primera sensación confusa de la ciudad; una masa de casas dormidas; de establecimientos cerrados, de faroles como centinelas borrachos de soledad. Una respiración grande, dificultosa, venía con el cuchicheo de la madrugada. Muy cerca, a mi espalda, enfrente de las callejuelas misteriosas que conducen al Borne, sobre mi corazón excitado, estaba el mar.

El olor especial, el gran rumor de la gente, la luces siempre tristes de la estación de tren, tenían para mí un gran encanto, ya que envolvían todas mis impresiones en la maravilla de haber llegado por fin a una ciudad grande, adorada en mis ensueños por desconocida.

7. ¿Cómo se siente la narradora al llegar a la ciudad?

(A) Perdida

(B) Encantada

(C) Cansada

(D) Tranquila

8. ¿Qué efecto producen en la narradora las luces de la estación?

(A) Le agradan mucho.

(B) Le dan vergüenza.

(C) La desorientan.

(D) La adormecen.

9. ¿Dónde está la ciudad a la que llega la narradora?

   (A) En la costa

   (B) En una cordillera

   (C) Al lado de un río

   (D) Cerca de un lago

Question 7 tests literal comprehension, and refers to how the protagonist feels upon her arrival in the city. In the second paragraph, she describes her impressions of the city using words such as *especial, encanto*, and *maravilla*. Later in the same paragraph, she also refers to *haber llegado por fin a una ciudad grande, adorada en mis ensueños* (…), so the correct answer is (B) *Encantada*. Choices (A), (C), and (D) are incorrect within the context of the passage.

Question 8 tests literal comprehension and refers to the effect that the lights of the station have on the protagonist. In the second paragraph, she specifically mentions them, saying *tenían un gran encanto*. Thus, the correct answer is (A) *Le agradan mucho*. Choices (B), (C), and (D) are incorrect within the context of the passage.

Question 9 tests literal comprehension and asks about the setting of the narrative. In the first paragraph, both the first line, *Un aire marino* (…) and the last sentence, *Muy cerca (…) estaba el mar*, refer to being close to the sea. The correct answer is (A) *En la costa*. Choices (B), (C), and (D) are incorrect within the context of the passage.

Spanish Test

The test that follows is an actual, recently administered SAT Subject Test in Spanish. To get an idea of what a real administration is like, take the test under conditions as close as possible to those of a national administration:

- Set aside an hour when you can take the test uninterrupted. Make sure you complete the test in one sitting.

- Sit at a desk or table with no other books or papers. Dictionaries, other books, or notes are not allowed in the test room.

- Time yourself by placing a clock or kitchen timer in front of you.

- Tear out an answer sheet from the back of this book and fill it in just as you would on the day of the test. One answer sheet can be used for up to three Subject Tests.

- Read the instructions that precede the practice test. During the actual administration you will be asked to read them before answering the test questions.

- After you finish the practice test, read the sections "How to Score the SAT Subject Test in Spanish" and "Reviewing Your Performance on the Spanish Subject Test."

- Actual test and answer sheets will indicate circles, not ovals.

Form K-3RAC

SPANISH TEST

The top portion of the section of the answer sheet that you will use in taking the Spanish test must be filled in exactly as shown in the illustration below. Note carefully that you have to do all of the following on your answer sheet.

1. Print SPANISH on the line under the words "Subject Test (print)."

2. In the shaded box labeled "Test Code" fill in four ovals:

   —Fill in oval 4 in the row labeled V.

   —Fill in oval 1 in the row labeled W.

   —Fill in oval 3 in the row labeled X.

   —Fill in oval B in the row labeled Y.

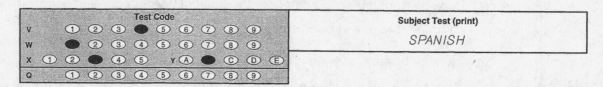

Please answer either Part I or Part II by filling in the specific oval in row Q. You are to fill in ONE and ONLY ONE oval, as described below, to indicate how you obtained your knowledge of Spanish. The information you provide is for statistical purposes only and will not influence your score on the test.

Part I   If your knowledge of Spanish does not come primarily from courses taken in grades 9 through 12, fill in oval 9 and leave the remaining ovals blank, regardless of how long you studied the subject in school. For example, you are to fill in oval 9 if your knowledge of Spanish comes primarily from any of the following sources: study prior to the ninth grade, courses taken at a college, special study, living in a home in which Spanish is the principal language spoken, or extensive residence abroad that includes significant experience in the Spanish language.

Part II   If your knowledge of Spanish does come primarily from courses taken in secondary school, fill in the oval that indicates the level of the Spanish course in which you are currently enrolled. If you are not now enrolled in a Spanish course, fill in the oval that indicates the level of the most advanced course in Spanish that you have completed.

First year:	first or second half	—Fill in oval 1.
Second year:	first half	—Fill in oval 2.
	second half	—Fill in oval 3.
Third year:	first half	—Fill in oval 4.
	second half	—Fill in oval 5.
Fourth year:	first half	—Fill in oval 6.
	second half	—Fill in oval 7.

Advanced Placement course
or a course at a level higher
than fourth year, second half
or
high school course work plus
a minimum of four weeks of
study abroad   —Fill in oval 8.

When the supervisor gives the signal, turn the page and begin the Spanish test. There are 100 numbered ovals on the answer sheet and 85 questions in the Spanish test. Therefore, use only ovals 1 to 85 for recording your answers.

SPANISH TEST

PLEASE NOTE THAT YOUR ANSWER SHEET HAS FIVE ANSWER POSITIONS MARKED A, B, C, D, E, WHILE THE QUESTIONS THROUGHOUT THIS TEST CONTAIN ONLY FOUR CHOICES. BE SURE <u>NOT</u> TO MAKE ANY MARKS IN COLUMN E.

Part A

<u>Directions:</u> This part consists of a number of incomplete statements, each having four suggested completions. Select the most appropriate completion and fill in the corresponding oval on the answer sheet.

---

1. Me encanta ------- en la sala porque las lámparas dan muy buena luz allí.

   (A) nadar
   (B) dormir
   (C) leer
   (D) pasear

2. Le dieron el palo al niño para que ------- la piñata.

   (A) rompiera
   (B) vendiera
   (C) pagara
   (D) quemara

3. Se alegró mucho al recibir la ------- de su madre.

   (A) letra
   (B) paliza
   (C) presencia
   (D) carta

4. Hasta el lunes, muchachos; espero ------- pasen un fin de semana fantástico.

   (A) y
   (B) aunque
   (C) pues
   (D) que

5. Cuando la abogada hizo la pregunta, ------- se la contestó.

   (A) nadie
   (B) nada
   (C) algún
   (D) algunos

6. Al soldado le dieron una condecoración por ser tan -------.

   (A) caro
   (B) valiente
   (C) triste
   (D) reservado

7. Elena no puede ir de vacaciones porque tiene que tomar un ------- de verano en la universidad.

   (A) sujeto
   (B) viaje
   (C) avión
   (D) curso

8. Las tenistas necesitan ------- más para jugar este partido.

   (A) una cuchara
   (B) un cuadro
   (C) un balón
   (D) una pelota

9. Recibí tu invitación y ------- de Isabel el mismo día.

   (A) la
   (B) suya
   (C) ella
   (D) cuya

10. Pepito, no se te olvide ------- la luz antes de salir del cuarto.

    (A) leer
    (B) salvar
    (C) cobrar
    (D) apagar

11. El niño está ------- porque se lastimó una rodilla.

    (A) cantando
    (B) ganando
    (C) llorando
    (D) pintando

K-3RAC

GO ON TO THE NEXT PAGE

12. Cuando ------- el ruido, recorrí la casa para asegurarme de que nadie había entrado.

    (A) oigo
    (B) oí
    (C) oiré
    (D) oía

13. Es necesario conducir con las luces ------- a causa de la niebla.

    (A) encendidas
    (B) abiertas
    (C) despiertas
    (D) extendidas

14. Elena, tienes que estudiar más si quieres ------- buenas calificaciones.

    (A) pasar
    (B) escoger
    (C) agarrar
    (D) sacar

15. Lo siento, señor. No se incluyen ------- con la comida.

    (A) pastillas
    (B) postres
    (C) datos
    (D) desiertos

16. Es imprescindible ------- por casa antes de ir al concierto.

    (A) pase
    (B) pasar
    (C) pasaré
    (D) pasara

17. Juan, es mejor que compres un billete -------.

    (A) sin querer
    (B) sin sentido
    (C) de ida y vuelta
    (D) de arriba abajo

18. ------- no tengo dinero porque se lo di todo a mi prima Diana ayer.

    (A) Nunca
    (B) Pronto
    (C) Ya
    (D) Más

19. Le darán la medalla a la ------- persona que termine el partido.

    (A) una
    (B) primera
    (C) primero
    (D) primaria

20. En 1956 el poeta español Juan Ramón Jiménez ganó ------- Nóbel de literatura.

    (A) el precio
    (B) la prisa
    (C) el premio
    (D) la prenda

21. No perder el vuelo a Santo Domingo es ------- importante ahora.

    (A) la
    (B) el
    (C) lo
    (D) le

22. Cuando ------- se oyó la explosión, todos se asustaron.

    (A) de repente
    (B) con ganas
    (C) muy despacio
    (D) de todos modos

23. Me daba muchísima lástima verla llorar tan -------.

    (A) claramente
    (B) amargamente
    (C) astutamente
    (D) personalmente

24. El Amazonas es el río más ------- del continente sudamericano.

    (A) mojado
    (B) gordo
    (C) grueso
    (D) ancho

GO ON TO THE NEXT PAGE

25. Pensaba que ese regalo era para ------, pero me equivoqué.

   (A) conmigo
   (B) yo
   (C) mí
   (D) me

26. Antes de una competencia deportiva, ------ a los participantes de cada equipo.

   (A) se presente
   (B) presentándose
   (C) hayan presentado
   (D) se presenta

27. Pocos saben que Colombia ------ el primer país que desarrolló la aviación comercial.

   (A) fue
   (B) era
   (C) será
   (D) sea

28. Cuando Cortés quemó sus barcos, sus hombres no pudieron ni huir, ni rebelarse ------.

   (A) además
   (B) tampoco
   (C) siempre
   (D) también

29. La industria automovilística requiere ------ toneladas de hierro.

   (A) miles de
   (B) ciento de
   (C) cientos
   (D) millones

30. A él y a mí nos ------ veinte minutos para terminar la tarea.

   (A) falta
   (B) faltan
   (C) faltamos
   (D) falten

31. Es verdad que el director ------ mañana.

   (A) vuelva
   (B) salió
   (C) terminaría
   (D) regresa

32. Carmencita, ------ la chaqueta gruesa porque hace mucho frío en las pistas de esquiar.

   (A) se ponga
   (B) te pongas
   (C) ponte
   (D) pusiste

GO ON TO THE NEXT PAGE

Part B

Directions: In each of the following paragraphs, there are numbered blanks indicating that words or phrases have been omitted. For each numbered blank, four completions are provided. First read through the entire paragraph. Then, for each numbered blank, choose the completion that is most appropriate given the context of the entire passage and fill in the corresponding oval on the answer sheet.

Fermina Daza se __(33)__ un vestido de seda, amplio y suelto, un collar de __(34)__ legítimas con seis vueltas largas y desiguales, unos zapatos con __(35)__ altos que sólo usaba en ocasiones muy __(36)__, pues ya los años no le daban para __(37)__ abusos. Aquel atuendo de moda no parecía __(38)__ para una abuela venerable, pero le __(39)__ muy bien a su cuerpo de huesos largos, todavía delgado y recto. Lo que le faltaba por la edad le alcanzaba por el carácter y le __(40)__ por la sabiduría.

33. (A) había puesto
    (B) haya puesto
    (C) pone
    (D) pondrá

34. (A) peras
    (B) perlas
    (C) papas
    (D) patas

35. (A) telones
    (B) tacones
    (C) hilos
    (D) suelos

36. (A) solemnes
    (B) capaces
    (C) deportivas
    (D) pacientes

37. (A) ningún
    (B) menos de
    (C) tantos
    (D) así como

38. (A) adecuar
    (B) adecuada
    (C) adecuando
    (D) adecuado

39. (A) vaya
    (B) fuera
    (C) irá
    (D) iba

40. (A) parecía
    (B) sobraba
    (C) buscaba
    (D) alarmaba

GO ON TO THE NEXT PAGE

Buenos Aires. — Un grupo de investigadores,

__(41)__ por el profesor Héctor Schenone, ha

localizado una __(42)__ del pintor español Francisco

de Goya en un depósito del Museo de Bellas Artes

de Argentina, a __(43)__ fue a parar hace dieciséis

años sin que los expertos __(44)__ el nombre de su

verdadero autor. El __(45)__ , titulado *Torero José*

Romero, ha sido valorado __(46)__ 300 y 600 millones

de pesetas, __(47)__ 90 por 75 centímetros y, __(48)__

el director del museo, es la obra de un Goya joven,

bohemio, que lo __(49)__ a finales del siglo XVIII o

__(50)__ del XIX.

41. (A) escrito
    (B) tomado
    (C) encabezado
    (D) abierto

42. (A) obra
    (B) cuadra
    (C) pinta
    (D) lata

43. (A) cual
    (B) cuanto
    (C) cuando
    (D) donde

44. (A) conocen
    (B) conocieran
    (C) conozcan
    (D) conocieron

45. (A) cuadro
    (B) palo
    (C) hombre
    (D) marco

46. (A) entre
    (B) como
    (C) contra
    (D) más

47. (A) vale
    (B) mide
    (C) queda
    (D) hace

48. (A) porque
    (B) sin
    (C) según
    (D) desde

49. (A) grabó
    (B) compró
    (C) oyó
    (D) pintó

50. (A) términos
    (B) salidas
    (C) principios
    (D) medidas

GO ON TO THE NEXT PAGE

Llevaba nada más una __(51)__ grande y muy pesada. Había __(52)__ sus libros, sus discos, sus adornos y se había traído __(53)__ lo más elemental y necesario. Caminaba por los pasillos del tren con ojos de angustia. El vagón donde ella se había subido iba __(54)__ . Uno de los empleados cogió su equipaje, miró su boleto y la __(55)__ hasta el último vagón, en la última alcoba, que era la que le correspondía.

Estela viajaba a Veracruz. Una de sus ilusiones había sido, __(56)__ de estudiar, irse a vivir con Rosario, a la que no veía __(57)__ que se casó. Las dos eran primas y crecieron juntas. __(58)__ muchísimo, tanto que cuando estaba cada quien por su parte las confundían a una con la otra.

51. (A) chuleta
    (B) muleta
    (C) maleta
    (D) raqueta

52. (A) dejado
    (B) dejados
    (C) dejando
    (D) dejarlos

53. (A) pero
    (B) tanto
    (C) solo
    (D) sólo

54. (A) lleno
    (B) distraído
    (C) sobrado
    (D) cansado

55. (A) mostró
    (B) multó
    (C) condujo
    (D) declaró

56. (A) mientras
    (B) además
    (C) aunque
    (D) durante

57. (A) cuando
    (B) casi
    (C) sin
    (D) desde

58. (A) Se parecían
    (B) Se admiraban
    (C) Se establecían
    (D) Se visitaban

GO ON TO THE NEXT PAGE

Part C

Directions: Read the following texts carefully for comprehension. Each is followed by a number of questions or incomplete statements. Select the answer or completion that is best according to the text and fill in the corresponding oval on the answer sheet.

Mi padre acababa de sentarse con más facilidad de la que había tenido. Permaneció unos momentos silencioso.

Línea
(5) Las muchachas lo miraban atemorizadas.

—Voy allá—exclamó él al fin—; voy al instante.

Buscó algo sobre la cama, y dirigiéndose a mí preguntó:

—Mi ropa . . . ¿Dónde está la ropa?

(10) —Es que no está aquí—le respondí—; han ido a traerla.

—¿Para qué se la han llevado?

—La habrán ido a cambiar por otra.

—Pero ¿qué tardanza es ésta?—dijo, secándose el
(15) sudor de la frente—. ¿Los caballos están listos?
—continuó.

—Sí, señor.

—Vaya y dígale a Efraín que lo espero para que montemos antes de que se haga tarde. ¡Muévase,
(20) hombre!

Y se acercaba al borde de la cama para saltar al suelo; María se aproximó a él diciéndole:

—No, papá; no haga eso.

—¿Qué?—le respondió con dureza.

(25) —Que si se levanta se impacientará el doctor, porque le hará a usted mal.

—¿Qué doctor?

—Pues el médico que ha venido a verlo, porque usted está enfermo.

(30) —¡Pero si estoy bueno! ¿Oyes? Bueno, y quiero levantarme.

59. Esta escena tiene lugar en

(A) la tienda de ropa
(B) la alcoba de una casa
(C) la oficina del médico
(D) el establo de una finca

60. ¿Cómo reaccionan las muchachas hacia el padre?

(A) Le tienen miedo.
(B) Lo dejan solo.
(C) No le hacen caso.
(D) Se burlan de él.

61. ¿Qué está buscando el padre en la cama?

(A) Unas medicinas
(B) Una almohada
(C) Algo para vestirse
(D) Algo para fumar

62. ¿Qué quiere el padre que haga Efraín?

(A) Que llame al médico
(B) Que monte a caballo con él
(C) Que le traiga la ropa
(D) Que lo visite al día siguiente

63. ¿Qué palabra describe mejor el comportamiento del padre en esta escena?

(A) Impaciente
(B) Vacilante
(C) Comprensivo
(D) Juguetón

64. ¿Cuál es la relación entre el narrador y el enfermo?

(A) Son padre e hijo.
(B) Son amo y criado.
(C) Son médico y paciente.
(D) Son amigos.

GO ON TO THE NEXT PAGE

La Televisión privada ya está aquí. A partir de ahora, se recomienda permanezcan en sus casas. Porque en Antena 3 Televisión usted podrá contemplar las apariciones más extraordinarias, los más formidables monstruos y los fenómenos más sorprendentes.

televisión
a3
antena 3
La Nueva Televisión

65. ¿De qué podrán disfrutar los televidentes?

(A) De una programación continua
(B) De las películas más recientes
(C) De programas llamativos
(D) De tres canales nuevos

GO ON TO THE NEXT PAGE

En el Uruguay, el carnaval es la fecha en que ríe el calendario. Las penas y alegrías se visten de colores y, detrás de la careta de cartón moldeado, se vuelca por

Línea espacio de días toda la población, a vivir con intensidad
(5) un mundo distinto . . . un mundo entre sueños, que a muchos ayuda a recordar y a otros a olvidar.

El color del carnaval uruguayo invade todos los barrios y las largas arterias de Montevideo, por donde se mueve la vida de todas sus gentes. Todo — la calle,
(10) el suburbio, la playa y el campo — se cubre de tonos alegres que se mueven al viento, en la serpentina o en el papelito que baila de ventana en ventana.

El carnaval del Uruguay llega a lo más hondo del corazón del pueblo, de un pueblo que se lanza frenético
(15) al mar de entusiasmo que inunda las calles, sobre todo en esa noche inolvidable en que, a través de una muralla de música, llega el Rey Momo para gobernar la fiesta. La fiesta atrae a cientos de viajeros que, mezclando idiomas, son bienvenidos a la contagiosa
(20) risa que la *mascarada* trae consigo. Y es que el carnaval, como si fuera un torneo de alegría, va formando en cada barrio una comparsa. Y todos se lanzan a esa ola de entusiasmo que cubre durante muchos días al país.

66. ¿De qué trata el artículo?

(A) Del impacto de una fiesta a nivel nacional
(B) Del significado de un festival regional
(C) Del espíritu festivo de un barrio
(D) Del entusiasmo religioso de una zona

67. ¿Cuál es el propósito del autor?

(A) Describir
(B) Burlarse
(C) Persuadir
(D) Entretener

68. Según el artículo, ¿qué efecto tiene el carnaval del Uruguay?

(A) Produce mucho dinero.
(B) Asusta a los turistas.
(C) Para el tráfico.
(D) Anima a la gente.

69. ¿Qué suele llevar la gente durante el carnaval?

(A) Vestimenta ordinaria
(B) Máscaras de cartón
(C) Disfraces infantiles
(D) Sombreros de colores vivos

70. El tono de esta selección es

(A) misterioso
(B) entusiasta
(C) enigmático
(D) filosófico

71. ¿Por cuánto tiempo dura la celebración?

(A) Una noche
(B) Un mes
(C) Muchos días
(D) Todo el año

GO ON TO THE NEXT PAGE

Se ha señalado que el horario español, con un almuerzo a las dos y media o tres de la tarde y una cena entre las diez y las once, trae complicaciones. Por ejemplo, las horas de trabajo, largamente interrumpidas,

Línea
(5) se prolongan durante casi todo el día. Pero cada vez me parece más interesante, y más favorable a la felicidad de la vida diaria, esa "mañana" española que llega hasta las dos, y esa interminable "tarde" que se extiende hasta las diez de la noche, y que deja tiempo libre para tanta

(10) conversación u otras ocupaciones agradables.

El horario norteamericano está en el extremo opuesto y tiene consecuencias más graves de lo que podría esperarse. En principio, se termina de trabajar a las cinco y se cena a las seis o seis y media; se entiende

(15) que no termina entonces el día, sino que empieza el tiempo libre o "propio". Después de la comida se hace lo que se quiere hacer, no lo que hay que hacer. Pero no ocurre así. El norteamericano, al salir de su trabajo, busca su coche donde está estacionado, conduce largo

(20) rato, por carreteras de intenso tráfico, hasta llegar a casa; o va a la estación, toma el tren suburbano, recorre muchas millas, encuentra su coche en la población donde vive y llega por fin a casa. Toma quizá una bebida, cena y . . . descubre que está cansado. No tiene

(25) ganas de volver al automóvil, volver a conducir largo rato por la carretera, hasta el espectáculo, el concierto o la casa de los amigos; y termina por encender la televisión y quedarse en casa. El día, que en teoría no termina con la cena, en realidad acaba con ella; la

(30) diferencia está en que, en lugar de terminar, como entre los españoles a las diez o diez y media, termina a las seis.

72. En comparación con las horas de las comidas en los Estados Unidos, ¿cómo es el horario español?

(A) Se come el almuerzo más temprano y la cena más tarde.
(B) Se come el almuerzo más tarde y la cena más temprano.
(C) Se comen el almuerzo y la cena más tarde.
(D) Se comen el almuerzo y la cena más temprano.

73. Se puede deducir de esta selección que los españoles tienen la costumbre de

(A) trabajar relativamente cerca de casa
(B) dejar poco tiempo para conversar
(C) disfrutar de profesiones agradables
(D) salir del trabajo a las once

74. Según el artículo, cuando los norteamericanos regresan a su casa, quieren

(A) salir otra vez
(B) descansar en su hogar
(C) reunirse con amigos
(D) seguir trabajando

75. Se puede deducir que el horario español favorece

(A) las actividades sociales
(B) la vida deportiva
(C) el cansancio prolongado
(D) los trabajos interminables

76. El punto de vista del autor sugiere que él prefiere

(A) el horario norteamericano
(B) el sistema español
(C) una combinación de ambos horarios
(D) una nueva alternativa

GO ON TO THE NEXT PAGE

Nací entre mangos, guayabas y almendras, en la casita que mi papá había construido con sus propias manos en la propiedad del club de cazadores. Papi era
Línea el encargado del club y, como tal, tenía que vivir en el
(5) local mismo para poder cuidarlo día y noche. Al casarse, mis padres se instalaron en la "casita vieja", como ha pasado a llamarse en nuestros recuerdos.

Dieciocho meses después de nacida yo, llegó mi hermano Pepín. ¡Qué dichosos éramos en los vastos
(10) terrenos del club! Vivíamos en un mundo de fantasía y. libertad absolutas, corriendo por el pasto recién cortado por papi, subiéndonos a los árboles de mango para saborear a plenitud el fruto delicioso, o jugando con Misula, nuestra fiel perrita.

(15) Hoy sigue transportándome al club de mi niñez el olor de las guayabas, los mangos y las almendras verdes. Pero el club es ahora un cuartel militar, y hombres vestidos de verde olivo ultrajan con sus pisadas duras la hierba que con tanto amor y sacrificio
(20) cortara mi padre. Desde el Norte miro hacia el Sur, y veo entre lágrimas el mar que me separa de ese terruño, paraíso de palomas nostálgicas. ¡Ay, el olor de la guayaba, el mango y las almendras tiernas! Hace unos cuarenta años que vengo nutriéndome de ese recuerdo.

77. ¿Por qué era tan especial la "casita vieja" (línea 6) para la narradora?

(A) Porque fue construida en el club
(B) Porque fue la casa donde nació
(C) Porque se llama así en sus recuerdos
(D) Porque era propiedad de su padre

78. ¿Cómo fue la niñez de la narradora?

(A) Despreocupada
(B) Rebelde
(C) Peligrosa
(D) Acomodada

79. Los niños subían a los árboles para

(A) tener más libertad
(B) cortarlos mejor
(C) jugar con sus amigos
(D) comer mangos

80. ¿Por qué vivían en el club?

(A) Porque sus padres nacieron allí
(B) Porque el transporte era malo
(C) Porque el padre lo atendía
(D) Porque allí eran dichosos

81. ¿Qué le trae recuerdos del club a la narradora?

(A) Ciertos aromas familiares
(B) Los hombres vestidos de verde
(C) Las memorias de su padre
(D) Las palomas que ve pasar

82. ¿Qué ha pasado con el club?

(A) Ha sido abandonado por todos.
(B) Ha sido ocupado por soldados.
(C) Se han construido muchas casas.
(D) Se mantiene igual que antes.

83. ¿Dónde vive la narradora ahora?

(A) En la costa norte de su país
(B) Cerca de un cuartel militar
(C) Lejos del lugar donde creció
(D) En un lugar donde hay árboles frutales

84. ¿Qué siente la narradora hacia los "hombres vestidos de verde olivo" (línea 18) ?

(A) Desprecio
(B) Indiferencia
(C) Compasión
(D) Envidia

85. ¿Cuándo ocurrió lo que recuerda la narradora?

(A) Hace unas semanas
(B) El mes anterior
(C) El año anterior
(D) Hace cuatro décadas

S T O P

IF YOU FINISH BEFORE TIME IS CALLED, YOU MAY CHECK YOUR WORK ON THIS TEST ONLY.
DO NOT TURN TO ANY OTHER TEST IN THIS BOOK.

How to Score the SAT Subject Test in Spanish

When you take an actual SAT Subject Test in Spanish, your answer sheet will be "read" by a scanning machine that will record your responses to each question. Then a computer will compare your answers with the correct answers and produce your raw score. You get one point for each correct answer. For each wrong answer, you lose one-third of a point. Questions you omit (and any for which you mark more than one answer) are not counted. This raw score is converted to a scaled score that is reported to you and to the colleges you specify

Worksheet 1. Finding Your Raw Reading Test Score

STEP 1: Table A lists the correct answers for all the questions on the SAT Subject Test in Spanish that is reproduced in this book. It also serves as a worksheet for you to calculate your raw score.

- Compare your answers with those given in the table.
- Put a check in the column marked "Right" if your answer is correct.
- Put a check in the column marked "Wrong" if your answer is incorrect.
- Leave both columns blank if you omitted the question.

STEP 2: Count the number of right answers.

Enter the total here: _____

STEP 3: Count the number of wrong answers.

Enter the total here: _____

STEP 4: Multiply the number of wrong answers by .333.

Enter the total here: _____

STEP 5: Subtract the result obtained in Step 4 from the total you obtained in Step 2.

Enter the result here: _____

STEP 6: Round the number obtained in Step 5 to the nearest whole number.

Enter the result here: _____

The number you obtained in Step 6 is your raw score.

TABLE A

Answers to the SAT Subject Test in Spanish, Form K-3RAC, and
Percentage of Students Answering Each Question Correctly

Question Number	Correct Answer	Right	Wrong	Percentage of Students Answering the Question Correctly*	Question Number	Correct Answer	Right	Wrong	Percentage of Students Answering the Question Correctly*
1	C			95	33	A			42
2	A			89	34	B			79
3	D			91	35	B			48
4	D			90	36	A			55
5	A			82	37	C			57
6	B			77	38	D			29
7	D			75	39	D			55
8	D			70	40	B			26
9	A			66	41	C			52
10	D			73	42	A			53
11	C			83	43	D			60
12	B			80	44	B			31
13	A			67	45	A			71
14	D			80	46	A			74
15	B			75	47	B			55
16	B			69	48	C			66
17	C			72	49	D			78
18	C			77	50	C			59
19	B			94	51	C			65
20	C			65	52	A			70
21	C			66	53	D			39
22	A			57	54	A			50
23	B			40	55	C			22
24	D			53	56	B			31
25	C			87	57	D			52
26	D			59	58	A			39
27	A			53	59	B			61
28	B			62	60	A			55
29	A			36	61	C			82
30	B			32	62	B			60
31	D			44	63	A			85
32	C			54	64	A			81

Table A continued on next page

Table A continued from previous page

Question Number	Correct Answer	Right	Wrong	Percentage of Students Answering the Question Correctly*	Question Number	Correct Answer	Right	Wrong	Percentage of Students Answering the Question Correctly*
65	C			52	76	B			66
66	A			48	77	B			40
67	A			84	78	A			38
68	D			77	79	D			83
69	B			56	80	C			69
70	B			89	81	A			60
71	C			68	82	B			79
72	C			82	83	C			28
73	A			55	84	A			50
74	B			65	85	D			88
75	A			68					

*These percentages are based on an analysis of the answer sheets for a random sample of 1,925 students who took this form of the test in May 1996 and whose mean score was 570. They may be used as an indication of the relative difficulty of a particular question. Each percentage may also be used to predict the likelihood that a typical SAT Subject Test in Spanish candidate will answer correctly that question on this edition of this test.

Finding Your Scaled Score

When you take SAT Subject Tests, the scores sent to the colleges you specify are reported on the College Board scale, which ranges from 200 to 800. You can convert your practice test score to a scaled score by using Table B. To find your scaled score, locate your raw score in the left-hand column of Table B; the corresponding score in the right-hand column is your scaled score. For example, a raw score of 53 on this particular edition of the SAT Subject Test in Spanish corresponds to a scaled score of 630.

Raw scores are converted to scaled scores to ensure that a score earned on any one edition of a particular Subject Test is comparable to the same scaled score earned on any other edition of the same Subject Test. Because some editions of tests may be slightly easier or more difficult than others, scaled scores are adjusted so that they indicate the same level of performance regardless of the edition of the test taken and the ability of the group that takes it. Thus, for example, a score of 400 on one edition of a test taken at a particular administration indicates the same level of achievement as a score of 400 on a different edition of the test taken at a different administration.

When you take the SAT Subject Tests during a national administration, your scores are likely to differ somewhat from the scores you obtain on the tests in this book. People perform at different levels at different times for reasons unrelated to the tests themselves. The precision of any test is also limited because it represents only a sample of all the possible questions that could be asked.

TABLE B

Scaled Score Conversion Table
Spanish Subject Test (Form K-3RAC)

Raw Score	Scaled Score	Raw Score	Scaled Score	Raw Score	Scaled Score
85	800	47	590	9	360
84	800	46	580	8	360
83	800	45	570	7	350
82	800	44	570	6	350
81	790	43	560	5	340
80	790	42	550	4	340
79	780	41	550	3	330
78	780	40	540	2	320
77	770	39	530	1	320
76	770	38	530	0	310
75	760	37	520	−1	310
74	760	36	520	−2	300
73	750	35	510	−3	290
72	750	34	500	−4	290
71	740	33	500	−5	280
70	730	32	490	−6	270
69	730	31	490	−7	260
68	720	30	480	−8	260
67	720	29	470	−9	250
66	710	28	470	−10	240
65	700	27	460	−11	230
64	700	26	460	−12	220
63	690	25	450	−13	220
62	680	24	450	−14	220
61	680	23	440	−15	210
60	670	22	430	−16	210
59	670	21	430	−17	210
58	660	20	420	−18	200
57	650	19	420	−19	200
56	650	18	410	−20	200
55	640	17	410	−21	200
54	630	16	400	−22	200
53	630	15	400	−23	200
52	620	14	390	−24	200
51	620	13	390	−25	200
50	610	12	380	−26	200
49	600	11	380	−27	200
48	590	10	370	−28	200

Reviewing Your Performance
on the Spanish Subject Test

After you score your test, analyze your performance—consider the following questions:

Did you run out of time before reaching the end of the test?

If so, you may need to pace yourself better. For example, maybe you spent too much time on one or two hard questions. A better approach might be to skip the ones you can't answer right away and try answering all the questions that remain on the test. Then if there's time, go back to the questions you skipped.

Did you take a long time reading the directions?

You will save time when you take the test by learning the directions to the Spanish Subject Test ahead of time. Each minute you spend reading directions during the test is a minute that you could use to answer questions.

How did you handle questions you were unsure of?

If you were able to eliminate one or more of the answer choices as wrong and guess from the remaining choices, your approach probably worked to your advantage. On the other hand, making haphazard guesses or omitting questions without trying to eliminate choices could cost you valuable points.

How difficult were the questions for you compared with other students who took the test?

Table A shows you how difficult the multiple-choice questions were for the group of students who took this test during its national administration. The right-hand column gives the percentage of students that answered each question correctly.

A question answered correctly by almost everyone in the group is obviously an easy question. For example, 94 percent of the students answered question 19 correctly. But only 22 percent answered question 55 correctly.

Keep in mind that these percentages are based on just one group of students and would probably be different if another group of students took the test.

If you missed several easy questions, go back and try to find out why: Did the questions cover material you haven't reviewed yet? Did you misunderstand the directions?

Spanish with Listening

The SAT Subject Test in Spanish with Listening is offered once a year only at designated test centers. To take the test you MUST bring an acceptable cassette player with earphones to the test center.

A cassette tape with listening questions is available for the practice Spanish Subject Test with Listening in this book. To receive your copy, complete and mail the postcard in this book. If the postcard has been removed, call 212 649-8424, or write to:

The College Board

Subject Tests Language Listening Cassette

45 Columbus Avenue

New York, New York 10023-6992

You must indicate the SAT Language Subject Test with Listening you plan to take.

Sample Listening Questions

Please note that the cassette does not start here. Begin using the cassette when you start the actual practice test on page 712.

Please note that your answer sheet has five answer positions marked A, B, C, D, E, while the questions throughout this test contain only four choices. Be sure NOT to make any marks in column E.

Part A

Directions: For each item in this part, you will hear four sentences designated (A), (B), (C), and (D), represented below in brackets ([ ]). The answer choices will not be printed in your test booklet. As you listen, look at the picture in your test booklet and select the choice that best reflects what you see in the picture or what someone in the picture might say. Then fill in the corresponding oval on the answer sheet. You will hear the choices only once. Now look at the following example.

You see:

You hear:

(Woman) [(A) Siento darles tan mala noticia.

(B) Tiene quince días para pagar la multa.

(C) Y aquí les mando la foto más reciente.

(D) Es preciso que se presente ante el juez.]

(7 seconds)

Choice (C), "Y aquí les mando la foto más reciente," best reflects what you see in the picture or what someone in the picture might say. Therefore, you would choose answer (C).

Now we will begin. Look at the first picture and listen to the four choices.

(Narrator)	[Número 1]
(Man)	[**(A)** ¡Otro micrófono, por favor!
	(B) La guitarra no tiene cuerdas.
	(C) Adiós, ya estoy aburrido.
	(D) ¡Cantemos todos juntos!]

(7 seconds)

Question 1 tests listening comprehension. Choice (D) *¡Cantemos todos juntos!* is the correct answer. To answer correctly, you need to recognize that (D) best reflects what the person in the photograph might say. The wrong choices, (A), (B), and (C), do not reflect what the singer might say in this instance.

Part B

Directions: In this part of the test you will hear several short conversations, or parts of conversations, followed by four choices designated (A), (B), (C), and (D). After you hear the four choices, choose the one that most logically continues or completes the conversation and mark your answer on your answer sheet. What you see in brackets ([ ]) will not be printed in your test booklet. Now listen to the following example.

You will hear:

(Man)	[Yo creo que leer es muy importante.]

You will also hear:

(Woman)	[(A) Pues no leas tanto.
	(B) Estoy totalmente de acuerdo.
	(C) No te acuerdas de nada.
	(D) No me importan esas leyes.]

(7 seconds)

The choice that most logically continues the conversation is (B), "Estoy totalmente de acuerdo." Therefore, you should choose answer (B). Now listen to the first conversation.

(Narrator)	[Número 2]
(Woman)	[Llegaste tarde; ¡ya no quedan entradas para esa obra!]
(Man)	(A) Qué entradas tan caras!
	(B) Hay otra puerta por aquí.
	(C) Perdona, se atrasó el autobús.
	(D) A la izquierda está la entrada.]

(7 seconds)

Question 2 tests listening comprehension. Choice (C) *Perdona, se atrasó el autobús.* is the correct choice. To answer correctly, you need to recognize that (C) is the most appropriate response to the woman's statement. The wrong choices, (A), (B), and (D), are inappropriate responses to the woman's statement that there are no tickets left for the performance.

Part C

Directions: You will now hear a series of selections. For each selection, you will see printed in your test booklet one or more questions with four possible answers. They will not be spoken. Select the best answer to each question from among the four choices printed and fill in the corresponding oval on your answer sheet. You will have 12 seconds to answer each question. There will be no example for this part. Now listen to the first selection.

(Narrator)	[Selección Número 1. Escuchen esta conversación en la recepción del Hotel California.]
(Man)	[Hola, buenas tardes, señorita. ¿Tiene Ud. una reservación a nombre de Escalante?
(Woman)	Déjeme ver. Mmm. . . No la veo, señor. ¿La hizo directamente con nosotros?
(Man)	Sí, con ustedes. Aquí tengo la confirmación.
(Woman)	Pues, señor, el problema es que el hotel está lleno y no quedan habitaciones.
(Man)	Pero, ¿qué hago yo? He pagado un depósito.
(Woman)	Un momento, por favor. Llamaré al gerente para solucionar el problema.]
(Narrator)	[Ahora contesten las preguntas 3 y 4.]

(24 seconds)

3. ¿Qué problema tiene el Sr. Escalante?

   (A) Perdió su confirmación.

   (B) No quiere alojarse en el Hotel California.

   (C) El hotel no tiene su reservación.

   (D) Olvidó pagar el depósito.

4. ¿Cómo trata la recepcionista al Sr. Escalante?

   (A) Bruscamente.

   (B) Respetuosamente.

   (C) Insolentemente.

   (D) Alegremente.

Question 3 tests listening comprehension. Choice (C) *El hotel no tiene su reservación.* is the correct choice. To answer correctly, you need to recognize that Sr. Escalante's problem is that the hotel does not have his reservation. He made a reservation, paid a deposit, and received a confirmation from the hotel; therefore (A), (B), and (D) are incorrect.

Question 4 tests listening comprehension. Choice (B) *Respetuosamente* is the correct answer. To answer correctly, you need to recognize that the receptionist treats Sr. Escalante respectfully in trying to help him. The wrong choices, (A), (C), and (D), do not accurately describe her manner towards him during the conversation.

Spanish Test with Listening

The test that follows is an actual, recently administered SAT Subject Test in Spanish with Listening. To get an idea of what a real administration is like, take the test under conditions as close as possible to those of a national administration:

- Set aside an hour when you can take the test uninterrupted. Make sure you complete the test in one sitting.

- Sit at a desk or table with no other books or papers. Dictionaries, other books, or notes are not allowed in the test room.

- Time yourself by placing a clock or kitchen timer in front of you.

- Tear out an answer sheet from the back of this book and fill it in just as you would on the day of the test. One answer sheet can be used for up to three Subject Tests.

- Read the instructions that precede the practice test. During the actual administration you will be asked to read them before answering test questions.

- After you finish the practice test, read the sections "How to Score the SAT Subject Test in Spanish with Listening" and "Reviewing Your Performance on the Spanish Subject Test with Listening."

- Actual test and answer sheets will indicate circles, not ovals.

Form 3QLC

SPANISH TEST WITH LISTENING

The top portion of the section of the answer sheet that you will use in taking the Spanish Test with Listening must be filled in exactly as shown in the illustration below. Note carefully that you have to do all of the following on your answer sheet.

1. Print SPANISH WITH LISTENING on the line under the words "Subject Test (print)."

2. In the shaded box labeled "Test Code" fill in four ovals:

    —Fill in oval 5 in the row labeled V.

    —Fill in oval 1 in the row labeled W.

    —Fill in oval 4 in the row labeled X.

    —Fill in oval B in the row labeled Y.

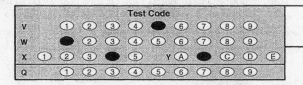

Please answer either Part I or Part II by filling in the specific oval in row Q. You are to fill in ONE and ONLY ONE oval, as described below, to indicate how you obtained your knowledge of Spanish. The information you provide is for statistical purposes only and will not influence your score on the test.

Part I   If your knowledge of Spanish does not come primarily from courses taken in grades 9 through 12, fill in oval 9 and leave the remaining ovals blank, regardless of how long you studied the subject in school. For example, you are to fill in oval 9 if your knowledge of Spanish comes primarily from any of the following sources: study prior to the ninth grade, courses taken at a college, special study, living in a home in which Spanish is the principal language spoken, or extensive residence abroad that includes significant experience in the Spanish language.

Part II   If your knowledge of Spanish does come primarily from courses taken in secondary school, fill in the oval that indicates the level of the Spanish course in which you are currently enrolled. If you are not now enrolled in a Spanish course, fill in the oval that indicates the level of the most advanced course in Spanish that you have completed.

First year:	first or second half	—Fill in oval 1.
Second year:	first half	—Fill in oval 2.
	second half	—Fill in oval 3.
Third year:	first half	—Fill in oval 4.
	second half	—Fill in oval 5.
Fourth year:	first half	—Fill in oval 6.
	second half	—Fill in oval 7.

Advanced Placement course
or a course at a level higher
than fourth year, second half
        or
high school course work plus
a minimum of four weeks of
study abroad.   —Fill in oval 8.

When the supervisor gives the signal, turn the page and begin the Spanish Test with Listening. There are 100 numbered ovals on the answer sheet and 85 questions in the Spanish Test with Listening. Therefore, use only ovals 1 to 85 for recording your answers.

SPANISH TEST WITH LISTENING

PLEASE NOTE THAT YOUR ANSWER SHEET HAS FIVE ANSWER POSITIONS, MARKED A, B, C, D, AND E, WHILE THE QUESTIONS THROUGHOUT THIS TEST CONTAIN ONLY FOUR CHOICES. BE SURE <u>NOT</u> TO MAKE ANY MARKS IN COLUMN E.

SECTION I

LISTENING

Approximate time—20 minutes

Questions 1-33

Part A

<u>Directions:</u> For each question in this part, you will hear four sentences, designated (A), (B), (C), and (D). They will not be printed in your test booklet. As you listen, look at the picture in your test booklet and select the choice that best reflects what you see in the picture or what someone in the picture might say. Then fill in the corresponding oval on the answer sheet. You will hear the choices only once. Now look at the following example.

You see:

You hear:

Statement (C), "Y aquí les mando la foto más reciente," best reflects what you see in the picture or what someone in the picture might say. Therefore, you would choose answer (C). Now we will begin. Look at the first picture and listen to the four choices.

GO ON TO THE NEXT PAGE

3QLC

1.

U. Welsch Photo Researchers, Inc.

2.

Reuters / Bettmann

3.

E. Stone/Photo Researchers, Inc.

4.

Reuters/Bettmann Newsphotos

GO ON TO THE NEXT PAGE →

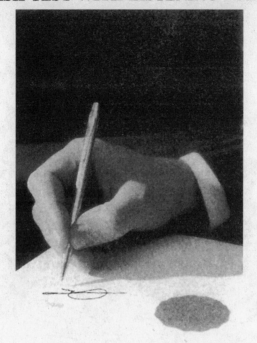

5.

G. Haling/Photo Researchers, Inc.

6.

UPI/Bettmann Newsphotos

GO ON TO THE NEXT PAGE

7.

R. Ellis Photo Researchers, Inc.

8.

Explorer/Photo Researchers, Inc.

GO ON TO THE NEXT PAGE ➤

9.

The Bettmann Archive

10.

T. Davis/Photo Researchers, Inc.

GO ON TO THE NEXT PAGE →

Part B

Directions: In this part of the test you will hear several short conversations or parts of conversations, followed by four choices, designated (A), (B), (C), and (D). After you hear the four choices, choose the one that most logically continues or completes the conversation and mark your answer on your answer sheet. Neither the conversations nor the choices will be printed in your test booklet. Now listen to the following example.

You will hear:

You will also hear:

The choice that most logically continues the conversation is (B), "Estoy totalmente de acuerdo." Therefore, you should choose answer (B). Now listen to the first conversation.

11. Mark your answer on your answer sheet.

12. Mark your answer on your answer sheet.

13. Mark your answer on your answer sheet.

14. Mark your answer on your answer sheet.

15. Mark your answer on your answer sheet.

16. Mark your answer on your answer sheet.

17. Mark your answer on your answer sheet.

18. Mark your answer on your answer sheet.

19. Mark your answer on your answer sheet.

20. Mark your answer on your answer sheet.

GO ON TO THE NEXT PAGE

Part C

Directions: You will now hear a series of selections. For each selection, you will see printed in your test booklet one or more questions with four possible answers. They will not be spoken. Select the best answer to each question from among the four choices printed and fill in the corresponding oval on your answer sheet. You will have twelve seconds to answer each question. There will be no example for this part. Now listen to the first selection.

Selección número 1.

21. ¿A quién llama la señora?

   (A) A la psiquiatra.
   (B) A la veterinaria.
   (C) A la cirujana.
   (D) A la dentista.

Selección número 2.

22. ¿Qué problema tiene Andrés?

   (A) No le gustan las fiestas de cumpleaños.
   (B) No quiere ir a la fiesta sin regalo.
   (C) No comprende a Melinda.
   (D) Teme llegar tarde.

23. ¿Qué pasó por fin?

   (A) Andrés decidió llevarle flores a Melinda.
   (B) Paula le sugirió a Andrés que comprara flores.
   (C) A Melinda no le gustaron las flores.
   (D) Melinda le llevó rosas a Andrés.

Selección número 3.

24. ¿Qué planes tiene el presidente de los Estados Unidos?

   (A) Ir de vacaciones a México.
   (B) Iniciar un intercambio cultural.
   (C) Firmar un tratado comercial.
   (D) Reunirse con representantes del gobierno mexicano.

25. ¿Qué resultados se esperan del viaje?

   (A) Establecer becas de estudio.
   (B) Pasar leyes contra las drogas.
   (C) Proteger el medio ambiente.
   (D) Mejorar el comercio.

Selección número 4.

26. Según la candidata, ¿qué deben hacer sus compatriotas?

   (A) Trabajar más.
   (B) Ser más patrióticos.
   (C) Elegirla a ella.
   (D) Combatir la inflación.

Selección número 5.

27. ¿Por qué está Silvia en la tienda de música?

   (A) Porque tiene una cita con Raúl.
   (B) Porque tiene que hacer una tarea para su clase.
   (C) Porque tiene mucho tiempo libre.
   (D) Porque va a tener una fiesta el sábado.

28. ¿Por qué escogió Silvia a Julio Iglesias?

   (A) Porque lo conoció años atrás.
   (B) Porque la tienda tiene muchos discos suyos.
   (C) Por el ritmo cautivador de su música.
   (D) Por su impacto en la música popular de hoy.

29. ¿Qué sabemos de Raúl?

   (A) Que prefiere la música clásica.
   (B) Que está muy interesado en la música popular.
   (C) Que es un gran aficionado de Julio Iglesias.
   (D) Que tiene que preparar una evaluación.

GO ON TO THE NEXT PAGE

<u>Selección número 6.</u>

30. ¿Cuándo tiene lugar este diálogo?

    (A) Por la mañana.
    (B) Al mediodía.
    (C) Por la tarde.
    (D) Al anochecer.

31. ¿Por qué le grita el padre a Eduardo?

    (A) Porque no le hace caso.
    (B) Porque su hermana está lista.
    (C) Para que se apure.
    (D) Para que vaya a almorzar.

<u>Selección número 7.</u>

32. ¿Quién propuso la solución al problema financiero?

    (A) El presidente del Gobierno.
    (B) El alcalde de Atenas.
    (C) El príncipe Constantino.
    (D) El padre del presidente.

33. ¿Qué se hizo con el dinero obtenido de la venta de los sellos?

    (A) Se hizo un sorteo de lotería.
    (B) Se le pagó al comité olímpico.
    (C) Se financió el pasaje de los atletas.
    (D) Se construyeron instalaciones en Atenas.

END OF SECTION I.
DO NOT GO ON TO SECTION II UNTIL YOU ARE TOLD TO DO SO.

SECTION II

READING

Time—40 minutes

Questions 34-85

WHEN YOU BEGIN THE READING SECTION, BE SURE THAT YOU MARK YOUR ANSWER TO THE FIRST READING QUESTION BY FILLING IN ONE OF THE OVALS NEXT TO NUMBER 34 ON THE ANSWER SHEET.

Part A

Directions: This part consists of a number of incomplete statements, each having four suggested completions. Select the most appropriate completion and fill in the corresponding oval on the answer sheet.

---

34. Por la mañana prefiero el café bien -------.

    (A) caluroso
    (B) cubierto
    (C) dulce
    (D) durable

35. Si mañana hace buen tiempo, pensamos ir de merienda al -------.

    (A) país
    (B) campo
    (C) teatro
    (D) cine

36. Felipe se acostó muy temprano porque tenía -------.

    (A) siesta
    (B) sal
    (C) sueño
    (D) sangre

37. ¿Tienes ------- para abrir la puerta?

    (A) llave
    (B) maleta
    (C) madera
    (D) vidrio

38. Para llegar al segundo piso, hay que ------- en ascensor.

    (A) elevarse
    (B) subir
    (C) corregir
    (D) saludar

39. ¿------- es el río más largo del mundo? ¿El Amazonas?

    (A) Cómo
    (B) Quién
    (C) Por qué
    (D) Cuál

40. La tienda estará abierta después ------- martes.

    (A) del
    (B) de la
    (C) de las
    (D) de

41. Me han dicho que ------- aquí sabe hablar quechua.

    (A) algún
    (B) algo
    (C) algunos
    (D) alguien

42. Voy a meter el regalo ------- de esta caja; no cabe en la otra.

    (A) después
    (B) dentro
    (C) antes
    (D) alrededor

GO ON TO THE NEXT PAGE

43. Tiene ------- y bigotes muy negros.

    (A) mostaza
    (B) barba
    (C) verbo
    (D) hielo

44. Todos fueron al baile menos -------.

    (A) nos
    (B) ella
    (C) le
    (D) me

45. El agua para el café ya ------- caliente.

    (A) está
    (B) tiene
    (C) es
    (D) hace

46. El no piensa alquilarlo ------- venderlo.

    (A) pero
    (B) mas
    (C) sino que
    (D) sino

47. Compraré una casa cuando ------- dinero.

    (A) tengo
    (B) tenga
    (C) tuviera
    (D) tuve

48. No ha llovido en varios meses y por eso la tierra está muy -------.

    (A) seca
    (B) salada
    (C) clara
    (D) pasada

49. Tienes que escoger una ------- otra.

    (A) a
    (B) o
    (C) u
    (D) e

50. La película empezará tan pronto como ------- las luces de la sala.

    (A) se apagaron
    (B) se apagarían
    (C) se apagan
    (D) se apaguen

GO ON TO THE NEXT PAGE

Part B

Directions: In each of the following paragraphs, there are numbered blanks indicating that words or phrases have been omitted. For each numbered blank, four completions are provided. First read through the entire paragraph. Then, for each numbered blank, choose the completion that is most appropriate given the context of the entire passage and fill in the corresponding oval on the answer sheet.

Questions 51-58

La posesión arqueológica más valiosa que Chile tiene es la Isla de Pascua que está a unas seis __(51)__ de vuelo comercial desde el territorio continental. En medio del Pacífico, visitada __(52)__ miles de turistas, la isla __(53)__ una visión del pasado de una civilización de la cual poco __(54)__.

Descrita como uno de los cinco misterios más antiguos de que la humanidad tiene memoria, las estatuas más prominentes que __(55)__ la isla miran __(56)__ el horizonte __(57)__ a la espera de algo o alguien que vendrá desde otra galaxia o universo.

Los nativos de la isla llaman a estas estatuas "Moais" o "Toros-Miros" y han sido duplicadas un infinito número de __(58)__ en postales, llaveros, adornos, prendas de vestir y publicaciones.

51. (A) horas
    (B) días
    (C) meses
    (D) ratos

52. (A) aún
    (B) hasta
    (C) para
    (D) por

53. (A) quita
    (B) mata
    (C) ofrece
    (D) encanta

54. (A) se extingue
    (B) se pierde
    (C) se destruye
    (D) se sabe

55. (A) habitaron
    (B) habitan
    (C) habitarán
    (D) habiten

56. (A) entre
    (B) bajo
    (C) hacia
    (D) tras

57. (A) tanto
    (B) como
    (C) luego
    (D) tan

58. (A) tiempos
    (B) datos
    (C) veces
    (D) lugares

GO ON TO THE NEXT PAGE

Questions 59-68

Estaba parada frente a la boletería, y pidió un pasaje de __(59)__ a San Isidro. No sé precisar qué fue lo que me __(60)__ la atención en ella. Fue __(61)__ esa leve sonrisa al pedir el boleto, quizá su mirada. Me agradó pensar que __(62)__ compañeras de viaje. De una manera inexplicable __(63)__ interesada por esa sensación de desconcierto que dejaba flotando a su paso. Salió rumbo al andén 4, y entró en el último vagón. __(64)__ que no deseaba compañía, sin embargo me senté del otro lado del pasillo. No creo que __(65)__ mi presencia; parecía estar absorta en sus pensamientos. Estoy segura de que para ella no existía más que __(66)__ que la sostenía y la ventanilla por __(67)__ miraba sin cesar; el resto, los demás pasajeros y yo, habíamos __(68)__ .

59. (A) lotería
    (B) ida y vuelta
    (C) aquí en adelante
    (D) avión

60. (A) llevó
    (B) trajo
    (C) indicó
    (D) llamó

61. (A) probablemente
    (B) al tanto
    (C) aunque
    (D) porque

62. (A) seremos
    (B) fuimos
    (C) somos
    (D) seríamos

63. (A) me senté
    (B) me sentí
    (C) me puse
    (D) me llevé

64. (A) Intuyera
    (B) Intuyo
    (C) Intuiré
    (D) Intuí

65. (A) advirtiera
    (B) advertiría
    (C) advierta
    (D) advirtiendo

66. (A) el padre
    (B) el boleto
    (C) el asiento
    (D) la compañía

67. (A) el que
    (B) la que
    (C) quien
    (D) cuales

68. (A) desaparecido
    (B) desaparecidos
    (C) desapareciendo
    (D) desaparecer

GO ON TO THE NEXT PAGE

Directions: Read the following texts carefully for comprehension. Each text is followed by a number of questions or incomplete statements. Select the answer or completion that is best according to the text and fill in the corresponding oval on the answer sheet.

Questions 69-72

Por primera vez he visto un cadáver. Es miércoles,
pero siento como si fuera domingo porque no he ido a
la escuela y me han puesto este traje de pana verde que
me aprieta en alguna parte. De la mano de mamá,
Línea
(5) siguiendo a mi abuelo que tantea con el bastón a cada
paso para no tropezar con las cosas (no ve bien en la
penumbra, y cojea), he pasado frente al espejo de la
sala y me he visto de cuerpo entero, vestido de verde y
con este blanco lazo almidonado[1] que me aprieta a un
(10) lado del cuello. Me he visto en la redonda luna
manchada y he pensado: *Ese soy yo, como si hoy fuera
domingo.*
　　Hemos venido al lugar donde está el muerto.
Siempre creí que los muertos debían tener sombrero.
Ahora veo que no.

[1]*almidonado* starched

69. ¿Quién narra este trozo?

(A) Un hombre de familia
(B) Un niño
(C) Un viejo
(D) Un hombre joven

70. El narrador lleva un

(A) sombrero nuevo
(B) bastón
(C) vestido blanco
(D) traje especial

71. Al referirse al abuelo, el narrador nos sugiere que éste

(A) está ciego
(B) está vestido de verde
(C) se siente incómodo
(D) camina con dificultad

72. Se podría inferir que el narrador, al mirarse en el espejo, se siente

(A) cansado
(B) extraño
(C) avergonzado
(D) angustiado

GO ON TO THE NEXT PAGE ▶

Questions 73-77

Bajo aquel sol tan intenso, está Mario ya bastante cansado de jugar a "El Tigre", juego de exclusiva invención suya y que consiste en perseguir subido por
Línea las ramas de los perales a su hermano Leo, que se
(5) defiende bravamente usando las peras verdes como proyectiles. El muchacho, cuidadoso de no caerse, se apoya en uno de los pilares del portón, asomándose momentáneamente a la calle, cuando un espectáculo inesperado le llena de agradable sorpresa.
(10) ¡Un potrillo! . . . Había que saber lo que significa para Mario, a la sazón, un potrillo, llegar a poseer un potrillo suyo, es su pasión, su eterno sueño . . .

Al instante, el joven que venía sobre el caballo le grita a Mario en voz alta una propuesta estupenda:
(15) — ¡Che, chiquitín . . .! ¡Si quieres este caballito te lo regalo!

Mario siente al oírle que el suelo se estremece, que sus ojos se nublan, que toda la sangre se le sube al cerebro, pero ¡ay! conoce tan a fondo las leyes de su
(20) casa, que no vacila ni un segundo y, rojo como un tomate, rehusa avergonzado. Y conformándose como otras tantas veces contempla platónicamente el paso de aquella maravilla.

73. Mario y su hermano estaban jugando

(A) en medio de la calle
(B) en los árboles
(C) en el parque
(D) dentro de la casa

74. La acción que aquí se narra tiene lugar

(A) temprano por la mañana
(B) por la noche
(C) hacia el mediodía
(D) al atardecer

75. Mario se emocionó muchísimo porque

(A) pudo ganarle fácilmente el juego a su hermano
(B) las leyes de su casa le permitían todo
(C) pudo vivir momentáneamente una gran ilusión
(D) vio llorar al dueño del potrillo

76. Mario se sintió avergonzado porque

(A) alguien le gritó en voz alta
(B) casi se cayó
(C) atacaba bravamente a su hermano
(D) no pudo aceptar lo que le ofrecían

77. ¿Cuál de los siguientes adjetivos describe mejor el carácter de Mario?

(A) Obediente
(B) Travieso
(C) Tranquilo
(D) Satisfecho

GO ON TO THE NEXT PAGE

Questions 78-79

"¡Llame al 213-688-ARTS y acompáñeme a los eventos del Festival Artes de México!"

Ricardo Montalbán

Asista a una gran celebración de la rica herencia cultural y artística de México en Los Angeles: Festival Artes de México, de septiembre a diciembre.

Asista a más de 250 eventos: • danza • música • exposiciones de arte • poesía • conferencias • cine y video • drama. Muchos de los eventos son *gratis*. Los demás, a precios módicos. Para informarse sobre el Festival llame al (213) 688-ARTS.

ARTES DE MEXICO

FESTIVAL

78. ¿Qué hace aquí Ricardo Montalbán, entre otras cosas?

(A) Solicita voluntarios para que ayuden en el festival.
(B) Invita a personalidades famosas a ir al festival.
(C) Indica cómo conseguir más información sobre el festival.
(D) Pide la colaboración de artistas folklóricos en el festival.

79. ¿Qué celebra el festival?

(A) La herencia cultural mexicana
(B) La riqueza agrícola de México
(C) Los dramas de Ricardo Montalbán
(D) La cinematografía de Los Angeles

GO ON TO THE NEXT PAGE

Questions 80-85

Esperanza y Claudia nacieron con minutos de diferencia. A partir de ese instante no han dejado de escuchar la misma frase: "Pero si son idénticas, *Línea* igualitas, como dos gotas de agua". Cierto, las dos
(5) tienen la misma cabellera pelirroja, la misma curva en la frente, la misma transparencia en la piel que de tan blanca, azulea. La sonrisa, las manos, son idénticas, como el gesto burlón que vuelve un poco irritante su presencia.
(10) Si siempre compartieron el espacio y los juegos, sus padres pensaron que lo más natural era inscribirlas en la misma escuela. Allí, al poco tiempo de haber entrado, se convirtieron en el terror de sus maestros que, incapaces de distinguir entre una y otra, terminaron por
(15) ser el blanco de las burlas infantiles. Tan crítica se volvió la situación, que luego de una asamblea la directora optó por separar a las gemelas. Las consecuencias fueron desastrosas: cada una por su lado desplegó las mayores posibilidades para perturbar a sus
(20) compañeros y cometer toda clase de indisciplinas. "Mientras están juntas se portan muy bien—aseguró su principal víctima: la prefecta—pero ya solas se convierten en la onda del diablo". Luego de otra asamblea las dos niñas, notablemente satisfechas y más poderosas que nunca, volvieron a ser vecinas de banca.

80. ¿Por qué dice la gente que Esperanza y Claudia son "como dos gotas de agua" (línea 4) ?

(A) Porque nacieron con dos minutos de diferencia
(B) Porque siempre andan juntas
(C) Porque son iguales en apariencia y carácter
(D) Porque sus bromas irritan a los maestros

81. ¿De qué color es el pelo de las dos hermanas?

(A) Blanco
(B) Rubio
(C) Rojo
(D) Azulado

82. Las gemelas iban a la misma escuela porque

(A) no querían separarse de sus padres
(B) sus padres lo consideraban lógico
(C) se portaban muy mal
(D) tenían miedo de separarse

83. En la escuela había constantemente problemas con las gemelas porque

(A) las chicas tenían muy mal carácter
(B) los maestros no las querían juntas
(C) los maestros no podían diferenciarlas
(D) los maestros se reían de las chicas

84. ¿Cómo decidió la directora arreglar la situación de las gemelas al principio?

(A) Separando a las dos chicas
(B) Apartando a las chicas de los demás
(C) Castigando a toda la clase
(D) Expulsando a las chicas del colegio

85. Las medidas tomadas por la directora fracasaron porque Esperanza y Claudia

(A) se fueron de la escuela
(B) se convirtieron en enemigas
(C) fueron el blanco de las burlas
(D) se portaron peor todavía

END OF SECTION II

STOP

IF YOU FINISH BEFORE TIME IS CALLED, YOU MAY CHECK YOUR WORK ON SECTION II OF THIS TEST.
DO NOT TURN TO ANY OTHER TEST IN THIS BOOK.

How to Score the SAT Subject Test in Spanish with Listening

When you take the SAT Subject Test in Spanish with Listening, you will receive an overall composite score as well as two subscores: one for the reading section, one for the listening section.

The reading and listening scores are reported on the College Board's 20-to-80 scale. However, the composite score, which is the most significant of the scores reported to the colleges you specify, is in the form of the College Board's 200-to-800 scale.

Worksheet 1. Finding Your Raw Listening Subscore

STEP 1: Table A lists the correct answers for all the questions on the SAT Subject Test in Spanish with Listening that is reproduced in this book. It also serves as a worksheet for you to calculate your raw Listening subscore.

- Compare your answers with those given in the table.
- Put a check in the column marked "Right" if your answer is correct.
- Put a check in the column marked "Wrong" if your answer is incorrect.
- Leave both columns blank if you omitted the question.

STEP 2: Count the number of right answers for questions 1–33.

Enter the total here: _____

STEP 3: Count the number of wrong answers for questions 1–33.

Enter the total here: _____

STEP 4: Multiply the number of wrong answers by .333.

Enter the product here: _____

STEP 5: Subtract the result obtained in Step 4 from the total you obtained in Step 2.

Enter the result here: _____

STEP 6: Round the number obtained in Step 5 to the nearest whole number.

Enter the result here: _____

The number you obtained in Step 6 is your raw Listening subscore.

Worksheet 2. Finding Your Raw Reading Subscore

STEP 1: Table A lists the correct answers for all the questions on the SAT Subject Test in Spanish with Listening that is reproduced in this book. It also serves as a worksheet for you to calculate your raw Reading subscore.

- Compare your answers with those given in the table.
- Put a check in the column marked "Right" if your answer is correct.
- Put a check in the column marked "Wrong" if your answer is incorrect.
- Leave both columns blank if you omitted the question.

STEP 2: Count the number of right answers for questions 34–85.

Enter the total here: _____

STEP 3: Count the number of wrong answers for questions 34–85.

Enter the total here: _____

STEP 4: Multiply the number of wrong answers by .333.

Enter the product here: _____

STEP 5: Subtract the result obtained in Step 4 from the total you obtained in Step 2.

Enter the result here: _____

STEP 6: Round the number obtained in Step 5 to the nearest whole number.

Enter the result here: _____

The number you obtained in Step 6 is your raw Reading subscore.

Worksheet 3. Finding Your Raw Composite Score*

STEP 1: Enter your unrounded raw Reading subscore from Step 5 of Worksheet 2 here: _____

STEP 2: Multiply your unrounded raw Reading subscore by 1.120.

Enter the product here: _____

STEP 3: Enter your unrounded raw Listening subscore from Step 5 of Worksheet 1 here: _____

STEP 4: Multiply your unrounded raw Listening subscore by .8810.

Enter the product here: _____

STEP 5: Add the results obtained in Step 2 to the result obtained in Step 4.

Enter the sum here: _____

STEP 6: Round the number obtained in Step 5 to the nearest whole number.

Enter the result here: _____

The number you obtained in Step 6 is your raw composite score.

*This weighting reflects the amount of time spent on the two sections of the test—40 minutes on the reading questions and 20 minutes on the listening questions. For those who are curious about how the calculation works, the weighting is done in standard deviation units, a measure of score variability. The weight given to the listening subscore is calculated by dividing the standard deviation of the reading subscore by two times the standard deviation of the listening subscore. Weights are then applied to both reading and listening sections so that the maximum raw composite score equals 85.

TABLE A

Answers to the SAT Subject Test in Spanish with Listening, Form 3QLC, and Percentage of Students Answering Each Question Correctly

Question Number	Correct Answer	Right	Wrong	Percentage of Students Answering the Question Correctly*	Question Number	Correct Answer	Right	Wrong	Percentage of Students Answering the Question Correctly*
1	D			99	33	D			41
2	D			71	34	C			35
3	A			85	35	B			85
4	B			88	36	C			60
5	C			83	37	A			81
6	A			81	38	B			51
7	C			75	39	D			88
8	B			66	40	A			60
9	B			50	41	D			72
10	A			41	42	B			60
11	A			78	43	B			65
12	B			61	44	B			73
13	A			49	45	A			79
14	B			57	46	D			32
15	B			40	47	B			33
16	B			55	48	A			78
17	C			38	49	C			28
18	A			40	50	D			26
19	D			46	51	A			69
20	D			41	52	D			60
21	D			76	53	C			86
22	B			90	54	D			58
23	A			72	55	B			70
24	D			79	56	C			37
25	C			53	57	B			59
26	C			41	58	C			49
27	B			76	59	B			45
28	D			80	60	D			47
29	A			86	61	A			54
30	A			68	62	D			38
31	C			30	63	B			58
32	C			42	64	D			45

Table A continued on next page

Table A continued from previous page

Question Number	Correct Answer	Right	Wrong	Percentage of Students Answering the Question Correctly*	Question Number	Correct Answer	Right	Wrong	Percentage of Students Answering the Question Correctly*
65	A			26	76	D			31
66	C			37	77	A			25
67	B			46	78	C			70
68	A			32	79	A			94
69	B			55	80	C			73
70	D			72	81	C			65
71	D			27	82	B			76
72	B			39	83	C			82
73	B			32	84	A			83
74	C			63	85	D			46
75	C			49					

*These percentages are based on an analysis of the answer sheets for a random sample of 6,847 students who took this form of the test in November 1994 and whose mean score was 525. They may be used as an indication of the relative difficulty of a particular question. Each percentage may also be used to predict the likelihood that a typical SAT Subject Test in Spanish with Listening candidate will answer correctly that question on this edition of this test.

Finding Your Scaled Score

When you take SAT Subject Tests, the scores sent to the colleges you specify are reported on the College Board scale, which ranges from 200 to 800. Subscores are reported on a scale which ranges from 20 to 80. You can convert your practice test scores to scaled scores by using Tables B, C, and D. To find your scaled score, locate your raw score in the left-hand column of the table; the corresponding score in the right-hand column is your scaled score. For example, in Table B a raw composite score of 58 on this particular edition of the SAT Subject Test in Spanish with Listening corresponds to a scaled score of 630.

Raw scores are converted to scaled scores to ensure that a score earned on any one edition of a particular Subject Test is comparable to the same scaled score earned on any other edition of the same Subject Test. Because some editions of tests may be slightly easier or more difficult than others, scaled scores are adjusted so that they indicate the same level of performance regardless of the edition of the test taken and the ability of the group that takes it. Thus, for example, a score of 400 on one edition of a test taken at a particular administration indicates the same level of achievement as a score of 400 on a different edition of the test taken at a different administration.

When you take the SAT Subject Tests during a national administration, your scores are likely to differ somewhat from the scores you obtain on the tests in this book. People perform at different levels at different times for reasons unrelated to the tests themselves. The precision of any test is also limited because it represents only a sample of all the possible questions that could be asked.

Your scaled composite score from Table B is _____ .

Your scaled listening score from Table C is _____ .

Your scaled reading score from Table D is _____ .

TABLE B
Scaled Score Conversion Table
Spanish Subject Test with Listening Composite Scores (Form 3QLC)

Raw Score	Scaled Score	Raw Score	Scaled Score	Raw Score	Scaled Score
85	800	47	560	9	360
84	800	46	560	8	350
83	800	45	550	7	350
82	800	44	550	6	340
81	790	43	540	5	340
80	790	42	540	4	330
79	780	41	530	3	330
78	770	40	530	2	320
77	770	39	520	1	320
76	760	38	520	0	310
75	760	37	510	−1	310
74	750	36	510	−2	300
73	750	35	500	−3	300
72	740	34	500	−4	300
71	730	33	490	−5	290
70	720	32	490	−6	290
69	720	31	480	−7	280
68	710	30	480	−8	280
67	700	29	470	−9	270
66	690	28	470	−10	270
65	680	27	460	−11	260
64	670	26	460	−12	260
63	670	25	450	−13	250
62	660	24	450	−14	250
61	650	23	440	−15	240
60	640	22	440	−16	230
59	640	21	430	−17	230
58	630	20	430	−18	220
57	620	19	420	−19	220
56	620	18	410	−20	210
55	610	17	410	−21	210
54	610	16	400	−22	200
53	600	15	400	−23	200
52	590	14	390	−24	200
51	590	13	380	−25	200
50	580	12	380	−26	200
49	570	11	370	−27	200
48	570	10	370	−28	200

TABLE C
Scaled Score Conversion Table
Spanish Subject Test with Listening Listening Subscore (Form 3QLC)

Raw Score	Scaled Score	Raw Score	Scaled Score	Raw Score	Scaled Score
33	78	18	53	3	34
32	76	17	52	2	33
31	74	16	51	1	32
30	72	15	50	0	30
29	70	14	49	−1	29
28	67	13	48	−2	28
27	65	12	46	−3	26
26	63	11	45	−4	25
25	62	10	44	−5	24
24	60	9	43	−6	22
23	59	8	41	−7	21
22	57	7	40	−8	20
21	56	6	38	−9	20
20	55	5	37	−10	20
19	54	4	36	−11	20

TABLE D
Scaled Score Conversion Table
Spanish Subject Test with Listening Reading Subscore (Form 3QLC)

Raw Score	Scaled Score	Raw Score	Scaled Score	Raw Score	Scaled Score
52	80	27	56	2	35
51	80	26	55	1	34
50	79	25	54	0	33
49	78	24	54	−1	33
48	78	23	53	−2	32
47	77	22	52	−3	32
46	76	21	51	−4	31
45	76	20	51	−5	31
44	75	19	50	−6	30
43	74	18	49	−7	30
42	73	17	48	−8	29
41	72	16	48	−9	28
40	70	15	47	−10	28
39	69	14	46	−11	27
38	68	13	45	−12	27
37	66	12	44	−13	26
36	65	11	43	−14	26
35	64	10	42	−15	25
34	63	9	41	−16	25
33	62	8	40	−17	24
32	61	7	39		
31	60	6	38		
30	59	5	37		
29	58	4	36		
28	57	3	35		

Reviewing Your Performance on the Spanish Subject Test with Listening

After you score your test, analyze your performance—consider the following questions:

Did you run out of time before reaching the end of the test?

If so, you may need to pace yourself better. For example, maybe you spent too much time on one or two hard questions. A better approach might be to skip the ones you can't answer right away and try answering all the questions that remain on the test. Then if there's time, go back to the questions you skipped.

Did you take a long time reading the directions?

You will save time when you take the test by learning the directions to the Spanish Test with Listening ahead of time. Each minute you spend reading directions during the test is a minute that you could use to answer questions.

How did you handle questions you were unsure of?

If you were able to eliminate one or more of the answer choices as wrong and guess from the remaining ones, your approach probably worked to your advantage. On the other hand, making haphazard guesses or omitting questions without trying to eliminate choices could cost you valuable points.

How difficult were the questions for you compared with other students who took the test?

Table A shows you how difficult the multiple-choice questions were for the group of students who took this test during its national administration. The right-hand column gives the percentage of students that answered each question correctly.

A question answered correctly by almost everyone in the group is obviously an easy question. For example, 99 percent of the students answered question 1 correctly. But only 26 percent answered question 65 correctly.

Keep in mind that these percentages are based on just one group of students and would probably be different if another group of students took the test.

If you missed several easy questions, go back and try to find out why: Did the questions cover material you haven't reviewed yet? Did you misunderstand the directions?

CollegeBoard SAT

SAT Subject Tests™

Your Name:
(Print)

Last _____ First _____ M.I. _____

ee to the conditions on the back of the SAT® Subject Tests book.

ature: _____ Date __/__/__

e Address: _____
Number and Street — City — State — Zip Code

er: _____
t) — City — State

YOUR NAME
st Name (4 Letters) | First Init. | Mid. Init.

3 SOCIAL SECURITY NUMBER

0 1 2 3 4 5 6 7 8 9

4 DATE OF BIRTH

MONTH	DAY	YEAR
Jan		
Feb		
Mar		
Apr		
May		
Jun		
Jul		
Aug		
Sep		
Oct		
Nov		
Dec		

5 SEX

○ Female   ○ Male

6 REGISTRATION NUMBER
(Copy from Admission Ticket.)

0 1 2 3 4 5 6 7 8 9

7 TEST CENTER
(Supplied by Test Center Supervisor.)

0 1 2 3 4 5 6 7 8 9

8 BOOK CODE
(Copy and grid as on back of test book.)

0 A 0
1 B 1
2 C 2
3 D 3
4 E 4
5 F 5
6 G 6
7 H 7
8 I 8
9 J 9
K L M N O P Q R S T U V W X Y Z

9 BOOK ID
(Copy from back of test book.)

10 BOOK SERIAL NUMBER
(Copy from front of test book.)

0 1 2 3 4 5 6 7 8 9

FOR OFFICIAL USE ONLY

0 1 2 3 4 5 6 7 8 9
0 1 2 3 4 5 6 7 8 9
0 1 2 3 4 5 6 7 8 9
0 1 2 3 4 5 6 7 8 9

11030-36392 • NS114E315 • Printed in U.S.A.
724844

Page 2

Use a No. 2 pencil only. Be sure each mark is dark and completely fills the intended circle. Completely erase any errors or stray marks.

If there are more answer spaces than you need, leave them blank.

Test Code

V	① ② ③ ④ ⑤ ⑥ ⑦ ⑧ ⑨
W	① ② ③ ④ ⑤ ⑥ ⑦ ⑧ ⑨
X	① ② ③ ④ ⑤ Y Ⓐ Ⓑ Ⓒ Ⓓ Ⓔ
Q	① ② ③ ④ ⑤ ⑥ ⑦ ⑧ ⑨

Subject Test (print)

1 Ⓐ Ⓑ Ⓒ Ⓓ Ⓔ   26 Ⓐ Ⓑ Ⓒ Ⓓ Ⓔ   51 Ⓐ Ⓑ Ⓒ Ⓓ Ⓔ   76 Ⓐ Ⓑ Ⓒ Ⓓ Ⓔ
2 Ⓐ Ⓑ Ⓒ Ⓓ Ⓔ   27 Ⓐ Ⓑ Ⓒ Ⓓ Ⓔ   52 Ⓐ Ⓑ Ⓒ Ⓓ Ⓔ   77 Ⓐ Ⓑ Ⓒ Ⓓ Ⓔ
3 Ⓐ Ⓑ Ⓒ Ⓓ Ⓔ   28 Ⓐ Ⓑ Ⓒ Ⓓ Ⓔ   53 Ⓐ Ⓑ Ⓒ Ⓓ Ⓔ   78 Ⓐ Ⓑ Ⓒ Ⓓ Ⓔ
4 Ⓐ Ⓑ Ⓒ Ⓓ Ⓔ   29 Ⓐ Ⓑ Ⓒ Ⓓ Ⓔ   54 Ⓐ Ⓑ Ⓒ Ⓓ Ⓔ   79 Ⓐ Ⓑ Ⓒ Ⓓ Ⓔ
5 Ⓐ Ⓑ Ⓒ Ⓓ Ⓔ   30 Ⓐ Ⓑ Ⓒ Ⓓ Ⓔ   55 Ⓐ Ⓑ Ⓒ Ⓓ Ⓔ   80 Ⓐ Ⓑ Ⓒ Ⓓ Ⓔ
6 Ⓐ Ⓑ Ⓒ Ⓓ Ⓔ   31 Ⓐ Ⓑ Ⓒ Ⓓ Ⓔ   56 Ⓐ Ⓑ Ⓒ Ⓓ Ⓔ   81 Ⓐ Ⓑ Ⓒ Ⓓ Ⓔ
7 Ⓐ Ⓑ Ⓒ Ⓓ Ⓔ   32 Ⓐ Ⓑ Ⓒ Ⓓ Ⓔ   57 Ⓐ Ⓑ Ⓒ Ⓓ Ⓔ   82 Ⓐ Ⓑ Ⓒ Ⓓ Ⓔ
8 Ⓐ Ⓑ Ⓒ Ⓓ Ⓔ   33 Ⓐ Ⓑ Ⓒ Ⓓ Ⓔ   58 Ⓐ Ⓑ Ⓒ Ⓓ Ⓔ   83 Ⓐ Ⓑ Ⓒ Ⓓ Ⓔ
9 Ⓐ Ⓑ Ⓒ Ⓓ Ⓔ   34 Ⓐ Ⓑ Ⓒ Ⓓ Ⓔ   59 Ⓐ Ⓑ Ⓒ Ⓓ Ⓔ   84 Ⓐ Ⓑ Ⓒ Ⓓ Ⓔ
10 Ⓐ Ⓑ Ⓒ Ⓓ Ⓔ   35 Ⓐ Ⓑ Ⓒ Ⓓ Ⓔ   60 Ⓐ Ⓑ Ⓒ Ⓓ Ⓔ   85 Ⓐ Ⓑ Ⓒ Ⓓ Ⓔ
11 Ⓐ Ⓑ Ⓒ Ⓓ Ⓔ   36 Ⓐ Ⓑ Ⓒ Ⓓ Ⓔ   61 Ⓐ Ⓑ Ⓒ Ⓓ Ⓔ   86 Ⓐ Ⓑ Ⓒ Ⓓ Ⓔ
12 Ⓐ Ⓑ Ⓒ Ⓓ Ⓔ   37 Ⓐ Ⓑ Ⓒ Ⓓ Ⓔ   62 Ⓐ Ⓑ Ⓒ Ⓓ Ⓔ   87 Ⓐ Ⓑ Ⓒ Ⓓ Ⓔ
13 Ⓐ Ⓑ Ⓒ Ⓓ Ⓔ   38 Ⓐ Ⓑ Ⓒ Ⓓ Ⓔ   63 Ⓐ Ⓑ Ⓒ Ⓓ Ⓔ   88 Ⓐ Ⓑ Ⓒ Ⓓ Ⓔ
14 Ⓐ Ⓑ Ⓒ Ⓓ Ⓔ   39 Ⓐ Ⓑ Ⓒ Ⓓ Ⓔ   64 Ⓐ Ⓑ Ⓒ Ⓓ Ⓔ   89 Ⓐ Ⓑ Ⓒ Ⓓ Ⓔ
15 Ⓐ Ⓑ Ⓒ Ⓓ Ⓔ   40 Ⓐ Ⓑ Ⓒ Ⓓ Ⓔ   65 Ⓐ Ⓑ Ⓒ Ⓓ Ⓔ   90 Ⓐ Ⓑ Ⓒ Ⓓ Ⓔ
16 Ⓐ Ⓑ Ⓒ Ⓓ Ⓔ   41 Ⓐ Ⓑ Ⓒ Ⓓ Ⓔ   66 Ⓐ Ⓑ Ⓒ Ⓓ Ⓔ   91 Ⓐ Ⓑ Ⓒ Ⓓ Ⓔ
17 Ⓐ Ⓑ Ⓒ Ⓓ Ⓔ   42 Ⓐ Ⓑ Ⓒ Ⓓ Ⓔ   67 Ⓐ Ⓑ Ⓒ Ⓓ Ⓔ   92 Ⓐ Ⓑ Ⓒ Ⓓ Ⓔ
18 Ⓐ Ⓑ Ⓒ Ⓓ Ⓔ   43 Ⓐ Ⓑ Ⓒ Ⓓ Ⓔ   68 Ⓐ Ⓑ Ⓒ Ⓓ Ⓔ   93 Ⓐ Ⓑ Ⓒ Ⓓ Ⓔ
19 Ⓐ Ⓑ Ⓒ Ⓓ Ⓔ   44 Ⓐ Ⓑ Ⓒ Ⓓ Ⓔ   69 Ⓐ Ⓑ Ⓒ Ⓓ Ⓔ   94 Ⓐ Ⓑ Ⓒ Ⓓ Ⓔ
20 Ⓐ Ⓑ Ⓒ Ⓓ Ⓔ   45 Ⓐ Ⓑ Ⓒ Ⓓ Ⓔ   70 Ⓐ Ⓑ Ⓒ Ⓓ Ⓔ   95 Ⓐ Ⓑ Ⓒ Ⓓ Ⓔ
21 Ⓐ Ⓑ Ⓒ Ⓓ Ⓔ   46 Ⓐ Ⓑ Ⓒ Ⓓ Ⓔ   71 Ⓐ Ⓑ Ⓒ Ⓓ Ⓔ   96 Ⓐ Ⓑ Ⓒ Ⓓ Ⓔ
22 Ⓐ Ⓑ Ⓒ Ⓓ Ⓔ   47 Ⓐ Ⓑ Ⓒ Ⓓ Ⓔ   72 Ⓐ Ⓑ Ⓒ Ⓓ Ⓔ   97 Ⓐ Ⓑ Ⓒ Ⓓ Ⓔ
23 Ⓐ Ⓑ Ⓒ Ⓓ Ⓔ   48 Ⓐ Ⓑ Ⓒ Ⓓ Ⓔ   73 Ⓐ Ⓑ Ⓒ Ⓓ Ⓔ   98 Ⓐ Ⓑ Ⓒ Ⓓ Ⓔ
24 Ⓐ Ⓑ Ⓒ Ⓓ Ⓔ   49 Ⓐ Ⓑ Ⓒ Ⓓ Ⓔ   74 Ⓐ Ⓑ Ⓒ Ⓓ Ⓔ   99 Ⓐ Ⓑ Ⓒ Ⓓ Ⓔ
25 Ⓐ Ⓑ Ⓒ Ⓓ Ⓔ   50 Ⓐ Ⓑ Ⓒ Ⓓ Ⓔ   75 Ⓐ Ⓑ Ⓒ Ⓓ Ⓔ   100 Ⓐ Ⓑ Ⓒ Ⓓ Ⓔ

Chemistry *Fill in circle CE only if II is correct explanation of I.

	I	II	CE*		I	II	CE*
101	Ⓣ Ⓕ	Ⓣ Ⓕ	○	109	Ⓣ Ⓕ	Ⓣ Ⓕ	○
102	Ⓣ Ⓕ	Ⓣ Ⓕ	○	110	Ⓣ Ⓕ	Ⓣ Ⓕ	○
103	Ⓣ Ⓕ	Ⓣ Ⓕ	○	111	Ⓣ Ⓕ	Ⓣ Ⓕ	○
104	Ⓣ Ⓕ	Ⓣ Ⓕ	○	112	Ⓣ Ⓕ	Ⓣ Ⓕ	○
105	Ⓣ Ⓕ	Ⓣ Ⓕ	○	113	Ⓣ Ⓕ	Ⓣ Ⓕ	○
106	Ⓣ Ⓕ	Ⓣ Ⓕ	○	114	Ⓣ Ⓕ	Ⓣ Ⓕ	○
107	Ⓣ Ⓕ	Ⓣ Ⓕ	○	115	Ⓣ Ⓕ	Ⓣ Ⓕ	○
108	Ⓣ Ⓕ	Ⓣ Ⓕ	○				

8 BOOK CODE
(Copy and grid as on back of test book.)

⓪	Ⓐ	⓪
①	Ⓑ	①
②	Ⓒ	②
③	Ⓓ	③
④	Ⓔ	④
⑤	Ⓕ	⑤
⑥	Ⓖ	⑥
⑦	Ⓗ	⑦
⑧	Ⓘ	⑧
⑨	Ⓙ	⑨
	Ⓚ	
	Ⓛ	
	Ⓜ	
	Ⓝ	
	Ⓞ	
	Ⓟ	
	Ⓠ	
	Ⓡ	
	Ⓢ	
	Ⓣ	
	Ⓤ	
	Ⓥ	
	Ⓦ	
	Ⓧ	
	Ⓨ	
	Ⓩ	

9 BOOK ID
(Copy from back of test book.)

10 BOOK SERIAL NUMBER
(Copy from front of test book.)

⓪	⓪	⓪	⓪	⓪	⓪
①	①	①	①	①	①
②	②	②	②	②	②
③	③	③	③	③	③
④	④	④	④	④	④
⑤	⑤	⑤	⑤	⑤	⑤
⑥	⑥	⑥	⑥	⑥	⑥
⑦	⑦	⑦	⑦	⑦	⑦
⑧	⑧	⑧	⑧	⑧	⑧
⑨	⑨	⑨	⑨	⑨	⑨

FOR OFFICIAL USE ONLY

R/C	W/S1	FS/S2	CS/S3	WS

PLEASE DO NOT WRITE IN THIS AREA

SERIAL #

Use a No. 2 pencil only. Be sure each mark is dark and completely fills the intended circle. Completely erase any errors or stray marks.

Subject Test (print)

here are more
swer spaces
n you need,
ve them blank.

Test Code

V	① ② ③ ④ ⑤ ⑥ ⑦ ⑧ ⑨
W	① ② ③ ④ ⑤ ⑥ ⑦ ⑧ ⑨
X	① ② ③ ④ ⑤ Y Ⓐ Ⓑ Ⓒ Ⓓ Ⓔ
Q	① ② ③ ④ ⑤ ⑥ ⑦ ⑧ ⑨

Ⓐ Ⓑ Ⓒ Ⓓ Ⓔ　26 Ⓐ Ⓑ Ⓒ Ⓓ Ⓔ　51 Ⓐ Ⓑ Ⓒ Ⓓ Ⓔ　76 Ⓐ Ⓑ Ⓒ Ⓓ Ⓔ
Ⓐ Ⓑ Ⓒ Ⓓ Ⓔ　27 Ⓐ Ⓑ Ⓒ Ⓓ Ⓔ　52 Ⓐ Ⓑ Ⓒ Ⓓ Ⓔ　77 Ⓐ Ⓑ Ⓒ Ⓓ Ⓔ
Ⓐ Ⓑ Ⓒ Ⓓ Ⓔ　28 Ⓐ Ⓑ Ⓒ Ⓓ Ⓔ　53 Ⓐ Ⓑ Ⓒ Ⓓ Ⓔ　78 Ⓐ Ⓑ Ⓒ Ⓓ Ⓔ
Ⓐ Ⓑ Ⓒ Ⓓ Ⓔ　29 Ⓐ Ⓑ Ⓒ Ⓓ Ⓔ　54 Ⓐ Ⓑ Ⓒ Ⓓ Ⓔ　79 Ⓐ Ⓑ Ⓒ Ⓓ Ⓔ
Ⓐ Ⓑ Ⓒ Ⓓ Ⓔ　30 Ⓐ Ⓑ Ⓒ Ⓓ Ⓔ　55 Ⓐ Ⓑ Ⓒ Ⓓ Ⓔ　80 Ⓐ Ⓑ Ⓒ Ⓓ Ⓔ
Ⓐ Ⓑ Ⓒ Ⓓ Ⓔ　31 Ⓐ Ⓑ Ⓒ Ⓓ Ⓔ　56 Ⓐ Ⓑ Ⓒ Ⓓ Ⓔ　81 Ⓐ Ⓑ Ⓒ Ⓓ Ⓔ
Ⓐ Ⓑ Ⓒ Ⓓ Ⓔ　32 Ⓐ Ⓑ Ⓒ Ⓓ Ⓔ　57 Ⓐ Ⓑ Ⓒ Ⓓ Ⓔ　82 Ⓐ Ⓑ Ⓒ Ⓓ Ⓔ
Ⓐ Ⓑ Ⓒ Ⓓ Ⓔ　33 Ⓐ Ⓑ Ⓒ Ⓓ Ⓔ　58 Ⓐ Ⓑ Ⓒ Ⓓ Ⓔ　83 Ⓐ Ⓑ Ⓒ Ⓓ Ⓔ
Ⓐ Ⓑ Ⓒ Ⓓ Ⓔ　34 Ⓐ Ⓑ Ⓒ Ⓓ Ⓔ　59 Ⓐ Ⓑ Ⓒ Ⓓ Ⓔ　84 Ⓐ Ⓑ Ⓒ Ⓓ Ⓔ
Ⓐ Ⓑ Ⓒ Ⓓ Ⓔ　35 Ⓐ Ⓑ Ⓒ Ⓓ Ⓔ　60 Ⓐ Ⓑ Ⓒ Ⓓ Ⓔ　85 Ⓐ Ⓑ Ⓒ Ⓓ Ⓔ
Ⓐ Ⓑ Ⓒ Ⓓ Ⓔ　36 Ⓐ Ⓑ Ⓒ Ⓓ Ⓔ　61 Ⓐ Ⓑ Ⓒ Ⓓ Ⓔ　86 Ⓐ Ⓑ Ⓒ Ⓓ Ⓔ
Ⓐ Ⓑ Ⓒ Ⓓ Ⓔ　37 Ⓐ Ⓑ Ⓒ Ⓓ Ⓔ　62 Ⓐ Ⓑ Ⓒ Ⓓ Ⓔ　87 Ⓐ Ⓑ Ⓒ Ⓓ Ⓔ
Ⓐ Ⓑ Ⓒ Ⓓ Ⓔ　38 Ⓐ Ⓑ Ⓒ Ⓓ Ⓔ　63 Ⓐ Ⓑ Ⓒ Ⓓ Ⓔ　88 Ⓐ Ⓑ Ⓒ Ⓓ Ⓔ
Ⓐ Ⓑ Ⓒ Ⓓ Ⓔ　39 Ⓐ Ⓑ Ⓒ Ⓓ Ⓔ　64 Ⓐ Ⓑ Ⓒ Ⓓ Ⓔ　89 Ⓐ Ⓑ Ⓒ Ⓓ Ⓔ
Ⓐ Ⓑ Ⓒ Ⓓ Ⓔ　40 Ⓐ Ⓑ Ⓒ Ⓓ Ⓔ　65 Ⓐ Ⓑ Ⓒ Ⓓ Ⓔ　90 Ⓐ Ⓑ Ⓒ Ⓓ Ⓔ
Ⓐ Ⓑ Ⓒ Ⓓ Ⓔ　41 Ⓐ Ⓑ Ⓒ Ⓓ Ⓔ　66 Ⓐ Ⓑ Ⓒ Ⓓ Ⓔ　91 Ⓐ Ⓑ Ⓒ Ⓓ Ⓔ
Ⓐ Ⓑ Ⓒ Ⓓ Ⓔ　42 Ⓐ Ⓑ Ⓒ Ⓓ Ⓔ　67 Ⓐ Ⓑ Ⓒ Ⓓ Ⓔ　92 Ⓐ Ⓑ Ⓒ Ⓓ Ⓔ
Ⓐ Ⓑ Ⓒ Ⓓ Ⓔ　43 Ⓐ Ⓑ Ⓒ Ⓓ Ⓔ　68 Ⓐ Ⓑ Ⓒ Ⓓ Ⓔ　93 Ⓐ Ⓑ Ⓒ Ⓓ Ⓔ
Ⓐ Ⓑ Ⓒ Ⓓ Ⓔ　44 Ⓐ Ⓑ Ⓒ Ⓓ Ⓔ　69 Ⓐ Ⓑ Ⓒ Ⓓ Ⓔ　94 Ⓐ Ⓑ Ⓒ Ⓓ Ⓔ
Ⓐ Ⓑ Ⓒ Ⓓ Ⓔ　45 Ⓐ Ⓑ Ⓒ Ⓓ Ⓔ　70 Ⓐ Ⓑ Ⓒ Ⓓ Ⓔ　95 Ⓐ Ⓑ Ⓒ Ⓓ Ⓔ
Ⓐ Ⓑ Ⓒ Ⓓ Ⓔ　46 Ⓐ Ⓑ Ⓒ Ⓓ Ⓔ　71 Ⓐ Ⓑ Ⓒ Ⓓ Ⓔ　96 Ⓐ Ⓑ Ⓒ Ⓓ Ⓔ
Ⓐ Ⓑ Ⓒ Ⓓ Ⓔ　47 Ⓐ Ⓑ Ⓒ Ⓓ Ⓔ　72 Ⓐ Ⓑ Ⓒ Ⓓ Ⓔ　97 Ⓐ Ⓑ Ⓒ Ⓓ Ⓔ
Ⓐ Ⓑ Ⓒ Ⓓ Ⓔ　48 Ⓐ Ⓑ Ⓒ Ⓓ Ⓔ　73 Ⓐ Ⓑ Ⓒ Ⓓ Ⓔ　98 Ⓐ Ⓑ Ⓒ Ⓓ Ⓔ
Ⓐ Ⓑ Ⓒ Ⓓ Ⓔ　49 Ⓐ Ⓑ Ⓒ Ⓓ Ⓔ　74 Ⓐ Ⓑ Ⓒ Ⓓ Ⓔ　99 Ⓐ Ⓑ Ⓒ Ⓓ Ⓔ
Ⓐ Ⓑ Ⓒ Ⓓ Ⓔ　50 Ⓐ Ⓑ Ⓒ Ⓓ Ⓔ　75 Ⓐ Ⓑ Ⓒ Ⓓ Ⓔ　100 Ⓐ Ⓑ Ⓒ Ⓓ Ⓔ

8 BOOK CODE
(Copy and grid as on back of test book.)

⓪ Ⓐ ⓪
① Ⓑ ①
② Ⓒ ②
③ Ⓓ ③
④ Ⓔ ④
⑤ Ⓕ ⑤
⑥ Ⓖ ⑥
⑦ Ⓗ ⑦
⑧ Ⓘ ⑧
⑨ Ⓙ ⑨
　Ⓚ
　Ⓛ
　Ⓜ
　Ⓝ
　Ⓞ
　Ⓟ
　Ⓠ
　Ⓡ
　Ⓢ
　Ⓣ
　Ⓤ
　Ⓥ
　Ⓦ
　Ⓧ
　Ⓨ
　Ⓩ

9 BOOK ID
(Copy from back of test book.)

10 BOOK SERIAL NUMBER
(Copy from front of test book.)

⓪ ⓪ ⓪ ⓪ ⓪ ⓪
① ① ① ① ① ①
② ② ② ② ② ②
③ ③ ③ ③ ③ ③
④ ④ ④ ④ ④ ④
⑤ ⑤ ⑤ ⑤ ⑤ ⑤
⑥ ⑥ ⑥ ⑥ ⑥ ⑥
⑦ ⑦ ⑦ ⑦ ⑦ ⑦
⑧ ⑧ ⑧ ⑧ ⑧ ⑧
⑨ ⑨ ⑨ ⑨ ⑨ ⑨

emistry　*Fill in circle CE only if II is correct explanation of I.

	I	II	CE*		I	II	CE*
	Ⓣ Ⓕ	Ⓣ Ⓕ	◯	109	Ⓣ Ⓕ	Ⓣ Ⓕ	◯
2	Ⓣ Ⓕ	Ⓣ Ⓕ	◯	110	Ⓣ Ⓕ	Ⓣ Ⓕ	◯
3	Ⓣ Ⓕ	Ⓣ Ⓕ	◯	111	Ⓣ Ⓕ	Ⓣ Ⓕ	◯
4	Ⓣ Ⓕ	Ⓣ Ⓕ	◯	112	Ⓣ Ⓕ	Ⓣ Ⓕ	◯
5	Ⓣ Ⓕ	Ⓣ Ⓕ	◯	113	Ⓣ Ⓕ	Ⓣ Ⓕ	◯
6	Ⓣ Ⓕ	Ⓣ Ⓕ	◯	114	Ⓣ Ⓕ	Ⓣ Ⓕ	◯
7	Ⓣ Ⓕ	Ⓣ Ⓕ	◯	115	Ⓣ Ⓕ	Ⓣ Ⓕ	◯
8	Ⓣ Ⓕ	Ⓣ Ⓕ	◯				

FOR OFFICIAL USE ONLY

R/C	W/S1	FS/S2	CS/S3	WS

PLEASE DO NOT WRITE IN THIS AREA

◻◯◯◯◯◯◯◯◯◯◯◯◯◯◯◯◯◯◯◯◯◯◯◯◯◯◯◯◯◯◯◯◯◯◯◯◯◯

SERIAL #

Page 4

If there are more answer spaces than you need, leave them blank.

Test Code

V ① ② ③ ④ ⑤ ⑥ ⑦ ⑧ ⑨
W ① ② ③ ④ ⑤ ⑥ ⑦ ⑧ ⑨
X ① ② ③ ④ ⑤ Y Ⓐ Ⓑ Ⓒ Ⓓ Ⓔ
Q ① ② ③ ④ ⑤ ⑥ ⑦ ⑧ ⑨

Subject Test (print)

1 Ⓐ Ⓑ Ⓒ Ⓓ Ⓔ   26 Ⓐ Ⓑ Ⓒ Ⓓ Ⓔ   51 Ⓐ Ⓑ Ⓒ Ⓓ Ⓔ   76 Ⓐ Ⓑ Ⓒ Ⓓ Ⓔ
2 Ⓐ Ⓑ Ⓒ Ⓓ Ⓔ   27 Ⓐ Ⓑ Ⓒ Ⓓ Ⓔ   52 Ⓐ Ⓑ Ⓒ Ⓓ Ⓔ   77 Ⓐ Ⓑ Ⓒ Ⓓ Ⓔ
3 Ⓐ Ⓑ Ⓒ Ⓓ Ⓔ   28 Ⓐ Ⓑ Ⓒ Ⓓ Ⓔ   53 Ⓐ Ⓑ Ⓒ Ⓓ Ⓔ   78 Ⓐ Ⓑ Ⓒ Ⓓ Ⓔ
4 Ⓐ Ⓑ Ⓒ Ⓓ Ⓔ   29 Ⓐ Ⓑ Ⓒ Ⓓ Ⓔ   54 Ⓐ Ⓑ Ⓒ Ⓓ Ⓔ   79 Ⓐ Ⓑ Ⓒ Ⓓ Ⓔ
5 Ⓐ Ⓑ Ⓒ Ⓓ Ⓔ   30 Ⓐ Ⓑ Ⓒ Ⓓ Ⓔ   55 Ⓐ Ⓑ Ⓒ Ⓓ Ⓔ   80 Ⓐ Ⓑ Ⓒ Ⓓ Ⓔ
6 Ⓐ Ⓑ Ⓒ Ⓓ Ⓔ   31 Ⓐ Ⓑ Ⓒ Ⓓ Ⓔ   56 Ⓐ Ⓑ Ⓒ Ⓓ Ⓔ   81 Ⓐ Ⓑ Ⓒ Ⓓ Ⓔ
7 Ⓐ Ⓑ Ⓒ Ⓓ Ⓔ   32 Ⓐ Ⓑ Ⓒ Ⓓ Ⓔ   57 Ⓐ Ⓑ Ⓒ Ⓓ Ⓔ   82 Ⓐ Ⓑ Ⓒ Ⓓ Ⓔ
8 Ⓐ Ⓑ Ⓒ Ⓓ Ⓔ   33 Ⓐ Ⓑ Ⓒ Ⓓ Ⓔ   58 Ⓐ Ⓑ Ⓒ Ⓓ Ⓔ   83 Ⓐ Ⓑ Ⓒ Ⓓ Ⓔ
9 Ⓐ Ⓑ Ⓒ Ⓓ Ⓔ   34 Ⓐ Ⓑ Ⓒ Ⓓ Ⓔ   59 Ⓐ Ⓑ Ⓒ Ⓓ Ⓔ   84 Ⓐ Ⓑ Ⓒ Ⓓ Ⓔ
10 Ⓐ Ⓑ Ⓒ Ⓓ Ⓔ   35 Ⓐ Ⓑ Ⓒ Ⓓ Ⓔ   60 Ⓐ Ⓑ Ⓒ Ⓓ Ⓔ   85 Ⓐ Ⓑ Ⓒ Ⓓ Ⓔ
11 Ⓐ Ⓑ Ⓒ Ⓓ Ⓔ   36 Ⓐ Ⓑ Ⓒ Ⓓ Ⓔ   61 Ⓐ Ⓑ Ⓒ Ⓓ Ⓔ   86 Ⓐ Ⓑ Ⓒ Ⓓ Ⓔ
12 Ⓐ Ⓑ Ⓒ Ⓓ Ⓔ   37 Ⓐ Ⓑ Ⓒ Ⓓ Ⓔ   62 Ⓐ Ⓑ Ⓒ Ⓓ Ⓔ   87 Ⓐ Ⓑ Ⓒ Ⓓ Ⓔ
13 Ⓐ Ⓑ Ⓒ Ⓓ Ⓔ   38 Ⓐ Ⓑ Ⓒ Ⓓ Ⓔ   63 Ⓐ Ⓑ Ⓒ Ⓓ Ⓔ   88 Ⓐ Ⓑ Ⓒ Ⓓ Ⓔ
14 Ⓐ Ⓑ Ⓒ Ⓓ Ⓔ   39 Ⓐ Ⓑ Ⓒ Ⓓ Ⓔ   64 Ⓐ Ⓑ Ⓒ Ⓓ Ⓔ   89 Ⓐ Ⓑ Ⓒ Ⓓ Ⓔ
15 Ⓐ Ⓑ Ⓒ Ⓓ Ⓔ   40 Ⓐ Ⓑ Ⓒ Ⓓ Ⓔ   65 Ⓐ Ⓑ Ⓒ Ⓓ Ⓔ   90 Ⓐ Ⓑ Ⓒ Ⓓ Ⓔ
16 Ⓐ Ⓑ Ⓒ Ⓓ Ⓔ   41 Ⓐ Ⓑ Ⓒ Ⓓ Ⓔ   66 Ⓐ Ⓑ Ⓒ Ⓓ Ⓔ   91 Ⓐ Ⓑ Ⓒ Ⓓ Ⓔ
17 Ⓐ Ⓑ Ⓒ Ⓓ Ⓔ   42 Ⓐ Ⓑ Ⓒ Ⓓ Ⓔ   67 Ⓐ Ⓑ Ⓒ Ⓓ Ⓔ   92 Ⓐ Ⓑ Ⓒ Ⓓ Ⓔ
18 Ⓐ Ⓑ Ⓒ Ⓓ Ⓔ   43 Ⓐ Ⓑ Ⓒ Ⓓ Ⓔ   68 Ⓐ Ⓑ Ⓒ Ⓓ Ⓔ   93 Ⓐ Ⓑ Ⓒ Ⓓ Ⓔ
19 Ⓐ Ⓑ Ⓒ Ⓓ Ⓔ   44 Ⓐ Ⓑ Ⓒ Ⓓ Ⓔ   69 Ⓐ Ⓑ Ⓒ Ⓓ Ⓔ   94 Ⓐ Ⓑ Ⓒ Ⓓ Ⓔ
20 Ⓐ Ⓑ Ⓒ Ⓓ Ⓔ   45 Ⓐ Ⓑ Ⓒ Ⓓ Ⓔ   70 Ⓐ Ⓑ Ⓒ Ⓓ Ⓔ   95 Ⓐ Ⓑ Ⓒ Ⓓ Ⓔ
21 Ⓐ Ⓑ Ⓒ Ⓓ Ⓔ   46 Ⓐ Ⓑ Ⓒ Ⓓ Ⓔ   71 Ⓐ Ⓑ Ⓒ Ⓓ Ⓔ   96 Ⓐ Ⓑ Ⓒ Ⓓ Ⓔ
22 Ⓐ Ⓑ Ⓒ Ⓓ Ⓔ   47 Ⓐ Ⓑ Ⓒ Ⓓ Ⓔ   72 Ⓐ Ⓑ Ⓒ Ⓓ Ⓔ   97 Ⓐ Ⓑ Ⓒ Ⓓ Ⓔ
23 Ⓐ Ⓑ Ⓒ Ⓓ Ⓔ   48 Ⓐ Ⓑ Ⓒ Ⓓ Ⓔ   73 Ⓐ Ⓑ Ⓒ Ⓓ Ⓔ   98 Ⓐ Ⓑ Ⓒ Ⓓ Ⓔ
24 Ⓐ Ⓑ Ⓒ Ⓓ Ⓔ   49 Ⓐ Ⓑ Ⓒ Ⓓ Ⓔ   74 Ⓐ Ⓑ Ⓒ Ⓓ Ⓔ   99 Ⓐ Ⓑ Ⓒ Ⓓ Ⓔ
25 Ⓐ Ⓑ Ⓒ Ⓓ Ⓔ   50 Ⓐ Ⓑ Ⓒ Ⓓ Ⓔ   75 Ⓐ Ⓑ Ⓒ Ⓓ Ⓔ   100 Ⓐ Ⓑ Ⓒ Ⓓ Ⓔ

8 BOOK CODE

(Copy and grid as on back of test book.)

⓪ Ⓐ ⓪
① Ⓑ ①
② Ⓒ ②
③ Ⓓ ③
④ Ⓔ ④
⑤ Ⓕ ⑤
⑥ Ⓖ ⑥
⑦ Ⓗ ⑦
⑧ Ⓘ ⑧
⑨ Ⓙ ⑨
Ⓚ
Ⓛ
Ⓜ
Ⓝ
Ⓞ
Ⓟ
Ⓠ
Ⓡ
Ⓢ
Ⓣ
Ⓤ
Ⓥ
Ⓦ
Ⓧ
Ⓨ
Ⓩ

9 BOOK ID

(Copy from back of test book.)

10 BOOK SERIAL NUMBER

(Copy from front of test book.)

⓪ ⓪ ⓪ ⓪ ⓪ ⓪
① ① ① ① ① ①
② ② ② ② ② ②
③ ③ ③ ③ ③ ③
④ ④ ④ ④ ④ ④
⑤ ⑤ ⑤ ⑤ ⑤ ⑤
⑥ ⑥ ⑥ ⑥ ⑥ ⑥
⑦ ⑦ ⑦ ⑦ ⑦ ⑦
⑧ ⑧ ⑧ ⑧ ⑧ ⑧
⑨ ⑨ ⑨ ⑨ ⑨ ⑨

Chemistry   *Fill in circle CE only if II is correct explanation of I.

	I	II	CE*		I	II	CE*
101	Ⓣ Ⓕ	Ⓣ Ⓕ	○	109	Ⓣ Ⓕ	Ⓣ Ⓕ	○
102	Ⓣ Ⓕ	Ⓣ Ⓕ	○	110	Ⓣ Ⓕ	Ⓣ Ⓕ	○
103	Ⓣ Ⓕ	Ⓣ Ⓕ	○	111	Ⓣ Ⓕ	Ⓣ Ⓕ	○
104	Ⓣ Ⓕ	Ⓣ Ⓕ	○	112	Ⓣ Ⓕ	Ⓣ Ⓕ	○
105	Ⓣ Ⓕ	Ⓣ Ⓕ	○	113	Ⓣ Ⓕ	Ⓣ Ⓕ	○
106	Ⓣ Ⓕ	Ⓣ Ⓕ	○	114	Ⓣ Ⓕ	Ⓣ Ⓕ	○
107	Ⓣ Ⓕ	Ⓣ Ⓕ	○	115	Ⓣ Ⓕ	Ⓣ Ⓕ	○
108	Ⓣ Ⓕ	Ⓣ Ⓕ	○				

FOR OFFICIAL USE ONLY

R/C	W/S1	FS/S2	CS/S3	WS

CERTIFICATION STATEMENT

Copy the statement below (do not print) and sign your name as you would an official docume

I hereby agree to the conditions set forth online at www.collegeboard.com and/or in the Registration Bulletin and certify that I am the person whose name and address appear on this answer sheet.

Signature _____   Date _____

CollegeBoard SAT

SAT Subject Tests™

Use a No. 2 pencil only. Be sure each mark is dark and completely fills the intended circle. Completely erase any errors or stray marks.

Your Name:
(Print)

Last _____ First _____ M.I. _____

ee to the conditions on the back of the SAT® Subject Tests book.

ature: _____ Date ___/___/___

Address: _____
Number and Street   City   State   Zip Code

er: _____
)   City   State

YOUR NAME
t Name (4 Letters) | First Init. | Mid. Init.

3 SOCIAL SECURITY NUMBER

4 DATE OF BIRTH

MONTH	DAY	YEAR
Jan		
Feb		
Mar		
Apr		
May		
Jun		
Jul		
Aug		
Sep		
Oct		
Nov		
Dec		

5 SEX

◯ Female   ◯ Male

6 REGISTRATION NUMBER
(Copy from Admission Ticket.)

7 TEST CENTER
(Supplied by Test Center Supervisor.)

8 BOOK CODE
(Copy and grid as on back of test book.)

9 BOOK ID
(Copy from back of test book.)

10 BOOK SERIAL NUMBER
(Copy from front of test book.)

FOR OFFICIAL USE ONLY

0 1 2 3 4 5 6 7 8 9
0 1 2 3 4 5 6 7 8 9
0 1 2 3 4 5 6 7 8 9
0 1 2 3 4 5 6 7 8 9

11030-36392 • NS114E315 • Printed in U.S.A.
724844

170192-001:654321   ISD5122

Page 2

Use a No. 2 pencil only. Be sure each mark is dark and completely fills the intended circle. Completely erase any errors or stray marks.

If there are more answer spaces than you need, leave them blank.

Test Code

V	① ② ③ ④ ⑤ ⑥ ⑦ ⑧ ⑨
W	① ② ③ ④ ⑤ ⑥ ⑦ ⑧ ⑨
X	① ② ③ ④ ⑤ Y Ⓐ Ⓑ Ⓒ Ⓓ Ⓔ
Q	① ② ③ ④ ⑤ ⑥ ⑦ ⑧ ⑨

Subject Test (print)

1 Ⓐ Ⓑ Ⓒ Ⓓ Ⓔ   26 Ⓐ Ⓑ Ⓒ Ⓓ Ⓔ   51 Ⓐ Ⓑ Ⓒ Ⓓ Ⓔ   76 Ⓐ Ⓑ Ⓒ Ⓓ Ⓔ
2 Ⓐ Ⓑ Ⓒ Ⓓ Ⓔ   27 Ⓐ Ⓑ Ⓒ Ⓓ Ⓔ   52 Ⓐ Ⓑ Ⓒ Ⓓ Ⓔ   77 Ⓐ Ⓑ Ⓒ Ⓓ Ⓔ
3 Ⓐ Ⓑ Ⓒ Ⓓ Ⓔ   28 Ⓐ Ⓑ Ⓒ Ⓓ Ⓔ   53 Ⓐ Ⓑ Ⓒ Ⓓ Ⓔ   78 Ⓐ Ⓑ Ⓒ Ⓓ Ⓔ
4 Ⓐ Ⓑ Ⓒ Ⓓ Ⓔ   29 Ⓐ Ⓑ Ⓒ Ⓓ Ⓔ   54 Ⓐ Ⓑ Ⓒ Ⓓ Ⓔ   79 Ⓐ Ⓑ Ⓒ Ⓓ Ⓔ
5 Ⓐ Ⓑ Ⓒ Ⓓ Ⓔ   30 Ⓐ Ⓑ Ⓒ Ⓓ Ⓔ   55 Ⓐ Ⓑ Ⓒ Ⓓ Ⓔ   80 Ⓐ Ⓑ Ⓒ Ⓓ Ⓔ
6 Ⓐ Ⓑ Ⓒ Ⓓ Ⓔ   31 Ⓐ Ⓑ Ⓒ Ⓓ Ⓔ   56 Ⓐ Ⓑ Ⓒ Ⓓ Ⓔ   81 Ⓐ Ⓑ Ⓒ Ⓓ Ⓔ
7 Ⓐ Ⓑ Ⓒ Ⓓ Ⓔ   32 Ⓐ Ⓑ Ⓒ Ⓓ Ⓔ   57 Ⓐ Ⓑ Ⓒ Ⓓ Ⓔ   82 Ⓐ Ⓑ Ⓒ Ⓓ Ⓔ
8 Ⓐ Ⓑ Ⓒ Ⓓ Ⓔ   33 Ⓐ Ⓑ Ⓒ Ⓓ Ⓔ   58 Ⓐ Ⓑ Ⓒ Ⓓ Ⓔ   83 Ⓐ Ⓑ Ⓒ Ⓓ Ⓔ
9 Ⓐ Ⓑ Ⓒ Ⓓ Ⓔ   34 Ⓐ Ⓑ Ⓒ Ⓓ Ⓔ   59 Ⓐ Ⓑ Ⓒ Ⓓ Ⓔ   84 Ⓐ Ⓑ Ⓒ Ⓓ Ⓔ
10 Ⓐ Ⓑ Ⓒ Ⓓ Ⓔ   35 Ⓐ Ⓑ Ⓒ Ⓓ Ⓔ   60 Ⓐ Ⓑ Ⓒ Ⓓ Ⓔ   85 Ⓐ Ⓑ Ⓒ Ⓓ Ⓔ
11 Ⓐ Ⓑ Ⓒ Ⓓ Ⓔ   36 Ⓐ Ⓑ Ⓒ Ⓓ Ⓔ   61 Ⓐ Ⓑ Ⓒ Ⓓ Ⓔ   86 Ⓐ Ⓑ Ⓒ Ⓓ Ⓔ
12 Ⓐ Ⓑ Ⓒ Ⓓ Ⓔ   37 Ⓐ Ⓑ Ⓒ Ⓓ Ⓔ   62 Ⓐ Ⓑ Ⓒ Ⓓ Ⓔ   87 Ⓐ Ⓑ Ⓒ Ⓓ Ⓔ
13 Ⓐ Ⓑ Ⓒ Ⓓ Ⓔ   38 Ⓐ Ⓑ Ⓒ Ⓓ Ⓔ   63 Ⓐ Ⓑ Ⓒ Ⓓ Ⓔ   88 Ⓐ Ⓑ Ⓒ Ⓓ Ⓔ
14 Ⓐ Ⓑ Ⓒ Ⓓ Ⓔ   39 Ⓐ Ⓑ Ⓒ Ⓓ Ⓔ   64 Ⓐ Ⓑ Ⓒ Ⓓ Ⓔ   89 Ⓐ Ⓑ Ⓒ Ⓓ Ⓔ
15 Ⓐ Ⓑ Ⓒ Ⓓ Ⓔ   40 Ⓐ Ⓑ Ⓒ Ⓓ Ⓔ   65 Ⓐ Ⓑ Ⓒ Ⓓ Ⓔ   90 Ⓐ Ⓑ Ⓒ Ⓓ Ⓔ
16 Ⓐ Ⓑ Ⓒ Ⓓ Ⓔ   41 Ⓐ Ⓑ Ⓒ Ⓓ Ⓔ   66 Ⓐ Ⓑ Ⓒ Ⓓ Ⓔ   91 Ⓐ Ⓑ Ⓒ Ⓓ Ⓔ
17 Ⓐ Ⓑ Ⓒ Ⓓ Ⓔ   42 Ⓐ Ⓑ Ⓒ Ⓓ Ⓔ   67 Ⓐ Ⓑ Ⓒ Ⓓ Ⓔ   92 Ⓐ Ⓑ Ⓒ Ⓓ Ⓔ
18 Ⓐ Ⓑ Ⓒ Ⓓ Ⓔ   43 Ⓐ Ⓑ Ⓒ Ⓓ Ⓔ   68 Ⓐ Ⓑ Ⓒ Ⓓ Ⓔ   93 Ⓐ Ⓑ Ⓒ Ⓓ Ⓔ
19 Ⓐ Ⓑ Ⓒ Ⓓ Ⓔ   44 Ⓐ Ⓑ Ⓒ Ⓓ Ⓔ   69 Ⓐ Ⓑ Ⓒ Ⓓ Ⓔ   94 Ⓐ Ⓑ Ⓒ Ⓓ Ⓔ
20 Ⓐ Ⓑ Ⓒ Ⓓ Ⓔ   45 Ⓐ Ⓑ Ⓒ Ⓓ Ⓔ   70 Ⓐ Ⓑ Ⓒ Ⓓ Ⓔ   95 Ⓐ Ⓑ Ⓒ Ⓓ Ⓔ
21 Ⓐ Ⓑ Ⓒ Ⓓ Ⓔ   46 Ⓐ Ⓑ Ⓒ Ⓓ Ⓔ   71 Ⓐ Ⓑ Ⓒ Ⓓ Ⓔ   96 Ⓐ Ⓑ Ⓒ Ⓓ Ⓔ
22 Ⓐ Ⓑ Ⓒ Ⓓ Ⓔ   47 Ⓐ Ⓑ Ⓒ Ⓓ Ⓔ   72 Ⓐ Ⓑ Ⓒ Ⓓ Ⓔ   97 Ⓐ Ⓑ Ⓒ Ⓓ Ⓔ
23 Ⓐ Ⓑ Ⓒ Ⓓ Ⓔ   48 Ⓐ Ⓑ Ⓒ Ⓓ Ⓔ   73 Ⓐ Ⓑ Ⓒ Ⓓ Ⓔ   98 Ⓐ Ⓑ Ⓒ Ⓓ Ⓔ
24 Ⓐ Ⓑ Ⓒ Ⓓ Ⓔ   49 Ⓐ Ⓑ Ⓒ Ⓓ Ⓔ   74 Ⓐ Ⓑ Ⓒ Ⓓ Ⓔ   99 Ⓐ Ⓑ Ⓒ Ⓓ Ⓔ
25 Ⓐ Ⓑ Ⓒ Ⓓ Ⓔ   50 Ⓐ Ⓑ Ⓒ Ⓓ Ⓔ   75 Ⓐ Ⓑ Ⓒ Ⓓ Ⓔ   100 Ⓐ Ⓑ Ⓒ Ⓓ Ⓔ

Chemistry *Fill in circle CE only if II is correct explanation of I.

	I	II	CE*		I	II	CE*
101	Ⓣ Ⓕ	Ⓣ Ⓕ	○	109	Ⓣ Ⓕ	Ⓣ Ⓕ	○
102	Ⓣ Ⓕ	Ⓣ Ⓕ	○	110	Ⓣ Ⓕ	Ⓣ Ⓕ	○
103	Ⓣ Ⓕ	Ⓣ Ⓕ	○	111	Ⓣ Ⓕ	Ⓣ Ⓕ	○
104	Ⓣ Ⓕ	Ⓣ Ⓕ	○	112	Ⓣ Ⓕ	Ⓣ Ⓕ	○
105	Ⓣ Ⓕ	Ⓣ Ⓕ	○	113	Ⓣ Ⓕ	Ⓣ Ⓕ	○
106	Ⓣ Ⓕ	Ⓣ Ⓕ	○	114	Ⓣ Ⓕ	Ⓣ Ⓕ	○
107	Ⓣ Ⓕ	Ⓣ Ⓕ	○	115	Ⓣ Ⓕ	Ⓣ Ⓕ	○
108	Ⓣ Ⓕ	Ⓣ Ⓕ	○				

8 BOOK CODE
(Copy and grid as on back of test book.)

⓪ Ⓐ ⓪
① Ⓑ ①
② Ⓒ ②
③ Ⓓ ③
④ Ⓔ ④
⑤ Ⓕ ⑤
⑥ Ⓖ ⑥
⑦ Ⓗ ⑦
⑧ Ⓘ ⑧
⑨ Ⓙ ⑨
Ⓚ
Ⓛ
Ⓜ
Ⓝ
Ⓞ
Ⓟ
Ⓠ
Ⓡ
Ⓢ
Ⓣ
Ⓤ
Ⓥ
Ⓦ
Ⓧ
Ⓨ
Ⓩ

9 BOOK ID
(Copy from back of test book.)

10 BOOK SERIAL NUMBER
(Copy from front of test book.)

⓪ ⓪ ⓪ ⓪ ⓪ ⓪
① ① ① ① ① ①
② ② ② ② ② ②
③ ③ ③ ③ ③ ③
④ ④ ④ ④ ④ ④
⑤ ⑤ ⑤ ⑤ ⑤ ⑤
⑥ ⑥ ⑥ ⑥ ⑥ ⑥
⑦ ⑦ ⑦ ⑦ ⑦ ⑦
⑧ ⑧ ⑧ ⑧ ⑧ ⑧
⑨ ⑨ ⑨ ⑨ ⑨ ⑨

FOR OFFICIAL USE ONLY

R/C	W/S1	FS/S2	CS/S3	WS

PLEASE DO NOT WRITE IN THIS AREA

SERIAL #

Use a No. 2 pencil only. Be sure each mark is dark and completely fills the intended circle. Completely erase any errors or stray marks.

ere are more
wer spaces
n you need,
e them blank.

Test Code

V	① ② ③ ④ ⑤ ⑥ ⑦ ⑧ ⑨	
W	① ② ③ ④ ⑤ ⑥ ⑦ ⑧ ⑨	
X	① ② ③ ④ ⑤ Ⓨ Ⓐ Ⓑ Ⓒ Ⓓ Ⓔ	
Q	① ② ③ ④ ⑤ ⑥ ⑦ ⑧ ⑨	

Subject Test (print)

Ⓑ Ⓒ Ⓓ Ⓔ 26 Ⓐ Ⓑ Ⓒ Ⓓ Ⓔ 51 Ⓐ Ⓑ Ⓒ Ⓓ Ⓔ 76 Ⓐ Ⓑ Ⓒ Ⓓ Ⓔ
Ⓑ Ⓒ Ⓓ Ⓔ 27 Ⓐ Ⓑ Ⓒ Ⓓ Ⓔ 52 Ⓐ Ⓑ Ⓒ Ⓓ Ⓔ 77 Ⓐ Ⓑ Ⓒ Ⓓ Ⓔ
Ⓑ Ⓒ Ⓓ Ⓔ 28 Ⓐ Ⓑ Ⓒ Ⓓ Ⓔ 53 Ⓐ Ⓑ Ⓒ Ⓓ Ⓔ 78 Ⓐ Ⓑ Ⓒ Ⓓ Ⓔ
Ⓑ Ⓒ Ⓓ Ⓔ 29 Ⓐ Ⓑ Ⓒ Ⓓ Ⓔ 54 Ⓐ Ⓑ Ⓒ Ⓓ Ⓔ 79 Ⓐ Ⓑ Ⓒ Ⓓ Ⓔ
Ⓑ Ⓒ Ⓓ Ⓔ 30 Ⓐ Ⓑ Ⓒ Ⓓ Ⓔ 55 Ⓐ Ⓑ Ⓒ Ⓓ Ⓔ 80 Ⓐ Ⓑ Ⓒ Ⓓ Ⓔ
Ⓑ Ⓒ Ⓓ Ⓔ 31 Ⓐ Ⓑ Ⓒ Ⓓ Ⓔ 56 Ⓐ Ⓑ Ⓒ Ⓓ Ⓔ 81 Ⓐ Ⓑ Ⓒ Ⓓ Ⓔ
Ⓑ Ⓒ Ⓓ Ⓔ 32 Ⓐ Ⓑ Ⓒ Ⓓ Ⓔ 57 Ⓐ Ⓑ Ⓒ Ⓓ Ⓔ 82 Ⓐ Ⓑ Ⓒ Ⓓ Ⓔ
Ⓑ Ⓒ Ⓓ Ⓔ 33 Ⓐ Ⓑ Ⓒ Ⓓ Ⓔ 58 Ⓐ Ⓑ Ⓒ Ⓓ Ⓔ 83 Ⓐ Ⓑ Ⓒ Ⓓ Ⓔ
Ⓑ Ⓒ Ⓓ Ⓔ 34 Ⓐ Ⓑ Ⓒ Ⓓ Ⓔ 59 Ⓐ Ⓑ Ⓒ Ⓓ Ⓔ 84 Ⓐ Ⓑ Ⓒ Ⓓ Ⓔ
Ⓑ Ⓒ Ⓓ Ⓔ 35 Ⓐ Ⓑ Ⓒ Ⓓ Ⓔ 60 Ⓐ Ⓑ Ⓒ Ⓓ Ⓔ 85 Ⓐ Ⓑ Ⓒ Ⓓ Ⓔ
Ⓑ Ⓒ Ⓓ Ⓔ 36 Ⓐ Ⓑ Ⓒ Ⓓ Ⓔ 61 Ⓐ Ⓑ Ⓒ Ⓓ Ⓔ 86 Ⓐ Ⓑ Ⓒ Ⓓ Ⓔ
Ⓑ Ⓒ Ⓓ Ⓔ 37 Ⓐ Ⓑ Ⓒ Ⓓ Ⓔ 62 Ⓐ Ⓑ Ⓒ Ⓓ Ⓔ 87 Ⓐ Ⓑ Ⓒ Ⓓ Ⓔ
Ⓑ Ⓒ Ⓓ Ⓔ 38 Ⓐ Ⓑ Ⓒ Ⓓ Ⓔ 63 Ⓐ Ⓑ Ⓒ Ⓓ Ⓔ 88 Ⓐ Ⓑ Ⓒ Ⓓ Ⓔ
Ⓑ Ⓒ Ⓓ Ⓔ 39 Ⓐ Ⓑ Ⓒ Ⓓ Ⓔ 64 Ⓐ Ⓑ Ⓒ Ⓓ Ⓔ 89 Ⓐ Ⓑ Ⓒ Ⓓ Ⓔ
Ⓑ Ⓒ Ⓓ Ⓔ 40 Ⓐ Ⓑ Ⓒ Ⓓ Ⓔ 65 Ⓐ Ⓑ Ⓒ Ⓓ Ⓔ 90 Ⓐ Ⓑ Ⓒ Ⓓ Ⓔ
Ⓑ Ⓒ Ⓓ Ⓔ 41 Ⓐ Ⓑ Ⓒ Ⓓ Ⓔ 66 Ⓐ Ⓑ Ⓒ Ⓓ Ⓔ 91 Ⓐ Ⓑ Ⓒ Ⓓ Ⓔ
Ⓑ Ⓒ Ⓓ Ⓔ 42 Ⓐ Ⓑ Ⓒ Ⓓ Ⓔ 67 Ⓐ Ⓑ Ⓒ Ⓓ Ⓔ 92 Ⓐ Ⓑ Ⓒ Ⓓ Ⓔ
Ⓑ Ⓒ Ⓓ Ⓔ 43 Ⓐ Ⓑ Ⓒ Ⓓ Ⓔ 68 Ⓐ Ⓑ Ⓒ Ⓓ Ⓔ 93 Ⓐ Ⓑ Ⓒ Ⓓ Ⓔ
Ⓑ Ⓒ Ⓓ Ⓔ 44 Ⓐ Ⓑ Ⓒ Ⓓ Ⓔ 69 Ⓐ Ⓑ Ⓒ Ⓓ Ⓔ 94 Ⓐ Ⓑ Ⓒ Ⓓ Ⓔ
Ⓑ Ⓒ Ⓓ Ⓔ 45 Ⓐ Ⓑ Ⓒ Ⓓ Ⓔ 70 Ⓐ Ⓑ Ⓒ Ⓓ Ⓔ 95 Ⓐ Ⓑ Ⓒ Ⓓ Ⓔ
Ⓑ Ⓒ Ⓓ Ⓔ 46 Ⓐ Ⓑ Ⓒ Ⓓ Ⓔ 71 Ⓐ Ⓑ Ⓒ Ⓓ Ⓔ 96 Ⓐ Ⓑ Ⓒ Ⓓ Ⓔ
Ⓑ Ⓒ Ⓓ Ⓔ 47 Ⓐ Ⓑ Ⓒ Ⓓ Ⓔ 72 Ⓐ Ⓑ Ⓒ Ⓓ Ⓔ 97 Ⓐ Ⓑ Ⓒ Ⓓ Ⓔ
Ⓑ Ⓒ Ⓓ Ⓔ 48 Ⓐ Ⓑ Ⓒ Ⓓ Ⓔ 73 Ⓐ Ⓑ Ⓒ Ⓓ Ⓔ 98 Ⓐ Ⓑ Ⓒ Ⓓ Ⓔ
Ⓑ Ⓒ Ⓓ Ⓔ 49 Ⓐ Ⓑ Ⓒ Ⓓ Ⓔ 74 Ⓐ Ⓑ Ⓒ Ⓓ Ⓔ 99 Ⓐ Ⓑ Ⓒ Ⓓ Ⓔ
Ⓑ Ⓒ Ⓓ Ⓔ 50 Ⓐ Ⓑ Ⓒ Ⓓ Ⓔ 75 Ⓐ Ⓑ Ⓒ Ⓓ Ⓔ 100 Ⓐ Ⓑ Ⓒ Ⓓ Ⓔ

nistry   *Fill in circle CE only if II is correct explanation of I.

I	II	CE*		I	II	CE*
Ⓣ Ⓕ	Ⓣ Ⓕ	◯	109	Ⓣ Ⓕ	Ⓣ Ⓕ	◯
Ⓣ Ⓕ	Ⓣ Ⓕ	◯	110	Ⓣ Ⓕ	Ⓣ Ⓕ	◯
Ⓣ Ⓕ	Ⓣ Ⓕ	◯	111	Ⓣ Ⓕ	Ⓣ Ⓕ	◯
Ⓣ Ⓕ	Ⓣ Ⓕ	◯	112	Ⓣ Ⓕ	Ⓣ Ⓕ	◯
Ⓣ Ⓕ	Ⓣ Ⓕ	◯	113	Ⓣ Ⓕ	Ⓣ Ⓕ	◯
Ⓣ Ⓕ	Ⓣ Ⓕ	◯	114	Ⓣ Ⓕ	Ⓣ Ⓕ	◯
Ⓣ Ⓕ	Ⓣ Ⓕ	◯	115	Ⓣ Ⓕ	Ⓣ Ⓕ	◯
Ⓣ Ⓕ	Ⓣ Ⓕ	◯				

8 BOOK CODE
(Copy and grid as on back of test book.)

⓪ Ⓐ ⓪
① Ⓑ ①
② Ⓒ ②
③ Ⓓ ③
④ Ⓔ ④
⑤ Ⓕ ⑤
⑥ Ⓖ ⑥
⑦ Ⓗ ⑦
⑧ Ⓘ ⑧
⑨ Ⓙ ⑨
Ⓚ
Ⓛ
Ⓜ
Ⓝ
Ⓞ
Ⓟ
Ⓠ
Ⓡ
Ⓢ
Ⓣ
Ⓤ
Ⓥ
Ⓦ
Ⓧ
Ⓨ
Ⓩ

9 BOOK ID
(Copy from back of test book.)

10 BOOK SERIAL NUMBER
(Copy from front of test book.)

⓪ ⓪ ⓪ ⓪ ⓪ ⓪
① ① ① ① ① ①
② ② ② ② ② ②
③ ③ ③ ③ ③ ③
④ ④ ④ ④ ④ ④
⑤ ⑤ ⑤ ⑤ ⑤ ⑤
⑥ ⑥ ⑥ ⑥ ⑥ ⑥
⑦ ⑦ ⑦ ⑦ ⑦ ⑦
⑧ ⑧ ⑧ ⑧ ⑧ ⑧
⑨ ⑨ ⑨ ⑨ ⑨ ⑨

FOR OFFICIAL USE ONLY				
R/C	W/S1	FS/S2	CS/S3	WS

PLEASE DO NOT WRITE IN THIS AREA

SERIAL #

Use a No. 2 pencil only. Be sure each mark is dark and completely fills the intended circle. Completely erase any errors or stray marks.

If there are more answer spaces than you need, leave them blank.

Test Code

V	① ② ③ ④ ⑤ ⑥ ⑦ ⑧ ⑨
W	① ② ③ ④ ⑤ ⑥ ⑦ ⑧ ⑨
X	① ② ③ ④ ⑤ Ⓨ Ⓐ Ⓑ Ⓒ Ⓓ Ⓔ
Q	① ② ③ ④ ⑤ ⑥ ⑦ ⑧ ⑨

Subject Test (print)

1 Ⓐ Ⓑ Ⓒ Ⓓ Ⓔ　26 Ⓐ Ⓑ Ⓒ Ⓓ Ⓔ　51 Ⓐ Ⓑ Ⓒ Ⓓ Ⓔ　76 Ⓐ Ⓑ Ⓒ Ⓓ Ⓔ
2 Ⓐ Ⓑ Ⓒ Ⓓ Ⓔ　27 Ⓐ Ⓑ Ⓒ Ⓓ Ⓔ　52 Ⓐ Ⓑ Ⓒ Ⓓ Ⓔ　77 Ⓐ Ⓑ Ⓒ Ⓓ Ⓔ
3 Ⓐ Ⓑ Ⓒ Ⓓ Ⓔ　28 Ⓐ Ⓑ Ⓒ Ⓓ Ⓔ　53 Ⓐ Ⓑ Ⓒ Ⓓ Ⓔ　78 Ⓐ Ⓑ Ⓒ Ⓓ Ⓔ
4 Ⓐ Ⓑ Ⓒ Ⓓ Ⓔ　29 Ⓐ Ⓑ Ⓒ Ⓓ Ⓔ　54 Ⓐ Ⓑ Ⓒ Ⓓ Ⓔ　79 Ⓐ Ⓑ Ⓒ Ⓓ Ⓔ
5 Ⓐ Ⓑ Ⓒ Ⓓ Ⓔ　30 Ⓐ Ⓑ Ⓒ Ⓓ Ⓔ　55 Ⓐ Ⓑ Ⓒ Ⓓ Ⓔ　80 Ⓐ Ⓑ Ⓒ Ⓓ Ⓔ
6 Ⓐ Ⓑ Ⓒ Ⓓ Ⓔ　31 Ⓐ Ⓑ Ⓒ Ⓓ Ⓔ　56 Ⓐ Ⓑ Ⓒ Ⓓ Ⓔ　81 Ⓐ Ⓑ Ⓒ Ⓓ Ⓔ
7 Ⓐ Ⓑ Ⓒ Ⓓ Ⓔ　32 Ⓐ Ⓑ Ⓒ Ⓓ Ⓔ　57 Ⓐ Ⓑ Ⓒ Ⓓ Ⓔ　82 Ⓐ Ⓑ Ⓒ Ⓓ Ⓔ
8 Ⓐ Ⓑ Ⓒ Ⓓ Ⓔ　33 Ⓐ Ⓑ Ⓒ Ⓓ Ⓔ　58 Ⓐ Ⓑ Ⓒ Ⓓ Ⓔ　83 Ⓐ Ⓑ Ⓒ Ⓓ Ⓔ
9 Ⓐ Ⓑ Ⓒ Ⓓ Ⓔ　34 Ⓐ Ⓑ Ⓒ Ⓓ Ⓔ　59 Ⓐ Ⓑ Ⓒ Ⓓ Ⓔ　84 Ⓐ Ⓑ Ⓒ Ⓓ Ⓔ
10 Ⓐ Ⓑ Ⓒ Ⓓ Ⓔ　35 Ⓐ Ⓑ Ⓒ Ⓓ Ⓔ　60 Ⓐ Ⓑ Ⓒ Ⓓ Ⓔ　85 Ⓐ Ⓑ Ⓒ Ⓓ Ⓔ
11 Ⓐ Ⓑ Ⓒ Ⓓ Ⓔ　36 Ⓐ Ⓑ Ⓒ Ⓓ Ⓔ　61 Ⓐ Ⓑ Ⓒ Ⓓ Ⓔ　86 Ⓐ Ⓑ Ⓒ Ⓓ Ⓔ
12 Ⓐ Ⓑ Ⓒ Ⓓ Ⓔ　37 Ⓐ Ⓑ Ⓒ Ⓓ Ⓔ　62 Ⓐ Ⓑ Ⓒ Ⓓ Ⓔ　87 Ⓐ Ⓑ Ⓒ Ⓓ Ⓔ
13 Ⓐ Ⓑ Ⓒ Ⓓ Ⓔ　38 Ⓐ Ⓑ Ⓒ Ⓓ Ⓔ　63 Ⓐ Ⓑ Ⓒ Ⓓ Ⓔ　88 Ⓐ Ⓑ Ⓒ Ⓓ Ⓔ
14 Ⓐ Ⓑ Ⓒ Ⓓ Ⓔ　39 Ⓐ Ⓑ Ⓒ Ⓓ Ⓔ　64 Ⓐ Ⓑ Ⓒ Ⓓ Ⓔ　89 Ⓐ Ⓑ Ⓒ Ⓓ Ⓔ
15 Ⓐ Ⓑ Ⓒ Ⓓ Ⓔ　40 Ⓐ Ⓑ Ⓒ Ⓓ Ⓔ　65 Ⓐ Ⓑ Ⓒ Ⓓ Ⓔ　90 Ⓐ Ⓑ Ⓒ Ⓓ Ⓔ
16 Ⓐ Ⓑ Ⓒ Ⓓ Ⓔ　41 Ⓐ Ⓑ Ⓒ Ⓓ Ⓔ　66 Ⓐ Ⓑ Ⓒ Ⓓ Ⓔ　91 Ⓐ Ⓑ Ⓒ Ⓓ Ⓔ
17 Ⓐ Ⓑ Ⓒ Ⓓ Ⓔ　42 Ⓐ Ⓑ Ⓒ Ⓓ Ⓔ　67 Ⓐ Ⓑ Ⓒ Ⓓ Ⓔ　92 Ⓐ Ⓑ Ⓒ Ⓓ Ⓔ
18 Ⓐ Ⓑ Ⓒ Ⓓ Ⓔ　43 Ⓐ Ⓑ Ⓒ Ⓓ Ⓔ　68 Ⓐ Ⓑ Ⓒ Ⓓ Ⓔ　93 Ⓐ Ⓑ Ⓒ Ⓓ Ⓔ
19 Ⓐ Ⓑ Ⓒ Ⓓ Ⓔ　44 Ⓐ Ⓑ Ⓒ Ⓓ Ⓔ　69 Ⓐ Ⓑ Ⓒ Ⓓ Ⓔ　94 Ⓐ Ⓑ Ⓒ Ⓓ Ⓔ
20 Ⓐ Ⓑ Ⓒ Ⓓ Ⓔ　45 Ⓐ Ⓑ Ⓒ Ⓓ Ⓔ　70 Ⓐ Ⓑ Ⓒ Ⓓ Ⓔ　95 Ⓐ Ⓑ Ⓒ Ⓓ Ⓔ
21 Ⓐ Ⓑ Ⓒ Ⓓ Ⓔ　46 Ⓐ Ⓑ Ⓒ Ⓓ Ⓔ　71 Ⓐ Ⓑ Ⓒ Ⓓ Ⓔ　96 Ⓐ Ⓑ Ⓒ Ⓓ Ⓔ
22 Ⓐ Ⓑ Ⓒ Ⓓ Ⓔ　47 Ⓐ Ⓑ Ⓒ Ⓓ Ⓔ　72 Ⓐ Ⓑ Ⓒ Ⓓ Ⓔ　97 Ⓐ Ⓑ Ⓒ Ⓓ Ⓔ
23 Ⓐ Ⓑ Ⓒ Ⓓ Ⓔ　48 Ⓐ Ⓑ Ⓒ Ⓓ Ⓔ　73 Ⓐ Ⓑ Ⓒ Ⓓ Ⓔ　98 Ⓐ Ⓑ Ⓒ Ⓓ Ⓔ
24 Ⓐ Ⓑ Ⓒ Ⓓ Ⓔ　49 Ⓐ Ⓑ Ⓒ Ⓓ Ⓔ　74 Ⓐ Ⓑ Ⓒ Ⓓ Ⓔ　99 Ⓐ Ⓑ Ⓒ Ⓓ Ⓔ
25 Ⓐ Ⓑ Ⓒ Ⓓ Ⓔ　50 Ⓐ Ⓑ Ⓒ Ⓓ Ⓔ　75 Ⓐ Ⓑ Ⓒ Ⓓ Ⓔ　100 Ⓐ Ⓑ Ⓒ Ⓓ Ⓔ

8 BOOK CODE
(Copy and grid as on back of test book.)

⓪	Ⓐ	⓪
①	Ⓑ	①
②	Ⓒ	②
③	Ⓓ	③
④	Ⓔ	④
⑤	Ⓕ	⑤
⑥	Ⓖ	⑥
⑦	Ⓗ	⑦
⑧	Ⓘ	⑧
⑨	Ⓙ	⑨
	Ⓚ	
	Ⓛ	
	Ⓜ	
	Ⓝ	
	Ⓞ	
	Ⓟ	
	Ⓠ	
	Ⓡ	
	Ⓢ	
	Ⓣ	
	Ⓤ	
	Ⓥ	
	Ⓦ	
	Ⓧ	
	Ⓨ	
	Ⓩ	

9 BOOK ID
(Copy from back of test book.)

10 BOOK SERIAL NUMBER
(Copy from front of test book.)

⓪ ⓪ ⓪ ⓪ ⓪ ⓪
① ① ① ① ① ①
② ② ② ② ② ②
③ ③ ③ ③ ③ ③
④ ④ ④ ④ ④ ④
⑤ ⑤ ⑤ ⑤ ⑤ ⑤
⑥ ⑥ ⑥ ⑥ ⑥ ⑥
⑦ ⑦ ⑦ ⑦ ⑦ ⑦
⑧ ⑧ ⑧ ⑧ ⑧ ⑧
⑨ ⑨ ⑨ ⑨ ⑨ ⑨

Chemistry *Fill in circle CE only if II is correct explanation of I.

	I	II	CE*		I	II	CE*
101	Ⓣ Ⓕ	Ⓣ Ⓕ	◯	109	Ⓣ Ⓕ	Ⓣ Ⓕ	◯
102	Ⓣ Ⓕ	Ⓣ Ⓕ	◯	110	Ⓣ Ⓕ	Ⓣ Ⓕ	◯
103	Ⓣ Ⓕ	Ⓣ Ⓕ	◯	111	Ⓣ Ⓕ	Ⓣ Ⓕ	◯
104	Ⓣ Ⓕ	Ⓣ Ⓕ	◯	112	Ⓣ Ⓕ	Ⓣ Ⓕ	◯
105	Ⓣ Ⓕ	Ⓣ Ⓕ	◯	113	Ⓣ Ⓕ	Ⓣ Ⓕ	◯
106	Ⓣ Ⓕ	Ⓣ Ⓕ	◯	114	Ⓣ Ⓕ	Ⓣ Ⓕ	◯
107	Ⓣ Ⓕ	Ⓣ Ⓕ	◯	115	Ⓣ Ⓕ	Ⓣ Ⓕ	◯
108	Ⓣ Ⓕ	Ⓣ Ⓕ	◯				

FOR OFFICIAL USE ONLY

R/C	W/S1	FS/S2	CS/S3	WS

CERTIFICATION STATEMENT

Copy the statement below (do not print) and sign your name as you would an official docum

I hereby agree to the conditions set forth online at www.collegeboard.com and/or in the Registration Bulletin and certify that I am the person whose name and address appear on this answer sheet.

Signature _____　Date _____

ollegeBoard SAT

SAT Subject Tests™

Use a No. 2 pencil only. Be sure each mark is dark and *completely fills the intended circle. Completely erase any errors or stray marks.*

Your Name:
(Print)

Last   First   M.I.

ee to the conditions on the back of the SAT® Subject Tests book.

ture: Date / /

Address:

Number and Street   City   State   Zip Code

r:

City   State

YOUR NAME

Name Letters) | First Init. | Mid. Init.

3 SOCIAL SECURITY NUMBER

5 SEX

○ Female   ○ Male

6 REGISTRATION NUMBER

(Copy from Admission Ticket.)

4 DATE OF BIRTH

MONTH | DAY | YEAR

○ Jan
○ Feb
○ Mar
○ Apr
○ May
○ Jun
○ Jul
○ Aug
○ Sep
○ Oct
○ Nov
○ Dec

7 TEST CENTER

(Supplied by Test Center Supervisor.)

8 BOOK CODE

(Copy and grid as on back of test book.)

9 BOOK ID

(Copy from back of test book.)

10 BOOK SERIAL NUMBER

(Copy from front of test book.)

FOR OFFICIAL USE ONLY

⓪①②③④⑤⑥⑦⑧⑨
⓪①②③④⑤⑥⑦⑧⑨
⓪①②③④⑤⑥⑦⑧⑨
⓪①②③④⑤⑥⑦⑧⑨

11030-36392 • NS114E315 • Printed in U.S.A.
724844

Page 2

If there are more answer spaces than you need, leave them blank.

Test Code

V	①	②	③	④	⑤	⑥	⑦	⑧	⑨	
W	①	②	③	④	⑤	⑥	⑦	⑧	⑨	
X	①	②	③	④	⑤	Y	Ⓐ	Ⓑ	Ⓒ	Ⓓ Ⓔ
Q	①	②	③	④	⑤	⑥	⑦	⑧	⑨	

Subject Test (print)

1 Ⓐ Ⓑ Ⓒ Ⓓ Ⓔ   26 Ⓐ Ⓑ Ⓒ Ⓓ Ⓔ   51 Ⓐ Ⓑ Ⓒ Ⓓ Ⓔ   76 Ⓐ Ⓑ Ⓒ Ⓓ Ⓔ
2 Ⓐ Ⓑ Ⓒ Ⓓ Ⓔ   27 Ⓐ Ⓑ Ⓒ Ⓓ Ⓔ   52 Ⓐ Ⓑ Ⓒ Ⓓ Ⓔ   77 Ⓐ Ⓑ Ⓒ Ⓓ Ⓔ
3 Ⓐ Ⓑ Ⓒ Ⓓ Ⓔ   28 Ⓐ Ⓑ Ⓒ Ⓓ Ⓔ   53 Ⓐ Ⓑ Ⓒ Ⓓ Ⓔ   78 Ⓐ Ⓑ Ⓒ Ⓓ Ⓔ
4 Ⓐ Ⓑ Ⓒ Ⓓ Ⓔ   29 Ⓐ Ⓑ Ⓒ Ⓓ Ⓔ   54 Ⓐ Ⓑ Ⓒ Ⓓ Ⓔ   79 Ⓐ Ⓑ Ⓒ Ⓓ Ⓔ
5 Ⓐ Ⓑ Ⓒ Ⓓ Ⓔ   30 Ⓐ Ⓑ Ⓒ Ⓓ Ⓔ   55 Ⓐ Ⓑ Ⓒ Ⓓ Ⓔ   80 Ⓐ Ⓑ Ⓒ Ⓓ Ⓔ
6 Ⓐ Ⓑ Ⓒ Ⓓ Ⓔ   31 Ⓐ Ⓑ Ⓒ Ⓓ Ⓔ   56 Ⓐ Ⓑ Ⓒ Ⓓ Ⓔ   81 Ⓐ Ⓑ Ⓒ Ⓓ Ⓔ
7 Ⓐ Ⓑ Ⓒ Ⓓ Ⓔ   32 Ⓐ Ⓑ Ⓒ Ⓓ Ⓔ   57 Ⓐ Ⓑ Ⓒ Ⓓ Ⓔ   82 Ⓐ Ⓑ Ⓒ Ⓓ Ⓔ
8 Ⓐ Ⓑ Ⓒ Ⓓ Ⓔ   33 Ⓐ Ⓑ Ⓒ Ⓓ Ⓔ   58 Ⓐ Ⓑ Ⓒ Ⓓ Ⓔ   83 Ⓐ Ⓑ Ⓒ Ⓓ Ⓔ
9 Ⓐ Ⓑ Ⓒ Ⓓ Ⓔ   34 Ⓐ Ⓑ Ⓒ Ⓓ Ⓔ   59 Ⓐ Ⓑ Ⓒ Ⓓ Ⓔ   84 Ⓐ Ⓑ Ⓒ Ⓓ Ⓔ
10 Ⓐ Ⓑ Ⓒ Ⓓ Ⓔ   35 Ⓐ Ⓑ Ⓒ Ⓓ Ⓔ   60 Ⓐ Ⓑ Ⓒ Ⓓ Ⓔ   85 Ⓐ Ⓑ Ⓒ Ⓓ Ⓔ
11 Ⓐ Ⓑ Ⓒ Ⓓ Ⓔ   36 Ⓐ Ⓑ Ⓒ Ⓓ Ⓔ   61 Ⓐ Ⓑ Ⓒ Ⓓ Ⓔ   86 Ⓐ Ⓑ Ⓒ Ⓓ Ⓔ
12 Ⓐ Ⓑ Ⓒ Ⓓ Ⓔ   37 Ⓐ Ⓑ Ⓒ Ⓓ Ⓔ   62 Ⓐ Ⓑ Ⓒ Ⓓ Ⓔ   87 Ⓐ Ⓑ Ⓒ Ⓓ Ⓔ
13 Ⓐ Ⓑ Ⓒ Ⓓ Ⓔ   38 Ⓐ Ⓑ Ⓒ Ⓓ Ⓔ   63 Ⓐ Ⓑ Ⓒ Ⓓ Ⓔ   88 Ⓐ Ⓑ Ⓒ Ⓓ Ⓔ
14 Ⓐ Ⓑ Ⓒ Ⓓ Ⓔ   39 Ⓐ Ⓑ Ⓒ Ⓓ Ⓔ   64 Ⓐ Ⓑ Ⓒ Ⓓ Ⓔ   89 Ⓐ Ⓑ Ⓒ Ⓓ Ⓔ
15 Ⓐ Ⓑ Ⓒ Ⓓ Ⓔ   40 Ⓐ Ⓑ Ⓒ Ⓓ Ⓔ   65 Ⓐ Ⓑ Ⓒ Ⓓ Ⓔ   90 Ⓐ Ⓑ Ⓒ Ⓓ Ⓔ
16 Ⓐ Ⓑ Ⓒ Ⓓ Ⓔ   41 Ⓐ Ⓑ Ⓒ Ⓓ Ⓔ   66 Ⓐ Ⓑ Ⓒ Ⓓ Ⓔ   91 Ⓐ Ⓑ Ⓒ Ⓓ Ⓔ
17 Ⓐ Ⓑ Ⓒ Ⓓ Ⓔ   42 Ⓐ Ⓑ Ⓒ Ⓓ Ⓔ   67 Ⓐ Ⓑ Ⓒ Ⓓ Ⓔ   92 Ⓐ Ⓑ Ⓒ Ⓓ Ⓔ
18 Ⓐ Ⓑ Ⓒ Ⓓ Ⓔ   43 Ⓐ Ⓑ Ⓒ Ⓓ Ⓔ   68 Ⓐ Ⓑ Ⓒ Ⓓ Ⓔ   93 Ⓐ Ⓑ Ⓒ Ⓓ Ⓔ
19 Ⓐ Ⓑ Ⓒ Ⓓ Ⓔ   44 Ⓐ Ⓑ Ⓒ Ⓓ Ⓔ   69 Ⓐ Ⓑ Ⓒ Ⓓ Ⓔ   94 Ⓐ Ⓑ Ⓒ Ⓓ Ⓔ
20 Ⓐ Ⓑ Ⓒ Ⓓ Ⓔ   45 Ⓐ Ⓑ Ⓒ Ⓓ Ⓔ   70 Ⓐ Ⓑ Ⓒ Ⓓ Ⓔ   95 Ⓐ Ⓑ Ⓒ Ⓓ Ⓔ
21 Ⓐ Ⓑ Ⓒ Ⓓ Ⓔ   46 Ⓐ Ⓑ Ⓒ Ⓓ Ⓔ   71 Ⓐ Ⓑ Ⓒ Ⓓ Ⓔ   96 Ⓐ Ⓑ Ⓒ Ⓓ Ⓔ
22 Ⓐ Ⓑ Ⓒ Ⓓ Ⓔ   47 Ⓐ Ⓑ Ⓒ Ⓓ Ⓔ   72 Ⓐ Ⓑ Ⓒ Ⓓ Ⓔ   97 Ⓐ Ⓑ Ⓒ Ⓓ Ⓔ
23 Ⓐ Ⓑ Ⓒ Ⓓ Ⓔ   48 Ⓐ Ⓑ Ⓒ Ⓓ Ⓔ   73 Ⓐ Ⓑ Ⓒ Ⓓ Ⓔ   98 Ⓐ Ⓑ Ⓒ Ⓓ Ⓔ
24 Ⓐ Ⓑ Ⓒ Ⓓ Ⓔ   49 Ⓐ Ⓑ Ⓒ Ⓓ Ⓔ   74 Ⓐ Ⓑ Ⓒ Ⓓ Ⓔ   99 Ⓐ Ⓑ Ⓒ Ⓓ Ⓔ
25 Ⓐ Ⓑ Ⓒ Ⓓ Ⓔ   50 Ⓐ Ⓑ Ⓒ Ⓓ Ⓔ   75 Ⓐ Ⓑ Ⓒ Ⓓ Ⓔ   100 Ⓐ Ⓑ Ⓒ Ⓓ Ⓔ

8 BOOK CODE (Copy and grid as on back of test book.)

⓪	Ⓐ	⓪
①	Ⓑ	①
②	Ⓒ	②
③	Ⓓ	③
④	Ⓔ	④
⑤	Ⓕ	⑤
⑥	Ⓖ	⑥
⑦	Ⓗ	⑦
⑧	Ⓘ	⑧
⑨	Ⓙ	⑨
	Ⓚ	
	Ⓛ	
	Ⓜ	
	Ⓝ	
	Ⓞ	
	Ⓟ	
	Ⓠ	
	Ⓡ	
	Ⓢ	
	Ⓣ	
	Ⓤ	
	Ⓥ	
	Ⓦ	
	Ⓧ	
	Ⓨ	
	Ⓩ	

9 BOOK ID (Copy from back of test book.)

10 BOOK SERIAL NUMBER (Copy from front of test book.)

⓪	⓪	⓪	⓪	⓪	⓪
①	①	①	①	①	①
②	②	②	②	②	②
③	③	③	③	③	③
④	④	④	④	④	④
⑤	⑤	⑤	⑤	⑤	⑤
⑥	⑥	⑥	⑥	⑥	⑥
⑦	⑦	⑦	⑦	⑦	⑦
⑧	⑧	⑧	⑧	⑧	⑧
⑨	⑨	⑨	⑨	⑨	⑨

Chemistry
*Fill in circle CE only if II is correct explanation of I.

	I	II	CE*		I	II	CE*
101	Ⓣ Ⓕ	Ⓣ Ⓕ	◯	109	Ⓣ Ⓕ	Ⓣ Ⓕ	◯
102	Ⓣ Ⓕ	Ⓣ Ⓕ	◯	110	Ⓣ Ⓕ	Ⓣ Ⓕ	◯
103	Ⓣ Ⓕ	Ⓣ Ⓕ	◯	111	Ⓣ Ⓕ	Ⓣ Ⓕ	◯
104	Ⓣ Ⓕ	Ⓣ Ⓕ	◯	112	Ⓣ Ⓕ	Ⓣ Ⓕ	◯
105	Ⓣ Ⓕ	Ⓣ Ⓕ	◯	113	Ⓣ Ⓕ	Ⓣ Ⓕ	◯
106	Ⓣ Ⓕ	Ⓣ Ⓕ	◯	114	Ⓣ Ⓕ	Ⓣ Ⓕ	◯
107	Ⓣ Ⓕ	Ⓣ Ⓕ	◯	115	Ⓣ Ⓕ	Ⓣ Ⓕ	◯
108	Ⓣ Ⓕ	Ⓣ Ⓕ	◯				

FOR OFFICIAL USE ONLY

R/C	W/S1	FS/S2	CS/S3	WS

SERIAL #

Use a No. 2 pencil only. Be sure each mark is dark and completely fills the intended circle. Completely erase any errors or stray marks.

here are more
swer spaces
n you need,
ve them blank.

Test Code

V	① ② ③ ④ ⑤ ⑥ ⑦ ⑧ ⑨
W	① ② ③ ④ ⑤ ⑥ ⑦ ⑧ ⑨
X	① ② ③ ④ ⑤ Ⓨ Ⓐ Ⓑ Ⓒ Ⓓ Ⓔ
Q	① ② ③ ④ ⑤ ⑥ ⑦ ⑧ ⑨

Subject Test (print)

Ⓐ Ⓑ Ⓒ Ⓓ Ⓔ 26 Ⓐ Ⓑ Ⓒ Ⓓ Ⓔ 51 Ⓐ Ⓑ Ⓒ Ⓓ Ⓔ 76 Ⓐ Ⓑ Ⓒ Ⓓ Ⓔ
Ⓐ Ⓑ Ⓒ Ⓓ Ⓔ 27 Ⓐ Ⓑ Ⓒ Ⓓ Ⓔ 52 Ⓐ Ⓑ Ⓒ Ⓓ Ⓔ 77 Ⓐ Ⓑ Ⓒ Ⓓ Ⓔ
Ⓐ Ⓑ Ⓒ Ⓓ Ⓔ 28 Ⓐ Ⓑ Ⓒ Ⓓ Ⓔ 53 Ⓐ Ⓑ Ⓒ Ⓓ Ⓔ 78 Ⓐ Ⓑ Ⓒ Ⓓ Ⓔ
Ⓐ Ⓑ Ⓒ Ⓓ Ⓔ 29 Ⓐ Ⓑ Ⓒ Ⓓ Ⓔ 54 Ⓐ Ⓑ Ⓒ Ⓓ Ⓔ 79 Ⓐ Ⓑ Ⓒ Ⓓ Ⓔ
Ⓐ Ⓑ Ⓒ Ⓓ Ⓔ 30 Ⓐ Ⓑ Ⓒ Ⓓ Ⓔ 55 Ⓐ Ⓑ Ⓒ Ⓓ Ⓔ 80 Ⓐ Ⓑ Ⓒ Ⓓ Ⓔ
Ⓐ Ⓑ Ⓒ Ⓓ Ⓔ 31 Ⓐ Ⓑ Ⓒ Ⓓ Ⓔ 56 Ⓐ Ⓑ Ⓒ Ⓓ Ⓔ 81 Ⓐ Ⓑ Ⓒ Ⓓ Ⓔ
Ⓐ Ⓑ Ⓒ Ⓓ Ⓔ 32 Ⓐ Ⓑ Ⓒ Ⓓ Ⓔ 57 Ⓐ Ⓑ Ⓒ Ⓓ Ⓔ 82 Ⓐ Ⓑ Ⓒ Ⓓ Ⓔ
Ⓐ Ⓑ Ⓒ Ⓓ Ⓔ 33 Ⓐ Ⓑ Ⓒ Ⓓ Ⓔ 58 Ⓐ Ⓑ Ⓒ Ⓓ Ⓔ 83 Ⓐ Ⓑ Ⓒ Ⓓ Ⓔ
Ⓐ Ⓑ Ⓒ Ⓓ Ⓔ 34 Ⓐ Ⓑ Ⓒ Ⓓ Ⓔ 59 Ⓐ Ⓑ Ⓒ Ⓓ Ⓔ 84 Ⓐ Ⓑ Ⓒ Ⓓ Ⓔ
Ⓐ Ⓑ Ⓒ Ⓓ Ⓔ 35 Ⓐ Ⓑ Ⓒ Ⓓ Ⓔ 60 Ⓐ Ⓑ Ⓒ Ⓓ Ⓔ 85 Ⓐ Ⓑ Ⓒ Ⓓ Ⓔ
Ⓐ Ⓑ Ⓒ Ⓓ Ⓔ 36 Ⓐ Ⓑ Ⓒ Ⓓ Ⓔ 61 Ⓐ Ⓑ Ⓒ Ⓓ Ⓔ 86 Ⓐ Ⓑ Ⓒ Ⓓ Ⓔ
Ⓐ Ⓑ Ⓒ Ⓓ Ⓔ 37 Ⓐ Ⓑ Ⓒ Ⓓ Ⓔ 62 Ⓐ Ⓑ Ⓒ Ⓓ Ⓔ 87 Ⓐ Ⓑ Ⓒ Ⓓ Ⓔ
Ⓐ Ⓑ Ⓒ Ⓓ Ⓔ 38 Ⓐ Ⓑ Ⓒ Ⓓ Ⓔ 63 Ⓐ Ⓑ Ⓒ Ⓓ Ⓔ 88 Ⓐ Ⓑ Ⓒ Ⓓ Ⓔ
Ⓐ Ⓑ Ⓒ Ⓓ Ⓔ 39 Ⓐ Ⓑ Ⓒ Ⓓ Ⓔ 64 Ⓐ Ⓑ Ⓒ Ⓓ Ⓔ 89 Ⓐ Ⓑ Ⓒ Ⓓ Ⓔ
Ⓐ Ⓑ Ⓒ Ⓓ Ⓔ 40 Ⓐ Ⓑ Ⓒ Ⓓ Ⓔ 65 Ⓐ Ⓑ Ⓒ Ⓓ Ⓔ 90 Ⓐ Ⓑ Ⓒ Ⓓ Ⓔ
Ⓐ Ⓑ Ⓒ Ⓓ Ⓔ 41 Ⓐ Ⓑ Ⓒ Ⓓ Ⓔ 66 Ⓐ Ⓑ Ⓒ Ⓓ Ⓔ 91 Ⓐ Ⓑ Ⓒ Ⓓ Ⓔ
Ⓐ Ⓑ Ⓒ Ⓓ Ⓔ 42 Ⓐ Ⓑ Ⓒ Ⓓ Ⓔ 67 Ⓐ Ⓑ Ⓒ Ⓓ Ⓔ 92 Ⓐ Ⓑ Ⓒ Ⓓ Ⓔ
Ⓐ Ⓑ Ⓒ Ⓓ Ⓔ 43 Ⓐ Ⓑ Ⓒ Ⓓ Ⓔ 68 Ⓐ Ⓑ Ⓒ Ⓓ Ⓔ 93 Ⓐ Ⓑ Ⓒ Ⓓ Ⓔ
Ⓐ Ⓑ Ⓒ Ⓓ Ⓔ 44 Ⓐ Ⓑ Ⓒ Ⓓ Ⓔ 69 Ⓐ Ⓑ Ⓒ Ⓓ Ⓔ 94 Ⓐ Ⓑ Ⓒ Ⓓ Ⓔ
Ⓐ Ⓑ Ⓒ Ⓓ Ⓔ 45 Ⓐ Ⓑ Ⓒ Ⓓ Ⓔ 70 Ⓐ Ⓑ Ⓒ Ⓓ Ⓔ 95 Ⓐ Ⓑ Ⓒ Ⓓ Ⓔ
Ⓐ Ⓑ Ⓒ Ⓓ Ⓔ 46 Ⓐ Ⓑ Ⓒ Ⓓ Ⓔ 71 Ⓐ Ⓑ Ⓒ Ⓓ Ⓔ 96 Ⓐ Ⓑ Ⓒ Ⓓ Ⓔ
Ⓐ Ⓑ Ⓒ Ⓓ Ⓔ 47 Ⓐ Ⓑ Ⓒ Ⓓ Ⓔ 72 Ⓐ Ⓑ Ⓒ Ⓓ Ⓔ 97 Ⓐ Ⓑ Ⓒ Ⓓ Ⓔ
Ⓐ Ⓑ Ⓒ Ⓓ Ⓔ 48 Ⓐ Ⓑ Ⓒ Ⓓ Ⓔ 73 Ⓐ Ⓑ Ⓒ Ⓓ Ⓔ 98 Ⓐ Ⓑ Ⓒ Ⓓ Ⓔ
Ⓐ Ⓑ Ⓒ Ⓓ Ⓔ 49 Ⓐ Ⓑ Ⓒ Ⓓ Ⓔ 74 Ⓐ Ⓑ Ⓒ Ⓓ Ⓔ 99 Ⓐ Ⓑ Ⓒ Ⓓ Ⓔ
Ⓐ Ⓑ Ⓒ Ⓓ Ⓔ 50 Ⓐ Ⓑ Ⓒ Ⓓ Ⓔ 75 Ⓐ Ⓑ Ⓒ Ⓓ Ⓔ 100 Ⓐ Ⓑ Ⓒ Ⓓ Ⓔ

nistry *Fill in circle CE only if II is correct explanation of I.

I	II	CE*		I	II	CE*
Ⓣ Ⓕ	Ⓣ Ⓕ	◯		109 Ⓣ Ⓕ	Ⓣ Ⓕ	◯
Ⓣ Ⓕ	Ⓣ Ⓕ	◯		110 Ⓣ Ⓕ	Ⓣ Ⓕ	◯
Ⓣ Ⓕ	Ⓣ Ⓕ	◯		111 Ⓣ Ⓕ	Ⓣ Ⓕ	◯
Ⓣ Ⓕ	Ⓣ Ⓕ	◯		112 Ⓣ Ⓕ	Ⓣ Ⓕ	◯
Ⓣ Ⓕ	Ⓣ Ⓕ	◯		113 Ⓣ Ⓕ	Ⓣ Ⓕ	◯
Ⓣ Ⓕ	Ⓣ Ⓕ	◯		114 Ⓣ Ⓕ	Ⓣ Ⓕ	◯
Ⓣ Ⓕ	Ⓣ Ⓕ	◯		115 Ⓣ Ⓕ	Ⓣ Ⓕ	◯
Ⓣ Ⓕ	Ⓣ Ⓕ	◯				

8 BOOK CODE
(Copy and grid as on back of test book.)

⓪	Ⓐ	⓪
①	Ⓑ	①
②	Ⓒ	②
③	Ⓓ	③
④	Ⓔ	④
⑤	Ⓕ	⑤
⑥	Ⓖ	⑥
⑦	Ⓗ	⑦
⑧	Ⓘ	⑧
⑨	Ⓙ	⑨
	Ⓚ	
	Ⓛ	
	Ⓜ	
	Ⓝ	
	Ⓞ	
	Ⓟ	
	Ⓠ	
	Ⓡ	
	Ⓢ	
	Ⓣ	
	Ⓤ	
	Ⓥ	
	Ⓦ	
	Ⓧ	
	Ⓨ	
	Ⓩ	

9 BOOK ID
(Copy from back of test book.)

10 BOOK SERIAL NUMBER
(Copy from front of test book.)

⓪	⓪	⓪	⓪	⓪	⓪
①	①	①	①	①	①
②	②	②	②	②	②
③	③	③	③	③	③
④	④	④	④	④	④
⑤	⑤	⑤	⑤	⑤	⑤
⑥	⑥	⑥	⑥	⑥	⑥
⑦	⑦	⑦	⑦	⑦	⑦
⑧	⑧	⑧	⑧	⑧	⑧
⑨	⑨	⑨	⑨	⑨	⑨

FOR OFFICIAL USE ONLY				
R/C	W/S1	FS/S2	CS/S3	WS

PLEASE DO NOT WRITE IN THIS AREA

SERIAL #

Use a No. 2 pencil only. Be sure each mark is dark and completely fills the intended circle. Completely erase any errors or stray marks.

If there are more answer spaces than you need, leave them blank.

Test Code

V	① ② ③ ④ ⑤ ⑥ ⑦ ⑧ ⑨
W	① ② ③ ④ ⑤ ⑥ ⑦ ⑧ ⑨
X	① ② ③ ④ ⑤ Ⓨ Ⓐ Ⓑ Ⓒ Ⓓ Ⓔ
Q	① ② ③ ④ ⑤ ⑥ ⑦ ⑧ ⑨

Subject Test (print)

1 Ⓐ Ⓑ Ⓒ Ⓓ Ⓔ 26 Ⓐ Ⓑ Ⓒ Ⓓ Ⓔ 51 Ⓐ Ⓑ Ⓒ Ⓓ Ⓔ 76 Ⓐ Ⓑ Ⓒ Ⓓ Ⓔ
2 Ⓐ Ⓑ Ⓒ Ⓓ Ⓔ 27 Ⓐ Ⓑ Ⓒ Ⓓ Ⓔ 52 Ⓐ Ⓑ Ⓒ Ⓓ Ⓔ 77 Ⓐ Ⓑ Ⓒ Ⓓ Ⓔ
3 Ⓐ Ⓑ Ⓒ Ⓓ Ⓔ 28 Ⓐ Ⓑ Ⓒ Ⓓ Ⓔ 53 Ⓐ Ⓑ Ⓒ Ⓓ Ⓔ 78 Ⓐ Ⓑ Ⓒ Ⓓ Ⓔ
4 Ⓐ Ⓑ Ⓒ Ⓓ Ⓔ 29 Ⓐ Ⓑ Ⓒ Ⓓ Ⓔ 54 Ⓐ Ⓑ Ⓒ Ⓓ Ⓔ 79 Ⓐ Ⓑ Ⓒ Ⓓ Ⓔ
5 Ⓐ Ⓑ Ⓒ Ⓓ Ⓔ 30 Ⓐ Ⓑ Ⓒ Ⓓ Ⓔ 55 Ⓐ Ⓑ Ⓒ Ⓓ Ⓔ 80 Ⓐ Ⓑ Ⓒ Ⓓ Ⓔ
6 Ⓐ Ⓑ Ⓒ Ⓓ Ⓔ 31 Ⓐ Ⓑ Ⓒ Ⓓ Ⓔ 56 Ⓐ Ⓑ Ⓒ Ⓓ Ⓔ 81 Ⓐ Ⓑ Ⓒ Ⓓ Ⓔ
7 Ⓐ Ⓑ Ⓒ Ⓓ Ⓔ 32 Ⓐ Ⓑ Ⓒ Ⓓ Ⓔ 57 Ⓐ Ⓑ Ⓒ Ⓓ Ⓔ 82 Ⓐ Ⓑ Ⓒ Ⓓ Ⓔ
8 Ⓐ Ⓑ Ⓒ Ⓓ Ⓔ 33 Ⓐ Ⓑ Ⓒ Ⓓ Ⓔ 58 Ⓐ Ⓑ Ⓒ Ⓓ Ⓔ 83 Ⓐ Ⓑ Ⓒ Ⓓ Ⓔ
9 Ⓐ Ⓑ Ⓒ Ⓓ Ⓔ 34 Ⓐ Ⓑ Ⓒ Ⓓ Ⓔ 59 Ⓐ Ⓑ Ⓒ Ⓓ Ⓔ 84 Ⓐ Ⓑ Ⓒ Ⓓ Ⓔ
10 Ⓐ Ⓑ Ⓒ Ⓓ Ⓔ 35 Ⓐ Ⓑ Ⓒ Ⓓ Ⓔ 60 Ⓐ Ⓑ Ⓒ Ⓓ Ⓔ 85 Ⓐ Ⓑ Ⓒ Ⓓ Ⓔ
11 Ⓐ Ⓑ Ⓒ Ⓓ Ⓔ 36 Ⓐ Ⓑ Ⓒ Ⓓ Ⓔ 61 Ⓐ Ⓑ Ⓒ Ⓓ Ⓔ 86 Ⓐ Ⓑ Ⓒ Ⓓ Ⓔ
12 Ⓐ Ⓑ Ⓒ Ⓓ Ⓔ 37 Ⓐ Ⓑ Ⓒ Ⓓ Ⓔ 62 Ⓐ Ⓑ Ⓒ Ⓓ Ⓔ 87 Ⓐ Ⓑ Ⓒ Ⓓ Ⓔ
13 Ⓐ Ⓑ Ⓒ Ⓓ Ⓔ 38 Ⓐ Ⓑ Ⓒ Ⓓ Ⓔ 63 Ⓐ Ⓑ Ⓒ Ⓓ Ⓔ 88 Ⓐ Ⓑ Ⓒ Ⓓ Ⓔ
14 Ⓐ Ⓑ Ⓒ Ⓓ Ⓔ 39 Ⓐ Ⓑ Ⓒ Ⓓ Ⓔ 64 Ⓐ Ⓑ Ⓒ Ⓓ Ⓔ 89 Ⓐ Ⓑ Ⓒ Ⓓ Ⓔ
15 Ⓐ Ⓑ Ⓒ Ⓓ Ⓔ 40 Ⓐ Ⓑ Ⓒ Ⓓ Ⓔ 65 Ⓐ Ⓑ Ⓒ Ⓓ Ⓔ 90 Ⓐ Ⓑ Ⓒ Ⓓ Ⓔ
16 Ⓐ Ⓑ Ⓒ Ⓓ Ⓔ 41 Ⓐ Ⓑ Ⓒ Ⓓ Ⓔ 66 Ⓐ Ⓑ Ⓒ Ⓓ Ⓔ 91 Ⓐ Ⓑ Ⓒ Ⓓ Ⓔ
17 Ⓐ Ⓑ Ⓒ Ⓓ Ⓔ 42 Ⓐ Ⓑ Ⓒ Ⓓ Ⓔ 67 Ⓐ Ⓑ Ⓒ Ⓓ Ⓔ 92 Ⓐ Ⓑ Ⓒ Ⓓ Ⓔ
18 Ⓐ Ⓑ Ⓒ Ⓓ Ⓔ 43 Ⓐ Ⓑ Ⓒ Ⓓ Ⓔ 68 Ⓐ Ⓑ Ⓒ Ⓓ Ⓔ 93 Ⓐ Ⓑ Ⓒ Ⓓ Ⓔ
19 Ⓐ Ⓑ Ⓒ Ⓓ Ⓔ 44 Ⓐ Ⓑ Ⓒ Ⓓ Ⓔ 69 Ⓐ Ⓑ Ⓒ Ⓓ Ⓔ 94 Ⓐ Ⓑ Ⓒ Ⓓ Ⓔ
20 Ⓐ Ⓑ Ⓒ Ⓓ Ⓔ 45 Ⓐ Ⓑ Ⓒ Ⓓ Ⓔ 70 Ⓐ Ⓑ Ⓒ Ⓓ Ⓔ 95 Ⓐ Ⓑ Ⓒ Ⓓ Ⓔ
21 Ⓐ Ⓑ Ⓒ Ⓓ Ⓔ 46 Ⓐ Ⓑ Ⓒ Ⓓ Ⓔ 71 Ⓐ Ⓑ Ⓒ Ⓓ Ⓔ 96 Ⓐ Ⓑ Ⓒ Ⓓ Ⓔ
22 Ⓐ Ⓑ Ⓒ Ⓓ Ⓔ 47 Ⓐ Ⓑ Ⓒ Ⓓ Ⓔ 72 Ⓐ Ⓑ Ⓒ Ⓓ Ⓔ 97 Ⓐ Ⓑ Ⓒ Ⓓ Ⓔ
23 Ⓐ Ⓑ Ⓒ Ⓓ Ⓔ 48 Ⓐ Ⓑ Ⓒ Ⓓ Ⓔ 73 Ⓐ Ⓑ Ⓒ Ⓓ Ⓔ 98 Ⓐ Ⓑ Ⓒ Ⓓ Ⓔ
24 Ⓐ Ⓑ Ⓒ Ⓓ Ⓔ 49 Ⓐ Ⓑ Ⓒ Ⓓ Ⓔ 74 Ⓐ Ⓑ Ⓒ Ⓓ Ⓔ 99 Ⓐ Ⓑ Ⓒ Ⓓ Ⓔ
25 Ⓐ Ⓑ Ⓒ Ⓓ Ⓔ 50 Ⓐ Ⓑ Ⓒ Ⓓ Ⓔ 75 Ⓐ Ⓑ Ⓒ Ⓓ Ⓔ 100 Ⓐ Ⓑ Ⓒ Ⓓ Ⓔ

Chemistry *Fill in circle CE only if II is correct explanation of I.

	I	II	CE*		I	II	CE*
101	Ⓣ Ⓕ	Ⓣ Ⓕ	◯	109	Ⓣ Ⓕ	Ⓣ Ⓕ	◯
102	Ⓣ Ⓕ	Ⓣ Ⓕ	◯	110	Ⓣ Ⓕ	Ⓣ Ⓕ	◯
103	Ⓣ Ⓕ	Ⓣ Ⓕ	◯	111	Ⓣ Ⓕ	Ⓣ Ⓕ	◯
104	Ⓣ Ⓕ	Ⓣ Ⓕ	◯	112	Ⓣ Ⓕ	Ⓣ Ⓕ	◯
105	Ⓣ Ⓕ	Ⓣ Ⓕ	◯	113	Ⓣ Ⓕ	Ⓣ Ⓕ	◯
106	Ⓣ Ⓕ	Ⓣ Ⓕ	◯	114	Ⓣ Ⓕ	Ⓣ Ⓕ	◯
107	Ⓣ Ⓕ	Ⓣ Ⓕ	◯	115	Ⓣ Ⓕ	Ⓣ Ⓕ	◯
108	Ⓣ Ⓕ	Ⓣ Ⓕ	◯				

8 BOOK CODE
(Copy and grid as on back of test book.)

⓪	Ⓐ	⓪
①	Ⓑ	①
②	Ⓒ	②
③	Ⓓ	③
④	Ⓔ	④
⑤	Ⓕ	⑤
⑥	Ⓖ	⑥
⑦	Ⓗ	⑦
⑧	Ⓘ	⑧
⑨	Ⓙ	⑨
	Ⓚ	
	Ⓛ	
	Ⓜ	
	Ⓝ	
	Ⓞ	
	Ⓟ	
	Ⓠ	
	Ⓡ	
	Ⓢ	
	Ⓣ	
	Ⓤ	
	Ⓥ	
	Ⓦ	
	Ⓧ	
	Ⓨ	
	Ⓩ	

9 BOOK ID
(Copy from back of test book.)

10 BOOK SERIAL NUMBER
(Copy from front of test book.)

⓪	⓪	⓪	⓪	⓪	⓪
①	①	①	①	①	①
②	②	②	②	②	②
③	③	③	③	③	③
④	④	④	④	④	④
⑤	⑤	⑤	⑤	⑤	⑤
⑥	⑥	⑥	⑥	⑥	⑥
⑦	⑦	⑦	⑦	⑦	⑦
⑧	⑧	⑧	⑧	⑧	⑧
⑨	⑨	⑨	⑨	⑨	⑨

FOR OFFICIAL USE ONLY

R/C	W/S1	FS/S2	CS/S3	WS

CERTIFICATION STATEMENT Copy the statement below (do not print) and sign your name as you would an official docum◄

I hereby agree to the conditions set forth online at www.collegeboard.com and/or in the Registration Bulletin and certify that I am the person whose name and address appear on this answer sheet.

Signature _____ Date _____

ollegeBoard SAT

SAT Subject Tests™

Your Name:
(Print)

Last _____ First _____ M.I. _____

ee to the conditions on the back of the SAT® Subject Tests book.

ture: _____ Date __/__/__

Address: _____
Number and Street _____ City _____ State _____ Zip Code

r: _____
City _____ State _____

YOUR NAME
(Name Letters) | First Init. | Mid. Init.

3 SOCIAL SECURITY NUMBER

5 SEX
○ Female ○ Male

6 REGISTRATION NUMBER
(Copy from Admission Ticket.)

7 TEST CENTER
(Supplied by Test Center Supervisor.)

4 DATE OF BIRTH
MONTH | DAY | YEAR
○ Jan
○ Feb
○ Mar
○ Apr
○ May
○ Jun
○ Jul
○ Aug
○ Sep
○ Oct
○ Nov
○ Dec

8 BOOK CODE
(Copy and grid as on back of test book.)

9 BOOK ID
(Copy from back of test book.)

10 BOOK SERIAL NUMBER
(Copy from front of test book.)

FOR OFFICIAL USE ONLY

11030-36392 • NS114E315 • Printed in U.S.A.
724844

Use a No. 2 pencil only. Be sure each mark is dark and completely fills the intended circle. Completely erase any errors or stray marks.

If there are more answer spaces than you need, leave them blank.

Test Code

V	① ② ③ ④ ⑤ ⑥ ⑦ ⑧ ⑨	
W	① ② ③ ④ ⑤ ⑥ ⑦ ⑧ ⑨	
X	① ② ③ ④ ⑤ Y Ⓐ Ⓑ Ⓒ Ⓓ Ⓔ	
Q	① ② ③ ④ ⑤ ⑥ ⑦ ⑧ ⑨	

Subject Test (print)

1 Ⓐ Ⓑ Ⓒ Ⓓ Ⓔ   26 Ⓐ Ⓑ Ⓒ Ⓓ Ⓔ   51 Ⓐ Ⓑ Ⓒ Ⓓ Ⓔ   76 Ⓐ Ⓑ Ⓒ Ⓓ Ⓔ
2 Ⓐ Ⓑ Ⓒ Ⓓ Ⓔ   27 Ⓐ Ⓑ Ⓒ Ⓓ Ⓔ   52 Ⓐ Ⓑ Ⓒ Ⓓ Ⓔ   77 Ⓐ Ⓑ Ⓒ Ⓓ Ⓔ
3 Ⓐ Ⓑ Ⓒ Ⓓ Ⓔ   28 Ⓐ Ⓑ Ⓒ Ⓓ Ⓔ   53 Ⓐ Ⓑ Ⓒ Ⓓ Ⓔ   78 Ⓐ Ⓑ Ⓒ Ⓓ Ⓔ
4 Ⓐ Ⓑ Ⓒ Ⓓ Ⓔ   29 Ⓐ Ⓑ Ⓒ Ⓓ Ⓔ   54 Ⓐ Ⓑ Ⓒ Ⓓ Ⓔ   79 Ⓐ Ⓑ Ⓒ Ⓓ Ⓔ
5 Ⓐ Ⓑ Ⓒ Ⓓ Ⓔ   30 Ⓐ Ⓑ Ⓒ Ⓓ Ⓔ   55 Ⓐ Ⓑ Ⓒ Ⓓ Ⓔ   80 Ⓐ Ⓑ Ⓒ Ⓓ Ⓔ
6 Ⓐ Ⓑ Ⓒ Ⓓ Ⓔ   31 Ⓐ Ⓑ Ⓒ Ⓓ Ⓔ   56 Ⓐ Ⓑ Ⓒ Ⓓ Ⓔ   81 Ⓐ Ⓑ Ⓒ Ⓓ Ⓔ
7 Ⓐ Ⓑ Ⓒ Ⓓ Ⓔ   32 Ⓐ Ⓑ Ⓒ Ⓓ Ⓔ   57 Ⓐ Ⓑ Ⓒ Ⓓ Ⓔ   82 Ⓐ Ⓑ Ⓒ Ⓓ Ⓔ
8 Ⓐ Ⓑ Ⓒ Ⓓ Ⓔ   33 Ⓐ Ⓑ Ⓒ Ⓓ Ⓔ   58 Ⓐ Ⓑ Ⓒ Ⓓ Ⓔ   83 Ⓐ Ⓑ Ⓒ Ⓓ Ⓔ
9 Ⓐ Ⓑ Ⓒ Ⓓ Ⓔ   34 Ⓐ Ⓑ Ⓒ Ⓓ Ⓔ   59 Ⓐ Ⓑ Ⓒ Ⓓ Ⓔ   84 Ⓐ Ⓑ Ⓒ Ⓓ Ⓔ
10 Ⓐ Ⓑ Ⓒ Ⓓ Ⓔ   35 Ⓐ Ⓑ Ⓒ Ⓓ Ⓔ   60 Ⓐ Ⓑ Ⓒ Ⓓ Ⓔ   85 Ⓐ Ⓑ Ⓒ Ⓓ Ⓔ
11 Ⓐ Ⓑ Ⓒ Ⓓ Ⓔ   36 Ⓐ Ⓑ Ⓒ Ⓓ Ⓔ   61 Ⓐ Ⓑ Ⓒ Ⓓ Ⓔ   86 Ⓐ Ⓑ Ⓒ Ⓓ Ⓔ
12 Ⓐ Ⓑ Ⓒ Ⓓ Ⓔ   37 Ⓐ Ⓑ Ⓒ Ⓓ Ⓔ   62 Ⓐ Ⓑ Ⓒ Ⓓ Ⓔ   87 Ⓐ Ⓑ Ⓒ Ⓓ Ⓔ
13 Ⓐ Ⓑ Ⓒ Ⓓ Ⓔ   38 Ⓐ Ⓑ Ⓒ Ⓓ Ⓔ   63 Ⓐ Ⓑ Ⓒ Ⓓ Ⓔ   88 Ⓐ Ⓑ Ⓒ Ⓓ Ⓔ
14 Ⓐ Ⓑ Ⓒ Ⓓ Ⓔ   39 Ⓐ Ⓑ Ⓒ Ⓓ Ⓔ   64 Ⓐ Ⓑ Ⓒ Ⓓ Ⓔ   89 Ⓐ Ⓑ Ⓒ Ⓓ Ⓔ
15 Ⓐ Ⓑ Ⓒ Ⓓ Ⓔ   40 Ⓐ Ⓑ Ⓒ Ⓓ Ⓔ   65 Ⓐ Ⓑ Ⓒ Ⓓ Ⓔ   90 Ⓐ Ⓑ Ⓒ Ⓓ Ⓔ
16 Ⓐ Ⓑ Ⓒ Ⓓ Ⓔ   41 Ⓐ Ⓑ Ⓒ Ⓓ Ⓔ   66 Ⓐ Ⓑ Ⓒ Ⓓ Ⓔ   91 Ⓐ Ⓑ Ⓒ Ⓓ Ⓔ
17 Ⓐ Ⓑ Ⓒ Ⓓ Ⓔ   42 Ⓐ Ⓑ Ⓒ Ⓓ Ⓔ   67 Ⓐ Ⓑ Ⓒ Ⓓ Ⓔ   92 Ⓐ Ⓑ Ⓒ Ⓓ Ⓔ
18 Ⓐ Ⓑ Ⓒ Ⓓ Ⓔ   43 Ⓐ Ⓑ Ⓒ Ⓓ Ⓔ   68 Ⓐ Ⓑ Ⓒ Ⓓ Ⓔ   93 Ⓐ Ⓑ Ⓒ Ⓓ Ⓔ
19 Ⓐ Ⓑ Ⓒ Ⓓ Ⓔ   44 Ⓐ Ⓑ Ⓒ Ⓓ Ⓔ   69 Ⓐ Ⓑ Ⓒ Ⓓ Ⓔ   94 Ⓐ Ⓑ Ⓒ Ⓓ Ⓔ
20 Ⓐ Ⓑ Ⓒ Ⓓ Ⓔ   45 Ⓐ Ⓑ Ⓒ Ⓓ Ⓔ   70 Ⓐ Ⓑ Ⓒ Ⓓ Ⓔ   95 Ⓐ Ⓑ Ⓒ Ⓓ Ⓔ
21 Ⓐ Ⓑ Ⓒ Ⓓ Ⓔ   46 Ⓐ Ⓑ Ⓒ Ⓓ Ⓔ   71 Ⓐ Ⓑ Ⓒ Ⓓ Ⓔ   96 Ⓐ Ⓑ Ⓒ Ⓓ Ⓔ
22 Ⓐ Ⓑ Ⓒ Ⓓ Ⓔ   47 Ⓐ Ⓑ Ⓒ Ⓓ Ⓔ   72 Ⓐ Ⓑ Ⓒ Ⓓ Ⓔ   97 Ⓐ Ⓑ Ⓒ Ⓓ Ⓔ
23 Ⓐ Ⓑ Ⓒ Ⓓ Ⓔ   48 Ⓐ Ⓑ Ⓒ Ⓓ Ⓔ   73 Ⓐ Ⓑ Ⓒ Ⓓ Ⓔ   98 Ⓐ Ⓑ Ⓒ Ⓓ Ⓔ
24 Ⓐ Ⓑ Ⓒ Ⓓ Ⓔ   49 Ⓐ Ⓑ Ⓒ Ⓓ Ⓔ   74 Ⓐ Ⓑ Ⓒ Ⓓ Ⓔ   99 Ⓐ Ⓑ Ⓒ Ⓓ Ⓔ
25 Ⓐ Ⓑ Ⓒ Ⓓ Ⓔ   50 Ⓐ Ⓑ Ⓒ Ⓓ Ⓔ   75 Ⓐ Ⓑ Ⓒ Ⓓ Ⓔ   100 Ⓐ Ⓑ Ⓒ Ⓓ Ⓔ

Chemistry *Fill in circle CE only if II is correct explanation of I.

	I	II	CE*		I	II	CE*
101	Ⓣ Ⓕ	Ⓣ Ⓕ	◯	109	Ⓣ Ⓕ	Ⓣ Ⓕ	◯
102	Ⓣ Ⓕ	Ⓣ Ⓕ	◯	110	Ⓣ Ⓕ	Ⓣ Ⓕ	◯
103	Ⓣ Ⓕ	Ⓣ Ⓕ	◯	111	Ⓣ Ⓕ	Ⓣ Ⓕ	◯
104	Ⓣ Ⓕ	Ⓣ Ⓕ	◯	112	Ⓣ Ⓕ	Ⓣ Ⓕ	◯
105	Ⓣ Ⓕ	Ⓣ Ⓕ	◯	113	Ⓣ Ⓕ	Ⓣ Ⓕ	◯
106	Ⓣ Ⓕ	Ⓣ Ⓕ	◯	114	Ⓣ Ⓕ	Ⓣ Ⓕ	◯
107	Ⓣ Ⓕ	Ⓣ Ⓕ	◯	115	Ⓣ Ⓕ	Ⓣ Ⓕ	◯
108	Ⓣ Ⓕ	Ⓣ Ⓕ	◯				

8 BOOK CODE
(Copy and grid as on back of test book.)

⓪ Ⓐ ⓪
① Ⓑ ①
② Ⓒ ②
③ Ⓓ ③
④ Ⓔ ④
⑤ Ⓕ ⑤
⑥ Ⓖ ⑥
⑦ Ⓗ ⑦
⑧ Ⓘ ⑧
⑨ Ⓙ ⑨
  Ⓚ
  Ⓛ
  Ⓜ
  Ⓝ
  Ⓞ
  Ⓟ
  Ⓠ
  Ⓡ
  Ⓢ
  Ⓣ
  Ⓤ
  Ⓥ
  Ⓦ
  Ⓧ
  Ⓨ
  Ⓩ

9 BOOK ID
(Copy from back of test book.)

10 BOOK SERIAL NUMBER
(Copy from front of test book.)

⓪ ⓪ ⓪ ⓪ ⓪ ⓪
① ① ① ① ① ①
② ② ② ② ② ②
③ ③ ③ ③ ③ ③
④ ④ ④ ④ ④ ④
⑤ ⑤ ⑤ ⑤ ⑤ ⑤
⑥ ⑥ ⑥ ⑥ ⑥ ⑥
⑦ ⑦ ⑦ ⑦ ⑦ ⑦
⑧ ⑧ ⑧ ⑧ ⑧ ⑧
⑨ ⑨ ⑨ ⑨ ⑨ ⑨

FOR OFFICIAL USE ONLY

R/C	W/S1	FS/S2	CS/S3	WS

PLEASE DO NOT WRITE IN THIS AREA

SERIAL #

Use a No. 2 pencil only. Be sure each mark is dark and completely fills the intended circle. Completely erase any errors or stray marks.

Page 3

here are more
swer spaces
an you need,
ave them blank.

		Test Code
V	①②③④⑤⑥⑦⑧⑨
W	①②③④⑤⑥⑦⑧⑨
X	①②③④⑤ Ⓨ ⒶⒷⒸⒹⒺ
Q	①②③④⑤⑥⑦⑧⑨

Subject Test (print)

ⒶⒷⒸⒹⒺ 26 ⒶⒷⒸⒹⒺ 51 ⒶⒷⒸⒹⒺ 76 ⒶⒷⒸⒹⒺ
ⒶⒷⒸⒹⒺ 27 ⒶⒷⒸⒹⒺ 52 ⒶⒷⒸⒹⒺ 77 ⒶⒷⒸⒹⒺ
ⒶⒷⒸⒹⒺ 28 ⒶⒷⒸⒹⒺ 53 ⒶⒷⒸⒹⒺ 78 ⒶⒷⒸⒹⒺ
ⒶⒷⒸⒹⒺ 29 ⒶⒷⒸⒹⒺ 54 ⒶⒷⒸⒹⒺ 79 ⒶⒷⒸⒹⒺ
ⒶⒷⒸⒹⒺ 30 ⒶⒷⒸⒹⒺ 55 ⒶⒷⒸⒹⒺ 80 ⒶⒷⒸⒹⒺ
ⒶⒷⒸⒹⒺ 31 ⒶⒷⒸⒹⒺ 56 ⒶⒷⒸⒹⒺ 81 ⒶⒷⒸⒹⒺ
ⒶⒷⒸⒹⒺ 32 ⒶⒷⒸⒹⒺ 57 ⒶⒷⒸⒹⒺ 82 ⒶⒷⒸⒹⒺ
ⒶⒷⒸⒹⒺ 33 ⒶⒷⒸⒹⒺ 58 ⒶⒷⒸⒹⒺ 83 ⒶⒷⒸⒹⒺ
ⒶⒷⒸⒹⒺ 34 ⒶⒷⒸⒹⒺ 59 ⒶⒷⒸⒹⒺ 84 ⒶⒷⒸⒹⒺ
ⒶⒷⒸⒹⒺ 35 ⒶⒷⒸⒹⒺ 60 ⒶⒷⒸⒹⒺ 85 ⒶⒷⒸⒹⒺ
ⒶⒷⒸⒹⒺ 36 ⒶⒷⒸⒹⒺ 61 ⒶⒷⒸⒹⒺ 86 ⒶⒷⒸⒹⒺ
ⒶⒷⒸⒹⒺ 37 ⒶⒷⒸⒹⒺ 62 ⒶⒷⒸⒹⒺ 87 ⒶⒷⒸⒹⒺ
ⒶⒷⒸⒹⒺ 38 ⒶⒷⒸⒹⒺ 63 ⒶⒷⒸⒹⒺ 88 ⒶⒷⒸⒹⒺ
ⒶⒷⒸⒹⒺ 39 ⒶⒷⒸⒹⒺ 64 ⒶⒷⒸⒹⒺ 89 ⒶⒷⒸⒹⒺ
ⒶⒷⒸⒹⒺ 40 ⒶⒷⒸⒹⒺ 65 ⒶⒷⒸⒹⒺ 90 ⒶⒷⒸⒹⒺ
ⒶⒷⒸⒹⒺ 41 ⒶⒷⒸⒹⒺ 66 ⒶⒷⒸⒹⒺ 91 ⒶⒷⒸⒹⒺ
ⒶⒷⒸⒹⒺ 42 ⒶⒷⒸⒹⒺ 67 ⒶⒷⒸⒹⒺ 92 ⒶⒷⒸⒹⒺ
ⒶⒷⒸⒹⒺ 43 ⒶⒷⒸⒹⒺ 68 ⒶⒷⒸⒹⒺ 93 ⒶⒷⒸⒹⒺ
ⒶⒷⒸⒹⒺ 44 ⒶⒷⒸⒹⒺ 69 ⒶⒷⒸⒹⒺ 94 ⒶⒷⒸⒹⒺ
ⒶⒷⒸⒹⒺ 45 ⒶⒷⒸⒹⒺ 70 ⒶⒷⒸⒹⒺ 95 ⒶⒷⒸⒹⒺ
ⒶⒷⒸⒹⒺ 46 ⒶⒷⒸⒹⒺ 71 ⒶⒷⒸⒹⒺ 96 ⒶⒷⒸⒹⒺ
ⒶⒷⒸⒹⒺ 47 ⒶⒷⒸⒹⒺ 72 ⒶⒷⒸⒹⒺ 97 ⒶⒷⒸⒹⒺ
ⒶⒷⒸⒹⒺ 48 ⒶⒷⒸⒹⒺ 73 ⒶⒷⒸⒹⒺ 98 ⒶⒷⒸⒹⒺ
ⒶⒷⒸⒹⒺ 49 ⒶⒷⒸⒹⒺ 74 ⒶⒷⒸⒹⒺ 99 ⒶⒷⒸⒹⒺ
ⒶⒷⒸⒹⒺ 50 ⒶⒷⒸⒹⒺ 75 ⒶⒷⒸⒹⒺ 100 ⒶⒷⒸⒹⒺ

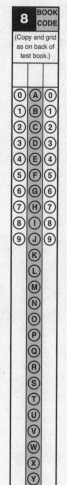

8 BOOK CODE
(Copy and grid as on back of test book.)

9 BOOK ID
(Copy from back of test book.)

10 BOOK SERIAL NUMBER
(Copy from front of test book.)

mistry *Fill in circle CE only if II is correct explanation of I.

	I	II	CE*		I	II	CE*
	ⓉⒻ	ⓉⒻ	○	109	ⓉⒻ	ⓉⒻ	○
	ⓉⒻ	ⓉⒻ	○	110	ⓉⒻ	ⓉⒻ	○
	ⓉⒻ	ⓉⒻ	○	111	ⓉⒻ	ⓉⒻ	○
	ⓉⒻ	ⓉⒻ	○	112	ⓉⒻ	ⓉⒻ	○
	ⓉⒻ	ⓉⒻ	○	113	ⓉⒻ	ⓉⒻ	○
	ⓉⒻ	ⓉⒻ	○	114	ⓉⒻ	ⓉⒻ	○
	ⓉⒻ	ⓉⒻ	○	115	ⓉⒻ	ⓉⒻ	○
	ⓉⒻ	ⓉⒻ	○				

FOR OFFICIAL USE ONLY				
R/C	W/S1	FS/S2	CS/S3	WS

PLEASE DO NOT WRITE IN THIS AREA

SERIAL #

Page 4

Use a No. 2 pencil only. Be sure each mark is dark and completely fills the intended circle. Completely erase any errors or stray marks.

If there are more answer spaces than you need, leave them blank.

Test Code

V	①	②	③	④	⑤	⑥	⑦	⑧	⑨	
W	①	②	③	④	⑤	⑥	⑦	⑧	⑨	
X	①	②	③	④	⑤	Y	Ⓐ	Ⓑ	Ⓒ	Ⓓ Ⓔ
Q	①	②	③	④	⑤	⑥	⑦	⑧	⑨	

Subject Test (print)

1. Ⓐ Ⓑ Ⓒ Ⓓ Ⓔ
2. Ⓐ Ⓑ Ⓒ Ⓓ Ⓔ
3. Ⓐ Ⓑ Ⓒ Ⓓ Ⓔ
4. Ⓐ Ⓑ Ⓒ Ⓓ Ⓔ
5. Ⓐ Ⓑ Ⓒ Ⓓ Ⓔ
6. Ⓐ Ⓑ Ⓒ Ⓓ Ⓔ
7. Ⓐ Ⓑ Ⓒ Ⓓ Ⓔ
8. Ⓐ Ⓑ Ⓒ Ⓓ Ⓔ
9. Ⓐ Ⓑ Ⓒ Ⓓ Ⓔ
10. Ⓐ Ⓑ Ⓒ Ⓓ Ⓔ
11. Ⓐ Ⓑ Ⓒ Ⓓ Ⓔ
12. Ⓐ Ⓑ Ⓒ Ⓓ Ⓔ
13. Ⓐ Ⓑ Ⓒ Ⓓ Ⓔ
14. Ⓐ Ⓑ Ⓒ Ⓓ Ⓔ
15. Ⓐ Ⓑ Ⓒ Ⓓ Ⓔ
16. Ⓐ Ⓑ Ⓒ Ⓓ Ⓔ
17. Ⓐ Ⓑ Ⓒ Ⓓ Ⓔ
18. Ⓐ Ⓑ Ⓒ Ⓓ Ⓔ
19. Ⓐ Ⓑ Ⓒ Ⓓ Ⓔ
20. Ⓐ Ⓑ Ⓒ Ⓓ Ⓔ
21. Ⓐ Ⓑ Ⓒ Ⓓ Ⓔ
22. Ⓐ Ⓑ Ⓒ Ⓓ Ⓔ
23. Ⓐ Ⓑ Ⓒ Ⓓ Ⓔ
24. Ⓐ Ⓑ Ⓒ Ⓓ Ⓔ
25. Ⓐ Ⓑ Ⓒ Ⓓ Ⓔ

26. Ⓐ Ⓑ Ⓒ Ⓓ Ⓔ
27. Ⓐ Ⓑ Ⓒ Ⓓ Ⓔ
28. Ⓐ Ⓑ Ⓒ Ⓓ Ⓔ
29. Ⓐ Ⓑ Ⓒ Ⓓ Ⓔ
30. Ⓐ Ⓑ Ⓒ Ⓓ Ⓔ
31. Ⓐ Ⓑ Ⓒ Ⓓ Ⓔ
32. Ⓐ Ⓑ Ⓒ Ⓓ Ⓔ
33. Ⓐ Ⓑ Ⓒ Ⓓ Ⓔ
34. Ⓐ Ⓑ Ⓒ Ⓓ Ⓔ
35. Ⓐ Ⓑ Ⓒ Ⓓ Ⓔ
36. Ⓐ Ⓑ Ⓒ Ⓓ Ⓔ
37. Ⓐ Ⓑ Ⓒ Ⓓ Ⓔ
38. Ⓐ Ⓑ Ⓒ Ⓓ Ⓔ
39. Ⓐ Ⓑ Ⓒ Ⓓ Ⓔ
40. Ⓐ Ⓑ Ⓒ Ⓓ Ⓔ
41. Ⓐ Ⓑ Ⓒ Ⓓ Ⓔ
42. Ⓐ Ⓑ Ⓒ Ⓓ Ⓔ
43. Ⓐ Ⓑ Ⓒ Ⓓ Ⓔ
44. Ⓐ Ⓑ Ⓒ Ⓓ Ⓔ
45. Ⓐ Ⓑ Ⓒ Ⓓ Ⓔ
46. Ⓐ Ⓑ Ⓒ Ⓓ Ⓔ
47. Ⓐ Ⓑ Ⓒ Ⓓ Ⓔ
48. Ⓐ Ⓑ Ⓒ Ⓓ Ⓔ
49. Ⓐ Ⓑ Ⓒ Ⓓ Ⓔ
50. Ⓐ Ⓑ Ⓒ Ⓓ Ⓔ

51. Ⓐ Ⓑ Ⓒ Ⓓ Ⓔ
52. Ⓐ Ⓑ Ⓒ Ⓓ Ⓔ
53. Ⓐ Ⓑ Ⓒ Ⓓ Ⓔ
54. Ⓐ Ⓑ Ⓒ Ⓓ Ⓔ
55. Ⓐ Ⓑ Ⓒ Ⓓ Ⓔ
56. Ⓐ Ⓑ Ⓒ Ⓓ Ⓔ
57. Ⓐ Ⓑ Ⓒ Ⓓ Ⓔ
58. Ⓐ Ⓑ Ⓒ Ⓓ Ⓔ
59. Ⓐ Ⓑ Ⓒ Ⓓ Ⓔ
60. Ⓐ Ⓑ Ⓒ Ⓓ Ⓔ
61. Ⓐ Ⓑ Ⓒ Ⓓ Ⓔ
62. Ⓐ Ⓑ Ⓒ Ⓓ Ⓔ
63. Ⓐ Ⓑ Ⓒ Ⓓ Ⓔ
64. Ⓐ Ⓑ Ⓒ Ⓓ Ⓔ
65. Ⓐ Ⓑ Ⓒ Ⓓ Ⓔ
66. Ⓐ Ⓑ Ⓒ Ⓓ Ⓔ
67. Ⓐ Ⓑ Ⓒ Ⓓ Ⓔ
68. Ⓐ Ⓑ Ⓒ Ⓓ Ⓔ
69. Ⓐ Ⓑ Ⓒ Ⓓ Ⓔ
70. Ⓐ Ⓑ Ⓒ Ⓓ Ⓔ
71. Ⓐ Ⓑ Ⓒ Ⓓ Ⓔ
72. Ⓐ Ⓑ Ⓒ Ⓓ Ⓔ
73. Ⓐ Ⓑ Ⓒ Ⓓ Ⓔ
74. Ⓐ Ⓑ Ⓒ Ⓓ Ⓔ
75. Ⓐ Ⓑ Ⓒ Ⓓ Ⓔ

76. Ⓐ Ⓑ Ⓒ Ⓓ Ⓔ
77. Ⓐ Ⓑ Ⓒ Ⓓ Ⓔ
78. Ⓐ Ⓑ Ⓒ Ⓓ Ⓔ
79. Ⓐ Ⓑ Ⓒ Ⓓ Ⓔ
80. Ⓐ Ⓑ Ⓒ Ⓓ Ⓔ
81. Ⓐ Ⓑ Ⓒ Ⓓ Ⓔ
82. Ⓐ Ⓑ Ⓒ Ⓓ Ⓔ
83. Ⓐ Ⓑ Ⓒ Ⓓ Ⓔ
84. Ⓐ Ⓑ Ⓒ Ⓓ Ⓔ
85. Ⓐ Ⓑ Ⓒ Ⓓ Ⓔ
86. Ⓐ Ⓑ Ⓒ Ⓓ Ⓔ
87. Ⓐ Ⓑ Ⓒ Ⓓ Ⓔ
88. Ⓐ Ⓑ Ⓒ Ⓓ Ⓔ
89. Ⓐ Ⓑ Ⓒ Ⓓ Ⓔ
90. Ⓐ Ⓑ Ⓒ Ⓓ Ⓔ
91. Ⓐ Ⓑ Ⓒ Ⓓ Ⓔ
92. Ⓐ Ⓑ Ⓒ Ⓓ Ⓔ
93. Ⓐ Ⓑ Ⓒ Ⓓ Ⓔ
94. Ⓐ Ⓑ Ⓒ Ⓓ Ⓔ
95. Ⓐ Ⓑ Ⓒ Ⓓ Ⓔ
96. Ⓐ Ⓑ Ⓒ Ⓓ Ⓔ
97. Ⓐ Ⓑ Ⓒ Ⓓ Ⓔ
98. Ⓐ Ⓑ Ⓒ Ⓓ Ⓔ
99. Ⓐ Ⓑ Ⓒ Ⓓ Ⓔ
100. Ⓐ Ⓑ Ⓒ Ⓓ Ⓔ

8 BOOK CODE
(Copy and grid as on back of test book.)

⓪	Ⓐ	⓪
①	Ⓑ	①
②	Ⓒ	②
③	Ⓓ	③
④	Ⓔ	④
⑤	Ⓕ	⑤
⑥	Ⓖ	⑥
⑦	Ⓗ	⑦
⑧	Ⓘ	⑧
⑨	Ⓙ	⑨
	Ⓚ	
	Ⓛ	
	Ⓜ	
	Ⓝ	
	Ⓞ	
	Ⓟ	
	Ⓠ	
	Ⓡ	
	Ⓢ	
	Ⓣ	
	Ⓤ	
	Ⓥ	
	Ⓦ	
	Ⓧ	
	Ⓨ	
	Ⓩ	

9 BOOK ID
(Copy from back of test book.)

10 BOOK SERIAL NUMBER
(Copy from front of test book.)

⓪	⓪	⓪	⓪	⓪	⓪
①	①	①	①	①	①
②	②	②	②	②	②
③	③	③	③	③	③
④	④	④	④	④	④
⑤	⑤	⑤	⑤	⑤	⑤
⑥	⑥	⑥	⑥	⑥	⑥
⑦	⑦	⑦	⑦	⑦	⑦
⑧	⑧	⑧	⑧	⑧	⑧
⑨	⑨	⑨	⑨	⑨	⑨

Chemistry *Fill in circle CE only if II is correct explanation of I.

	I	II	CE*		I	II	CE*
101	Ⓣ Ⓕ	Ⓣ Ⓕ	◯	109	Ⓣ Ⓕ	Ⓣ Ⓕ	◯
102	Ⓣ Ⓕ	Ⓣ Ⓕ	◯	110	Ⓣ Ⓕ	Ⓣ Ⓕ	◯
103	Ⓣ Ⓕ	Ⓣ Ⓕ	◯	111	Ⓣ Ⓕ	Ⓣ Ⓕ	◯
104	Ⓣ Ⓕ	Ⓣ Ⓕ	◯	112	Ⓣ Ⓕ	Ⓣ Ⓕ	◯
105	Ⓣ Ⓕ	Ⓣ Ⓕ	◯	113	Ⓣ Ⓕ	Ⓣ Ⓕ	◯
106	Ⓣ Ⓕ	Ⓣ Ⓕ	◯	114	Ⓣ Ⓕ	Ⓣ Ⓕ	◯
107	Ⓣ Ⓕ	Ⓣ Ⓕ	◯	115	Ⓣ Ⓕ	Ⓣ Ⓕ	◯
108	Ⓣ Ⓕ	Ⓣ Ⓕ	◯				

CERTIFICATION STATEMENT

Copy the statement below (do not print) and sign your name as you would an official docum

I hereby agree to the conditions set forth online at www.collegeboard.com and/or in the Registration Bulletin and certify that I am the person whose name and address appear on this answer sheet.

Signature _____   Date _____

CollegeBoard SAT

SAT Subject Tests™

Your Name:
(Print)

Last   First   M.I.

ee to the conditions on the back of the SAT® Subject Tests book.

ture: Date   /   /

Address:

Number and Street   City   State   Zip Code

r:

City   State

YOUR NAME

Name (Letters)	First Init.	Mid. Init.

3	SOCIAL SECURITY NUMBER

5	SEX

○ Female   ○ Male

6	REGISTRATION NUMBER

(Copy from Admission Ticket.)

8	BOOK CODE

(Copy and grid as on back of test book.)

9	BOOK ID

(Copy from back of test book.)

10	BOOK SERIAL NUMBER

(Copy from front of test book.)

4	DATE OF BIRTH

MONTH	DAY	YEAR

○ Jan
○ Feb
○ Mar
○ Apr
○ May
○ Jun
○ Jul
○ Aug
○ Sep
○ Oct
○ Nov
○ Dec

7	TEST CENTER

(Supplied by Test Center Supervisor.)

FOR OFFICIAL USE ONLY

11030-36392 • NS114E315 • Printed in U.S.A.
724844

Page 2

Use a No. 2 pencil only. Be sure each mark is dark and completely fills the intended circle. Completely erase any errors or stray marks.

If there are more answer spaces than you need, leave them blank.

Test Code

V ① ② ③ ④ ⑤ ⑥ ⑦ ⑧ ⑨
W ① ② ③ ④ ⑤ ⑥ ⑦ ⑧ ⑨
X ① ② ③ ④ ⑤ Y Ⓐ Ⓑ Ⓒ Ⓓ Ⓔ
Q ① ② ③ ④ ⑤ ⑥ ⑦ ⑧ ⑨

Subject Test (print)

1 Ⓐ Ⓑ Ⓒ Ⓓ Ⓔ   26 Ⓐ Ⓑ Ⓒ Ⓓ Ⓔ   51 Ⓐ Ⓑ Ⓒ Ⓓ Ⓔ   76 Ⓐ Ⓑ Ⓒ Ⓓ Ⓔ
2 Ⓐ Ⓑ Ⓒ Ⓓ Ⓔ   27 Ⓐ Ⓑ Ⓒ Ⓓ Ⓔ   52 Ⓐ Ⓑ Ⓒ Ⓓ Ⓔ   77 Ⓐ Ⓑ Ⓒ Ⓓ Ⓔ
3 Ⓐ Ⓑ Ⓒ Ⓓ Ⓔ   28 Ⓐ Ⓑ Ⓒ Ⓓ Ⓔ   53 Ⓐ Ⓑ Ⓒ Ⓓ Ⓔ   78 Ⓐ Ⓑ Ⓒ Ⓓ Ⓔ
4 Ⓐ Ⓑ Ⓒ Ⓓ Ⓔ   29 Ⓐ Ⓑ Ⓒ Ⓓ Ⓔ   54 Ⓐ Ⓑ Ⓒ Ⓓ Ⓔ   79 Ⓐ Ⓑ Ⓒ Ⓓ Ⓔ
5 Ⓐ Ⓑ Ⓒ Ⓓ Ⓔ   30 Ⓐ Ⓑ Ⓒ Ⓓ Ⓔ   55 Ⓐ Ⓑ Ⓒ Ⓓ Ⓔ   80 Ⓐ Ⓑ Ⓒ Ⓓ Ⓔ
6 Ⓐ Ⓑ Ⓒ Ⓓ Ⓔ   31 Ⓐ Ⓑ Ⓒ Ⓓ Ⓔ   56 Ⓐ Ⓑ Ⓒ Ⓓ Ⓔ   81 Ⓐ Ⓑ Ⓒ Ⓓ Ⓔ
7 Ⓐ Ⓑ Ⓒ Ⓓ Ⓔ   32 Ⓐ Ⓑ Ⓒ Ⓓ Ⓔ   57 Ⓐ Ⓑ Ⓒ Ⓓ Ⓔ   82 Ⓐ Ⓑ Ⓒ Ⓓ Ⓔ
8 Ⓐ Ⓑ Ⓒ Ⓓ Ⓔ   33 Ⓐ Ⓑ Ⓒ Ⓓ Ⓔ   58 Ⓐ Ⓑ Ⓒ Ⓓ Ⓔ   83 Ⓐ Ⓑ Ⓒ Ⓓ Ⓔ
9 Ⓐ Ⓑ Ⓒ Ⓓ Ⓔ   34 Ⓐ Ⓑ Ⓒ Ⓓ Ⓔ   59 Ⓐ Ⓑ Ⓒ Ⓓ Ⓔ   84 Ⓐ Ⓑ Ⓒ Ⓓ Ⓔ
10 Ⓐ Ⓑ Ⓒ Ⓓ Ⓔ   35 Ⓐ Ⓑ Ⓒ Ⓓ Ⓔ   60 Ⓐ Ⓑ Ⓒ Ⓓ Ⓔ   85 Ⓐ Ⓑ Ⓒ Ⓓ Ⓔ
11 Ⓐ Ⓑ Ⓒ Ⓓ Ⓔ   36 Ⓐ Ⓑ Ⓒ Ⓓ Ⓔ   61 Ⓐ Ⓑ Ⓒ Ⓓ Ⓔ   86 Ⓐ Ⓑ Ⓒ Ⓓ Ⓔ
12 Ⓐ Ⓑ Ⓒ Ⓓ Ⓔ   37 Ⓐ Ⓑ Ⓒ Ⓓ Ⓔ   62 Ⓐ Ⓑ Ⓒ Ⓓ Ⓔ   87 Ⓐ Ⓑ Ⓒ Ⓓ Ⓔ
13 Ⓐ Ⓑ Ⓒ Ⓓ Ⓔ   38 Ⓐ Ⓑ Ⓒ Ⓓ Ⓔ   63 Ⓐ Ⓑ Ⓒ Ⓓ Ⓔ   88 Ⓐ Ⓑ Ⓒ Ⓓ Ⓔ
14 Ⓐ Ⓑ Ⓒ Ⓓ Ⓔ   39 Ⓐ Ⓑ Ⓒ Ⓓ Ⓔ   64 Ⓐ Ⓑ Ⓒ Ⓓ Ⓔ   89 Ⓐ Ⓑ Ⓒ Ⓓ Ⓔ
15 Ⓐ Ⓑ Ⓒ Ⓓ Ⓔ   40 Ⓐ Ⓑ Ⓒ Ⓓ Ⓔ   65 Ⓐ Ⓑ Ⓒ Ⓓ Ⓔ   90 Ⓐ Ⓑ Ⓒ Ⓓ Ⓔ
16 Ⓐ Ⓑ Ⓒ Ⓓ Ⓔ   41 Ⓐ Ⓑ Ⓒ Ⓓ Ⓔ   66 Ⓐ Ⓑ Ⓒ Ⓓ Ⓔ   91 Ⓐ Ⓑ Ⓒ Ⓓ Ⓔ
17 Ⓐ Ⓑ Ⓒ Ⓓ Ⓔ   42 Ⓐ Ⓑ Ⓒ Ⓓ Ⓔ   67 Ⓐ Ⓑ Ⓒ Ⓓ Ⓔ   92 Ⓐ Ⓑ Ⓒ Ⓓ Ⓔ
18 Ⓐ Ⓑ Ⓒ Ⓓ Ⓔ   43 Ⓐ Ⓑ Ⓒ Ⓓ Ⓔ   68 Ⓐ Ⓑ Ⓒ Ⓓ Ⓔ   93 Ⓐ Ⓑ Ⓒ Ⓓ Ⓔ
19 Ⓐ Ⓑ Ⓒ Ⓓ Ⓔ   44 Ⓐ Ⓑ Ⓒ Ⓓ Ⓔ   69 Ⓐ Ⓑ Ⓒ Ⓓ Ⓔ   94 Ⓐ Ⓑ Ⓒ Ⓓ Ⓔ
20 Ⓐ Ⓑ Ⓒ Ⓓ Ⓔ   45 Ⓐ Ⓑ Ⓒ Ⓓ Ⓔ   70 Ⓐ Ⓑ Ⓒ Ⓓ Ⓔ   95 Ⓐ Ⓑ Ⓒ Ⓓ Ⓔ
21 Ⓐ Ⓑ Ⓒ Ⓓ Ⓔ   46 Ⓐ Ⓑ Ⓒ Ⓓ Ⓔ   71 Ⓐ Ⓑ Ⓒ Ⓓ Ⓔ   96 Ⓐ Ⓑ Ⓒ Ⓓ Ⓔ
22 Ⓐ Ⓑ Ⓒ Ⓓ Ⓔ   47 Ⓐ Ⓑ Ⓒ Ⓓ Ⓔ   72 Ⓐ Ⓑ Ⓒ Ⓓ Ⓔ   97 Ⓐ Ⓑ Ⓒ Ⓓ Ⓔ
23 Ⓐ Ⓑ Ⓒ Ⓓ Ⓔ   48 Ⓐ Ⓑ Ⓒ Ⓓ Ⓔ   73 Ⓐ Ⓑ Ⓒ Ⓓ Ⓔ   98 Ⓐ Ⓑ Ⓒ Ⓓ Ⓔ
24 Ⓐ Ⓑ Ⓒ Ⓓ Ⓔ   49 Ⓐ Ⓑ Ⓒ Ⓓ Ⓔ   74 Ⓐ Ⓑ Ⓒ Ⓓ Ⓔ   99 Ⓐ Ⓑ Ⓒ Ⓓ Ⓔ
25 Ⓐ Ⓑ Ⓒ Ⓓ Ⓔ   50 Ⓐ Ⓑ Ⓒ Ⓓ Ⓔ   75 Ⓐ Ⓑ Ⓒ Ⓓ Ⓔ   100 Ⓐ Ⓑ Ⓒ Ⓓ Ⓔ

Chemistry *Fill in circle CE only if II is correct explanation of I.

	I	II	CE*		I	II	CE*
101	Ⓣ Ⓕ	Ⓣ Ⓕ	○	109	Ⓣ Ⓕ	Ⓣ Ⓕ	○
102	Ⓣ Ⓕ	Ⓣ Ⓕ	○	110	Ⓣ Ⓕ	Ⓣ Ⓕ	○
103	Ⓣ Ⓕ	Ⓣ Ⓕ	○	111	Ⓣ Ⓕ	Ⓣ Ⓕ	○
104	Ⓣ Ⓕ	Ⓣ Ⓕ	○	112	Ⓣ Ⓕ	Ⓣ Ⓕ	○
105	Ⓣ Ⓕ	Ⓣ Ⓕ	○	113	Ⓣ Ⓕ	Ⓣ Ⓕ	○
106	Ⓣ Ⓕ	Ⓣ Ⓕ	○	114	Ⓣ Ⓕ	Ⓣ Ⓕ	○
107	Ⓣ Ⓕ	Ⓣ Ⓕ	○	115	Ⓣ Ⓕ	Ⓣ Ⓕ	○
108	Ⓣ Ⓕ	Ⓣ Ⓕ	○				

8 BOOK CODE
(Copy and grid as on back of test book.)

⓪ Ⓐ ⓪
① Ⓑ ①
② Ⓒ ②
③ Ⓓ ③
④ Ⓔ ④
⑤ Ⓕ ⑤
⑥ Ⓖ ⑥
⑦ Ⓗ ⑦
⑧ Ⓘ ⑧
⑨ Ⓙ ⑨
Ⓚ
Ⓛ
Ⓜ
Ⓝ
Ⓞ
Ⓟ
Ⓠ
Ⓡ
Ⓢ
Ⓣ
Ⓤ
Ⓥ
Ⓦ
Ⓧ
Ⓨ
Ⓩ

9 BOOK ID
(Copy from back of test book.)

10 BOOK SERIAL NUMBER
(Copy from front of test book.)

⓪ ⓪ ⓪ ⓪ ⓪ ⓪
① ① ① ① ① ①
② ② ② ② ② ②
③ ③ ③ ③ ③ ③
④ ④ ④ ④ ④ ④
⑤ ⑤ ⑤ ⑤ ⑤ ⑤
⑥ ⑥ ⑥ ⑥ ⑥ ⑥
⑦ ⑦ ⑦ ⑦ ⑦ ⑦
⑧ ⑧ ⑧ ⑧ ⑧ ⑧
⑨ ⑨ ⑨ ⑨ ⑨ ⑨

PLEASE DO NOT WRITE IN THIS AREA

SERIAL #

Use a No. 2 pencil only. Be sure each mark is dark and completely fills the intended circle. Completely erase any errors or stray marks.

here are more
swer spaces
n you need,
ve them blank.

Test Code

V	① ② ③ ④ ⑤ ⑥ ⑦ ⑧ ⑨
W	① ② ③ ④ ⑤ ⑥ ⑦ ⑧ ⑨
X	① ② ③ ④ ⑤ Ⓨ Ⓐ Ⓑ Ⓒ Ⓓ Ⓔ
Q	① ② ③ ④ ⑤ ⑥ ⑦ ⑧ ⑨

Subject Test (print)

Ⓐ Ⓑ Ⓒ Ⓓ Ⓔ   26 Ⓐ Ⓑ Ⓒ Ⓓ Ⓔ   51 Ⓐ Ⓑ Ⓒ Ⓓ Ⓔ   76 Ⓐ Ⓑ Ⓒ Ⓓ Ⓔ
Ⓐ Ⓑ Ⓒ Ⓓ Ⓔ   27 Ⓐ Ⓑ Ⓒ Ⓓ Ⓔ   52 Ⓐ Ⓑ Ⓒ Ⓓ Ⓔ   77 Ⓐ Ⓑ Ⓒ Ⓓ Ⓔ
Ⓐ Ⓑ Ⓒ Ⓓ Ⓔ   28 Ⓐ Ⓑ Ⓒ Ⓓ Ⓔ   53 Ⓐ Ⓑ Ⓒ Ⓓ Ⓔ   78 Ⓐ Ⓑ Ⓒ Ⓓ Ⓔ
Ⓐ Ⓑ Ⓒ Ⓓ Ⓔ   29 Ⓐ Ⓑ Ⓒ Ⓓ Ⓔ   54 Ⓐ Ⓑ Ⓒ Ⓓ Ⓔ   79 Ⓐ Ⓑ Ⓒ Ⓓ Ⓔ
Ⓐ Ⓑ Ⓒ Ⓓ Ⓔ   30 Ⓐ Ⓑ Ⓒ Ⓓ Ⓔ   55 Ⓐ Ⓑ Ⓒ Ⓓ Ⓔ   80 Ⓐ Ⓑ Ⓒ Ⓓ Ⓔ
Ⓐ Ⓑ Ⓒ Ⓓ Ⓔ   31 Ⓐ Ⓑ Ⓒ Ⓓ Ⓔ   56 Ⓐ Ⓑ Ⓒ Ⓓ Ⓔ   81 Ⓐ Ⓑ Ⓒ Ⓓ Ⓔ
Ⓐ Ⓑ Ⓒ Ⓓ Ⓔ   32 Ⓐ Ⓑ Ⓒ Ⓓ Ⓔ   57 Ⓐ Ⓑ Ⓒ Ⓓ Ⓔ   82 Ⓐ Ⓑ Ⓒ Ⓓ Ⓔ
Ⓐ Ⓑ Ⓒ Ⓓ Ⓔ   33 Ⓐ Ⓑ Ⓒ Ⓓ Ⓔ   58 Ⓐ Ⓑ Ⓒ Ⓓ Ⓔ   83 Ⓐ Ⓑ Ⓒ Ⓓ Ⓔ
Ⓐ Ⓑ Ⓒ Ⓓ Ⓔ   34 Ⓐ Ⓑ Ⓒ Ⓓ Ⓔ   59 Ⓐ Ⓑ Ⓒ Ⓓ Ⓔ   84 Ⓐ Ⓑ Ⓒ Ⓓ Ⓔ
Ⓐ Ⓑ Ⓒ Ⓓ Ⓔ   35 Ⓐ Ⓑ Ⓒ Ⓓ Ⓔ   60 Ⓐ Ⓑ Ⓒ Ⓓ Ⓔ   85 Ⓐ Ⓑ Ⓒ Ⓓ Ⓔ
Ⓐ Ⓑ Ⓒ Ⓓ Ⓔ   36 Ⓐ Ⓑ Ⓒ Ⓓ Ⓔ   61 Ⓐ Ⓑ Ⓒ Ⓓ Ⓔ   86 Ⓐ Ⓑ Ⓒ Ⓓ Ⓔ
Ⓐ Ⓑ Ⓒ Ⓓ Ⓔ   37 Ⓐ Ⓑ Ⓒ Ⓓ Ⓔ   62 Ⓐ Ⓑ Ⓒ Ⓓ Ⓔ   87 Ⓐ Ⓑ Ⓒ Ⓓ Ⓔ
Ⓐ Ⓑ Ⓒ Ⓓ Ⓔ   38 Ⓐ Ⓑ Ⓒ Ⓓ Ⓔ   63 Ⓐ Ⓑ Ⓒ Ⓓ Ⓔ   88 Ⓐ Ⓑ Ⓒ Ⓓ Ⓔ
Ⓐ Ⓑ Ⓒ Ⓓ Ⓔ   39 Ⓐ Ⓑ Ⓒ Ⓓ Ⓔ   64 Ⓐ Ⓑ Ⓒ Ⓓ Ⓔ   89 Ⓐ Ⓑ Ⓒ Ⓓ Ⓔ
Ⓐ Ⓑ Ⓒ Ⓓ Ⓔ   40 Ⓐ Ⓑ Ⓒ Ⓓ Ⓔ   65 Ⓐ Ⓑ Ⓒ Ⓓ Ⓔ   90 Ⓐ Ⓑ Ⓒ Ⓓ Ⓔ
Ⓐ Ⓑ Ⓒ Ⓓ Ⓔ   41 Ⓐ Ⓑ Ⓒ Ⓓ Ⓔ   66 Ⓐ Ⓑ Ⓒ Ⓓ Ⓔ   91 Ⓐ Ⓑ Ⓒ Ⓓ Ⓔ
Ⓐ Ⓑ Ⓒ Ⓓ Ⓔ   42 Ⓐ Ⓑ Ⓒ Ⓓ Ⓔ   67 Ⓐ Ⓑ Ⓒ Ⓓ Ⓔ   92 Ⓐ Ⓑ Ⓒ Ⓓ Ⓔ
Ⓐ Ⓑ Ⓒ Ⓓ Ⓔ   43 Ⓐ Ⓑ Ⓒ Ⓓ Ⓔ   68 Ⓐ Ⓑ Ⓒ Ⓓ Ⓔ   93 Ⓐ Ⓑ Ⓒ Ⓓ Ⓔ
Ⓐ Ⓑ Ⓒ Ⓓ Ⓔ   44 Ⓐ Ⓑ Ⓒ Ⓓ Ⓔ   69 Ⓐ Ⓑ Ⓒ Ⓓ Ⓔ   94 Ⓐ Ⓑ Ⓒ Ⓓ Ⓔ
Ⓐ Ⓑ Ⓒ Ⓓ Ⓔ   45 Ⓐ Ⓑ Ⓒ Ⓓ Ⓔ   70 Ⓐ Ⓑ Ⓒ Ⓓ Ⓔ   95 Ⓐ Ⓑ Ⓒ Ⓓ Ⓔ
Ⓐ Ⓑ Ⓒ Ⓓ Ⓔ   46 Ⓐ Ⓑ Ⓒ Ⓓ Ⓔ   71 Ⓐ Ⓑ Ⓒ Ⓓ Ⓔ   96 Ⓐ Ⓑ Ⓒ Ⓓ Ⓔ
Ⓐ Ⓑ Ⓒ Ⓓ Ⓔ   47 Ⓐ Ⓑ Ⓒ Ⓓ Ⓔ   72 Ⓐ Ⓑ Ⓒ Ⓓ Ⓔ   97 Ⓐ Ⓑ Ⓒ Ⓓ Ⓔ
Ⓐ Ⓑ Ⓒ Ⓓ Ⓔ   48 Ⓐ Ⓑ Ⓒ Ⓓ Ⓔ   73 Ⓐ Ⓑ Ⓒ Ⓓ Ⓔ   98 Ⓐ Ⓑ Ⓒ Ⓓ Ⓔ
Ⓐ Ⓑ Ⓒ Ⓓ Ⓔ   49 Ⓐ Ⓑ Ⓒ Ⓓ Ⓔ   74 Ⓐ Ⓑ Ⓒ Ⓓ Ⓔ   99 Ⓐ Ⓑ Ⓒ Ⓓ Ⓔ
Ⓐ Ⓑ Ⓒ Ⓓ Ⓔ   50 Ⓐ Ⓑ Ⓒ Ⓓ Ⓔ   75 Ⓐ Ⓑ Ⓒ Ⓓ Ⓔ   100 Ⓐ Ⓑ Ⓒ Ⓓ Ⓔ

8 BOOK CODE (Copy and grid as on back of test book.)

9 BOOK ID (Copy from back of test book.)

10 BOOK SERIAL NUMBER (Copy from front of test book.)

nistry   *Fill in circle CE only if II is correct explanation of I.

I	II	CE*		I	II	CE*
Ⓣ Ⓕ	Ⓣ Ⓕ	◯				
Ⓣ Ⓕ	Ⓣ Ⓕ	◯	109	Ⓣ Ⓕ	Ⓣ Ⓕ	◯
Ⓣ Ⓕ	Ⓣ Ⓕ	◯	110	Ⓣ Ⓕ	Ⓣ Ⓕ	◯
Ⓣ Ⓕ	Ⓣ Ⓕ	◯	111	Ⓣ Ⓕ	Ⓣ Ⓕ	◯
Ⓣ Ⓕ	Ⓣ Ⓕ	◯	112	Ⓣ Ⓕ	Ⓣ Ⓕ	◯
Ⓣ Ⓕ	Ⓣ Ⓕ	◯	113	Ⓣ Ⓕ	Ⓣ Ⓕ	◯
Ⓣ Ⓕ	Ⓣ Ⓕ	◯	114	Ⓣ Ⓕ	Ⓣ Ⓕ	◯
Ⓣ Ⓕ	Ⓣ Ⓕ	◯	115	Ⓣ Ⓕ	Ⓣ Ⓕ	◯
Ⓣ Ⓕ	Ⓣ Ⓕ	◯				

FOR OFFICIAL USE ONLY

R/C	W/S1	FS/S2	CS/S3	WS

PLEASE DO NOT WRITE IN THIS AREA

SERIAL #

Page 4

Use a No. 2 pencil only. Be sure each mark is dark and completely fills the intended circle. Completely erase any errors or stray marks.

If there are more answer spaces than you need, leave them blank.

Test Code

V	① ② ③ ④ ⑤ ⑥ ⑦ ⑧ ⑨
W	① ② ③ ④ ⑤ ⑥ ⑦ ⑧ ⑨
X	① ② ③ ④ ⑤ Y Ⓐ Ⓑ Ⓒ Ⓓ Ⓔ
Q	① ② ③ ④ ⑤ ⑥ ⑦ ⑧ ⑨

Subject Test (print)

1 Ⓐ Ⓑ Ⓒ Ⓓ Ⓔ 26 Ⓐ Ⓑ Ⓒ Ⓓ Ⓔ 51 Ⓐ Ⓑ Ⓒ Ⓓ Ⓔ 76 Ⓐ Ⓑ Ⓒ Ⓓ Ⓔ
2 Ⓐ Ⓑ Ⓒ Ⓓ Ⓔ 27 Ⓐ Ⓑ Ⓒ Ⓓ Ⓔ 52 Ⓐ Ⓑ Ⓒ Ⓓ Ⓔ 77 Ⓐ Ⓑ Ⓒ Ⓓ Ⓔ
3 Ⓐ Ⓑ Ⓒ Ⓓ Ⓔ 28 Ⓐ Ⓑ Ⓒ Ⓓ Ⓔ 53 Ⓐ Ⓑ Ⓒ Ⓓ Ⓔ 78 Ⓐ Ⓑ Ⓒ Ⓓ Ⓔ
4 Ⓐ Ⓑ Ⓒ Ⓓ Ⓔ 29 Ⓐ Ⓑ Ⓒ Ⓓ Ⓔ 54 Ⓐ Ⓑ Ⓒ Ⓓ Ⓔ 79 Ⓐ Ⓑ Ⓒ Ⓓ Ⓔ
5 Ⓐ Ⓑ Ⓒ Ⓓ Ⓔ 30 Ⓐ Ⓑ Ⓒ Ⓓ Ⓔ 55 Ⓐ Ⓑ Ⓒ Ⓓ Ⓔ 80 Ⓐ Ⓑ Ⓒ Ⓓ Ⓔ
6 Ⓐ Ⓑ Ⓒ Ⓓ Ⓔ 31 Ⓐ Ⓑ Ⓒ Ⓓ Ⓔ 56 Ⓐ Ⓑ Ⓒ Ⓓ Ⓔ 81 Ⓐ Ⓑ Ⓒ Ⓓ Ⓔ
7 Ⓐ Ⓑ Ⓒ Ⓓ Ⓔ 32 Ⓐ Ⓑ Ⓒ Ⓓ Ⓔ 57 Ⓐ Ⓑ Ⓒ Ⓓ Ⓔ 82 Ⓐ Ⓑ Ⓒ Ⓓ Ⓔ
8 Ⓐ Ⓑ Ⓒ Ⓓ Ⓔ 33 Ⓐ Ⓑ Ⓒ Ⓓ Ⓔ 58 Ⓐ Ⓑ Ⓒ Ⓓ Ⓔ 83 Ⓐ Ⓑ Ⓒ Ⓓ Ⓔ
9 Ⓐ Ⓑ Ⓒ Ⓓ Ⓔ 34 Ⓐ Ⓑ Ⓒ Ⓓ Ⓔ 59 Ⓐ Ⓑ Ⓒ Ⓓ Ⓔ 84 Ⓐ Ⓑ Ⓒ Ⓓ Ⓔ
10 Ⓐ Ⓑ Ⓒ Ⓓ Ⓔ 35 Ⓐ Ⓑ Ⓒ Ⓓ Ⓔ 60 Ⓐ Ⓑ Ⓒ Ⓓ Ⓔ 85 Ⓐ Ⓑ Ⓒ Ⓓ Ⓔ
11 Ⓐ Ⓑ Ⓒ Ⓓ Ⓔ 36 Ⓐ Ⓑ Ⓒ Ⓓ Ⓔ 61 Ⓐ Ⓑ Ⓒ Ⓓ Ⓔ 86 Ⓐ Ⓑ Ⓒ Ⓓ Ⓔ
12 Ⓐ Ⓑ Ⓒ Ⓓ Ⓔ 37 Ⓐ Ⓑ Ⓒ Ⓓ Ⓔ 62 Ⓐ Ⓑ Ⓒ Ⓓ Ⓔ 87 Ⓐ Ⓑ Ⓒ Ⓓ Ⓔ
13 Ⓐ Ⓑ Ⓒ Ⓓ Ⓔ 38 Ⓐ Ⓑ Ⓒ Ⓓ Ⓔ 63 Ⓐ Ⓑ Ⓒ Ⓓ Ⓔ 88 Ⓐ Ⓑ Ⓒ Ⓓ Ⓔ
14 Ⓐ Ⓑ Ⓒ Ⓓ Ⓔ 39 Ⓐ Ⓑ Ⓒ Ⓓ Ⓔ 64 Ⓐ Ⓑ Ⓒ Ⓓ Ⓔ 89 Ⓐ Ⓑ Ⓒ Ⓓ Ⓔ
15 Ⓐ Ⓑ Ⓒ Ⓓ Ⓔ 40 Ⓐ Ⓑ Ⓒ Ⓓ Ⓔ 65 Ⓐ Ⓑ Ⓒ Ⓓ Ⓔ 90 Ⓐ Ⓑ Ⓒ Ⓓ Ⓔ
16 Ⓐ Ⓑ Ⓒ Ⓓ Ⓔ 41 Ⓐ Ⓑ Ⓒ Ⓓ Ⓔ 66 Ⓐ Ⓑ Ⓒ Ⓓ Ⓔ 91 Ⓐ Ⓑ Ⓒ Ⓓ Ⓔ
17 Ⓐ Ⓑ Ⓒ Ⓓ Ⓔ 42 Ⓐ Ⓑ Ⓒ Ⓓ Ⓔ 67 Ⓐ Ⓑ Ⓒ Ⓓ Ⓔ 92 Ⓐ Ⓑ Ⓒ Ⓓ Ⓔ
18 Ⓐ Ⓑ Ⓒ Ⓓ Ⓔ 43 Ⓐ Ⓑ Ⓒ Ⓓ Ⓔ 68 Ⓐ Ⓑ Ⓒ Ⓓ Ⓔ 93 Ⓐ Ⓑ Ⓒ Ⓓ Ⓔ
19 Ⓐ Ⓑ Ⓒ Ⓓ Ⓔ 44 Ⓐ Ⓑ Ⓒ Ⓓ Ⓔ 69 Ⓐ Ⓑ Ⓒ Ⓓ Ⓔ 94 Ⓐ Ⓑ Ⓒ Ⓓ Ⓔ
20 Ⓐ Ⓑ Ⓒ Ⓓ Ⓔ 45 Ⓐ Ⓑ Ⓒ Ⓓ Ⓔ 70 Ⓐ Ⓑ Ⓒ Ⓓ Ⓔ 95 Ⓐ Ⓑ Ⓒ Ⓓ Ⓔ
21 Ⓐ Ⓑ Ⓒ Ⓓ Ⓔ 46 Ⓐ Ⓑ Ⓒ Ⓓ Ⓔ 71 Ⓐ Ⓑ Ⓒ Ⓓ Ⓔ 96 Ⓐ Ⓑ Ⓒ Ⓓ Ⓔ
22 Ⓐ Ⓑ Ⓒ Ⓓ Ⓔ 47 Ⓐ Ⓑ Ⓒ Ⓓ Ⓔ 72 Ⓐ Ⓑ Ⓒ Ⓓ Ⓔ 97 Ⓐ Ⓑ Ⓒ Ⓓ Ⓔ
23 Ⓐ Ⓑ Ⓒ Ⓓ Ⓔ 48 Ⓐ Ⓑ Ⓒ Ⓓ Ⓔ 73 Ⓐ Ⓑ Ⓒ Ⓓ Ⓔ 98 Ⓐ Ⓑ Ⓒ Ⓓ Ⓔ
24 Ⓐ Ⓑ Ⓒ Ⓓ Ⓔ 49 Ⓐ Ⓑ Ⓒ Ⓓ Ⓔ 74 Ⓐ Ⓑ Ⓒ Ⓓ Ⓔ 99 Ⓐ Ⓑ Ⓒ Ⓓ Ⓔ
25 Ⓐ Ⓑ Ⓒ Ⓓ Ⓔ 50 Ⓐ Ⓑ Ⓒ Ⓓ Ⓔ 75 Ⓐ Ⓑ Ⓒ Ⓓ Ⓔ 100 Ⓐ Ⓑ Ⓒ Ⓓ Ⓔ

8 BOOK CODE (Copy and grid as on back of test book.)

⓪	Ⓐ	⓪
①	Ⓑ	①
②	Ⓒ	②
③	Ⓓ	③
④	Ⓔ	④
⑤	Ⓕ	⑤
⑥	Ⓖ	⑥
⑦	Ⓗ	⑦
⑧	Ⓘ	⑧
⑨	Ⓙ	⑨
	Ⓚ	
	Ⓛ	
	Ⓜ	
	Ⓝ	
	Ⓞ	
	Ⓟ	
	Ⓠ	
	Ⓡ	
	Ⓢ	
	Ⓣ	
	Ⓤ	
	Ⓥ	
	Ⓦ	
	Ⓧ	
	Ⓨ	
	Ⓩ	

9 BOOK ID (Copy from back of test book.)

10 BOOK SERIAL NUMBER (Copy from front of test book.)

⓪	⓪	⓪	⓪	⓪	⓪
①	①	①	①	①	①
②	②	②	②	②	②
③	③	③	③	③	③
④	④	④	④	④	④
⑤	⑤	⑤	⑤	⑤	⑤
⑥	⑥	⑥	⑥	⑥	⑥
⑦	⑦	⑦	⑦	⑦	⑦
⑧	⑧	⑧	⑧	⑧	⑧
⑨	⑨	⑨	⑨	⑨	⑨

Chemistry *Fill in circle CE only if II is correct explanation of I.

	I	II	CE*		I	II	CE*
101	Ⓣ Ⓕ	Ⓣ Ⓕ	◯	109	Ⓣ Ⓕ	Ⓣ Ⓕ	◯
102	Ⓣ Ⓕ	Ⓣ Ⓕ	◯	110	Ⓣ Ⓕ	Ⓣ Ⓕ	◯
103	Ⓣ Ⓕ	Ⓣ Ⓕ	◯	111	Ⓣ Ⓕ	Ⓣ Ⓕ	◯
104	Ⓣ Ⓕ	Ⓣ Ⓕ	◯	112	Ⓣ Ⓕ	Ⓣ Ⓕ	◯
105	Ⓣ Ⓕ	Ⓣ Ⓕ	◯	113	Ⓣ Ⓕ	Ⓣ Ⓕ	◯
106	Ⓣ Ⓕ	Ⓣ Ⓕ	◯	114	Ⓣ Ⓕ	Ⓣ Ⓕ	◯
107	Ⓣ Ⓕ	Ⓣ Ⓕ	◯	115	Ⓣ Ⓕ	Ⓣ Ⓕ	◯
108	Ⓣ Ⓕ	Ⓣ Ⓕ	◯				

FOR OFFICIAL USE ONLY

R/C	W/S1	FS/S2	CS/S3	WS

CERTIFICATION STATEMENT

Copy the statement below (do not print) and sign your name as you would an official docum

I hereby agree to the conditions set forth online at www.collegeboard.com and/or in the Registration Bulletin and certify that I am the person whose name and address appear on this answer sheet.

Signature _____   Date _____